AF528256

First published in 2025 by Hachette India
(Registered name: Hachette Book Publishing India Pvt. Ltd)
An Hachette UK company
www.hachetteindia.com

1

Information in the book has been updated to 31 August 2024, except in the Science and Technology, Education, Business and Economy, Medical Sciences, The Natural World, Visual Arts, and Sports chapters, where select information relates to later dates.

All maps in this work are pictorial representations, not to scale, and are not meant to represent exact political boundaries. They are for general illustration only, and are not intended to be used for reference purposes or reproduction elsewhere. It is clarified that the representation of a particular theme, or data set across regions with colour demarcations do not reflect political boundaries. It is also reiterated that such pictorial maps do not either represent or contradict India's national sovereignty, jurisdiction, or the recognition of political regions as mandated by the Surveyor General of India for maps showing political boundaries.

Old place names (such as Madras, Calcutta, and Bombay) may have been used to retain the historicity of the information as well as avoid confusion with earlier presidencies and provinces of the same name.

All efforts have been made to verify the copyright ownership of photographs as well as the correctness of the information included in this edition. Any omissions are unintentional and regretted, and, following written communication, will be rectified in the next edition.

Subsequent edition/reprint specifications may be subject to change, including but not limited to cover or inside finishes, paper, text colour, and/or colour sections.

Hardback edition ISBN 978-93-5731-496-1
Ebook edition ISBN 978-93-5731-966-9

Hachette Book Publishing India Pvt. Ltd
4th & 5th Floors, Corporate Centre
Plot No. 94, Sector 44, Gurugram 122003, India

Designed and typeset
by Syed Salahuddin

Printed and bound in India
by Manipal Technologies Limited

LIMCA BOOK of RECORDS

India at Her Best

2025

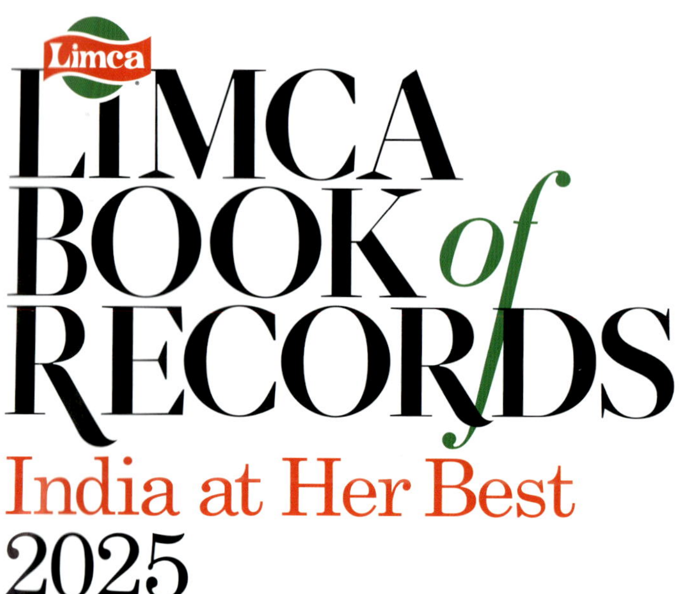

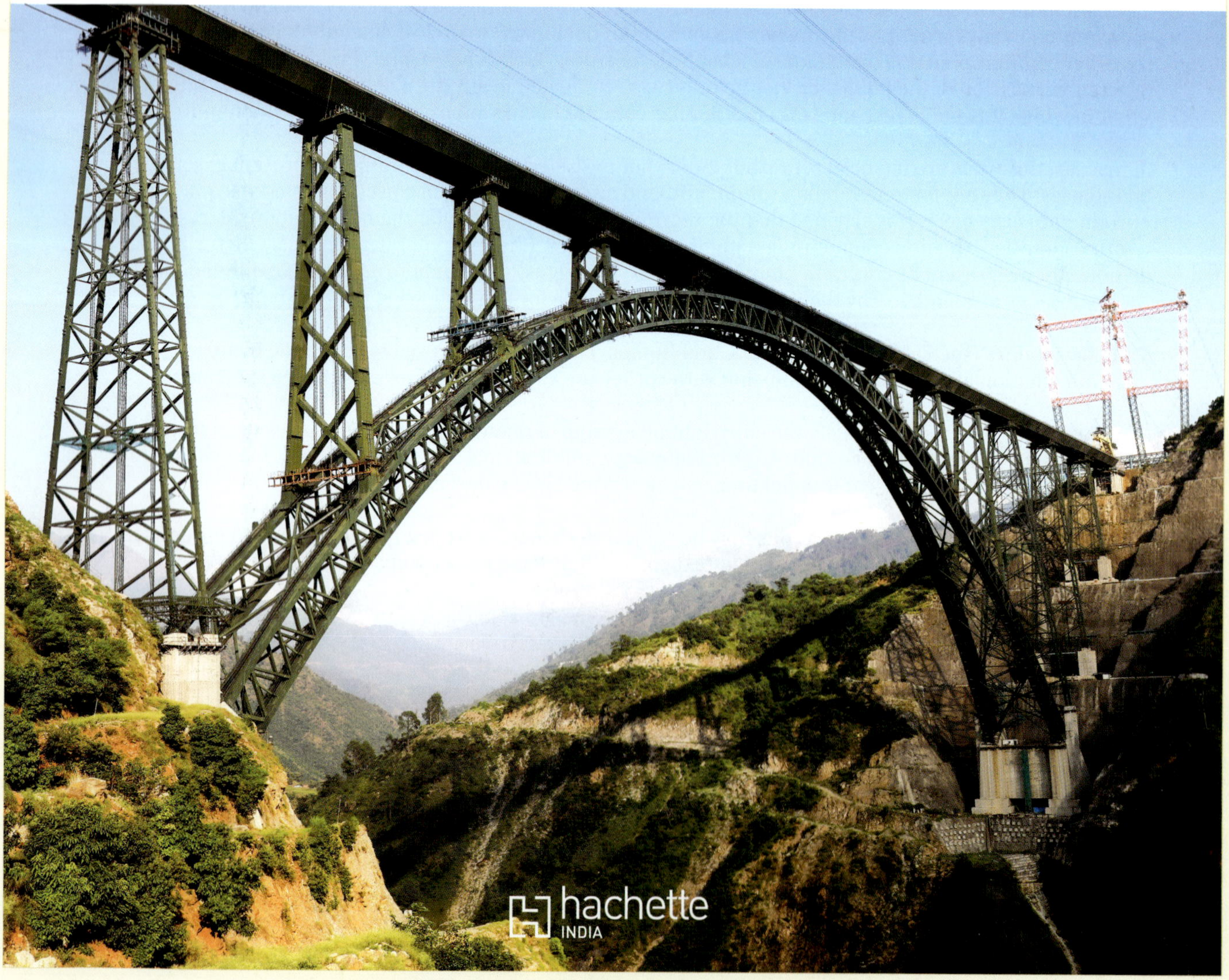

hachette INDIA

Dear Readers,

For thirty-five years, India's first and most prestigious record book has been curating achievements of Indians who determinedly seek their place in the sun, its light shining on their incredible achievements that surpass all that came before. This year too, many of our fellow countrypeople have scripted history with their stellar performances in varied fields.

Why not begin with the 2024 Olympics! Aman Sehrawat, 21 years and 24 days old, became India's youngest-ever Olympic medallist by winning the bronze in the men's freestyle 57 kg wrestling event in Paris. Manu Bhaker's stunning performances in both the 10 m pistol mixed event (with Sarabjot Singh) and the 10 m air pistol event won India its first ever Olympic medal in women's shooting. Bhaker is also the only Indian woman, and the only Indian athlete since Independence, to win two medals in a single edition of the Olympics.

The year 2024 also saw India's most successful campaign ever in the Paralympic Games, with a tally of 29 medals including 7 golds. Para shooter Avani Lekhara became the first Indian woman to bag 2 gold medals in this mega sports event, with her win in the women's 10 m air rifle standing SH1 event at the Tokyo 2020 Paralympic Games, and again in Paris, setting a new record of 249.7 points in 2024. Sharing the glory on the podium were Sumit Antil, Navdeep Singh, Harvinder Singh, and Mariyappan Thangavelu. The list goes on ...

Back home, showing both stamina and fortitude, B. Srinivasan from Chennai, Tamil Nadu, completed 301 half-marathons (beating the previous record of 164), the most by an individual, covering 7,037.77 km. Kavita Singh from the capital achieved new heights by performing yoga asanas at Umling La, at an altitude of 19,024 ft, breaking the record for performance at the highest altitude.

In the field of medical sciences too, India and Indians went from strength to strength. In April 2024, President Droupadi Murmu launched India's first home-grown CAR-T cell therapy for the treatment of cancer, developed by IIT Bombay, Tata Memorial Centre, and ImmunoACT. While it is a first for India, it is also being deemed as the most affordable CAR-T cell therapy in the world.

Keeping the spirit of Indian culture alive, the Nrityachakra team of the Prerana Foundation from Pune, Maharashtra, performed Kathak with a record-setting 1,188 participants at Maharashtriya Mandal's Chandrashekhar Agashe College Grounds, Pune, in February 2024.

Marking commendable strides in defence and security, the first private military aircraft facility was inaugurated in October 2024 at Vadodara, Gujarat – the result of a partnership between Tata Advanced Systems Limited and Airbus Defence and Space.

Closer to our everyday lives, the record for the world's largest office building now belongs to India! Surat Diamond Bourse, Gujarat, has surpassed the record of the Pentagon, USA.

Chronicling these feats and many more, the *Limca Book of Records* 2025 offers, as always, not just a collection of records but a unique celebration of the triumphs of India and Indians.

Please join us in congratulating and applauding all those who have set glorious new records and made the country proud!

LBR Marketing Team
Coca-Cola India

HACHETTE INDIA LBR TEAM

Consulting Editor: Vatsala Kaul Banerjee

Managing Editor: Anirban Sarkar

Research and Editorial Team:
Shubhali Chopra, Arunima Dharanipragada, Yukta Vats

Administrative Executive: Susheel Kapoor

CONSULTANTS

ADVENTURE
Ajeet Bajaj

CINEMA
Diptakirti Chaudhuri

EDUCATION
Dr Alpana Neogy

MEMORY
Squadron Leader Jayasimha Ravirala

BUSINESS AND ECONOMY
Suparna Pathak

SPORTS
Kamesh Srinivasan: Shooting

K. Arumugam: Hockey

Rakesh Rao: Chess, Golf, and Table Tennis

Aditya K. Halder: Archery, Athletics, Badminton, Basketball, Boxing, Cricket, Cue Sports, Football, Gymnastics, Kabaddi, Powerlifting, Squash, Swimming and Water Sports, Tennis, Weighlifting, Wrestling, General Sports, and Sports Statistics

LAST DATE FOR NEW ENTRIES (COMPLETE WITH DOCUMENTATION) FOR THE *LIMCA BOOK OF RECORDS* 2026 EDITION:

31 MAY 2025

Please see the revised and updated 'Rules and Guidelines' section for details.

Limca Book of Records does not have any branch offices or representatives.

General and Sales enquiries: **sales@hachetteindia.com**

Record applications/queries: **lbr.entries@hachetteindia.com**

Dear Readers,

As we put the final lustrous cover on the *Limca Book of Records*, we marvel once again at the spirit and zeal of people fired by the imagination and the will to raise the bar and rise above it; to defy not only the expectations of others but also their own.

Take, for instance, India's historic double gold victory – both in the open and women's events – at the Chess Olympiad in Budapest, Hungary, which comes as a glowing testimony to the country's leading place in the game!

Then again, on the global stage, at the Paris Paralympic Games, Sumit Antil became the first Indian to successfully defend his gold medal in the men's javelin throw in the F64 category while Navdeep Singh secured a historic first-ever gold in the men's javelin throw in the F41 category. Harvinder Singh brought home India's maiden gold medal in para archery with a thumping 6–0 victory in the men's individual recurve open final. Mariyappan Thangavelu became the first Indian para athlete to win medals at three consecutive Paralympic Games with his bronze in high jump (1.85 m).

Indians have also made groundbreaking strides in medical science. This year, a record has been registered for the highest spectacle power corrected surgically (–32.5 D) by Dr Rahil Chaudhary of Eye7 Eye Hospital, New Delhi.

Efforts for environment welfare have naturally made it to the book too. India's largest climate clock was installed and activated by the Council of Scientific & Industrial Research (CSIR) at the CSIR Headquarters Building in New Delhi, as a part of the Earth Day celebrations on 23 April 2024. The aim was to spread awareness about climate change and its ill effects.

This edition is underpinned by our team's painstaking research as always. Pushpendra Saroj, a Samajwadi Party candidate who won the Lok Sabha election 2024 from UP, was widely hailed as the youngest member of the Lok Sabha. However, our deep dive into data showed that Prakash Chandra from Bihar was younger by a day when he became a member of the eighth Lok Sabha in 1984 – an unbroken Parliament record we retrieved from oblivion.

And now there are a couple of important notes to share with you ...

First, a significant change in our policy. We have stopped considering record attempts by minors (children below 18 years) for review. However, records related to official sports events (associated with only officially recognized national or international bodies such as the BCCI, IOA, ICC, and FIFA) and medical science where the minor is not an active participant (heaviest baby, lightest baby, and similar records) may be considered.

Second, we have introduced a new icon to mark all public domain records added or significantly updated 2025 edition onwards: .

Finally, please remember that while pursuing records, record applicants have to be watchful of risks and damage to both their life and those of others while attempting records. A case in point is the hoarding put up by Ego Media at Ghatkopar, Mumbai, which held the record as the largest hoarding in India. When it collapsed and took 17 lives, and Ego Media was accused of flouting the law, we wrote to them for a satisfactory explanation. In the absence of a response, we cancelled the record.

We have a zero-tolerance policy towards non-compliance with the law and issues that threaten or impact public health and safety. The onus is on the applicants to get a full understanding of all the compliance required for a particular attempt and fulfil the same.

The *LBR* Team looks forward to your continued support and participation, and wishes you all a joyous year full of aspirations and achievements.

Anirban Sarkar
Managing Editor, *Limca Book of Records*
(Reference Division, Hachette India)

CONTENTS

40

THE HUMAN STORY

14 SKILLS
14 ENDEAVOUR
14 YOGA
17 PHYSICAL FEATS
24 LARGEST
28 SMALLEST
30 COMMUNITY DEVELOPMENT
34 CURRENCY, COINS, AND STAMPS
39 MEMORY
40 ENDURANCE
41 TALLEST
41 MOST
45 FASTEST
45 LONGEST
45 COLLECTIONS

STRUCTURES

60 EARLY TIMES
61 MEDIEVAL AND MODERN ERAS
64 FORTS AND PALACES
68 RELIGIOUS STRUCTURES
73 STATUES AND IDOLS
75 BRIDGES
78 DAMS
79 LIGHTHOUSES
79 AMUSEMENT ZONES
79 MECHANICAL AND GENERAL STRUCTURES
81 MODERN STRUCTURES
81 SPECIALIZED STRUCTURES

AGRICULTURE

86 GENERAL
86 HISTORY
89 AWARDS AND HONOURS
89 FARMLANDS AND PRINCIPAL CROPS
92 HORTICULTURE
93 ANIMAL HUSBANDRY
97 CLONING RECORDS
97 POULTRY AND FISHERIES
98 FERTILIZERS, PESTICIDES, AND MACHINERY

98

71

62

EDUCATION

102 LITERACY
102 SCHOOLS
104 HIGHER EDUCATION
111 ARCHIVES AND LIBRARIES
113 MUSEUMS
118 QUIZZES

PERFORMING ARTS

122 DANCE
125 MUSIC
132 THEATRE

VISUAL ARTS

138 CINEMA
152 PHOTOGRAPHY
155 PAINTING AND CRAFT

LITERATURE

162 BOOKS
165 PUBLISHING AND BOOK SELLING
171 AWARDS AND HONOURS

178

MEDIA AND COMMUNICATIONS

176 PRINT
180 RADIO
184 TELEVISION
187 POST AND PHILATELY
192 TELECOM
194 INTERNET, SOCIAL MEDIA, AND APPS

CONTENTS

GOVERNMENT

198 HISTORICAL PERSPECTIVE
199 PARTIES AND ELECTIONS
208 PRESIDENTS AND VICE PRESIDENTS
208 UNION GOVERNMENT
209 PRIME MINISTERS
210 THE STATES
211 GOVERNANCE
212 AADHAAR
212 LAW AND ORDER
213 LEGAL MATTERS
215 THE CENSUS
215 PARLIAMENT RECORDS

205

214

DEFENCE AND MILITARY AFFAIRS

220 ARMY
230 NAVY
237 AIR FORCE
242 COAST GUARD

240

227

247

SCIENCE AND TECHNOLOGY

246 FORMAL SCIENCES
247 PHYSICAL SCIENCES
256 OCEAN STUDIES
256 LIFE SCIENCES
258 INTERDISCIPLINARY AND APPLIED SCIENCES
260 METALLURGY
261 SPACE

248

235

MEDICAL SCIENCES

266 GENERAL
266 FERTILITY, CHILDBIRTH, AND BABIES
267 MEDICAL INSTITUTIONS AND LABORATORIES
270 PUBLICATIONS AND INNOVATION
270 DOCTORS
271 MEDICINE AND SURGERY
273 MEDICAL MARVELS
274 TRANSPLANTS

275

273

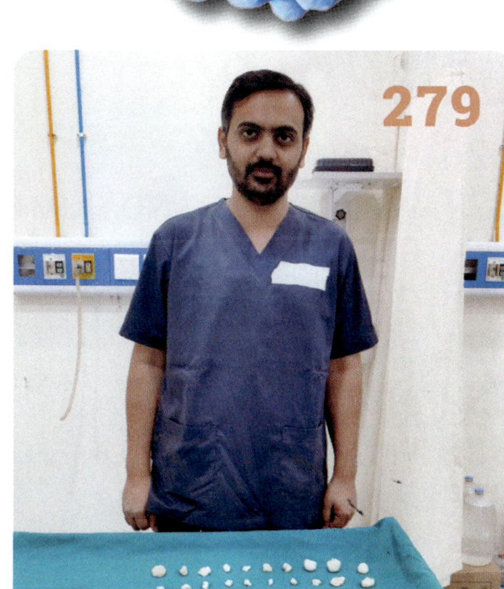

279

THE NATURAL WORLD

282 PHYSICAL FEATURES
285 FOSSILS
285 MAMMALS
287 BIRDS
288 BUTTERFLIES
289 AMPHIBIANS
289 REPTILES
294 TORTOISES AND TURTLES
294 FISH AND MOLLUSCS
295 PLANTS
296 CONSERVING NATURE AND WILDLIFE
298 GARDENING
300 ENVIRONMENT AND SUSTAINABILITY
305 CLEANEST IN INDIA!

296

294

291

287

CONTENTS

TRANSPORT

308 AIR
312 RAIL AND METRO
317 ROAD
322 WATER

BUSINESS AND ECONOMY

326 PLANNING
327 WORKFORCE AND HUMAN RESOURCES
328 COINS AND CURRENCY
329 BANKING
332 INSURANCE
333 FINANCIAL INSTRUMENTS
333 POWER AND ENERGY
336 FINANCIAL INSTITUTIONS
339 MINING
340 INDUSTRIES AND COMPANIES
343 RETAIL
344 ADVERTISING

ADVENTURE

348 AERO SPORTS
352 ROAD EXPEDITIONS
361 WATER SPORTS
367 MARATHONS
369 MOUNTAIN ADVENTURES
370 TREKKING
371 THE POLES

361

SPORTS

374 GENERAL
378 ARCHERY
381 ATHLETICS
385 BADMINTON
389 BASKETBALL
390 BOXING
392 CHESS
397 CRICKET
404 CUE SPORTS
406 FOOTBALL
413 GOLF
417 GYMNASTICS
418 HOCKEY
421 KABADDI
422 LUGE
423 MARTIAL ARTS
423 POWERLIFTING
424 SHOOTING
428 SQUASH
429 SWIMMING
431 TABLE TENNIS
434 TENNIS
438 WEIGHTLIFTING
439 WRESTLING

390

409

393

417

India @ Paris Olympics 2024 444

India @ Paris Paralympics 2024 448

449

452 INDEX
476 IMAGE COPYRIGHT INFORMATION
485 RULES AND GUIDELINES

Images are representative

Search...

SKILLS

Most juggling patterns on a balance board

Jaykishan Vimalbhai Hingu from Jetpur, Gujarat, performed 28 juggling patterns using 3 balls while balancing on a balance board on 5 May 2021 at Radha Park, Jetpur. The patterns were cascade, columns, fake columns, the machine, crossed columns, one going over the top, half shower, false shower, behind the back, box, clawed catches, Mangham's mangle, 'M', infinity, reverse infinity, Georgian shuffle, real tennis, tennis, yo-yo, oy-oy, outside throws, Statue of Liberty, shower, Ripley's rainbow, wiper, 'W', the weave, and Mill's mess.

Jaykishan Vimalbhai Hingu

Fastest to form the English alphabet on Rubik's cubes while blindfolded

Affan Kutty from Thane, Mumbai, formed all 26 letters of the English alphabet from A to Z, while blindfolded, on 7 x 7 Rubik's cubes on 30 May 2020 at Noori Garden, Mumbai, in 5 mins 6 secs 55 microseconds. Each letter was formed on all six sides of the Rubik's cube.

Most football rolls from eye to eye

Satish Kasi from Bengaluru, Karnataka, performed 164 football rolls from eye to eye in 1 min. from 9:36 a.m. to 9:37 a.m. on 16 May 2019 at Sree Kanteerava Stadium, Bengaluru. He shifts the football from eye to eye while balancing the ball on the forehead.

Satish Kasi

Most tie knots tied – 1 min

Dr Deepak M. Sharma from Ahmedabad, Gujarat, knotted a tie around the neck seven times in 1 min. on 12 February 2020 at a stage performance in Surat.

Longest duration of non-stop hitting of a dangling cricket ball

Dr Arjun Anand Shirsath from Ahmednagar, Maharashtra, knocked a dangling cricket ball with a 1.83 m (6 ft) cord length non-stop 10,332 times with a bat for 4 hrs 34 mins 35 secs on 24 April 2020.

Longest basketball shot

Manisha Satyajit Dange from Thane made a 21.4 m long basketball shot in 2 secs 72 millisecs at 10:03 a.m. on 22 May 2021 at the Central Railway Sport Complex, Parel, Mumbai.

Longest time balancing a hockey stick on the middle finger

Arun Kumar Kannan Murthy from Kanchipuram, Tamil Nadu, balanced an on-field hockey stick on his middle finger for 3 hrs 11 mins 50 secs on 18 August 2019 at Neat Trust, Vellore.

Longest time balancing a hockey stick on the little finger

Gagandeep Singh from Fatehgarh Sahib, Punjab, balanced a hockey stick weighing 660 g on his little finger for 1 hr from 4:00 p.m. to 5:00 p.m. on 10 May 2019 in Sirhind, Fatehgarh.

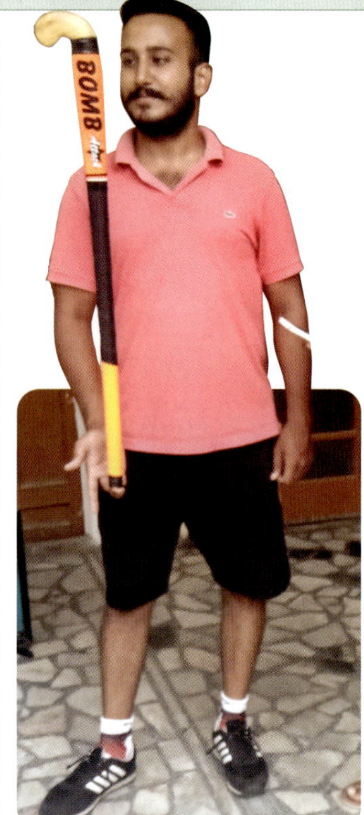

Gagandeep Singh

ENDEAVOUR

Marathon Knitting – solo

Sazida Khan from New Delhi knitted woollen caps for a duration of 27 hrs 28 mins. She started knitting with a number 4 needle at 7:00 a.m. on 26 September 2023 and finished at 10:28 a.m. on 27 September 2023 at Tejas Camp Race Course, New Delhi. She knitted 16 woollen caps as part of the event.

YOGA

Longest *setubandhasana*

Prof. Dr S. Ramesh Babu from Bengaluru, Karnataka, performed setubandhasana (bridge pose) for 24 mins from 8:00 a.m. to 8:24 a.m. on 9 July 2019 at Vidyanjali Academy for Learning, Bengaluru.

Longest *ashtavakrasana*

Adesh Motiramji Karnase from Gurugram, Haryana, performed ashtavakrasana (eight-angle pose) for 1 min. 4 secs on 10 June 2020 in Morshi, Maharashtra.

Longest *vishvamitrasana*

Nitin Mohanrao Prajapat from Gurugram, performed vishvamitrasana

Mangal Raj

for 1 min. 13 secs on 10 June 2020 in Morshi, Maharashtra.

Longest *padma mayurasana*
Mangal Raj from Sitamarhi, Bihar, performed padma mayurasana (lotus in peacock pose) for 4 mins 14 secs starting at 5:49 p.m. to 5:54 p.m. on 19 November 2021 at Raj Classic Park, Versova, Mumbai.

Longest *purvattanasana*
Sandeep Krishna Murthy Karupakala and Aruna K.S. from Chintamani, Karnataka, held purvattanasana (upward plank pose) for 2 mins 10 secs on 10 April 2021 at Lalitha Nivas, Chintamani.

Longest *mandukasana*
Swapan Kumar Sur from Faridabad, Haryana, performed mandukasana (frog pose) for 47 mins 11 secs starting at 8:33 p.m. to 9:21 p.m. on 14 April 2021 in Chhinamore, Hooghly, West Bengal.

Longest *parshva poorna dhanurasana*
Amrutha Anand from Chidambaram, Tamil Nadu, performed parshva poorna dhanurasana (full side bow pose) for 15 mins 10 secs, starting at 2:00 p.m., on 2 March 2019 at the Great Wall of China, Beijing.

Longest *mayurasana* – with one hand
Mangal Raj from Sitamarhi, Bihar, performed mayurasana (peacock pose) with one hand for 56 secs on 4 February 2022 at Raj Classic Park, Versova, Mumbai.

Longest *Hanumanasana*
Dr Narendra Kumar Sharma from Jaipur, Rajasthan, performed Hanumanasana (monkey pose) for 23 mins 36 secs on 22 June 2020 in Malviya Nagar, Jaipur.

Longest *ekapada shirshasana*
Virendra Vikram Singh (b. 2 December 1954) from Balrampur, Uttar Pradesh, performed ekapada shirshasana (foot behind the head pose) for 10 mins from 10:00 a.m. to 10:10 a.m. on 20 February 2019 at M.L.K. PG College, Balrampur.

Longest *Bakasana*
Virendera Vikram Singh from Balrampur, Uttar Pradesh, performed the Bakasana (crane pose) for 5 mins from 6: 10 p.m. to 6:15 p.m. on 16 May 2022 at M.P.P. Inter College, Balrampur.

Amrutha Anand

Longest *Janu Shirshasana*
Virendera Vikram Singh from Balrampur, performed the janu shirshasana (head to knee pose) for 1 hour from 9:00 a.m. to 10:00 a.m. on 24 February 2021 at Late Ravindra Singh Memorial, Balrampur.

Longest *Paschimottanasana*
Virendera Vikram Singh from Balrampur, performed the paschimottanasana (seated forward bend pose) for 40 mins from 9:00 a.m. to 9:40 a.m. on 19 May 2020 at Bagh Palace, Balrampur.

Longest *supta pandangushthasana*
Virendera Vikram Singh from Balrampur, performed the supta pandangushthasana (reclining hand to big toe pose) for 20 mins from 9:50 a.m. to 10:10 a.m. on 19 May 2020 at Late Maharaj Dharmendra Prasad Singh Memorial, Balrampur.

Arooj. K

Longest *padahastasana*
Arooj. K from Thiruvananthapuram, Kerala, performed the padahastasana (forward bending pose) for 3 min 24 sec from 8:26 a.m. to 8:29 a.m. on 24 April 2024 at his home.

Longest *karnapidasana*
Adarsh Pandey from Rewa, Madhya Pradesh, performed the karnapidasana (lifting legs over head and bending knees

Yoga at the highest altitude

Kavita Singh from New Delhi has performed yogasanas at Umling La Ladakh on 20 April 2024 at an altitude of 19,024 ft for 1 hour 9 mins 34 secs. She performed these asanas along with Surya namaskar at an extremely cold temperature at –17 degree Celsius with 40 per cent less oxygen than average.

towards ears) for 30 mins on 14 May 2024 at Dekhaha, Rewa, Madhya Pradesh.

Longest *niralamba ushtrasana*
Dr Narendra Kumar Sharma from Jaipur, Rajasthan, performed niralamba ushtrasana (unsupported camel pose) for 10 mins 38 secs on 30 May 2021 in Bharatpur, Rajasthan.

Dr Narendra Kumar Sharma

Longest *padma vrischikasana*
Shyam Shamraoji Gawande from Wardha, Maharashtra performed the padma vrischikasana (scorpion in lotus pose) for 2 mins and 8 sec on 18 February 2024 at his home in Wardha.

Longest *sirsasana*
Puran Singh from Mathura, performed the sirsasana (headstand) for 4 hours from 6:15 a.m. to 10:15 a.m. on 29 October 2023 at the Chandralekha Stadium.

PHYSICAL FEATS

Most alternative squats – 1 min.
Gaurav Singh Bhatti of Mandi Dabwali, Haryana, attempted 122 alternative squats in 1 min. at Big Gym on 7 July 2018.

Gaurav Singh Bhatti

Most squats – 1 min.– women
Priyanka Prasher from Gurugram, Haryana, performed 97 squats in 1 min. from 12:09 p.m. to 12:10 p.m. on 10 May 2019 at H2O Fitness Gym, Gurugram.

Most squats – 1 min.
Apoorv Ashok Mathur performed 96 squats in 1 min. at H2O Fitness Gym, Gurugram, Haryana, on 28 April 2018.

Most sit-ups – 1 min.
Sandeep Arya of Kolkata, attempted 67 sit-ups in 1 min. at Tivoli Court, Kolkata, at 9.30 a.m. on 28 April 2018.

Most abdominal sit-ups – 1 min.– women
Shreya Bhardwaj performed 85 abdominal sit-ups in 1 min. from 12:05 p.m. to 12:06 p.m. on 23 May 2019 at H2O Fitness Gym, Gurugram.

Most burpees – 1 min.– women
Ankita Nagpal from Gurugram, Haryana, performed 48 burpees in 1 min. from 12:05 p.m. to 12:06 p.m. on 23 May 2019 at H2O Fitness Gym, Gurugram.

Most jumping jacks – 1 min. – women
Richa Maheshwari from New Delhi performed 115 jumping jacks in 1 min. from 12:07 p.m. to 12:08 p.m. on 25 May 2019 at H2O Fitness Gym, Gurugram.

Most jumping jacks – 1 hr
Jasjeet Singh from New Delhi performed 4,479 jumping jacks in 1 hr from 9:12 a.m. to 10:12 a.m. on

Jasjeet Singh

17 February 2021 at his residence in Vikaspuri, Delhi.

Most jumping jacks – 1 min.
Venkata Sairam Reddy Pulusu from Hyderabad, Telangana, performed 127 jumping jacks in 1 min. from 12:05 p.m. to 12:06 p.m. on 23 May 2019 at H2O Fitness Gym, Gurugram.

Most lunges – 1 hr
Kapil Arora from Mumbai, Maharashtra, performed 948 lunges in 1 hr between 8:16 a.m. and 9:16 a.m. on 28 June 2020 at his residence.

Most abdominal crunches – 1 min.
Mohit Bhardwaj from Gurugram, Haryana, performed 108 abdominal crunches in 1 min. from 12:06 p.m. to 12:07 p.m. on 23 May 2019 at H2O Fitness Gym, Gurugram.

Longest plank
Abhishek Sihag from Sikar, Rajasthan, performed the longest plank for 8 hrs 5 mins from 6:51 a.m. to 2:56 p.m. at the Railway Community Centre, Sikar, on 1 January 2019.

Most parallel dips – 1 min.
Ashish Lohia from Gurugram, Haryana, performed 75 parallel dips in 1 min. from 12:05 p.m. to 12:06 p.m. on 28 May 2019 at H2O Fitness Gym in Gurugram.

Most pistol squats – alternating legs – 1 min.
Shivam from Lucknow, Uttar Pradesh, performed 45 pistol squats in 1 min. using legs alternately on 4 September 2019 at his residence.

Highest unassisted martial arts kick
Chinmay Sharma, from New Delhi, has performed the highest unassisted martial arts 360 degree kick on 4 August 2024. The kick reached a height of 6 ft 9 inches setting a new benchmark.

Most bicycle crunches – 1 min. (woman)
Sunita Chhabra from Jaipur, Rajasthan, performed 88 bicycle crunches in 1 min. from 7:32 p.m. to 7:33 p.m. on 18 February 2020 at the office of JVP Media Group, Jaipur.

Most jump squats – 1 min.
Himanshu Jadon from Gurugram, Haryana, performed 82 jump squats in 1 min. from 12:05 p.m. to 12:06 p.m. on 28 May 2019 at H2O Fitness Gym, Gurugram.

Most reverse dips – 1 min.
Ankush Gurjar from Gurugram,

Most of push-ups

Arya Rishabh Rameshchandra

Most two-finger push-ups – both arms – 1 min.
Arya Rishabh Rameshchandra from Ahmedabad, Gujarat, performed 65 two-finger push-ups (index and middle finger) in 1 min. on 19 May 2019 at I-Can Gym, Ahmedabad.

Most side-jump push-ups – 1 min.
Anand S. from Chennai, Tamil Nadu, performed 42 side-jump push-ups in 1 min. from 1:00 p.m. to 1:01 p.m. on 20 October 2021 in Potheri, Chennai.

Most superman push-ups – 1 min.
Kuwar Amritbir Singh from Gurdaspur, Punjab, performed 52 superman push-ups in 1 min. from 12:05 p.m. to 12:06 p.m. on 5 May 2021 in Umarwala, Punjab.

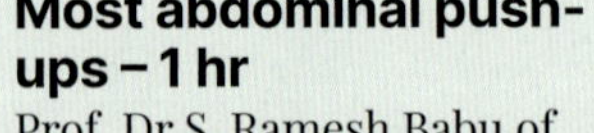

Most abdominal push-ups – 1 hr
Prof. Dr S. Ramesh Babu of Bengaluru, Karnataka, did 1,700 non-stop abdominal push-ups in 1 hr, at Prof. Satish Dhawan Park, from 9:00 a.m. on 14 April 2018.

Shaikh Rejaul Haque

Most clap push-ups – 1 min.
Jatin Goel from Gurugram, Haryana, performed 85 clap push-ups in 1 min. from 12:05 p.m. to 12:06 p.m. on 10 May 2019 at H2O Fitness Gym, Gurugram.

Most fingertip push-ups – one arm – 1 min.
Shaikh Rejaul Haque of Ulhasnagar, Maharashtra, performed 45 one-arm fingertip push-ups in 1 min. on 20 May 2015.

Mandeep Singh Karir

Most tandem push-ups – 1 min.
Mandeep Singh Karir and Baldeep Singh of Singhbhum, Jharkhand, performed 28 tandem push-ups in 1 min. at Paul Fitness and Yoga Hub on 6 July 2022.

Haryana, performed 137 reverse dips in 1 min. from 12:06 p.m. to 12:07 p.m. on 4 May 2019 at H2O Fitness Gym, Gurugram.

Most crunches*
Nitin Arora of Ghaziabad, Uttar Pradesh, performed 1,000 abdomen crunches in 8 mins from 8:45 a.m. to 8:53 a.m. on 6 May 2018.

Most full-contact kicks on a kickpad – alternate legs – 1 hr
Naman Bhardwaj from Ghaziabad, Uttar Pradesh, performed 6,170 full-contact kicks in 1 hr from 10:20 a.m. to 11:20 a.m. on 26 May 2021 at Vasundhara Taekwondo Academy, Ghaziabad, Uttar Pradesh.

Naman Bhardwaj

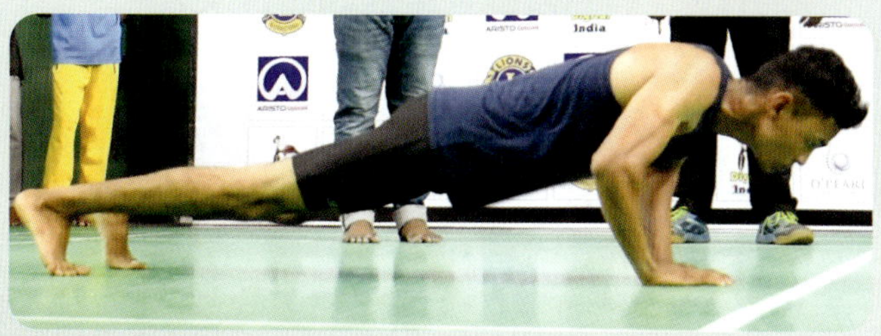

V. Kaliraj

Most diamond push-ups – 1 min.
V. Kaliraj from Virudhunagar, Tamil Nadu, did 112 diamond push-ups in 1 min. on 26 May 2019 at D'Pearl Sport Academy, Ramapuran, Chennai.

Most half-knuckle push-ups – 1 min.
Ashif Khan from Gurugram, Haryana, did 145 half-knuckle push-ups in 1 min. from 12:05 p.m. to 12:06 p.m. on 23 May 2019 at H2O Fitness gym, Gurugram.

Most half push-ups – 1 hr
Umesh Sopan Vyavahare of Adhegaon, Tal Madha, Solapur District, Maharashtra, performed 2,993 half push-ups in 1 hr from 5:30 to 6:30 p.m. on 13 July 2017.

Most decline push-ups – 1 min. – women
Shaleni Banthia from New Delhi performed 55 decline push-ups in 1 min. on 24 May 2023 from 5:00 p.m. to 5:01 p.m. at Feet Fit Gym, New Delhi.

Shaleni Banthia

Most incline push-ups – 1 min.
Jasjeet Singh from New Delhi performed 90 incline push-ups in 1 min. on 25 August 2023 from 7:39 a.m. to 7:40 a.m. at MMA Warriors Fight Club and Fitness Hub, Delhi.

Most two-thumb push-ups – 1 min.
Harpreet Singh of Sultanpuri Lodhi, Kapurthala District, Punjab, performed 69 two-thumb push-ups in 1 min. at Lyallpur Khalsa College for Women on 17 April 2017.

Most push-ups – 1 min. – women
Sunita Chhabra of Jaipur, Rajasthan, performed 34 full push-ups at Manav Seva Trust's head office in 1 min. on 25 March 2018.

Most contortion push-ups – 1 min.
Rajendra Bishnoi from Bikaner, Rajasthan, performed 132 unique contortion push-ups in 1 min. on 17 March 2019 at Swargiya Shri Balasaheb Thackeray Maidan, Mumbai.

* This record has been revised after updates in the rules regarding this category.

The Skipping Guys

Aman Baburam Verma

Aman Baburam Verma of Kalyan West, Maharashtra, created three skipping records at Birla College in Kalyan, Maharashtra:

- 320 alternative skips in 1 minute on 5 May 2018
- 163 doubles in 1 minute on 22 June 2018
- 70 buttock jumps in 30 sec on 26 June 2018

One-leg skipping – most in 1 min.

Dr Raghuvir Gangjibhai Dayatar of Keshod, Junagadh District, Gujarat, skipped 248 times in 1 min. on his right leg at his physiotherapy clinic on 18 March 2017.

Two-leg skipping – most in 1 min.

Amit Pal of Janakpuri, New Delhi, skipped 256 times in 1 min. on 2 March 2018.

Dishant Rawal

Dishant Rawal of Charkhi Dardi, Haryana, performed 5 skipping records of 1 min. each:

- 140 reverse cross skips on 2 legs
- 137 reverse cross skips on 1 leg
- 94 cross skips with joggers on 2 legs
- 102 reverse cross skips with joggers on 2 legs
- 149 reverse skips on 1 leg

LARGEST

Largest raj kachori

A team of five chefs, Vaibhav Nehra, Rudra Pratap Singh, Gireesh Kumar, Bipin Rawat, and Rahul, from Bird Airport Hotel Pvt. Ltd, Roseate House, Hospitality District, Aerocity, New Delhi, made the largest raj kachori (an Indian chaat dish), measuring 76.2 cm (2.5 ft) in diameter. The raj kachori was appropriately filled with stuffing, curd, and chutneys, and was made in 40 minutes on 22 May 2024 at Roseate House, Aerocity, New Delhi.

Largest decorative display using currency*

Sri Sathya Ganapathi Shirdi Sai Trust (R) created the largest decorative display, covering an area of 13,000 sq ft using Indian currency on 18 September 2023 for Ganesh Chaturthi. The impressive display was created over a period of 18 days by 150 artisans under CCTV surveillance. The value of coins and notes used for making the display was ₹7,00,000, and included ₹1, ₹10, and ₹20 coins, and ₹20, ₹50, ₹100, ₹200, and ₹500 notes.

*This is a one-time category. Further and future applications for this record will not be accepted.

Largest flag – recycled material

Coca-Cola India created the largest flag from recycled material, which was displayed during the ICC Men's Cricket World Cup 2023. They created the Indian national flag from approximately 11,000 PET bottles. It measured 35 metres (114.83 ft) in length and 20 metres (65.62 ft) in width, and weighed 115.55 kg.

SMALLEST

Smallest rugby stadium model

Shaminder Singh from Coventry, UK, constructed a model of the Ricoh Arena rugby stadium, 122 cm (48 in.) long, 76 cm (29.9 in.) wide, and 41 cm (16.1 in.) high, with 45,000 toothpicks. He worked on the model for a total of 900 hours over six months between 1 September 2017 and 2 March 2018.

Smallest rugby stadium

Smallest scissors

Mattewada Ajay Kumar of Warangal, Telangana, created a miniature working pair of gold scissors in 3 hrs in 2015. It is 11 mm (0.43 in.) long and weighs 0.18 mg.

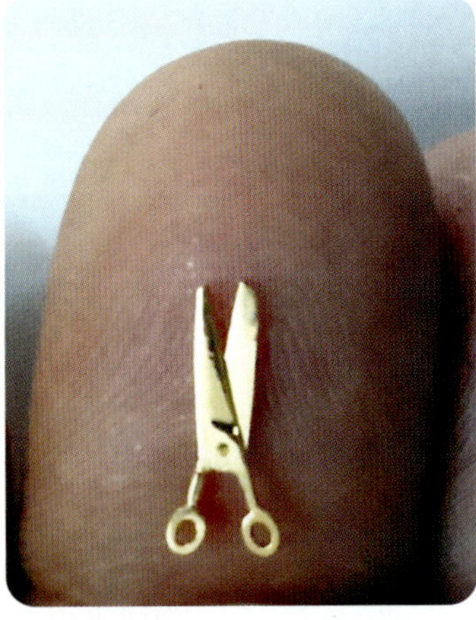

Smallest scissors

Smallest microwave oven

Salvendar Ghansheed Baba from Vijayawada, Andhra Pradesh, made the smallest microwave oven, 80 mm (3.15 in.) long, 35 mm (1.38 in.) wide, and 40 mm (1.57 in.) high in 15 days, from 11 to 25 December 2018. He used plywood cardboard, green and orange LED lights of 3 volts, 1,000-ohm resistor, small wires, Nichrome wire, aluminium foil, Fevicol glue, a small switch, a design sticker, a 3.7-volt phone battery and a connecting pin to make the oven.

Smallest gold violin

Mattewada Ajay Kumar of Warangal, Telangana, created a 20 mm (0.78 in) long miniature gold violin, weighing 0.74 mg, in 12 hrs in 2009.

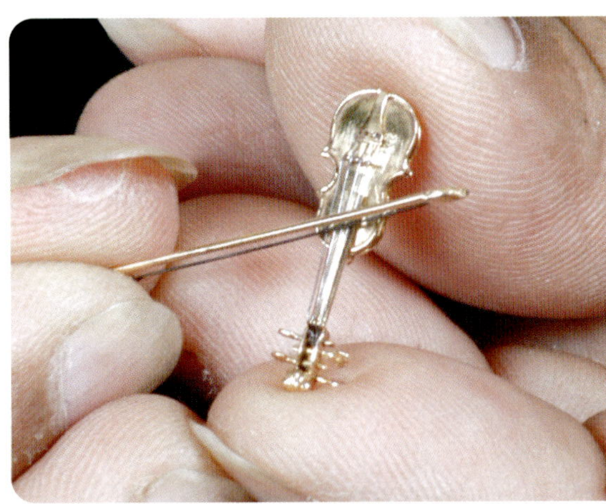

Smallest gold violin

Smallest spinning wheel

Jayant Natthuji Tandulkar from Nagpur, Maharashtra, designed the smallest spinning wheel (charkha) to spin yarn from cotton measuring 2.94 mm (0.12 in.) in length, 2.40 mm (0.09 in.) in width, 2.74 mm (0.11 in.) in height, and weighing 0.03 g on 22 April 2023. It took him 8 hrs to make it. He used materials

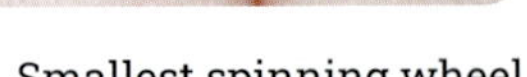

Smallest spinning wheel

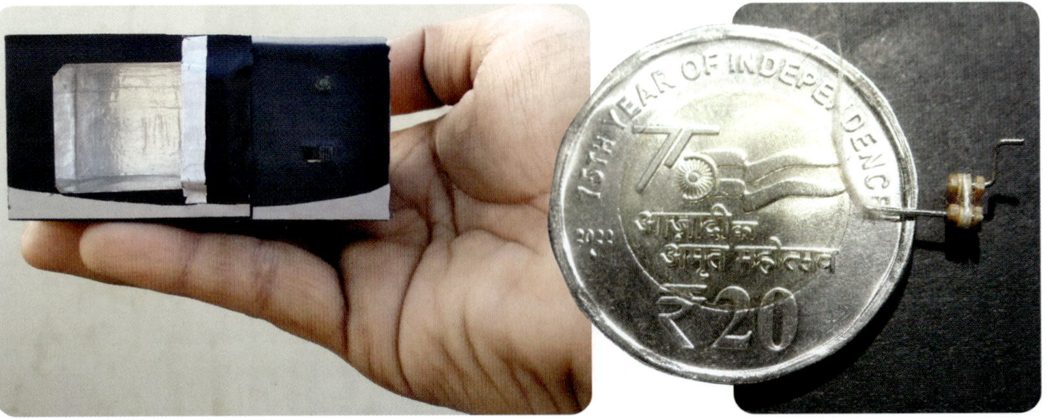

Smallest microwave oven

such as steel wire, wooden sticks, and cotton thread to make it. The charkha was measured using a vernier caliper and a digital scale.

Smallest Wimbledon Centre Court model

Shaminder Singh of Coventry, UK, made a replica of the Wimbledon Centre Court using 12,000 toothpicks over 40 hours each week in 03 months from 2 July to 25 September 2017. The structure is 36 in (91.44 cm) long, 28 in (71.12 cm) wide, and 12 in (30.48 cm) in height.

Smallest Wimbledon Centre Court model

Smallest iron

Pawan Sharma of Surat, Gujarat, made the smallest electric iron of 17 mm (0.67 in.) height, 9 mm (0.35 in.) width, and 2.5 mm (0.10 in.) thickness, which he completed in seven days spending 1 hr every day until 17 October 2012. The iron is made using aluminium, a plastic handle, asbestos, tungsten wire, a steel stand, and a mobile charger with a 12V DC connection.

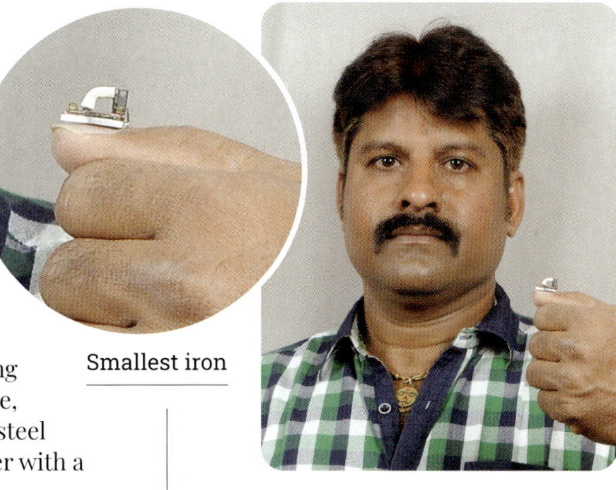

Smallest iron

Smallest model of Belur Math

Sudhakar Raghunath Shinde from Pune, Maharashtra, carved the smallest model of the Belur Math, out of wood, measuring 218.5 cm (86 in.) in length, 102 cm (40 in.) in width, and 98 cm (38.6 in.) in height. The design included details such as carving of elephants, balconies, blooming lotuses, domes, pillars, Lord Ganesha, and Lord Hanuman. He has never visited the Belur Math and made this model using images downloaded from the internet.

Smallest model of Belur Math

COMMUNITY DEVELOPMENT

Largest shoe donation

INC.5 Shoes Pvt. Ltd in Mumbai, Maharashtra, distributed 5,000 pairs of shoes to women, girls, and the underprivileged in Mumbai and Navi Mumbai between 10:00 a.m. and 5:00 p.m. on 15 March 2019.

Most food donated in a single day – multiple venues

The ISKCON Temple in Dwarka, Delhi, under the chairmanship of Pradyumna Priya Das, in coordination with the district magistrate of south-west Delhi, Rahul Singh, cooked and distributed food to migrant labourers and other needy persons during the lockdown. Beginning in the third week of March 2020 with 5,000 meals a day, they increased the meals to 10,000 and subsequently 100,000 a day.

Most food packets distributed

Swami Sunil Das Prabhakaran, chairman of the Muthalamada Charitable Trust in Palakkad, Kerala, has been distributing 1,000 food packets every day to the poor since 1992. He distributed nine million food packets and seventy million litres of drinking water to the poor up to September 2018.

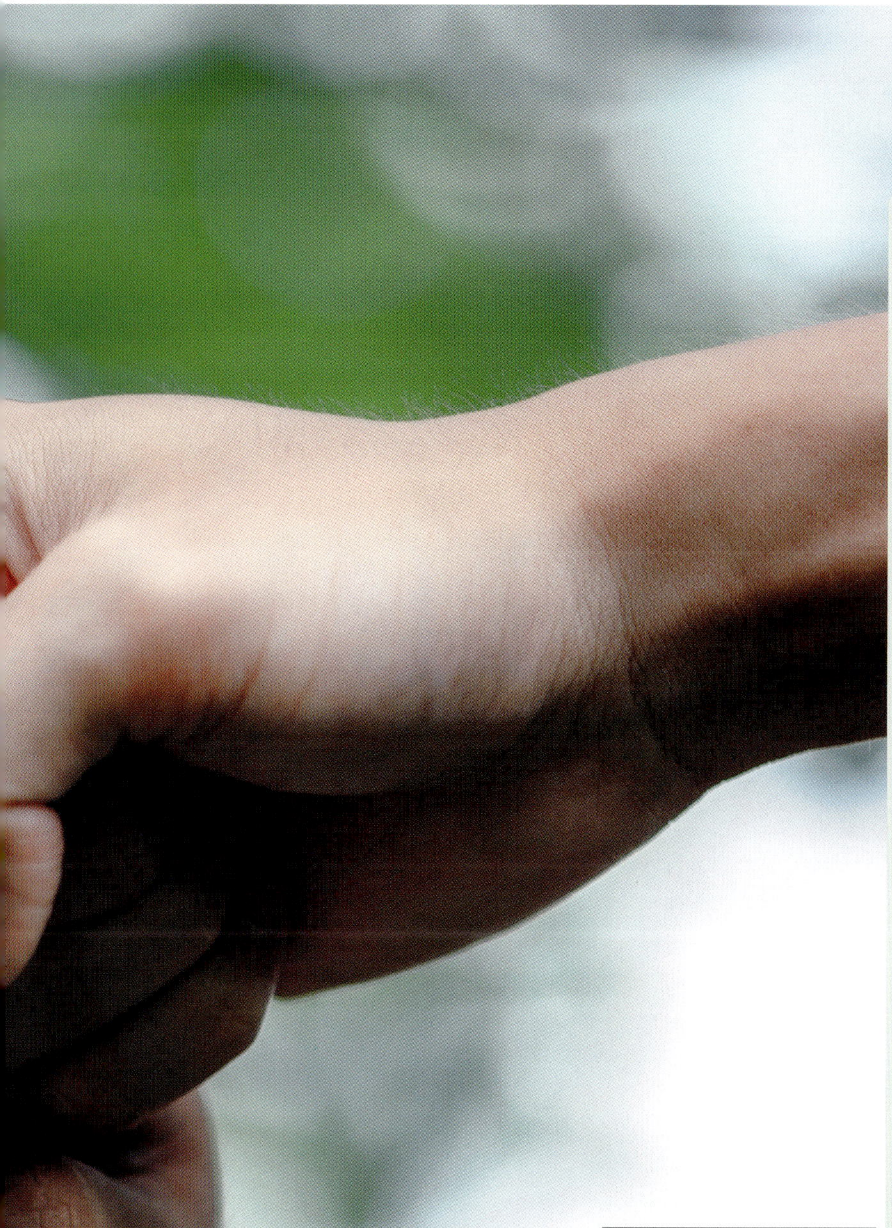

Most toys donated – single day

Children's University, Gandhinagar, Gujarat, has donated 5,100 toys on a single day, 12 May 2022, on its campus between 9:00 a.m. and 11:00 a.m. The toys were distributed to eight organizations and schools, as well as NGOs working with children. The donation drive was organized by the University's Departments of Toy Innovations and Social Work, and around 30 people participated in the drive.

Most benches donated – 1 year

The Ghanshyamdas Saraf Trust, a charitable trust in Mumbai, Maharashtra, donated 127 three-seater RCC pink benches to temples and police stations in and around Mumbai, between July 2021 and July 2022. A team of eight people were employed in making the benches and it took a week to make 20 benches.

Most ramps constructed – single day

J.K. Cement Ltd, Uttar Pradesh, set a record by constructing 249 cemented ramps for the specially abled on 5 August 2021 at different government schools around Jaipur, Rajasthan. The ramps were constructed for government schools of Jotwara City and Rural, and Sanganer City and Rural.

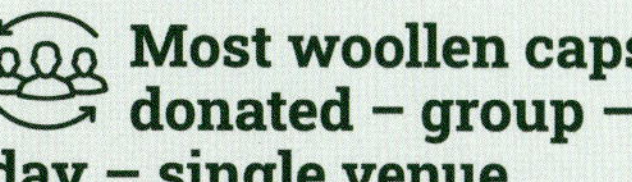

Most woollen caps donated – group – single day – single venue

The Air Force Wives Welfare Association (AFWWA) from New Delhi donated 9,071 woollen caps to Safe Approach, a shelter home in Delhi on 28 October 2022 between 9:55 a.m. and 12:51 p.m. Nineteen people participated in the event as organizers. Each cap measured 22.86–26.67 cm (9–10.5 in.) in length and 43.18–50.8 cm (17–20 in.) in circumference.

Woollen caps for everyone!

Most craft pieces made out of waste – solo – single day

Ratnamala Rao from Jabalpur, Madhya Pradesh, made the most number of handmade craft pieces from waste in a day. She made 53 craft pieces in total and her craftworks included a variety of items, including table, chair, handbag, lamp, bracelet, necklace, cake, and samosa.

CURRENCY, COINS, AND STAMPS

Largest collection of currency notes with birth dates of presidents and prime ministers of India

Ajay Mehta of Bhopal, Madhya Pradesh, has the largest collection of Indian currency notes, with serial numbers matching the birth dates of all Indian presidents and prime ministers so far. There are 32 currency notes in total in his collection.

Largest collection of specimen currency notes

Ajay Singh Rawat from Dehradun, Uttarakhand, has 165 unduplicated specimen currency notes from 165 internationally recognized countries. The total notes in his collection, including multiple notes from a single country are 313. Some of them are also from unrecognized countries including Bermuda, Cayman Islands, and Transnistria.

Specimen Currency Note

A specimen currency note is a limited-edition sample of a real banknote that is denoted by the word 'SPECIMEN' to make it obvious that it is not legal tender and cannot be used for transactions. These notes are used to familiarize people and authorities with the newly issued currency, to display new banknote designs, or to allow collectors to examine various currency variations.

Specimen currency notes

Largest collection of high denomination currency notes

Putsa Krishna Kameshwar from Amalapuram, Andhra Pradesh, has the largest collection of high denomination currency notes with 306 unduplicated high denomination currency notes of 49 different denominations from 100 to 100 quadrillion from 91 countries. He has been collecting these since 2007. The oldest note in his collection is from Portugal with a face value of 12,800 Réis, printed in 1799, and the latest note is from Iran, 10,000 rials, released in 2022.

Largest collection of ₹5 stamps

Putsa Krishna Kameshwar from Amalapuram, Andhra Pradesh, has the largest collection of ₹5 stamps with 360 unduplicated stamps released by India Post. His collection includes famous personalities of India, places, animals, birds, trees, forts, festivals, institutions, zodiac signs, movie artists, Indian cuisine, Indian fashion and so on. He has collected these over a period of 25 years.

Largest collection of 7-digit currency notes

Sagi Satya Narayana Raju from Visakhapatnam, Andhra Pradesh, has the largest collection of unduplicated 7-digit Indian currency notes. There are 116 notes in total in his collection.

Largest collection of COVID-19 themed coins

Paravathina Venkata Narayana from Yedidha, Andhra Pradesh, has the largest collection of unduplicated COVID-19 themed international currency coins which consists of 40 coins from 23 countries and 2 British Overseas Territories. These coins were released between 2020 and 2023.

Largest collection of COVID-19 themed coins

Largest collection of postcards – matchbox theme

Samirkumar Hasmukhbhai Arya from Valsad, Gujarat, has the largest collection of unduplicated matchbox-themed postcards with 170 unused postcards featuring matchbox label art. He believes that his collection showcases art, history, and diversity, and this collection is his way of preserving heritage.

Largest collection of matchbox themed postcards

Largest collection of star series currency notes

Sagi Satya Narayana Raju from Visakhapatnam, Andhra Pradesh, has the largest collection of unduplicated star series Indian currency notes. There are 5,100 notes in total in his collection.

ANDORRA
ANDORRA
ALGERIA
AFGHANISTAN
BAHRAIN
BANGLADESH
BHUTAN
CEYLON
COMOROS ISLAND
CYPRUS
CROATIA
COOK ISLANDS
Eastern Caribbean
EGYPT
FIJI
GUYANA
GUINEA BISSAU
GHANA
HUNGARY
ISLE OF MAN
ITALY
INDONESIA
JAMAICA
KOREA NORTH
MACEDONIA
MALDIVES
MALI
MYANMAR
MOROCCO
NEPAL
NICARAGUA
NAMIBIA
OMAN
PORTUGAL
PANAMA
PARAGUAY
PARAGUAY
PHILIPPINES
SAMOA
SAN MARINO
SAN MARINO
SOMALIA
SRI LANKA
SEYCHELLES
SYRIA
SPAIN
SWAZILAND
SWAZILAND
SAO TOME AND PRINCIPE
TUNISIA
TONGA
TONGA
TONGA
TONGA
TRINIDAD AND TOBAGO
TURKEY
UGANDA
URUGUAY
UNITED ARAB EMIRATES
WEST AFRICAN STATES

Largest collection of FAO coins

Narasimha Baba Durga Dara from Hyderabad, Telangana, has the largest collection of unduplicated Food and Agriculture Organization (FAO) coins that consists of 152 international currency coins in different denominations from more than 60 countries across the world. He started collecting these coins in 2020, and his collection has been increasing since then.

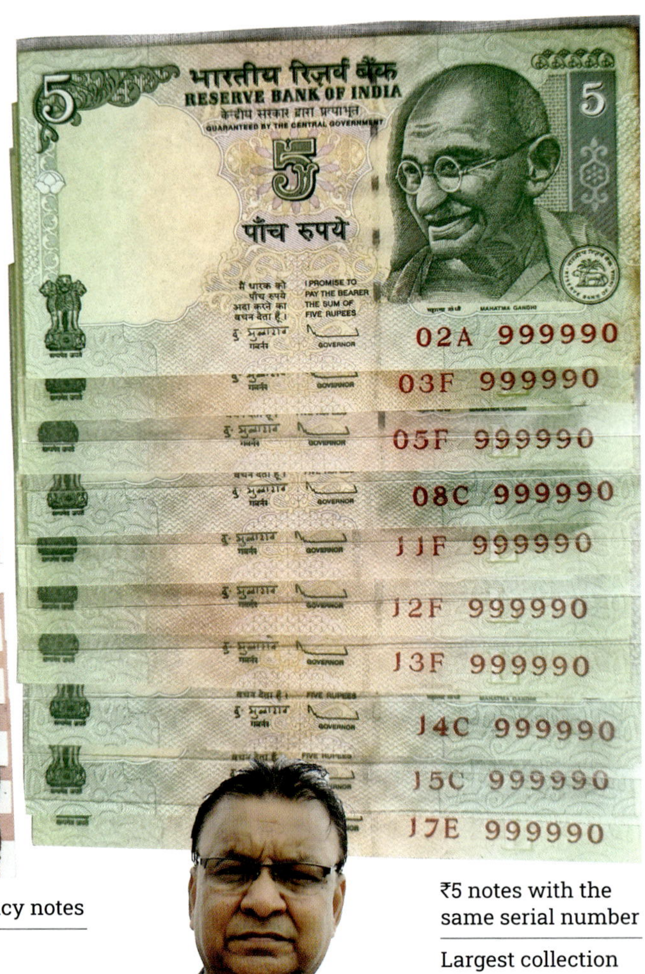

Solid number currency notes

₹5 notes with the same serial number

Largest collection of one-quarter British anna coins

Largest collection of solid number currency notes
Sagi Satya Narayana Raju from Vishakapatnam, Andhra Pradesh, has the largest collection of unduplicated solid number Indian currency notes. There are 1,116 notes in total in his collection.

Largest collection of 5-rupee notes with the same serial number
Raj Kishore Mahanta from Keonjhar, Odisha, has the largest collection of 5-rupee currency notes with the same serial number. He has 108 notes in his collection with the serial number 999990. All notes have the signature of the former RBI governor D. Subbarao.

Largest collection of one-quarter British anna coins
Rajendra Agrawal 'Shashi' from Satna, Madhya Pradesh, has collected 10 varieties of one-quarter British anna coins issued between 1835 and 1942. His collection has 90 coins and includes the East India Company, Queen Victoria, King Edward II, King George V, and King George VI.

Fastest to identify the capitals of all the countries of the world*

Abheer Dinesh Bang from Nanded, Maharashtra identified the capitals of all the countries in the world in 15 minutes on 8 October 2023 at Brilliant Commerce Academy, Nanded.

Abheer Dinesh Bang

* The rules regarding the age of participants have been modified. Please see *Rules and Guidelines*.

Memory Mania

Fastest to identify the flags of all the countries of the world*

Taha Ammar Kheyroolla from Chennai, Tamil Nadu, identified the flags of all the countries (195) of the world in 3 mins 1 millisec. on 16 May 2021 at Club Mahindra Resort, Puducherry.

Fastest to identify all the bones in the human body

Kudrat Kukreja from Shimla, Himachal Pradesh, set a new record by identifying all the bones in the human body in 1 min. 53 secs on 21 August 2020 at Hotel Siddharth, Ram Bazar, Shimla.

Fastest solving of mirror cube while blindfolded*

Mohammed Aiman Koli from Mumbai, Maharashtra, solved a mirror cube (3 x 3), blindfolded, in 1 min. 0.8 sec. on 26 December 2017 at Veermata Jijabai Technological Institute, Mumbai.

Fastest to recall 2,500 digits of π

Vimosh Venugopal from Thrissur, Kerala, recalled 2,500 digits of the value of π correctly in 12 mins 18 secs 90 microseconds on 27 October 2019 at Hotel Joys Palace, Thrissur.

Fastest identification of all elements of the periodic table

Jag Prasad Bhattarai from Dehradun, Uttarakhand, identified all 118 elements of the periodic table by looking at the atomic numbers arranged in random order in 1 min. 30 secs on 19 February 2019 at the Choice Coaching Institute, Kaulagarh, Dehradun.

Most 2-digit numbers multiplied correctly – 1 min.*

Abhilakshya Arora, a student of Trendz Abacus, Kota, Rajasthan, solved 29 tasks of multiplication of a 2-digit number by a 2-digit number in 1 min. in an event held during 23–26 May 2019.

Most number of national anthems sung by an individual*

Yathaarth Murthy from Bengaluru, Karnataka, sang the national anthems of 260 countries, as confirmed on 31 May 2019.

Most Rubik's cubes solved – 1 hr*

Satya Sudhai Kolipaka from Hyderabad, Telangana, solved 93 scrambled Rubik's cubes (3 x 3) in 1 hr on 23 July 2019 in Hyderabad.

Most squares correctly calculated – 3-digit numbers – 1 min.*

Virat Maken from Ranchi, Jharkhand, correctly identified the squares of 24 three-digit numbers in 1 min. from 10:24 p.m. to 10:25 p.m. on 22 May 2023 at the Namkum Police Station, Ranchi.

Most cubes correctly calculated – 3-digit numbers – 1 min.*

Viraj Maken from Ranchi, Jharkhand, correctly identified the cubes of 22 three-digit numbers in 1 min. from 9:36 p.m. to 9:37 p.m. on 22 May 2023 at the Namkum Police Station, Ranchi.

Most dinosaur names identified – 1 min.*

Reyaansh Pardeshi from Doha, Qatar, correctly identified 85 dinosaurs by name in 1 min. on 28 May 2021 at the Indian Cultural Centre (ICC), Doha.

Reyaansh Pardeshi

ENDURANCE

Longest duration of non-stop hitting a table tennis ball on a table tennis racket

Mahir Kumar from Gurugram, Haryana, set the record for the longest duration of non-stop hitting a table tennis ball on a table tennis racket by performing it for 3 hours 44 mins from 2:18 p.m. to 6:02 p.m. on 9 December 2022 at the Chenab Boys Hostel, IIT Ropar main campus, Punjab.

Mahir Kumar

* The rules regarding the age of participants have been modified. Please see *Rules and Guidelines*.

TALLEST

Tallest Man

Dharmendra Pratap Singh from Meerut, Uttar Pradesh, is the tallest man in India. Standing 8 ft 1 in. tall, he is a feet taller than the Great Khali.

Tallest Mannequin

Shoppers Stop Ltd (SSL) made the tallest mannequin, 35 ft tall with 74 rft (running feet) circumference out of metal and finished in paper, and installed it at the SSL Store in GIP Mall, Noida, UP, on 10 July 2015.

Tallest Santa Claus

Shoppers Stop Ltd made the tallest Santa Claus, 75.4 ft, at Inorbit Mall in Malad, Mumbai, for Christmas. Work on the Santa started on 10 December 2015 and was completed on 4 January 2016. Over 30 people worked round the clock to construct it.

Tallest Ravana effigy

Rana Tejinder Singh Chauhan is the founder of Shri Ram Leela Club, Barara, Ambala, Haryana. For Dussehra 2014 the Club made a 64 m (210 ft) tall Ravana effigy and burnt it with fire crackers on 3 October that year. The structure weighed 5 tonnes and used hardware like iron pipes, rods, and angles accounting for 3.5 tonnes while the bamboo, cloth, rope, and paper constituted the remaining 1.5 tonnes. The effigy was burnt as a symbolic representation of the destruction of social vices such as terrorism, communalism, casteism, corruption, foeticide, and adulteration.

Tallest Snowman

Shoppers Stop Ltd made the tallest snowman, 28 ft tall and weighing 200 kg. It was displayed in three metros – Inorbit Mall, Malad, Mumbai; Rajouri Garden, Delhi; and Banerghatta, Bengaluru – from 12 December 2014 to 2 January 2015. Twenty people were involved in its making, and it took 15 days to complete.

Tallest man-made Christmas tree

Delhi International Airport Ltd, New Delhi, commissioned India's tallest man-made Christmas tree, 30.7 m (101 ft) tall (including the 2.4 m [8 ft] star on top). It had over 16,000 Christmas ornaments and 60,000 pine twigs as decoration. The 12 tonne installation was made in 23 days by a team of 80 members from Karmic Events India. It was inaugurated on 23 December 2019.

Effigy

An effigy is often the sculptural representation especially of a person. These are usually for negative representations and are made to be burned or destroyed.

Tallest stacked coin tower

Gandhi Institute of Engineering & Technology (GIET), Gunupur, Rayagada, Odisha, organised a Science and Tech Expo from 21 to 23 February, 2014 wherein around 350 social and technical models were demonstrated by the students. Sanjeev Kumar Pal, a fourth-semester student of BTech, and his friends used 47,000 ₹1 coins to make a 3.66 m (12 ft) high, 2.74 m (9 ft) long and 1.83m (6 ft) wide replica of India Gate, which was displayed at the expo.

MOST

Most kites on a single line

Dharampal Satyapal Foods Limited in association with MOMS Outdoor Media Solutions flew a train of 1,150 kites on a single line between 1:00 p.m. and 2:16 p.m. on 25 February 2023 at the Rann of Kachchh, Gujarat. The thread measured 1,155 m, and around 10 people participated in the event.

Most diyas lit – single venue – group – single day

Sanjay Vilas Narvekar and Amrutrao Patankar, both from Mumbai, have been celebrating Kojagari Purnima (Sharad Purnima) for the past 12 years by lighting two lakh diyas, except for the first year, at Swami Gagangiri Maharaj Manori Ashram, Malad, Mumbai. In 2011, it was celebrated on 11 October. Starting from 6.00 pm, over 5,000 sevaks (helpers) lit the lamps and about 2–4 lakh people visited it by midnight.

Most diyas lit – multiple venues – group – Single day

The Department of Tourism, Government of Uttar Pradesh, District Administration, Ayodhya and Dr Rammanohar Lohia Avadh University displayed 2,512,585 oil lamps at the ghats in Ayodhya including Ram ki Paudi ghat on 30 October 2024.

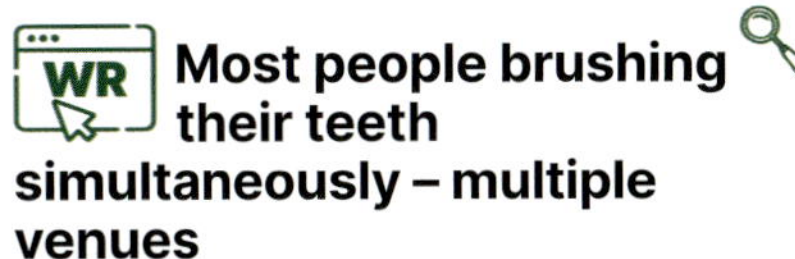

Most people brushing their teeth simultaneously – multiple venues

Colgate-Palmolive (India) Ltd in

Most kites on a single line

Handy Eggs!

Most eggs held in one hand – palm down

Lakshmi Manohar Reddy Mavuru from Vijayawada, Andhra Pradesh, equalled the record of holding the most eggs in one hand with the palm facing downwards on 16 April 2024 by holding 13 eggs. Earlier the world record was set by Marcus Loscher from Australia in 2020.

Most eggs held in one hand – palm up

Rajender Singh Mathru of Tilak Nagar, Delhi, held 32 eggs in his right hand for 3 mins 50 secs on 23 September 2017. The eggs were of average size with 59 mm length and 42 mm diameter.

Most saree styles draped

Kalpana Bhagwandas Shah from Mumbai, draped a total of 226 unduplicated saree styles in 24 hrs on 9 April 2022. The sarees used varied from chiffon to georgette and crepe to Benarasi silk. A total of 3,914 ft of saree material was draped. The fastest saree drape was done within 1 min.

association with Indian Dental Association organized most people brushing their teeth simultaneously – a total of 177,003 participants in 380 locations – on 9 October 2007.

Most people sweeping the floor simultaneously – multiple venues

Prayagraj Mela Authority, Government of India, organized the most people sweeping the floor across multiple venues in locations across Prayagraj, Uttar Pradesh, on 2 March 2019. As many as 10,180 people participated in the event.

Most varieties of siddu prepared*

Him Anchal Chefs Association (HIMCA) prepared and displayed 451 varieties of siddu (a traditional form of bread from Himachal Pradesh) on 19 March 2024 at the Peterhoff Shimla.

Most varieties of pakoras prepared*

School of Hospitality Management, RIMT University prepared 225 varieties of pakoras on 28 May 2024. Nineteen people participated in the event. The pakoras were prepared between 11:03 a.m and 12:13 p.m.

Most mannequins displayed – single day – single venue

Max Fashion, Lifestyle International displayed 100 full body mannequins on 30 september 2023 from 11:00 a.m. to 7:00 p.m. at the Nexus Forum Mall, Hyderabad.

FASTEST

Fastest assembling of cycles

Hindustan Petroleum Corporation Ltd organized the 'Velocipede Challenge', where 313 participants simultaneously assembled 60 bicycles from different segregated components in 45 mins at the Yuvantage 3.0 Grand Finale on 7 January 2019 at Ramoji Film City, Hyderabad.

Fastest time to travel to all seven continents

Dr Ali Irani and Sujoy Kumar Mitra hold the record for fastest time to travel to all seven continents for 3 days 1 hour 5 mins and 4 secs. in Melbourne, Australia on 7 December 2022.

LONGEST

Longest sandwich

The St. Soldier Institute of Hotel Management and Catering Technology, Jalandhar, Punjab, made the longest sandwich on 22 December 2021. Led by Sandeep Lohani, the principal, 5 faculty chefs and 15 students prepared a sandwich, measuring 223 ft 2.4 in. in length and 8 in. in width, in 35 mins from 11:13 a.m. to 11:48 a.m. They used 123 slices of loaf spread with a combination of vegetables, noodles, cheese, pasta, and dressings for it.

Longest charcuterie platter

Spectra, a restaurant at the Leela Ambience Gurugram Hotel and Residences, Gurugram, Haryana, displayed a 9.448 m (31 ft) long and 30 cm (11.8 in.) wide Christmas charcuterie platter on 24 December 2018. It had a variety of cheeses, meats, compotes, crudités, sandwiches, canapés, truffles, and chocolates, among other dishes.

Longest paper chain

Vimin M. Vincent from Thiruvananthapuram, Kerala, made the longest paper chain measuring 956.20 m (3,137 ft 1.6 in.) in 24 hours on 11 February 2022.

Longest kebab

NIMS University-Jaipur in Jaipur, Rajasthan, made a kebab measuring 49 ft 8.4 in. in length with a team of 45 participants under the supervision of Prof. Manoj Srivastava in 9 hrs 53 mins on 6 April 2022. The vegetarian *tawa* kebab was made on a customized tawa, 50 ft long and 2.5 ft wide, using seven industrial gas cylinders with 4 mm hot plate tawa with rail burners underneath. It was displayed at the Sundervan Garden of NIMS University. The kebab was made with 16 kg potatoes, 5 kg chickpea flour, 2 kg green peas, 2 kg ghee, 1 kg mint leaves, 5 kg onion garlic paste, 2 kg capsicum, 1 kg green chillies, 5 kg soya nuggets, 7 kg spinach, and 900 gm ground garam masala.

Longest and largest human chain

The Government of Bihar, as part of its 'Jan Jeevan Hariyali' campaign, organized an 18,034 km long human chain with 5.16 crore (51.6 million) people on 19 January 2020. It took 7 helicopters and over 100 drones to take aerial images of the human chain. The event championed the cause of conservation of environment along with other social causes.

Longest bill

Sanjay Dodrajka from New Delhi ordered 420 burgers from the Burger King outlet in Dhaula Kuan for children of MCD School, Nangal Punya, New Delhi, on 7 December 2019. As a result, Sanjay got a 12 ft (144 in.) long bill.

Longest hair

Akanksha Yadav from Thane, Maharashtra, has the longest hair, which is 3.01 m (9 ft 10.5 in.) long.

Akanksha Yadav

COLLECTIONS

Credit cards

Manish Kumar Dhameja from Lucknow, Uttar Pradesh, has a collection of 1,638 valid credit cards from 25 banks. His first credit card was issued by the State Bank of India in 2014. The collection includes prepaid cards and add-on supplementary cards. His collection was exhibited from 10:00 a.m. to 11:00 a.m. on 30 August 2022 at the Telecommunications Consultants India Limited (TCIL) Southern Regional Office, Hyderabad.

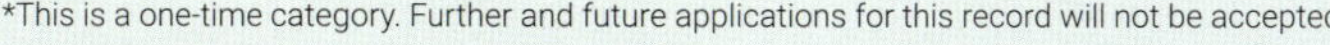

*This is a one-time category. Further and future applications for this record will not be accepted.

Maps

Ravindranath Vishnu Newadkar from Thane, Maharashtra, has a collection of 365 maps up to 31 May 2022. These include 100 maps of various countries and 265 maps of different cities.

PAKISTAN
ADMINISTRATIVE DIVISIONS
SVERIGE
SWEDEN
SAINT LUCIA
The Map of Singapore
St Kitts
УКРАИНА
UKRAIN
PAPUA NEW GUINEA
PORTUGAL
PHILIPPINES
RUSSIA
Tourist scheme
MAPA
ESPAÑA
sri lanka
Tourist Map of Sri Lanka
South Africa
Routekaart
Groot-Brittannië en Ierland
UK+
N. Ireland
United States
MAP OF QATAR
Sultanate of Oman Maps
Kingdom of Saudi Arabia Map
SLOVENIA TOURIST MAP
WELCOME TO PANAMA
ENJOY THE TASTE OF OUR PEOPLE
Monaco plan • map
2017-2018
NORWAY
In Your Pocket
MAP OF MALAYSIA
San Marino
World Heritage
Swiss Travel Map
explorer
UAE
mini map
ABU DHABI
WORLD MAP
Thailand
MAP OF INNER & OUTER ISLANDS
Poland
Tourist Map
Road Map & Guide
New Zealand Touring Map
Rwanda Culture
TOURIST MAP
Mexico
TANZANIA
NATIONAL PARKS
Quick Reference
Tourist Map
SERBIA
Tourist Map
Holland
NETHER LAND.
VIET NAM
TOURIST MAP
TOUR MONGOLIA.com
Map of Maldives
Map of MAURITIUS
2019
RAVINDRA NEWADKAR
www.holland.com
21.4.22
Mosaique Malgache
Madagascar Mozaic Tour
Român

Amitabh Bachchan memorabilia

Mohan Rajgopal Iyer from Nagpur, Maharashtra, an ardent admirer of superstar Amitabh Bachchan, has a collection of his photographs, articles, press clippings, filmography, and correspondences and articles from the internet. The total number of items were 8,650 up to 31 May 2019.

Playing cards

Aditi Shailesh Agarwal from Ahmedabad, Gujarat, has 6,000 sets of Indian and foreign playing cards, the largest such collection, which she started when she was 15 years old. The collection varies in theme, form, size, shape, and material. Aditi has a card deck that was used for a code during the First World War and a celebrity collection on Lady Diana, George Bush, Nelson Mandela, and Bollywood stars Amitabh Bachchan, Madhuri Dixit, Shah Rukh Khan, and others.

Owl-shaped jewellery

Dr Prashant Laxman Wagh from Nashik, Maharashtra, has a collection of owl-shaped jewellery, which he started in 2016. He has 717 items in his collection – 478 pendants, 129 brooches, 62 earrings, and 48 rings. The jewellery is made of materials like zinc alloy, stainless steel, rhinestone, synthetic turquoise stone, and semi-precious metals, among others.

Models of owls

Ramesh Kumar Bhatia from Mumbai, Maharashtra, has a collection of 351 owl models (up to 31 May 2020) since 2013. The models of owls are from different countries including

Owl-shaped jewellery

India, Bhutan, China, New Zealand, Australia, Iceland, Uzbekistan, and Morocco, among others.

Matchboxes featuring horses

Sudhir Jain from Satna, Madhya Pradesh, has a collection of 235 matchboxes featuring a horse in the design. None of the matchboxes in the collection is duplicated.

Ties

Dr Deepak M. Sharma from Ahmedabad, Gujarat, has a collection of 4,589 ties including 2,611 theme-based ones.

Airmail envelopes

Jinesh Joseph from Bengaluru, has a collection of 1,858 airmail envelopes from 338 regions including recognized countries, disputed territories, and autonomous republics.

Stickers

Nidhi Bansal from Fatehgarh Sahib, Punjab, had collected 1,03,800 stickers, a hobby since 2007. She had categorized her collection into subjects like smiley faces, flowers, footballs, birds, trains, and cartoons, among others.

Autographs – national awardees

Praful Thakkar has more than 4,300 autographs of Indian and world celebrities, collected in more than 40 years and arranged thematically into 50 categories. The collection includes autographs of 519 Padma Shri awardees and 101 Nobel laureates.

Chitra Kathayen comics

Ninad Jadhav from Barkuhi, Chhindwara District, Madhya Pradesh, has the largest collection of Hindi-film *Chitra Kathayen*, numbering 123, a collection since 1997. Most of the comics feature Mithun Chakraborty, Dimple Kapadia, Madhuri Dixit, Vinod Khanna, Rajesh Khanna, Shah Rukh Khan, and Navin Nischol. All *Chitra Kathayen* are from Diamond Comics. Amit Jain from Berasia, Bhopal, an ardent fan of Amitabh Bachchan, helped Ninad build this collection.

Hair clips

Sana Fathima from Pudukkottai, Tamil Nadu, has 1,200 hair clips, a collection started on 24 October 2017 and completed on 24 March 2018.

Napkins

Napkins

Parveen Gupta, his wife Anuradha Gupta, and daughter Dr Kanika Gupta from New Delhi have collected 12,246 commercial and 9,325 non-commercial paper napkins from countries like Romania, Egypt, Slovakia, the UK, the US, the UAE, Germany, Australia, Switzerland, and India. They started their collection in 2014.

Autographs of Ajit Laxman Wadekar

Satish Laxman Chaphekar from Dombivli, Maharashtra, has 39 autographs of the late cricketer Ajit Laxman Wadekar, who played 39 international matches during his career including 37 Tests and 2 ODIs. Satish collected Wadekar's bats, balls, and gloves, among other things.

Obituaries – from a single family

Ninad Jadhav from Chhindwara, Madhya Pradesh, has the most obituary news clippings of the Kapoor family (of Hindi cinema) from 272 multi-language newspapers. The obituaries are of Shammi Kapoor (111), Shashi Kapoor (68), Rishi Kapoor (19) and Rajiv Kapoor (74).

Seer (Indian weights)

Ranjeet Kumar Jha from Bhopal, Madhya Pradesh, has a collection of

250 'seer' or 'ser', old Indian weights in various shapes from different Indian princely states like Bhopal, Gwalior, Mewar, Agra, Rajkot, and Indore. In total there are 25 kinds of seer. The scales carry different state seals with different values in different languages.

WR Aircraft models

Vikram Rajkumar Tirkannad from Chennai, Tamil Nadu, has collected 719 models of aircraft over the last 38 years. The first model in his collection was an Air India Boeing 747. The largest are the Airways Concorde and a Jet Airways Boeing 737-800 Winglet, both measuring 0.6 m (2 ft). The smallest is the Air India ATR 42-320 measuring only 6 cm (2.36 in.).

Nokia handsets

Jayesh Umesh Kale from Thane, Maharashtra, has a collection of 1,600 Nokia handsets, a hobby he started in 2013. All the mobile handsets are in working condition.

Cinema press booklets – on a single personality

Ninad Jadhav from Chhindwara, Madhya Pradesh, has a collection of 105 cinema press booklets on actor Mithun Chakraborty. The oldest booklet is of the film *Mera Rakshak*, which was released in 1978.

Soap covers – single brand

Mohanan Vareeth Vattapparuthayl from Ernakulam, Kerala, who has been using only Medimix brand soap at home, started a collection of the soap covers in 1994. Since then he has collected as many as 1,300 soap covers of that single brand till 10 December 2021.

Cinema Press Booklets

Cinema press booklets are booklets that contain images and information related to a film project. These are part of the marketing and publicity efforts to introduce the project to the viewers. They are not as prevalent in contemporary times.

Cinema press booklets

मुजरिम
ANNU MALIK'S PAPPU-VINAY SHUKLA
DIRECTED BY VIJAY SADANAH
MUSIC LAXMIKANT PYARELAL
STORY/LYRICS S.H.BIHARI PHOTOGRAPHY S.L.SHARMA
NARAK YAHAN
PRODUCED BY RAJEEV KUMAR
DIRECTED BY VIMAL KUMAR
MUSIC RAJESH ROSHAN
TULIKA
DEVAR FILMS
Mera Rakshak
मेरा रक्षक
Picture Perfect
Qaidi
Produced by Sunil Bohra-Randeep Arya
Directed by T.L.V. Prasad
Music Bappi Lahiri
SENMIT MOVIE VISUAL'S
Shaukeeen
SCREENPLAY DIRECTION BASU CHATTERJI
MUSIC R.D. BURMAN
SHREERAM GOYAL & MAHESH GARG PRESENTS
PYAR KE NAAM QURBAN
B. SUBHASH
HERO FILMS
RANGBAAZ
WRITTEN AND DIRECTED BY KANTI SHAH
KANTI SHAH-P.L. AHUJA
MUSIC BAPPI LAHIRI
TRISHAKTI FILMS
उस्तादों के उस्ताद
USTADON KE USTAD
PRODUCED BY D.N. JOSHI DIRECTED BY T.L.V. PRASAD MUSIC DILIP SEN • SAMEER S
SURI ART INTERNATIONAL'S
RAJOO DADA
राजू दादा
DIRECTED BY D.S.AZAD
RAJ KUMAR KOHLI'S

Soap wrappers (alphabetical)
Jayadevan Rajagopala from Thrissur, Kerala, has 1,840 unique bath-soap wrappers, a collection spanning more than 30 years. No two covers are the same in his collection, although the same brand might have more than one cover.

Toothpaste wrappers
Mankeerat Kaur from Gurugram, Haryana, has toothpaste wrappers from different countries, a collection started in April 2020. She has 178 unduplicated toothpaste wrappers from India, the United Arab Emirates (UAE), and the United States of America (US). Her complete collection comprises 204 wrappers.

Pradhan Mantri Yojana matchboxes
Alok Mehrotra from Kanpur, Uttar Pradesh, has a collection of 1,550 matchboxes of 21 Pradhan Mantri Yojanas including the Awas Yojana, the Amrit Kosh Yojana, the Garib Kalyan Yojana, the Sukanya Samriddhi Yojana, the Namami Gange programme, the Swachh Bharat Mission, the Pradhan Mantri Jan Aarogya Yojna, the National Sports Talent Yojana, the UMANG Yojana, the Jal Shakti Yojana, and the Sovereign Gold Bond Yojana, among others. He started his collection in 2019.

Lapel pins
Arvind Sinha from Mumbai, Maharashtra, has been collecting lapel pins since 1998 and had 53,228 lapel pins as on 31 March 2015. He exhibits his collection to create awareness on history through lapel pins. The world wars, development of guns, aviation history, space programmes – all these are depicted through his lapel pins.

Lighters
Hamed Husein Patel from Mumbai, Maharashtra, has a collection of 1,042 gas and petrol lighters (till 30 June 2018). The most expensive lighter is the 2008 limited edition St Dupont priced at ₹2,00,000. He also possesses a Dunhill lighter which was once owned by Elvis Presley.

Railway platform tickets
Naveen Kumar from New Delhi has a collection of 100 unduplicated railway platform tickets. These tickets have been collected from Uttar Pradesh, Uttarakhand, Delhi, Haryana, Maharashtra, and Rajasthan between 30 April 2023 and 10 June 2023.

Magazines – Hindi
Dr Jawahar Karnavat from Bhopal, Madhya Pradesh, has 93 Hindi magazines, a collection that started in 2002. The oldest magazine in his collection is the *India Opinion* published in 1903 in South Africa in Gujarati, Tamil, English, and Hindi. In all, there are 25 weekly, 3 fortnightly, 40 monthly, 18 quarterly, and 7 half-yearly magazines. The Deepawali special issue of *Shanti Doot* published from Fiji contains as many as 120 pages.

Magazines
Daria Singh Yadav from Haryana has a collection of over 3,000 different magazines and periodicals. The magazines, which are not necessarily first issues, are in 17 languages covering 6 continents.

Magazines – regional languages
A. Ramanan from Vellore, Tamil Nadu, has collected over 1,706 Tamil magazines, some of which have now stopped publication. The oldest *Varthaga Mitran* is dated 1917, and the second oldest is *Ramanujan* dated 1919.

Magazines – first issues
Mudappalam M. Sukumar from Mumbai, has been collecting first issues of magazines since May 1979. He has a total of 662 issues of weekly, fortnightly, monthly, and bimonthly magazines in English, Tamil, and Hindi. There are 488 Tamil, 30 Hindi, 112 English, and 32 in other languages. His collection started with the very first issue of the Tamil magazine *Chaavi*.

Airline magazines
Mallikarjun M. Umadi from Nashik, Maharashtra, has been collecting magazines printed by various airlines since 2006; and as of 30 June 2016, he had 175 different magazines of 33 different airlines, both national and international.

Magazines – personality covers – featuring a single personality
Anuradha Gupta from New Delhi has collected 317 different magazines in various languages with Prime Minister Narendra Modi on the cover. The collection began in 2017.

Badges – political theme
Ranjeet Kumar Jha from Bhopal, Madhya Pradesh, has 250 badges from different years and of different shapes, sizes, material, and logos of political parties, such as the Congress, BJP, and BSP, in his collection. He started the collection on 9 April 2003 and completed it on 9 April 2021.

Antique matchbox labels – uncut sheets
Samirkumar Hasmukhbhai Arya from Valsad, Gujarat, has a collection of 225 uncut antique matchbox labels.

Bindi
A. Kalaivani has the largest bindi collection with 3,000 unique bindis as verified on 1 February 2016.

Scales
Ameya Gupta of Delhi has a collection of 2,072 scales (including 1,890 duplicates) from countries like India, UAE, Japan, China, South Korea, Taiwan, Germany, Malaysia, and Egypt as on 30 June 2015. They are made of different materials like aluminium, steel, wood, paper and plastic. The tallest scale is 6 ft (1.83 m) in length and the smallest is just 3 inches (7.62 cm).

Spoons
Shubhangi Apte of Raipur, Chhattisgarh, has 1,852 small and big spoons, a collection started in April 1995. The collection has silver, gold, ceramic, steel, copper, and wooden spoons in a variety of sizes, shapes, and colours. The biggest spoon was 18 inch and smallest measured 1 inch.

WR Airline boarding passes
K. Ullas Kamath has a collection of 3,030 airline boarding passes as verified on 15 August 2014.

Antique clocks
S. Robert Kennedy of Chennai, Tamil Nadu, has been collecting antique clocks (2,200 by March 2018) since 1983. The oldest clock in his collection is 285 years old from the UK. His collection has mechanical and wind-up clocks,

Pencils

Tushar Lakhanpal from New Delhi has the largest unduplicated pencil collection that started in 2001. The collection from 62 countries has over 50 scented pencils in various fragrances, pencils that show temperature variations, pencils depicting the crowns of various Austrian and English kingdoms, and a spoon-like pencil, among others. His collection grew to 16,795 as on 30 June 2017.

Toothbrushes

Dr Yogesh Chandrana from Vadodra, Gujarat, has a collection of toothbrushes numbering a total of 2,371 items as on 21 January 2024. The collection has rare pieces from the 19th century as well.

pendulum wall clocks, ship clocks, carriage clocks, skeleton clocks, alarm clocks, table clocks, pocket watches, and wristwatches.

Dice

Ankit Shah of Mumbai has the largest collection of dice numbering to 3,131 items. His collection has dices in all shapes and sizes.

Candles

Johnson Nayankara of Irinjalakuda, Kerala, has the largest collection of candles. By 30 June 2011, his collection grew to 3,309 candles of different sizes and shapes, and even fragrant ones. He collected them from different parts of the world.

Pens

V.T. Jolly of Kochi, Kerala, has 13,000 used pens, both ball-point and fountain, in his possession. Among the many novel pens in his collection, there is a unique golden crown pen, a perfume spraying pen, pens with cigarette lighter, double-sized pen, and more. He has pens from 16 countries.

Same-day newspapers

Shiju Thomas from Bengaluru, Karnataka, has the largest collection of Mahatma Gandhi's 150th birth anniversary newspapers, dated 2 October 2019. His collection comprises 603 newspapers, which includes 301 newspapers with different titles and 302 newspapers with different place editions in 17 Indian languages. The collection includes weekly, fortnightly, and monthly publications.

Sequential same-day newspaper

Akanksha Jain from Vadodara, Gujarat, has the longest unbroken sequential collection of the same-day newspaper, *The Times of India*, dated 20 July for 16 years, right from 1994 to 2009.

Newspaper clippings featuring Lata Mangeshkar – solo

Dr Anil Patiram Meshram from Nagpur, Maharashtra, has the largest collection of information and items related to Bharat Ratna Lata Mangeshkar. He has 2,200 newspaper photos, 318 photo clippings with information, and 144 news information pieces without a photo.

Newspaper clippings featuring Lata Mangeshkar – group

Gaurav Sharma and Manju Lata Sharma have collected 11,505 news clippings on the late singer Lata Mangeshkar. The oldest press clipping dates back to 1955. There are various original press articles on her from 1959 onwards in various languages – Hindi, Marathi, Odia, Bangla, Gujarati, Konkani, Tamil, Telugu, Assamese, Malayalam, Punjabi, Urdu, and English. There are also original newspaper articles on her from Finland, the UK, and Bangladesh.

Newspaper clippings featuring Sridevi – solo

Anuradha Gupta from New Delhi has a collection of 1,270 press clippings about late actor Sridevi from newspapers and magazines in many languages starting from 24 February 2018.

Newspaper clippings featuring Atal Bihari Vajpayee – solo

Anuradha Gupta from New Delhi has collected 612 newspaper clippings of former prime minister Atal Bihari Vajpayee. The clippings are in many languages including Hindi, English, Marathi, Gujarati, Tamil, and Telugu.

Newspaper clippings featuring Mahatma Gandhi – solo

Shiju Thomas from Bengaluru, Karnataka, has a collection of 860 news clippings on Mahatma Gandhi in various Indian languages.

Newspaper clippings on cinema

Swarnlata Vishwafool from Katihar, Bihar, has collected 100,147 clippings related to Hindi cinema from various Hindi newspapers from 1998 to 2019.

Newspaper clippings featuring deities

Rekha Gore of Raipur, Chhattisgarh, has been collecting pictures or likenesses of Ganesha since 1950. She has 31,517 such items including 18,309 wedding cards, 9,430 newspaper cuttings, 78 magazine cuttings, 219 books, 102 photographs (foreign), and 3,379 of these from her relatives. She has held an exhibition of these at Raipur on 19 April 2009.

It's in the News!

Newspapers

Dayanand N. Manchanda of Lajpat Nagar, Delhi, collected about 1,20,000 newspapers in English and Hindi over the last 15 years. He has been collecting at least 22 papers every day since 1996. He collected them originally as reference material for his research on numerology. He also has a collection of 2,500 magazines on astrology over the last 15 years.

Foreign newspapers

Manu Parkash Jindal of Jalandhar has a collection of 3,216 newspapers from 76 countries in 54 languages (including 29 foreign languages). The entire collection is indexed giving detailed explanations on the papers.

Newspapers from most countries

Shashanka Sekhar Dash from Jajpur, Odisha, has a collection of 981 newspapers in 63 languages from 102 countries. Started in 2005, his collection has newspapers from countries including Lesotho, Seychelles, Peru, Palestine, East Timor, and Papua New Guinea, and in languages including Estonian, Yakut, Tok Pisin, Tetum, Hebrew, Dari, and Pashto.

Newspapers in most languages

Shashanka Sekhar Dash popularly known as 'Paperboy Shashank' of Jajpur, Odisha, has the largest collection of newspapers totalling 5,000 since 2001. His collection has 3,584 different newspapers from 76 countries in 66 languages.

Hindi-language newspapers

Dr Ashok Pandey 'Gulshan' from Bahraich, Uttar Pradesh, has a collection of 12,634 different Hindi newspapers under 655 titles from Indian states, Nepal, China, and Thailand, all received by India Post in Uttar Pradesh since 1990. He has bound volumes alphabetically as Daily, Tri-weekly, Biweekly, Weekly, Fortnightly, Monthly, Bimonthly, Tri-monthly, and Annual Special Issues.

Regional-language newspapers

A.S. Muhammed from Kottayam District, Kerala, has been collecting old Malayalam publications like newspapers and magazines, including the 1890 first edition of *Malayalam Manorama*, and the new edition of *Suprabhaatham* published in 2014. His archival collection includes 150 newspapers and over 2,000 journals.

Search...

EARLY TIMES

Earliest village settlement
A 4,000-year-old village settlement of the Chalcolithic period (Copper Age), along with remnants of subsequent Iron Age occupation, was unearthed at Balathal near Udaipur, Rajasthan. It included a massive mud rampart. It is the oldest village settlement in India outside of Harappan sites.

First architect on record
Maha Govinda is considered the first architect on record. He designed many north Indian cities in the fifth century BCE. He has been mentioned in the Buddhist work *Dhammapada.*

Oldest rust-free iron pillar
The iron pillar in the Qutb (Minar) complex in Mehrauli, Delhi, has stood strong since the fifth century CE—during the Gupta period. Udayagiri in what is now Madhya Pradesh is most likely where it was built (some also believe Mathura was the place where it was made), before it was moved to Delhi. A solid iron shaft, 7.2 m (23 ft 7.4 in.) high, it has many inscriptions in Sanskrit, among which the oldest, a six-line inscription, states that the pillar was built for a Vishnu temple and at the order of a king called Chandra (often believed to be Chandragupta II).

Rampart

A wall that is wide enough for people to walk on it and is built to protect a town or castle.

First to Win

First architect to win the Pritzker Prize
Dr Balkrishna Vithaldas Doshi (b. 26 August 1927) won the famed Pritzker Architecture Prize on 12 March 2018, the first Indian to do so in the award's 40-year history. The Pritzker Prize is referred to as the Nobel Prize in architecture.

First Indian winner of the Aga Khan Award for architecture
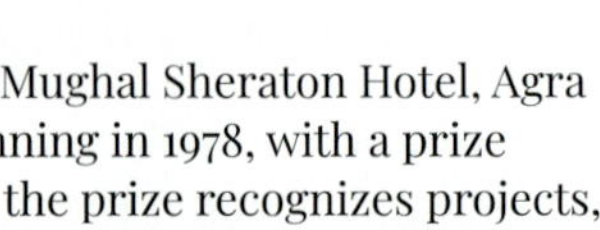

The first Indian winner of the award was the Mughal Sheraton Hotel, Agra in 1980. Presented in three-year cycles, beginning in 1978, with a prize money of 1 million USD (approx. ₹8.25 crore), the prize recognizes projects, stakeholders, buildings and teams that translate aspirations of the Muslim society through design and architecture.

First architects to win JK Architecture of the Year Awards (AYAs)
The first architects to win the JK Architecture of the Year Awards (AYAs), when it was started in 1990:

a) Laurie Baker (2 March 1917–1 April 2007), a British-born Indian architect from Thiruvananthapuram, was the first to win the Great Master's Award. He is often considered a pioneer of sustainable architecture.

b) Anant D. Raje (17 September 1929–27 June 2009) from Ahmedabad was the first to win the Architect of the Year Award. He taught architecture at various universities across the world, including CEPT University, Ahmedabad, and University of New Mexico, US.

Earliest open-air theatre
The earlier open-air theatre was made in the third century BCE at Nagarjunakonda in Guntur District, Andhra Pradesh. It is similar to ancient Greek and Roman amphitheatres – has a pit with tiers on all four sides, which could seat at least 1,000 spectators. It encloses a rectangular room of 16.5 m x 13.7 m (54 ft 1.5 in. x 44 ft 11.4 in.). The structure has good acoustic properties.

Earliest extensive drainage system
The Harappan towns of Lothal in Gujarat and Mohenjo-daro (now in Pakistan); with rectangular houses, chessboard streets, brick-lined bathrooms, drainage pipes, and cesspits; were unique in the ancient world. The toilets were equipped with water chutes, which carried dirty water away to covered street drains. The main sewer, about 1.5 m (4 ft 11 in.) deep and 91 cm (2 ft 11 .8 in.) across, is connected to north-south and east-west sewers.

Oldest palace site excavated
Kumrahar in Patna, Bihar, dating to 250 BCE, is said to be one of Emperor

Drainage systems in the Indus Valley Civilization

Earliest extant book on architecture

Several references are found in different literatures including the Rigveda, epics, Puranas, and the *Arthasastra*. However, the earliest separate treatise on architecture that is still available is *Manasara*. It is the culmination of all architectural traditions and treatises that were available before. It is believed to have been composed by a person known as Shilpin, a practising architect in roughly 500–700 CE. The exact authorship and date are unknown. Another treatise on housing architecture from the same period is the *Mayamata*.

Ashoka's palaces. The remains of the columns at the site indicate that the palace had an 84-pillar hall, originally made of wood.

Oldest man-made lake

Sudarshan Lake at the foot of Girnar Hills in Junagadh District, Gujarat, was built during the reign of Chandragupta Maurya (c. 321–297 BCE), according to the epigraph engraved on the Ashokan pillar a kilometre from the lake. It was restored by Emperor Ashoka around 273 BCE. Now the lake has shrunk due to silt and debris.

Oldest Dockyard

The most substantial remains of the prehistoric Harappan culture in India have been discovered at Lothal – the oldest dockyard near the Gulf of Cambay (now Gulf of Khambhat) in Gujarat. Built in 2300 BCE, the dock is a long, rectangular tank of 218 m x 37 m (715 ft x 121 ft) and about 16 km from its nearest seaport.

Largest stupa

The great stupa at Sanchi in Madhya Pradesh, built with bricks by Emperor Ashoka between 273 and 232 BCE, was later enlarged and enclosed within another stone stupa. In its present form, the stupa now has a diameter of 37 m (121 ft 5 in.) and a height of 16 m (52 ft 6 in.).

Deepest stepwell

Chand Baori, located at Abhaneri in Dausa District, Rajasthan, is the deepest stepwell in India, extending to 30 m (98 ft 5 in.) down from the ground. It is also considered to be the largest ancient stepwell in the country and among the oldest wells in the world. Its oldest parts were constructed in the 8th century by King Chand and the upper storeys were built during the reign of the Mughals in the 18th century. The stepwell has 13 levels and 3,500 narrow steps. The temperature at the bottom of the well remains 6°C lower than the temperature at its surface.

Earliest graveyard

The largest necropolis of pre-urban era, which is the earliest graveyard discovered in India to date, is located in a Harappan site near Kutch, Gujarat. This 40-acre Harappan burial site predates Dholavira. The graveyard exhibits the transition from earth-mound burials to stone graves – being functional for about 500 years (between 3,200 BCE and 2,600 BCE). The oldest grave here is 5,200 years old. The excavation began in 2019 and involved more than 150 national and international scientists.

MEDIEVAL AND MODERN ERAS

Largest silver article

A 1.8 m (5 ft 11 in.) tall silver jug at the City Palace in Jaipur, Rajasthan, was made for the maharaja of Jaipur to store drinking water during his visit to England in 1901 for the coronation of King Edward VII.

Largest corbelled cornice dome

The Gol Gumbaz, built in 1659 in the tomb complex of the Adil Shahi sultans at Bijapur in Karnataka, features a dome that measures 42 m (137 ft 9.5 in.) in diameter. Its corbelled cornice (the ornamental projection that crowns a building) projects more than 3 m (9 ft 10 in.). The dome is the largest of its kind in the world.

Gol Gumbaz: largest corbelled cornice dome

Earliest known monumental tomb

The Sultan Garhi tomb in Delhi was built over a garhi (cave) in 1231 for Prince Nasiruddin Mahmud by his father Iltutmish, the third sultan of the Slave dynasty, who ruled in Delhi from 1212 to 1236. The octagonal tomb is like a fortress with a courtyard-like layout, uncommon for a tomb.

Largest silver article

Largest bas-relief

The 'Descent of the Ganga' bas-relief, also known as 'Arjuna's Penance', in Mamallapuram in Chengalpattu District, Tamil Nadu, is 27 m (88 ft 7 in.) long and 9 m (29 ft 6 in.) high. Created during the Pallava period in the seventh century CE, it features over 30 large and small sculptures of animals, humans, sages, and gods.

Descent of the Ganga: the largest bas-relief

Largest vaulted hall

The Bara Imambara in Lucknow, Uttar Pradesh, is not only India's but also Asia's largest hall without any external support of wood, iron, or stone beams. The hall measures 49.4 m x 16.2 m (162 ft x 53 ft 2 in.). The ceiling is more than 15 m (49 ft 2.5 in.) high.

Largest maze

The Bhul-Bhulaiya, which is a set of passages on the top terrace of the Bara Imambara building in Lucknow, Uttar Pradesh, is a labyrinth of over 1,000 interconnected passages that can be approached through a narrow flight of steps but seem to lead nowhere. These passages reduced the load on the walls, which support the massive 4.88 m (16 ft) thick roof with an estimated weight of about 20,000 tonnes. It was built by Asaf-ud-Daula, Nawab of Awadh, in 1784.

Bhul-Bhulaiya: largest maze

Largest brick minaret

The Qutb Minar in Delhi, made in fluted sandstone carved with verses from the Quran, is 72 m (236 ft) high with 379 steps inside leading to the top. It is a tapering tower of five storeys, with a base diameter of 14.3 m (47 ft), which reduces to 2.74 m (9 ft) at the top. Its construction began under Qutbuddin Aibak in 1193 CE, and his successor Iltutmish added three storeys. Firuz Shah Tughlaq completed the last storey in 1383 CE.

Qutb Minar: largest brick minaret

First garden tomb

The tomb of Sikandar Lodi (r. 1489–1517) of the Lodi dynasty is located in Lodi Garden near Lodi Road in New Delhi and was built during 1517–18 by his son Ibrahim Lodi.

Forts and Palaces

Oldest forts

Though it is difficult to say which is the oldest fort in India, forts found at Harappan sites are surely the earliest. Several parts of a Harappan fort, including its gateways, still exist at Dholavira. Parts of earlier forts that pre-date the Harappan civilization are also found at Dholavira and Kalibangan, which are datable to the last part of the fourth millennium.

Oldest surviving fort

Quila Mubarak in Bhathinda is the oldest surviving fort of India. The fort consists of bricks that date back to the era of the Kushan rulers (believed to be built between 90 CE and 110 CE). The original fort was a mud structure built by Raja Dhab. Razia Sultan was imprisoned here, and Guru Govind Singh visited this fort in 1705 CE.

Oldest extant marble structure

The white marble structure over Hoshang Shah Ghori's tomb, built by his son c.1440, at Mandu, Dhar District, Madhya Pradesh, is the oldest extant marble structure known.

Only palace with just a facade wall

Hawa Mahal ('the palace of winds') in Jaipur, Rajasthan, has a facade built on to a wall of the main palace compound. Royal ladies seated in its 953 niches and windows could look down at the street below.

Largest fort in India

The Mehrangarh Fort, sprawling over and area of 1,200 acres and perched on sandstone hills about 400 ft (122 m) above the Thar Desert, was built in the 15th century by Rao Jodha, the 15th Rathore ruler of Marwar. The fort has 7 gates, and the maximum height of the walls is 120 ft (36 m). The walls are about 65 ft (20m) wide at places.

Mehrangarh Fort

Longest fortification wall

A 36 km (22.37 miles) long fortification wall was built by Rana Kumbha (r. 1433–68) along the Aravallis in Rajasthan to protect his kingdom of Mewar. It enclosed 34 fortresses. At its widest sections, the wall is 15 m (49 ft) thick and has stone-brick masonry and decorative flourishes along the top.

Kumbhalgarh Fort with the largest fortification wall, built by Rana Kumbha

Fort with largest metal ordnance

The Bijapur Fort in Bijapur District, Karnataka, houses the famous bell metal cannon Malik-e-Maidan ('lord of the battlefield'). It is the largest piece of medieval bell-metal ordnance, which is 4.45 m (14 ft 7 in.) long, and has a diameter of 1.5 m (4 ft 11 in.). It weighs 55 tonnes and has a bore of 0.71 m (2 ft 4 in.) from which an iron ball of over a tonne could be fired.

Tallest gateway

Buland Darwaza, the tallest gateway in India, is 53.5 m (175 ft 6 in.) high. It was built by Mughal emperor Akbar (r. 1550–1605) at Fatehpur Sikri, about 40 km from Agra in Uttar Pradesh, and commemorated his conquest of Ranthambore Fort and Khandesh.

Palace with the largest chandelier

The durbar hall of Jai Vilas Mahal of Gwalior, Madhya Pradesh, has two chandeliers, each 12.5 m (41 ft) high and weighing 3.5 tonnes. It is said that three (or eight!) elephants were hoisted to the roof (or suspended from it!) to make sure it would withstand the weight of the chandeliers.

RELIGIOUS STRUCTURES

Earliest extant structural temple

A third century BCE circular brick-and-timber shrine excavated at Bairat (now Viratnagar) in Jaipur District, Rajasthan, is considered to be the earliest surviving structural temple. The shrine, with a diameter of 8.23 m (27 ft), was built with lime-plastered panels of brickwork alternating with 26 octagonal wooden pillars. The shrine, portico, and a 2 m (6 ft 6.7 in.) wide ambulatory were enclosed in a rectangular compound that measures 305 m x 21 m (1,000 ft 7.8 in. x 68 ft 10.7 in.).

Oldest functional Hindu temple

The Mundeshwari Devi temple, in Kaimur District of Bihar, is believed to the oldest functional Hindu temple in the world. Per the Archaeological Survey of India (ASI), this temple was built in 108 CE. The temple is dedicated to Shiva and Shakti and also has other deities like Ganesha, Surya, and Vishnu in it.

Earliest mosque

The Cheraman Jama Masjid in Kodungallur, Thrissur District, Kerala, is said to have been built in 629 CE. It is considered the first mosque in India and the second in the world where Juma prayers were started. Malik Ibn Dinar, who made this mosque under instructions from Maharaja Chereman Perumal, used Kerala style of architecture to build this mosque. He also became its first ghazi. The mosque is still in use. In the 1970s, it was reconstructed in a way that changed its look completely. In 2021, further renovation took place which brought back the original look.

First revolving minaret

The minaret of the 55-year-old Masjid-e-Chini ki Burj, also known as Chhoti Masjid in Jaipur, Rajasthan, was the first revolving minaret in India. The 10-tonne dome of the 30.5 m (100 ft) high minaret, with a 3 m (9 ft 10 in.) diameter, completed one round in a minute, running on a 1.5 HP motor.

First Baha'i house of worship

The Baha'i house of worship, or 'Lotus Temple', in Kalkaji, New Delhi, the first such structure in Asia, is built on 26 acres (10.52 hectares) of land. Built between 1980 and 1986, it is designed as a blossoming lotus. The main structure has three folds of nine concrete petals, each covered with Grecian marble. The temple rises to 35 m (114 ft 10 in.) and is surrounded by pools of water.

Oldest Buddhist monument

A stupa, which was estimated to be 2,500 years old, was excavated in 1898 in Piprahwa in Siddharthnagar District, Uttar Pradesh, by British colonial engineer and landowner W.C. Peppe. The solid brickwork stupa was 7 m (23 ft) high and its cupola measured 35 m (114 ft 10 in.) in diameter. Most of the other surviving stupas are from the reign of Emperor Ashoka (c. 273 to 232 BCE).

Largest monastery

The largest Buddhist monastery in the country, and a functioning one, is located in Tawang District, Arunachal Pradesh. The three-storey structure spread over 140 sq m (1,507 sq ft) has 65 residential buildings that can house up to 450 lamas. This monastery's Tibetan name – Galden Namgey Lhatse – translates as 'celestial paradise on a clear night'.

Oldest Buddhist monument

Largest monastery

Biggest temple lamp

A lamp with 1,000 wicks at the Chettikulangara Devi Temple in Alappuzha District, Kerala, is made of 1,500 kg of gunmetal. It is 3.3 m (10 ft 10 in.) high with 13 tiers. The lowest rung is 2.1 m (6 ft 10.7 in.) in circumference and holds 101 wicks. The topmost is over 1 m wide with 53 wicks.

Biggest bathing tank

The Brahma Sarovar at Thanesar in Kurukshetra District, Haryana, is 1,370 m x 762 m (4,495 ft x 2,500 ft) and attracts thousands of pilgrims during solar eclipses. Its ancient water reservoir finds mention in the Mahabharata.

Oldest active synagogue

The Paradesi Synagogue in Mattancherry in Kochi, Kerala, was built by the descendants of the European Jews in 1568 CE. The synagogue is also the first one known to be built in a Commonwealth country.

Biggest queue complex

The Vaikuntam queue complex at the Venkateswara Temple complex, Tirumala, Tirupati, Andhra Pradesh, permits the free flow of around 35,000 pilgrims daily. It has a two-tier seating gallery, two corridors, and a floor at the ground level with amenities within a semicircular length of 238 m (781 ft). A new complex was added later for sarvadarshan, or free entry of devotees.

Only rat temple

The 575-year-old temple of Karni Devi (one of the nine incarnations of Goddess Durga) has a large number of rats called kaba, believed to be the offspring of the presiding deity. Located at Deshnok, 35 km from Bikaner, Rajasthan, this temple is devoted exclusively to the 'holy' rats, which have the run of the place.

Meenakshi Sundareswar Temple

Most sculptures in a temple

The Meenakshi Sundareswar Temple in Madurai, Tamil Nadu, has more than 30 million sculptures in its shrines, halls, and colonnades. It covers an area of 243 m x 228 m (797 ft x 748 ft).

Largest cave temple complex

The cave temples in Ellora in Aurangabad District, Maharashtra, were built between the fifth and tenth centuries CE. There are 12 Buddhist, 17 Hindu, and 5 Jain cave temples and monasteries. The Kailasa or Kailasanatha Temple in cave 16 is the largest single monolithic rock excavation in the world.

Biggest temple bell

The 110-year-old bronze bell at Tirumala Devaswom, Kochi, Kerala, is more than 1.8 m (5 ft 11 in.) high and weighs over 3 tonnes. The bell is suspended from a huge wooden frame that rests over four massive granite pillars.

Only shaking minarets

At the Sidi Bashir Mosque in Ahmedabad, Gujarat, the minarets, which are three storeys high and have carved balconies, are known as the jhulta, or shaking, minarets. Dated to

Karni Devi: only rat temple

Ellora: largest cave temple complex

1452 CE, the mosque was built either by Sidi Bashir, a slave of Sultan Ahmed Shah, or by Malik Sarang, a noble in the court of Sultan Mahmud Begada. The shaking of either minaret results in the other minaret vibrating after a few seconds, a fact that was first observed in the 19th century by an Englishman and Sanskrit scholar, Monier M. Williams. One minaret has been partly taken down to prevent it from falling over.

Largest synagogue

Located on Moledina Street in Pune, Maharashtra, the Ohel David Synagogue is a 30 m (98 ft 5 in.) high tower, built in the Gothic style with a spire and four giant clocks.

Largest sun temple

Built by Narasimha Deva I in 1200 CE, the Sun Temple in the historic town of Konark, Odisha, represents a huge chariot with 12 pairs of ornamental wheels, drawn by seven horses rearing up to the east. The original temple consisted of a sanctum sanctorum with a lofty curvilinear shikhara, a 34.14 m (112 ft) long and 38.4 m (126 ft) high jagmohana (assembly hall), and a dance hall. Along with many subsidiary structures, the Sun Temple, which is now the largest extant sun temple, was enclosed within a compound wall 264 m (866 ft) long and 165 m (541 ft) wide, with three gates.

Largest collection of temples

There are as many as 1,000 Jain temples and 12,000 idols in the Shatrunjai Hills of Palitana in Bhavnagar District of Gujarat.

Largest mosque

The Taj-ul-Masjid, or Taj-ul-Masajid, in Bhopal, Madhya Pradesh, was built by Sultan Shah Jehan Begum between 1868 and 1901. Constructed over decades, the mosque was completed in 1985 by Maulana Sayed Hashmat Ali Sahab and Allama Mohammad Imran Khan Nadwi Azhari. Its name means 'the crown of mosques' and it has an interior area of 23,000 sq m (247,570 sq ft). The mosque is made of red stone and can accommodate 1,75,000 worshippers.

Largest Imambara 

The Nizamat Imambara located in the Nizamat Kila in Murshidabad, West Bengal, was first built by Nawab Siraj ud-Daulah in 1740. But it was completely destroyed by fire in 1846. Nawab Nazim Mansur Ali Khan built a new structure in 1847. This new Nizamat Imambara, India's largest, is 680 feet long and has varying width at different places. Bara Imambara in Lucknow is the second largest of the country. (See largest vaulted hall on page 62.)

Largest chaitya hall

The Karla Caves near Lonavala, Maharashtra, house the largest known chaitya (Buddhist prayer hall) cave. Its dimensions are 37 m x 14 m x 14 m (121 ft 5 in. x 46 ft x 46 ft).

WR Tallest single-stone shikhara

The 80-tonne single-piece granite shikhara atop the Brihadeeswarar

Imambara

An imambara is a place to carry out majlis-e-Hussain—where Shia Muslim devotees gather to commemorate and mourn the martyrdom of Prophet Muhammad's grandson, Hussain.

Below: Nizamat Imambara Murshidabad
Bottom: Bara Imambara

Temple at Thanjavur, Tamil Nadu, is the heaviest single-stone object on top of any temple in the world. This marvel of engineering was constructed from 1004 CE, during the reign of Rajaraja Chola, to 1009 CE. It is the world's first temple built with granite. Its *vimana* (a pyramidal tower built over the central shrine of a temple) is also the highest, at 66 m (216 ft 6 in.).

Only mosque entirely of marble

Moti Masjid (the Pearl Mosque), built by Mughal emperor Shah Jahan in the 17th century CE within the Agra Fort, is made entirely of marble.

Moti Masjid: only mosque entirely of marble

Tallest temple tower

The 13-storey Sri Ranganathaswamy Temple, built between 1982 and 1987 at Srirangam in Tiruchirappalli District, Tamil Nadu, has a 72 m (236 ft) high *rajagopuram* (main gateway).

Tallest temple tower

Highest gurdwara

The gurdwara at Hemkund in Chamoli District, Uttarakhand, stands at a height of 4,328.16 m (14,200 ft) above mean sea level. The place Hemkund finds mention in the Guru Granth Sahib and in Guru Gobind Singh's memoir, *Bachittar (or Bichittar) Natak.*

Tallest hollow stone structure

The Global Vipassana Pagoda at Gorai in Mumbai, Maharashtra, is one of the world's largest structures enshrining the relics of the Buddha. It was donated by the Sri Lankan government and the Mahabodhi Society, Bodhgaya, Bihar. Inaugurated on 8 February 2009, it contains the largest and tallest pillar-less hollow stone pagoda in the world. The height of the dome is 29 m (95 ft 1.7 in.), and the height of the building is 96.12 m (315 ft 4.2 in.). It took around 11 years and 2.5 million tonnes of stone to complete it.

Highest monastery

The Tangyud Monastery at Komic Village near Hikkim in Spiti Valley, Himachal Pradesh, is India's highest monastery at an altitude of around 4,572 m (15,000 ft). Built like a fortified castle, it lies on the edge of the Kibber Wildlife Sanctuary.

Below: Highest gurdwara
Far right: Highest monastery

Oldest church

St Thomas Syro-Malabar Church, located in Palayoor in Thrissur District, Kerala, is believed to be built by St Thomas, one of the 12 apostles of Jesus Christ, in 52 CE. It was rebuilt in the 17th century by the Reverend Fenichi. The original altar survives. It is also known as the Malankara Mar Thoma Syrian Church, or the Mar Thoma Church.

Mar Thoma

Mar Thoma, in Aramaic, means 'St Thomas'.

Tallest church

The Gothic-style Basilica of Our Lady of Dolours, known locally as Puthanpally, is a minor basilica of the Syro-Malabar Catholic Church in Thrissur, Kerala. Its construction started in 1929. Its two front towers are 45 m (147 ft 8 in.) tall, and the central tower is 79 m (259 ft 2 in.) tall.

Largest church

The 76.2 m x 55 m (250 ft x 180 ft 5 in.) Se Cathedral at Old Goa, around 10 km from Panaji, is the largest in India. It was constructed between 1562 and 1619. It was consecrated in 1640. It had two towers, but one collapsed in 1776 and was not rebuilt.

STATUES AND IDOLS

Tallest monolithic statue

The Gommateshwara statue at Shravanabelagola, Karnataka, is the world's tallest monolithic statue. Dedicated to Bahubali and venerated by the Jains, it is 17.37 m (57 ft) high. It was carved from a single block of granite and weighs 80 tonnes. It was built between 978 and 993 CE by Chavundaraya, a minister of the Western Ganga dynasty.

Tallest shivalinga

The tallest shivalinga in the world was created by Maheswaram Sri Sivaparvathi Temple Trust, Thiruvananthapuram, Kerala. It measures 33.85 m (111 ft) and was constructed in six years and one day between 31 December 2012 and 31 December 2018.

Tallest Shani Dev statue

The Shani Dev Sewa Samiti, Shani Dham, Jammu, built and installed the world's tallest Shani Dev statue, which is 11.88 m (39 ft) high, including its 1.83 m (6 ft) base, in Jourian Village, Akhnoor District, Jammu and Kashmir. It weighs around 2,100 kg.

Tallest Ganesha Idol

A 6 m (19 ft 8 in.) high and 3.35 m (11 ft) wide Ganesha, weighing 190 tonnes and carved out of a single block of stone, was installed at the Mundhi Vinayagar Temple at Puliakulam, Coimbatore District, Tamil Nadu. Its *abhisheka* ritual needs 3 litres of oil and is performed using a ladder.

Tallest Durga structure

Nuruddin Ahmed from Bishnupur Village in Chirang District, Assam, built the tallest Durga structure, measuring 30 m x 14.5 m x 8 m (98 ft 5 in. x 47 ft 7 in. x 26 ft 3 in.), using only bamboo materials (including 5,000 bamboo sticks). No other material was used except cotton cloth as rope. It was made to promote the bamboo sector in Assam.

Largest Nandi statue

Largest sculpture of a mythical creature

Jatayu, the largest sculpture of a mythical creature in India, is located at the Jatayu Earth's Centre (also known as Jatayu Rock or Jatayu Nature Park) in Chadayamangalam, Kollam District, Kerala. The sculpture, conceptualized and built by sculptor and film-maker Rajiv Anchal, is 60.96 m (200 ft) long, 45.72 m (150 ft) wide, and 21.33 m (70 ft) high. It houses a digital museum and a multidimensional theatre, making it a 'functional' sculpture.

Largest Nandi statue

Nandi is the sacred bull and Lord Shiva's vehicle in Hindu mythology. The Nandi statue, about 200 m (656 ft) from the Veerabhadra Temple at Lepakshi Village in Anantapur District, Andhra Pradesh, is 4.57 m (15 ft) tall and 8.23 m (27 ft) long. It is carved from a single piece of granite.

Largest bust

Inaugurated on 24 February 2017, the 34.1 m (112 ft) tall 'Adiyogi' Lord Shiva statue made of steel and located in Coimbatore, Tamil Nadu, at the Isha Yoga Centre, has been funded by the Isha Foundation, and set up by Sadhguru Jaggi Vasudev. Built over eight months, the structure reportedly weighs 500 tonnes. Its height signifies the 112 chakras in the human system to explore the 112 dimensions of life.

Largest shivalinga

Located in Bhojpur, on the outskirts of the city of Bhopal in Madhya Pradesh, the Bhojeshwar Temple, built by Raja Bhoj (r. 1010–53 CE), houses the largest shivalinga, 5.5 m (18 ft) high and 2.5 m (8 ft 2 in.) in circumference.

Jatayu Centre, Chadayamangalam, Kerala: largest bird sculpture

TALLEST STATUES OF INDIA (TOP 10)

Statue	Place	Height	Description
1. Statue of Unity' of Sardar Vallabhbhai Patel	Sadhu Bet Island in the Narmada River near Rajpipla, Narmada District, Gujarat	182 m (597 ft)	Designed by sculptor Ram V. Sutar, it took nearly four years to build and cost an estimated ₹29.89 billion (2,989 crore). It is the world's tallest statue.
2. Statue of Belief (Bishwas Swaroopam)	Nathdwara, Rajasthan	112.4 m (369 ft)	It is a statue of Lord Shiva. It is the world's tallest sitting statue.
3. Statue of Equality of Sri Ramanujacharya	Hyderabad, Telangana	65.8 m (216 ft)	The Statue is made of panchaloha, a combination of five metals: gold, silver, copper, brass, and zinc.
4. Staue of Social Justice	Vijaywada, Andhra Pradesh	62.78 m (206 ft)	This Dr B. R. Ambedkar statue project incurred a cost of ₹404.35 crore.
5. Hanuman Statue	Beside Vamsadhara River, Madapam, Andhra Pradesh	52 m (171 ft)	This is the world's tallest Hanuman statue.
6. Panchamukhi Hanuman Statue	Bidanagere, Karnataka	49 m (161 ft)	It is a five-faced Hanuman statue.
7. Hanuman Statue	Manav Bharti University, Solan, Himachal Pradesh	47 m (155 ft)	The statue is made of reinforced cement and has a design life of 100 years.
8. Muthumalai Murugan Statue	Salem, Tamil Nadu	44.5 m (146 ft)	This is the world's tallest Murugan statue.
9. Maa Vaishno Devi Statue	Vrindavan, Uttar Pradesh	43 m (141 ft)	Around 400 tonnes of steel and concrete was used to build this statue.
10. Veera Abhaya Anjaneya Hanuman Swami	Paritala, near Vijayawada, Andhra Pradesh	41 m (135 ft)	The Paritala Anjaneya Temple is located in the hollow at the statue's base.

1 2 3 5 6 8 9

BRIDGES

First iron bridge

The first iron bridge was built by Jessop and Company Limited in 1815 over the Gomti River in Lucknow in Uttar Pradesh. Designed by the Scottish engineer John Rennie the Elder, it was made at Butterfly Iron Works, England, for the nawab of Awadh.

First cable-stayed road bridge

The Akkar Bridge in Jorethang, over the Rangit River in Sikkim, is an all-concrete, cable-stayed road bridge built in 1988. It spans a 1.5 km (0.93 mile) wide and nearly 20 m (65 ft 7 in.) deep valley. The bridge consists of two 77 m (252 ft 7 in.) symmetrical spans supported from a single central pylon. With 17 pairs of cable stays, the 55 m (180 ft) high pylon supports the decking 21 m (69 ft) above the river bed.

Only bascule bridge

The only bascule bridge in the country is constructed on Tolly's Nullah (or Adiganga) at Khidirpur in Kolkata, West Bengal. Operated by the Kolkata Port Trust, it is built in two halves, each of which goes up to allow ships to pass through. The bridge has a span of about 35 m (114 ft 10 in.) and was built by Wagner Biro AG, Austria. It was commissioned on 5 November 1966 and replaced a swing bridge built in 1892.

Longest bridge of India

The Mumbai Trans Harbour Link (MTHL) (later named Atal Bihari Vajpayee Sewri–Nhava Sheva Atal Setu) in Mumbai, Maharashtra, the longest bridge in India, is 21.8 km (13.55 mile) long. This six-lane bridge has about 16.5 km length over the sea. About 5.5 km of the bridge lies on land. It connects Mumbai International Airport and Navi Mumbai International Airport. Travelling to Pune, Goa, and south India will now be faster too.

Longest balanced cantilever bridge

The 3,015 m (9,892 ft) road bridge across the Brahmaputra River at Tezpur, Assam, called Kolia Bhomora Setu, is the longest bridge that has been provided with a central suspended span of 15 m (49 ft 2.5 in.) length because of its geographical location in a seismic zone. The bridge consists of 24 spans of 120 m (393 ft 8 in.) each and two shore spans of 67.5 m (221 ft 5 in.) each. With a carriageway of 7.5 m (24 ft 7 in.) width, it was constructed between October 1981 and April 1987.

Longest river bridge

The Bhupen Hazarika Setu, also referred to as the Dhola–Sadiya Bridge, connecting Dhola in Dibrugarh District and Sadiya in Lakhimpur District, Assam, is the longest river bridge. The 9.15 km (5.7 miles) long bridge on the Brahmaputra River was inaugurated on 26 May 2017 by Prime Minister Narendra Modi. It is named after Bhupen Hazarika, a well-known Assamese musician and film-maker, who died in 2011.

Bhupen Hazarika Setu: longest river bridge

Longest Bailey bridge

The 182.8 m (600 ft) long suspension bridge over the Chubi River in Wokha, Nagaland, connects the Mokokchung District and the Dimapur District of Nagaland.

Widest double-decker steel bridge

The North–South corridor of Nagpur Metro Rail Project comprises an 18.9 m (62 ft) wide double-decker viaduct: the lower level has a highway flyover and the upper level has a double-line metro rail. It is a two-level bridge over existing railway lines, crossing the Indian Railways tracks at Gaddigodam at a skew angle of 19 degrees. The span is straight with an effective dimension of 80 m (262 ft) centre to centre of pier. The project was commissioned on 13 May 2022 and commercial operations began on 11 December 2022.

Atal Setu: longest bridge of India

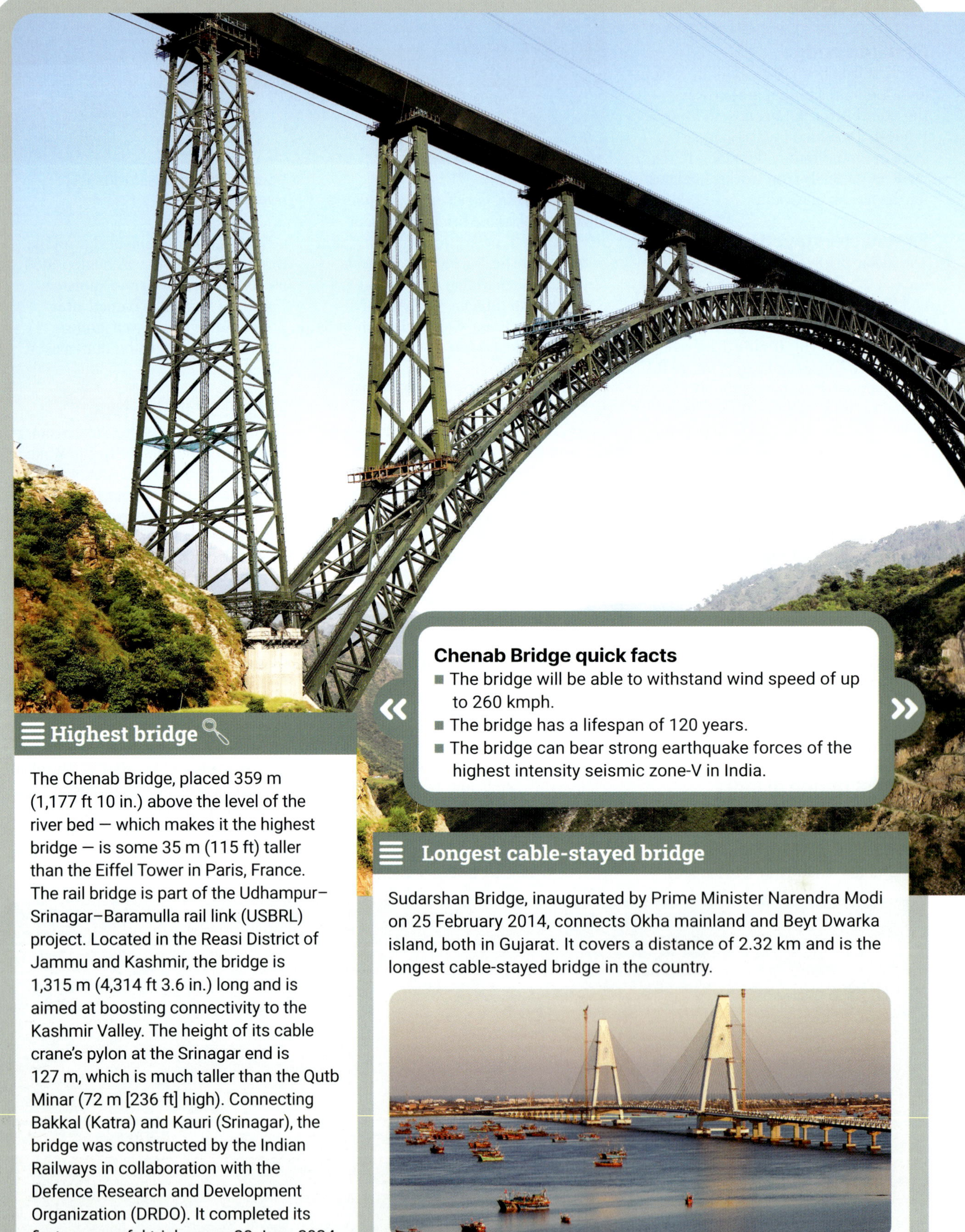

Chenab Bridge quick facts

- The bridge will be able to withstand wind speed of up to 260 kmph.
- The bridge has a lifespan of 120 years.
- The bridge can bear strong earthquake forces of the highest intensity seismic zone-V in India.

Highest bridge

The Chenab Bridge, placed 359 m (1,177 ft 10 in.) above the level of the river bed — which makes it the highest bridge — is some 35 m (115 ft) taller than the Eiffel Tower in Paris, France. The rail bridge is part of the Udhampur–Srinagar–Baramulla rail link (USBRL) project. Located in the Reasi District of Jammu and Kashmir, the bridge is 1,315 m (4,314 ft 3.6 in.) long and is aimed at boosting connectivity to the Kashmir Valley. The height of its cable crane's pylon at the Srinagar end is 127 m, which is much taller than the Qutb Minar (72 m [236 ft] high). Connecting Bakkal (Katra) and Kauri (Srinagar), the bridge was constructed by the Indian Railways in collaboration with the Defence Research and Development Organization (DRDO). It completed its first successful trial run on 20 June 2024.

Longest cable-stayed bridge

Sudarshan Bridge, inaugurated by Prime Minister Narendra Modi on 25 February 2014, connects Okha mainland and Beyt Dwarka island, both in Gujarat. It covers a distance of 2.32 km and is the longest cable-stayed bridge in the country.

Highest railway bridge

The Chenab Bridge, the highest bridge in India, is also the highest railway bridge in the world.

First blast-proof bridge

The Chenab Bridge, made of 28,660 tonnes of steel, is India's first blast-proof bridge.

The Chenab Bridge

Longest cantilever bridge

The Howrah Bridge (or Rabindra Setu) is India's longest cantilever bridge. It spans the Hooghly River in Kolkata, West Bengal. It was completed in 1943. It is the seventh longest cantilever bridge in the world.

Official name: Rabindra Setu; **design:** suspension type balanced cantilever and truss arch; **total length:** 705 m (2,313 ft); **length of the suspended span:** 457 m (1,499 ft); **width:** 21.6 m (71 ft) with two footpaths of 4.6 m (15 ft) on either side; **opened:** 3 February 1943

Busiest bridge

With over 1,00,000 vehicles and over 1,50,000 pedestrians using this bridge a day, Rabindra Setu is also India's busiest bridge.

Bridge at the highest location

The bridge at the highest location in the country lies at a height of 5,602 m (18,380 ft) at Khardung La in Ladakh. The 30 m (98 ft 5 in.) long Bailey bridge rests on ice. It consists of square diamond-braced panels that can be assembled on approach and then pushed or pinned together at the corners to form a girder.

Longest road-and-rail bridge

Bogibeel Bridge on the Brahmaputra River, between Dhemaji and Dibrugarh Districts, Assam, is the longest road-and-rail bridge, with a length of 4.94 km. The bridge has a double-line 1.676 m (5 ft 6 in.) broad-gauge railway on the lower deck and a three-lane road on the upper one. It is India's first bridge with fully welded steel-concrete support beams to withstand earthquakes of magnitudes up to 7 on the Richter scale.

First cable-stayed rail bridge

India's first cable-stayed rail bridge, Anji Khad Bridge, is in Jammu and Kashmir. It spans across the Chenab River. The total length of cable strand used to build this bridge is 653 km.

Bogibeel Bridge: longest road-and-rail bridge

DAMS

Earliest canal system
Canal systems have existed since the pre-Harappan era (around 2500 BCE). Excavations at Dholavira in Gujarat have revealed ingenious systems for diverting water from seasonal nullahs.

Longest canal
The Indira Gandhi Canal, or Rajasthan Canal, which starts in Punjab and ends in Rajasthan, is 649 km long, and is the world's second longest canal. Its schemes include 6,308 km of distributary canals.

Earliest dam
The earliest dam discovered was built on Sudarshan Lake in Junagadh (then Girinagar) in Gujarat. It dates to 326 BCE.

Oldest extant dam
The Grand Anicut Dam, also known as the Kallanai Dam, built on the Kaveri River, 24 km from Tiruchirappalli in Tamil Nadu, is the oldest extant dam known in India. This masonry dam, which was built in the second century CE by the Chola king Aditha Karikalan (or Aditya II), is 330 m (1,083 ft) long, 5.49 m (18 ft) high, and 12–18 m (39–59 ft) wide. The ancient dam was remodelled, repaired, and fitted with sluice gates in 1899–1902. For centuries, it has irrigated more than a million acres (0.4 million hectares) of land.

Longest breakwater
The V.O. Chidambaranar Port (earlier Tuticorin Port) North Breakwater in Tamil Nadu is the longest at 4.14 km.

First hydroelectric project
Shivanasamudra Falls hydroelectric project in Chamarajanagar District, Karnataka, opened in 1902 and involved the harnessing of the Kaveri River to supply electrical energy to run the machinery at the Kolar goldfields. The power station is still a functioning one.

Tehri Dam

Largest river dam
The Sardar Sarovar Dam is a gravity dam on the Narmada River near Navagam in Surat District, Gujarat. One of the 30 dams planned on the Narmada River, it is the largest such structure to be built and among the largest dams in the world. Four Indian states – Gujarat, Madhya Pradesh, Maharashtra, and Rajasthan – receive water and electricity supplied from the dam.

Highest dam
The Tehri Dam, near Pratapnagar in Tehri Garhwal District in Uttarakhand, is situated on the Bhagirathi River with a maximum height above foundation of 260.5 m (854 ft and 8 in). It's a rock-fill structure and its reservoir holds 21,00,000 acre-feet of water. It also ranks among the world's top ten dams.

Largest water reservoir
Indira Sagar Dam is a multipurpose project on the Narmada River in East Nimar District of Madhya Pradesh. The reservoir has a capacity of 12.2 billion cubic metre (98,90,701 acre feet) and, in terms of water storage, stands as the largest reservoir in India.

Largest barrage
The Farakka Barrage on the Ganga River was opened in 1972 to help maintain navigable depths in Shyama Prasad Mookerjee Port (earlier Kolkata Port). Its length of 2,245 m (7,365 ft 6 in.) contains 108 gated bays of 18 m (59 ft) each and two 8 m (26 ft) fish locks.

Left: Sardar Sarovar Dam
Right: Farakka Barrage

LIGHTHOUSES

Oldest lighthouses

In 1766, two signal houses were built, one on Old Woman's Island (now part of Colaba) and the other at Malabar Point, in Bombay, Maharashtra. The former was replaced by the first proper lighthouse built in 1768–71. This threw a beam seven leagues seaward in clear weather at 45.72 m (150 ft). It was repaired in 1828 and 1853 but stopped operating when the Prongs Lighthouse was installed in 1874. Prongs Lighthouse is situated in a military area, so it has restricted access.

Oldest functional lighthouses

The lighthouse built in 1821 on Sagar Island, at the mouth of the Hooghly River in West Bengal, was renovated in 1911. Its elevation from mean sea level is 26 m (85 ft 4 in.) and the tower is 25 m (82 ft) high. Its flashing light has a range of 31 km in clear weather.

Highest lighthouse

The highest lighthouse from mean sea level is at Dolphin's Nose at Visakhapatnam, Andhra Pradesh. Its masonry tower rises 19 m (62 ft 4 in.) up from the ground level, and it has an elevation of 173 m (567 ft 7 in.) from mean sea level – which makes it the highest in India.

First unmanned lighthouse

Near Thalassery (earlier Tellicherry) in Kannur District, Kerala, stands the first unmanned lighthouse. It was built in 1835 and renovated in 1924. It is at an altitude of 27 m (89 ft) from mean sea level, and its range is 8 km.

Lighthouse in Thalassery, Kerala: first unmanned lighthouse

Tallest lighthouse

The Jakhau Lighthouse in Gujarat is the tallest at 45 m (147.63 ft); from mean sea level it is 46 m (151 ft) high. It was established in 1957, and the present tower was built in 1965. Located on the main quay of Jakhau, a fishing port in western Kachchh, the lighthouse has a range of 33 km.

AMUSEMENT ZONES

First indoor amusement play station

Funky Orbit at Ansal Plaza Mall on Khel Gaon Marg in New Delhi was launched on 15 June 2000 by Panoramic Entertainment Pvt. Ltd. The multi-tiered play station had an 8.53 m (28 ft) long curly slide and a ball pool. It closed down in 2011.

First amusement park

Appu Ghar at Pragati Maidan, New Delhi, the first family entertainment centre in India, opened during the 1982 Asian Games in Delhi. It was named after the Games' mascot – Appu the elephant. Shutting down in 2008, it has reopened in Gurugram, Haryana.

MECHANICAL AND GENERAL STRUCTURES

First elevator

The first elevator was installed at Raj Bhavan, in Calcutta (now Kolkata), West Bengal in 1892. It used Otis's first design of an electric lift.

First hand-operated crane

The first hand-operated crane was built by Jessop & Company in 1850. The 5-tonne crane was installed at the then Calcutta Port (now Shyama Prasad Mookerjee Port) Customs.

First marine amusement park

In 1998, Dolphin City was set up by Amusements and Picnic Resorts Pvt. Ltd in Chennai, Tamil Nadu, with three performing dolphins and a performing sea lion show. Following the death of the performing dolphins, the marine amusement park featured sea lion performances, underwater viewing, and leisure boating.

First houseboat

The first houseboat, named *Victory*, was built in 1888 and stationed at the Dal Lake in Srinagar, Jammu and Kashmir.

First live entertainment, theatre, and leisure destination

Kingdom of Dreams in Gurugram, Haryana, is India's first live entertainment, theatre, and leisure destination. Spread over 6 acres (2.4 hectares), it is run by the Great Indian Nautanki Company (GINC).

Most names engraved on a monument

India Gate in Delhi carries the names of 13,516 British and Indian soldiers of the British Indian Army, who died during 1914–21 at various fronts of the First World War and the Third Anglo-Afghan War. This constitutes the largest number of names inscribed on a monument. Designed by architect Edwin Lutyens, the arch was completed in 1921. It is 42.3 m (139 ft) high and 9.1 m (30 ft) wide.

First floating restaurant

The first floating restaurant was built at Sirhind, Punjab, on the Bhakra Canal in 1979. The eight-room air-conditioned restaurant was part of a tourist complex.

First space-frame concrete structure

The first space-frame structure in reinforced concrete was the Hall of Nations at the Trade Fair Authority of India exhibition grounds in Pragati Maidan, New Delhi. Built during 1971–72, the hall offered an uninterrupted exhibition area of 6,700 sq m (72,120 sq ft) in a 82 m x 82 m x 27 m (269 ft x 269 ft x 88 ft 7 in.) pyramid supported at eight points.

First revolving restaurant

Neelkanth Patang at Ahmedabad, Gujarat, was the first revolving restaurant at 67.4 m (221 ft) above ground level. Opened in 1984, it has a 90-minute rotation, which unfolds a view of the old and new city of Ahmedabad.

Sri Shanmukhananda Hall

Largest auditorium
Sri Shanmukhananda Hall, inaugurated on 22 August 1963 in Bombay (now Mumbai), Maharashtra, has a total capacity of 3,012 seats. The ground floor seats 1,552, the first balcony 896 and the second balcony 564 people. The stage has a depth and width of 16 m (52 ft) and a height of 6.4 m (21 ft).

Largest table
The teakwood table in the Banquet Hall at the Rashtrapati Bhavan in Delhi can seat 104 people at a time.

First water park
Shanku's Water Park on the Ahmedabad–Mahesana Highway in Gujarat was launched by Shankarbhai Chaudhary in 1993, on a 75-acre (30.35 hectares) campus. It introduced a giant 15.24 m (50 ft) speed slide that ended in a shallow water pool, a spiral ride, a wave pool that simulated sea waves, and a kids' corner.

Largest cooking vessel
The original badi deg (big vessel), christened Deg-i-Chittor-Kusba, or the 'Chittor-conquering vessel', said to be presented by the Mughal emperor Akbar to the dargah of Khwaja Moinuddin Chishti in Ajmer, Rajasthan, could hold 4,000 kg of food at a time that was enough for 12,000 people.

Largest official residence
The Rashtrapati Bhavan in New Delhi, the official residence of the president of India, has 340 rooms, 18 staircases, 74 lobbies, 37 salons, 1 km of corridors, 37 fountains, and 190 acres (76.9 hectares) of gardens. The residence covers 50 acres (20.2 hectares) of a 330-acre (133.5 hectare) estate.

Largest retractable roof
Kunta International Ltd, Noida, Uttar Pradesh, designed, built, installed, and commissioned an electrically driven retractable roof on a reusable structure on the presidential dais on Rajpath (now Kartavya Path), New Delhi, for Republic Day 2018. Made of steel and polycarbonate sheets with inbuilt sensors, it was 30.5 m (100 ft) wide and 6.4 m (21 ft) deep.

Tallest chimney
The 275.2 m (903 ft) tall chimney of the Reliance Dahanu Thermal Power Station, Dahanu, in Palghar District, Maharashtra, is India's tallest RCC chimney. The base diameter of the chimney is 7 m (23 ft).

Largest glasshouse
A glass-covered hall in Davanagere, Karnataka, completed in 2018, covers 7,334 sq m (78,942.5 sq ft). It houses a horticultural information centre and a botanical garden.

Longest conveyor
The longest single-belt international conveyor stretches from Nongtrai Village near Shella, East Khasi Hills District, Meghalaya, in India, to a cement factory at Chhatak in Sunamganj District, Bangladesh. It is about 17 km long (7 km in India and 10 km in Bangladesh) and conveys limestone and shale at 960 tonnes/hr. The conveyor was engineered by AUMUND France and Larsen & Toubro and installed by Beltpro. Its rollers are unusually designed to deal with both horizontal and vertical terrain curves.

Largest multiplex
Mayajaal in Kanathur in Chennai, Tamil Nadu, has the largest movie multiplex with 16 screens and a seating capacity of 2,600. It is part of an entertainment centre that houses a shopping mall, a sports complex, and a resort.

Longest underground pipeline
The Hazira–Bijapur–Jagdishpur (HBJ) gas pipeline is India's first cross-country gas pipeline. This project by GAIL (India) Ltd began in 1986 to supply gas to fertilizer plants in Uttar Pradesh. The first phase, consisting of a non-branched 1,750 km grid, was later expanded to supply gas for industrial and domestic use in Rajasthan, Haryana, and the National Capital Territory (NCT). This extended the grid length to 3,474 km.

Oldest ice-skating rink
The ice-skating rink near Lakkar

Largest glasshouse: A glass-covered hall in Davanagere

Bazaar in Simla (now Shimla), Himachal Pradesh, was founded in 1920 by one Mr Blessington. Initially out of bounds for Indians during British rule, it is now managed by the Shimla Ice-Skating Club and is open for skating between the winter months of December and February.

MODERN STRUCTURES

First skyscraper

The first skyscraper Usha Kiran, an apartment building of 26 storeys in Bombay was the first of high-rise buildings. It was built between 1964 and 1967.

Tallest building

Lokhandwala Minerva, a 300.6 m (986 ft), 78-floor (above ground, below ground 2) skyscraper in Mumbai is the tallest completed building in India. Developed by Lokhandwala Kataria Construction Pvt. Ltd, the building was completed in 2023.

First reinforced-concrete structure

The Golconde dormitory at Sri Aurobindo Ashram in Pondicherry (now Puducherry) was designed by Czech-American architect Antonin Raymond (1888–1976) and completed in 1948. It is the first reinforced-concrete structure in India. All its features evolved from a study of the local climatic conditions and the occupants' needs.

First underground market

First underground market Palika Bazaar, the air-conditioned underground market at Connaught Place (now Rajiv Chowk) in New Delhi, was set up in 1978.

Largest office building

Surat Diamond Bourse (SDB), Surat, Gujarat, covers a built-up area of 6,22,450 sq m (67,00,000 sq ft) and can accommodate over 4,500 offices and 67,000 professionals. This 15-storey interconnected building has 131 lifts to connect different floors and has surpassed the Pentagon, US, by almost 55,000 sq ft to become the world's largest office building. SDG was inaugurated by Prime Minister Narendra Modi on 17 December 2023.

First all-steel building

The ICICI headquarters in Mumbai, Maharashtra, designed by Raja Aederi and built in 1995, have a superstructure area of 39,948 sq m (4,30,000 sq ft), two-level basements with a total area of 21,368 sq m (2,30,000 sq ft), and a structural area of 14,000 sq m (1,50,700 sq ft).

First underground market: Palika Bazaar

Tallest escalator

The Janakpuri West metro station on the Magenta Line of the Delhi Metro features India's tallest escalator. The escalator is 15.6 m (51 ft 2 in.) high.

SPECIALIZED STRUCTURES

Oldest slide

The rock-cut slide at Mamallapuram in Chengalpattu District, Tamil Nadu, is said to be the world's oldest children's slide.

First floating cottages

Kabeer Khader and M.R. Narayanan's Floatels India in 1999 launched 20 floating cottages at Poovar Island Resort in Thiruvananthapuram District, Kerala. Designed by architect N. Mahesh, they are built on laminated ferro-cement platforms.

Largest tent structure

The largest permanent tent structure stood at the Osho International Commune in Pune, Maharashtra. Oval in shape – with a 62.75 m (205 ft 10 in.) major axis and a 32.8 m (107 ft 7 in.) minor axis – it had a floor area of 1,582 sq m (17,029 sq ft).

The roof, which was 3.9 m (12 ft 9.5 in.) high, was a free-spanning, tensile structure on a three-hinged steel arch covering 45.5 m (149 ft 3 in.). It used nylon reinforced PVC material, weighing 1,990 kg.

First igloo stay

Keylinga's Manali Igloo Stay, near Sethan Village, about 16 km from Manali in Himachal Pradesh, was opened in 2017 by Vikas Kumar and Tashi Dorje of Keylinga Himalayan Adventures. Starting with two fully functional igloos, the duo provide guests sleeping bags with extra fleece, and hot-water bottles.

Largest pillar-less dome

The World Peace Monument is located at the Maharashtra Institute of Technology's World Peace University (MIT -WPU) campus at Loni Kalbhor near Pune, Maharashtra. At a height of 29 m (95 ft), the world's biggest pillar-less dome is built on top of the World Peace Prayer Hall and Library and has a diameter of 48.7 m (160 ft), larger than the dome of the Vatican 42.5 m (139 ft 5 in.). Completed in 2018, the dome has a bell hanging from the centre.

World Peace Monument: largest pillar-less dome

The Rani ki Vav: most elaborate stepwell

Most elaborate stepwell

The Rani ki Vav ('queen's stepwell') at Patan, Gujarat, was built by Rani Udayamati, the queen of King Bhimadeva I (r. 1022–64 CE) of the Chalukya dynasty, in memory of her husband. It measures 65 m x 20 m (213 ft 3 in. x 65 ft 7 in.) and is over 28 m (91 ft 10 in.) deep. Originally, over 800 sculptures decorated it.

Supertech Emerald Court Housing Society: India's biggest demolition

India's Biggest Demolition

Two illegally constructed towers at the Supertech Emerald Court Housing Society in Sector 93A, Noida, Uttar Pradesh, made headlines on 28 August 2022. The 103 m (338 ft) high towers were demolished by the 'waterfall implosion' technique in a mere 12 seconds! The demolition of these twin residential towers was ordered by the Supreme Court and carried out by a Mumbai-based company, Edifice Engineering, along with the South African firm Jet Demolitions as their expert partner. With the grounding of Apex (32 storeys) and Ceyane (29 storeys) towers, India joined the club of countries that have razed buildings taller than 100 m (328 ft).

Largest underground aquarium

The Bagh-e-Bahu Aquarium at the Bagh-e-Bahu Garden that surrounds Bahu Fort in Jammu in Jammu and Kashmir is the largest underground aquarium in India. At more than

First ropeway

India opened its first ropeway service in Rajgir, Bihar. It was inaugurated on 25 October 1969 by the then president V. V. Giri.

Highest ropeway

The Gulmarg Gondola, a gondola lift that covers 2,540 m (8,333 ft), is a joint venture of the Jammu and Kashmir government and the French firm Pomagalski SA. Its first stage transfers people from Gulmarg at 2,600 m (8,530 ft) to Kongdori Station in Kongdori Valley. The second stage goes to 3,747 m (12,293 ft) on Kongdori Mountain, with the highest point at 4,200 m (13,780 ft).

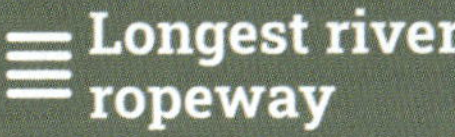

Longest river ropeway

A 1.8 km (5,906 ft) long ropeway was opened in August 2020 across the Brahmaputra River in Guwahati, Assam. It connects the southern and northern parts of the city, cutting down travel time from an hour to eight minutes.

220 m (721 ft 9 in.) in length, this fish-shaped aquarium has freshwater and saltwater fish species in 24 caves with 13 smaller caves.

First eco-hotel

Asia's first certified eco-hotel, the Orchid, opened in Mumbai, Maharashtra, in 1997.

Longest transportation railway tunnel

The 11.21 km long Pir Panjal or Banihal Railway Tunnel is the longest transportation tunnel in India. It connects Bichleri Valley, Banihal, to Qazigund in the Kashmir Valley. The first train here was flagged off on 26 June 2013.

Pir Panjal or Banihal Railway Tunnel

Search...

GENERAL

First fully organic state

Sikkim was officially declared India's first fully organic state on 18 January 2016. It has succeeded in converting around 75,000 hectares (1,85,329 acres) of its agricultural land to certified organic land by implementing organic practices as per the guidelines of the National Programme for Organic Production.

First nationwide farm loan waiver

The first nationwide farm loan waiver in independent India was the Agricultural and Rural Debt Relief Scheme (ARDRS), announced by the then finance minister Madhu Dandavate, under the V.P. Singh government and implemented in 1990–91. It cost the exchequer ₹10,000 crore (100 billion).

Madhu Dandavate

Biggest farm loan waiver

The Agricultural Debt Waiver and Debt Relief Scheme of 2008 under the UPA government was the biggest farm loan waiver in India by value. It costed the exchequer ₹60,000 crore (600 billion) and benefitted over 3 crore small and marginal farmers.

First agricultural theme park

N.K. Kurian, a civil engineer, is the person behind Mango Meadows. It is the world's first man-made agricultural theme park, spread on 12 hectares (29.65 acres) of land, in Kottayam, Kerala. Work on the park began in 2004, and it was opened to the public in December 2016. With saplings and seeds collected from 15 countries, currently the park has 4,500 species of plants, including 1,900 medicinal plants, 700 trees, and 900 flowering plants.

First fruit train

A train exclusively carrying fruit – 890 tonnes of locally grown bananas – was flagged off from Tadipatri railway station in Anantapur District, Andhra Pradesh. It reached the Jawaharlal Nehru Port in Mumbai, Maharashtra, on 31 January 2020. The train was laden with 43 refrigerator containers of bananas that had been despatched for export to international markets.

First state/UT to regulate crops

Telangana became the first state in the country to stipulate when and how much of which crops to grow for its farmers. From the beginning of the kharif season in 2020, the state decided to regulate the cropping pattern with the help of a detailed cropping map and a seed regulation authority. The emphasis has been to drive supply according to the market demand.

First state/UT to enact a law on contract farming

Tamil Nadu became the first state in the country to pass a law on contract farming called the Agricultural Produce and Livestock Contract Farming and Services (Promotion and Facilitation) Act in February 2019. Contract farming enables more transparency, and legally safeguards the interests of farmers, producer companies, and purchasers. The Act covers the produce of agriculture, sericulture, horticulture, apiculture, animal husbandry, and forest activities.

HISTORY

Earliest ploughed field

Archaeologists B.B. Lal and B.K. Thapar of the Archaeological Survey of India (ASI) found a ploughed field dated to c. 2450–2300 BCE during excavations at Kalibangan in Pilibangan Tehsil in Hanumangarh District, Rajasthan.

Earliest irrigation

Evidence of irrigation on agricultural land in the Indian subcontinent dates to the Chalcolithic period (3000–1000 BCE). The Inamgaon area of Maharashtra has a prehistoric mud embankment structure with a stone foundation. This was connected to the Ghod River by a number of channels. Floodwater was used effectively to irrigate the surrounding regions during the dry months by storing it and then distributing it.

Mango Meadows, Kottayam, Kerala

Earliest cotton cultivation

The earliest evidence for cotton production comes from the Harappan civilization (2500–1700 BCE). The earliest sample of cotton material was discovered by archaeologist Daya Ram Sahni during 1921–22 in Mohenjo-daro (now in Pakistan). It was a small fragment of cotton clinging to the side of a vase and dyed red with madder pigment (*Rubia tinctorum*).

First famine commission

The Campbell Commission set up in 1866 after the famine in 1865–66 (also known as the Odisha famine since it was most severe there), was the first famine commission in the country. Under the chairmanship of Sir George Campbell, it was followed by the appointment of a committee. It blamed the government machinery for the famine and its tragic effects.

Sir George Campbell

First agricultural society

William Carey, a British Christian missionary, social reformer, translator, and anthropologist, founded the Agri-Horticultural Society of India in September 1820 in Calcutta (now Kolkata), West Bengal. It was set up to help disseminate scientific information among the people.

William Carey

Cryobanks are facilities that store living tissue at very low temperatures. The temperature is maintained at −196°C using liquid nitrogen.

First society of soil sciences

The Indian Society of Soil Sciences was formed on 22 December 1934 in Calcutta with 28 members. It was formally inaugurated on 3 January 1935 at the Presidency College (now Presidency University). Sir Bryce C. Burt, then agricultural commissioner in the Imperial (now Indian) Council of Agricultural Research (ICAR), was its first president and Prof. J.N. Mukherjee its first secretary.

First agricultural university

The G.B. (Govind Ballabh) Pant University of Agriculture and Technology (GBPUA&T), also known as Pantnagar University, was the first agricultural university in India. It was inaugurated on 17 November 1960 as the Uttar Pradesh Agricultural University (UPAU). Later, in 1972, its name was changed to Govind Ballabh Pant University of Agriculture and Technology after the first chief minister of Uttar Pradesh and Bharat Ratna recipient Pandit Govind Ballabh Pant.

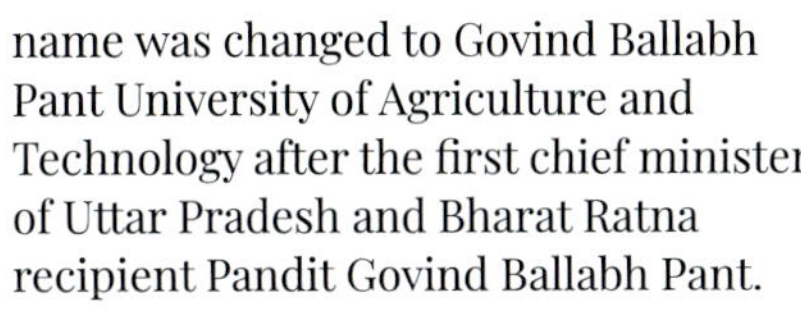

G.B. Pant University of Agriculture and Technology

First pollen cryobank

The first pollen cryobank (frost bank) was established in 1983 at the Indian Institute of Horticultural Research, Bengaluru, Karnataka, to conserve genetic biodiversity among plants and support the work of crop breeders.

First spices research institute

The regional station for spice research, set up at Kozhikode, Kerala, in 1975 is the apex research organization for spices in the country. It later evolved into the Indian Institute of Spices Research in 1986.

Oldest locust control programme

The Locust Warning Organization (LWO), set up in 1939 in Karachi (now in Pakistan) by the British, is the oldest locust control programme in the world. In 1946, the LWO moved to Delhi under the Directorate of Plant Protection, Quarantine and Storage, Ministry of Agriculture and Farmers' Welfare, Government of India. It surveys locust populations and issues bulletins.

A locust on a leaf

First agricultural research institute

The Imperial Agricultural Research Institute, established in 1905 at Pusa, Samastipur District, Bihar, was India's first agricultural research institute. After the building was damaged in an earthquake in 1934, the institute was moved to New Delhi in 1936. It is now known as the Indian Agricultural Research Institute (IARI) and is the oldest agricultural institute in India.

Groundwater irrigation system: pumping groundwater to rice fields

Tocklai Experimental Station, Jorhat, Assam

Central Tuber Crops Research Institute, Sreekariyam, Thiruvananthapuram, Kerala

Largest groundwater irrigation system

India has the largest groundwater irrigation system in the world with 39 million hectares (96.4 million acres) of land under this kind of irrigation. Besides groundwater, India's irrigation depends on canals from rivers, well-based systems, tanks, and other rainwater harvesting systems. About two-thirds of farmlands in the country still depend on the monsoon.

Oldest tea research station

Set up in 1911, the Tocklai Experimental Station in Jorhat, Assam, is the world's oldest and largest tea research station. Its many contributions include the invention of tea machinery and the development of 30 vegetative clones. The transfer of innovative technology to its member estates is carried out through its advisory network. This network covers 1,076 tea estates occupying 3,41,049 hectares (8,42,750.4 acres) of land spread over the Brahmaputra Valley, the Barak Valley, Tripura, the Dooars, Darjeeling, and the Terai areas. Tocklai has its regional R&D centre at Nagrakata in Jalpaiguri District, West Bengal.

Only weed research centre

The Directorate of Weed Science Research (DWSR), Jabalpur, Madhya Pradesh, set up the National Research Centre for Weed Science on 22 April 1989 – the only one in the world for weed management research.

Only research centre for tropical tuber crops

The Central Tuber Crops Research Institute at Sreekariyam in Thiruvananthapuram District, Kerala, is the only institute in the world dedicated to research on tropical tuber crops. It was established in 1963.

Research institute located at the highest altitude

The Defence Institute of High Altitude Research (DIHAR), situated at 3,505 m (11,499 ft) in Leh, Ladakh, is a laboratory of the Defence Research Development Organization (DRDO). It was established in 1962 to help Indian defence troops as well as farmers of the region with appropriate agro-animal technologies.

AWARDS AND HONOURS

First Indian scientist to receive the Ramon Magsaysay Award

Geneticist Dr M.S. Swaminathan received the Ramon Magsaysay award in 1971 for community leadership and became the first Indian scientist to do so. Known as the 'Father of the Green Revolution' for his leading role in food self-sufficiency in India, he was the director of the Indian Agricultural Research Institute in Delhi at the time. Dr Swaminathan advocates environmentally sustainable agriculture as well as preservation of biodiversity, culminating in what he has termed an 'evergreen' revolution.

Dr M.S. Swaminathan

First Indian fellow of the Royal Society

Dr Benjamin Peary Pal, the first director of the Indian Council of Agricultural Research, was also the first Indian agricultural scientist to become a Fellow of the Royal Society of London, UK, while in office, in 1972. He was also awarded the top national civilian awards: the Padma Shri (1959), the Padma Bhushan (1968), and the Padma Vibhushan (1987).

First Indian president of the International Society of Soil Sciences

Dr J.S. Kanwar was elected president of the International Society of Soil Sciences for the period 1978–82. The Society was founded in 1924, mainly by European agro-pedologists interested in establishing standardized methods of soil analysis.

First winner of the World Food Prize

In 1987, Dr M.S. Swaminathan became the first Indian to win the World Food Prize. He was an agronomist, agricultural scientist, and plant geneticist. This global award is given to outstanding individuals who have advanced human development by improving the quality, quantity, or availability of food in the world. So far, eight Indians have won the World Food Prize and the most recent was Dr Rattan Lal, an Indian-born British scientist from the USA, in 2020.

Dr Rattan Lal

FARMLANDS AND PRINCIPAL CROPS

Largest single farm

The Central State Farm at Suratgarh in Rajasthan, with an area of 6,296 hectares (15,557.8 acres), is said to be the largest farm in Asia.

Largest average farm holdings in a state/UT

As per the 2015–16 agricultural census, Nagaland has the largest farm holdings, with 4.87 hectares (12.03 acres) as the average size of an operational unit.

First tea estate

In 1837, the British East India Company set up the first tea estate at Chabua in Dibrugarh District, Assam. Now the estate is owned by Amalgamated Plantations Private Ltd. The first Tea Committee in India was set up in 1834 by the then Governor General of India, William Bentinck.

Highest tea garden

The Korakundah Tea Estate of the United Nilgiri Tea Estates Co. Ltd, near Coonoor in the Nilgiris in Tamil Nadu, has its highest tea garden at an altitude of 2,471 m (8,107 ft).

First hybrid Basmati rice

The IARI, New Delhi, developed and released RH-10 in 2001, the first hybrid superfine-grained, aromatic rice in the world. The optimum yield of this variety of rice, with typical Basmati traits, is 7 tonnes/hectare.

Tallest sugar cane

Vedant Rajendra Yadav (b. 28 January 1998) from Fursungi Village in Pune District, Maharashtra, grew a sugar cane plant that was 13.1 m (43 ft) tall in January 2021.

Tallest paddy plant

Tanaji Nikam, a farmer in Vannur Village in Kolhapur, Maharashtra, grew a paddy plant 2.8 m (9 ft 2 in.) tall in 2005, using organic manure.

Only producer of five commercial silk varieties

India is the only producer of all five commercial varieties of silk, viz., mulberry, oak tussore, tropical tussore, *eri*, and *muga*. Golden muga is produced only in India. During 2018–19, India produced 31,906 tonnes of raw silk.

Handwoven pure golden muga silk

Korakundah Tea Estate, Nilgiris, Tamil Nadu

ALL INDIA PROJECTED COST OF PRODUCTION FOR PADDY AND WHEAT

COST (in ₹ per quintal)

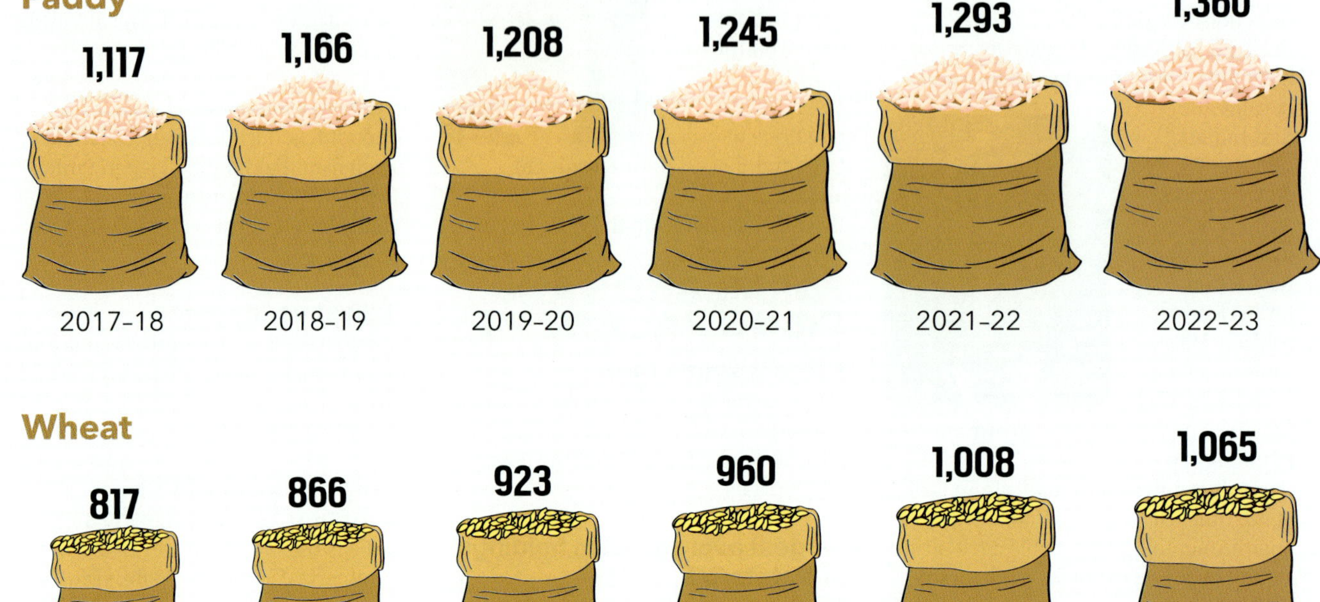

SOURCE: Commission for Agricultural Costs and Prices, Agricultural Statistics at a Glance 2022, Ministry of Agriculture & Farmers Welfare, Government of India

SHARE OF AREA UNDER ORGANIC CULTIVATION IN INDIA

AREA (in thousand hectare)

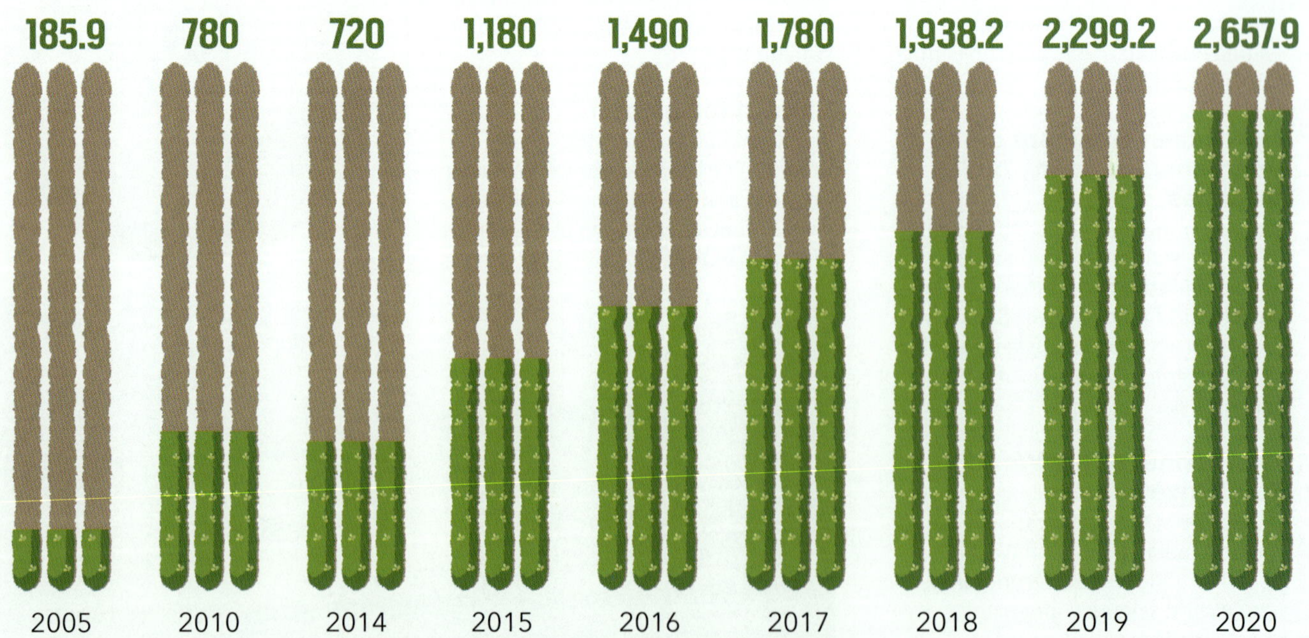

SOURCE: World Food And Agriculture Statistical Yearbook 2022

FLOW OF INSTITUTIONAL CREDIT TO AGRICULTURE SECTOR
(in ₹ crore)

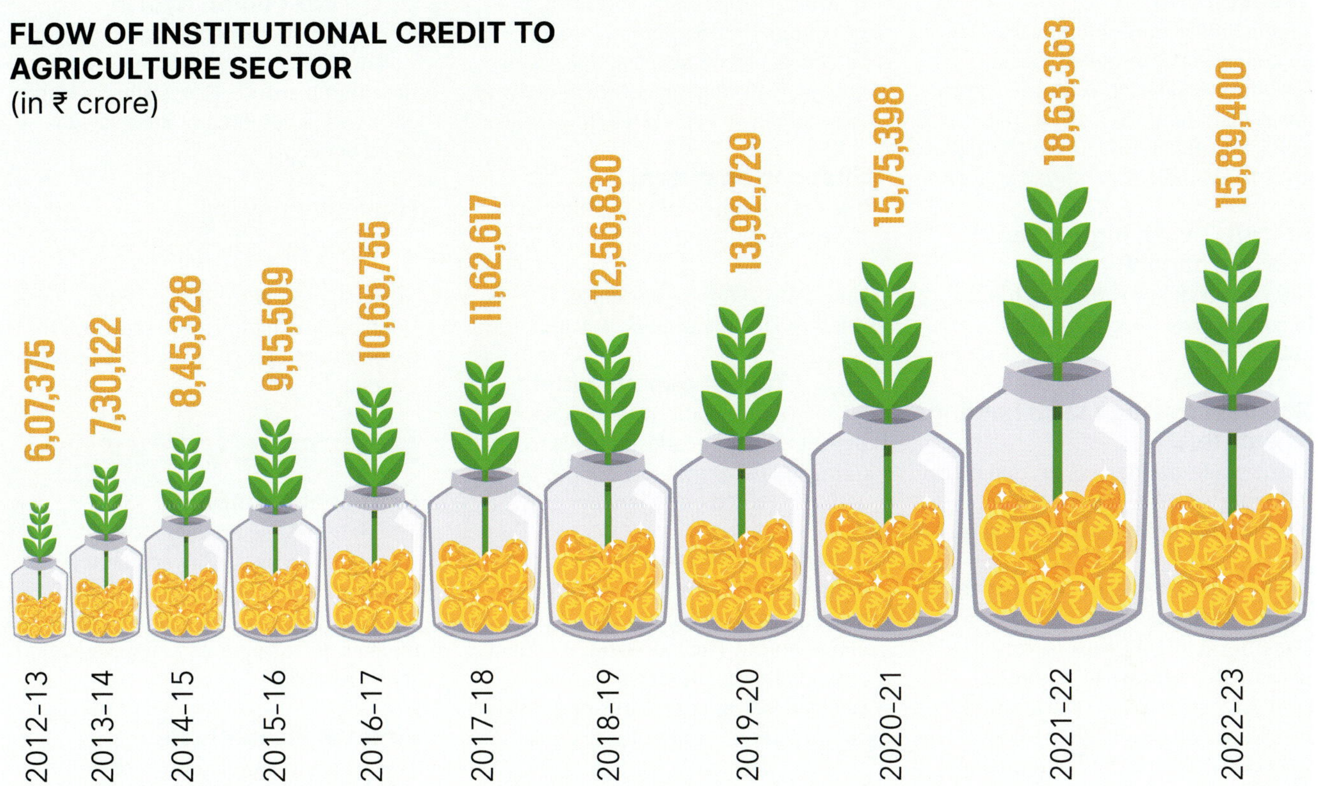

SOURCE: ENSURE Portal of NABARD, Agricultural Statistics at a Glance 2022, Ministry of Agriculture & Farmers Welfare, Government of India

GROSS VALUE ADDED IN AGRICULTURE PER WORKER
VALUE (in ₹)

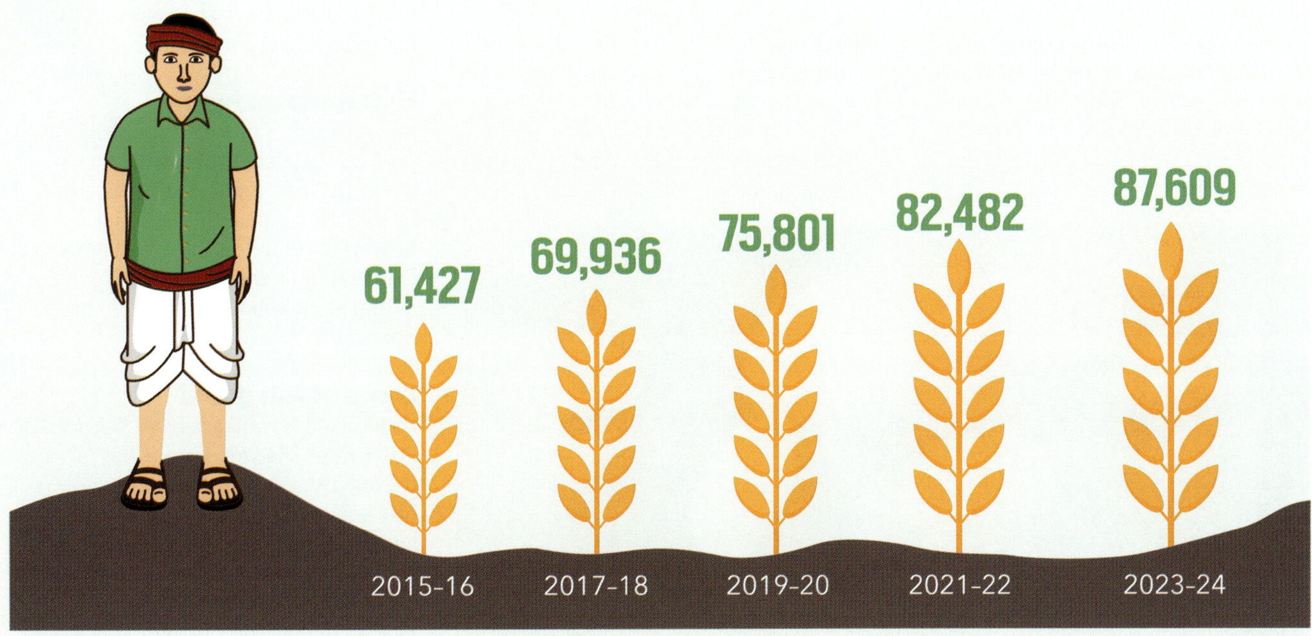

SOURCE: SDGs National Indicator Framework Progress Report 2024, MoSPI, GOI

AGRICULTURE

Tallest jowar
Dodda Ramachandra Reddy (b. 20 January 1951) from Peddapalli, Karimnagar District, Telangana, grew a jowar plant that was 5.3 m (17 ft 4 in.) tall as on 27 October 2018. It took 161 days to grow to this height.

State/UT with highest cold storage capacity
Uttar Pradesh has 1,48,34,695 tonnes of cold storage capacity as on 31 January 2022.

Smallest average farm holdings in a state/UT
The average size of an operational farm in Kerala is 0.18 hectares (0.44 acres) as per the 2015–16 Agricultural Census.

First pigeon pea (arhar) hybrid
The International Crops Research Institute for Semi-Arid Tropics (ICRISAT) released the world's first hybrid pigeon pea, ICPH-8, in 1991. This variety recorded a yield potential of 2,057 kg/hectare.

First genetically modified cash crop approved for commercial cultivation
Bt (*Bacillus thuringiensis*) cotton was the first genetically modified (GM) crop approved for commercial cultivation in 2002 by the Government of India. The Genetic Engineering Appraisal Committee (GEAC) has also approved confined field trials of 20 GM crops for the generation of bio-safety data from both private and public sector institutions. The crops are cotton, mustard, brinjal, okra, sorghum, groundnut, maize, potato, tomato, chickpea, pigeon pea, banana, castor, papaya, watermelon, sugar cane, wheat, rice, rubber tree, and Indian wormwood.

First cotton hybrid
The first commercial cotton hybrid in the country, named H-4 or Sankar-4, was developed at the Gujarat Agricultural University in 1970 by agricultural scientist Dr Chandrakant T. Patel.

Tallest papaya plant
Jhantu Paul from Kolkata, West Bengal, owns the tallest papaya tree (*Carica papaya*) measuring 14.07 m (46 ft 2 in.) as verified on 22 January 2017.

Heaviest jackfruit
Kaithakkoli Kurichiya's family found a jackfruit weighing 57.9 kg on their compound in Thallappuzha, Wayanad District, Kerala, in May 2020. The jackfruit was 67 cm (26 in.) long, with a circumference of 1.35 m (4 ft 5 in.).

Longest and biggest coconut
Dr Dilip Kumar Vitthaldas Patil, a scientist at the Central Institute for Cotton Research, Nagpur, Maharashtra, preserved for 12 years, the largest and biggest coconut (and the longest preserved) seen in India. Dr Patil found this giant coconut in a farm in Pilicode Village, Kasaragod District, Kerala. Even in the dried state, it was 27 cm (10.63 in.) from stalk to tip and its equitorial length was 67.5 cm (26.57 in.) as against normal green coconuts, which are 14 to 20 cm (5.51 to 7.87 in.) horizontally and 25 to 45 cm (9.84 to 17.72 in.) long. In its dried state the coconut weighed 1,450 g against an average of 300–500 g.

Bt cotton crop

First onion hybrid
The world's first onion hybrid was developed at the Indian Agricultural Research Institute, New Delhi, in March 2002 with a potential of increasing yield by 20 per cent.

Highest vineyard
At 1,585 m (5,200 ft) above mean sea level, Kookkal Vineyards (Domaine Kookkal) at Kookkal Village, near Udhagamandalam, Tamil Nadu, are the highest commercial-scale vineyards in the country.

HORTICULTURE

First seed company
The National Seeds Corporation, set up in 1963 by the Government of India, undertakes the production of certified seeds of nearly 600 varieties of 60 crops through its 8,000 registered seed growers.

First vanilla cultivation
The first cultivation centres of vanilla were set up more than a century ago at the Kallar Fruit Research Station, Thiruvananthapuram District, and the Ambalavayal Horticultural Research Station, Wayanad District, Kerala.

First non-narcotic poppy
Sujata, a poppy variety developed in 1998 at the Central Institute of Medicinal and Aromatic Plants, Lucknow, Uttar Pradesh, was the first poppy variety free of opium and opium alkaloids.

First mustard hybrid
In 2008, NRC Sankar Sarson (NRCHB 506), an Indian hybrid of mustard, was developed by a team of scientists led by Dr K.H. Singh at the National Research Centre on Rapeseed-Mustard (NRCRM; now called the Directorate of Rapeseed Mustard Research) in Bharatpur, Rajasthan.

Longest ash gourd
Dr Johnson Nayankara from Mapranam in Thrissur District, Kerala, has grown the longest ash gourd as verified on 11 November 2020. It was 47.3 cm (18.62 in.) long, with a 6.2 cm (2.4 in.) stalk.

First coconut hybrids
Researchers at the Coconut Research Station, now called the Central Plantation Crops Research Institute

Central Plantation Crops Research Institute (CPCRI), Kasaragod, Kerala

(CPCRI), Kasaragod, Kerala, produced the first coconut hybrids between the tall and dwarf palms in 1932, with two to three times more nuts than in each of the parent palms.

First castor hybrid

The Castor and Mustard Research Station in Sardarkrushinagar in Banaskantha District, Gujarat, developed the first castor hybrid named GCH 3 and released it in 1968–69 on a commercial scale. GCH 7, released in 2006, has the highest potential productivity (3,000 kg/hectare) in India.

Hottest chilli

The *bhut jolokia*, or 'ghost chilli', is the hottest chilli in India. Rated at 10,41,427 Scoville heat units (SHUs), this variety is cultivated in the north-eastern states of Arunachal Pradesh, Assam, Nagaland and Manipur.

Bhut jolokia

Capsaicin

Capsaicin is the chemical present in chilli that gives chilli its heat. The level of capsaicin concentration in a chilli is measured through the Scoville scale, that uses Scoville heat units (SHUs) to depict it. The SHUs in the scale range from 0 (no heat) to over 16 million (pure capsaicin).

ANIMAL HUSBANDRY

Early vet research

Research on animal healthcare began with the setting up of the Imperial Bacteriological Laboratory at Poona (now Pune), Maharashtra, on 9 December 1889, with Dr Alfred Lingard as the first bacteriologist in 1890. It was moved to Mukteshwar, Uttarakhand, in 1895. The Indian Veterinary Research Institute (IVRI) later began in 1913 at Izatnagar, Bareilly District, Uttar Pradesh.

Dr Alfred Lingard

First veterinary surgeon

William Moorcroft (1767–1825), a Britisher who was appointed veterinary surgeon in 1808 at the Pusa Stud Farm, Bihar, is the first one on record in India.

First frozen semen bank for bulls

The first frozen semen bank for bulls was established in 1963 in Mattupetty, Idukki, Kerala, with Indo-Swiss collaboration. The objective was to evolve a new breed of cattle adapted to the local environment. The bank dealt with the collection, processing, storage, and transportation of the semen of bull breeds.

First artificial insemination in bulls

Artificial insemination was successfully attempted for the first time in 1939 by Sampath Kumaran, who crossed the Indian Hallikar breed with Holstein Friesian bulls.

First dairy research institute

Established in 1923 as the Imperial Dairy Institute of Animal Husbandry and Dairying in Bangalore (now Bengaluru), Karnataka, it was renamed National Dairy Research Institute (NDRI) after Independence. In 1955, its headquarters was moved to Karnal, Haryana. It undertakes research, teaching, and extension activities in dairy development.

India: The Largest Producer

Largest producer of spices

India is the largest producer of spices and spice products. In 2020–21, India produced 16.6 million tonnes of spices.

Largest number of organic producers in the world

According to the World of Organic Agriculture Report 2022, India has the largest number of organic producers in the world. With 15,99,010 certified organic producers, the country is home to more than 47.02 per cent of the total number of organic producers (3.4 million) worldwide. However, when it comes to the total area under certified organic cultivation, India has only 1.5 per cent of its entire agricultural area under organic cultivation.

Largest producer of mangoes

According to the first estimates for 2020–21, India's mango production stood at 20.82 million tonnes. Andhra Pradesh turned out to be the top mango-producing state with the production of 50,01,740 tonnes of mangoes.

Top milk-producing country

India has led the world in milk production since 1997. Milk production in the country increased to 209.96 million tonnes during 2021. India contributes 21 per cent of the global milk production. The top milk-producing states are Uttar Pradesh, Rajasthan, and Madhya Pradesh.

Largest producer of coconuts

India produces 34.73 per cent of the global production of coconuts. As per 2020–21 reports, the area and production of coconuts in the country is 2.18 million hectares (5.8 million acres) and 14.57 million tonnes, respectively. The four southern states of Kerala, Tamil Nadu, Karnataka, and Andhra Pradesh account for 88.97 per cent of the area under coconut cultivation and 89.67 per cent of the coconut production in the country.

Camels in National Research Centre on Camel, Bikaner, Rajasthan

Only camel farm

The National Research Centre on Camel (NRCC), also a camel-breeding farm, was set up in Bikaner, Rajasthan, in 1957 for conducting scientific research on camels. The centre aims to study ways of optimizing the working capacity of camels. It is the only camel farm in the country.

First lamb from frozen embryo

Scientists at the Central Sheep and Wool Research Institute in Avikanagar in Tonk District, Rajasthan, implanted a cryo-preserved Bharat Merino embryo into a Kheri surrogate ewe, which birthed a lamb on 20 January 1999.

Highest stud farm

The Zanskar Pony Breeding and Training Centre at Partapur in Nubra Block, Ladakh, is located at 3,146 m (10,321 ft) above mean sea level.

Most piglets in a single litter

An artificial insemination field project by scientists at the National Research Centre on Pig in Guwahati, Assam, achieved the largest litter size of 19 piglets in a single delivery in 2012.

First test-tube yak calf

The first test-tube yak calf in the world, a male weighing 19 kg, was born at the Nyukmadung farm of the National Research Centre on Yak (NRCY), Dirang Dzong, West Kameng District, Arunachal Pradesh, on 15 July 2013. The yak calf was named Norgayal.

First cross-bred cow

The first cross-bred cow breed in India, called Taylor, was named after an Englishman, William Taylor, who was the one to initiate cattle cross-breeding in Patna, Bihar, in the mid-19th century.

First buffalo-milk powder

The Kaira District Cooperative Milk Producers Union (Amul Dairy), Anand, Gujarat, produced whole and skimmed milk powder from buffalo milk in 1955. They were also the first in the world to commercially produce cheese and baby food from buffalo milk in 1960.

Largest population of livestock

India had the largest population of livestock, with an estimated 536.76 million heads of cattle by 2019, making up as much as 31 per cent of the world's livestock population.

Heaviest goat

Asif Ali from Bhopal, Madhya Pradesh, reared the heaviest goat named King on his R.K. Goat Farm. King weighed 171 kg on 25 July 2019.

Heaviest and highest-priced bull

In March 2018, Haryana's first Murrah Ratan Award was won by a buffalo called Shahenshah, which weighed between 1,100 and 1,200 kg and was owned by Narender Singh from Didwari Village, Panipat, Haryana.

State with the most veterinary institutions

Rajasthan leads Indian states and UTs with 7,897 veterinary institutions (as on 31 March 2018).

Largest cattle farm

Mathigiri Cattle Farm and District Livestock Centre near Hosur in Krishnagiri District, Tamil Nadu, is India's and Asia's largest cattle farm. It is spread over 480 hectares (1,200 acres).

Dr Verghese Kurien

Largest dairy development programme

Project Operation Flood, launched in 1970 by the National Dairy Development Board (NDDB) and led by Dr Verghese Kurien, general manager and later chairman, AMUL, and chairman, NDDB and the Institute of Rural Management Anand (IRMA), Gujarat. It involved forming a National Milk Grid that connected milk producers to consumers in over 700 towns and cities in India.

Oldest cow

Ruby, a cow owned by Dr Dipa Panjuani of Pune, Maharashtra, crossed 35 years in 2017. It was milking till six months before it turned 32 years old.

CLONING RECORDS

First cloned pashmina goat

Noori, the first cloned pashmina goat, was born at the Faculty of Veterinary Sciences and Animal Husbandry, Sher-e-Kashmir University of Agricultural Sciences and Technology, Srinagar, Jammu and Kashmir, on 9 March 2012. With a birthweight of 1.3 kg, she was cloned by a team headed by Dr Riaz Ahmad Shah, using somatic cell nuclear transfer technique.

First cloned buffalo

On 6 February 2009, a team of six scientists – S.K. Singla, M.S. Chauhan, R.S. Manik, P. Palta, R.A. Shah, and A. George – all from the Animal Biotechnology Centre at the National Dairy Research Institute (NDRI), Karnal, Haryana, cloned the first female water buffalo calf in the world from a year-old buffalo of the Murrah breed. Although the calf died five days later, the team of scientists succeeded in testing the cloning and other technologies that helped them achieve one of their objectives of getting the desired gender of the cloned animal.

First calf cloned from frozen semen

In July 2014, a male calf named Rajat was cloned by the National Dairy Research Institute, Karnal, using a donor cell from the frozen semen of a highly ranked Murrah buffalo bull. This was the first time frozen semen was used for cloning a farm animal.

First cloned female buffalo by hand-guided technique

In June 2014, scientists of the National Dairy Research Institute, Karnal, produced the world's first female cloned buffalo calf through 'hand-guided' cloning, using a donor cell from the ear of a high-yielding Murrah buffalo. The calf was named Lalima.

Most calves cloned from a single bull

The Central Institute for Research on Buffaloes (CIRB), located in Hisar, Haryana, achieved the cloning of seven calves from a single superior breeding bull, named M-29, between October 2019 and January 2020.

Ganga–the first cloned cow in India

On 16 March 2023, Ganga, the first cloned cow in India, was born. The scientists at NDRI created her. The process of cloning a cow took much longer due to religious sentiments as the technology available back then was invasive. However, in 2018, the scientists got access to a non-invasive technology called ovum pick up that is used to separate oocytes from the cow without harming her. They chose Gir breed as it could withstand harsh weather and produce 2–3 times more milk, i.e., 15 to 20 litres per day.

POULTRY AND FISHERIES

First broiler chicken variety

B-77, the first broiler variety of chicken, was released by the IVRI in Izatnagar in Bareilly District, Uttar Pradesh, in 1977.

Largest poultry company

Suguna Foods Pvt. Ltd, which achieved a sales turnover of over ₹8,700 crore (87 billion) during 2019–20, is the largest broiler chicken company in India. Based in Coimbatore, Tamil Nadu, it ranks among the top 10 poultry enterprises worldwide and operates in 18 states in India, covering over 40,000 farmers in over 15,000 villages. Its products and services include hatcheries, feed mills, processing plants, value-added eggs, and broiler and frozen chicken.

Representative image

Central Marine Fisheries Research Institute (CMFRI) building

Oldest fisheries research institutes

The oldest fisheries research institutes are the Central Marine Fisheries Research Institute (CMFRI), established in 1947, and the Central Inland Capture Fisheries Research Institute (CICFRI), also set up in 1947 under the name of Central Inland Fisheries Research Institute (CIFRI) in Calcutta (now Kolkata), West Bengal.

Biggest hen egg

A hen at the Dev Research and Breeding Farms of Sukhbir Singh of Ramrai Khera in Jind, Haryana, laid an egg weighing 167 g on 28 September 2014. It was 8.35 cm (3.3 in.) long and 5 cm (2 in.) wide.

First deep-sea fishing station

The Deep-Sea Fishing Station, Bombay (now Mumbai), Maharashtra, was set up in October 1946. It was renamed the Exploratory Fisheries Project (EFP) in 1974 when it systematically surveyed the coastal and offshore waters up to a depth of 70 m (230 ft). Engaged in oceanic surveys of Exclusive Economic Zones, it was renamed the Fishery Survey of India in 1979.

First transgenic rohu fish

During 2004–05, a team of scientists led by Dr T.J. Pandian at the Madurai Kamaraj University, Madurai, Tamil Nadu, developed a genetically modified rohu fish that could grow 6–7 times faster than a normal one.

Rohu fish

First marine aquarium for ornamental fish

An aquarium for ornamental fish breeding and multiplication was established in 1998 in Vizhinjam, near Kovalam in Kerala.

Top shrimp-producing state/UT

Andhra Pradesh led with 6,34,672 million tonnes, followed by West Bengal with 35,392 million tonnes, in 2020–21.

Indian white shrimp

First and only licensed fisherwoman

In 2017, K.C. Rekha from Thrissur, Kerala, became India's only licensed deep-sea fisherwoman. Rekha accompanies her husband Karthikeyan to work every day.

First research institute for freshwater aquaculture

The Central Institute of Freshwater Aquaculture, Bhubaneswar, Odisha, began in the Pond Culture Division of the Central Inland Fisheries Research Institute, at Cuttack, Odisha, in 1949. The division was later upgraded as the Freshwater Aquaculture Research and Training Centre in 1976. It became an independent institute on 1 April 1987.

First pearl culture

The first cultured pearls, using the Akoya pearl oyster, were produced in 1973 at the Tuticorin Research Centre at the Central Marine Fisheries Research Institute (CMFRI) in Thoothukudi, Tamil Nadu, in collaboration with the Tamil Nadu State Fisheries Department.

FERTILIZERS, PESTICIDES, AND MACHINERY

Earliest soil treatment experiments

The earliest methods to find out the effects of inorganic fertilizers on the soil – its physical, chemical, and biological properties vis-à-vis crop yields – were started at the Agricultural College and Research Institute, Coimbatore, Tamil Nadu, in 1909.

First institute for farm machinery training and testing

The Central Farm Machinery Training and Testing Institute (CFMTTI), established in 1959 in Budni, Sehore District, Madhya Pradesh, was the first of the four FMTTI centres in India. Since its inception and up to March 2020, the centre has trained a total of 69,056 trainees from across India.

First fertilizer factory

The first SSP (single superphosphate) factory that produced fertilizer mixtures, insecticides, and fungicides was set up in 1906 in Ranipet District in Tamil Nadu by East India Distilleries Parry Ltd.

First pesticide
Benzene hexachloride (BHC) was first commercialized by the Imperial Chemical Industries Ltd (ICI) in 1952 at Rishra in Hooghly District, West Bengal. A factory was set up in Calcutta.

First attempt at weed control using herbicides
The earliest attempt to control weeds in India with herbicides was made in 1937 in Punjab for controlling Carthamus oxyacantha by using sodium arsenite. 2,4-dichlorophenoxyacetic acid was first tested in India in 1946 to kill weeds and control plant growth.

First neem-based biocide
The first neem-based biocide was tested and commissioned by the National Tree Growers Cooperative Federation during 1997–98.

First use of lift irrigation
In 1926, an experimental lift irrigation system on 1,012 hectares (2,500 acres) of wasteland was started in the Rachna Doab region of Gangapur Village in Punjab (now in Pakistan) by Sir Ganga Ram, a member of the Regional Commission on Agriculture.

State/UT with the highest use of fertilizers per hectare
With a total consumption of 312.04 kg/hectare in 2021, Puducherry is the largest consumer of fertilizers (N, P & K).

First synthetic pesticide
DDT (Dichlorodiphenyltrichloroethane) was introduced in 1946 for vector control and used in 1948. Its use was banned in May 1989.

DDT molecule

DDT
$C_{14}H_9Cl_5$

- Carbon
- Chlorine
- Hydrogen

All about Indian tractors

Most sold farm equipment with largest market share
Tractors have the biggest share of the farm machinery market in India, at 80 per cent. In 2020–21, overall tractor sales in the country were 8,42,266 units.

Earliest use of tractors
Sardar Sir Jogendra Singh (1877–1946) experimented with steam tractors for wasteland reclamation in 1914 at Aira estate in Lakhimpur, Uttar Pradesh, and at Iqbal Nagar (now in Pakistan) in Punjab.

First semi-autonomous tractor
In April 2018, Mahindra and Mahindra Ltd rolled out a high-tech tractor, the Pack 1. This is an 'intelligent' tractor with a driver-assist system.

WR Largest seller of tractors
Mahindra and Mahindra Ltd is the largest-selling tractor brand in India, with total sales of 3,37,052 units in the financial year ended March 2022. It exported 17,646 units in the same period.

State/UT with most tractor exports
Maharashtra with exports worth US $186 million was the state with the most tractor exports in the year 2019–20. According to data from the Directorate General of Commercial Intelligence and Statistics, Punjab exported tractors worth US $178 million in 2019–20, while Tamil Nadu exported tractors worth US $156 million.

Mahindra – the largest seller of tractors

First agri-plane
Hindustan Aeronautics Ltd's HA-31 Basant monoplane was built in 1972 for agricultural needs. Its use was discontinued in 1980.

First biocontrol agents
The ladybird beetle of Australia was introduced in 1898 to control mealy bugs on fruit crops.

Ladybird beetle

LITERACY

First state/UT to achieve 100 per cent literacy

On 18 April 1991, also the 81st birthday of Dr Malcolm S. Adiseshiah, the doyen of adult education in India, Kerala was declared 100 per cent literate.

First 100 per cent literate district

In 1990, Ernakulam, Kerala, with a population of three million then, became the first completely literate district in the country, with a literacy rate of 98.34 per cent in the age group of 5–60 years.

First national education council

The All India Council for Secondary Education (AICSE) was set up in 1955.

State/UT with the highest literacy rate

Kerala, with 96.2 per cent, has the highest rate of literacy among all states, according to the 75th round of the National Sample Survey (NSS) conducted from July 2017 to June 2018.

State/UT with the lowest literacy rate

Andhra Pradesh, with 66.4 per cent, has the lowest rate of literacy among all states, according to the 75th round of the National Sample Survey.

State/UT with highest and lowest female literacy rate

The female literacy rate in Kerala was 95.2 per cent while Rajasthan recorded 57.6 per cent, according to the 75th round of the National Sample Survey.

State/UT with the highest percentage of graduates

Out of a total of around 68 million graduates in the country, Chandigarh, with 24.65 per cent, has the highest percentage of its population as graduates, according to the Census 2011.

First minister of education

Independent India's first minister of education was Maulana Abul Kalam Azad (1888–1958), during 1947–58. Besides establishing the first Indian Institute of Technology (IIT), the Indian Institute of Science (IISc), the School of Planning and Architecture (SPA) and the University Grants Commission (UGC), he set up key cultural and literary organizations like the Sangeet Natak Akademi, the Lalit Kala Akademi, the Sahitya Akademi, and the Indian Council for Cultural Relations.

State/UT with the lowest percentage of graduates

Assam has the lowest percentage of graduate population, with only 4.83 per cent as per Census 2011.

SCHOOLS

Earliest schools for girls

St. Thomas School for Girls, which was founded in 1789 for the English-speaking community of Calcutta, Bengal (now Kolkata, West Bengal), was the first girls-only school in India.

Oldest extant school

St. George's Anglo-Indian Higher Secondary School, founded as the Military (later Madras) Male Orphan Asylum, was established in 1715 in Madras (now Chennai), Tamil Nadu.

First school for the hearing-impaired

Established in 1893, the Calcutta Deaf and Dumb School in Calcutta, was the first school for the hearing-impaired.

WR Largest open school

Set up as an autonomous institution under the Ministry of Human Resource Development in 1989, the National Institute of Open Schooling (NIOS) has a cumulative enrolment of 4.13 million students. It works through a network of 23 regional centres, two subregional centres, five departments, two NIOS cells, and over 7,400 study centres (accredited institutions and accredited vocational institutions). These centres are located in various parts of the world, viz., India, Nepal, and the Middle East.

First Indian school abroad

The Indian High School, Dubai, set up in 1957, was the first Indian educational institution situated in a foreign country.

Oldest extant institute for the blind

The Institute for the Blind – Andh Vidyalaya – was established in Lahore (now in Pakistan) in 1939 and shifted to Delhi after Independence in 1947.

Largest school science fair – single venue – single day

iScience World, a science club formed by science communicators in Prayagraj, Uttar Pradesh, in collaboration with Shri Mahaprabhu Public School, organized a science fair on 14 December 2019 at Delhi Public School, Prayagraj, in which 4,272 students from over 35 schools participated.

Largest chain of government schools

The Kendriya Vidyalaya Sangathan, an autonomous body under the Ministry of Human Resource Development, Government of India, since 15 December 1963, administers 1,252 schools, including three abroad, with 14,28,619 students, as of February 2023.

Kendriya Vidyalaya Sangathan

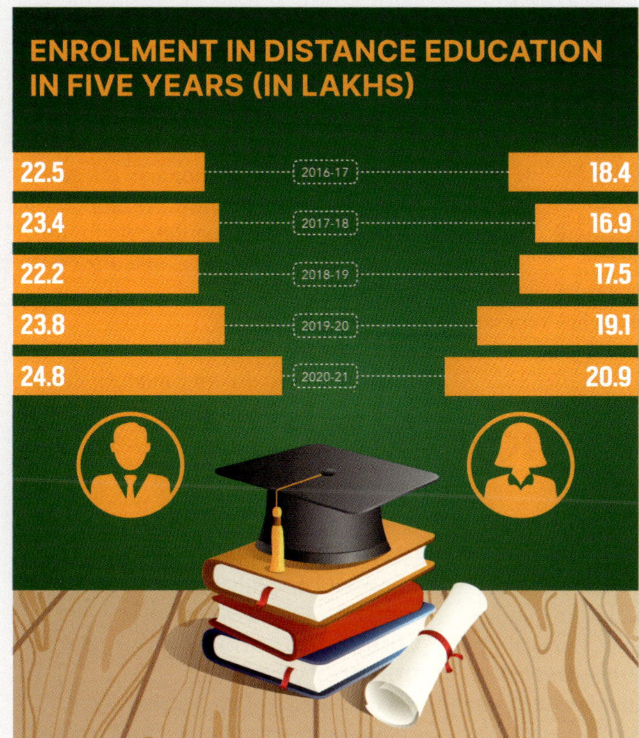

SOURCE: Annual Report 2022-23, Ministry of Education

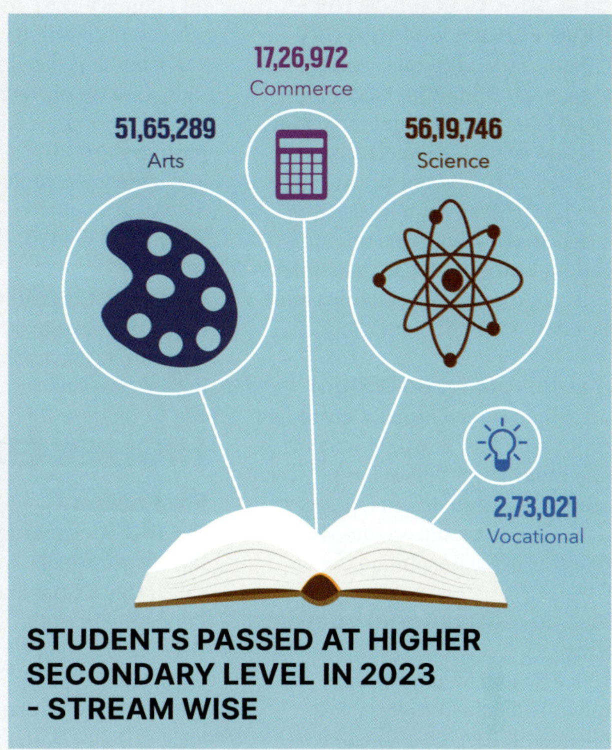

SOURCE: Annual Report 2022-23, Ministry of Education

SOURCE: Annual Report 2022-23, Ministry of Education

POST-GRADUATE LEVEL TURN-OUT – SUBJECT-WISE (IN LAKHS)

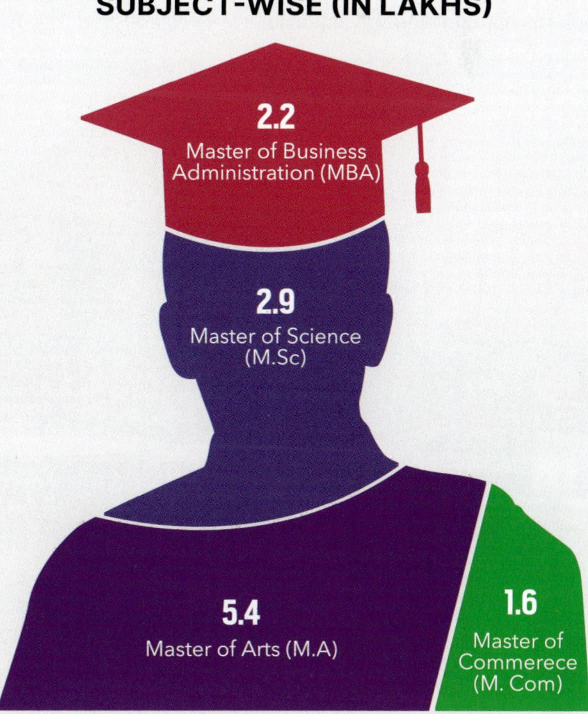

SOURCE: Annual Report 2022-23, Ministry of Education

Largest school science fair – multiple venues – single day

More than 22,500 students from 637 upper primary schools of Bastar District, Chhattisgarh, conducted more than 35,000 scientific experiments at 116 centres on 18 January 2017. The Bastar Vigyan Mela, an annual event, was organized by the Department of Education, Bastar District. The students demonstrated scientific activities and displayed innovative science models.

First solar-powered school

Sri Aurobindo International Centre for Education in White Town, Puducherry, became India's first fully solar-powered educational institute in 2014. It was set up in 1943 by Mirra Alfassa, the spiritual collaborator of Sri Aurobindo.

Oldest co-educational boarding school

Lawrence School Sanawar, near Kasauli in Himachal Pradesh, was established in 1847. It is is the oldest co-educational boarding school in India founded by Sir Henry Lawrence, and was initially intended for the children of British soldiers.

First Sainik school for girls opens in Vrindavan

The Samvid Gurukulam Girls Sainik School was inaugurated in Vrindavan on 1 January 2024. Alongside a CBSE curriculum, military training by ex-servicemen is provided to the students. The Ministry of Defence plans to establish 100 new Sainik schools in partnership with NGOs, private entities, and state government schools.

The first Gondi language school

In 2019, the Gond Adivasi community established a primary school in Mohagaon, Gadchiroli, Maharashtra, to teach children in their first language, Gondi.

HIGHER EDUCATION

First steps

The first educational policy in colonial India was articulated in a document called the 'Dispatch of 1854 on "General Education in India"' sent by Sir Charles Wood to the then Governor General Lord Dalhousie. Sir Charles stressed the adoption of vernacular languages in local primary schools, Anglo-vernacular language in high schools and English-medium education in colleges.

First Sanskrit university

The Sampurnanand Sanskrit Vishwavidyalaya in Varanasi, Uttar Pradesh, was the first Sanskrit university in India and is said to have been established in 1791 as a Sanskrit college during the East India Company rule. It has 628 affiliated colleges across India.

First modern university

William Carey, a British Christian missionary, opened the Serampore College, the first missionary college at Serampore, Bengal (now Srirampur, Hooghly District, West Bengal), in 1818. It was granted the status of a university in 1829.

First modern college

The first college to offer modern education in India was the Hindu College of Calcutta, Bengal, established in 1817. Scottish watchmaker and philanthropist David Hare was its first principal. It was renamed Presidency College in 1855. It became Presidency University on 7 July 2010.

Longest functioning ancient university

Nalanda Mahavihara, located about 95 km south-east of present-day Patna in Bihar, functioned uninterrupted as a university from the Buddha's time in the sixth century BCE up to the 13th century CE, when it was destroyed by Muhammad bin Bakhtiyar Khilji. The university's curriculum then included many subjects such as logic,

Ruins of the ancient Nalanda university

Mastering a Language

Oldest centre for German Studies

The University of Mumbai, the oldest centre for German Studies in India, introduced a BA in German in 1913 and an MA in German before 1916. It offers full-time programmes in German Studies (BA, MA, MA (Hons), and PhD) focused on language, literature, culture, translation, and intercultural studies, designed to be research and job-oriented.

First University to introduce Japanese language courses

In 1954, Visva-Bharati University (Shantiniketan) established a Japanese department, making it the first university in India to introduce Japanese language courses.

The oldest centre for Chinese Studies

Cheena Bhavana, founded in 1937 at Visva-Bharati University, is the oldest centre for Chinese studies in the subcontinent, offering undergraduate and postgraduate courses in Chinese literature, philosophy, politics, and Buddhist literature.

Centre of Spanish, Portuguese, Italian and Latin American Studies (CSPILAS)

The Centre of Spanish Studies was originally established in the 1970s. It was later expanded to include Portuguese, Italian, and Latin American Studies and was renamed CSPILAS in 2004. It is part of the School of Language, Literature and Culture Studies at Jawaharlal Nehru University in New Delhi. The CSPILAS is one of the leading centres for Spanish and Latin American Studies in South-east Asia and is the first in the country to introduce graduate, master's, and Doctoral programmes in Spanish.

The only place to teach ancient Greek

The School of Languages in the Ramakrishna Mission Institute of Culture, Golpark, Kolkata, is the only place in India where ancient Greek is taught. The course is popular among students, teachers, and retired professionals.

medicine, metaphysics, grammar, and the sciences. In an effort to emulate the ancient centre of learning, Nalanda University, an exclusively postgraduate and doctoral institution, was started in 2014 in Rajgir, Bihar.

First university act

The Indian Universities Act, 1904, was the first set of educational reforms, which stipulated that universities should offer more teaching and research opportunities and exert more control over affiliated colleges.

First intermediate colleges

The University of Punjab (now in Chandigarh) and the University of Allahabad (now in Prayagraj) were the first to establish intermediate colleges in 1917, offering two-year courses between high school and degree college, as proposed by the Sadler Commission.

First medical school

Established on 24 January 1857, the University of Calcutta was the first multidisciplinary and Western-style educational institution in Asia. It was also the first university in Asia to teach European classics, English literature, Indian philosophy, and Occidental and Oriental history. At the time of establishment, it had a catchment area ranging from Lahore to Burma (now Myanmar) and Ceylon (now Sri Lanka).

The first medical school, the Calcutta Medical College, was affiliated to the university in 1857. Five Nobel laureates (the highest number in South Asia) are associated with the university. They are Sir Ronald Ross, Rabindranath Tagore, Sir C.V. Raman, Amartya Sen, and Abhijit Vinayak Banerjee.

First rural university

Mahatma Gandhi Chitrakoot Gramoday University, established in 1991 in Chitrakoot, Madhya Pradesh, to promote rural education, was the first rural university in the country.

First pharmacy education course

A chemists and druggists course was initiated in Madras Medical College in 1874. It gained popularity and in 1898, a separate department of chemists and druggists was established at the college. The College of Pharmacy at Madras Medical College is the first institution in India to provide pharmacy education and training by offering a one-year certificate course called the 'Chemist and Druggist Course' training personnel for drug dispensing. However, formal pharmacy education in India was started in 1932 at the Banaras Hindu University (BHU) by Mahadeva Lal Schroff with the support of the vice chancellor of the university, Pandit Madan Mohan Malaviya. Initially, the course was known as B. Pharm (Bachelor of Pharmacy) and in April 1940 the first M. Pharm course was started at BHU.

First five universities

The University of Calcutta, the University of Madras, and the University of Bombay (now renamed as the University of Mumbai), which were modelled on London University, were established in 1857 as non-teaching examining bodies. The University of Punjab in Lahore, Pakistan), was set up in 1881, and the University of Allahabad in 1887.

First medical school to offer degrees in oncology

The Cancer Institute (WIA–Women's' Indian Association), also known as the Adyar Cancer Institute, is a renowned non-profit treatment and research centre located in Chennai, Tamil Nadu. It was established in 1954 under the leadership of Muthulakshmi Reddy, with the motto 'Service to All'. The institute has played a vital role in cancer research and oncology in India. It is the first medical school to offer degrees in various sub-specialities of oncology like radiotherapy, medical oncology, surgical oncology, etc. The Cancer Institute (WIA) is affiliated to both the University of Madras and Anna University, where it offers research programmes leading to MPhil and PhD degrees in areas of medical physics, psycho-oncology, and molecular oncology. It has also established the first department of nuclear medical oncology in the country and the first ever medical physics department.

Oldest dentist college in South-east Asia

In 1920, the legendary visionary Dr Rafiuddin Ahmed (1890–1965) set up the first Dental College in Calcutta, and since 1949 it is affiliated to Calcutta University, the same year that Dr Ahmed donated his college to the West Bengal government. Dr Ahmed served as principal of the college from 1920 to 1950. He established the Bengal Dental Association, which became the forerunner for the Indian Dental Association. He also started the *Indian Dental Journal* in 1925 and was its editor till 1946. Dr Ahmed helped draft the Bengal Dentists Act in 1939, the first governmental dental regulation in India. It became the model for the Indian Dental Act passed in 1948.

First institute to teach modern architecture

The first course in architecture can be traced to the founding of a draftsman's class at the Sir J.J. School of Art (established in 1856), Bombay (now Mumbai), Maharashtra, in 1896. In 1913, the course was reorganized, and an independent Department of Architecture was formed.

Only school of tropical medicine

The School of Tropical Medicine, Kolkata, also known as Calcutta School of Tropical Medicine (CSTM) was established in 1914 by Leonard Rogers. It is the only institution in the country dedicated exclusively in research, post-graduate education, and healthcare for tropical diseases. The institute is presently under the governance of West Bengal University of Health Sciences. The institute focuses on advanced research on HIV/HBV co-infection and Hepatitis B anti-viral therapy.

Tropical Medicine

The branch of medicine that focuses on the prevention, diagnosis, and treatment of diseases that are prevalent in tropical and subtropical regions where areas are often characterized by hot and humid climates.

First virtual medical university
The first virtual medical university, Medvarsity, established in 2000, is an initiative of the Apollo Hospitals Group.

First energy studies university
The University of Petroleum and Energy Studies in Dehradun, Uttarakhand, established in 2003, is India's first university specializing in petroleum, energy, and power.

First five residential universities
In 1915, the Banaras Hindu University (BHU) was established as a teaching and residential university, followed by the Universities of Mysore (1916), Patna (1917), and Osmania (1918), and the Aligarh Muslim University (1920).

First science college
The Government Science College, Jabalpur, Madhya Pradesh, was the first Indian science college and was affiliated to the Calcutta University from 1836 to 1890.

First college of nursing
The Christian Medical College (CMC) and Hospital, Vellore, is a private educational institute with a network of hospitals in and around Vellore, Tamil Nadu. It was started in 1902 by Dr Ida Scudder, a third-generation American missionary. In 1903, she began training women compounders and started the first school of nursing at CMC in 1909.

First technical university
The Thomason College of Engineering, established in 1847 at Roorkee (now in Uttarakhand), was India's first technical university. Its civil engineering department is the oldest one. It is now the Indian Institute of Technology (IIT), Roorkee.

First railway university
The National Rail and Transport University was established on 5 September 2018 at the Pratap Vilas Palace in Vadodara, Gujarat. It has now been subsumed by the Gati Shakti Vishwavidyalaya, announced as a central university in July 2022. It provides education and training in the latest technological applications related to the railways, such as radio frequency identification, artificial intelligence, and satellite-based tracking. It offers graduate degrees in subjects such as transportation management, transportation technology, rail infrastructural engineering, and electronics and communication engineering.

First women's university
The Shreemati Nathibai Damodar Thackersey (SNDT) Women's University was established in Pune, Maharashtra, by D.K. Karve (its first principal) on 5 July 1916. Dr R.P. Paranjpye was its first vice chancellor.

First college for women
The Bethune School of Calcutta, Bengal, set up in 1849, was reorganized after it merged with Banga Mahila Vidyalaya. In 1879, Bethune College classes started with one student, Kadambini Bose.

First college alumni association
Dr William Miller, principal of Madras Christian College, Madras, Tamil Nadu, formed the first alumni association in 1891.

First technical university for women
The Indira Gandhi Delhi Technical University for Women (IGDTUW), New Delhi, was founded in 1998.

First IIT
The first Indian Institute of Technology (IIT) was established in 1951 at Kharagpur, West Bengal, at the site of the Hijli Detention Camp. There are 23 approved IITs in India currently.

First metro technology institute
The Institute of Metro and Rail Technology (IMRT) opened in October 2013 in Hyderabad, Telangana. It offers short- and long-term courses to design, build, and manage modern rail systems.

First institute for population sciences
The Institute for Population Sciences in Mumbai, Maharashtra, earlier known as the Demographic Training and Research Centre, was established in 1956 to prepare students for administrative, teaching, research, and consultancy careers in population sciences.

First school of mines
The Indian School of Mines – now renamed the Indian Institute of Technology – in Dhanbad, Jharkhand, opened in 1926.

First university of fisheries and ocean studies
The College of Fisheries in Panangad, Cochin (now Kochi), Kerala, established in 1979, was a constituent college of the Kerala Agricultural University. The Kerala University of Fisheries and Ocean Studies (KUFOS) was established in 2010 with its headquarters at the College of Fisheries.

First institute of oceanography
The National Institute of Oceanography, which was founded on 1 January 1966, is

IIT Kharagpur: first IIT

MISSION POSSIBLE: KNOW YOUR EXAMS

Important exams conducted in India	Conducted by	The purpose
Joint Entrance Exam (JEE)	National Testing Agency (NTA)	For admission to different engineering colleges in India
National Eligibility cum Entrance Test (NEET)	National Testing Agency (NTA)	For admission to any graduate or postgraduate medical course in government or private colleges
Common Admission Test (CAT)	National Testing Agency (NTA)	For admission to management programmes offered by the IIMs and other prestigious business schools
Graduate Pharmacy Aptitude Test (GPAT)	National Board of Examinations in Medical Sciences (NBEMS)	For admission to M.Pharma programmes
National Eligibility Test (UGC NET)	National Testing Agency (NTA)	For those who wish to become assistant professors or to seek a junior research fellowship in universities
Council of Scientific and Industrial Research (CSIR-UGC NET)	National Testing Agency (NTA)	For those who wish to pursue lecturership or seek a junior research fellowship in the field of science
Common University Entrance Test (CUET)	National Testing Agency (NTA)	For admission to specific programmes of participating central universities across India
National Council for Hotel Management Joint Entrance Examination (NCHM JEE)	National Testing Agency (NTA)	For admission to various undergraduate programmes in the field of hospitality and hotel management
Indian Institute of Foreign Trade (IIFT)	National Testing Agency (NTA)	For admission to MBA in international business and MBA in business analytics programmes
Jawaharlal Nehru University Entrance Examination (JNUEE)	National Testing Agency (NTA)	For admission to different undergraduates and postgraduate courses at Jawaharlal Nehru University
Union Public Service Commission Civil Services Examination (UPSC)	Union Public Service Commission (UPSC)	To recruit and appoint civil servants for various government services
Graduate Aptitude Test in Engineering (GATE)	Indian Institute of Technology (IIT) and Indian Institute of Science (IISc)	For admission to MTech and PhD courses
National Defence Academy exam (NDA)	Union Public Service Commission	To recruit candidates as officers in the Indian Navy, Indian Army and Indian Air Force
Common Law Admission Test (CLAT)	Consortium of National Law Universities (NLUs)	For admission to various national law universities in India
Chartered Accountant (CA)	Institute of Chartered Accountants of India (ICAI)	For ICAI membership and the title of chartered accountant
Staff Selection Commission – Combined Graduate Level Exam (SSC CGL)	Staff Selection Commission (SSC)	To recruit candidates into various organizations, departments, offices under Government of India
Actuarial Common Admission Test (ACET)	The Institute of Actuaries of India (IAI)	For admission to actuarial programmes at Indian institutions
NID Entrance Examination	National Institute of Design (NID)	For admission to various undergraduate and postgraduate courses at NID colleges
Combined Defence Exam (CDS)	Union Public Service Commission	To join the Indian armed forces including army, navy, and air force
Central Armed Police Force Exam (UPSC-CAPF)	Union Public Service Commission	To select candidates for the role of assistant commandant in Central Armed Police Forces

an autonomous research organization that undertakes scientific research and studies of special oceanographic features of the northern Indian Ocean. The institute has its main campus in Dona Paula, Goa, and regional centres have been set up in Mumbai, Kochi, and Visakhapatnam.

First statistical institute

The Indian Statistical Institute (ISI) was established in 1931 in Calcutta, Bengal, by scientist and statistician P.C. Mahalanobis.

First university for the study of outer space

The Indian Institute of Space Science and Technology (IIST) in Thiruvananthapuram, Kerala, is the first university in Asia to be solely dedicated to the study and research of outer space. It was set up by the Indian Space Research Organization (ISRO) under the Department of Space, Government of India, in 2007. The institute offers undergraduate, postgraduate, and doctorate programmes with a focus on space science, space technology, geoinformatics, earth system sciences, and their applications.

First gemmological institute

The Gemmological Institute of India (GII), a non-profit public institution founded by the Gem and Jewellery Exporters Association, was established in Bombay in 1971 to promote the scientific knowledge of gemmology.

First institute of mass communication

The first institute to provide a formal education in mass communication was the Indian Institute of Mass Communication (IIMC). Set up by the Government of India in 1965, it is now located in the Jawaharlal Nehru University (JNU) campus in New Delhi. It is an autonomous institution under the Ministry of Information and Broadcasting, and offers courses related to different media.

First institute of fashion technology

The Ministry of Textiles, Government of India, set up the National Institute of Fashion Technology (NIFT) in Delhi on 24 August 1987 to provide professional human resources for the textile industry. There are currently 18 NIFT campuses in the country.

First home science college

Lady Irwin College, established in 1932 in New Delhi, was the country's first home science college.

First institute for studying footwear design

The Footwear Design and Development Institute (FDDI), set up in 1986 at Noida, Uttar Pradesh, trains students in footwear technology, computer-aided designing, and pattern making.

First law university

The National Law School of India University (NLSIU) in Bangalore was established on 29 August 1987. Currently, there are 23 such national law universities in India.

First national institute of management

The Indian Institute of Management, Calcutta, was established for the pursuit of postgraduate studies in management on 17 November 1961 by the Government of India, in collaboration with the Sloan School of Management, Massachusetts Institute of Technology (MIT), US, the Government of West Bengal, the Ford Foundation, and several Indian industries.

First model-training school

Catwalk, set up in Bombay in 1990 by leading model Lubna Adams, was the first training school in India for fashion models.

> The Rashtriya Indian Military College began due to the demands of Indian nationalists to have more Indians in the officer cadre of British Indian Army. The first concrete step towards this aim came from Lord Curzon, who established the Indian Cadet Corps first at Meerut and then at Dehradun in 1901. The Imperial Cadet Corps was the forerunner for the RIMC.

First military school

The Prince of Wales Royal Indian Military College in Dehradun, Uttarakhand, now called the Rashtriya Indian Military College (RIMC), was inaugurated on 13 March 1922 by Prince Edward VIII, the Prince of Wales, to provide training to Indian boys to become officers in the armed forces. In a landmark move in 2021, women were allowed admission to the institute.

First college of physical education

The YMCA College of Physical Education in Madras, established in 1920 by Harry Crowe Buck of Pennsylvania, US, was Asia's first college for physical education. It is now affiliated to the Tamil Nadu Physical Education and Sports University, and is considered a pioneer in the promotion of sports for persons with disabilities.

First college for the hearing-challenged

The St. Louis Institute for the Deaf and Blind in Madras, Tamil Nadu, which opened on 8 September 1993, was the first college for the hearing-impaired in the country. It is affiliated to the University of Madras and offers graduate degrees.

First radio jockey training academy

The Academy of Broadcasting in Chandigarh, set up in July 2003, was the first academy for training radio jockeys.

First yoga institute

The Bihar School of Yoga, later the Bihar Yoga Bharati in Munger, Bihar, an institute for advanced studies in yoga, set up in 1964, was the first of its kind in Asia.

First defence academy

The National Defence Academy at Khadakwasla, Maharashtra, was opened on 16 January 1955, to give its students a military orientation to join any of the three services of the Indian armed forces.

First university for the disabled

The Jagadguru Rambhadracharya Handicapped University (now renamed as the Jagadguru Rambhadracharya Divyang State University) in Chitrakoot, Uttar Pradesh, was established as a private university on 27 September 2001 to provide higher and professional education only to persons with disabilities in four categories – the visually impaired, the hearing-impaired, the mobility-impaired, and the mentally impaired, as defined in the Persons with Disability Act, 1995.

First correspondence courses

The University of Delhi introduced non-formal education in 1962 with its first correspondence course.

First national institute for the visually impaired

The National Institute for the Visually Impaired was established in Dehradun, Uttarakhand, in 1979.

First college for sanitation workers

The Harpic World Toilet College, located in Aurangabad (now Chhatrapati Sambhajinagar), in Maharashtra, was established in August 2018. It is the first of its kind in the country and has trained more than 3,200 sanitation workers. It trains workers in the required skills and also makes them aware of the occupational hazards related to the job. It is run by British consumer goods company Reckitt Benckiser.

First university only for tribal students

The Kalinga Institute of Social Sciences, founded by Achyuta Samanta in Bhubaneswar, Odisha, became India's first exclusively 'tribal' university when it was granted university status by the Ministry of Human Resources Development in 2017. It admits students only from indigenous communities and is the only known university in the world to do so.

First National Institute of Watersports (NIWS)

The National Institute of Watersports (NIWS) was established in 1990 at Caranzalem, near Dona Paula Circle, Panaji, Goa, under the Ministry of Tourism. It is the first Institute of its kind in South-east Asia. NIWS serves as a centre for training, education, consultancy, and research for various watersports disciplines, including life-saving, power boat handling, sailing, windsurfing, scuba-diving, river rafting, and kayaking. The institute offers 20 courses designed for watersports professionals and tourists visiting Goa. Certification and licensing from NIWS are mandatory for operators handling different watercraft for tourists, swimming pools, water theme parks, etc.

First master's programme in Hindu studies

Two central universities, Banaras Hindu University (BHU) and Shri Lal Bahadur Shastri National Sanskrit University, have jointly launched a master's course in Hindu studies in 2022. The curriculum, developed by BHU, aims to provide a comprehensive understanding of the foundational principles underlying Hindu civilization, society, and culture, despite the endless variety. The course is interdisciplinary and covers various subjects, including Hindu philosophy, Mimamsa, the antiquity of Hinduism, and the meaning of the word *Hindu*. The programme is aligned with the recently introduced National Education Policy (NEP).

Oldest school of art

Sir J.J. School of Art in Bombay, was founded by Sir Jamsetjee Jeejeebhoy in 1833.

First postgraduate degree

Calcutta University in Kolkata, West Bengal, conferred the first postgraduate degree (MA) in India in 1862.

First Indian to receive a PhD from a foreign university

Agostino Lourenco of Margao, Goa, is considered to have received his PhD in chemistry in Paris, France, in 1860.

First woman Bachelor of Medicine

Anandibai Joshi was the first Indian woman to obtain a Bachelor of Medicine degree in 1886 from the University of Philadelphia in the US, but she did not practise medicine.

First woman doctor

Kadambini Ganguly née Bose obtained the graduate degree from Calcutta Medical College to become the first woman doctor in 1888. She was the first woman to receive the degree from India as well as the first woman to practise medicine in the country.

First women graduates

Kadambini Ganguly née Bose and Chandramukhi Basu passed the BA examination from Calcutta University in 1883.

First woman to receive a PhD in a scientific discipline

Kamala Sohonie (1912–98), a biochemist, received her PhD at the Indian Institute of Science (IISc) Bangalore, Karnataka, in 1939, for her work on vitamins and the nutritive values of pulses, paddy, and groups of food items consumed by the poorer sections of society.

First Indian vice chancellor

In 1890, Gurudas Banerjee became the vice chancellor of Calcutta University, Bengal.

First woman vice chancellor

Hansa Jivraj Mehta (1897–1995) made history when she became the first vice chancellor of the Maharaja Sayajirao University of Baroda, Vadodara, Gujarat, in 1949.

The entrance to NALSAR

First gender-neutral certificate

The National Academy of Legal Studies and Research (NALSAR), Hyderabad, Telangana, issued the first gender-neutral graduation certificate in June 2015.

First woman law graduate

Cornelia Sorabji 1866-1954 graduated in law from the University of Bombay (now University of Mumbai) in 1894.

First to pass the Indian Medical Service examination

Surjo Kumar Chakraborty (1826–74),

MRCS (Member of the Royal College of Surgeons), was the first Indian to pass the Indian Medical Service (IMS) examination in 1855. He subsequently became the first Indian professor of Materia Medica at Calcutta Medical College.

First to obtain a doctorate

In 1904, Annoda Prasad Sircar became the first to obtain a doctorate when the University of Allahabad (established in 1887) awarded him a DSc.

First to score 100 per cent in NEET

Kota-based ALLEN Career Institute's student Soyeb Aftab scored 720/720 with all- India rank no.1 at the National Eligibility-cum-Entrance Test (NEET) 2020 (UG).

Most PhDs awarded by a university in a year

Delhi University awarded 910 PhD degrees (512 females and 398 males) at its 99th Convocation on 25 February 2023.

Most master's degrees obtained – woman

Vandana Agrawal (b. 12 November 1954) from Alwar, Rajasthan, has 10 MA degrees, the highest number of postgraduate degrees attained by a woman in India.

Postgraduate qualifications from most number of universities

Dr Anil Kumar Yadav (b. 4 June 1968) from Chandigarh holds 32 postgraduate qualifications (PhD, MPhil and PG degrees and diplomas) from 20 universities across 17 states and Union Territories. His record begins with MA (sociology) from Annamalai University in May 1995 and his latest degree is MA (sociology) from the University of Mumbai, Maharashtra, in May 2022.

First chartered scientist in aviation

Dr Bishnujee Singh (b. 27 October 1972), the chief executive officer of Cayley Aerospace Inc., from Lynnwood, Washington, US, became the world's first chartered scientist in aviation, with the Science Council, UK, in association with the Royal Aeronautical Society, on 26 September 2006.

First woman director of Indian Statistical Institute (ISI)

Dr Sanghamitra Bandyopadhyay, a computer scientist specializing in computational biology, currently serves as director of the Indian Statistical Institute (ISI). She oversees all the five centres of ISI located in Kolkata, Delhi, Bengaluru, Chennai, and Tezpur.

Youngest chancellor

Dileep K. Nair became the youngest chancellor of a university in the country when he took office at the North East Frontier Technical University (NEFTU) in Along (now Aalo), West Siang District, Arunachal Pradesh, in April 2017. He was 38 years old at the time.

Largest open university

The Indira Gandhi National Open University (IGNOU) at Maidan Garhi, New Delhi, has the distinction of being the largest open university in the world, serving more than three million enrolled students through its 21 schools of studies, and a network of 67 regional centres, around 2,000 learner support centres and 25 overseas partner institutions in 15 countries.

First foreign branch campus set up in India

Australia's Deakin University inaugurated a branch campus in GIFT city, Gujarat, on 10 January 2024. This is the first-ever foreign university branch campus in India. Indian students can pursue Master of Business Analytics and Master of Cybersecurity (Professional) from July 2024 without leaving the country.

First university for journalism and mass communication

Makhanlal Chaturvedi National University of Journalism and Communication (MCNUJC) was established in 1992 in Bhopal. It is the country's first university for journalism and mass communication and offers bachelor's, master's and PhD degrees.

ARCHIVES AND LIBRARIES

Oldest library

The Calcutta Public Library (established in 1836) was merged with the Imperial

Calcutta Public Library

Library Firsts

First library

Christian missionaries at Serampore set up their first library (later the William Carey Library) in 1800, which became the hub of their educational activities. The Reverend John Fountain, sent to India in 1796 to assist William Carey, a missionary, was its first librarian.

First operational digital library network

DELNET was the first operational digital library network. It was started as a project of the India International Centre, New Delhi, in 1988 and registered as a society in 1992.

First online Braille library

Launched in 2012 by the National Institute for the Visually Handicapped (NIVH), Dehradun, Uttarakhand, to commemorate the birth anniversary of Louis Braille on 4 January, the online Braille library provides access to 12,000 books in 10 languages in a user-friendly format.

First university library

The first university library began functioning at the University of Calcutta in 1870.

First mobile library

A bullock cart (in the shape of a small stall), laden with books at Melavasal, a village near Mannargudi in Tamil Nadu, on 21 October 1931, was possibly the first mobile library in the country. The brainchild of Rao Bahadur S.V. Kanagasabai Pillai, a Mannargudi-based engineer, the library was inaugurated by S.R. Ranganathan, called the father of library science in India. The mobile library carried books that dealt with bee-keeping and other cottage industries, aimed at providing vocational training to farmers. The cart would visit neighbouring villages in the months when there was less farming activity. A replica of the cart is now displayed in Tamil University in Thanjavur, Tamil Nadu.

First sports library

The Kanga Library at Wankhede Stadium, Mumbai has a collection of 13,000 books on sports. Around 10,000 of these are on cricket, including the entire collection of *Wisden Cricketers' Almanack* from 1864.

First national medical library

This library was initially conceived as a departmental library with a small collection of books for the use of officers of the erstwhile Directorate General of Indian Medical Services (DGIMS). In 1947, DGIMS was merged with the Office of the Public Health Commission and the Directorate General of Health Services (DGHS), and the library became DGHS Library. As the need for a central library grew to support academic, research, and clinical work by medical and health science professionals in the country, the DGHS Library was developed and was renamed Central Medical Library. In 1966, this library, located in New Delhi, was declared as the National Medical Library.

First boat library

The Young Readers' Boat Library was set up on a boat by the West Bengal Transport Corporation in collaboration with a heritage bookshop. It was launched on 26 January 2021, and houses a collection of over 500 titles in English and Bengali. The boat library conducts three-hour ferries on the Hooghly River, starting from Millennium Park to Belur Math Jetty and back. It also offers free Wi-Fi facilities and various readership activities, and conducts three trips on all weekdays.

Library (established in 1891) in 1903. In 1953, it was inaugurated as the National Library with B.S. Kesavan as its first librarian.

Biggest public library system

The Delhi Public Library, started as a UNESCO project in 1951 by the Government of India, is the biggest public library system in India and reportedly the busiest set of public libraries in South Asia. The library network consists of a central library, one zonal library, three branch libraries, 18 sub-branch libraries, one community library, seven resettlement colony libraries, one Braille library, 104 mobile library service points and 30 book-reading centres in the Union Territory of Delhi and the NCR. It has a collection of over 1.8 million books in English and other Indian languages.

Only underground library

In Bhadariya Village in Jaisalmer District, Rajasthan, is an underground library 16 ft (4.88 m) below ground level. Above this library is a temple of Devi Bhadariya Mata. The library can seat 4,000 persons and is maintained by the trustees of the temple. Housing around 9,00,000 books, the library was started by Harbansh Singh Nirmal, an avid reader, popularly known as Bhadariya Maharaj.

Largest university library

The Maulana Azad Library, the central library of Aligarh Muslim University in Aligarh, is the largest university library in Asia. The current seven-floor library houses about 14,00,000 books, periodicals, and pamphlets, 43,000 e-journals and manuscripts, and also paintings and photographs. It was inaugurated by Jawaharlal Nehru, the first prime minister of India, in 1960.

Only bookshop-cum-library on a lake

Gulshan Books, a bookshop-cum-library set up in May 2016, has a reading room, a cafe and over 80,000 books. Located on Nehru Park Island on the Dal Lake in

Ghoda library

Shubham Badhani has created a unique *'Ghoda Library'* initiative in the Himalayan mountains with a commitment to literacy, education, and cultural preservation. This initiative features mobile libraries carried by specially trained horses to the remote villages of Nainital. The *Ghoda* library focuses on preserving and promoting the unique Himalayan culture.

Srinagar, Jammu and Kashmir, it can be reached by a shikara.

Largest film archives

The National Film Archives were set up in 1964 in Poona (now Pune), Maharashtra, as a media unit of the Ministry of Information and Broadcasting, Government of India. Besides over 1,00,000 films, it has 1,57,687 photographs, 23,748 film posters, 14,210 song booklets, over 1,00,000 press clippings, and more.

The oldest public library

Krishnadas Shama Goa State Central Library in Panaji, inaugurated on 15 September 1832 by the Portuguese viceroy of Goa, is the first public library in India. Initially called the Publica Livaria of the Academia Militar de Goa, it was later renamed Central Library.

Largest library

- *By built-up area:* The Anna Centenary Library in Chennai, Tamil Nadu, is the largest in terms of constructed area – close to 3,30,000 sq ft (3.07 hectares). It houses around 1 million books.
- *By number of books:* The National Library, Kolkata, with more than 2.6 million books and over 5,00,000 manuscripts, is the largest library by number of books. The campus of the library is spread over 30 acres (12.14 hectares). However, the actual built-up area is around 1.5 lakh sq. ft (1.39 hectares).

MUSEUMS

Largest and oldest museum

The Indian Museum in Kolkata, West Bengal, one of the oldest museums in the world, founded by the Asiatic Society of Bengal in 1814 and has rare collections of antiques, armour and ornaments, fossils, skeletons, mummies, and Mughal paintings.

First public museum in a university

Established in 1937, the Ashutosh Museum of Indian Art, located in the main campus of the University of Calcutta, West Bengal, is the first public museum in any university in India. It is named after Sir Ashutosh Mukherjee, the great educationist, who introduced the study of Indology – including Indian art and archaeology – at the university level and was the vice chancellor of the university from 1906 to 1914 and 1921 to 1923. The museum houses more than 25,000 sculptures, paintings, folk-art objects, textiles, and terracotta items, among other artefacts from various phases of Indian art, with special emphasis on the art of Bengal.

First museum of textiles

The Calico Museum of Textiles in Ahmedabad, Gujarat, was set up by Gautam Sarabhai, chairman of Calico Mills, in 1949, at the suggestion of the pioneering art historian and philosopher Dr Ananda Coomaraswamy. The museum has a comprehensive collection of Indian textiles. The foundation of modern Indian textile studies was laid here and the catalogues of the Calico Museum textile collection are an indispensable reference.

First transport museum

Opened on 7 December 2013, the Heritage Transport Museum at Tauru, Nuh District, Haryana, has a rich collection of 2,500 objects, including howdahs, bullock carts, palanquins, a 1924 Ford, vintage scooters, a 1946 Piper aircraft, transport toys from the 1920s to now, and other related artefacts.

First national museum of Indian cinema

The country's first National Museum of Indian Cinema (NMIC) was inaugurated in Mumbai in January 2019. Conceived in 1997, it has been designed by the National Council of Science Museums and implemented by the Films Division, under the Ministry of Information and Broadcasting, Government of India. It is placed in a period 19th century heritage bungalow called Gulshan Mahal, and extends to another new high-technology five-floor building with two mezzanine floors. On display are projectors, recording equipment, cameras, archival posters of old films, and biographies of actors and other film personalities.

First railway museum

Inaugurated by Kamalapati Tripathi, the then minister of railways, on 1 February 1977, the Rail Transport Museum at Chanakyapuri, New Delhi, was the first rail museum in India. It was renamed the National Rail Museum in 1995 and features historical exhibits and artefacts related to the history of rail transport in India.

First Partition museum

The Arts and Cultural Heritage Trust, set up on 24 October 2016 in Amritsar, Punjab, is the world's first museum on partition of India. Housed in a restored portion of the Town Hall, it is dedicated to partition of the subcontinent in 1947. The museum commemorates Partition's victims, its survivors and its legacy. On display are photographs, clothes, utensils, and other memorabilia of the time.

Only kite museum

A museum dedicated to the rarest kites in the world is housed in Ahmedabad, Gujarat, a city popular for its annual International Kite Festival. Established in 1985, the museum was the brainchild of Bhanubhai Shah, who donated his rare collection of over 50 years to the Ahmedabad Municipal Corporation. The only kite museum in the country, it is located in the basement of Sanskar Kendra and boasts of kites of many shapes and sizes, with some that measure up to 6.7 m x 4.88 m (22 ft x 16 ft).

First underground museum

India's first underground museum opened in the Rashtrapati Bhavan on 2 October 2016. The museum showcases a collection of artefacts associated with each of the past presidents of India, including their personal belongings and vehicles, with a range of materials highlighting the history of India's freedom struggle. The museum displays more than 2,000 artefacts in a sprawling 12,077.39 sq m (1,30,000 sq ft) space.

First sports museum – personal collection

Fanattic Sports Museum is located over 6,700 sq ft (622.45 sq. m) at Ecospace in New Town, Rajarhat, around 25 km from central Kolkata. Opened in 2017, this multi-sports museum displays memorabilia from cricket, hockey, football, the Olympics, and Paralympics. It houses memorabilia collected by cricket historian Boria Majumdar for over 25 years. Highlights include Sachin Tendulkar's gloves, Lionel Messi's shoes, Didier Drogba's Chelsea jersey, and many artefacts donated by Olympic gold medallist Abhinav Bindra, Paralympics silver medallist Deepa Malik, and bronze medallist Devendra Jhajaria, among others.

First sports museum – organization

The National Institute of Sports, also known as the Netaji Subhas National Institute of Sports (NSNIS) in Patiala, Punjab, houses within the campus a sports museum. Established in 1972, which showcases a remarkable collection of rare photographs, kits, and medals of renowned Indian sportsmen including the gold medal won by Dhyan Chand at the Amsterdam Olympics in 1928, the Adidas spikes worn by Milkha Singh during the Rome Olympics in 1960, P.T. Usha's shoes, and a doughnut-shaped exercise equipment used by Gama Pehalwan, among others. There is a cricket bat on display signed by the Indian cricket team led by Kapil Dev which won the World Cup in 1983. The museum also houses replicas of different national awards given for sports, like the Arjuna Award and the Dronacharya Award. A part of the museum displays numerous rare photographs and personal items contributed by the royal family of Patiala.

First wax museum

Madame Tussauds Delhi, located in the vintage Regal Theatre in Rajiv Chowk, New Delhi, was part of the famed international chain of wax museums, the first of which opened in London in 1835. Set up in December 2017, the Delhi wax museum had on display over 40 life-size wax sculptures of political leaders and celebrities from sports, music, Bollywood, and Hollywood. The

Madame Tussauds, Delhi

23rd location for Tussauds museums, it was moved to DLF Mall of India, Noida, Uttar Pradesh, in 2022.

First museum of toilets

The Sulabh International Museum of Toilets at Mahavir Enclave in New Delhi, a museum dedicated to toilets, has 300 objects with a mix of originals, models, and photographs. The museum traces 4,500 years of the history of toilets.

First solar observatory

The Kodaikanal Solar Observatory, operational since 1889, was initially established by the British East India Company in 1792 as the Madras Solar Observatory.

Only election museum

Inaugurated in 2016, the Election Museum, located in the office premises of the chief electoral officer at Kashmiri Gate, Delhi, depicts the election journey of the largest democracy in the world. The four sections – library, audio-visual, photo gallery, and electoral management – display more than 200 archived photographs, maps, artefacts, and references. Possibly the largest of its kind in the world, the museum showcases the electoral journey of India since the first general election in 1952.

First insect museum

An insect museum was unveiled by Tamil Nadu chief minister Edappadi K. Palaniswami, at the Tamil Nadu Agricultural University in Coimbatore, Tamil Nadu, in March 2018. Covering 621.61 sq. m (6,691 sq. ft), this museum displays insect specimens starting from the early 20th century. It has live butterflies in a natural setting, termite mounds, bee species, and insect-eating plants, along with images, video, and models of their behaviour and habitats.

First dinosaur museum

The Dinosaur Museum at the Balasinor Dinosaur Park in Raiyoli Village in Balanisor Taluka in Gujarat's Mahisagar District was inaugurated in June 2019. With an enhanced version of the Dinosaur Museum already existing there, the facility is equipped with modern technology like 3D projection, virtual-reality presentations, interactive kiosks, and life-size dinosaur replicas. Its 10 galleries exhibit dinosaur remains and fossil records from the area as well as other regions of Gujarat and some other states of India, and show the history of these dinosaurs (such as the *Rajasaurus narmadensis*) from their origin to extinction.

First interactive museum of music

The Indian Music Experience (IME), established in 2018 in Bengaluru, Karnataka, is a rare museum that offers an interactive musical journey during which the visitor is encouraged to touch and feel the instruments on display to create one's own music. IME features a sound garden with 10 playable musical sculptures. It also has touchscreens, musical instruments, small theatres, and audio-video kiosks as well as a learning centre that offers music classes and workshops on a regular basis.

First science museum

The first science museum was set up by the industrialist Ghanshyam Das Birla at Birla Institute of Technology and Science (BITS), Pilani, Jhunjhunu District, Rajasthan, in 1954. Located in a hall 185 sq. m (1,991 sq. ft) of the Tower Building, it depicts the industries and business enterprises of the Birla family along with curricular scientific concepts and shows on current trends in science and technology. It is the only museum of industry and technology located inside a university campus.

First archaeological site museum

The first archaeological site museum was established adjacent to the excavated site of Sarnath, near Varanasi, in Uttar Pradesh. The Archaeological Museum Sarnath is the oldest site museum of the Archeological Survey of India and houses the findings and excavations from the Sarnath archaeological site. The idea of archaeological site museums was first proposed by Sir John Marshal, the then director general of archaeology in India, in 1905. Today there are 46 archaeological site museums spread over the length and breadth of the country displaying excavated antiquities in close proximity to their original site.

First culinary arts museum

Michelin-starred Indian chef Vikas Khanna opened India's first living culinary museum, the Museum of Culinary Arts, at his alma mater, the Welcomgroup Graduate School of Hotel Administration in Manipal, Karnataka, in April 2018. Over 2,000 utensils and artefacts from all over India and dating back centuries are housed in the museum, which is in the shape of a giant pot (similar to Harappan ones). It is spread over 2,322 sq m (25,000 sq. ft), as a part of the Department of Culinary Arts.

Largest chain of science museums

The National Council of Science Museums (NCSM), under the Ministry of Culture, Government of India, is the largest chain of science centres/museums under a single administrative umbrella in the world. There are 24 science centres or museums and an R&D laboratory and training centre of NCSM, located in different states in India.

First museum of utensils

Vechaar (Vishalla Environmental Centre for Heritage of Art, Architecture and Research), a museum that archives heritage utensils, including more than 5,400 pots, pans, serving vessels, nutcrackers, and other kitchen equipment, is housed in a village-like complex called Vishalla in Ahmedabad, Gujarat. The museum was set up in April 1981 by its collector and owner, Surendra C. Patel, and anthropologist Jyotindra Jain.

Largest terracotta museum – by collection

Formerly called the Allahabad Museum, it was established in 1931 by the Allahabad Municipal Board. The museum has the largest collection of terracoata artefacts in the country. Additionally, its rock art gallery showcases the largest collection of prehistoric paintings dating to 2000 BCE. The museum has achieved self-reliance in power generation by utilizing a solar power system, making it the first museum in the country to do so.

The prime ministers' museum

The Pradhanmantri Sangrahalaya, located on the Teen Murti Estate in New Delhi, is a museum dedicated to celebrating all former prime ministers of India. It was inaugurated on 14 April

AUDITORIUM
TOILET

Smritivan earthquake memorial and museum

Smritivan Earthquake Memorial and Museum, Bhuj District, Gujarat, covering an area of 470 acres, was created for the families of the earthquake victims from 2001. This memorial has 50 check-dam reservoirs that have the name plates of almost 13,000 victims and these reservoirs increase the surrounding water levels that help the surrounding forests. The museum is 11,500 sq. m and has 7 different blocks named – Rebirth, Rediscover, Restore, Rebuild, Rethink, Relive, Renew. The museum was inaugurated by Prime Minister Narendra Modi on 28 August 2022.

India's first sunken museum

India's first sunken museum was built at the Humayun's tomb site, Delhi. It was built by the Aga Khan Trust for Culture on behalf of Archaeological Survey of India and displays the legacy of Emperor Humayun along with lesser known details about his life. It also shows the heritage of Nizamuddin area over the last few centuries. The immersive gallery offers a 270-degree screen, and includes an animated feature on the evolution of Humayun's tomb over 500 years.

2022 by Prime Minister Narendra Modi, marking 75 years of Independence. This museum consists of 43 galleries showcasing the lives and tenures of former prime ministers. It offers various interactive experiences like holograms, virtual reality, augmented reality, and more. The exhibits include personal items, gifts and memorabilia, and medals and commemorative stamps, provided by families of former prime ministers.

Only leprosy museum

The Acworth Leprosy Museum is located at Wadala Acworth Municipal General Hospital in Mumbai. The museum, inaugurated in 2003, showcases the early history of leprosy and honours the contributions by Mahatma Gandhi, Vinobha Bhave, and Ramachandra Vitthal Lad (also called Bhau Daji Lad) towards eradicating the disease and fighting against the discriminations and prejudices associated with leprosy. It is the only leprosy museum in the country and houses panels documenting the history of leprosy, therauptic experiments conducted by Mumbai doctors, social and legal histories related to leprosy, and the efforts of notable figures in the fight against leprosy.

Conflictorium

The Conflictorium, a museum in Ahmedabad, Gujarat, was inaugurated on 14 April 2013. It is housed in the Gool Lodge, a two-storey building, located between the Progressive West and the Historical East of the Sabarmati River. The museum was designed by Avni Sethi in collaboration with Janvikas, Centre for Social Justice, and Navsarjan, aiming to document the violent and oppressive history of the state of Gujarat since its establishment in 1960. Originally owned by a Parsi lady, Bachuben Nagarwala, who was the first trained beautician and hairstylist of Ahmedabad, the building is now divided into several galleries each expressing people's voices and thoughts. The purpose of the museum is to enable people to engage in various topics of conflict through artistic and creative ways in various forms of art and culture. It serves as a space for dialogue, reflection, and exploration of conflicts in society. Avni Sethi was declared the recipient of the Jane Lombard Prize for Art and Social Justice for 2020–22 by the Vera List Center for Arts and Politics.

QUIZZES

First live quiz on TV

Neil O'Brien, called the 'father of quizzing', brought the concept of quizzes to India in 1967, after watching them on TV in the UK in the 1960s. He moderated the *Eddie Hyde Memorial Quiz Contest* 1967 in the parish hall of the Church of Christ the King in Calcutta before a 40-strong audience. The open live quiz had four teams with members from all walks of life.

First quiz show on radio

On 12 April 1972, the *Cadbury Bournvita Quiz Contest* for high-school students became the first English quiz show to be broadcast on radio (Vividh Bharati) in India. It became one of India's most famous quiz contests. It ran for over a decade and was later revived as a television quiz in June 1992. The original quizmaster on the radio show was Hamid Sayani, a prominent broadcast personality.

Longest-running open quiz

Instituted in 1992 in Chennai, Tamil Nadu, by the Landmark Bookstores, the annual *Landmark Quiz* is the longest-running open quiz in the country. A preliminary round of about 40 questions that come up on a screen is held due to the huge turnout. The quiz is hosted by Dr Navin Jayakumar and his team (which included his mother) since its inception, with the exception of 2006 when Derek O'Brien was the quizmaster.

Longest-running school quiz

The *Cadbury Bournvita Quiz Contest* was a weekly televised show that started in 1992 as the first televised school quiz in India. Anchored by reputed quizmaster Derek O'Brien, it ran continuously on Zee TV till 2001, after which it moved to the TV channel Sony, followed by Colors. Now it is conducted in a mobile application format.

Quizmaster Derek O'Brien who hosted the *Cadbury Bournvita Quiz*

First national TV quizmaster

Raman Kumar was the first quizmaster on national television. He hosted *Mashoor Mahal* during 1985–86 in the quiz genre, featuring famous personalities.

Longest-running televised quiz

Prashnottari, a twice-a-week (previously fortnightly) quiz, with participants from schools, colleges, and a general live TV audience, was first telecast on Prasar Bharati's Jaipur Doordarshan Kendra on 23 July 1993. Hosted by former IAS officer Dr Mahendra Surana since it began, it continued without break on the same channel, completing 900 episodes on 15 March 2020.

Longest-running state-level quiz

Initiated in 1986 by Vijaya Bank, Karnataka's oldest quiz competition, titled *VGenUth Quiz Contest* (now called the *Baroda Champ Annual Quiz Contest*), is open to all high-school students across Karnataka. Its 34th edition was held on 2 February 2020 in Bengaluru, in which more than 400 students from over 200 schools participated.

Most participants in an online quiz – single day

An e-quiz based on the theme 'AatmaNirbhar Bharat: Strengthen the Future', organized by the School of Entrepreneurship Skills, Bharatiya Skill Development University, Jaipur, Rajasthan, and conducted in association with The Employers Association of Rajasthan and the Global Foundation for Skill Development and Entrepreneurship, had 5,058 participants on 1 June 2020. The purpose of this quiz was to disseminate knowledge about the AatmaNirbhar Bharat Abhiyan or self-reliance movement.

Most participants in an offline quiz – single venue – single day

Under the aegis of Deendayal Vichar Manch, Bhartiya Janata Yuva Morcha conducted 'Jaane Humara Madhya Pradesh', the largest one-day general knowledge quiz with 15,000 participants from all walks of life at Nanakheda Stadium, Ujjain, Madhya Pradesh, on 11 February 2013. Conducted between 9:30 a.m. to 11:00 a.m., there were 80 objective questions with over 900 invigilators present.

Most participants in an offline quiz – multiple venues – single day

The Haryana Police organized an hour-long state-level quiz competition on 8 November 2016 on the theme of road safety. As many as 24,47,744 students participated in it.

ONLINE

Longest lesson - online

Priyanka Sankurushetti (8 January 1995) from Suryapet, Telangana, delivered a marathon lecture on Clinical Research and Clinical Data Management for 24 hours. She began at 9:30 a.m. on 11 December 2022 and ended on 9:30 a.m. on 12 December 2022, on Zoom from Vaagdevi College of Pharmacy, Hanamkonda, Telangana.

Quizzing in India

Quizzing in India was first popularized by Neil O'Brien who conducted a formal quiz in Calcutta. The city was the hub for 'quiz wars' during the late 1970s and early 1980s. However, today very few quizzing competition exists in Kolkata and are more prominent in Chennai which has taken the crown.

The *Bournvita Quiz Contest* first went on air on 12 April 1972 on Vividh Bharati and quickly became very popular. It was hosted by Hamid Sayani and his brother Ameen and the show saw numerous school kids take part. It was Derek O'Brien who later built his brand image and popularized the *Bournvita Quiz contest*. Another famous quiz competition during this time was the 'North Star Quiz' sponsored by Bata and initially hosted by Sadhan Banerjee.

Siddhartha Basu was another important quizmaster who hosted the national level inter-collegiate 'Quiz Time' in the late 1980s and it was followed by 'India Quiz.' Eventually one of the most popular shows on Indian television was *Kaun Banega Crorepati* hosted by Amitabh Bachchan. It was a success from the start and still continues on prime-time TV.

Quizzes are now an integral part of the nation's curriculum and most schools, colleges, and offices have their dedicated teams. The love for quizzing in India is perennial.

Amitabh Bachchan hosted *KBC*

DANCE

Earliest scriptural mention of dancers

The first known textual mention of dancers can be traced back to the Rig Veda (composed between c. 1500 and 1200 BCE), which has references to mythical *apsaras* (divine dancers) in the story of the celestial dancer Urvashi and the mortal king Pururava.

Earliest known treatise on the performing arts

The *Natyashastra*, said to be the work of Bharata Muni, is dated variously between the second and third centuries BCE and the fourth and fifth centuries CE. It is the earliest known treatise on the performing arts. The *Natyashastra* has 37 chapters with 5,569 slokas. It is the basis of classical Indian dance, music and drama, and is often referred to as the fifth Veda.

Earliest evidence of formalized dancing

The statuette of a dancing girl from Mohenjo-Daro in the Indus Valley that dates to 2500 BCE is the earliest evidence of formal dance.

Earliest sculptures of Odissi

Sculptures depicting dancers in the Jain cave temples of Khandagiri and Udayagiri, such as the Machapuri and Hathigumpha caves (second century BCE) in present-day Odisha, show the existence of a dance form in the region in which the dance of the female temple dancers called *maharis* (devadasis) formed a ritual during worship. Hundreds of figures depicting dance movements are carved on the walls of the Parashurameshwara, Kapileshwara, Brahmeshwara, Mukteshwara, Rajarani, and Lingaraj temples in Bhubaneswar, Puri, and Konark in Odisha, displaying the complex vocabulary of Odissi.

Oldest surviving dance drama form

Mudiyettu from Kerala, now incorporated in Kathakali, is the oldest extant dance drama form. It is traced back to the ninth century CE.

First known dance drama form

In the early 17th century, Manaveda Raja, Zamorin of Calicut (now Kozhikode), Kerala, was inspired by Jayadeva's *Gita Govinda* to compose the *Krishna Geeti* in Sanskrit. He set it to a new dance drama form known as Krishnanattam – 'the dance of Krishna'. It combined ancient theatre traditions such as Kutiyattam, ritual performances like Theyyam, and folk dances like Kaikottikali.

Earliest text to mention Odissi

Odissi has been traced to a dance form that prevailed in present-day Odisha and Bihar. In ancient times it was in a region referred to as Odhra-Magadha and was first mentioned in the *Natyashastra*. The dance was performed by maharis and male temple acolytes called *gotipuas*. It is also later mentioned in Maheswar Mahapatra's *Abhinaya Chandrika* (15th–16th century CE). This dance form, which includes the *tandava* style and the *lasya* style, has its own repertoire, costumes, music, and grammar.

First modern translation of the *Natyashastra*

In 1950, Manmohan Ghosh translated the *Natyashastra* into English for the Asiatic Society. This was the first successful attempt at translating the definitive text on Indian performing arts.

Mudiyettu from Kerala: oldest surviving dance drama form

First English periodical on Carnatic music and dance

Sruti, a periodical on music, was first published in October 1983 in Madras (now Chennai), Tamil Nadu, and gained 30,000 readers in its very first year. It was published by P.N. Sundaresan and edited by N. Pattabhiraman. It was the first known English periodical on Carnatic music and dance.

First dance schools

- Santiniketan, which was founded in 1901 in Bolpur, Birbhum District, Bengal (now West Bengal) by Rabindranath Tagore, had a department of dance to which he invited gurus from regions as far-flung as Manipur and Kerala to live on the campus and teach their dance forms to students. Santiniketan, which later evolved into the Visva-Bharati University, now has an institute of dance, drama and music, called the Sangit Bhavan.
- Kalakshetra, a premier school for classical dance, was established in 1936 at Adyar, Madras, Tamil Nadu, by Indian classical dancer Rukmini Devi Arundale. Initially called the International Academy of Arts, it was renamed Kalakshetra on the suggestion of Sanskrit and Tamil scholar Pandit P.S. Subrahmanya Sastri. Its first dance production was titled *Kutrala Kuravanji*.

First classical dance to be revived

The British colonial rule saw the decline of various dance forms, and the devadasi culture associated with Odissi was discouraged by the Christian missionaries and British officials. Odissi was rediscovered by dancer Indrani Rehman, who then popularized it abroad in the early 1940s, though it was recognized as a classical dance form only from the 1960s.

First national dance seminar

The Sangeet Natak Akademi held the first national seminar on dance from 30 March to 7 April 1958. Dr P.V. Rajammar was the Akademi's chairman then. The seminar's inaugural dance was performed by leading Kathak exponent Pandit Shambhu Maharaj.

Kerala Kalamandalam: first revivalist dance school

First revivalist dance school

The Kerala Kalamandalam in Trichur (now Thrissur) Kerala was founded in 1930 by the poet Vallathol Narayana Menon to re-establish Kathakali as a major regional theatre art and to revive Mohiniattam, a classical dance form from Kerala. These art forms flourished briefly under Maharaja Swathi Thirunal in the 19th century and then languished, until they were revived by Vallathol Narayana Menon.

First modern work on dance

The book titled *Classical Indian Dance in Literature and the Arts* by scholar Dr Kapila Vatsyayan, published in 1968 by the country's premier institution of dance and music, the Sangeet Natak Akademi, was the first definitive modern work on dance, written in English. Dr Vatsyayan received the Sangeet Natak Akademi fellowship in 1970.

WR Thickest make-up

The *chutti*, used in Kathakali, is a three dimensional mask-like attachment made of rice paste and paper, which may extend to 15 cm (6 in.) from the face. It is the thickest make-up used in any dance form in the world.

First Kuchipudi dance couple to receive the Padma Shri

Raja and Radha Reddy were the first couple to receive the Padma Shri award for a single cause, individually and together, in 1984. Widely travelled, they popularized the Kuchipudi form of dance in India and abroad. They also won the Padma Bhushan in 2000.

First Sangeet Natak Akademi award for creative dance

Dance pioneer Uday Shankar was the first to be honoured by the Sangeet Natak Akademi with an award for creative dance in 1960. Two years later, he received the Sangeet Natak Akademi fellowship. In 1971, Uday Shankar became the first modern dancer to receive the Padma Vibhushan.

Earliest reference to musical performances

The grammarian Panini (c. fourth century BCE) in his comments on *nritya* (dancing) mentions composers of sutras on dancing. The *Pali Pitaka* (c. 300 BCE) mentions two disciples of Gautama Buddha attending one such recital.

First woman to perform Chhau

Sonal Mansingh, the well-known exponent of Kuchipudi, was the first woman to learn the Chhau dance form. It is a semi-classical dance with martial and folk origins, and is found in three styles drawing their names from the regions where they are traditionally performed – Puralia Chhau (performed in West Bengal), Seraikella Chhau (performed in Jharkhand), and Mayurbhanj Chhau (performed in Odisha).

There are seven basic make-up styles used in Kathakali – Pacha (green make-up for noble and divine characters), Pazhuppu (ripe make-up), Kathi (knife make-up used for villainous males), Kari (black make-up), Thadi (beard make-up), Minukku (radiant make-up for women, sages, and Brahmins) and Teppu (red make-up).

First campaign for revival of Bharatanatyam

E. Krishna Iyer, a lawyer based in Madras, was the first to fight the anti-nautch campaigns of the 1920s by learning the dance form Bharatanatyam in 1926 from the famous Natesa Iyer from Melattur, Kerala. For six years, he lectured and wrote for his cause, and presented devadasis in public performances outside of temples. Finally, it was with T. Balasaraswati's dance performance at the All-India Music Conference in Varanasi, Uttar Pradesh, in 1935, that the dance became accepted as a respectable art form.

First Kuchipudi solo

Vedantam Lakshminarayana Sastri (1886–1956) performed the first solo recital in the traditional dance drama form of Kuchipudi. He learnt the dance form from Sri Vempati Venkatanarayana. He also introduced the popular *tarangam* into the form, during which the dancers have to balance themselves on the edges of a thali.

First Sangeet Natak Akademi award winners for dance

T. Balasaraswati and Shambhu Maharaj won the first Sangeet Natak Akademi awards for dance in 1955 for their contribution to Bharatanatyam and Kathak, respectively. The awards were instituted in 1952 to honour performing artistes.

First known Kathak teacher

Pandit Birju Maharaj (1938–2022) is the first known Kathak teacher. Born in Lucknow, Uttar Pradesh, to Shri Achhan Maharaj, a Kathak exponent, he was the popular face of the dance form globally. He was invited to teach Kathak at the age of 13 at Sangeet Bharati, and later at the Bharatiya Kala Kendra, New Delhi. He received the Sangeet Natak Akademi award in 1966 and the Padma Vibhushan in 1986.

First ballet film

Classical-folk fusion guru Uday Shankar's film *Kalpana*, released in 1948, used the ballet form for a major part of its narration, making it the country's first ballet film.

First dance theatre form recognized by UNESCO: Kutiyattam

Kutiyattam, a traditional Sanskrit performing art form originating in Kerala, is recognized by UNESCO as a 'Masterpiece of the Oral and Intangible Heritage of Humanity'. It is considered to be at least 2,000 years old and the oldest living theatre tradition globally. UNESCO usually considers only monuments and heritage sites, and this was the first art form recognized for its exceptional value. Mizhavu, a large percussion instrument, is the primary musical instrument that accompanies Kutiyattam. Considered to be sacred, Kutiyattam was traditionally performed only in temple theatres, called *koothambalam*.

First to win an international dance competition

Madame Menaka (1899–1947), whose real name was Leila Sokhey, was the first Indian to win an international dance competition at the Berlin Dance Olympiad in July 1936. Her troupe, which featured on two days, performed Menaka's original ballet, *Deva Vijaya Nritya*, and won the first three individual prizes, along with the first prize in the competition.

First celebrity dance competition

Ten famous television couples participated in the first ever celebrity dance competition, *Nach Baliye*, on TV channel Star One. The show premiered on 11 October 2005. The judges were choreographer Saroj Khan, film-maker Farhan Akhtar, and VJ-and-model Malaika Arora Khan. TV stars Sachin and Supriya Pilgaonkar were the first winners of the contest.

First Indian–European fusion

Versatile dancer Uday Shankar (1900–77), who was born in Udaipur, Rajasthan, is known as the father of modern dance in India. He combined European theatrical dance techniques with the classical and folk dance forms of India. Uday Shankar danced with Anna Pavlova, the Russian ballerina, during the 1920s and created *Hindu Wedding* as well as the duet *Radha and Krishna*, which was included in Pavlova's performance *Oriental Impressions*. In 1971, he was awarded the Padma Vibhushan, the second highest civilian award in India.

Kutiyattam: recognized by UNESCO

Only extant pre-Vedic dances

Bhutam and Theyyam are ritual dances of Karnataka and Kerala, respectively. The dancers represent local gods and ancestral spirits, based on a pre-Vedic belief system.

Only pan-Indian dance text

Jayadeva's Sanskrit book of verse, the *Gita Govinda* (12th century CE), has been choreographed in all major Indian dance styles. It is sung in both Hindustani and Carnatic modes, and has been translated into many European languages.

Oldest recipient of President's Award

Asan Chandu Panikkar (1873–1969), a pioneer of 20th-century Kathakali, received the President's Award in 1958 at 84 years. He danced at the award ceremony, in front of the then prime minister Jawaharlal Nehru and the then president Dr Rajendra Prasad.

Only dance form varied in three states

Chhau, the classical folk dance with martial overtones, has three versions based on the regions it is performed in – Seraikela Chhau in Jharkhand (masked), Mayurbhanj Chhau in Odisha, and Purulia Chhau in West Bengal.

Only dance drama performed by women alone

Kuravanji, a form of musical play popular at the beginning of the 18th century, was meant only for devadasis and was performed at the annual festivals of some temples in Tamil Nadu.

Only Asthana Nartaki

In 1978, Bharatanatyam exponent Yamini Krishnamurthy was awarded the title of 'Asthana Nartaki', meaning 'resident dancer' of Lord Venkateswara Temple, Tirupati, Andhra Pradesh.

Only classical dancer with an artificial foot

Accomplished Bharatanatyam dancer Sudha Chandran, who lost a leg in a car crash in 1981, resumed her dancing career with a prosthetic Jaipur Foot in 1984. She was rehabilitated by Dr P.K. Sethi of the Sawai Man Singh Hospital in Jaipur, Rajasthan.

Only Persianized classical dance

Kathak is a classical dance form that derives its name from the female professional storytellers or *kathikas* who recited verses from the Ramayana and the Mahabharata, along with explanatory gestures, appropriate choreography, and music, as part of a system of ritualistic worship. This dance form, with its fast and intricate movements, attracted the attention of the Mughal rulers. Over time, the dance form split into two main schools: 'Temple Kathak', with its emphasis on *bhava* (or emotion), and a court dance or 'Darbari Kathak', with its focus on rhythmic display.

Largest Bharatanatyam ensemble

The Department of Tourism, Government of Tamil Nadu, organized the largest Bharatanatyam ensemble

with 10,176 dancers on 8 February 2020. The event 'Sathir 10,000', which based the dance on the famous Tamil text *Thirukkural*, was held at S.I.V.E.T College in Chennai.

Largest arts festival

Soorya Festival, organized annually by the Soorya Stage and Film Society, Thiruvananthapuram, Kerala, is the largest of its kind in India, both in terms of membership and the number of activities. The festival is held across 111 days between September and January each year. The 30,000-plus members of Soorya Society, founded in 1978, conduct around 200 programmes annually.

Largest Kathak ensemble

Keeping the spirit of Indian culture alive, the Nrityachakra team of the Prerana Foundation from Pune, Maharashtra, organized a Kathak event where a total number of 1,188 participants came forward to perform the classical Kathak dance for a duration of 20 minutes. This event was held at Maharashtriya Mandal's Chandrashekhar Agashe College Grounds in Pune on 25 February 2024.

MUSIC

First raga

The first raga is believed to be the Carnatic Mayamalavagowla (equivalent to the Hindustani raga Bhairavi) that Purandara Dasa (c. 1484–1564), the Bhakti poet and musician, also known as Adi Guru, used as the teaching scale. Called Adi Raga, it is said to have emanated from Lord Shiva.

Purandara Dasa: the Bhakti poet and musician

Earliest form of classical song

The Dhrupad, originally called Dhruvapada, was the prevailing mode of music until medieval times. While this form traces its roots to the *Natyashastra,* it was developed by Swami Haridas and the legendary singer Tansen in the 15th century.

Only multilingual classical songs

Manipravalam *kriti*s are songs in the Carnatic tradition in which two or even three languages are used and the lines are sung alternately in these languages, which include Tamil and Sanskrit.

Earliest form of music

The Rig Veda has references to *saman* hymns, the earliest form of music in India. Saman singing is also mentioned in the *Brahmana*s as well as the Upanishads, and features as a part of spiritual observances and exercises.

Earliest known royal composer of ragas

Maharaja Swathi Thirunal (r. 1813–46), the ruler of the erstwhile princely state of Travancore (now in Kerala), created more than 400 classical compositions in both the Carnatic and Hindustani modes.

Maharaja Swathi Thirunal: one of the earliest royal composers

Earliest musical notes

The Sama Veda, which is believed to date to c. 1200–1000 BCE, mentions seven musical notes in saman singing, viz., Krushta, Prathama, Dvitiya, Tritiya, Chaturtha, Mandra/Panchama and Antya/Atisvara.

First medieval treatise on music

The Chalukyan king, Someshvara III, who ruled in the Karnataka region in the 12th century CE, wrote the *Manasollasa*, an encyclopaedic work in Sanskrit on a variety of topics, including music, with 2,500 verses dedicated to the topic. The music section, one of the largest sections in the book, is considered the earliest treatise on music.

Earliest ballad singing

Both Vedic and epic literature mentions minstrels singing *akhyana*s (texts narrated by professional storytellers), sung to the veena, in the *marga* style of singing. While the Vedas mentions both instrumental music and akhyana recitation in yagnas, the Ramayana also has several references to the singing of ballads.

A stamp honouring Ramanuja Iyengar: first codifier of the Carnatic concert format

Earliest mention of raga

The word *raga* in its modern connotation appears first in the classical Sanskrit text *Brihaddeshi* by Matanga (eighth century CE). It is described as 'a combination of tones which, with beautiful illuminating graces, pleases people'.

Earliest Prakrit (popular) songs

The *Natyashastra* mentions *dhruvas*, i.e., songs of five different kinds that were an integral part of drama. These songs indicate the context, place, and people in a scene. Dhruvas were originally in Prakrit and were mostly sung by a choir.

First to standardize music

Purandara Dasa (1484–1564) is revered as Sangeet Pitamaha (grandfather of music). He standardized Carnatic music for teaching, besides classifying 35 types of *tala*. He pioneered a musical notation system that is still being used.

Most prolific composer

Purandara Dasa (1484–1564), the philosopher-saint and Bhakti poet, is credited with as many as 4,75,000 compositions.

First codifier of Carnatic concert format

Ariyakudi Ramanuja Iyengar (1890–1967) was the architect of modern Carnatic concert music. He pioneered the transition of the Carnatic concert from temples and courts to modern concert halls, codifying and adapting its format, order, and duration. He introduced the largest number of compositions from the trinity of Thyagaraja, Muthuswamy Dikshitar and Syama Sastri to the concert

Indian Dance

Indian dance is a rich and diverse tradition with deep cultural and religious significance reflecting the country's vast heritage. It encompasses both classical and folk forms. Some prominent classicals include:

Bharatanatyam – originating from Tamil Nadu, and known for its precision and grace, it conveys stories from Hindi epics.
Kathak – originating in north India it is known for its intricate footwork, spins and storytelling.
Kathakali – originating in Kerala it is a dramatic form of dance-drama incorporating movements from ancient Indian martial arts and athletic traditions of south India.
Kuchipudi – originating in Andhra Pradesh, it is a blend of dance and drama known for its fluid movements and theatrical elements.
Odissi – originating in Odisha, it is one of the oldest classical dances recognized for its lyrical graceful movements.
Manipuri – originating in Manipur, it is often related to stories of Radha and Krishna.

India also has numerous folk dances where every state has its own folk dance forms such as Garba, Bhangra, Thirayattam, Ghoomer, Bacha Nagma, Domkach, Chholiya, Dolly Kunitha, etc.

Kathak

Kuchipudi

Navarasas

Bharata Muni wrote about the *rasas* in *Natyasastra*. In the Indian performing arts, a rasa is a sentiment or emotion evoked in each member of the audience by the art. There are nine rasas or nine essential emotional states are depicted through facial expressions, body language and gestures to convey the mood and emotion of a performance. The Navarasas are:

Sringara – the rasa of love or attraction
Hasya – the rasa that represents joy, laughter, and mirth
Raudra – the rasa that signifies intense emotions like anger, wrath, or ferocity
Karuna – the rasa that evokes feelings of sympathy, compassion, and sadness
Bibhatsa – the rasa that represents disgust, revulsion, or loathing
Bhayanaka – the rasa that conveys fear, anxiety, or apprehension
Veera – the rasa that shows bravery, heroism, and valour
Adbhuta – the rasa that expresses surprise, awe, or amazement
Santa – the rasa that represents serenity, calmness, and spiritual contentment

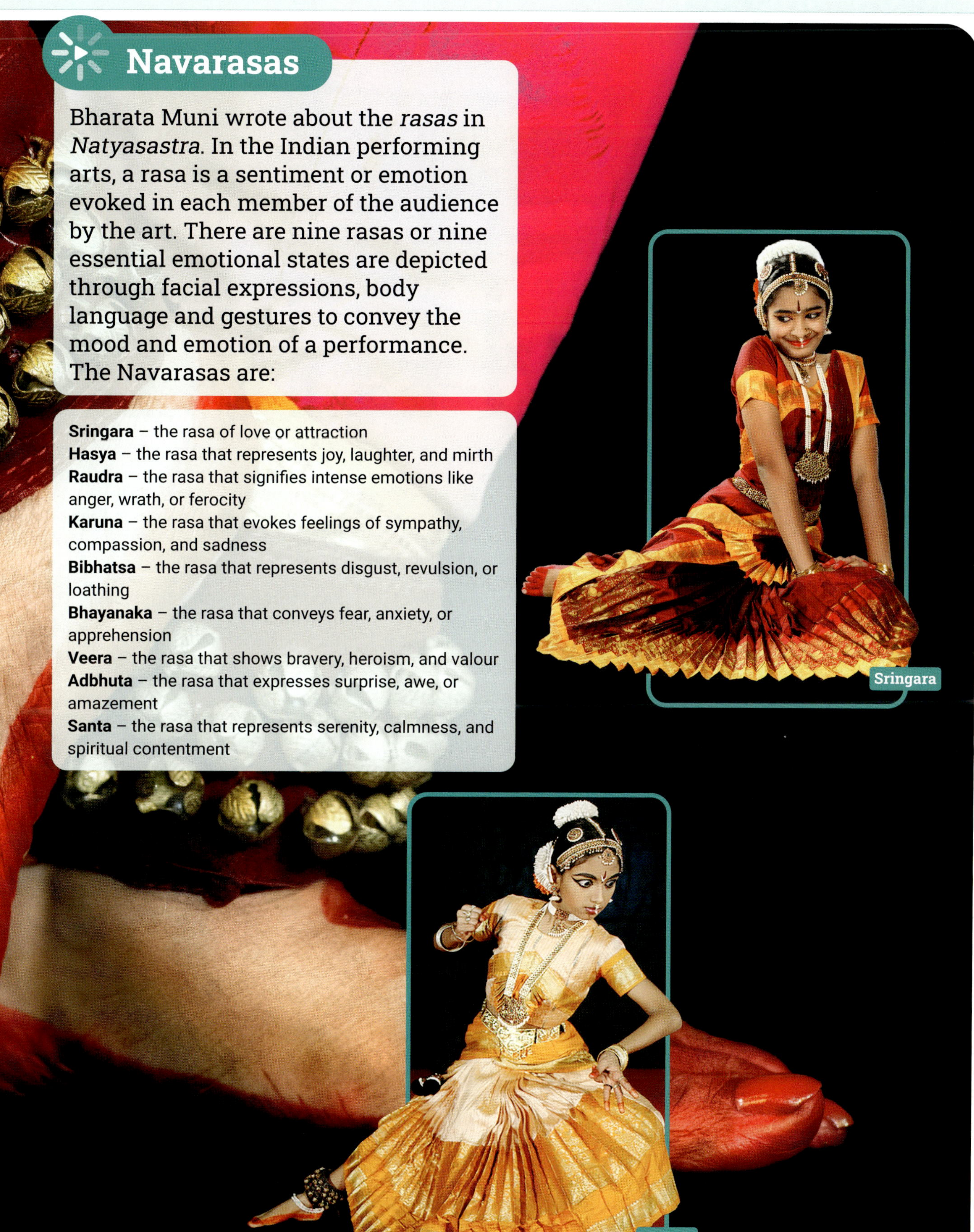

Sringara

Raudra

repertoire, new *pallavis* (opening phrase of a song), the order of *tukkadas* (composition played towards the end of a Carnatic concert) and *padams* (other songs) that follow the main item of *ragam-thanam-pallavi*.

Early treatise on Carnatic music
Rama Amatya, a royal composer at the court of King Ramaraja of Vijayanagar, gave the first detailed exposition of the Carnatic system of music in his text titled *Swaramela Kalanidhi*, around 1550 BCE. He described the first collection of ragas.

First fusion melody
The 14th century saw the introduction of Persian models into Indian music. Amir Khusrau (1253–1325), the famous singer at the court of Alauddin Khilji (r. 1296–1316), introduced the qawwali mode of singing, a mixture of Persian and Indian music. He also introduced the sitar, a modification of the veena.

Oldest gharana
The Gwalior gharana was founded in the 16th century by Nathan Khan Pir Bakhsh.

Oldest sabha for dance and music
Sri Parthasarathy Swami Sabha at Triplicane, Madras, was established in 1900. The Bangalore Gayana Sabha, Bangalore (now Bengaluru), Karnataka, set up on 5 August 1905, is the second oldest private cultural organization with programmes in dance and music.

Oldest south Indian stringed instrument
The *yazh*, a seven-stringed lute is mentioned in Tamil Sangam literature (first to fourth century CE), making it the oldest south Indian stringed instrument known.

Oldest known percussion instrument
The *ghatam* or mud pot, still in vogue in Carnatic concerts, is mentioned in the Ramayana. It was used in folk music for centuries and later elevated to concert status by maestro Palani Krishna Iyer (1876–1908). This tradition continued with maestros such as Kodandarama Iyer and T.H. 'Vikku' Vinayakram, who popularized it.

A lithophone

Oldest musical instrument
A lithophone (stone chimes comparable to a xylophone), 3,000–4,000 years old, was identified by German archaeologists in Sankarjang Village in Angul District, Odisha. All the 20 similar-shaped polished basalt stones found possibly formed fragments of a lithophone, with excellent acoustic quality, as the edges were ground thin to achieve a specific pitch.

First mention of the drum
The *Mahajanaka Jataka* (c. second century BCE) mentions the drum, along with horns, gongs, and cymbals.

Earliest extant musical instruments
Drums came into being during the Vedic period. The earliest drums included the *dundubhi* and *adambara*, ordinary drums; *bhumi dundubhi*, an earth drum made by digging a hole in the ground and covering it with hide; and *vanaspati*, a wooden drum. Early stringed instruments included the *skanda veena* and *karkari*, ordinary lutes; *vana*, a lute with a hundred strings; and the veena (similar to the present-day one). Wind instruments included the *tunava*, a wooden flute; the *nadi*, a reed flute; and *bakura*, whose shape is unknown.

First Indian performer at the Royal Albert Hall
The first Indian singer to perform at the iconic venue, the Royal Albert Hall, in London, UK, was Bollywood playback singer Lata Mangeshkar, who gave a performance at the venue in 1974. Other Indians who have also performed here include sitar players Pandit Ravi Shankar and Anoushka Shankar, flautist Hariprasad Chaurasia, and singer Shreya Ghoshal.

First three-in-one classical instrument
The *mridanga veenai*, a stand-up instrument that is framed in wood and played sitting on a chair, was invented by Audanoor P. Haridass, who demonstrated it on 23 September 1984 at the Purasawalkam Arts Academy, Madras. Played with bamboo sticks, it not only reproduces the sounds of percussion and strings, but also simulates the sound of cymbals used in *natuvangam* (rhythmic sound play) and the tinkle of *gajjai* (ankle bells).

Earliest use of the Carnatic veena
Govinda Dikshitar modified the Saraswati veena into the Carnatic veena to enable the playing of all ragas. He was a minister of King Raghunatha Naik of Thanjavur (r. 1614–32 CE), Tamil Nadu.

First singer to be recorded on gramophone
Gauhar Jaan (1873–1930) was selected to sing when Fred Ginsberg introduced the gramophone in India with the first disc being cut in Calcutta (now Kolkata), West Bengal, in 1902. She was paid ₹3,000 for the recording session.

First recorded song
Sashimukhi of Classic Theatre in

Gramophone recording in India

Gramophone records were introduced in India in 1902 and many short-lived Indian and foreign companies made recordings. These recordings were made on brittle and perishable shellac records. Since the recordings made in the beginning of the 20th century were made without electricity the singers had to sing loudly into the horn of the gramophone recorder to make a satisfactory recording and ultimately very few copies of the record were released. Carnatic music, Hindustani music, devotional songs and abridged forms of musical drama were some of the recordings made, and the companies that were popular for the recording were The Wellington Cycle Co., Bombay; The Binapani Recording Co., Calcutta; The Gramophone Co., Calcultta; The Kamala recording Co., Calcutta; Valabhdas Runchordas & Co., Bombay.

Calcutta recorded the first song 'Kanha Jeevan Dhan' in 1902, from the play *Srikrishna* on a 22.86 cm (9 in.), one-sided disc made by the Gramophone and Typewriter Ltd.

First voices recorded on gramophone

The voices of Dr Harnamdas and Ahmed were recorded by the Gramophone Company in 1899 in London, UK. They sang songs based on the Ramayana and recited the *aayat*s of the Quran for the recordings.

First gramophone company

On 7 July 1901, J. Watson Harrod opened a branch of the Gramophone Company Ltd at Calcutta, which was further developed by T.W. Gainsberg. In 1908, the first factory to process and press records was set up in Beliaghata, Calcutta.

First female professional saxophone players

Sisters M.S. Lavanya and M.S. Subbulakshmi from Chennai, have given a new dimension to Carnatic music by playing ragas on the saxophone. Daughters of mridangam exponent M.R. Sainath, the duo, called the 'Saxophone Sisters', learnt the instrument from Padma Shri Dr Kadri Gopinath. They performed at venues such as the Soorya Festival in Thiruvananthapuram, Kerala, the Sri Thyagaraja Festival at Thiruvaiyaru, Tamil Nadu, and the Malleswaram Sangeetha Sabha, Bengaluru, Karnataka. They have also performed at the 'One City One World Festival' in Nottingham and the Bath International Music Festival in the UK.

Only gramophone museum

Discs and Machines – Sunny's Gramophone Museum and Records' Archive in Kottayam, Kerala, is a unique repository of around 1,10,000 records and more than 260 gramophones. Owner Sunny Matthew has been collecting them for the last 33 years and opened the museum to public on 25 January 2015. A copy of the first recorded song in India is also on display here. The museum may be visited by appointment.

First gramophone record

Indian music was first produced on a gramophone record in 1898 at the Beliaghata factory of the Gramophone and Typewriter Ltd. In July 1908, the production of disc records was started at the Sealdah factory located on Beliaghata Road, Calcutta. In 1928, the Sealdah factory was closed and building work commenced at the new factory on Jessore Road, Dum Dum, Calcutta.

First electronic instrument

The first electronic tala aid called talometer was invented by M.G. Raj Narayan of Bangalore, in June 1978. It helps musicians to get a precise, unerring, and continuous course of cycles in all the talas.

First duo to introduce jugalbandi

Pandit Ravi Shankar and Ustad Ali Akbar Khan formed the first musical duo to introduce instrumental duets popularly known as jugalbandi. Shankar and Khan performed the jugalbandi for the first time at the debut performance of the former in 1939, with Shankar playing the sitar and Khan playing the sarod. The duo was also among the first to popularize Indian classical music abroad.

First use of shehnai in Hindustani classical music

The shehnai, like the *sundari* and *surnayi,* was originally a folk instrument that was played on festive occasions. It was Ustad Bismillah Khan (1916–2006) who brought it into the realm of classical music, at par with other classical instruments.

First harp player

Meagan Pandian from Mumbai, Maharashtra, is the first harp player from India and the first Indian harpist to participate in A.R. Rahman's concerts. She received the 'Young Musician of the Year' award from the Olga and Jules Craen Foundation in 2014.

First woman instrumentalist

Renowned sarod player Sharan Rani Backliwal (1929–2008) was a leading exponent of Hindustani instrumental music and the first female instrumentalist to give a public recital in the 1930s. She trained under sarod maestros Baba Allauddin Khan and Ustad Ali Akbar Khan. Popularly known as Sarod Rani, she was given the Sahitya Kala Parishad award and the Sangeet Natak Akademi award for classical Hindustani instrumental music in 1974. She received the Padma Shri in 1968.

First woman shehnai player

Bageswari Gamar was crowned 'Shehnai Queen' at Chandigarh in 1983, the year she made her debut. A disciple of Ustad Bismillah Khan, she recorded a jugalbandi with the maestro, besides releasing solo cassettes.

She represented India at the Bharat Mahotsav in Russia in 1988.

First woman nadaswaram player

Madurai M.S. Ponnuthayi from Madurai, Tamil Nadu, was the first professional woman player of the nadaswaram, long considered a male bastion. Born into a family of musicians, she was introduced to the instrument by her father. After receiving training under Natesa Pillai, she gave her first performance at the age of nine in the 1940s.

Nadaswaram

First woman ghatam player

Sukanya Ramgopal (b. 13 June 1957) from Bengaluru, became the first woman to play the ghatam in the Carnatic music tradition. Among many of her innovations are the 'Ghata Tarang', a melody created out of six ghatams, and the 'Sthree Taal Tarang', an all-woman percussion ensemble, experiments that have taken her to stages across India and abroad. She received the Sangeet Natak Akademi Award in 2014.

First to perform at the UN

M.S. Subbulakshmi (1916–2004) was the first Indian to perform at the United Nations (UN) in a concert at the UN General Assembly on UN Day, 23 October 1966. She received the Padma Bhushan in 1954 and the Padma Vibhushan in 1975 and became the first musician to be awarded the Bharat Ratna in 1998. Subbulakshmi was also the first Indian musician to receive the Ramon Magsaysay Award for Public Service in 1974.

First music school

Pandit Vishnu Digambar Paluskar (1872–1931) set up the Gandharva Mahavidyalaya – India's first known music school – in Lahore (now in Pakistan) on 5 May 1901. It was run on public donations and funds raised by his concerts. Another branch was opened by him in Bombay in September 1908, and Pandit Vinayakrao Patwardhan started a branch in Poona (now Pune), Maharashtra, on 8 May 1932. Later, the Lahore school was moved to Bombay after Independence in 1947.

Most recorded artiste

Asha Bhosle is the most recorded artiste in the history of music. Having begun her career in 1948 with the Hindi film *Chunariya*, she had recorded 11,000 solo, duet, and chorus songs by 2011. In a career spanning more than six decades, she has sung in over 20 Indian and foreign languages. She received the Dadasaheb Phalke Award in 2000 and the Padma Vibhushan in 2008. She was also the first Indian singer to be nominated for the Grammy Awards.

First foreign concert tour by a woman instrumentalist

According to a report in *Amrita Bazar Patrika*, dated 11 September 1912, Satyabala Devi, an 18-year-old Bengali girl, had gone to America in the summer of 1911 to play the veena. The article stated that she was the first Indian woman to have gone abroad to perform in an instrumental music concert, and it was declared a great success.

Ancient veena

First recorded music

In the 1930s, an organization called Shining Star Society recorded sets of discs with mythological themes. A mix of music and dialogue, the sets ran into several records. A-10 disc *Ramayana* by Saraswati Stores was very popular, followed by other drama sets like *Tukaram* (four discs), *Purandara Dasa* (five discs), *Siruthondar* (three discs) and *Thirugnana Sambandhar* (four discs). Their recording was supervised by the Katcheri set pioneer, Thuraiyur Rajagopala Sharma.

First compact disc

Pankaj Udhas's album titled *Shagufta* was the first to be formally released in a compact disc (CD) format by Music India in December 1987.

First fusion album

Violinist Yehudi Menuhin and sitar maestro Pandit Ravi Shankar collaborated on a double album called *West Meets East*, which was released in Britain in January 1967, where both played Western and Indian classical pieces alternately.

First set of records

Renowned businessman H. Bose's Talking Machine Hall, a recording shop in Calcutta, released the first set of phonograph records on 19 March 1906. The set featured eight songs by Rabindranath Tagore and four by D.L. Roy.

First portable digital audio player

Carvaan, by Saregama India Ltd, is the world's first portable digital audio player with over 5,000 inbuilt songs. The songs are categorized based on singers, lyricists, music composers, and moods. Using a jog dial, music stations can be selected, from Kishore Kumar classics and R.D. Burman's hits to timeless love songs and soulful Sufi tracks. Carvaan can function as an FM radio, and also has Bluetooth and USB features.

Carvaan, by Saregama India Ltd

First all-woman Hindustani–Carnatic music band

Tabla soloist Anuradha Pal from Mumbai, founded Stree Shakti, the first all-woman Hindustani–Carnatic music band, in 1996. It performed in India as well as other countries, including in international festivals such as BBC Music Live and Rhythm Sticks.

Grammy Award for the Best World Music Album

Music composer and tabla player Sandeep Das won a Grammy Award for the Best World Music Album in 2017 for his collaboration with Yo-Yo Ma and the Silk Road Ensemble on the album *Sing Me Home*.

First Indo-jazz (fusion) albums

Indo-jazz came into its own in India in the 1970s with Shakti, a group formed by jazz guitarist John McLaughlin, along with L. Shankar on the electric double violin (which he invented), Zakir Hussain on the tabla and T.H. 'Vikku' Vinayakram on the ghatam.

First Grammy Award–winning Indian percussionist

T.H. 'Vikku' Vinayakram was the first Indian percussionist to win the Grammy Award in 1991. He won it for his participation in *Planet Drum* by Mickey Hart. Vinayakram, well-known for playing the ghatam and popularizing Carnatic music, was honoured with the Padma Shri in 2002 and the Padma Bhushan in 2014. He also won the Sangeet Natak Akademi fellowship in 2012.

Only Indian to win both an Oscar and a Grammy Award

Composer and singer A.R. Rahman won two Grammys following his Oscar wins for the soundtrack from Danny Boyle's *Slumdog Millionaire*, becoming the first Indian to win an individual Grammy. He won the first Grammy in the Best Compilation Soundtrack for the Motion Picture category. The second was for the song '*Jai Ho*' in the Best Motion Picture Song category for the same in 2009.

Shankar Mahadevan and Zakir Hussain are part of the fusion band Shakti which received the 'Best Global Music Album' award at the Grammy Awards. They got the award for their latest album *This Moment*.

First Asian to win the Golden Reel Award

Resul Pookutty was the first Asian to win the 63rd American Motion Picture Sound Editor's Golden Reel Award in 2016 for best sound for the documentary *India's Daughter*. A sound designer, editor, and mixer who works in Hollywood and Indian cinema, he also won the Academy Award (Oscar) in 2009 for best sound mixing for the movie *Slumdog Millionaire*, along with Richard Pryke and Ian Tapp. He was awarded the Padma Shri in 2010 and the National Film Award for best audiography in the same year.

First whistling LP

An album of Carnatic and Hindustani ragas entirely whistled by Siva Prasad from Hyderabad (now in Telangana) was released on 15 June 1985.

First Indian band on MTV

Rana Banerjee and Sanjoy Sengupta's band, Extinct, was the first Indian group to be featured on MTV Asia, in September 1993.

India's only music director couple

Samir and Mana Raval from Ahmedabad, Gujarat, are India's first and only music director couple, having composed music for more than 100 songs in 35 feature films in Gujarati and Hindi. Having started with music direction for *Teenagers Gang*, a Gujarati film, in 2013, the couple continues to compose music for Hindi and other films, TV serials, and jingles.

First female rapper

Taran Kaur Dhillon (b. 29 July 1979), aka Hard Kaur, was the first female rapper of Indian origin. A British citizen, she topped the UK charts with her song, 'Ek Glassy' in 2007. Her first solo album *Supawoman* released the same year had 11 tracks. She marked her Bollywood debut with the title track (which she co-wrote) of the film *Johnny Gaddaar* (2007).

A.R. Rahman: only Indian to win both an Oscar and a Grammy Award

First disabled DJ

Varun Khullar, aka DJ Aamish, from New Delhi, is the first disabled professional disc jockey (DJ) in India. He began his career in May 2017 and is currently a resident DJ with Kitty Su, New Delhi, a part of the Lalit Group and Hotels. He has performed at festivals like Time Out 72 and Greeshma Utsav.

Longest innings as a conductor

Western music maestro Zubin Mehta (b. 29 April 1936) from Bombay spent over 13 years as the music director and principal conductor of the New York Philharmonic Orchestra from 1978 to 1991. Currently, he is the music director of the Israel Philharmonic Orchestra.

First virtual music festival

Sunburn Home Festival, a two-day virtual music festival, was organized from 11 to 12 July 2020. The festival featured a line-up of international stars such as Bassjackers, Vini Vici, and Ummet Ozcan. The highlight of the event was the application of extended reality (XR) technology offering a mixed reality and holistic environment, also used for the first time.

Longest ravanhatha

Praveen Singh Rathore along with Shiv Pal Ram, Sugana Ram, and Manwari from Jodhpur, Rajasthan, made the longest ravanhatha, a folk string instrument of Rajasthan. The ravanhatha, measuring 224 cm (7 ft 4.19 in.), was made in two weeks at Bhakrasani, Jodhpur, using bamboo, mango wood, goat leather, bull horn, iron, cotton threads, plastic threads, *baval* (babul) wood, *ghungroo* (bells) and fabric.

Marathon flute performance

Ananthakrishnan S.R., a flautist from Thiruvananthapuram, Kerala, played the flute for 33 hrs 36 mins, from 6:30 a.m. on 13 July to 6:30 p.m. on 14 July 2017 in Thrissur, Kerala, with a total break time of 2 hrs 24 mins.

Marathon qawwali performance

Haji Mohammad Idris and Mohammad Ilyas, known as the Qutbi brothers of Dargah Hazrat Qutbuddin, performed Sufi qawwali for 12 hrs. They began at 9:00 p.m. on 12 November 2016 and ended at 9:00 a.m. on 13 November 2016 at the Sangeet Natak Akademi in Delhi. Sixteen singers accompanied them.

Marathon duet singing

Venkatesh and Sangeetha Rajeshkumar from Chennai, sang duets for 28 hours at the Akshaya Mahalakshmi Mahal, Chennai, during 28–29 January 2017. They sang 342 Tamil film songs starting at around 4:00 a.m. on 28 January and ended by 12:30 p.m. the next day. The total break time was 4 hrs 30 mins.

Most events in a day

Pernod Ricard India Pvt. Ltd organized 104 musical events on a single day – 29 November 2019. These events were held at different venues across 27 cities in the country, including Delhi, Mumbai, Pune, Chennai, Visakhapatnam, and Chandigarh. Titled 'Play for a Cause', this campaign raised awareness on issues such as pollution, nature, plastic use, and meals for the underprivileged. Bands and artistes including Perfect Strangers (Bengaluru), Parikrama (Gurugram), Ankur Tiwari and the Ghalat Family (Mumbai), Cherry Singh (Chandigarh), and Usha Uthup (Kolkata) performed at these events.

Marathon Carnatic vocal performance

Sajna Sudheer (b. 1 August 1984) from Thiruvananthapuram, Kerala, performed a marathon Carnatic vocal recital for 37 hrs 50 mins at the Ganesham Natakakalari of Soorya Stage and Film Society. She began her performance at 3:15 a.m. on 21 January 2019 and ended at 9:15 p.m. on 22 January 2019, with a total break time of 4 hrs 10 mins.

Most people playing the harmonica together

Hindustan Petroleum Corporation Ltd, as part of its mega festival – Yuvantage BLITZ during 6–7 January 2019 – set a record for most people playing the harmonica simultaneously. The music was played by 457 of the company's employees on their harmonicas for 6 mins 17 secs on 6 January 2019 at Ramoji Film City, Hyderabad, Telangana.

THEATRE

First modern Indian plays (translations)

Gerasim Lebedev, a Russian adventurer, founded the first European-style proscenium drama theatre in Calcutta, in 1795. He was helped by the local intellectuals. Along with his Bengali tutor, Goloknath Das, he presented the plays *The Disguise* and *Love Is the Best Doctor* on 7 November 1795. These English comedies, translated into Bengali, were the first urban theatrical performances.

Marathon nukkad natak performance

The Mayaar Group of the Bhopal School of Social Sciences in Bhopal, Madhya Pradesh, organized a street-play marathon to celebrate Mahatma Gandhi's 150th birth anniversary. A

Parikrama

Indian plaque showing the story of Shakuntala

record was set with a team of 17 members performing 151 street plays from 5:00 a.m. on 3 March 2019 to 3:56 a.m. on 4 March 2019 at different locations in the city. The performance time added up to 22 hours 56 mins, with a break time of 2 hrs 26 mins. The plays conveyed the importance of the Swachh Bharat Mission of the Government of India.

First foreign translation of a Sanskrit play

Poet Kalidasa's *Abhijnana Shakuntalam* was translated into German in 1791 by revolutionary Georg Forster and into English by Anglo-Welsh philologist Sir William Jones in 1795.

First 'protest play'

Nīl Darpan, a play in Bengali about the plight of indigo farmers, was written by Dinabandhu Mitra in 1860. The play was banned by the British authorities.

First full-fledged opera

The Fakir of Benares, an Indo-French opera, was staged at the Siri Fort Auditorium, New Delhi, on 27 February 2002. The opera was directed by Muzaffar Ali while his wife Meera Ali designed the costumes.

First public theatre hall

The Star Theatre in Calcutta, was inaugurated on 21 July 1883 with the play *Daksha Yajna*. Among the first to produce plays here was the acclaimed playwright, novelist, theatre director, and actor Girish Chandra Ghosh. The theatre moved to its present site on Bidhan Sarani in 1888 and now mainly functions as a cinema hall with plays also being staged.

First dramatic club

The first dramatic club was the Parsi Natak Mandali established in 1853 in Bombay. They performed their first play *Roostum Zabooli and Sohrab* that year, followed by *King Afrasiab and Rustom Pehlvan* and *Padshah Faredun*. Other Parsi theatre clubs were the Elphinstone, established in 1860, and the Victoria, established in 1867. These drama clubs inspired Gujarati theatre.

First and only play on Broadway and West End

The Ramayana by Gopal Sharman, enacted in a one-woman tour de force by Jalabala Vaidya, was played at the Barbizon Plaza Theatre, Manhattan, New York, in February 1975. The play was also performed at other venues, such as the Smithsonian Institution, Washington DC, the United Nations headquarters, New York, USA, and Sedler's Wells Theatre, London, UK.

First Marathi musical

Shakuntala was staged as a Sangeet play on 31 October 1880 by Balwant Pandurang 'Annasaheb' Kirloskar and his Kirloskar Natak Mandali. Written in Marathi, it featured simple songs. This format was followed by Marathi stage in the musical drama genre called Sangeet plays. It attracted giants like Bal Gandharva (Narayanrao Rajahansa) and Keshavrao Bhonsle.

Bal Gandharva

Play performed in most languages – single day

Yugpurush – Mahatma's Mahatma, a two-hour play based on the relationship between Mahatma Gandhi and his spiritual guide, Shrimad Rajchandra-ji, was performed in five languages, viz., English, Hindi, Bengali, Gujarati, and Tamil, on 11 August 2017. It was organized by the Shrimad Rajchandra Mission in Dharampur, Valsad District, Gujarat, as one of the 808 performances for the 150th birth anniversary celebrations of Shrimad Rajchandra-ji.

First commercial theatre

The first commercial theatre, generally known as the 'Parsi theatre', started by Pestonji Framji in 1870, was aimed at mass entertainment, while dealing with social problems. Though based in Bombay, the theatre company travelled widely all over north India.

First opera in English by an Indian

Well-known author Vikram Seth's *Arion and the Dolphin*, which premiered in the UK in June 1994, was the first opera written in English by an Indian. Commissioned by the English National Opera, it was performed at the 964-seat drill shed of HMS *Drake*, a high-security naval base. The opera was directed by Rebecca Meitlis.

WR Most theatrical performances

The Gujarati stage actor Pransukhlal Nayak (1910–89) had 22,455 theatrical performances to his credit by December 1986. He had played 241 roles in stage productions in a career he started at the age of nine.

Most stage plays performed in a day - solo

Akash Bhadsavle (9 February 1996) has performed a total of 12 shows in 3 plays of 45 minutes each on Sunday, 9 October 2022. The plays were performed in Gadkari Rangayatan, Thane, in two sessions from 8:00 a.m. to

Regional Folk Theatre of India

Folk Theatre of India has a fusion of different elements of music, dance, pantomime, versification, epic and ballad recitations, and religious tales. The folk theatre has roots in native culture and has its foundations in local identity and social values. This form of theatre also talks about political and cultural issues to create awareness among people. Some of the types of regional theatre:

Yakshagana

Tamasha – It is a traditional form of theatre from Maharashtra that began in the early 18th century. Originally performed to entertain armies that were encamped, it is a form of theatre that often talks about social and political themes.
Bhavai – It is a traditional folk theatre form from Indian states of Gujarat and Rajasthan, and is a combination of music, dance, and skits, or *vesha* that are performed by men from Bhavaiyya community. It comes from the Sanskrit words bhava meaning emotion.

Bhavai

Saang

Yakshagana – This is a traditional theatre form developed in Udupi, Shivamogga, and western parts of Chikmagalur districts. It combines dance, music, dialogue, costume, make-up, and stage techniques with a unique style and form.
Karyala – It is a theatre form from Himachal Pradesh and it is a fusion of dance, music, and versification. It is usually played during Diwali and doesn't require a stage. Here men play female roles and it includes interactive conversations, skits, and performances that comment on local politics, domesticity, and social relations.
Saang – It is a popular folk dance-theatre form in Haryana, Rajasthan, Uttar Pradesh, and the Malwa region of Madhya Pradesh. It is a dialogue-oriented form of theatre and has mimicry, song, and theatrics. It depicts religious stories, folk tales, and tales of humour, valour, and sacrifice.

11:00 p.m. and 11:00 a.m. to 2:30 p.m.; in Dada Kondake Amphi theatre, Thane, from 4:00 p.m. to 7:30 p.m.; and in Mahakavi Kalidas Natya Mandir Mulund from 8:30 p.m. to 11:45 p.m.

Asia's biggest theatre festival

Bharat Rang Mahotsav, the annual theatre festival of the National School of Drama (NSD), is the biggest theatre festival in Asia. Established in 1999, the Bharat Rang Mahotsav includes theatre groups from around the world. The 23rd edition of the Bharat Rang Mahostav was conducted in February 2024 and featured around 150 performances, and also included workshops, discussions, and master classes.

Most performances as a personality – stage and screen

Deepak Madhukant Antani (b. 20 August 1964) from Ahmedabad, Gujarat, is a professional actor who has performed the most times as Mahatma Gandhi on screen and stage. His maiden venture enacting the role of the Mahatma was on 20 June 2000 in *Sardar Patel*, a play written by him for Sardar Vallabhbhai Patel's 125th birth anniversary celebrations. As a Gandhi lookalike, he has performed in one advertisement, two feature films, 21 short films, one TV serial, 190 stage plays, three documentaries, four voice-overs, and a 200-km *padyatra* completed in nine days.

Most performances as a character (mythological) – stage

V.S. Narayanan (b. 20 November 1943) from Mumbai, has been performing the role of Hanuman for the annual Ramnavami festival held by the Mulund Bhajana Samaj, Mumbai, since 1967. He has performed each year for 53 years.

Longest-serving director of the NSD

Ebrahim Alkazi (1925–2020) was appointed as the second director of the National School of Drama (NSD) in 1962 and served till 1977.

First recipient of the Kalidas Samman (theatre)

Shambhu Mitra (1915–1997) from Kolkata, was the first recipient of the Kalidas Samman for his contribution to Bengali theatre.

The Earliest and Oldest

Early dramatic references

There are references to drama, dancing, music, and acting in the Ramayana, the Mahabharata, and the Puranas. Buddhist and Jain texts mention that monks were forbidden from watching dramatic performances. Panini (c. fourth century BCE) mentions dramatic works in his *Ashtadhyayi*. Patanjali (variously dated from second century BCE to the fourth century CE), describes the conditions of dramatic performers. Kautilya also refers to music, dance, and drama in the *Arthashastra*.

Earliest plays

• Patanjali mentions plays such as *Kamavadha*, *Balibandhan*, and *Sariputra-Prakarana* in his text *Mahabhashya* (c. third century BCE).
• Bharatamuni also mentions plays such as *Devasura Sangrama*, *Amrita Manthana*, and *Tripuradaha* in his *Natyashastra.*
• *Uparupaka*s (secondary dramas) are found in the Rig Veda in the form of dialogue hymns. The most famous one tells the story of Pururava and Urvashi. Eighteen such uparupakas are mentioned in *Sahitya Darpana*, a book on rhetoric and dramaturgy from the 14th century, authored by Pandit Vishwanath Kaviraj. These plays pre-date even the *Natyashastra.* Uparupakas were probably enacted before the public on royal occasions and temple festivals.

Early political plays

Mrichchhakatika by Shudraka (dated between the third and the fifth century CE) and Vishakhadatta's *Mudrarakshasa* (dated between late fourth and the eighth century CE), both depict clashes between different powers, political intrigue, espionage, and counter-espionage. They are considered to be the first plays with political themes.

Earliest playwright

Bhasa (third to fourth century CE) of the Chola era in south India is believed to be the earliest playwright. Well-known plays by him include *Abhisheka*, *Swapnavasavadattam*, and *Pratimanatakam*.

Earliest street plays

Therukoothu, a theatre form originating during 200 BCE–200 CE in ancient Tamilakam, literally means 'street play'. It was performed on streets on an improvised stage with very few props and hardly any special costumes. Themes were taken from the epics. Therukoothu as well as other forms of street plays like Pallu, Kuravanji, and Nandi Natakam are still performed in south India.

Oldest extant play

Palm-leaf fragments belonging to the Kushana period (around first century CE) feature a nine-act Buddhist play titled *Sariputra Prakarana*, by Ashvaghosha, the court poet of King Kanishka. It follows all the rules for drama laid down in the *Natyashastra.*

Oldest cave theatre

The cave theatres at Sita Bengra and Jogimara in the Surguja District of Chhattisgarh are estimated to be around 3,000 years old. Sita Bengra, which pre dates the Lomas Rishi caves of the Mauryan period (322–187 BCE), was chiefly used for dance and drama.

Oldest children's theatre

Children's Little Theatre, the oldest children's theatre in the country, was founded in Calcutta, by Samar Chatterjee (1908–86) in May 1951. It included dance, drama, music, and puppetry.

DEVELOPMENT OF
PHOTOGRAPHY
फोटोग्राफी का विकास
PHENAKISTOSCOPE
फेनाकिस्टोस्कोप

Search...
THAUMATROPE
थमाट्रॉप
PERSISTENCE
OF VISION
दृष्टि की जड़ता

CINEMA

PIONEERS

First film shot in India

Coconut Fair is said to be the first short film shot in India in 1897, and it was made by an unknown foreign photographer. Shortly after, another 'film' made in India, a short dancing scene from the Bengali opera *The Flower of Persia* was exhibited at the Star Theatre, Calcutta (now Kolkata), West Bengal, on 9 February 1898.

First female actor of the talkies

After silent performances in 36 movies, Zubeida Begum acted in the first Indian talkie *Alam Ara* (1931).

Zubeida Begum

First advertisement for a film

The first advertisement for a film appeared in *The Times of India*, Bombay (now Mumbai), on 7 July 1896. It gave the night's programme for the screening of the six short films by the Lumière Brothers and called the event, 'the marvel of the century' and 'the wonder of the world'.

LANGUAGE

First Indian film in English

Ardeshir Irani's *Noor Jahan*, directed by Ezra Mir in 1931, starring Mazhar Khan, Nayampally, Mubarak, and Vimala, was given an English version a year later for foreign markets.

Ardeshir Irani

First film in multilingual versions

J.B.H. Wadia's *Court Dancer* (*Raj Nartaki*), directed by Madhu Bose and featuring Sadhana Bose and Prithviraj Kapoor, was shot in Hindi, Bengali, and English in 1941.

Left: A stamp commemorating Prithvi Raj Kapoor
Above: Sadhana Bose

Films edited in most languages/ dialects

A. Sreekar Prasad (b. 12 March 1963) from Chennai, Tamil Nadu, has edited films in 17 languages/ dialects: English, Hindi, Tamil, Telugu, Malayalam, Kannada, Odia, Assamese, Bengali, Punjabi, Nepali, Marathi, Sinhalese, Karbi, Mishing, Bodo, and Pangchenpa.

FIRSTS

First film concern

Royal Bioscope Company was started in 1898 by Hiralal Sen and his brother Motilal. Initially they bought films that were made in England and showcased them in India.

First film serial

Ram Vanvas (The Exile of Rama) was made by Patankar Friends and Company and released on 14 September 1918. It was shown in four parts, each running for a period of a few weeks.

First Film review

In 1899, *The Times of India* started a film review column.

First one-actor, one-set film

Sunil Dutt made *Yaadein* in 1964, the first experiment of its kind in the world with only one actor (himself) emoting on only one set. In 2005, Kannada film *Shanthi* became the second movie with a single actor.

The Pan-India Film

For most of Indian film history, language was seen to be an insurmountable barrier. At one count, a dozen Hindi superstars acted in different remakes of Uttam Kumar's Bengali superhits but when Uttam Kumar tried to enter Hindi films, he failed. On the North–South axis, hit films from both sides of the Vindhyas made it to the other side – but as remakes, with a new starcast. Most of Jeetendra's filmography was Hindi versions of Tamil and Telugu hits. In the reverse direction, many of Rajinikanth's hits were remakes, originally starring Amitabh Bachchan. The audiences didn't accept southern superstars in Hindi films – barring exceptions.

Uttam Kumar

Mani Ratnam's *Roja* (1992) and *Bombay* (1995) were dubbed in Hindi to massive success – making stars out of Arvind Swamy and Madhu, though the latter film was also boosted by the presence of the Hindi star Manisha Koirala. Several of Salman Khan's successes were remakes of Tamil and Telugu

Bombay poster

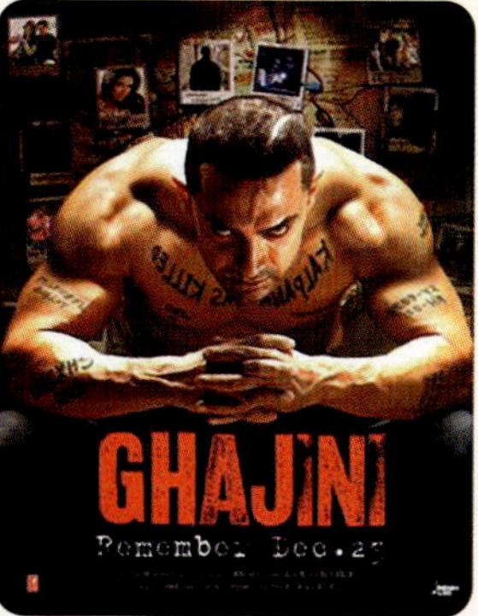

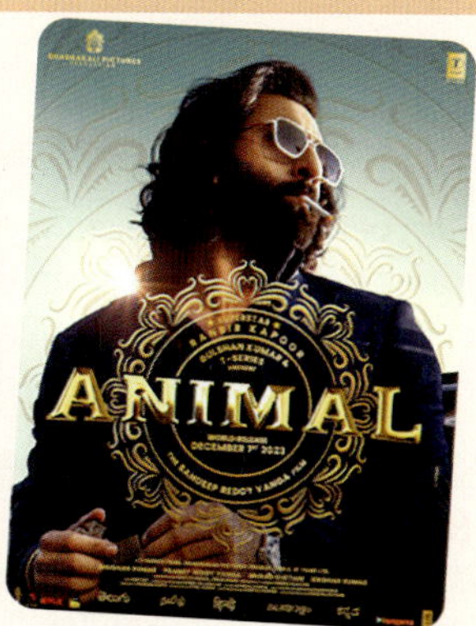

From left to right, top row: Posters of *Ghajini* (Tamil), *Ghajini* (Hindi), *Jawan, Animal; bottom*: *Gadar 2* poster

hits (e.g. *Wanted* from *Pokkiri*, *Ready* from *Ready*, *Jai Ho* from *Stalin*, etc.)

With the spread of movie channels on satellite television from the early twenty-first century, movie libraries were expanded by dubbing superhits from the south into Hindi and running them repeatedly – thus finding audiences in smaller centres who seemed to appreciate the masala, even if the lips spewing the whistle-inducing dialogues didn't match perfectly! Telugu star Chiranjeevi's 2002 superhit *Indra* was dubbed in Hindi as *Indra: The Tiger* and ran on TV for more than a decade. Several other Tamil, Telugu, and Kannada films were also milked by the television channels. In the 2010s, when mainstream Bollywood took to a more sophisticated style of cinema catering to metro audiences, small-town theatres often ran these dubbed films to great (but localized) success.

The clincher came with the advent of streaming platforms when audiences could watch any film in any language, and became more open to accepting stars from any industry. One could say the *Baahubali* franchise broke down the doors for Telugu stars to take over the national box office.

Till 2014, only one non-Hindi film ever managed to become the highest-grossing film of India: Shankar and Rajinikanth's *Enthiran* (2010). Only two remakes – *Tohfa* (1984) and *Ghajini* (2008) – reached the No. 1 position. But in the last decade (2015 to 2024), the tables have turned completely. Only three Hindi films – *Dangal*, *Tanhaji*, and *Jawan* – were the highest - grossing films of the respective years, that too on the back of mostly Hindi box office. The south Indian films, on the other hand, garnered a much larger collection from the Hindi belt and even in states other than their own.

The biggest blockbusters – with charismatic stars, great action, popular music, and large canvases – now have a market all over India, and are called the 'Pan-India film'. Also, the formula for this kind of national success has mostly been cracked by the south Indian film-makers, who have even cleverly used Hindi stars in major roles to boost the prospects of their films. The south-to-north crossover has well and truly happened, and we are waiting for the first big hit in the other direction.

The top 10 pan-India films in terms of domestic box office collection*

Film	Original language	Total domestic collection (in INR Crores)	Year of Release
Baahubali 2: The Conclusion	Telugu	1,430	2017
*Pushpa 2: The Rule***	Telugu	1,352	2024
KGF: Chapter 2	Kannada	1,008	2022
RRR	Telugu	944	2022
Kalki 2898 AD	Telugu	741–98	2024
Jawan	Hindi	762	2023
Animal	Hindi	662	2023
2.0	Tamil	519	2018
Baahubali: The Beginning	Telugu	515.77	2015
Dangal	Hindi	511.58	2016

*Based on domestic gross revenue estimates (not adjusted for inflation) from Wikipedia and other sources. Source information may not be exact.; **Currently running in theatres at the time of publication.

Film Censor

Film censorship is exercised through requesting the edits of certain frames or scenes or deeming it unsuitable for audiences. The censorship board categorizes the film as per its content into various categories and then they are released as such.

First adult film

Social Evil, a docudrama, was made by the Social Purity League of Bombay, Maharashtra, in 1929 to provide information about sex problems. It was also the first sex educational film. It was shown free of cost and was the first film given the label 'For adults only'.

First cinema hall

Elphinstone Picture Palace was started by J.F. Madan in Calcutta, West Bengal, in 1905. It was first renamed the Minerva Theatre and then Chaplin Cinema. This piece of history was demolished in 2013 by the Kolkata Municipal Corporation (which owned it).

First studio

Khan Bahadur Ardeshir Irani (1886–1969) started his first studio – Star Films – in 1920.

First censor boards

- The first film censor boards were set up in Bombay, Calcutta, and Madras (now Chennai) in 1920.
- Film censorship was centralized under a central board, the Central Board of Film Certification (CBFC) in Bombay, Maharashtra, in 1951.

First box office hit

Dadasaheb Phalke's *Lanka Dahan* (1917), which ran for 23 weeks, was India's first box office hit. It is on record that the money collected at the ticket counters had to be transported in bullock carts protected by armed guards!

INTERNATIONAL

First Academy Award for Best Documentary (short subject)

The Elephant Whisperers, directed by Kartiki Gonsalves, was awarded the Best Documentary (short subject) award at the 95th Academy Awards held on 13 March 2023 in Los Angeles, US.

First Academy Award

Bhanu Athaiya (1929–2020) became the first Indian to win an Academy Award (Oscar) in 1983. She designed the costumes for the acclaimed film *Gandhi* (1982), directed by Sir Richard Attenborough.

First Indian winner of the Legion d'Honneur

Satyajit Ray is the only Indian film personality to be awarded the Commandeur level of France's highest civilian award, the Legion d'Honneur, on 2 February 1989 – one of only two film-makers in the world to have received it. He is also the only Indian film-maker to receive the Magsaysay Award.

Satyajit Ray

A poster of *Seeta*

First to act in a Hollywood film

The first Indian actor to feature in a role that was credited in a Hollywood movie was Dastagir, who was also known as 'Sabu' in the film world. He hailed from the princely state of Mysore (now Mysuru), Karnataka. He acted in Robert Flaherty's film *Elephant Boy* (1937). His other films included *The Thief of Baghdad* (1940), and *Jungle Book* (1942).

Most awards won by a film*

Kaho Naa... Pyaar Hai, featuring Hrithik Roshan and Amisha Patel in lead roles and a production of Rakesh Roshan's Film Kraft Production (I) Pvt. Ltd, bagged an unprecedented 89 awards between 2000 and 2001 in various categories. The millennium's biggest blockbuster swept awards in both the national and international arena including nine Filmfare awards, 14 Zee Cine awards, four Zee Sangeet awards, 10 Screen awards, 11 Sansui awards, and nine International Indian Film Academy (IIFA) awards among others.

First foreign film award

The film *Seeta* (1934) by East India Films Co., Calcutta, which was directed by Debaki Bose, was the first film from India to win the gold medal at the Third International Exhibition of

* This record has been revised after updates in the rules regarding this category.

Cinematographic Art in Venice, Italy, in 1935.

First South Asian to win the Pardo alla Carriera

Shah Rukh Khan won the coveted Pardo alla Carriera award, the first south asian to win it, on 10 August 2024. He received it at the 77th Locarno Film Festival in Switzerland. Also known as the Career Leopard, it is a lifetime achievement award for contributions to cinema and collective imagination.

Shah Rukh Khan

PERFORMANCE

First woman stunt actor

Nadia, India's legendary woman stunt actor, has been described as 'Zorro, Tarzan, and John Wayne rolled into one'. Born Mary Evans, she swung from chandeliers, jumped from moving trains, and performed many other incredible stunts that earned her the title of 'Fearless Nadia'. Her best-known film is the 1935 hit, *Hunterwali*.

Fearless Nadia in the film *Hunterwali*

CENTRAL BOARD OF FILM CERTIFICATION (CBFC) STATISTICS 2023–24*

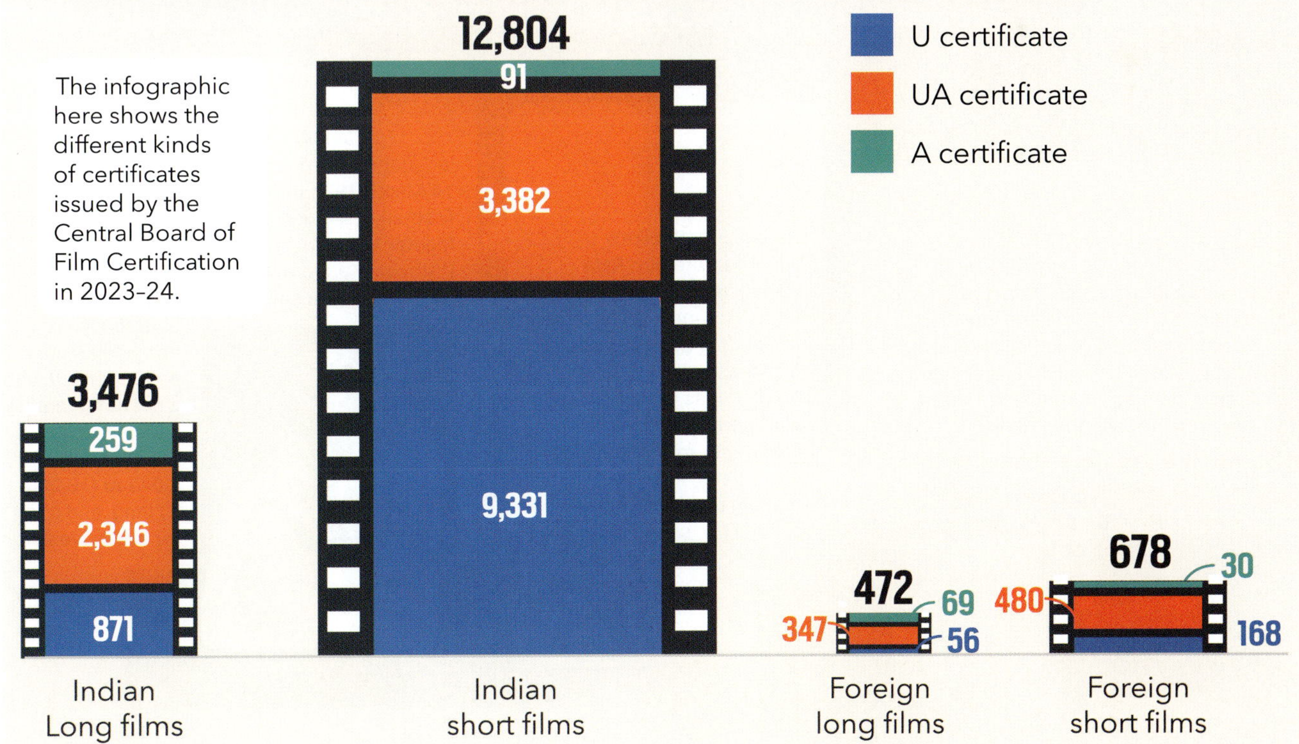

* S certificates were not issued in any category (S certificates are issued for restricted to specialized audiences, such as doctors or scientists)
Source: CBFC website

Timeline of Technical Advances in Films

The Indian Film Industry has come a long way from the humble early beginnings to the massive global reach they have now. This journey would not have been possible without the aid of technological advancements on the way. Here's a look at some milestones in that journey from the 20th century...

1896

7 July: First films exhibited

The first screening of six short films, by France's famed Lumière Brothers, Louis and Auguste, was held on 7 July 1896. They were *Entry of Cinematographe, Arrival of a Train at la Ciotat Station, Sea Bath, Workers Leaving the Factory, A Demolition,* and *Ladies and Soldiers on Wheels.*

1899

November: First film shot by an Indian

H.S. Bhatavadekar was the first to import a Riley camera from the UK. He shot two short films – *The Wrestlers*, which featured a wrestling match, and *Man and Monkey*, which was about a juggler training his monkeys – both released in November 1899.

1912

First 'trick' effects

Ankurachi Wadh (1912) by Dadasaheb Phalke showed a bud bursting into a flower with the single-frame exposing technique.

1913

3 May: First indigenous feature film

Dadasaheb Phalke's silent feature film *Raja Harishchandra* was released at the Coronation Theatre in Bombay (now Mumbai), Maharashtra, on 3 May 1913. It was a fully Indian venture and was shown along with four imported short films, together making up a 90-minute show. It ran for 23 days and was screened again later at multiple venues.

1920

7 February: First feature film to be shot on indigenous camera

Baburao Painter (and his brother Anandrao) were inspired by Phalke and they built a camera entirely by themselves and shot *Sairandhari* that was released in 1920 after a lot of hardship. (This film was also the first time a film was censored as the themes were perceived to be anti-British by the censors)

1931

14 March: First talkie

Alam Ara, made in Hindustani language by Ardeshir Irani and released on 14 March 1931 in Bombay, became India's first talkie feature. The first talkie stars were Master Vithal as hero, Zubeida as heroine, Prithviraj Kapoor in a supporting role, and W.M. Khan as a singing fakir. The first music directors were Pirojshah Mistry and B. Irani. It was a costume fantasy with seven songs. The film reel was 3,048 m (10,000 ft) long, and it ran for seven weeks.

A still from *Alam Ara*

First recorded film song

The song 'De de Khuda ke Naam Pyaare' from *Alam Ara* was the first recorded song and was sung by W.M. Khan.

First animated film

Directed by R.C. Boral, *On a Moonlit Night* (1934) was the first Indian animated film with a soundtrack.

First film with background music

The film *Chandidas* (Bengali) introduced the concept of background music in 1932.

First film in 70 mm

• The first Indian film in 70 mm (using the blowing-up method) was director Pachhi's *Around the World*, starring Raj Kapoor and Rajshree, in 1967. It was in Technicolor and had stereophonic sound.

• G.P. Sippy's multi-starrer blockbuster *Sholay* in 1975 was shot on the 70 mm format in India, along with stereophonic soundtrack, the four channels of which could be connected to amplifiers in cinema theatres. Those not equipped for it were provided flat (35 mm) single-track prints.

• Tarachand Barjatya's *Maine Pyar Kiya* (1989) was made in Cinemascope with a new system of four-track magnetic stereophonic sound. This could be fitted in theatres. Later, mobile equipment was provided for the stereophonic effect in small towns and touring cinemas.

1932

1934

1959

1967

1984

First experiments with colour

The very first colour venture was by Madan Theatres of Calcutta in 1932. Their talkie feature *Bilwamangal* was sent abroad for printing. Prabhat Company under V. Shantaram tried a colour-processed film *Sairandhri* (1935), which was taken to Germany for printing. Ardeshir Irani tried a local process called Cine Colour in his *Kisan Kanya* (1937) and *Mother India* (1938). Bhavnani's *Ajit* (1948) and Mehboob's *Aan* (1952) were shot in 16 mm Kodachrome and processed abroad. *Aan* had the first Technicolour prints. Sohrab Modi's *Jhansi ki Rani* (1953) was the first Technicolour film shot in India by foreign technicians and printed abroad. Ambalal Patel's *Pamposh* (1954) was the first film in Gevacolour to be completely shot and processed in India. The first Technicolour film to be completely shot by an Indian was V. Shantaram's *Jhanak Jhanak Payal Baaje* (1955) with prints made abroad.

First cinemascope films

• Guru Dutt made *Kaagaz Ke Phool* in 1959 in black-and-white Cinemascope.

• Mahesh Kaul made *Pyar Ki Pyaas* in Cinemascope and colour in 1961.

First 3D film

My Dear Kuttichathan (1984), produced by M.C. Punoos and directed by his son, Jijo, was the first Indian 3D. It was a Malayalam-language film.

First use of surround sound

Khuda Gawah (1992), when screened in big cities, used stereophonic four-track sound with special gadgets fitted into theatre walls and ceilings. This gave the impression of sound surrounding the audience, to give more impact to scenes of fights, horse riding, and the Afghan game of *buzkashi*, among others.

Role Models!

First Double Role

Dadasaheb Phalke's discovery, A. Salunke is the first artiste to have played both hero and heroine in the same film. He played Rama and Sita in Phalke's *Lanka Dahan* in 1917. In the talkie era Sahu Modak played the double role of a prince and a pauper in *Awara Shahzada* (Vagabond Prince) directed by Master Vithal in 1933. Neetu Singh, then known as Baby Sonia, is the only child star of India to have played a full-length double role of twin sisters in *Do Kaliyan* made in 1968.

Most roles in a single film

- Harish Raj enacted 16 roles in the Kannada film *Shri Sathyanarayana*, which released on 11 March 2016. He essayed the role of the lead character named Sathyanarayana as well as 15 other cameo roles with screen time ranging from one to five minutes for each.
- Priyanka Chopra played 12 roles (one for each sign of the zodiac) in Ashutosh Gowariker's *What's Your Raashee?* (2009).
- Kamal Haasan played 10 different roles in K.S. Ravikumar's *Dasavathaaram* (2008), including one as former US president George W. Bush.

Most films as a lead

Prem Nazir, born as Abdul Kadar in Chirayinkeezhu, Kerala, played the lead role in as many as 600 films. He starred in Malayalam, Tamil, Kannada, and Telugu films, and co-starred in films with at least 85 female actors.

WR Roles in most films

- *Women*: Manorama, a popular Tamil heroine of the 1950s and '60s, who later became a character actor, acted in over 1,000 films. Her first film was *Malayitta Mangai* (1958). Her real name was Gopishantha. She received the Padma Shri in 2002.
- *Men*: Brahmanandam Kanneganti, a well-known comedian of Telugu cinema, has received credits for acting in 1,178 films. He achieved this feat over an acting career of more than 30 years and he is still going strong. He received the Padma Shri in 2009.

WR Most pairings

Actors Prem Nazir and Sheila paired together in 107 films and hold a world record for the highest number of movies done together. They did 92 films more than the Hollywood husband–wife pair of Charles Bronson and Jill Ireland, who starred together in 15 films.

Oldest debut actor in a film

Ninety-three-year-old Chinnakrishnan Kaliyaperumal from Ariyalur, Tamil Nadu, acted as the lead in the Tamil short (20-minute) film, *93* Not Out* (2016), directed by engineer-turned-film-maker Arudra Saravanakumar. It is the story of an old man who, after a pacemaker implant, has the desire to ride a cycle and to buy a book, and how he finally achieves it at the age of ninety-three. The film has won several awards, for editing, direction and more, besides a jury mention at the Dadasaheb Phalke Film Festival 2017, and has been showcased at national and international film festivals.

LENGTH

Most episodic films in a single feature film

BSB Films, a film-making company from Jaipur, Rajasthan, made a Hindi-language film, titled *Prabhu Mahaveer Ki Divyavani*, under their banner. The film features 23 episodic films as part of it, the highest in a single feature film. The film has a total duration of 157 mins and 27 secs and was released on 30 September 2021.

Longest use of reused archival footage

Camellia Productions Pvt Ltd, a film production company in Kolkata used recycled footage of Uttam Kumar from his previous films for 24 minutes 48 seconds in their film, *Oti Uttam* (2024). It was directed by Srijit Mukherji.

Films with longest footage

- Vithalbhai Jhaveri's documentary on Mahatma Gandhi, *Mahatma: Life of Gandhi, 1869–1948* (1968), was 5 hrs 30 mins long, and was broken up into many segments for general screening.
- R.K. Films' productions *Mera Naam Joker* (1970) that had a run time of 248 minutes, along with *Sangam* (1964) with a run time of 238 minutes, were the first to be run with two intervals.

Debut

A debut is the event/occassion when a performer presents something to the general public for the first time. It originates from the mid 18th century, French word *début*, which came from *débuter* that means 'lead off'.

MUSIC

Most songs recorded in a day

In 1993, playback singer Kumar Sanu recorded 28 songs in a single day at the Musicians Studio in the Juhu area in Mumbai, Maharashtra. The session was made for Sterling Records and Cassettes and the chief recordist was Vishram More, who was on the machines for 24 hours.

WR Most number of songs in a Hindi film

Indra Sabha, made in 1932, featured 71 songs. Based on an Urdu play and opera written by Agha Hasan Amanat and first staged in 1853, the 211-minute-long film was made by Jamshedji Framji Madan's company, Madan Theatre.

WR Most prolific lyricist

Shitala Pande, better known as Sameer 'Anjaan', holds the world record for writing lyrics for the most number of songs. Starting in 1983 with the Hindi film *Bekhabar*, he had written lyrics for 3,524 songs for Hindi and Bhojpuri films

First Things First!

First Films in Different Languages/Dialects

LANGUAGE/DIALECTS	FILM	YEAR OF RELEASE
Assamese	*Joymoti*	1935
Bengali	*Dena Paona*	1931
Bruj	*Brij Bhumi*	1982
Garhwali	*Jagwal*	1983
Haryanvi	*Bahurani*	1983
Hindi	*Raja Harishchandra*	1913
Kashmiri	*Naizraat*	1964
Konkani	*Suzanne*	1982
Maithili	*Mamta Gawae Geet*	1982
Odia	*Sita Bibaha*	1934
Rajasthani	*Jeevi Rabaran*	1981

First women on screen

Durgabai Gokhale and her daughter Kamalabai Gokhale were the first women to feature as actors as part of Dadasaheb Phalke's film, *Mohini Bhasmasur* (1913). Prior to this, male actors played female roles as well, such as A. Salunke in *Raja Harishchandra*.

Kamalabai Gokhale

First Woman Film-Maker

The first woman to produce, direct and script a film in the silent era was Fatma Begum. She formed the Fatma Film Corporation and made *Bulbule Paristan* in 1926.

Fatma Begum

National Film Awards 2024*	
Award	**Recipient**
Swarna Kamal	
Best Feature Film	*Aattam* (Malayalam) directed by Anand Ekarshi
Best Director	Sooraj R. Barjatya for *Uunchai* (Hindi)
Best Popular Film Providing Wholesome Entertainment	*Kantara* (Kannada) directed by Rishab Shetty
Best Film in Animation, Visual Effects, Gaming, Comics (AVGC (Best Animation Film)	*Brahmastra: Part One – Shiva* (Hindi) directed by Ayan Mukerji
Best Non-Feature Film	*Ayena* (Hindi, Urdu) directed by Siddhant Sarin
Best Direction (Non-Feature Film)	Miriam Chandy Menacherry for *From The Shadows* (English, Bengali, Hindi)
Best Book on Cinema	*Kishore Kumar: The Ultimate Biography* by Anirudha Bhattacharjee and Parthiv Dhar
Rajat Kamal	
Best Actor in a Leading Role	Rishab Shetty for *Kantara*
Best Actress in a Leading Role	Nithya Menon for *Thiruchtrambalam* (Tamil) and Manasi Parekh for *Kutch Express* (Gujarati)
Best Documentary	*Murmurs of the Jungle* (Marathi) directed by Sohil Vaidya
Best Non-Feature Film Promoting Social and Environmental Values	*On the Brink – Season 2 – Gharial* (English) directed by Akanksha Sood Singh
Best Cinematography	Ravi Varman for *Ponniyin Selvan: I* (Tamil)

*Selected categories

Nithya Menon

Sooraj Barjatya

Ayan Mukerji

Rishab Shetty

Akanksha Sood Singh

Manasi Parekh

by 15 December 2015. He has also written lyrics for music albums. He has done the highest number of films (146) with the music director duo Anand–Milind, writing around 899 songs for them.

MAKERS

Most film-making aspects handled

Narasimha Raju (b. 4 March 1955) from Bengaluru, Karnataka, handled 18 segments of film-making for the Kannada film *The Fire* (2017). He was credited for direction, story, screenplay, dialogues, fight, stunt, direction of cinematography, editing, special effects, grading, Digital intermediate (DI), sound, dubbing, voice dubbing, Background music (BGM) placing, re-recording, poster design, and acting in the film. The 113-minute film participated in the 10th Bengaluru International Film Festival in March 2018.

Tallest film cut-out

The world's tallest cut-out – 65.5 m (215 ft) high – advertised a film in Thiruttani town, Tiruvallur District, Tamil Nadu. It featured actor Suriya (in a folded *veshti*, holding a flaming torch) to promote his film *Nandha Goalan Kumaran (NGK)* in 2019.

Largest film poster

Global United Media Co. Ltd, in collaboration with Impresario Event Management (I) Ltd, unveiled a 75.28 m (247 ft) long and 63.39 m (208 ft) wide poster of *Baahubali*, to mark the launch of the film's Malayalam audio, at the Sacred Heart College football field in Thevara, Kochi, Kerala, on 27 June 2015. The poster, designed by the director of the movie, S.S. Rajamouli, and made by Sign Maker Digital Solution at Vyttila, Kochi, took 30 hrs to print.

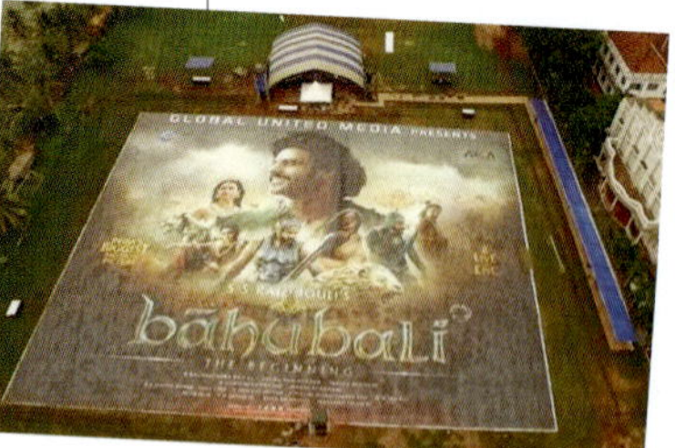

Baahubali

Most films produced

Well-known director and producer of Telugu films, Dr D. Ramanaidu holds the record of having produced 110 films (including 11 dubbed films) in six languages over a span of 36 years. He started his career with *Anuragam* in 1963.

Largest film city/studio

Ramoji Film City in Hyderabad, Telangana, spread over a little more than 1,666 acres (674 hectares), is the largest film city/studio in the world. It has sound stages and permanent sets ranging from railway stations and temples to gardens and residential streets, among others. It is also a tourist attraction because of its unique cinema-like experience.

Most tickets booked in advance

BookMyShow, a ticket-booking app, saw a record sale of advance tickets when it sold over a million tickets online in a day. The tickets for Marvel's *Avengers: Endgame* were booked in a manic frenzy as soon as they were available on 22 April 2019. The sale averaged about 18 tickets per second!

Film Fraternity MPs: A Selection of Those Who Went from the Glitz and Glamour of Cinema to the Hustle and Bustle of Politics

Year	Member of Parliament	Party, constituency	Film credentials
2024	Kangana Ranaut	BJP, Mandi (Himachal Pradesh)	Three-time National Award winner (*Queen, Tanu Weds Manu Returns, Panga, Manikarnika: The Queen of Jhansi*) with a significant body of critical and commercial successes.
2024	Arun Govil	BJP, Meerut (Uttar Pradesh)	Known for playing Lord Ram in the Doordarshan show *Ramayana*.
2024	Suresh Gopi	BJP, Thrissur (Kerala)	National Award-winner for Best Actor (*Kaliyattam*), he has acted in over 250 films across south Indian languages but mostly in Malayalam.
2019	Sunny Deol	BJP, Gurdaspur (Punjab)	The rabble-rousing, adrenaline-pumping star of *Gadar*, *Border*, *Damini,* and *Ghayal* made a foray into politics like his father and stepmother (Dharmendra and Hema Malini respectively)
2014	Hema Malini	BJP, Mathura (Uttar Pradesh)	One of the biggest stars of the 1970s, who even became an action heroine with *Seeta Aur Geeta*, she followed her husband into the Parliament.
2014	Dev	Trinamool Congress, Ghatal (West Bengal)	Star of the three highest-grossing Bengali films of all times (*Amazon Obhijan, Chander Pahad, Projapoti*), Dev has a passionate fan base and a long list of superhits.
2009	Shatrughan Sinha	BJP, Patna Sahib (Bihar)	Major star of the 1970s, he started his career as a villain but soon graduated to leading roles and made his name for his dramatic dialogue delivery.
2004	Dharmendra	BJP, Bikaner (Rajasthan)	Often called 'He-Man' for the action roles in the 1980s, he built an impressive range of roles since the 1960s, which included comedies, tragedies, romances, and thrillers.
2004	Govinda	Indian National Congress, Mumbai North (Maharashtra)	Dubbed as '*Virar ka chhokra*' for literally being an outsider, Govinda was the biggest star of the 1990s, who gained notoriety for signing an unprecedented number of films on achieving success but managed to deliver hits in an astounding number of them.
1998	Vinod Khanna	BJP, Gurdaspur (Punjab)	A handsome and charismatic star of the 1970s, he started as a villain but soon moved to becoming the hero. His film career is punctuated by a spiritual break, when he joined Osho Rajneesh's ashram.
1992	Rajesh Khanna	Indian National Congress, New Delhi (Delhi)	The biggest heart-throb of Hindi cinema and also its first superstar, he was called The Phenomenon and had once delivered 15 consecutive hits between 1969 and 1972.
1984	Vyjayanthimala	Indian National Congress, Chennai South (Tamil Nadu)	Apart from being an accomplished classical dancer, she is also a leading star of the 1950s and '60s. She has acted in superhits with the trio of superstars – Raj Kapoor, Dilip Kumar, and Dev Anand – holding her own and more.
1984	Amitabh Bachchan	Indian National Congress, Allahabad (Uttar Pradesh)	Bachchan's story of initial struggle and stupendous success from his 13th film (*Zanjeer*) is the stuff of cinema folklore.
1984	Sunil Dutt	Indian National Congress, Mumbai North West (Maharashtra)	Popular star, crowd favourite, untiring fighter and unflinching patriot, Dutt sa'ab (as he was called) acted in and produced both commercially successful and critically acclaimed films – the last of which was the classic *Munna Bhai MBBS* (and also the only time he shared screen with his son). He won the constituency five times (1984, 1989, 1991, 1999, and 2004).

From left to right: Kangana Ranaut, Hema Malini, Shatrughan Sinha, Vyjanthimala, Dharmendra, and Govinda

Evolution of the Most Expensive Film

Kalki 2898 AD – the biggest grosser among Indian films in 2024 – is also the new record-holder of the most expensive film ever made in India. The commercial film-maker's instinct has always been to push the boundaries of star-cast, location, technology, and market. Every film-maker has tried to go where no one has gone before and some of the biggest names from showbiz mounted these super-expensive films in a bid to go double or quits. It used to be even more adventurous in older times, when betting big often meant betting your last shirt on the film. In recent times, with pan-India and global releases in multiple languages, the earning potential of films have gone up manifold, financing has become easier and so has increased the appetite to push the boundaries of spectacular (read: expensive!) film-making. Which is why you see the mantle of the most expensive film changing hands much more frequently.

Year	Film	Budget (In INR Cr.)	Reasons
2024	*Kalki 2898 AD*	600	Creation of a post-apocalyptic world and the salaries of two of the biggest yesteryear stars (Amitabh Bachchan and Kamal Haasan) and two of the biggest current stars (Prabhas and Deepika Padukone) made it a film that made jaws drop with both its visuals and its collections.
2022	*RRR*	550	Telugu cinema's two biggest stars – Jr NTR and Ram Charan – come together in a period drama with authentic costumes, grand locales, and eye-popping set pieces requiring cutting-edge visual effects (VFX).
2017 & 2015	*Baahubali: The Conclusion and The Beginning*	250 + 180	S.S. Rajamouli, already known for his imaginative and grand vision, got a canvas like no other when he punched together familiar characters and storylines into a grand spectacle that wowed all of India and created the genre of 'pan-India films'.
2013	*Dhoom 3*	175	The finanical muscle of Yash Raj Films was fully utilized when they took their successful fanchise to yet another spectacular locale and threw in all the bells and whistles required to make a crime thriller pop! The star power of Aamir Khan probably added both to the bill and the collections, making the film one of the biggest hits when it released.
2011	*Ra.One*	150	Shah Rukh Khan pretty much started his extremely successful VFX venture – Red Chillies – when he produced a superhero film that would rub shoulders with the Marvels and DCs of the world. The stunning effects (including a scene in which Mumbai's C.S.T. station collapses) were propped by a marketing campaign like no other and the film made a ton of money as well, but probably not enough for superhero G.One to become a franchise.
2010	*Enthiran*	132	Director Shankar used a level of special effects, hitherto unseen in Indian cinema and used Rajinikanth's star power to build a world of gadgets and gizmos.
2009	*Blue*	80	Touted as India's first 'underwater action film', the multi-starrer had a lot of stunning action in grand locales but the story was too derivative and the Indian audience too exposed to similar levels of effects to make an impact. The film wasn't successful in recovering its substantial investment.
2008	*Dasavatharam*	60	Kamal Haasan played 10 roles – including the US President George W. Bush, a Punjabi pop singer, and a giant – based on Lord Vishnu's ten incarnations. The locations, the action, the special effects, and even the make-up required hefty investments that were matched by Haasan's involvement and efforts.

Year	Film	Budget (Rs Cr.)	Reasons
2002	*Devdas*	50	A diamond merchant turned film financier turned producer, Bharat Shah bankrolled *Devdas*, a maximalist version directed by Sanjay Leela Bhansali who would make this his signature style in the years to come. The sets (by Nitin Desai) took nearly a year to make and cost about ₹20 crore, almost the budget of many blockbusters of the time. Everything else was as spectacular and created a stir in the box office, with the budget generating as much curiosity as the rest of the film.
2001	*Lagaan*	25	A cricket film set in nineteenth-century British India needed a massive cast staying for months in a remote village in Gujarat, where the entire film's sets were erected for perfect authenticity. The film went on to become a massive success, an Oscar nominee and an all-time classic – justifying actor-producer Aamir Khan's confidence in a topic everyone predicted to be a failure.
1996	*Indian*	15	Kamal Haasan played the role of a former soldier of the Azad Hindu Fauj who turns into a vigilante, aided with Hollywood-level special effects (where a young Haasan shook hands with Subhas Bose) and one of the first uses of prosthetic make-up in India. Director Shankar helmed his risky, expensive venture that went on to become one of the biggest hits of the year as well. It was released as *Hindustani* in Hindi.
1995	*Trimurti*	11	In the year Shah Rukh Khan delivered *Dilwale Dulhaniya Le Jayenge*, the longest-running Indian film, he acted in producer Subhash Ghai and director Mukul S. Anand's star-studded outing that had everything except a good script. It flopped miserably, making it one of Ghai's rare disasters and a setback for Anand, who had just come off a string of well-regarded films.
1991	*Ajooba*	8	An Indo-Russian co-production was an Arabian Nights–style fantasy with India's biggest stars and an international crew, but it got caught in the middle of the Soviet Union's collapse and the spiralling costs got loaded on to the Indian producer (Shashi Kapoor). The massive costs didn't translate well on screen and it became one of India's biggest flops.
1983	*Razia Sultan*	7	Hema Malini as the first queen regent of Delhi Sultanate was directed by Kamal Amrohi, already known for his spectacular picturization of period topics. The palaces, the battlefields, the costumes – all conceptualized over a long period of gestation – didn't make much of an impact on the audience and it crashed at the box office.
1980	*Shaan*	6	Fresh from Indian cinema's biggest hit, the Sippys mounted an even bigger film in the mould of James Bond capers – set in international locales, with an enviable star cast and excellent production values. The budget was double of their previous venture but made only about half the revenue. It was not a flop, but it felt like one.
1975	*Sholay*	3	Producer G.P. Sippy – buoyed by two superhits – wanted to make a 'big film' and his young son Ramesh wanted to bring the world's best cinematic action to India. An entire village set was constructed far away from Bombay, to and from where the entire cast and crew were ferried. The film's budget ballooned three times from the original estimate, but the father–son duo never compromised their vision to create the 'greatest film ever made'. It was also the biggest hit ever made.
1960	*Mughal-e-Azam*	1.5	Artisans, costumers, jewellers, technicians, and three of India's biggest stars came together to bring alive a perfectionist director's vision. K. Asif's demands were so big that an industrialist group had to produce it, since the budget was bigger than the film industry's appetite for risk. They were rewarded with the biggest box office collection of Indian cinematic history.

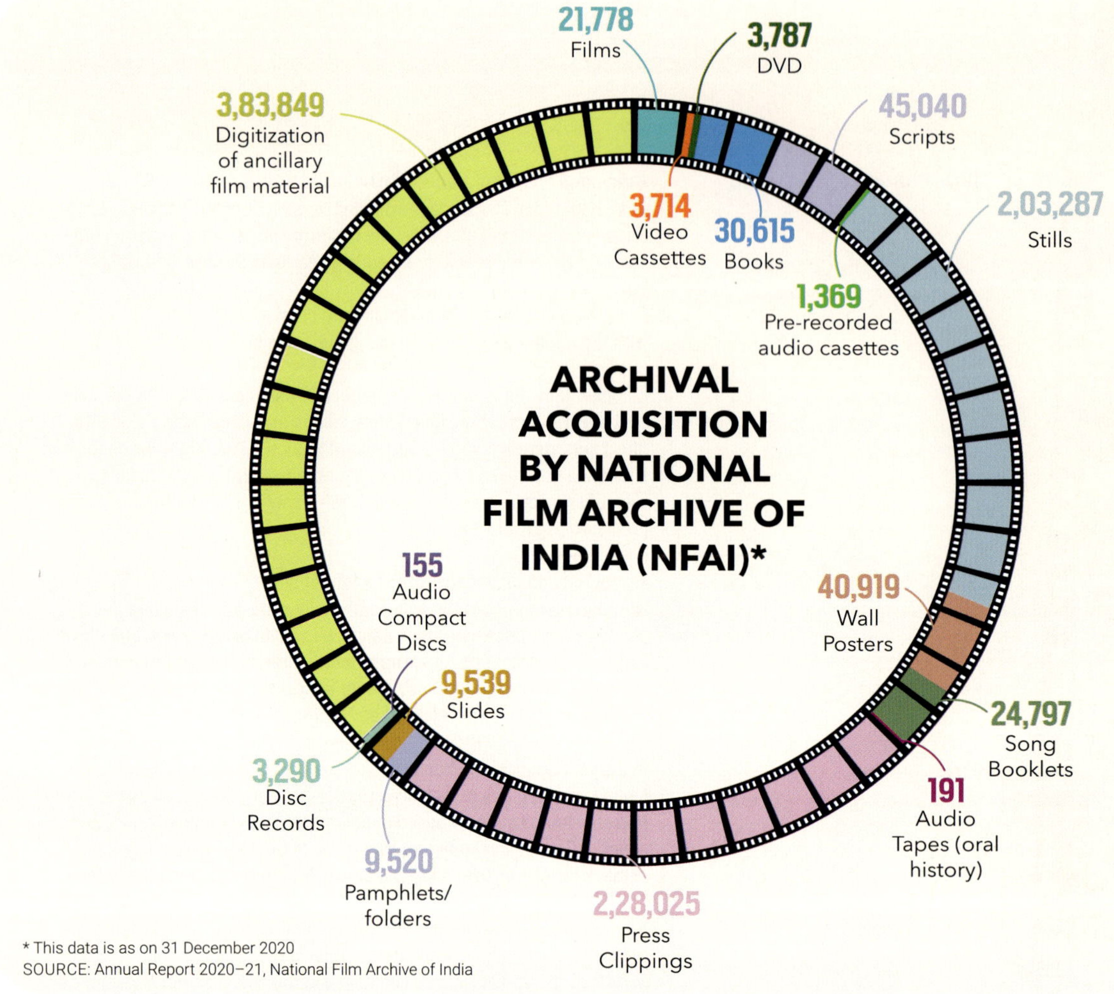

* This data is as on 31 December 2020
SOURCE: Annual Report 2020–21, National Film Archive of India

TOP 10 STATES WITH MOST AVGC EDUCATIONAL INSTITUTIONS IN INDIA – FEDERATION OF INDIAN CHAMBERS OF COMMERCE AND INDUSTRY (FICCI) ESTIMATES 2021

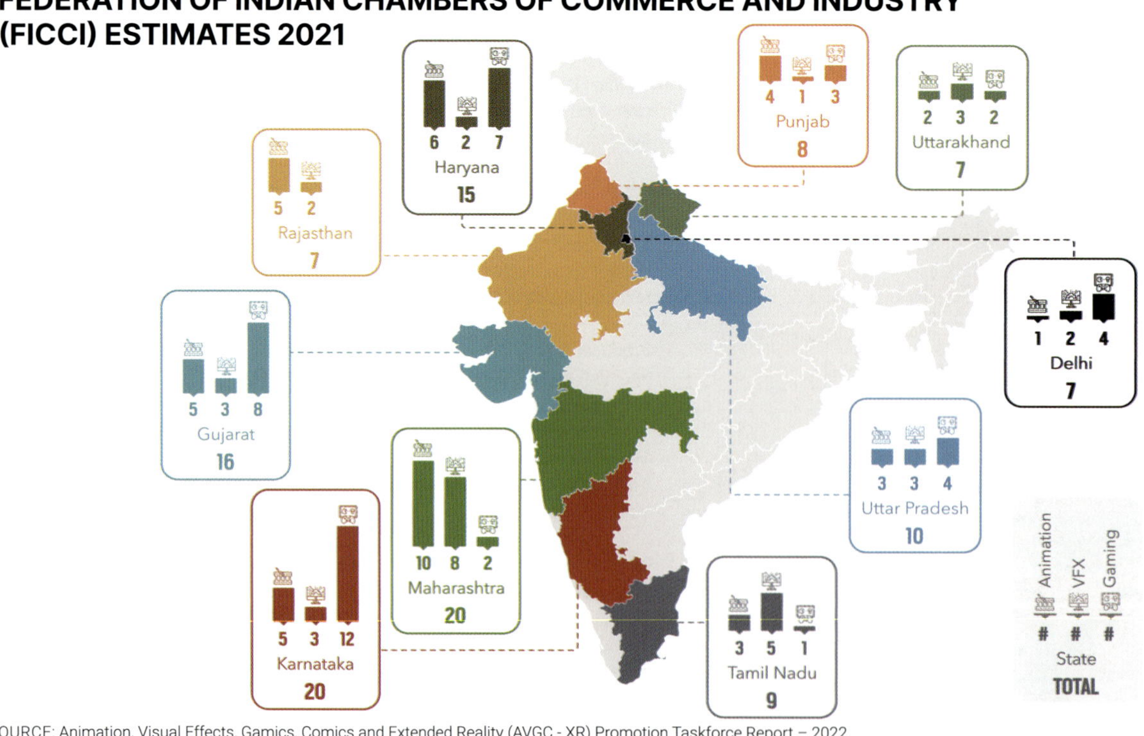

SOURCE: Animation, Visual Effects, Gamics, Comics and Extended Reality (AVGC - XR) Promotion Taskforce Report – 2022

DETAILS OF EMPLOYMENT IN MEDIA AND ENTERTAINMENT (M&E) SECTOR - FICCI ESTIMATES

Year	Television	Film	Events and Live Performances	Art and Culture	Sound and Music	Advertisement and Out-of-home (OOH) Advertisement	Digital and Over-the-top (OTT)	Total
FY 2025 Estimates (E)	7,64,646	3,30,298	2,39,403	1,40,116	73,935	53,782	1,25,689	17,27,869
FY 2024E	6,94,565	3,03,026	2,10,003	1,29,737	66,013	48,019	1,00,551	15,51,914
FY 2023E	6,30,906	2,78,005	1,84,213	1,20,127	58,940	42,722	80,441	13,95,354
FY 2022E	5,78,813	2,57,412	1,56,112	1,11,229	51,253	37,247	61,878	12,53,944
FY 2021E	5,41,858	2,42,842	1,39,386	1,02,989	45,761	32,860	49,502	11,55,198
FY 2020E	5,27,510	2,38,080	1,32,749	97,160	41,983	30,147	38,673	11,06,302
2019	5,80,000	2,56,000	1,76,998	1,21,450	48,817	36,800	29,298	12,49,363

SOURCE: AVGC-XR Promotion Taskforce Report – 2022

Highest number of screens

RRR – a period drama about two legendary revolutionaries and their journeys and directed by S.S. Rajamouli – was released worldwide on over 10,200 screens.

Most feature films directed

Dr Dasari Narayana Rao (1947–2017) has directed 148 films. Among women, Vijaya Nirmala has directed 35 films in Telugu and Tamil.

Left: Dr Dasari Narayana Rao
Right: Vijaya Nirmala

Most horror films produced

The seven Ramsay brothers – Kumar, Keshu, Tulsi, Kiran, Shyam, Gangu, and Arjun - made more than 30 horror films on low budgets, of which the well-known ones are *Purana Mandir* (1984), *Veerana* (1988), and *Purani Haveli* (1989).

Clockwise from top: Posters of *Purana Mandir*, *Veerana*, and *Purani Haveli*

Longest-running film

Yash Raj Films' *Dilwale Dulhania Le Jayenge* (*DDLJ*) is still running at Mumbai's Maratha Mandir theatre – twenty-eight years after the film premiered there. The single show at 11:30 a.m. is the result of an arrangement between Yash Raj and the theatre, which agreed to run the film there for (what seems like) eternity. But even before the arrangement, *DDLJ* ran to semi-packed houses for over two decades, making it the longest-running film in the world.

A cut out from *DDLJ* at Mt Titlis, Switzerland

PHOTOGRAPHY

First commercial photographer

Lala Deen Dayal of Hyderabad, the 'photographer of kings', is India's best-known photographer from the British times. His career began in the mid-1870s, and he went on to set up studios in three cities in three different states – Indore, Madhya Pradesh; Bombay, Maharashtra; and Hyderabad (now in Telangana). He was appointed the photographer to the viceroy of India in 1885. His lens captured India's rich culture, architecture, and landscapes.

Earliest recorded commercial album

A gilded and bound album of a hundred photographs of Indian buildings, scenery, races, costumes, and bazaar incidents was sold for ₹12 in Bombay in 1884. It used to be a popular souvenir among the British.

Earliest book on photography

Pagoda Hallibee written by R.B. Gakley in 1859 was the first book on photography published in India.

First use of the daguerreotype

Within a year of its first use in England, the daguerreotype (early photography process using an iodine-sensitized silvered plate and mercury vapour) was used in Calcutta, in January 1840. It was brought to document India's architecture and landscape.

First photo exhibition

The first All-India Photographic Exhibition was organized by the Photographic Society of India in Bombay, in 1856. The exhibition was inaugurated by the then governor general of India, Lord Canning.

First woman photojournalist

Homai Vyarawalla (1913–2012), born into a priestly family in Navsari, Gujarat, in December 1913, was the first Indian woman photojournalist to document Indian life. Her very first photographs were published in *Bombay Chronicle* in 1936. She and her husband even covered wartime activities for *The Illustrated Weekly of India* and the *Far Eastern Bureau* of the British Information Service. *Life* and *Time* magazines also featured her photographs of the Indian independence movement.

Largest camera museum

The Museo Camera Centre for the Photographic Arts, Gurugram, Haryana, houses more than 2,500 cameras, which is the world's largest collection of vintage and other cameras on display. Inaugurated on 27 September 2019, it is spread over 1,672.2 sq m (18,000 sq ft) of built-up space and can accommodate up to 200 visitors at a time. It is a collaboration between acclaimed photographer Aditya Arya and the Municipal Corporation of Gurugram.

Bourne and Shepherd

Earliest commercial studio
Bourne and Shepherd was well known for its studio portraits of the ruling classes, both Indian and British. Its photographers attended royal events, state visits and the imperial durbars of 1877, 1903, and 1911. After Independence, Bourne and Shepherd was bought over by Indian proprietors, who operated under the same name in Calcutta. The studio was closed down on 20 April 2016 after 176 years of operations.

First Kodak Express outlet
Established in 1978, Skylab was the first colour lab in suburban Bombay. Initially the lab catered to advertising agencies, but gradually the focus shifted to providing a photo colour lab and studio for amateurs and ordinary people.

First photo film-manufacturing company
Hindustan Photo Films Manufacturing Co. (HPF), a public sector unit, was set up in 1960 at Ooty (now Udhagamandalam), Tamil Nadu, to make photosensitive materials for the Indian film industry, still photography, and X-ray films for medical and industrial use. It introduced the Indu brand of raw film.

First personal studio
Maharaja Sawai Man Singh of Jaipur, Rajasthan, was a 19th-century amateur photographer. Thousands of photographic plates of his work were discovered in the 1980s in the storerooms of the City Palace in Jaipur. He recorded the life of the people in his state.

Oldest extant portrait studio
Sir Victor Sassoon, who was passionate about photography and constructed many public buildings in Bombay, set up Hamilton Studios in the E.D. Sassoon Building, which he owned, in 1928. Photography sessions at these studios were held by appointment, and the rich and famous personalities of Bombay were seen coming for quick and glamorous shoots. Currently, the studios are run by Ajita Madhavji and can be found in Ballard Estate.

First photographic society
The Bombay Photographic Society was founded in October 1854 with British captain Harry J. Barr as its first president. It had more than 200 people as members, many of them Indian. Divisions in Madras and Bengal followed in 1856.

First course in photography
The first photography course began in Elphinstone College, Bombay, in 1855.

Elphinstone College, Bombay

The J.J. School of Art, Bombay, and the Madras School of Art, Madras, Tamil Nadu, began similar courses around the same time.

Largest unit for photo production/distribution

The Photo Division, Press Information Bureau, under the Ministry of Information and Broadcasting, Government of India, provides photographs to media units, and Central and state government departments. In the year 2023– 24, it acquired 6,95,776 digital images in-house and supplied 2,541 digital prints.

Largest collection of cameras

Dilish Parekh, a photojournalist from Mumbai, has a collection of 4,425 cameras, some dating back to 1906. It includes brands such as Leica, Nikon, Kodak, Canon, Hasselblad, and Royal Mail Postage, besides types such as watch, binocular, and button cameras. He began the collection in 1977 with 600 cameras given to him by his grandfather.

Most people in a selfie

On 26 March 2016, during Ragam, the annual cultural festival at the National Institute of Technology Calicut (NITC) in Kozhikode, Kerala, actor Sreenath Bhasi clicked a selfie with a camera mounted on a selfie stick at the open-air theatre on the campus, with 2,151 students.

Most people in a selfie

Marathon photography – models

Photographer Vivek Ashok Somani (b. 7 August 1995) from Surat, Gujarat, conducted a marathon photo shoot on 12 May 2019. He clicked 11,076 photographs in 15 hrs 55 mins. Using a Nikon D5300 camera, and an 18–55 mm lens, he photographed 70 models at Future Dance Studio, Surat.

Marathon photography – city/structures

Hariohm N. Gurjar from Vadodara, Gujarat, set out to document his city's various dimensions at 7:00 a.m. on 14 March 2014. He travelled 95 km in the city, shooting for 13 hrs. He captured 3,555 unduplicated images of people, architecture, markets, monuments, and more.

AWARDS AND HONOURS

First to receive the Hasselblad Award

Dayanita Singh from New Delhi became the first Indian and the first South Asian laureate to receive the Hasselblad Award. She was handed the award on 14 October 2022 in a ceremony held in Gothenburg, Sweden. She won two million Swedish krona, becoming the first to receive the prize since it was upgraded. Awarded annually since 1982, the Hasselblad Award is considered to be one of the most prestigious awards in photography worldwide. Dayanita received commendation for her 'mobile museums' (she uses objects that

Dayanita Singh

allow for the artwork to be constantly arranged and rearranged) in the official citation for the award.

First Indian fellow of the British Photographic Society

Sir Prodyot Coomar Tagore (1873–1942), a prominent landowner of the time in Calcutta, was an art collector besides being a keen photographer. He was the first Indian to be elected a Fellow of the British Photographic Society in 1896. He had a studio in his Tagore Castle home and exhibited his works. He was the founder and first president of the Academy of Fine Arts, Calcutta.

First Asian to win the International Photography Awards

Sharad Haksar from Chennai, Tamil Nadu, won one gold, one silver, two bronzes, and 21 nominations in the International Photography Awards 2004. India finished fourth behind the US, the UK, and Canada.

First winner of the Wildlife Photographer of the Year title

The Wildlife Photographer of the Year, organized by the Natural History Museum, London, UK, is one of the most famed contests in the world. Rajesh Bedi became the first Indian to win the

Rajesh Bedi

grand title in 1986 for his photograph of the Asiatic black bear.

First winners of the Pulitzer Prize for feature photography

- Anushree Fadnavis and Adnan Abidi were part of the Reuters team that won in the 'Breaking News Photography' category of the Pulitzer Prize for photography in 2020, for their work on the Hong Kong protests.
- Dar Yasin, Mukhtar Khan, and Channi Anand from Associated Press won in the 'Feature Photography' category of the Pulitzer Prize for photography in 2020 for their coverage of Jammu and Kashmir.

WR First winner of the Académie des Beaux-Arts Photography Award – William Klein

Raghu Rai won the first-ever Académie des Beaux-Arts Photography Award – William Klein (Fine Arts Academy award for Photography). He was named the laureate and was awarded the prize at the Palais de l'Institut de France on 30 October 2019. The award carries a prize money of € 1,20,000 (approximately ₹10.79 crore). It was instated in honour of William Klein, a celebrated US-born French photographer and film-maker.

WR First permanent photo exhibition in space

Dr Hersh Chadha (b. 27 November 1957) is the first person to organize a permanent photo exhibition in space on the International Space Station (ISS). Five images of different flowers were sent to the ISS on 16 October 2016 with the ISS 49/50 team. The purpose of this was to help the astronauts staying in space for months to remain connected with nature. On 1 March 2017, Dr Chadha was honoured by the Yuri Gagarin Cosmonaut Training Centre, Russia, for this.

PAINTING AND CRAFT FIRSTS

Earliest use of tempera method

The Ajanta Caves are rock-cut Buddhist cave monuments in Aurangabad, Maharashtra, dating back from the 2nd century BCE to about 650 CE. The paintings in these caves used the tempera method. In this technique the rough mud plaster containing some organic matter like cow dung and animal hair was first pressed on the surface of the rocks and then a coat of fine lime plaster was laid all over it. This layer was allowed to dry thoroughly before applying colour on it. The scenes represented in these caves are mostly from Buddhist texts and events from the Buddha's life.

Earliest paintings discovered

Painted pottery, mostly in fragments, excavated at Mohenjo-Daro, Chanhu-Daro, Harappa, and other places in the Indus Valley, are dated to 3000–2250 BCE.

Painted pottery from Mohenjo-Daro

Paintings of the Ajanta Caves

First Mughal illuminated manuscript

Emperor Humayun engaged Mir Sayyid Ali and a group of painters to paint the *'Dastan-i-Amir'* (the story of Amir Hamza), which featured as many as 1,375 miniatures painted on cotton cloth in the Persian Safavid style. The work on the manuscript was under way in the 1560s.

First auction of contemporary Indian paintings abroad

Sotheby's hosted the first-ever auction of contemporary Indian paintings in New York, US, on 12 June 1995. The 38 artists whose works were displayed included Jogen Chowdhury, M.F. Husain, Arpita Singh, Ganesh Pyne, S.H. Raza, and Jamini Roy.

Oldest extant murals

Two 1,000-year-old Chola paintings, which were found at the Brihadeeswarar Temple in Thanjavur, Tamil Nadu, are believed to be the oldest existing mural paintings. They depict two women who are watching a procession from a balcony.

First modern art school

The Mechanical Institute was founded by Frederik Corbyn and Tarapada Chakrabarty in Calcutta, on 2 February 1839. First named Society for the Promotion of Industrial Art, it was finally called the School of Industrial Art on 16 August 1854. It held its first exhibition from 22 January to 3 February 1855.

First fine arts exhibition

The first fine arts exhibition was held in the Public Library, Calcutta, on 1 February 1831, by the Brush Club, with paintings drawn by foreign artists in India.

First art summit

The first India Art Summit was held at Pragati Maidan, New Delhi, during 22–24 August 2008. The 34 exhibition galleries exhibited over 550 artworks and sold more than half of them. The summit was brought to India by Hanmer MS&L Communications Pvt. Ltd.

First realist painter

Raja Ravi Varma (1848–1906) from the princely state of Travancore (now in Kerala) painted themes mainly from Indian mythology and legends in the realistic style of the West, making him the first realist painter in the country and the pioneer of a new movement in Indian art. In 1904, the then viceroy Lord Curzon bestowed the Kaisari-i-Hind Gold Medal on him.

First painting gallery

Maharaja Ram Singh, a 19th-century king of Jaipur, built a unique hall in the garden of the Ram Niwas Bagh Palace. It was fully displayed with paintings and called the Ram Vilas. The walls of this hall were covered with imitations of several Greek, Roman, Persian, and Chinese paintings.

Paintings from the Brihadeeswarar Temple

Maharaja Ram Singh

Earliest rock paintings

The largest and the oldest collection of rock paintings in India is at Bhimbetka, about 46 km from Bhopal, Madhya Pradesh. The paintings, found in more than 700 rock shelters dated to around 30,000 years ago, depict people's everyday lives such as hunting, dancing, and decoration of bodies.

First academy for visual arts

The Lalit Kala Akademi, which was established in Delhi in 1954, started its work by organizing national exhibitions of contemporary Indian art. It also gives awards and honours and conducts Triennale-India (a global art show) and a Rashtriya Kala Mela (national art fair), where artists from across the country come together to present their work.

First art bank

The Art Bank, set up in 2007 and started by curator Adishwar Puri, primarily for novice collectors apprehensive of making bad choices, now has corporations, government institutions, banks, and hospitals as clients. The artists who register benefit by receiving 50 per cent of the rental value of the work.

First officially recognized female graffiti artist

Kajal Singh from New Delhi, who goes by the moniker 'Dizy', is the first recognized female graffiti artist from India. Her art form includes the use of bright colours and different font styles that instantly pop out. Besides India, she has left her signature in countries like Germany, China, the United States, Russia, and Indonesia. She was part of the Indo-German Hip-Hop Urban Art Project (2012), Each One Teach One (2013), 25 Years of the Berlin Wall (2014), Hip-Hop Cultural Exchange (2015), and On The Run Exhibition (2016). She was honoured as the 'First Lady' of graffiti in India by the Ministry of Women and Child Development, Government of India on 20 January 2018.

First cartoon gallery

The Indian Institute of Cartoonists opened its 186 sq m (2,000 sq ft) gallery, the Indian Cartoon Gallery, at Midford House, Bangalore (now Bengaluru), Karnataka, on 16 August 2007. It has a seminar hall, a library, and a cartoon bibliography from across the world.

GENERAL

Highest price at an auction for a work of Indian art

Vasudeo S. Gaitonde

Vasudeo S. Gaitonde (1924–2001) was regarded as India's leading abstract painter. On 11 March 2021, a 1961 untitled painting by him was auctioned at the Saffronart Spring Live Auction for ₹39.98 crore (US $5.5 million) – a new record for the highest price achieved for a work of Indian art in an auction worldwide. It broke the painter's earlier record from 2020, when another of his untitled oil-on-canvas made in 1974 was sold for ₹36.8 crore at an auction by Pundole's.

Most National Awards won in a family

Nine members of the Jangid family have won the Master Craftsman Award, the national award for artisans and craft people between 1971 and 2017. Mal Chand Jangid, Richotmal Jangid, Vinod Kumar Jangid, Mahesh Chand Jangid, Sitaram Jangid, Kamlesh Jangid, Pawan Kumar Jangid, Navatmal Jangid, and Om Prakash Jangid won these awards.

First public art district

The Lodhi Art District in New Delhi, inaugurated by the Central Public Works Department on 1 March 2019, is the first public art district in the country. Conceptualized and realized by the St+Art India Foundation, a not-for-profit that works on art projects in open spaces, the artistic transformation of the district began in 2015. With the support of the local community and civic and cultural bodies, more than 50 artists of 23 nationalities have reimagined the area's facades by creating murals that bring the viewer into a contemporary urban art museum. A total of 56 walls with an area of approximately 16,310 sq m (1,75,565 sq ft) have been painted by the artists. This was followed by the Mahim (East) art district in Mumbai, Maharashtra; the Maqta art district in Hyderabad, Telangana; and the Panjim (Panaji) art district in Goa.

LARGEST, SMALLEST, AND MARATHON ARTWORK

Largest collage – group

Forty-four students and three teachers from Christ University, Bengaluru, created the largest collage on 2 March 2018. The collage, which measured 85.34 m x 9.14 m (280 ft x 30 ft), was made in 2 hrs 12 mins.

Largest Zentangle Art

Twenty-five students from the National Institute of Fashion Technology – Tiruppur Exporters Association (NIFT-TEA) College of Knitwear Fashion, Tiruppur, Tamil Nadu, created the largest Zentangle artwork measuring 185.8 sq m (2,000 sq. ft), with 'Make in India' as its theme. The students completed the artwork in 34 hrs during 17–18 August 2018.

Largest drawing – pencils – solo

Megha Harsha (b. 12 July 1992) from Bikaner, Rajasthan, created the largest pencil drawing by an individual. The

Largest pencil drawing – solo

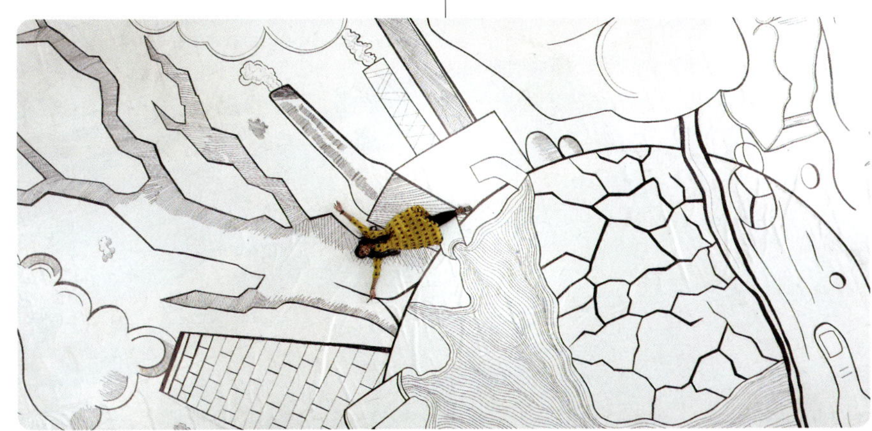

artwork measured 455.21 sq m (4,900 sq ft) and was completed in 86 hrs over the course of 17 days from 16 October to 1 November 2019 at Bikaner Boys School, Bikaner. The artwork created awareness regarding the United Nations' Sustainable Development Goals (SDGs) related to climate change, safety of women, and pollution, among others.

Largest mandala artwork – solo
Radha Shankar Narayanan (b. 11 April 1977) from Bengaluru, created a 58.06 sq m (625 sq ft) mandala artwork in 89 hrs 20 mins over 14 days at BGS National Public School, Bengaluru. He started his painting on 15 June 2021 and finished on 28 June 2021.

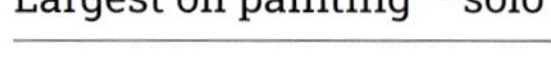

Largest oil painting – solo

Largest mandala artwork – solo

Largest mandala artwork – group
NIFT-TEA College of Knitwear Fashion in Tiruppur, Tamil Nadu, created a mandala artwork, which was 101.17 sq m (1,089 sq ft) in area, in 25 hrs over two days in the college premises. The participants began the artwork on 27 February 2021 and finished on 28 February 2021.

Largest quilling artwork – solo
Dr Jiji S. Deepak from Thrissur, Kerala, created a 6.71 m x 3.66 m (22 ft x 12 ft) artwork, using the paper-quilling technique. It took her 45 hrs 10 mins over a period of nine days. The artwork is based on the theme 'Mother Earth'.

Largest painting – oil paints – solo
Sandeep Sinha (b. 6 January 1982), an artist from Pune, Maharashtra, made an oil-on-canvas painting titled 'HiMakhan'. The artwork measures 48.78 sq m (525.06 sq ft) and is a single-scene painting of the Himalayas. He began in August 2018 and completed the work by October 2018. His painting was exhibited at the Raja Ravi Varma Art Gallery, Pune. Sinha dedicated this work to acid attack survivors.

Largest quilling artwork – solo

Largest wall painting – single wall – solo
NIFT-TEA College of Knitwear Fashion, Tiruppur, Tamil Nadu, created a wall painting measuring 46.82 sq m (504 sq ft) in 250 hrs over 25 days in the college premises. The painting was made by R. Sanjay Kumar for the college. He started his painting on 17 June 2020 and finished on 11 July 2020.

Largest portrait – pencils – solo
Aman Gulati from Lakhimpur, Uttar Pradesh, created the largest pencil portrait, which measured 410.25 sq m (4,416 sq ft) in area. The portrait of Mahatma Gandhi was completed on 2 October 2019 to mark Gandhiji's 150th birth anniversary.

Largest portrait – acrylic paints – solo

Rajeev Ranjan (b. 1 March 1977) from Purnea, Bihar, who is popularly known as Rajeev Raj, created a painting of former prime minister Atal Bihari Vajpayee with acrylic paints on canvas. He began painting on 3 December 2018 at 4:43 p.m. and completed the artwork at 11:18 p.m. on 4 December 2018 at the Vidya Vihar Residential School. He took 30 hrs 35 mins and used 225 pieces of canvas, each 0.762 m x 0.762 m (2.5 ft x 2.5 ft). The artwork covered a total area of 130.6 sq m (1,406 sq ft).

Largest painting – natural colours – solo

Sangeeta Gupta (b. 25 May 1958) from New Delhi created a painting using natural indigo and titled 'Aadiyogi Shiv – A Journey in Cosmic Indigo'. The artwork measures 169.16 sq m (1,820.78 sq ft) and is painted on *khadidar* fabric. She began the artwork on 25 February 2020 and completed it on 4 March 2020 at the Shilpi Sansthan, Rataliya Village, Jaipur, Rajasthan. The artwork was made to create awareness for sustainable living, using natural colours and dyes.

Smallest pencil-lead carving

Tribeni Kachari (b. 30 April 1997) from Kamrup, Assam, created the smallest pencil-lead carving of 'India Gate' on a graphite pencil lead. The artwork measures 5 mm (0.196 in.) in length and 3 mm (0.118 in.) in width. It was made on 31 August 2020.

Tallest sand castle

Sudarsan Pattnaik (b. 15 April 1977) from Puri, Odisha, created the tallest sand castle, 14.86 m (48 ft 9 in.) tall, to symbolize the message of world peace in 2017.

Marathon Mania

Marathon sand painting

Neha Umak (b. 22 December 1990) from Thane, Maharashtra, completed 133 pieces of sand painting artwork in 24 hrs 49 mins 19 secs from 9:16 a.m. on 30 June 2019 to 10:05 a.m. on 1 July 2019 at Kundan Talent Academy, Thane. The total break time was 1 hr 37 mins 40 secs. The artworks were a mix of portraits and sceneries.

Marathon pencil-art session

Dinesh K. Gupta (b. 22 May 1978) from Mumbai, completed 201 drawings in a marathon pencil-art session, starting at noon on 5 April 2019 and ending at noon on 6 April 2019. Using 6B pencils, he sketched famous people, natural sceneries, religious figures, and still life on A3 sheets. The event took place at Dr Babasaheb Ambedkar Art Gallery, Kalyan. The total break time was 1 hr 50 mins.

Marathon portrait making – marker and ink – solo

Srushti Sandeep Ingale (b. 14 March 2000) from Kolhapur, Maharashtra, completed 157 portraits in a marathon marker-and-ink session, starting at 7:00 a.m. on 20 November 2021 and ending at 8:00 p.m. on the same day. Using four Montex Mega Tap black ball pens, she sketched portraits of political and sports personalities, among others, on A3 sheets. The event took place at Hotel Pearl, Kolhapur. The total break time was 50 mins.

Marathon painting – acrylic colours – solo

Ramita Bhaduri (b. 27 September 1971) from Nazir Bagan, Kolkata, completed 213 artworks, using acrylic paints in 24 hrs from 4:05 p.m. on 5 June 2018 to 7:35 p.m. on 6 June 2018. The total break time was 3 hrs 30 mins.

Marathon sculpture-making

Ramita Bhaduri (b. 27 September 1971) from Nazir Bagan, Kolkata, West Bengal, completed a marathon sculpture-making session during 29–30 April 2019, using clay and cement. She logged 15 hrs of sculpting and 3 hrs break time (30 mins after every 3 hrs), making 29 sculptures in all. The average dimensions of the sculptures were 30.48 cm x 30.48 cm x 33.02 cm (12 in. x 12 in. x 13 in.) for standing figures, 25.4 cm x 30.48 cm x 38.1 cm (10 in. x 12 in. x 15 in.) for lying down ones, and 25.4 cm x 25.4 cm x 30.48 cm (10 in. x 10 in. x 12 in.) for sitting figures.

Origami

Origami is the Japanese art of folding papers to create resultant artworks that are two-dimensional and three-dimensional without using glue or cuts. It comes from the Japanese word *oru* meaning 'to fold' and *kami* meaning 'paper'.

Largest single-item origami (widest) – solo

Glendale Academy International created the largest single-item origami artwork on 21 February 2019. Radhika Chintalapati, a teacher from the school, created a butterfly with nine folds in 15 mins at Glendale International School, Hyderabad. The width of the butterfly was 2.438 m (8 ft), and the wing-to-wing length was 4.267 m (14 ft).

Most leaf artworks – solo*

Durga Unhale from Bhopal, Madhya Pradesh, has crafted 500 leaf artworks from dry bean pods of the subabul tree.

Most leaf artworks – solo

*This is a one-time category. Further and future applications for this record will not be accepted.

Search...

BOOKS

Oldest living language
Tamil, which belongs to the Dravidian group of languages, is the oldest living language of India. *Tholkappiyam,* the oldest known work in Tamil, is a work on Tamil grammar. Its composition has been variously dated to between the second century BCE and the fifth century CE.

Oldest surviving book
The oldest surviving Indian book is the Tamil work *Christiya Vanakkam,* a revised edition of the *Doctrina Christiana.* It was first published in 1560 in Goa and followed by its Tamil version published in 1564.

First known printed book
The first known printed book in India, titled *Conclusoes e Outras Coisas,* was printed in Portuguese in Goa by Joao de Bustamante, a Christian missionary.

Earliest known grammar text
The Sanskrit grammar treatise *Ashtadhyayi,* which was composed around 500 BCE by Panini, a grammarian, is said to be the earliest formalized book on Sanskrit grammar. It contains 4,000 precise rules of grammar in as many sutras, expounding an array of topics such as syntax, root derivatives and moods.

Below: *Therigatha:* Earliest known anthology
Bottom: *Ashtadhyayi*: earliest known grammar text

Anthology
The term anthology refers to a selected collection of stories or poems, or other literary works that have been contributed by different authors and published together in one book. The term comes from influences of the French term *anthologie* and the Greek *anthologia* which stood for flower-gathering.

Earliest known anthology
Therigatha, the ninth book of the *Khuddaka Nikaya,* is the earliest known anthology. This Buddhist scripture, written in Pali, consists of short poems that were recited by the early members of the Buddhist sangha. It has 73 poems, which are organized into 16 chapters, and the text comprises 522 stanzas.

First printed book to use Bengali type
A Grammar of the Bengal Language written in 1778 by Nathaniel Brassey Halhed constitued the first grammar book in Bengali. It was printed in Hoogly, Bengal (now West Bengal).

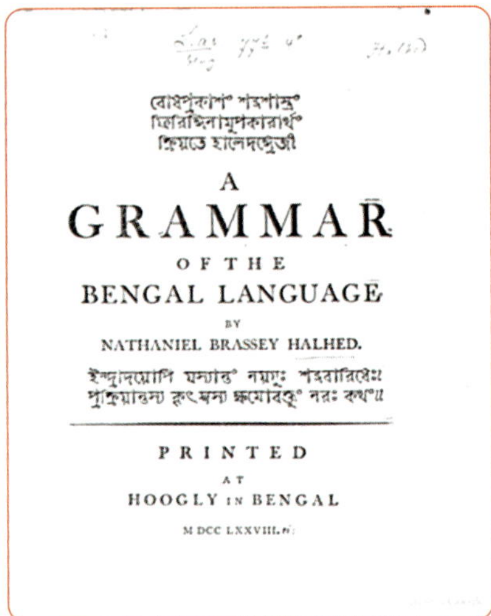

A
GRAMMAR
OF THE
BENGAL LANGUAGE
BY
NATHANIEL BRASSEY HALHED.

PRINTED
AT
HOOGLY IN BENGAL
M DCC LXXVIII.

First printed book to use Bengali type

First printed book in Bengali
Krister Mangal Samacar (*The New Testament*) published in 1819, written by William Carey was the first translation of the Bible in Bengali. It was printed by the Serampore Mission Press, Serampore, Bengal (now Srirampur, West Bengal).

First known printed books in local languages
- **Assamese:** An early translation of the New Testament, titled *Dharmapustak,* printed by the Serampore Mission Press, Serampore, Bengal, in 1813.
- **Devanagari/Hindi:** *Grammar of Sanskrit and Grammar of the Hindustani Language,* published by the Chronicle Press, Calcutta (now Kolkata), in 1796.
- **Dogri:** *Valmiki Ramayana,* published by Sri Saraswati Press, Jammu, in Jammu and Kashmir, in 1858.
- **Gujarati:** *Dabestan-e-Mazaheb,* the

Gujarati translation of a Persian book, published by Fardoonjee Marazban in Bombay (now Mumbai), Maharashtra, in 1815.

- **Kannada:** *A Grammar of the Karnatic Language* by William Meckerell, published by the Serampore Mission Press, Serampore, Bengal, in 1820.
- **Konkani:** *Doutrina Crista,* printed at the Society of Jesus Press, Goa, in 1556.
- **Maithili:** *Krishna Janma,* edited by Grierson, published by Vidyapati Press, Laheriasarai, Bihar, in 1936.
- **Malayalam:** *The Bible,* printed at the Courier Press, Bombay, Maharashtra, in 1811.
- **Odia:** A translation of the New Testament by Pandit Mrityunjaya Vidyalankar, printed at the Serampore Mission Press, Serampore, Bengal, in 1807.
- **Tamil:** *A Book of Prayers,* published by the Society of Jesus Press, Goa, around 1560.
- **Telugu:** *A Grammar of Telugu,* printed at the Serampore Mission Press, Serampore, Bengal, in 1813.
- **Urdu:** Halhed's Urdu translation of Kannada laws, published by Honourable Company Press in Calcutta, in 1792.

First poet in English in India

Henry Louis Vivian Derozio, assistant headmaster of Hindu College, (now Presidency University, Kolkata), West Bengal, is considered to be the first Indian poet who wrote in English. The poems that he submitted to the newspaper *India Gazette* under the pseudonym 'Juvenis' were published as a collection in 1827. The second edition of the collection was released in the following year and included his most famous poem, 'The Fakeer of Jungheera', which featured aspects of life in colonial India.

A stamp commemorating Henry Louis Vivian Derozio

First official sign language dictionary

Bridging the gap for the deaf and speech-disabled communities, *The Indian Sign Language Dictionary,* a first-of-its-kind book, was launched on 23 March 2018. Developed by the Delhi-based Indian Sign Language Research and Training Centre, it contains 3,000 words in Hindi and English, and their corresponding graphic representations. Available in both print and video formats, it brings uniformity to the various sign languages used. It divides the words into five categories: Everyday, Legal, Academic, Medical and Technical terms.

Most translated Indian work

The most translated Indian work is the Bhagavadgita, which is an integral part of the Mahabharata. The Bhagavadgita was first translated into English in 1785 by British typographer

Earliest known works in different languages

Earliest known Malayalam work

Samkshepa Vedartham, a catechism book by the Reverend Clement Pianius, was printed in movable type in Rome in 1772.

Earliest original Odia work

Lavanyavati, the first Odia epic, was an original work featuring the love story of a prince of Karnataka and a princess of Sri Lanka, by Upendra Bhanja (1680– 1720), who belonged to a ruling feudatory family in Ghumsar in Bhanjanagar in present-day Odisha. Called *'Kavi Samrat',* he is said to have written many books.

Earliest known Gujarati work

The earliest work in Gujarati prose was *Balavabodha,* written by Tarunaprabha and dated to 1355 CE.

Earliest known Kannada works

- The earliest extant work in Kannada, the second oldest living language in India, is the *Kavirajamarga,* which was written (possibly in parts) by a Rashtrakuta king – Nrupatunga Amoghavarsha I (r. 814–78 CE). It is a work on the rhetoric, poetics and grammar of Kannada.
- The Kannada text in prose, titled *Vaddaradhane* (sixth to ninth century CE), which is believed to have been written by Shivakotiacharya, consists of inspiring stories of 19 great Jain saints.

Earliest known Marathi works

- *Viveka Sindhu* was written by Mukundraj (1128–1200 CE) in Marathi verse, and preached Advaita bhakti. Mukundraj was a follower of Adi Shankaracharya's philosophy of Advaita or 'non-dualism', which inspired him to write this religious composition.
- *Leela Charitra* by Mahim Bhat is a biography of Chakradhara, a 13th century saint who founded the Mahanubhava sect and socio-religious movement. The work contains more than a hundred stories on the subject.

Earliest extant English work

Cavelly Venkata Boriah's *Account of the Jains,* published in 1809, is the first extant evidence of Indian writing in English.

Earliest known Tamil work

Tholkappiyam, a treatise on the grammar of the Tamil language, is the earliest known extant work in Tamil. It has been dated to between the second century BCE and the fifth century CE. The authorship is loosely attributed to the sage Tholkappiyar.

Earliest known Telugu work

The first printed prose work in Telugu, which was a part of the New Testament, was translated by Reverend Benjamin Schultze in the early 18th century.

Largest Book

and founder of the Asiatic Society, Charles Wilkins. Since then, it has been translated into as many as 55 languages.

Longest audiobook

The longest audiobook, titled *Shree Haricharitramrut Sagar*, was voiced by Gyanjivandasji Swami – 'Kundaldham' and Ishwarcharandasji Swami – 'Kundaldham', and published on 27 October 2017. The audiobook is 146,444 mins 52 secs long.

Only Shakespeare folio

A rare copy of Shakespeare's First Folio (1623) was found at the Mahatma Gandhi Central Library, University of Roorkee, Uttar Pradesh (now IIT-Roorkee, Uttarakhand) as reported in 2019. The 900-page volume titled *Mr William Shakespeare's Comedies, Histories and Tragedies* was found in an old trunk in the librarian's office. It contains 36 of Shakespeare's 37 plays.

Shakespeare's First folio

Longest novel

Avakasikal, written by M.K. Menon in Malayalam, runs into 3,958 pages, in four volumes, making it the longest novel in any Indian language. Menon received the Sahitya Akademi Award in 1981 and the Vayalar Award in 1983 for the novel.

First pseudonym

'Sujatha' was the pseudonym of the popular Tamil author S. Rangarajan (1935–2008), who wrote more than 100 novels, 250 short stories, 10 books on science, 10 stage plays and a volume of poems. He was a regular contributor to topical columns in Tamil periodicals such as *Ananda Vikatan, Kumudam* and *Kalki.* He served for a brief period as the editor of *Kumudam,* and also wrote screenplays and dialogues for Tamil movies.

Longest novel

Largest book

A special edition of the Bhagavadgita at the ISKCON temple in New Delhi is the largest-sized book. The book measures 2.8 m x 2 m (9 ft 2.2 in. x 6 ft 6.7 in.) and has 670 pages. Weighing 800 kg, it was printed in Milan, Italy, on YUPO synthetic paper, making it untearable and waterproof. It was unveiled on 26 February 2019.

Thickest book

Povitr Pustokantlem Bhanddar (*Roman Konkani Biblical Concordance*) is the thickest book. It is 149.09 cm (58.7 in.) thick, and measures 30.5 cm (12 in.) in length and 43.2 cm (17 in.) in width. The book was launched on 28 February 2021 at the Our Lady of Carmel Chapel, Navelim, Goa. The copyright owner of the book is Ives Joaquim Tavares.

Smallest book

B. Jameela from Madras (now Chennai), Tamil Nadu, had a copy of the Quran, which is 27 mm (1.06 in.) long, 19 mm (0.74 in.) wide and 10 mm (0.39 in.) thick, and weighed only 4.4 g.

Pseudonym

A pseudonym is a name adopted by somebody, especially an artist or writer that they wish to use instead of their name. Some examples of pseudonyms are Rabindranath Tagore's 'Bhanu Singha' and Sampooran Singh Kalra's 'Gulzar'.

PUBLISHING AND BOOK SELLING

Largest trade publishing house

Penguin Random House India is the subcontinent's largest English-language trade publisher. It publishes more than 300 new titles every year and has an active backlist of over 3,000 titles.

Publisher

A publisher is a person or a business that is involved in making books, magazines, periodicals, or electronic products available to the general public for commercial purposes.

Largest literary publisher

DC Books in Kottayam, Kerala, started in 1974 by Dominic Chacko Kizhakemuri, is considered the publishing hub of south India. The translation programme of DC Books is considered to be the largest in India. It publishes around 1,500 books in a year (2024).

First children's literary festival

Co-founded by Swati Roy, Jo Williams, and Venkatesh M. in 2008, Bookaroo was the first children's literary festival in India, with its first edition held in New Delhi.

First book fair

The First International Book Fair opened at New Delhi's Pragati Maidan on 18 March 1972 during the International Book Year. Around a hundred Indian publishers took part, displaying about 10,000 books in English and local Indian languages. Foreign participants included those from the USSR, the USA, France, New Zealand, Turkey and Sri Lanka.

First comic book convention

The Annual Indian Comic Book Convention (Comic Con) was organized for the first time on 19 February 2011 by Twenty Onwards Media at Dilli Haat, New Delhi. Fifty publishers participated in it, bringing together writers, gamers, cosplayers, games and films.

First Comic book convention (Comic Con) India

Biggest retail bookshop chain – high street

Crossword Bookstores Ltd, a wholly owned subsidiary of Shoppers Stop Ltd, is the largest high-street bookstore chain in India. Established in October 1992, the company had 88 stores, including franchises, across India by August 2023. These stores are across the country in cities such as Mumbai, Bengaluru, Ahmedabad, Gurugram, Delhi, Chennai, and Pune, among others.

Crossword Bookstores

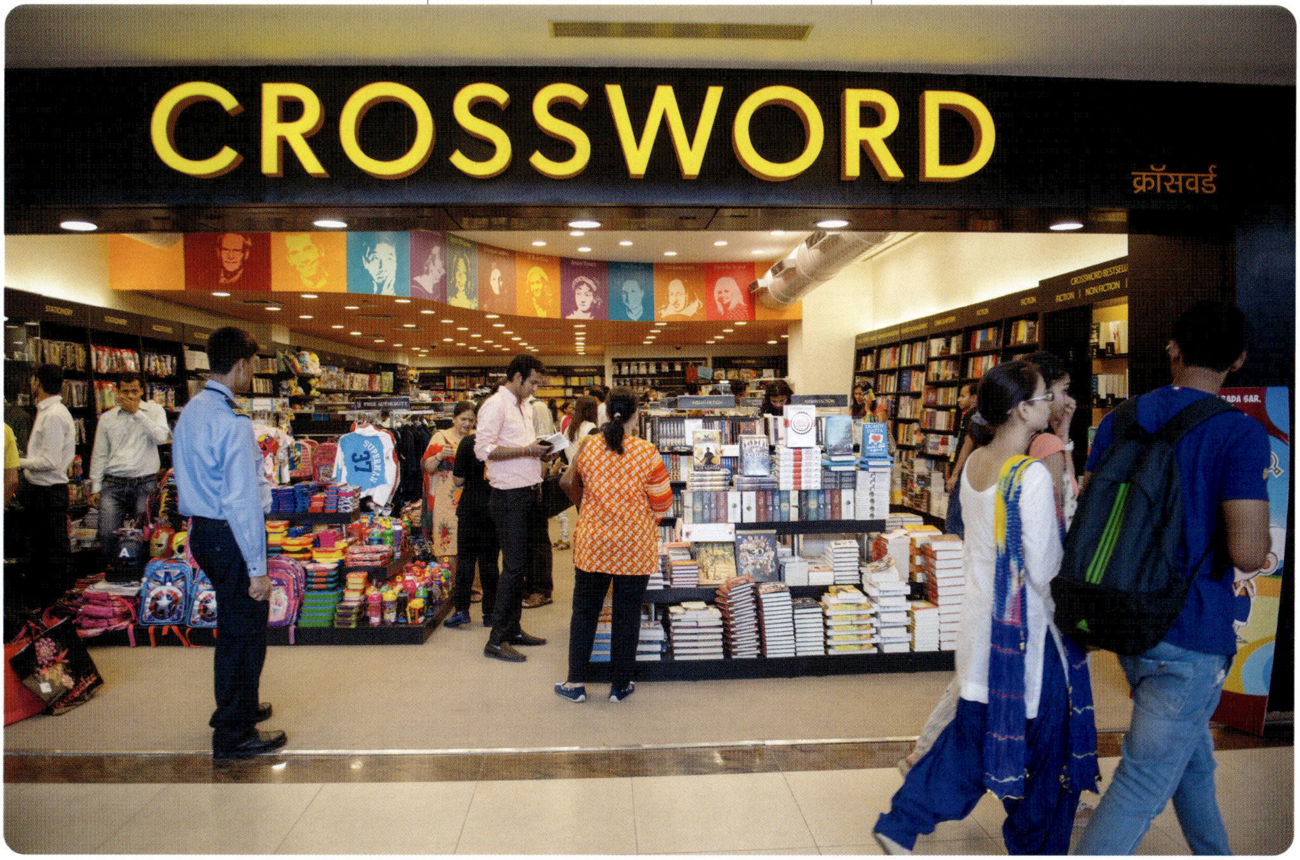

Oldest Bookshop

Higginbothams, the oldest bookshop in the country, was opened in 1844 by Abel Joshua Higginbotham in Madras, Tamil Nadu. It has a subscription division that helps educational institutions, corporate bodies and professionals to get journals and periodicals from more than 3,000 publishing houses abroad. It currently has 22 branches in India.

ாதம்ஸ்
THAMS
BOOKSELLERS AND STATIONERS

First virtual literary festival

LitFest X, organized between 23 October and 1 November 2015 was the country's first virtual literary festival. The event used multiple platforms like YouTube, Google Hangouts, Facebook and Twitter to present the interactive sessions to readers including book launches and book readings.

First literary agency

Neville Tuli of Osian, Rajasthan, set up the first professional agency for authors on 9 April 2007. The first author they signed on was Omair Ahmad on 1 June 2007. The literary agency was a division of Osian's Connoisseurs of Art Pvt. Ltd.

First independent publisher

The first Indian publisher to set up a press was Gangakishor Bhattacharya in 1821 in Calcutta, West Bengal, a former employee of the Serampore Press, Serampore, Bengal. He published 18th century ballads in Bengali and adaptations from classics.

First book village

Bilhar, located in Satara District of Maharashtra, was identified as the first book village in India on 4 May 2017. Known as *Pustakanch Gaav*, the village has genre-specific libraries in 25 locations, housing more than 15,000 books, mostly in Marathi. The village is decorated with murals, paintings and artworks on the theme of books. The aim of the initiative is to share a passion for books and an appetite for knowledge.

Largest book market

College Street in Kolkata, West Bengal, is the venue of the largest book market in the country and possibly the largest used-books market in the world. Known locally as *boi para* (the neighbourhood of books), this 1.5 km long street sees a large number of book lovers and buyers every day.

Largest sales for a children's book – hardback

Harry Potter and the Cursed Child (Parts One and Two) is the official script book for the play of the same name written by J.K. Rowling, John Tiffany, and Jack Thorne. It is the eighth story in the Harry Potter book series. Released in India by Hachette India, Gurugram, Haryana, in July 2016, it sold 2,59,537 print copies (as of October 2017), making it the largest-selling children's book in India.

Largest sales on release for a fiction title – hardback

Dan Brown is a best-selling American author of thrillers. His book *Origin* was the fifth in his Robert Langdon series, following *Angels & Demons, The Da Vinci Code, The Lost Symbol,* and *Inferno.* It was released in India on 3 October 2017 by Penguin Random House India, with an initial subscription of 1,25,000 copies, breaking all records in the fiction hardback category.

Largest adult non-fiction seller – hardback

Cricket legend Sachin Tendulkar's autobiography, *Playing It My Way,* co-authored with Boria Majumdar, was published in India by Hachette India, Gurugram, Haryana, and released on 6 November 2014. It broke all previous records in the adult non-fiction (hardback) category

Pavement bookshop in College Street, Kolkata

TOP 5 FRONTLIST TITLES* 2023

ADULT FICTION		
Title	*Author*	*Volume*
The Hidden Hindu (Book 3)	*Akshat Gupta*	*39,684*
Never Never	*Colleen Hoover and Tarryn Fisher*	*11,874*
Lessons in Chemistry	*Bonnie Garmus*	*9,107*
Victory City	*Salman Rushdie*	*8,724*
Before the Coffee Gets Cold	*Toshikazu Kawaguchi*	*8,645*

Salman Rushdie

K.J.S. Dhillon

ADULT NON-FICTION		
Energize Your Mind: Learn the Art of Mastering Your Thoughts, Feelings and Emotions	*Gaur Gopal Das*	*1,47,528*
8 Rules of Love: How To Find It, Keep It, and Let It Go	*Jay Shetty*	*37,646*
Kitne Ghazi Aye Kitne Ghazi Gaye: My Life Story	*K.J.S. Dhillon*	*28,061*
Beyond the Story: 10-Year Record of BTS	*BTS and Myeongseok Kang*	*20,485*
The Power of One Thought: Master Your Mind, Master Your Life	*Brahma Kumari Shivani*	*20,118*

CHILDREN'S FICTION		
Diary of a Wimpy Kid: No Brainer	*Jeff Kinney*	*21,192*
Percy Jackson and the Olympians: The Chalice of the Gods	*Rick Riordan*	*12,359*
From the World of Percy Jackson: The Sun and the Star: A Nico Di Angelo Adventure	*Rick Riordan and Mark Oshiro*	*11,611*
The Gita for Children: Limited Celebratory Edition	*Roopa Pai*	*6,158*
Five Survive	*Jackson, Holly*	*5,537*

CHILDREN'S NON-FICTION		
The Miracle Makers: Indian Cricket's Greatest Epic	*Bharat Sundaresan with Gaurav Joshi*	*2,258*
The Yoga Sutras for Children	*Roopa Pai*	*2,230*
The Monkey Who Fell From the Future	*Ross Welford*	*1,438*
A Complete History of India	*Roshen Dalal*	*1,221*
They Meant Business: 50 Inspiring Stories from Indian Biz	*Rosemary Marandi*	*760*

Frontlist

In the publishing industry, 'Frontlist' is a term that is applied to titles that are released recently, usually in the current year. Titles become 'backlist' after a year of publication.

**NOTE: Titles published between 1 January and 31 December 2023. Data sourced from Nielsen BookScan retail panel market and © Nielsen BookData. Volume indicates the number of copies sold. The list includes new re-issues, changes in format or any other change by publishers.*

with 1,50,289 copies confirmed on order subscriptions.

Largest lifetime sales – hardback

The Secret by Rhonda Byrne, published by Simon and Schuster, US, in 2006, is a best-selling self-help book, based on the pseudoscientific 'law of attraction', which claims that a person's thoughts can change the world directly. The book has sold over 7,00,000 copies in India and has also been translated into 50 languages.

First feminist publishing house

Kali for Women, a not-for-profit trust, publishing a wide variety of books by women and on women, was started in 1984 by Urvashi Butalia and Ritu Menon in New Delhi.

Largest-selling bilingual dictionary

The *English–English–Malayalam*

Largest bookshop

Sapna Book House in Gandhinagar, Bengaluru, Karnataka, was started in 1967 by Suresh C. Shah. Spread over 3,716 sq m (40,000 sq ft), it has more than 2,20,000 titles covering many genres and topics. Sapna Book House has four more branches in Bengaluru and Mysuru – adding up to retail space of about 9,290.3 sq m (1,00,000 sq ft).

Most travel bookshops

Wheeler (A.H. Wheeler and Co. Pvt. Ltd) owns a bookshop chain co-founded by Emile Moreau and T.K. Banerjee in Allahabad (now Prayagraj), Uttar Pradesh, in 1877, with around 900 popular bookshops selling magazines and books at as many as 264 railway stations.

Dictionary by T. Ramalingam Pillai was first published in May 1983. Published by DC Books, based in Kottayam, Kerala, it is in its 55th impression now. As on September 2019, around 2.4 million copies had been sold.

Largest literary festival

The Jaipur Literature Festival, founded in 2006, is an annual literary festival in Jaipur, Rajasthan, which brings together some of the most prominent thinkers and writers from across the world every January. The festival directors are authors Namita Gokhale and William Dalrymple, and it has been produced by Sanjoy Roy of Teamwork Arts since 2008. The festival has seen a footfall of 4,31,000 people, conducted 238 sessions in over 46 languages by around 370 speakers in 2023.

AWARDS AND HONOURS

First recipients of the Sahitya Akademi Award

• *Man*: Makhanlal Chaturvedi (1889–1968), a poet, was the first person to receive this award for *Him Tarangini* (Hindi) in 1955.

• *Woman*: The Punjabi poet and writer Amrita Pritam (1919–2005) received the award in 1956, the year after its inception, for *Sunehre* (Punjabi), a collection of poems.

First Sahitya Akademi Bhasha Samman Award

The Bhasha Samman Awards are given annually for contribution towards the development of a language. The first of these awards were given in 1996 to:

• Dharikshan Mishra for Bhojpuri,
• Bansi Ram Sharma and M.R. Thakur for Pahari (Himachali),
• K. Jathappa Rai and Mandara Keshava Bhat for Tulu (Karnataka), and
• Chandra Kanta Murasingh for Kokborok (Tripura).

First to win the DSC Prize for South Asian Literature

• *Man*: Poet and novelist Jeet Thayil won the DSC Prize for South Asian Literature 2013 for his novel *Narcopolis* (Faber & Faber).

• *Woman*: Jhumpa Lahiri was judged as the winner of the DSC Prize for South Asian Literature 2015 for her book *The Lowland*. The US $ 50,000 prize and the specially designed trophy was awarded to her on 22 January 2015.

First Winners of the Sahitya Akademi Translation Prize

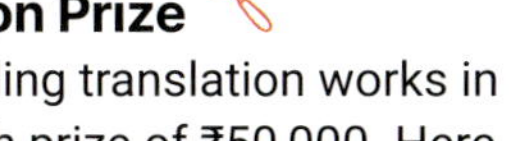

Established in 1989, the award is presented for outstanding translation works in 24 languages. The awardees receive a plaque and a cash prize of ₹50,000. Here is a list of the first winners:

Language	Translator	Translation Title	Year
Assamese	Narendranath Sarma	*Atmajivan Charit*	1990
Bengali	Nilina Abraham	*Patummar Chhagal O Balyaskhi*	1989
Bodo	Pramila Narzary	*Aswini Solo*	2005
Dogri	Ram Nath Shastri	*Mitti Di Gaddi*	1989
English	Bikram K. Das	*Paraja*	1989
Gujarati	Nagindas Parekh	*Na Hanyate*	1989
Hindi	Noor Nabi Abbasi	*Malabar Se Masko Tak*	1989
Kannada	S.V. Parameshwara Bhatta	*Kannada Kalidasa Mahasamputa*	1990
Kashmiri	Syed Rasool Pompur	*Pranwaar*	1991
Konkani	Ravindra Kelekar	*Ani Tankan Manshant Hadle*	1990
Maithili	Upendranath Jha 'Vyas'	*Vipradas*	1990
Malayalam	K. Ravi Verma	*Ganadevata*	1989
Manipuri	T. Thoibi Devi	*Drishtipath*	1989
Marathi	Uma Virupax Kulkarni	*Vamsavriksha*	1989
Nepali	Karna Thami	*Sakanta Ka Kavitaharu*	1994
Odia	Basanta Kumari Devi	*Ganadebata, Parts I and II (Panchagram)*	1989
Punjabi	Rattan Singh Jaggi	*Tulasi Ramayan (Ramcharitmanas)*	1989
Rajasthani	Deo Dutta Nag	*Sapano*	1990
Sanskrit	Ganesha Sharma	*Vijananam Samajasca*	1990
Santhali	Sobha Nath Beshra	*Rahla Raybar*	2010
Sindhi	Jagat Assudomal Advani	*Rolak Ji Atam Kahani*	1989
Tamil	M.G. Jagannatharaja	*Aamukta Malyada*	1990
Telugu	B. Gopala Reddi	*Ravindruni Natikalu*	1989
Urdu	Hameed Almas	*Farmoodat*	1989

Cover images for some Indian writers' DSC Prize winning books: *From left*: *Half the Night is Gone* by Amitabha Bagchi, *Chronicle of a Corpse Bearer* by Cyrus Mistry, *Sleeping on Jupiter* by Anuradha Roy and *No Presents Please* by Jayant Kaikini

First recipients of the Jnanpith Award

The Jnanpith Award is presented annually by the Bharatiya Jnanpith to an Indian author for their contribution to literature. The first winners were:

• *Man*: Malayalam poet G. Sankara Kurup (1901–78) was the recipient of the first Jnanpith Award in 1965, the year of its inception, for his anthology of poems, *Odakkuzhal*.

• *Woman*: Ashapurna Devi (1909–95), Bengali novelist and poet, was the first woman author to receive the Jnanpith Award in 1976 for her novel *Pratham Pratishruti* (which was published in 1965), the first of a trilogy that included *Subarnalata* and *Bakul Katha*.

First Sahitya Akademi Fellowship

• *Man:* Former Indian president and eminent scholar Dr S. Radhakrishnan (1888–1975) was the first to receive this honour in 1968 for his contribution to Indian thought and universal humanism.

• *Woman:* The first woman to be elected Fellow of the Akademi was the poet Mahadevi Varma in 1979.

First Indian winner of the Neustadt Prize

The Neustadt International Prize (given for an author's body of work) is one of the few international prizes for which poets, novelists, and playwrights are all eligible. Raja Rao was the first Indian to win it in 1988. Indian-Canadian writer Rohinton Mistry won the prize in 2012.

First Indian citizen to win the Booker Prize

Arundhati Roy (b. 24 November 1961) won the prestigious Booker Prize in 1997 for her first novel, *The God of Small Things.*

First novel in an Indian language to win the International Booker Prize

Tomb of Sand by Geetanjali Shree became the first Indian-language (Hindi) novel to win the prestigious International Booker Prize in 2022. Translated from *Ret Samadhi* into English by Daisy Rockwell, it is set in north India and follows the story of an 80-year-old woman.

First Indian winner of Newbery Medal

Dhan Gopal Mukerji (1890–1936), who was born in a village near Calcutta, West Bengal, and later went to the US, was the first Indian winner of the Newbery Medal for his novel, *Gay-Neck, the Story of a Pigeon,* in 1928.

The cover of *Gay-Neck, the Story of a Pigeon*

First Indian winner of the Ondaatje Prize

Sports journalist Rahul Bhattacharya's *The Sly Company of People Who Care* won the Royal Society of Literature Ondaatje Prize in 2012. It also won the Hindu Literary Prize (2011) and was the Kirkus Fiction Book of the Year in the USA.

First winners of the Saraswati Samman

The Saraswati Samman was instituted by the K.K. Birla Foundation in 1991. Award winners receive ₹15 lakh along with a citation and a plaque. The first winners are:

• *Man*: Harivansh Rai Bachchan for

COUNTRIES WITH MOST SAHITYA AKADEMI FELLOWS*

(Recipients of the Premchand Fellowship and the Anandcoomaraswamy Fellowship)

Country	Premchand Fellowship	Anandacoomaraswamy Fellowship
Bangladesh	3	0
Sri Lanka	4	2
Pakistan	2	0
Maldives	2	0
Nepal	1	0
Singapore	0	1
Afghanistan	0	1
China	0	1
Israel	0	1
Jordan	0	1
Thailand	0	2
Japan	0	3
Philippines	0	1
Vietnam	0	1
Uzbekistan	0	1

SOURCE: Sahitya Akademi website

Autobiography in four volumes (Hindi) in 1991.

• *Woman*: Balamani Amma for *Nivedyam* (Malayalam) in 1995.

First Indian winner of the Commonwealth Writers' Prize

Author Nayantara Sahgal won the Commonwealth Writers' Prize for Best Book in 1987, for her novel *Plans for Departure.*

First winner of Grinzane Cavour Prize

Anita Desai won the lifetime achievement award of the Grinzane Cavour Prize in Piedmont, Italy, on 18 July 2005.

First Indian-origin winner of the Pulitzer Prize – fiction

Jhumpa Lahiri's *Interpreter of Maladies* (Mariner Books/Houghton Mifflin) won the Pulitzer Prize for Fiction in 2000.

First winner of the Rabindranath Tagore Literary Prize

The Rabindranath Tagore Literary Prize, started in 2018, is awarded annually for valuable contributions to literature and poetry. Kabir (awarded posthumously) was the first awardee for *One Hundred Poems of Kabir* in 2018.

First winners of the JCB prize

The JCB Prize was established in 2018 and is awarded annually. The first winners were:

• *Man*: Benyamin for *Jasmine Days* in 2018.

• *Woman*: Madhuri Vijay for *The Far Field* in 2019.

Highest monetary prize

• *Fiction:* The JCB Prize, established in 2018, is the most valuable prize in Indian literature, amounting to ₹25 lakh (2.5 million). Funded by JCB, a British manufacturing firm, the prize is awarded to the best work of fiction by an Indian citizen in English or translated from another language into English. Each of the five shortlisted books is awarded ₹1 lakh (0.1 million) and a separate prize of ₹5 lakh (0.5 million) is given if the winning entry is a translation. Mita Kapur, founder and CEO of Siyahi, a literary consultancy organization, now serves as its director.

• *Non-Fiction:* The richest prize for non-fiction writing is the New India Foundation Prize, valued at ₹15 lakh (1.5 million).

First Indian to win Prestigious Erasmus Prize

Amitav Ghosh was awarded with the 'Erasmus Prize' 2024 on 7 March 2024 for highlighting the climate change crisis. The award is given by the Premium Erasmianum Foundation of the Netherlands that has been giving the award for outstanding contribution to the humanities, social sciences and arts in Europe and beyond since 1958. He was also awarded a cash prize of ₹1.5 lakh.

First winners of the Kamaladevi Chattopadhyay NIF Book Prize

Established in 2018, the Kamaladevi Chattopadhyay NIF Book Prize is an annual award for non-fiction books published in the preceding year. The first winner of the award was Milan Vaishnav in 2018 for *When Crime Pays: Money and Muscle in Indian Politics*.

First winners of the Yuva Puruskar Award

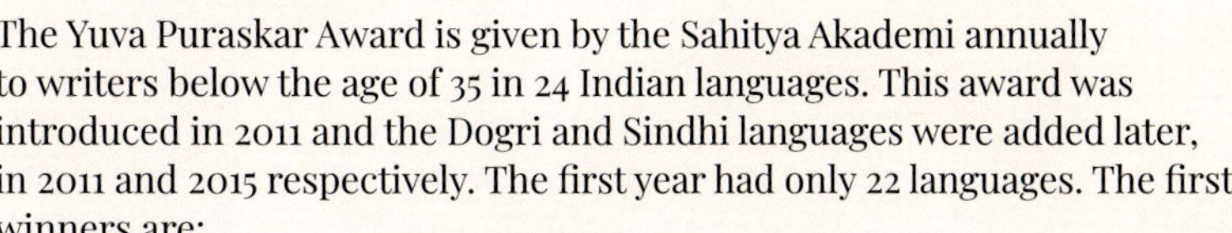

The Yuva Puraskar Award is given by the Sahitya Akademi annually to writers below the age of 35 in 24 Indian languages. This award was introduced in 2011 and the Dogri and Sindhi languages were added later, in 2011 and 2015 respectively. The first year had only 22 languages. The first winners are:

Assamese: Arindam Borkataki for *Anusilon.*

Bengali: Binod Ghosal for *Danaowla Manus.*

Bodo: Jaishree Baro for *Jeu Saharani Beduin.*

Dogri: Yash Raina for *Do Kandhe* in 2012.

English: Vikram Sampath for *My Name is Gauhar Jaan! – The Life and Times of a Musician.*

Gujarati: Dhwanil Parekh for *Antim Yuddha.*

Hindi: Uma Shankar Choudhary for *Kahte Hain Tab Shanshaah So Rahe The.*

Kannada: Veeranna Madiwalara for *Nelada Karuneya Dani.*

Kashmiri: Nisar Azam for *Patte Leji Zoon Daras.*

Konkani: Jofa Gonsalves for *Nirnay.*

Maithili: Anand Kumar Jha for *Hathat Parivartan.*

Malayalam: Sushmesh Chandroth for *Marana Vidyalayam.*

Manipuri: Devchand for *Nongthangna Mutkhrabada.*

Marathi: Aishwarya Patekar for *Bhuishastra.*

Nepali: Kamal Regmi for *Srijana Ra Abhista.*

Odia: Gayatribala Panda for *Gaan.*

Punjabi: Paramveer Singh for *Amrit Vela.*

Rajasthani: Dula Ram Saharan for *Peer.*

Sanskrit: Paramanand Jha for *Kavyakaveri.*

Santali: Satilal Murmu for *Jagron.*

Sindhi: Manoj Chawla 'Tanha' for *Pinjraa* in 2015.

Tamil: M. Thavasi for *Sevalkattu.*

Telugu: Vempalli Gangadhar for *Jumma.*

Urdu: Vishal Khullar for *Dhund Mein Amaan.*

MEDIA AND COMMUNICATIONS

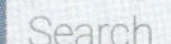

PRINT

First printing press

The first printing press came to India accidentally, in 1556, when the patriarch designate of Abyssinia (now Ethiopia, Africa) broke his journey at Goa and later died there. The printing press was left behind. The printers were a Spaniard named João de Bustamante and his Indian assistant, whose name is not known.

First paper-making machine

William Carey (1761–1834), a British Christian missionary, translator, social reformer, and cultural anthropologist, who founded Serampore College in Bengal, first set up a paper-making machine in Calcutta (now Kolkata), West Bengal in 1830.

First lithographic printing

Lithographic printing was introduced by the Calcutta Art Studio in 1878 in Calcutta (now Kolkata), West Bengal.

First multilingual press

A multilingual press for all the main local Indian languages was first set up in Serampore, Bengal (Srirampur, West Bengal), in 1800 by Christian missionaries.

Earliest type

The first types in any Indian language were cast in Goa in 1577 by João Gonçalves reportedly assisted by Father Pero Luis, who was a Tamil Jesuit priest.

First typewriters

The first typewriters were imported into India in 1896.
First indigenous typewriters:

- Godrej & Boyce Manufacturing Company Ltd manufactured India's first manual typewriter in 1955. It was designed and created entirely by Indian engineers.
- Blackwood India Ltd in Calcutta, established in 1960 and renamed J.K. Business Machines in 1961, were the first makers of portable typewriters in the country.
- The first indigenous electronic typewriters were manufactured by Hindustan Teleprinters Ltd in 1975.

Lithograph

A lithograph is a type of print made by drawing on a flat stone or metal plate with a special greasy crayon. The artist then uses ink and presses the design on to paper to create multiple copies. It's a common technique for making art prints.

First news agency

The Press Trust of India (PTI), which is a non-profitsharing cooperative of Indian newspapers, was established on 27 August 1947. It took over the Associated Press of India and the Indian operations of Reuters. It provided news, photographs, features, and infographics from February 1949 onwards.

First press regulation

The Censorship of Press Act of 1799 was the first censorship regulation to enforce wartime restrictions on the press. It was enacted by the then Governor General Lord Wellesley, who anticipated a French invasion of India. All news was scrutinized, including 'pre-censorship' before publication, by a special security administration unit with a view to preventing information leaks.

General Lord Wellesley

Press Trust of India office, New Delhi: first news agency

First newspaper

Hicky's Bengal Gazette or the *Original Calcutta General Advertiser*, India's and Asia's first newspaper, was launched on 29 June 1780 by James Augustus Hicky, an Irishman.

WR First newspaper for visually impaired people

Swagat Thorat's *Sparshdnyan*, launched in February 2008, is India's first newspaper for visually challenged people. Its name means 'knowledge by touch', and it is published in Marathi on the 1st and 15th of every month.

First news agency to supply news in Urdu

On 5 June 1992, the United News of India (UNI) became the first agency in the world to supply Urdu news. It remains the only agency to do so.

First non-English newspaper

In 1794, the Reverend Harutyun Shmavonyan edited and published *Azdarar* in the Armenian script in

Madras (now Chennai), Tamil Nadu. This was the first Armenian journal in the world and the first non-English one in India.

The only handwritten newspaper

The Musalman, the oldest Urdu language daily newspaper, published from Chennai, Tamil Nadu, is the only handwritten newspaper in the world. It is a four-page evening paper handwritten by four calligraphers or *katibs*, and printed. Established in 1927 by Syed Azmatulla, it has not missed a single day's publication. The paper has correspondents all over India and sells at 75 paise a copy to around 25,000 subscribers.

English daily with the largest readership

The Times of India, headquartered in Mumbai, Maharashtra, has a recorded readership of 1,73,44,000 (2019 Q4; Indian Readership Survey [IRS]).

First newsprint factory

The first paper mill in India to manufacture newsprint was a factory at Nepanagar, Burhanpur District, Madhya Pradesh, set up in January 1955.

First vernacular paper

Samachar Darpan was published in Bengali from Serampore, Bengal, by William Carey and John Clark Marshman from May 1818 onwards.

Samachar Darpan

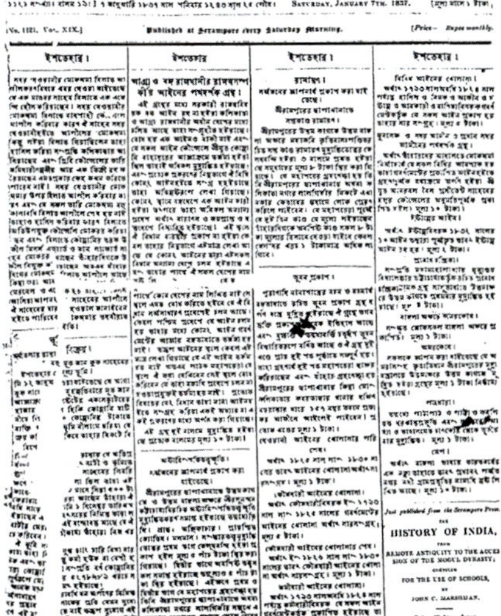

Saturday, January 7th, 1837.

Published at Serampore every Saturday Morning.

HISTORY OF INDIA,

Selling the Smell of Mangoe

On 2 June 2024, *The Times of India* partnered with Swiggy Instamart to welcome the mango season. The front page featured a beautiful photo of mangoes and invited readers to 'read this ad with your nose. The page was imbued with the aroma of mangoes. The ad was intended to promote Swiggy's instamart feature of delivering home-essentials within 10 minutes. Around 8,00,000 copies of this special edition newspaper were distributed.

Marshman was a British journalist, historian, and publisher of the *Friend of India* from which *The Statesman* newspaper descended.

First Hindi newspaper

Banaras Akhbar began in 1845, under the editorship of Govind Narayan Thatte, as the first Hindi newspaper.

First financial daily

The Economic Times, India's first financial daily, was launched by the Times of India Group in March 1961. Like the London-based *Financial Times*, it too was printed on salmon-pink paper.

First magazine in Hindi

Saraswati, India's first Hindi monthly magazine, was published in January 1900. Its founder was the well-known printer and publisher Chintamani Ghosh and the magazine was published by the Indian Press, which was based in Allahabad (now Prayagraj), Uttar Pradesh.

Chintamani Ghosh

First daily with an international edition

In February 1994, India's global newspaper *The Asian Age* was launched simultaneously from Delhi, Mumbai, and London. It has a Kolkata edition too.

First newspaper run entirely by women

Khabar Lahariya is the first newspaper in India that is entirely staffed, edited, and published by women. The eight-page rural weekly newspaper in Hindi is sold in 600 villages in its print form and on multiple digital platforms. It was launched in 2002 in Chitrakoot District, Uttar Pradesh. In 2009, it was awarded the UNESCO King Sejong Literary Prize for its contribution to literacy.

First women's magazine in English

The Indian Ladies' Magazine was first published in English in 1901 by Kamala Satthianadhan in Madras.

First women's magazine in an Indian language

Masik Patrika in Bengali, published from Calcutta, in 1854, was the first women's magazine in an Indian language.

First magazine for visually challenged people

White Print was the first lifestyle magazine in English in India for visually challenged people. It was launched in May 2013 by Upasana Makati, a former communications student from the University of Ottawa, Canada. This 64-page monthly, printed at the National Association for the Blind, Mumbai, Maharashtra, and circulated across India, features articles about sports, politics, culture, fashion, and technology, besides short stories and reader contributions. *White Print* has also released Braille-tactile alphabet books in Braille, in both English and Hindi, which are called 'Tactabet'.

Hindu office front

Chandamama front cover

First newspaper to be printed in colour

The Hindu, with its headquarters in Madras began as a weekly in 1878 and turned into a daily in 1889. A family-run newspaper, it was the first to be printed in colour in 1940. It was also the first Indian newspaper to own aeroplanes to distribute newspapers (1963), and the first newspaper to digitize and be available online (1995).

First vernacular periodical

Digdarshan, a Bengali monthly, first appeared in April 1818.

First letters to the editor column

The letters to the editor column was introduced in the biweekly magazine *Calcutta Journal*, first published in 1878 in Bengal.

Multi-edition daily with the largest readership

Dainik Jagran, which has its headquarters in Kanpur, Uttar Pradesh, leads with 37 editions across 11 states and a readership of 6,86,67,000 (2019 Q4; IRS).

Daily with largest readership – Hindi

Dainik Jagran, which is headquartered in Kanpur, Uttar Pradesh, has a readership of 6,86,67,000 (2019 Q4; IRS).

State/UT with the most newspaper and periodical publications

Uttar Pradesh, with 21,166 publications, leads with the maximum number of publications in India. It is followed by Maharashtra, with 19,796 publications, and Delhi with 16,351 of them as of 2020–21.

State/UT with the most Indian-language publications

Delhi leads among all states and UTs in the most number of Indian language publications in as many as 15 languages. It is followed by Maharashtra, Uttarakhand, and Tamil Nadu with publications in 14 languages each. Gujarat comes after that with publications in 11 languages as of 2020–21.

State/UT with most registered newspapers

Uttar Pradesh, with 21,336 registered publications, is the state with the most registered newspaper publications.

Most read English magazine

India Today, a weekly published from Noida, Uttar Pradesh, by the India Today Group, has a readership of 94,93,000 (2019 Q4; IRS).

Largest read regional-language daily

Malayala Manorama, with its headquarters in Kottayam, Kerala, has a readership of 1,77,63,000 (2019 Q4; IRS).

Malyala Manorama newspaper

Oldest children's magazine

Chandamama, founded by Telugu film-makers B. Nagi Reddy and Aluri Chakrapani was launched in July 1947 in Telugu. It was edited by Kodavatiganti Kutumba Rao. The magazine ceased publication in 1998. In 2007, it was acquired by Geodesic Ltd. Its last edition came out in March 2013 and since then its status is unknown. In its heyday, *Chandamama* was published in 13 languages and had a readership of around 2,00,000 across the country.

Most circulated government publication

Employment News, an English weekly

published from New Delhi by the Publications Division, Ministry of Information and Broadcasting, Government of India, has the highest circulation of 2,39,498 among government publications (as of 2019).

Most read Hindi magazine

India Today (Hindi), a weekly published from Noida, Uttar Pradesh, by the India Today Group, has a total readership of 66,41,000 (2019 Q4; IRS).

Most read magazine in a regional language

Vanitha, a Malayalam fortnightly magazine, published from Kottayam, Kerala, by the Malayala Manorama Group, has a readership of 58,86,000 (2019 Q4; IRS).

State/UT with most publications in a single language

Uttar Pradesh, with 16,557 publications in Hindi, leads among all states and UTs with the most publications in a single language (Hindi).It is followed by Madhya Pradesh, with 11,973 Hindi-language publications, and Maharashtra, with 9,982 publications in Marathi.

First Indian-origin journalist to win the Pulitzer Prize

Gobind Behari Lal (1889–1982), a science journalist in the USA, won the Pulitzer Prize in 1937.

Gobind Behari Lal: first Indian-origin journalist to win the Pulitzer Prize

Longest spell as editor

Tushar Kanti Ghosh (1898–1994) was editor of the *Amrita Bazar Patrika*, based in Kolkata for 64 years. He had founded the newspaper in 1928.

Amrita Bazar Patrika

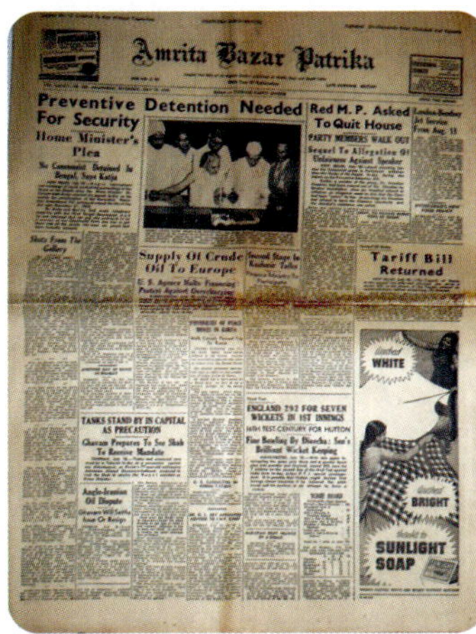

Amrita Bazar Patrika

Preventive Detention Needed For Security

Home Minister's Plea

Red M.P. Asked To Quit House

PARTY MEMBERS WALK OUT

Supply Of Crude Oil To Europe

Tariff Bill Returned

TANKS STAND BY IN CAPITAL AS PRECAUTION

ENGLAND 292 FOR SEVEN WICKETS IN 1ST INNINGS

WHITE

SUNLIGHT SOAP

Longest-running women's magazine

Femina, which started in July 1959 with Frene Talyarkhan as its first editor, continues to be published. It is now published by Worldwide Media, which is owned by the Times Group. It was also the first lifestyle magazine of the country in English, and has the highest circulation in its category (1,08,560 in August 2019).

A popular feature of *The Times of India* is 'The Common Man' cartoon created by R.K. Laxman. 'The Common Man' began in 1952 and represents the average Indian. He is seen wearing a dhoti and a jacket and often makes sharp and cutting observations on the Indian political and social situation. 'The Common Man' first appeared in the daily comic strip 'You Said It' in the newspaper.

Oldest extant newspaper – regional language

The *Bombay Samachar*, now titled *Mumbai Samachar*, is the oldest continuously published newspaper in any language in India, and continues to be published. Launched on 1 July 1822 by Fardoonjee Marazban (1787–1847), the daily is published in both Gujarati and English. Marazban, who was from Bombay (now Mumbai), Maharashtra, was a printer and a newspaper editor. He established vernacular journalism in India and initiated the production of Gujarati types.

Oldest extant newspaper – English

The Times of India began on 3 November 1838 as a biweekly, initially called *Bombay Times and Journal of Commerce*. It was renamed *The Times of India* in 1850, with J.E. Brennan as its editor.

Most pages in a newspaper supplement

Kannada daily *Vijayavani*'s Mysuru edition brought out a special issue with 320 pages in 10 volumes on 25 March 2020. This supplement was dedicated to Shri Mayakara Madappa, a social reformer and spiritual leader of the 16th century. The newspaper was sold at a price of ₹4.

Most articles published in a year – single publication

Dr Prem Kumar Sharma (b. 9 November 1958) has been writing columns for *Hindustan Times* for a long time. He has written a total number of 415 articles in HT City in the year 2019, containing 362 daily horoscopes, 52 weekly astro queries, and 1 yearly horoscope.

Longest career as a journalist

B.P. Sharma, a journalist from Jammu and Kashmir, who died in 2005 at the age of 97, was an active journalist for over 70 years. He established the Jammu station of Radio Kashmir (All India Radio), and was its first director. He also worked with the news agency Reuters, *The Times of India, Hindustan Times* and *The Tribune*. Later, he served as the principal information officer of Jammu and Kashmir.

Longest letter to the editor

Vinod Chandrashekhar Dixit (b. 1 December 1964) from Ahmedabad, Gujarat, wrote the longest letter to the editor, which was published in *Free Press*, Gujarat, on 30 April 2024. He wrote a total of 3,646 words on the topic '*Modi hai to mumkin hai? –* PM Narendra Modi's Journey of Leadership and Vision'.

Most pages in a newspaper
Dainik Bhaskar's Indore edition brought out a special issue with 128 pages on 17 September 2020. This issue was on the theme 'AatmaNirbhar Indore'.

Most columns published in a year – multiple publications
Dr Prem Kumar Sharma (b. 9 November 1958) has the most number of columns published in a year. He has written nearly 1275 columns for multiple publications. His columns have been published in *Haribhoomi, Punjab Kesari, Voice Weekly, Hindustan Times* and other dailies.

Most articles published in a year – multiple publications
Vinod Chandrashekhar Dixit (b. 1 December 1964) from Ahmedabad, Gujarat, published the most number of articles in newspapers and magazines in a year. The total number of articles published by him between 1 March 2022 and 28 February 2023 was 1,846.

RADIO

First broadcasting service
The Madras Presidency Radio Club, under the stewardship of C.V. Krishnaswamy Chetty, started a broadcasting service in 1924, using a tiny 40-watt transmitter with an effective range of only 8 km.

First controller of broadcasting
Lionel Fielden took over as the first controller of broadcasting for the Indian State Broadcasting Service (ISBS) on 30 August 1935 in British India. A senior BBC producer, he spent five years in India, establishing a countrywide radio service. On 8 June 1936, the ISBS was renamed All India Radio.

First direct relay
A historic occasion, the first direct relay coincided with India's 'freedom at midnight' from British colonial rule. The ceremonies for the transfer of power from Britain to an independent India on the night of 14–15 August 1947 at the Central Hall of the Parliament House in Delhi were relayed by AIR.

Longest running commentary
Melville de Mellow's running commentary on the last journey of Mahatma Gandhi on 31 January 1948, a day after his assassination, lasted for more than seven continuous hours.

First private radio station
On 10 September 1935, Akashvani Mysore, a private radio station, was set up in present-day Karnataka by Dr M.V. Gopalaswamy, professor of psychology and principal of the Maharaja's College, at his residence.

First private FM broadcaster
Times FM from Times Group commenced operations in 1993 from Ahmedabad, Gujarat. It ran till June 1998 and was relaunched as Radio Mirchi in 2000. Over the years, Radio Mirchi has expanded its presence across 63 cities in India and multiple stations in the UAE and the US.

First private FM station
Radio City Bangalore, based in Bengaluru in Karnataka, started on 3 July 2001, becoming the country's first private FM radio station, after the Government of India opened up the FM broadcasting industry to private companies and competition.

Largest media organization
All India Radio, established in 1936, today reaches almost the entire population across the length and breadth of the country and nearly 92 per cent of the total area, making it the largest media organization by reach. It broadcasts in 23 languages and 179 dialects. Programmes of its External Services Division are broadcast in 11 Indian and 16 foreign languages.

First frequency modulation (FM) service
AIR inaugurated the first ever FM service from Madras, on 23 July 1977.

First broadcast
In June 1923, the Radio Club of Bombay made the first ever broadcast in the country from Bombay. This was followed by the setting up of the Calcutta Radio Club in West Bengal around five months later.

First national broadcast of music
AIR broadcast its first national music programme on 20 July 1952 with sitar maestro Pandit Ravi Shankar as the music conductor.

Ravi Shankar

Funeral of Mahatma Gandhi (Commentary of Melville de Mellow)

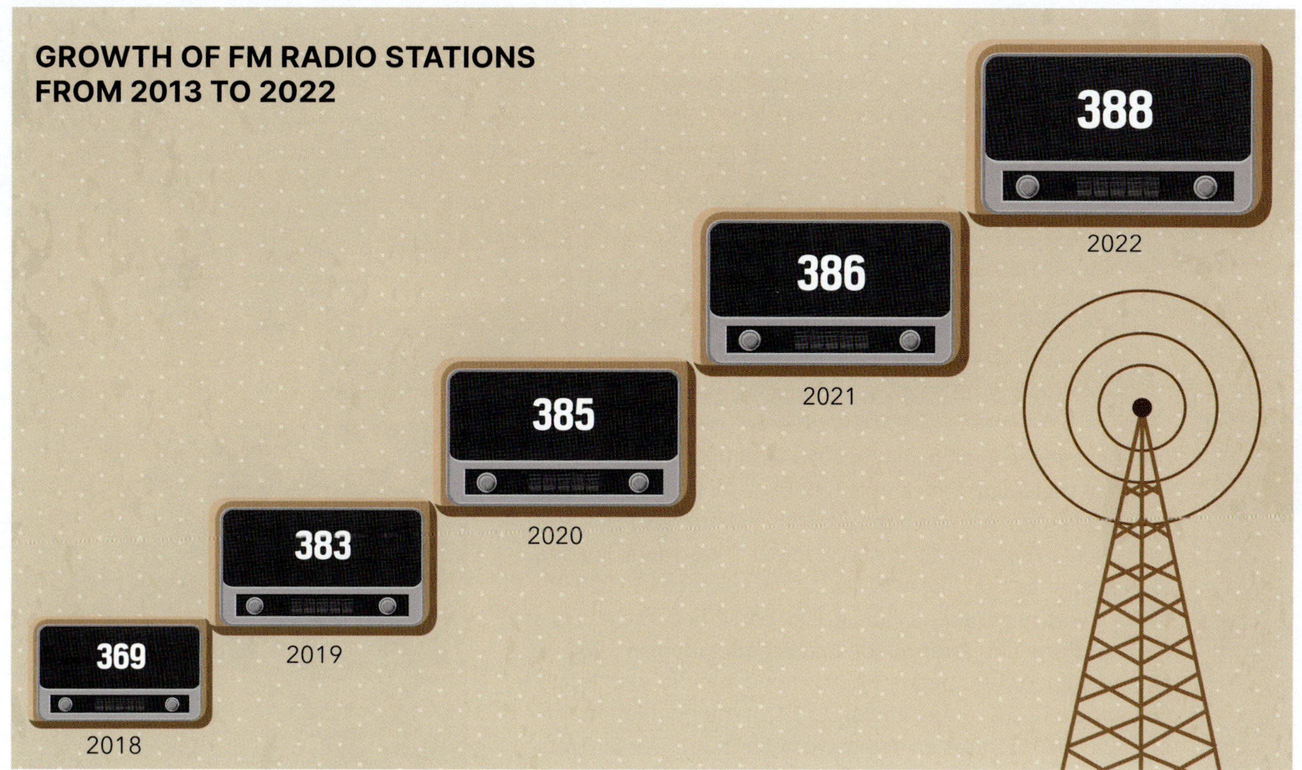

Source: Statistical Handbook on Media and Entertainment Sector 2022-23, Ministry of Information and Broadcasting

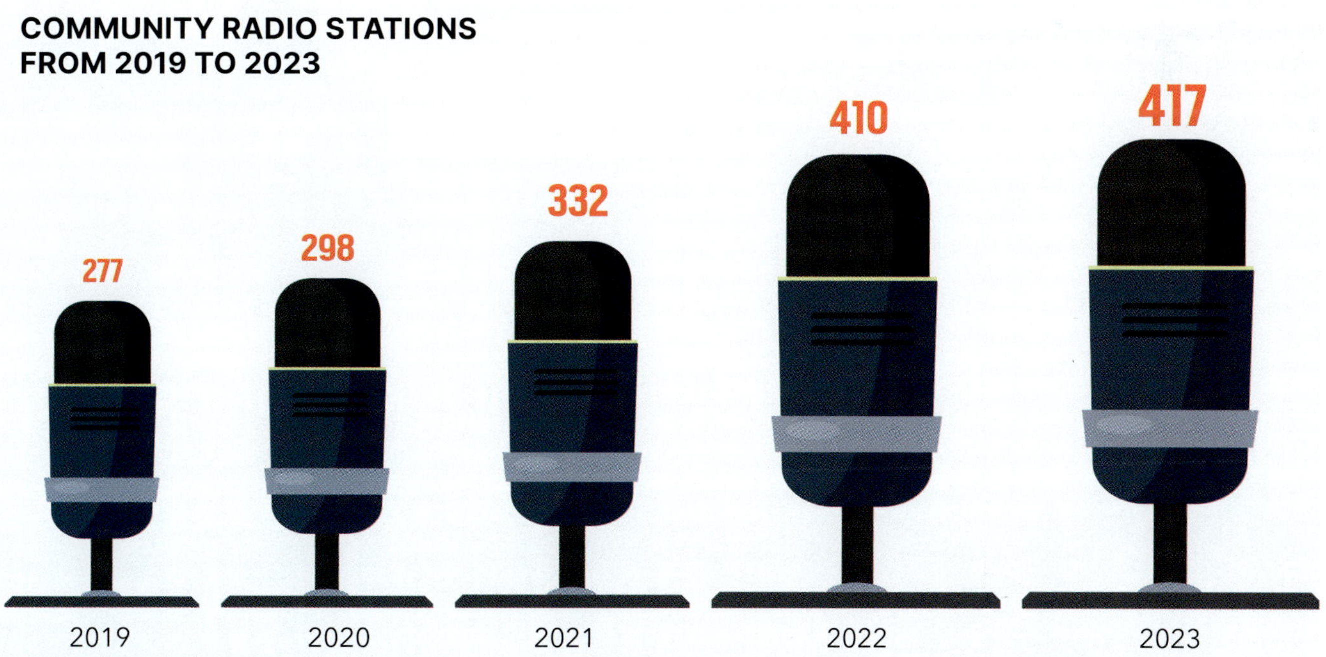

Source: Statistical Handbook on Media and Entertainment Sector 2022-23, Ministry of Information and Broadcasting

History of All India Radio

Broadcasting in India began in 1923 with the Radio Club of Bombay, preceding the establishment of All India Radio by over a decade. The Indian Broadcasting Company (IBC) was formed in 1927 but it dissolved in under three years, leading to the experimental Indian Broadcasting Service in 1930. By 1936, it was renamed All India Radio, and it became a part of the Department of Information and Broadcasting in 1941. At independence, AIR operated six stations in India, with limited coverage of 2.5% of the area and 11% of the population. As of 2024, AIR operates an extensive network of over 500 radio stations and is working toward complete digitization of its broadcasting services. Approximately 900 million people in India have access to DRM broadcasts, and over 6 million DRM-compatible car receivers are already in use. This expansion aligns with the government's efforts to enhance radio accessibility and quality across urban and rural areas.

Akashvani Bhawan, All India Radio headquarters, New Delhi

First broadcasting company

The Indian Broadcasting Company (IBC) was set up in Bombay, on 23 July 1927, with a medium-wave transmitter that had a range of 50 km.

First national broadcast of a play

In July 1956, AIR first aired a play that was broadcast countrywide. The play was *Prafulla* by Girish Chandra Ghosh. It was a Bangla stage play.

First news bulletin

The first news bulletin over radio was aired in English on 23 July 1927 from the Indian Broadcasting Company's station in Mumbai. As the station did not have a news bureau, the bulletin was based on news supplied by Reuters.

First sponsored programme

A musical programme, *Saridon Ke Saathi*, sponsored by Saridon, was aired on 3 May 1970 on the Mumbai–Pune–Nagpur radio network.

First cricket commentary

On 1 January 1936, Bertie Meyer provided commentary for a match between the All-India XI and the maharaja of Patiala's Australian XI, from the Bombay station of AIR from 12:46 p.m. to 1:00 p.m.

Highest radio station

The Himbotingla station of AIR in Ladakh, located at an altitude of 4,053.84 m (13,300 ft) above mean sea level, is the highest radio station in the world. The 10 kW, high-power transmitters were inaugurated on 25 September 2021.

Most commercial radio programmes anchored

The legendary radio announcer and programme anchor Ameen Sayani started his broadcasting career in 1951. During his career, he compèred more than 10,000 commercial radio programmes, and voiced 12,000 spots and jingles. He produced more than 38,920 publicity programmes for feature films.

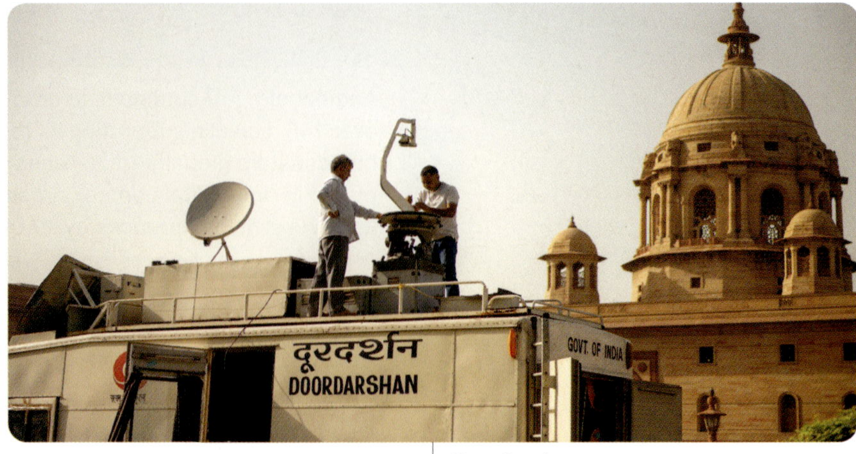

Doordarshan

First phone-in programme

Phone-in programmes were introduced on 10 January 1993 at AIR, Delhi.

First national programme of talks

On 29 July 1953, AIR aired the first national programme of talks in English.

First relay between radio stations

On 18 January 1939, an inter-station relay took place between Delhi and Bombay.

TELEVISION

First simultaneous tele-broadcast

Om Namah Shivay, directed by Dheeraj Kumar, was the first tele-serial to be telecast and broadcast at the same time on television and radio from March 1999.

First national telecast

Doordarshan (DD) started nationwide telecasts on 15 August 1982 from its TV studio in Mandi House New Delhi.

Longest running non-fiction TV series

Krishi Darshan, a TV programme aimed at disseminating useful information on farming to rural areas and agricultural communities, started on 26 January 1967 on DD National and still continues on the channel as well as on DD Kisan. It is considered to be the longest-running non-fiction TV series.

First private producer of national news

In February 1995, New Delhi Television Ltd (NDTV) became the first private producer of national news with the show titled *The News Tonight*, which was hosted by Prannoy Roy at 8:00 p.m. They were the first private broadcasters for news on Doordarshan.

First central production centre

Set up in 1989 at the Siri Fort Complex, New Delhi, the Central Production Centre began with two large studios

Ameen Sayani

Dheeraj Kumar

Siri Fort Auditorium

equipped with modern facilities to produce high-quality, well-researched programmes.

First director general of Doordarshan

P.V. Krishnamoorthy became the first director general of Doordarshan on 1 April 1976, the day Doordarshan and AIR were each given separate status.

Tallest TV tower

The tallest TV tower in India is located in Rameswaram, Tamil Nadu. The height of the tower is 323 m (1,060 ft). The tower was built in 1995 and is used by Doordarshan for television broadcasting. It is made of reinforced cement concrete, and the mast is of lattice steel.

Rameswaram TV tower

First newsreader

Doordarshan began a five-minute news bulletin in 1965 with Pratima Puri as the first TV newsreader.

First high-definition channel

The first high-definition (HD) channel was introduced in India by Discovery Communications in March 2010.

First in Television

First telecast

The first experimental telecast was carried out in Delhi on 15 September 1959 from a makeshift studio with the help of a single transmitter of 500W, which carried signals up to 25 km for an operational time of an hour a day. The studio was relocated to Rajpath for the first live telecast of the Republic Day parade in 1960.

First colour TVs

In 1982, the year India hosted the Asiad (Asian Games), colour TVs were introduced in India.

First colour transmission

An experimental telecast was conducted from the Madras TV station on 18 July 1980 for one hour. It was transmitted to Delhi viewers.

First TV station to get a second channel

Delhi was the first TV station to get a second channel on 17 September 1984.

First satellite linkage

The first satellite linkage experiment was launched on 1 August 1975 in six states in the country for one year. Later, satellite channels were available for the first time in 1991 to a select few who had access to the powerful dish antennas in embassies and five-star hotels.

First private channel

Zee TV, the first private television channel in the country, was launched in October 1992 in collaboration with Star TV and Zee Telefilms Ltd.

First business channel

Asia Business News International (ABNI), a 24/7 business channel, was launched on 14 February 1996 by the Hinduja Group in collaboration with Asia Business News (ABN) and TV18.

First private satellite channel

Aaj Tak was the first private satellite channel permitted in 2000.

First 24-hour news channel

Star News, India's first 24-hour news channel, started on 3 February 1998, with news updates every hour from 6:00 a.m.

First infotainment channel

DD-3, which was Doordarshan's dedicated channel for infotainment, was launched on 14 November 1995.

First teleshopping programme

Shopping through TV was introduced on 1 January 1995, with an hour-long home-shopping show on Doordarshan's Metro channel in Delhi.

First serial

Teesra Rasta was the first fiction serial telecast from Doordarshan Kendra, New Delhi, starting from 2 May 1962.

First Indian animation serial

Featuring Ghayab, the do-gooder ghost, *Ghayab Aya* was the first fully 'made-in-India' serialized animation film telecast on Doordarshan in 1986. The animator director was the well-known painter-illustrator Suddhasattwa Basu.

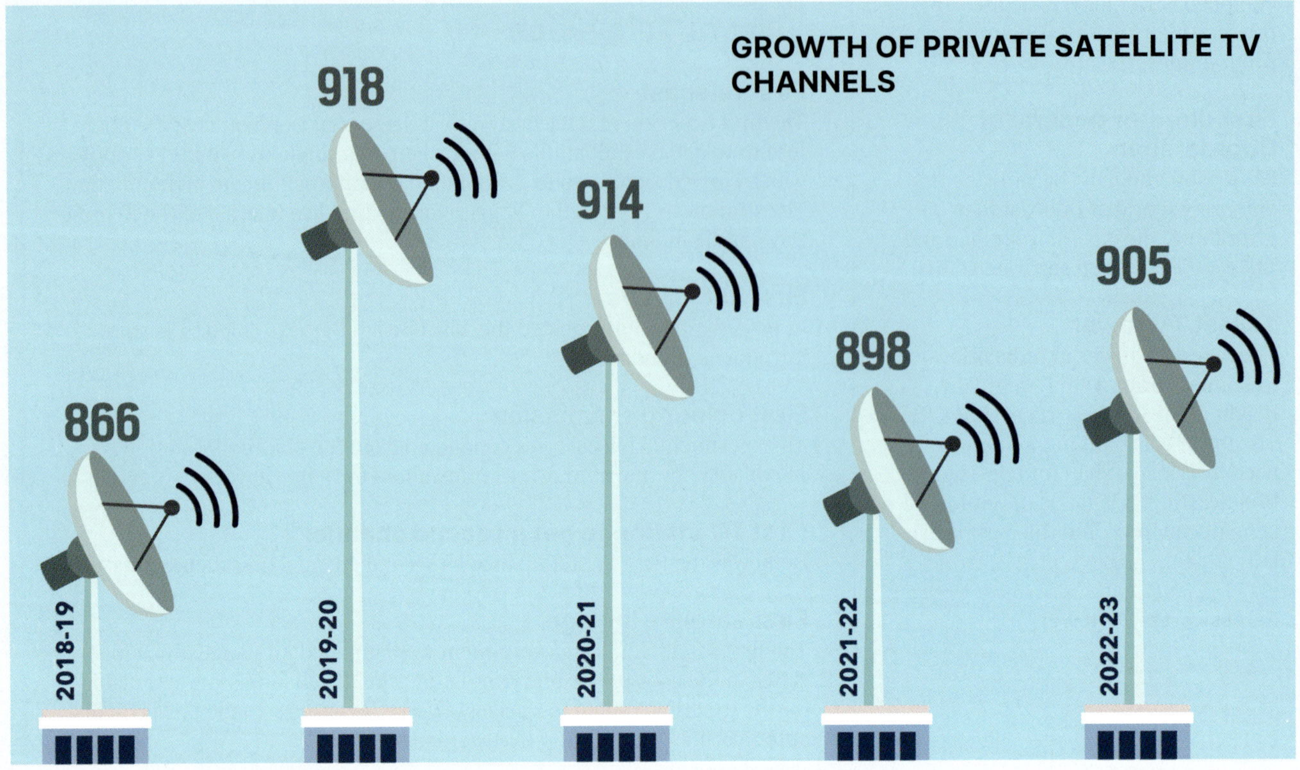

Source: Statistical Handbook on Media and Entertainment Sector 2022-23, Ministry of Information and Broadcasting

GROWTH TRENDS IN MEDIA AND ENTERTAINMENT SECTOR*

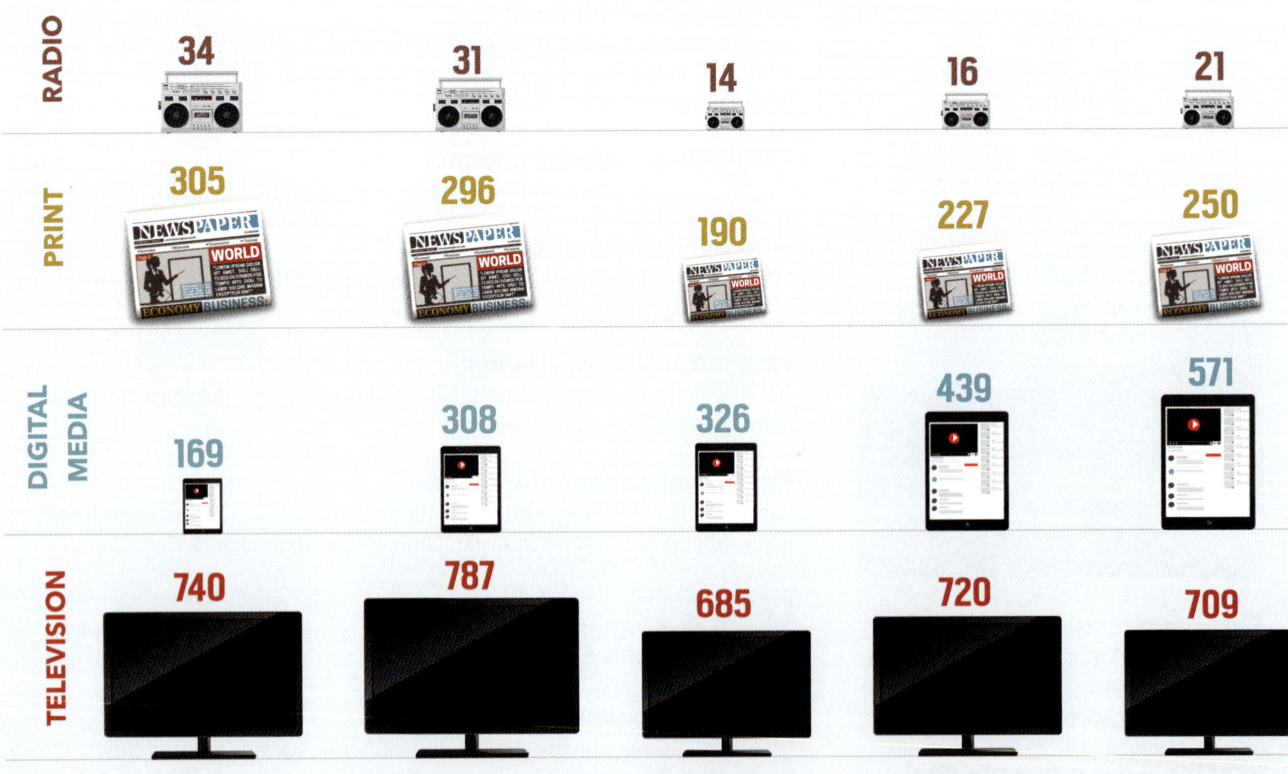

*Figures are in gross of taxes (INR billion) for calendar years

Source: Statistical Handbook on Media and Entertainment Sector 2022-23, Ministry of Information and Broadcasting

History of Television in India

Television came to India in 1959 and was transmitted from Delhi. It had a makeshift audio, a low-power transmitter and only twenty-one community television sets. In 1972 services were expanded to Mumbai, and by 1975 stations popped up in Calcutta, Chennai, Srinagar, Amritsar, and Lucknow. Prasar Bharati, a board formed by the Government of India ran a public broadcast television channel called Doordarshan (DD) and it is now one of the largest broadcasting organizations in the world in terms of infrastructure of studios and transmitters. DD became national when it began to telecast national programmes in the year 1982, and this was the same year when colour TVs were introduced to the Indian market.

First DTH service

Launched on 2 October 2013, Dish TV was the first Direct-to-Home (DTH) service in India.

First sci-fi serial

Space City Sigma, produced by Studio Ifekt, was telecast from 21 May 1989.

Most watched daily soap

Anupamaa, starring Rupali Ganguly and Sudhanshu Panday, is the most watched daily soap in India between 21 and 27 October, according to the Broadcast Audience Research Council (BARC).

Satyajit Ray

First video film

Teri Meri Kahani, the first video film, was produced by B.R. Chopra in 1981.

B.R.Chopra

First telefilm

Satyajit Ray's *Sadgati* was telecast on the national network on 13 April 1981. This 52 min. telefilm was based on Munshi Premchand's short story. Produced by Doordarshan, it starred well-known actors, such as Om Puri and Smita Patil.

Dialogue writer with most credited episodes – tv series – fiction

Munisha Rajpal, from Andheri West, Mumbai has been the dialogue writer for the tv show Yeh Rishta Kya Kehlata Hai for over ten years, eleven months, and fourteen days. She has been credited with 2,863 episodes.

POST AND PHILATELY

Earliest postal communication

- In India, the earliest evidence of a systematic mail service is found during the reign of Chandragupta Maurya (r. 321–297 BCE), who ruled from Magadha (now in southern Bihar). In his empire, confidential reports were dispatched from the emperor to the outlying provinces, and from the provinces back to the ruler.
- The first recorded mention of a postal service was made by Ziauddin Barani, who wrote that Alauddin Khilji (r. 1296–1316) organized a regular foot-runner service, called *harkara*, as early as 1296. These harkaras carried a baton with bells and ran across allotted territory, carrying mail in a relay system with the runners changing every mile. Harkaras have faded with the advent of railways in the 19th century, but continue to work in remote areas.
- Sikandar Lodi (r. 1488–1518), a ruler of the Lodi dynasty set up small posts across his kingdom and sent firmans daily to his armies.
- Babur (r. 1483–1530), the founder of the Mughal Empire, set up horse couriers from his capital at Agra up to Kabul, maintaining a regular 'postal' system.

First mail by steamboat

In 1828, mail was sent by a steamboat service between Calcutta (now Kolkata), West Bengal and Allahabad (now Prayagraj), Uttar Pradesh, along 1,266 km of the Ganga River. This is the earliest instance of mail delivery by steamer in Asia.

First Indian to host the Emmy awards

Stand-up comedian and Indian actor Vir Das is scheduled to be the host for the 2024 International Emmy Awards by the International Academy of Television Arts and Sciences. It marks Das's return to the International Emmy stage after he won the best comedy award for his Netflix stand-up special Vir Das: Landing, in 2023.

Post under British rule

- The first superintendent of post offices was appointed in Allahabad, Uttar Pradesh, in 1870.
- British India became the first non-founding member of the General Postal Union in 1876.

First window delivery of letters

The Madras General Post Office or GPO (now in Chennai, Tamil Nadu) began the window delivery of letters from 1 June 1786 in the then Fort St George Square.

Madras General Post Office

First postal training centre

Established on 2 April 1951, the postal training centre at Saharanpur, Uttar Pradesh, was the first training centre in Asia, set up exclusively for postal and telegraph personnel.

First electronic Indian Postal Order

On 22 March 2013, the first electronic Indian Postal Order (E-IPO) was introduced for Indian nationals living abroad. On 14 February 2014, the service was also extended to all Indian citizens.

Largest postal network

With a network of 1,56,434 post offices, the Indian Department of Posts has the world's largest postal network as recorded till 31 March 2021.

First postcard

The Postal and Telecommunications Department issued the first postcard on 1 July 1879.

First hot-air balloon carrying mail

A special postal cover was carried in a hot-air balloon carrier of India Post from Sakthi Mills Ground, Pollachi, Coimbatore District, Tamil Nadu, to the postmaster of Kovipalayam, Pollachi, on 3 January 2016.

First delivery peons

- Men: Postmen or delivery peons were first engaged on a security bond with a specific responsibility, as part of postal reforms carried out in Bengal in 1840. They were dressed in uniform and wore badges supplied by post offices. They were allowed to earn baksheesh of 2 pies (1 pie = 1/192 of a rupee) on each letter delivered, in addition to the collection of postage due to the post office.
- Women: K. Padmakshi Amma, who worked in the Thiruvananthapuram postal division in Kerala, joined service on 19 February 1959 as the country's first postwoman.

First Indian postmaster general

- *Man:* Rai Bahadur Saligram became the first Indian postmaster general for the North-Western Provinces in 1881.
- *Woman:* Sushila Chaurasia, who was born in Bijapur, Karnataka, in 1923, was the first woman to become postmaster general in the country. She assumed charge of the Madhya Pradesh circle on 24 May 1979.

First woman postal inspector

R. Santhakumari, who was from the Thiruvananthapuram postal division, Kerala, passed the inspector's examination in 1968 to become the first woman postal inspector.

First letter by airmail

The first airmail letter was introduced in the country in November 1944. Priced at six annas, the airmail letter was called an 'aerogramme' and could be sent to the UK and other countries under the British Empire.

First aerial post image

General Post Office, a building built in colonial architectural style in the B.B.D. Bagh area of Calcutta

First insured mail service

The system of insurance post for letters and parcels, which was then called the 'insured mail service', was introduced on 1 January 1878.

First dead letter office

A post office for undelivered, unclaimed letters and letters with incomplete addresses was set up during 1834–37 in Benson Town in Bangalore. It was also called a Returned Letter Office.

First post office savings bank account

The post office savings bank, which started on 1 April 1882, introduced the then revolutionary concept of banking with a post office instead of a bank, which had been the usual method of keeping one's savings.

First all-woman post office

• Avinashilingam Home Science College post office in Coimbatore, Tamil Nadu, which opened in January 1966, was the first all-woman post office in India.

• A post office, which started functioning at Manoramaganj in Indore, Madhya Pradesh, on 31 March 1976, is also fully run by women employees only.

First computerized registration centre

The first computerized registration centre (CRC) was opened in June 1996 at the Market Road wing of the New Delhi General Post Office (GPO).

Mahatma Gandhi stamps

Stamps from most countries in honour of a person

Stamps in honour of Mahatma Gandhi have been issued from over 150 countries up to 2019.

First drive-in post office

A drive-in post office was inaugurated on 11 November 1975 in Pune, Maharashtra.

First mobile post office

On 1 November 2011, the Department of Post, Government of India, launched the Post Office on Wheels initiative with its first mobile van running in Pune, Maharashtra. The van worked from 8:00 a.m. to 8:00 p.m. daily covering 30 locations in a week, stopping at each location for two hours. The van offered all types of postal services, including e-enabled services, selling postcards, opening a new savings account, and selling postal life insurance, among others. The services were resumed during the lockdown period in 2020 due

India's first 3D post office

India's first 3D post office was inaugurated in Cambridge Layout near Ulsoor Bazaar, Bengaluru. The construction of the building began in April 2023 and was completed in a period of 45 days. The building was constructed using 3D printing technology and was carried out by Larsen and Toubro Limited while IIT Madras guided them in structural design.

to Covid-19, to deliver pensions and provide mobile services in states such as Kerala and Uttar Pradesh.

First parcel service

Originally known as Bhangy post, parcel service was introduced on 2 December 1884. Its name came from the *bhangy* or bamboo stick with parcels on either end that the parcel carriers balanced on their shoulders.

First registered mail service

The first mention of a system of registration being adopted by a post office to secure the safety of coins or documents in transit was found in an advertisement published on 20 February 1795. Actual registered post was introduced in Bombay Presidency on 1 November 1849 with a postal notice on 16 October 1849. In Bengal, it was established at Calcutta GPO on 1 January 1851 and later at Madras GPO. The fee was eight annas for registering a letter.

First fully-computerized post office

The Head Post Office located at Sansad Marg, New Delhi, became fully computerized on 24 June 1998.

First letter boxes away from post offices

A great reform in the history of Indian post took place in October 1854 with the introduction of letter boxes located away from post offices.

First automatic mail processing centre (AMPC)

The first AMPC was launched at the Mumbai GPO, Maharashtra, on 29 April 1993, and a second one was established at Chennai, Tamil Nadu, in October 1995.

Longest-serving postmaster

Brother K.V.S.J. Peter, who received a Padma Shri in 1983, was the longest - serving postmaster, for 68 years. He took charge of the Shenbaganur post office in Dindigul District, Tamil Nadu, on 12 September 1913, and was in service till 8 February 1982.

First express mail service

Speed Post was introduced by the Government of India on 1 August 1986, connecting seven cities in the country, and five other countries to India.

Stamps to commemorate festival of India in the USSR

First stamp to be jointly issued with another country

India and the erstwhile USSR issued a set of two stamps on the Festival of India in the USSR, which was held in August 1990. Both countries issued the stamp with similar designs.

First stamp

The Scinde Dawk (Provincial), India's first half-anna stamp, was issued with the help of Edward Lees Coffey, the postmaster of Karachi, on 1 July 1852 in Scinde District, Karachi (now in Pakistan). It was embossed on circular red wafers used as seals on letters, with the East India Company emblem and the legend Scinde District Dawk around the circumference. It was Asia's first ever adhesive stamp. It was withdrawn in 1854.

First airmail

India became the first country in the world to send mail by plane when 6,500 letters and postcards were flown from Allahabad to Naini (a distance of only 18 km!) in Uttar Pradesh in a Humber-Sommer biplane by Henri Pequet on 18 February 1911. A pictorial postmark showing the aeroplane was used.

First Indian stamp featuring a woman

The Indian saints and poets series, issued on 1 October 1952, featured Mirabai, the 16th-century Bhakti poet-saint.

First customization of stamps

Initially introduced in India during the World Philatelic Exhibition 'INDIPEX-2011', 'My Stamp' is the scheme for personalized sheets of postage stamps of India Post. Such a sheet has a thumbnail image, for example–the customer's photograph, logos of institutions, artwork, famous tourist places, historical cities, heritage buildings, or wildlife, on a selected template sheet featuring postage stamps. The facility is available for both non-corporate and corporate entities.

Stamp printed for Indipex-2011

First state to issue a stamp (pre-1947)

Kathiawar state in Saurashtra (later Gujarat) issued a one-anna stamp in November 1864 with the inscription 'Saurashtra Post 1864–65'.

First differently shaped stamps

- **Polygonal:** The four-anna indigo-and-red stamp of India, issued on 15 October 1854, was polygonal, with the top and side panels raised from the main frame, which was slightly curved.
- **Circular:** The earliest circular stamp was the Scinde Dawk, though only the first printing was circular in the true sense since the later versions were issued on sheets that were usually cut square. It was the first circular stamp issued not only in India but in all of Asia. Later, the states of Indore (1889) and Jammu and Kashmir (1866–78) issued similar circular stamps.
- **Triangular:** Stamps of this shape were issued on 10 October 1985 by the Border Roads Organization.
- **Oval:** The half-anna red

Triangular stamp of India

stamp, issued by the Indian state of Bhor (now in Maharashtra) in 1879, was oval in a horizontal format. It was imperforate and had to be cut out.

- **Diamond-shaped:** Depicting Raja Ram Mohan Roy, these stamps were issued on 27 September 1964.
- **Trimmed:** These revenue stamps, reissued for postal use in 1866, had their inscriptions cut off at the top and bottom.
- **Octagonal:** A set of six octagon-shaped commemorative stamps to mark the 150th birth anniversary of Mahatma Gandhi was released on 2 October 2019 for the first time.

First stamp designer (pre-Independence)

Captain H.E.L. Thuillier, the deputy surveyor general of India, who was then stationed in Calcutta designed the first lithographic stamps, which were issued in 1854 and said to be engraved by an artist called Munirooddin.

First stamp of independent India

A 3.5-anna stamp with the inscription 'Jai Hind' was issued on 21 November 1947.

First one-rupee charity stamp

The first charity stamps were issued on 26 January 1950. Three 'Healthy India' charity stamps were brought out in denominations of one anna, four annas, and one rupee.

First miniature sheet

To commemorate the India International Philatelic Exhibition 1973 in Delhi, a miniature sheet with a face value of ₹4.65 was issued on 14 November 1973.

First national philatelic museum

The National Philatelic Museum of India was established in New Delhi on 6 July 1968. It has large collections of postage stamps printed and issued by India and former princely states of India, early essays, proofs, and colour trials, Indian stamps used abroad, early Indian postcards, postal stationery, and other thematic collections. It also has a philatelic bureau and postal objects such as letter boxes from Victorian times.

First autograph-inscribed stamp

A stamp issued on 7 May 1961 to commemorate the birth centenary of Nobel laureate Rabindranath Tagore had his signature inscribed on it.

Rabindranath Tagore stamp

First philatelic society

The Philatelic Society of India, the country's first philatelic society, was formed in Mumbai on 6 March 1897.

First stamp featuring wildlife

The first Indian stamp depicting an animal was released in 1962, and it was a 15-paisa stamp showing the Indian rhinoceros. Next year, five more such stamps came out, featuring the Indian gaur (10 paise), the red panda (15 paise), the Indian elephant (30 paise), the Bengal tiger (50 paise), and the Asiatic lion (one rupee).

Rhino stamp

First Indian president of Federation Internationale de Philatelie (FIP)

Late D.N. Jatia, a reputed philatelist, was elected president at the 59th Congress of the FIP in London, UK, on 14 May 1990.

Largest philatelic bureau

Mumbai General Post Office Philatelic Bureau also an international philatelic bureau, is the largest in the country.

First philatelic exhibition

The Philatelic Society of Bengal held an exhibition of postage stamps at the art gallery of the Government School of Art (now renamed the Government College of Art and Craft) in Calcutta in December 1894.

First commemorative stamps

A set of six stamps was issued on 9 February 1931 on the laying of the foundation of New Delhi as the new capital of India. These were the first pictorial stamps depicting the important landmarks of the city.

First Indian to design a stamp for the United Nations

Dipok Dey (b. 1938) from Calcutta was the first Indian to design a stamp for the UN in 1985. The stamp was based on the theme of child survival.

First international stamp exhibition

'India 80' was the first international stamp exhibition held in Asia under the patronage of the Federation Internationale de Philatelie (FIP), held from 25 January 1980 to 3 February 1980.

National Philatelic Museum

TELECOM

First Indian radio telegraphy company

The Indian Radio Telegraphy Co. was established in 1923, which ushered in the era of wireless telegraphy.

First Indo-European telegraph line

The first independent double line of telegraph from London, UK, to Karachi via Tehran, and Iran, which was constructed by M/s Siemens and Co., was opened for operations on 31 January 1870.

First fibre-optic link

India's first fibre-optic link was made in 1979 when Hindustan Cables Ltd's office at Shivaji Nagar, Pune, Maharashtra, was linked to the Cotton Telephone Exchange, a distance of 4 km.

First submarine cable link

Madras was linked to Penang, Malaysia, in 1886 with a submarine telegraph cable.

First director general of the telegraph service

Sir William O'Shaughnessy was appointed as chief superintendent of telegraphs in 1857 in colonial India.

William Brooke O'Shaughnessy

First manufacturer of telephones

- A telecommunication maintenance and repair shop was set up at Alipore, Calcutta, in 1860. The manufacture of minor components that were needed for the Baudot Telegraph and Line stores was initiated at the P&T workshop in 1913.
- The Indian Telephone Industries Ltd was established at Doorvaninagar near Bangalore, in July 1948 for manufacturing automatic and carrier equipment. The local assembly of phones from imported parts began in 1948, and the first phone off-the-line was produced on 26 January 1949.
- The first telephone with indigenous components was made in 1951.

A radio telephone

First radio phone link

On 1 May 1933, Sir Samuel Hoare, the then Secretary of State for India under British rule, spoke from London, UK, to Sir Frederick Sykes, governor of Bombay, on radio phone, thus establishing a communication network between Britain and India.

First STD service

The facility for subscriber trunk dialling (STD) was first started between Lucknow and Kanpur in Uttar Pradesh on 26 November 1960.

Last telegram

India's 163-year-old telegram service ended at 11:45 p.m. on 14 July 2013. Its last message was booked at the Central Telegraph Office, Janpath, New Delhi, by Ashwani Mishra, who sent telegrams to Congress leader Rahul Gandhi and the DD news director general S.M. Khan.

First known use of SOS signal

On 1 November 1977, the duty operator in the astral wireless station at Ennore, near Madras, received a weak SOS call from a cargo ship in the Bay of Bengal, stating that its engine room was on fire. The call was acknowledged and rescue ships reached in an hour.

First ISD service

The Arvi earth station for satellite communication, set up in 1971 in Arvi near Poona (now Pune), Maharashtra, marked the introduction of the first operator dialled service to international subscribers. The first intercontinental telephone exchange was commissioned in 1973, and the first international subscriber dialling (ISD) telephone service was introduced between Bombay, and London in 1976.

First SMS provider

Hutchison Max Telecom Ltd. offered a global text messaging service (SMS) in India in 2001.

First automatic telephone exchange

The first automatic telephone system in the country was commissioned at Simla (now Shimla), Himachal Pradesh, in 1914. The exchange had 400 working lines and another 300 lines in reserve.

First push-button telephone

The first Indian firm to manufacture electronic push-button phone answering machines was Bharti Telecom Ltd. It was also the first Indian company to launch cordless phones that were called 'Beetel'.

First call using a mobile phone

On 31 July 1995, the then Union telecom minister Sukh Ram and the then West Bengal chief minister Jyoti Basu spoke to each other using hand-held mobile phones, over Modi Telstra's MobileNet service.

First carrier to demonstrate 5G service capability

Bharti Airtel became the first carrier to successfully demonstrate live 5G service over a commercial network on 28 January 2021 in Hyderabad, Telangana. The carrier was capable

Bharti Airtel store, Udaipur

> The Oriental Telephone Company was established on 25 January 1881. It was an agreement between Thomas Edison, Alexander Graham Bell, the Oriental Bell Telephone Company of New York and the Anglo-Indian Telephone Company Ltd. The company was licensed to sell telephones in Greece, Turkey, South Africa, India, Japan, China, and other Asian countries.

of delivering 10x speed, 10x latency (the time it takes for data to pass from one point on a network to another), and 100x concurrency (the execution of multiple instruction sequences at the same time) in comparison with existing technologies.

First cellular operators' association

The Cellular Operators Association of India (COAI), Delhi, was set up in 1995.

Mobile tower at the highest altitude

Installed by BSNL with the help of the Indian Army's Trishul Signallers, the highest mobile tower is located at 4,877 m (16,000 ft) in Chongtash in Ladakh. With this tower, even the remotest regions of Ladakh are connected by a communication link.

First circle launch

In 1996, Bharti Mobile Ltd, which was a joint venture of Bharti Enterprises with Telia Company of Sweden, launched Airtel, the first to provide services in a circle (outside metros) in Himachal Pradesh.

Service area with largest access subscriber base

Uttar Pradesh (East), with 98.14 million (9.814 crore) wireless and wireline subscribers, has the largest subscriber base (September 2020).

First national/international roaming service

On 12 September 1997, the Department of Telecommunications (DoT), Ministry of Communications, Government of India, cleared a national automatic roaming facility for cellular operators in Delhi, Mumbai, Calcutta and Chennai. International roaming facility was approved on 12 January 1998.

Largest wireline service provider

Reliance Jio is the largest wireline service provider in India with a market share of approximately 34.7 per cet as of December 2023. Airtel is the second-largest provider with a market share of 25.24 per cent.

First net fax service

Satyamfax, launched by Satyam Infoway on 25 April 2000 at Chennai, Tamil Nadu, in technical association with Singapore Telecom, was the first to provide fax to fax, web to fax, email to fax, and PC desktop to fax services.

First telephone exchange

In 1881, the Government of India licensed the Oriental Telephone Company to set up telephone exchanges

BSNL office, Delhi

in Calcutta, Bombay, Madras, and Karachi. A 50-line exchange was set up in Calcutta in 1881 as one of the oldest exchanges in the world. It was set up only five years after the invention of the telephone.

First internet telephony service

On 25 July 2018, government-owned Bharat Sanchar Nigam Limited launched India's first internet telephony service that allows users to dial any phone number in India through its mobile app.

Telstra headquarters, Australia

First cellular service

Modi Telstra, a joint-venture company of the B.K. Modi Group and the Telstra Corporation of Australia, inaugurated the first commercial cellular service in India on 23 August 1995. The network was constructed by Telecommunication Engineering Centre and the Modi Telstra team.

State/UT with highest tele-density

Delhi has the highest tele-density (number of fixed landline telephone connections) with over 278 telephones per 100 people as of December 2023.

Largest wireless service provider

Reliance Jio was the leading wireless service provider with 459.81 million subscribers, followed by Bharti Airtel with 381.73 million subscribers, as of 2024.

Service provider with number of rural subscribers – wireless

Reliance Jio has 179.31 million rural subscribers, which amounts to 33.47 per cent of total rural wireless subscribers. It is followed by Bharti Airtel with 168.63 million rural subscribers and Vodafone Idea with 149.93 rural subscribers up till March 2021.

INTERNET, SOCIAL MEDIA, AND APPS

First provider of Internet services

Videsh Sanchar Nigam Limited (VSNL), under Department of Telecommunications (DoT), Ministry of Telecommunications, Government of India, was the first provider of Internet services in the country. It was launched on 15 August 1995.

First 3G operators

- The public sector telecom service provider Mahanagar Telephone Nigam Limited (MTNL) first provided 3G mobile service to parts of Delhi. This service started on 11 December 2008.
- Tata Docomo launched its 3G mobile service in many states – Rajasthan, Uttar Pradesh (West), Gujarat, Maharashtra (except Mumbai), Haryana, Punjab, Kerala, Karnataka, and Madhya Pradesh – on 5 November 2010. It was he first private 3G operator in India.

First private Internet service provider (ISP)

Satyam Infoway (Sify) became the country's first private internet service provider company on 22 November 1998.

First mobile app store

Airtel App Central was the first Indian mobile application store in the country. It was launched by Bharti Airtel Ltd on 9 February 2010.

First Aadhaar-based payment app

The Government of India launched Bharat Interface for Money (BHIM) app, an Aadhaar-based mobile app for digital payments, on 30 December 2016.

First free email service

Conceived by Sabeer Bhatia (and colleague Jack Smith), Hotmail was the first free email service that took the whole world by storm in 1996. Bhatia was a Bengaluru-born Indian-American businessman and led Hotmail as its president and CEO, until its eventual acquisition by Microsoft in 1998.

TCS headquarters, previously called VSNL

Top Internet subscription – service areas – both wired and wireless

The highest-subscription service areas in the country are the states of Uttar Pradesh (East+ West) (87.88 million/8.78 crore), Maharashtra (61.42 million/ 6.14 crore), Andhra Pradesh (56.73 million/5.67 crore), Tamil Nadu (50.42 million/ 5.04 crore) and Madhya Pradesh (47.23 million/4.72 crore).

Reliance and Disney merger

The Competition Commission of India approved a merger between Disney Star and Reliance Industries. The joint venture is valued at ₹70, 350 crore and it will combine various media assets including channels such as Colors, Star Plus, and Star Gold, along with OTT platforms such as JioCinema and Hotstar and will gain exclusive rights to distribute Disney films and productions in India.

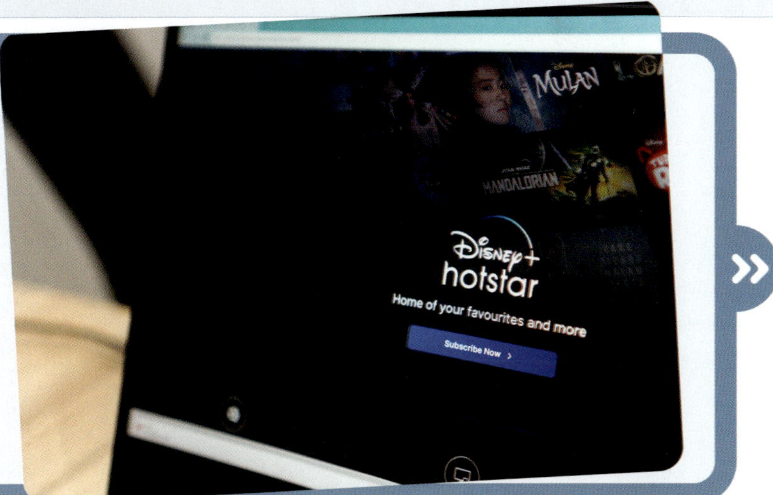

Largest WhatsApp user base in the world

India remained WhatsApp's biggest market with 40 crore (400 million) monthly active users, who exchange around 6,000 crore (60 billion) messages daily (as of July 2019). The country has been the biggest market for WhatsApp since November 2015.

Largest Facebook user base

With 310 million (31 crore) active users, India emerged as Facebook's largest audience in July 2020.

Highest data consumption

India has the highest data consumption of 11 gigabyte/month per user on an average.

Most number of mobile app downloads

India had the most number of mobile app downloads, 7 billion (700 crore), on the Apple iOS Appstore as well as on Google Playstore in the second quarter of 2020. It is followed by the USA with 375 crore (3.75 billion) and Brazil with 300 crore (3 billion).

Most popular search engine

Google, with a user base of 93.4 per cent, is the favourite search engine in India.

Most popular mobile operating system

The favourite mobile operating system in India is Android with 62 per cent usage; next is Windows with 19.4 per cent usage.

Most viewed Indian video on YouTube

'Phonics Song with TWO Words', an alphabet learning video by ChuChu TV has garnered 4,348,214,171 views on YouTube as on 14 December 2021. The video was posted on 7 March 2014.

Most popular browser

The most popular browser in India is Google Chrome, with a share of 51.91 per cent among all browsers.

First and only 4G, all-Internet protocol network

Reliance Jio, which revolutionized the mobile Internet market in India when it rolled out 4G services in 2016, is the only network in the world to rely solely on 4G Long-Term Evolution (LTE) network, based on Internet telephony, without the backing of the legacy 3G/2G services.

Most subscribed YouTube channel

T-Series (Super Cassettes Industries Pvt. Ltd), a music record label and film production company, became the first YouTube channel in the world to reach 100 million subscribers in May 2019. As of October 2022, it had 226 million (22.6 crore) subscribers.

T-Series: most subscribed YouTube channel

Fastest 4G service provider

Vodafone Idea Ltd is the provider of the fastest 4G network in the country with a download speed of 13.74 megabyte per second and an upload speed of 6.19 Mbps. It is followed by Bharti Airtel and Reliance Jio.

Highest concurrent video viewership

A new world record of 2.57 crore (25.7 million). concurrent viewers was set by Jio Cinema, the official digital streaming partner of the India Premier League (IPL). The record was set for the IPL 2023 match. Viewers came to watch Chennai Super Kings play with the Royal Challengers Bangalore. The previous record was held by Disney+Hotstar which had a record of 2.53 crore (2.53 million).

Most downloaded mobile application

Aarogya Setu, a COVID-19 contact-tracing app launched by the Government of India became the most downloaded application in India and the seventh most downloaded application in the world. It recorded 127.6 million (12.76 crore) installations up till July 2020.

Largest social network penetration

India is the world's second largest market with 34.997 crore (349.97 million) users in 2020. While there are many apps available to the Indian public, YouTube leads with 82 per cent market penetration. It is closely followed by Facebook (76 per cent), WhatsApp (70 per cent), Instagram (64 per cent), and Facebook Messenger (53 per cent), according to the 2019 Q3 figures.

Search...

HISTORICAL PERSPECTIVE

Earliest republic on the subcontinent

Vrijji, a mahajanapada (republic) of ancient India, dating to the sixth century BCE, is believed to be the earliest republic on the Indian subcontinent. It did not have a monarch, but instead a popular assembly of elders carried on the business of state. Vrijji was formed by the union of several clans, including the Lichchhavis, Jnatrikas, and Videhas. Its capital was at Vaishali, in the present-day region of Mithila, Bihar.

First Indo-European alliance

Chandragupta Maurya met Alexander III of Macedon in 327 BCE – after the battle with Porus (or Puru) and the capture of Punjab – and teamed up with him for the capture of Magadha in what may be termed the first Indo–European treaty.

The last act of Malik Naib Kafur, 1316 CE. – 20th century artist's impression

Shortest reign—monarchy

Following the death of Alauddin Khilji (Khilji dynasty) in 1316, Malik Kafur captured the throne of Delhi. His reign lasted between 25 and 30 days. He was ousted by Alauddin's son, Shihabuddin Omar.

First colonial rule

Dom Francisco de Almeida was appointed the first Portuguese viceroy in India by King Manuel I of Portugal in 1505 – marking the first colonial rule in India.

Longest colonial rule

Goa, Daman, and Diu were under colonial rule for the longest period in Indian history – over 450 years. For over a decade after the British had left India, the Portuguese ruled these pockets as 'Estado da India Portuguesa' (the Portuguese State of India). They were liberated by the Indian Army on 19 December 1961.

First woman rulers

- Nayanika from the Satavahana dynasty (first century BCE) is considered the first woman ruler of India. She was a queen regent, who was holding the fort for her son, Satakarni II, when he was a child. She was also the first woman ruler to have coins struck in her name. Nayanika was the wife of King Satakarni I.
- In 1236 CE, when Razia Sultan of the Mamluk dynasty ascended the Delhi throne, she became the first queen regnant in India. Unlike a queen regent, Razia ruled her territory in her own right. She was also the only woman ruler of the Delhi Sultanate.

First Republic Day parade

India became an independent nation on 15 August 1947, and declared itself a sovereign and democratic republic with the promulgation of the Constitution of India on 26 January 1950. The first Republic Day parade was held in 1950 at Irwin Stadium (now known as Major Dhyan Chand National Stadium) in New Delhi. Five years later in 1955 the R-Day parade found a new and permanent venue at Rajpath (now Kartavya Path), New Delhi.

PARTIES AND ELECTIONS

First political organization

The first recorded political organization in the country was the Zamindari Association of Calcutta (now Kolkata), West Bengal. Formally launched in 1838, it was a body of landlords, which changed its name to Landholders' Association shortly after its inception. Its principal organizers were Radhakanta Deb and Prasanna Kumar Tagore. It was set up to defend the landlords against government policies that the Zamindars thought were against their interest. It became defunct in 1851.

Oldest political party

Allan Octavian Hume (1829–1912), a member of the Imperial Civil Service, initiated the events that led to the formation of the first political party in India. Speaking out against British policies in India, in 1883, he exhorted Calcutta University graduates to form their own national political movement. This led to the first session of the Indian National Congress in Bombay (now Mumbai), Maharashtra, in 1885.

A.O. Hume: one of the founders of the first political party

First electoral win by an Indian political party

In the elections held under the provisions of the Government of India Act, 1935, the Indian National Congress formed governments in seven states, in addition to a coalition ministry in Assam. They lasted till October–November 1939, after which they unanimously resigned in protest against the inclusion of Indians in the Second World War.

First chief election commissioner

Sukumar Sen (1898–1963) was India's first chief election commissioner, in office from 21 March 1950 to 19 December 1958. Under his leadership,

The Long and the Short

Longest tenure as president

Dr Rajendra Prasad (1884–1963), a lawyer and freedom fighter who became the first president of India, remained in office for 12 years, 3 months, and 18 days – from 26 January 1950 to 13 May 1962.

Dr Zakir Hussain: shortest tenure as president

Shortest tenure as president

Dr Zakir Hussain (1897–1969), the third president of India, held the office of president from 13 May 1967 until his death, for a little less than two years. He was also the first president to die in harness.

Longest tenure as vice president

This record is shared by Sarvepalli Radhakrishnan and Hamid Ansari. Both were in office for 10 years – May 1952 to May 1962 and August 2007 to August 2017 respectively.

Shortest tenure as vice president

V.V. Giri (1894–1980) was vice president for two years during 1967–69, making his tenure the shortest for a vice president. He was elevated to the post of (acting) president on 24 August 1969, following the death of Dr Zakir Husain, the third president of India.

Jawaharlal Nehru: longest tenure as prime minister

Longest tenure as prime minister

Jawaharlal Nehru (1889–1964), the first prime minister of India served as prime minister until he died on 27 May 1964. His tenure lasted 16 years and 286 days.

Shortest tenure as prime minister

- Chaudhary Charan Singh (1902–87) was prime minister for 171 days from 28 July 1979 to 14 January 1980, making him the shortest-tenured prime minister on record. He was the only prime minister of India who never faced the Parliament.
- Gulzari Lal Nanda had two shorter tenures as acting prime minister, once from 27 May to 9 June 1964, after Jawaharlal Nehru's death, and again from 11 to 24 January 1966, following Lal Bahadur Shastri's demise.

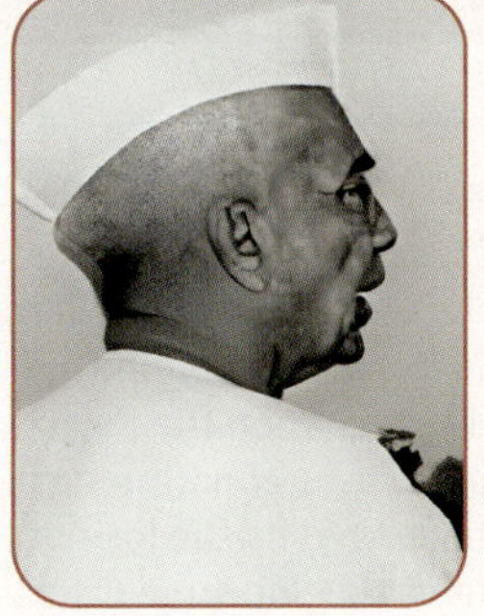

Chaudhary Charan Singh: shortest tenure as prime minister

Longest tenure as chief minister

Pawan Kumar Chamling (former chief minister of Sikkim) has been India's longest-serving chief minister, having served in that post for five terms from 12 December 1994 to 26 May 2019 (24 years and 165 days). He has surpassed the record of Jyoti Basu, who held the office of chief minister of West Bengal from 1 June 1977 to 6 November 2000 (23 years 137 days).

Shortest tenure as chief minister

Jagdambika Pal was chief minister of Uttar Pradesh for one day – on 21 February 1998. Harish Rawat's second term as chief minister of Uttarakhand also lasted a day – 21 April 2016.

the Election Commission of India conducted India's first two general elections, in 1951–52 and 1957. He also administered the first parliamentary elections in Sudan in 1953.

Longest tenure as chief election commissioner

K.V.K. Sundaram (1904–92), India's second chief election commissioner, served for eight years, nine months, and eleven days, from 20 December 1958 to 30 September 1967.

Shortest tenure as chief election commissioner

V.S. Ramadevi (1934–2013), the first woman chief election commissioner (acting) of the country, held the post of chief election commissioner for only 17 days from 26 November 1990 to 12 December 1990.

First general election

First general election

India went to the polls as an independent country for the first time during 1951–52, with 314 constituencies with 1 seat, 86 constituencies with 2 seats, and 1 with 3 seats. There were also 2 nominated Anglo-Indian members. At the time, the Election Commission of India recognized 14 political parties as multi-state parties and 39 parties as state parties. Voting in the election was based on the 'balloting system', i.e., casting votes in ballot boxes allotted to the respective candidates.

National party with most votes

The Congress (I) secured a record 11,52,21,078 votes (78.5 per cent of the total votes) and won 412 out of the 513 parliamentary seats in the elections held in December 1984. This is the largest victory margin of any political party on record.

First use of single ballot paper and single ballot box

The general election of 1962 introduced the single ballot paper system, in which the voter had to mark one choice from the candidates and drop the paper in a ballot box. Earlier, during the 1951–52 and 1957 general elections, there were separate ballot boxes for each candidate with their name and party symbol on them.

First electronic voting machines

Electronic voting machines (EVMs) were used for the first time in the assembly by-elections in Kerala in April 1982. The Election Commission of India (ECI) used EVMs on a trial basis at 50 of 84 polling stations in the Paruvar constituency by-election that year. The machines were developed by the Electronics Corporation of India Ltd (ECIL). However, when the Parur (a village in the Paruvar constituency) contest was challenged by the losing side in the courts, the Supreme Court annulled the elections on account of the use of EVMs, saying the Representation of the People Act, 1951, clearly laid out that votes were to be cast by ballots, not voting machines.

Persisting with its recommendation for EVMs, the ECI recommended an amendment to the said law, which came through in 1989–even though a general consensus about their use came about nearly a decade later in 1998. That year a pilot run was carried out in 25 assembly constituencies in Delhi, Madhya Pradesh, and Rajasthan. The first state assembly elections to have EVMs operationalized in all constituencies were held in 2001 in Kerala, Pondicherry (now Puducherry), Tamil Nadu, and West Bengal. The first general elections to see EVMs deployed (more than a million) in all 543 Lok Sabha constituencies was that of 2004.

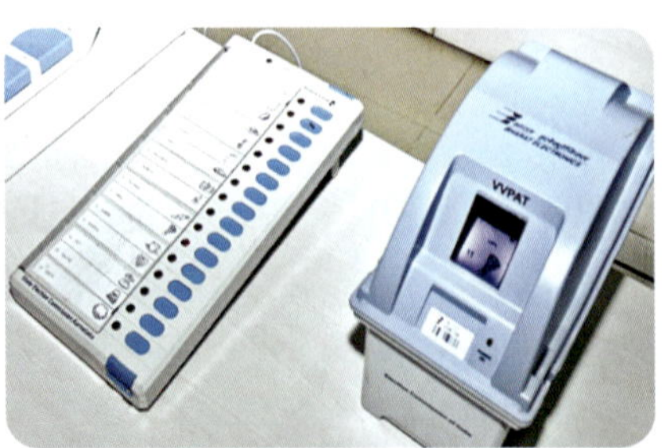

EVM and VVPAT for fair elections

Indelible ink

First use of indelible ink

It is generally believed that indelible ink was used for the first time in the third Lok Sabha elections in 1962. Mysore Paints and Varnish Ltd, based in Mysore (now Mysuru), Karnataka, was authorized to manufacture the ink. The company continues to supply this ink to this date. However, there are sources that date similar use of indelible ink back to the 1952 general election.

First app launched for voter vigilance

For the first time in elections, an application called 'cVIGIL' was launched for citizens to report any malpractice or violation of the model code of conduct before or during elections. This app includes a combination of live photo/ video and time-stamping with auto-location. A government official is bound to respond within 100 minutes. Launched in July 2018, the app was rolled out across India before the 2019 Lok Sabha election.

First 'Others' category of voters
A third gender category of voters, called 'Others', was introduced in the electoral rolls in 2014. As many as 28,314 voters enrolled in this category in 2014 and 38,970 voters in 2019.

First teenage vote
The 61st amendment of the Constitution of India in 1989 lowered the voting age for election to the Lok Sabha and the state legislatures from 21 years to 18 years. As a result, 35.7 million voters in the age group of 18–21 years voted.

First NOTA option

The 2014 general elections were the first to offer Indian voters the option of choosing 'None of the Above' (NOTA), also known as the 'against all' or a 'scratch' vote internationally. The NOTA option provides a neutral vote to those electors who do not wish to vote for any candidate on the electoral ballot. Around 1.04 per cent of voters polled NOTA in the 2019 elections – NOTA received 65.2 lakh votes. However, the number dipped significantly in 2024 to a meagre 1.48 lakh votes.

Lowest voter turnout in the Lok Sabha general election
In the 1951–52 general election, which was the first election to be held in independent India, only 44.87 per cent of the electorate was recorded as having cast their votes.

Highest voter turnout in the Lok Sabha general election
The 2019 general election had the largest voter turnout to date with 61,31,36,854 voters, constituting 67.1 per cent of the total electorate of the country.

Fewest women elected in a general election
Only 19 women were elected in the 1977 general election, which was the fewest ever in the history of general elections.

Most independent candidates elected in a general election
In the history of Indian elections, independent candidates had the most successful run in the 1957 general election, winning 42 seats.

First voter of independent India

Shyam Saran Negi (1 July 1917–5 November 2022), a schoolteacher in Kalpa of Himachal Pradesh, was declared by the Election Commission in 2012 to have been the first to cast his vote in the first general elections of independent India.

Youngest winning candidate in Lok Sabha

Prakash Chandra (b. 29 September 1959) won the Lok Sabha election from Bihar's Barh constituency in 1984. He was 25 years, 3 months, and 3 days old when the eighth Lok Sabha began its term on 31 December 1984. He was a member of the Indian National Congress. His father Ram Lakhan Singh Yadav was a freedom fighter and also a politician of independent India from Bihar.

Samajwadi Party (SP) member Pushpendra Saroj (b. 1 March 1999) is a close contender for the record and lost it just by a day—he was 25 years, 3 months, and 4 days old when the eighteenth Lok Sabha began its term. He contested and won the Kaushambi Lok Sabha seat in Uttar Pradesh in the 2024 general election.

Most women elected in a Lok Sabha general election
Seventy-eight women were elected in the 2019 Lok Sabha general election, making it the election with the highest number of successful female candidates. The number slipped to 74 in 2024.

Most independent candidates in a general election
The 1996 general election had a total of 10,636 independent candidates, the highest ever to date.

Most voter IDs distributed – 1 hr
The district administration of Allahabad (now Prayagraj), Uttar Pradesh, led by District Magistrate Sanjay Kumar and Chief Development Officer Andra Vamsi, conducted the largest ever voter ID distribution camp on 16 February 2017, distributing 12,594 voter ID cards in one hour. The distribution event took place from 11:00 a.m. to 12:00 noon at the Parade Ground in the city.

Fewest independent candidates elected in a general election
Only 3 of the 3,235 independent candidates in the 2014 general election were successful, the lowest win by independents in the history of general elections in India.

Voters with their voter IDs

Lok Sabha Election 2024

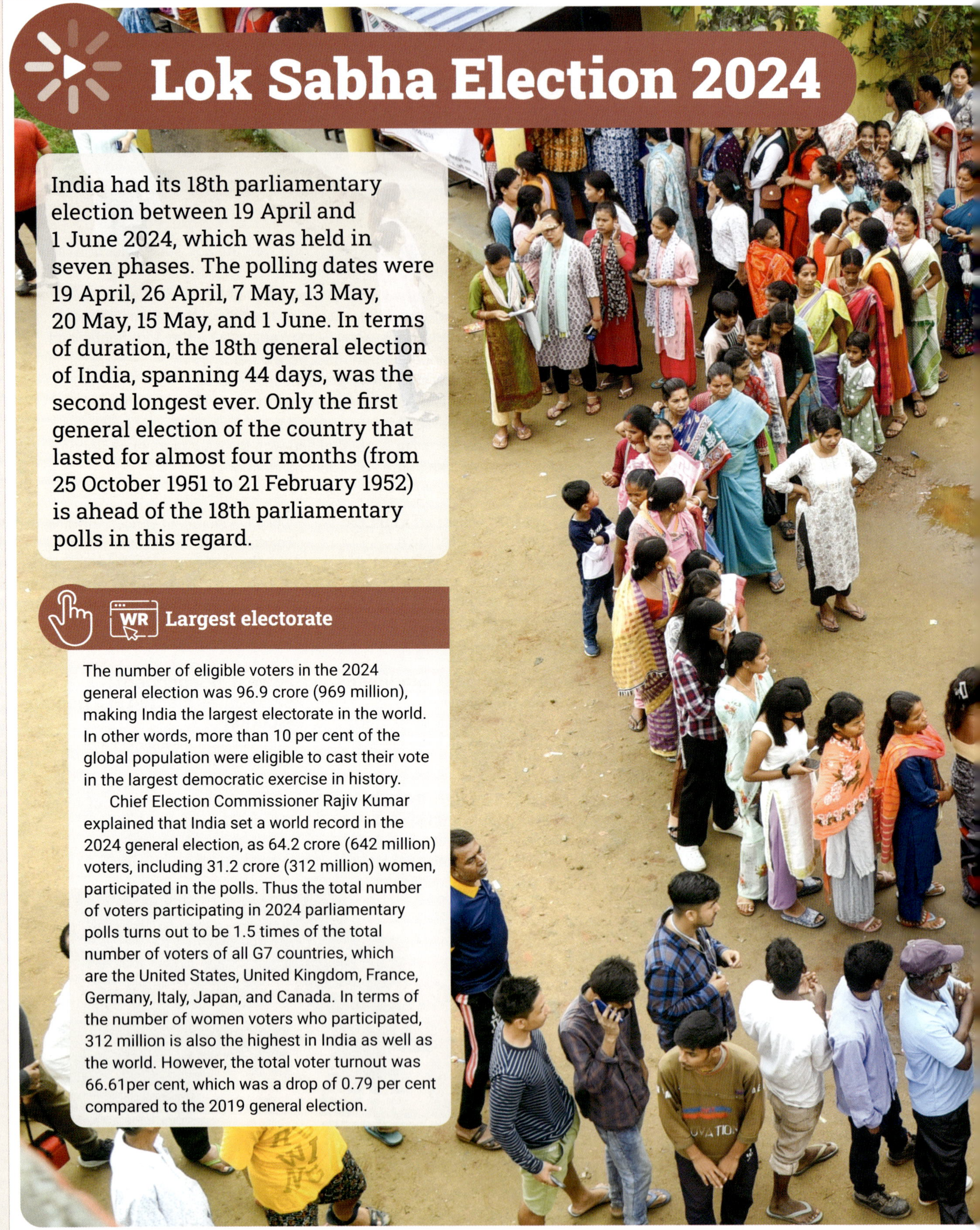

India had its 18th parliamentary election between 19 April and 1 June 2024, which was held in seven phases. The polling dates were 19 April, 26 April, 7 May, 13 May, 20 May, 15 May, and 1 June. In terms of duration, the 18th general election of India, spanning 44 days, was the second longest ever. Only the first general election of the country that lasted for almost four months (from 25 October 1951 to 21 February 1952) is ahead of the 18th parliamentary polls in this regard.

Largest electorate

The number of eligible voters in the 2024 general election was 96.9 crore (969 million), making India the largest electorate in the world. In other words, more than 10 per cent of the global population were eligible to cast their vote in the largest democratic exercise in history.

Chief Election Commissioner Rajiv Kumar explained that India set a world record in the 2024 general election, as 64.2 crore (642 million) voters, including 31.2 crore (312 million) women, participated in the polls. Thus the total number of voters participating in 2024 parliamentary polls turns out to be 1.5 times of the total number of voters of all G7 countries, which are the United States, United Kingdom, France, Germany, Italy, Japan, and Canada. In terms of the number of women voters who participated, 312 million is also the highest in India as well as the world. However, the total voter turnout was 66.61per cent, which was a drop of 0.79 per cent compared to the 2019 general election.

State/UT with the largest electorate

Uttar Pradesh had the largest electorate in the 2024 general election, with 15,41,03,670 eligible voters. This is the largest ever in India.

State/UT with most Lok Sabha seats

Uttar Pradesh had 80 Lok Sabha seats up for grab in the 2024 general election. There were 9 states with just 1 seat each.

State/UT with the smallest electorate

The Union Territory of Lakshadweep had the smallest electorate in the 2024 general election, comprising a total of 57,784 eligible voters. The UT also holds the record for being the constituency with the smallest ever electorate in the country.

Most women candidates in an election

In the 2024 election, 797 women contested (up by 81 candidates from 2019), constituting 9.6 per cent of the total 8,337 candidates.

Despite an increase in the number of women candidates, the total number of women elected to the 18th Lok Sabha dipped to 74 from what was 78 in 2019.

Among states, West Bengal is leading with 11 women MPs. The All India Trinamool Congress fielded 11 women candidates and all of them won the election.

Among political parties, the BJP tops the list, having 31 elected women MPs out of 69 women candidates they fielded.

Almost 1.8 million Voter-Verifiable Paper Audit Trail (VVPAT) systems and 1.7 million control units were deployed for 2024 polls in 1.05 million polling stations across India. The VVPAT system is attached to the EVM to confirm the vote of every voter. It prints a small slip of paper carrying the symbol and name of the candidate voted for. This is visible to every voter and can be later used by the Election Commission of India (ECI) to verify the votes.

WR Highest polling station

A small village, Tashigang, in Himachal Pradesh is the world's highest polling station. Only 62 voters were registered to vote at the station that is located 15,256 ft (4,650 m) above sea level. The polling personnel along with Electronic Voting Machines (EVMs), VVPAT systems, and other gadgets and papers had to use helicopter to reach this remote areas. The polling station is situated near the Indo-China border in the Spiti Valley. The polling centre of Tashigang falls under the Mandi parliamentary constituency, one of the four Lok Sabha seats in Himachal Pradesh.

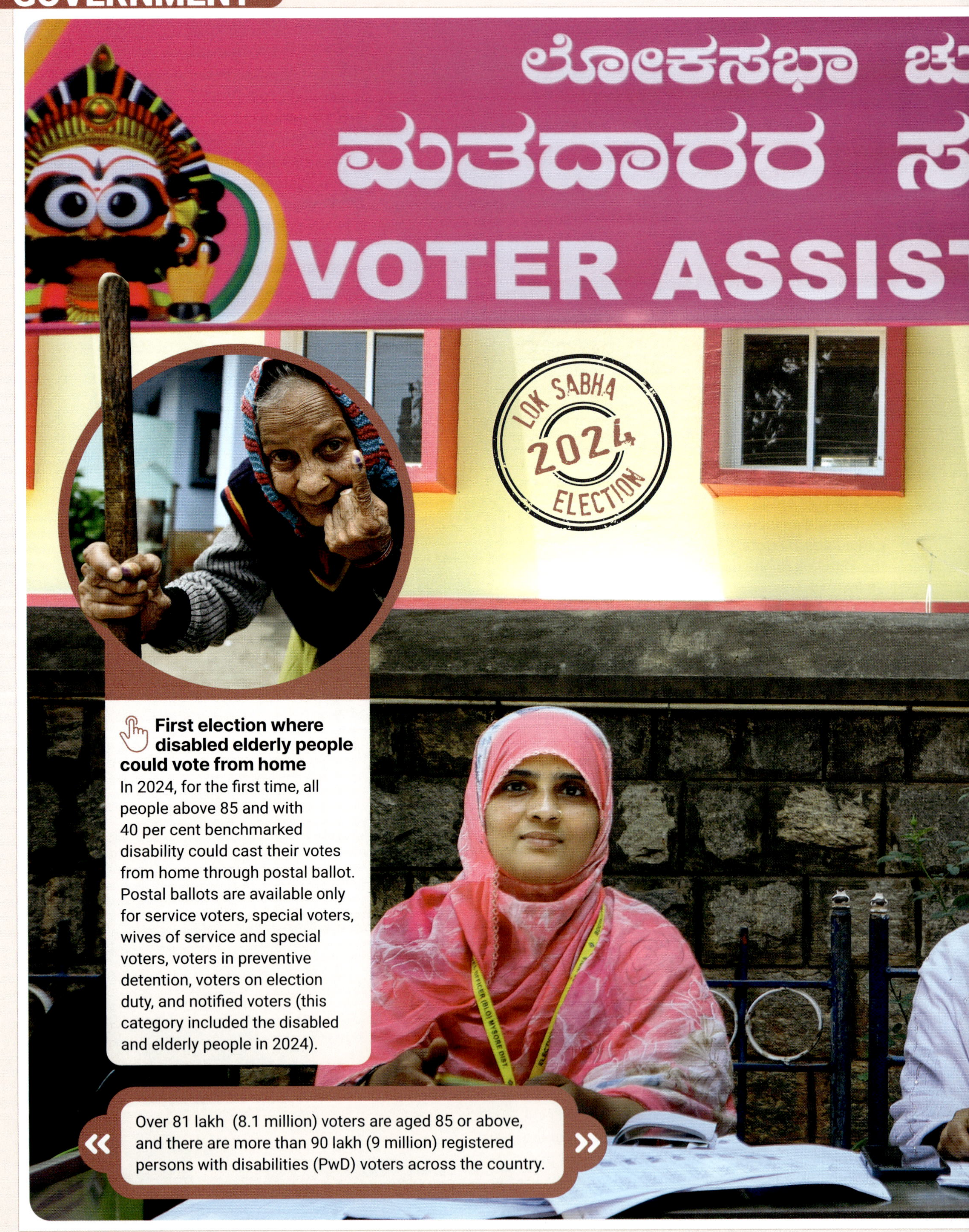

First election where disabled elderly people could vote from home

In 2024, for the first time, all people above 85 and with 40 per cent benchmarked disability could cast their votes from home through postal ballot. Postal ballots are available only for service voters, special voters, wives of service and special voters, voters in preventive detention, voters on election duty, and notified voters (this category included the disabled and elderly people in 2024).

« Over 81 lakh (8.1 million) voters are aged 85 or above, and there are more than 90 lakh (9 million) registered persons with disabilities (PwD) voters across the country. »

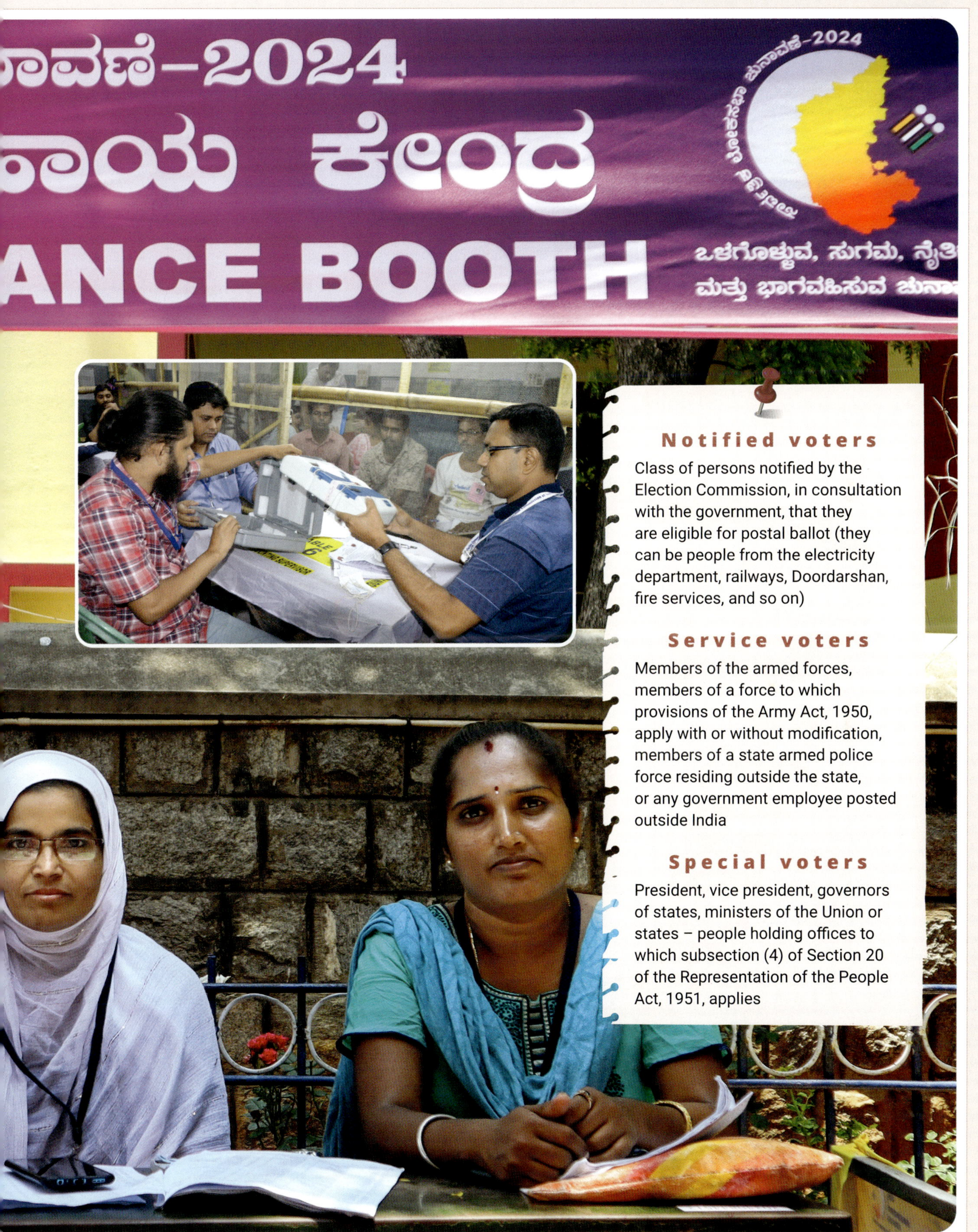

Notified voters

Class of persons notified by the Election Commission, in consultation with the government, that they are eligible for postal ballot (they can be people from the electricity department, railways, Doordarshan, fire services, and so on)

Service voters

Members of the armed forces, members of a force to which provisions of the Army Act, 1950, apply with or without modification, members of a state armed police force residing outside the state, or any government employee posted outside India

Special voters

President, vice president, governors of states, ministers of the Union or states – people holding offices to which subsection (4) of Section 20 of the Representation of the People Act, 1951, applies

2024 LOK SABHA ELECTION RESULT PARTYWISE

LOK SABHA 2024 ELECTION

Party	Number of Seats Won	Vote share
Bharatiya Janata Party (BJP)	240	36.56%
Indian National Congress (INC)	99	21.19%
Samajwadi Party (SP)	37	4.58%
All India Trinamool Congress (AITC)	29	4.37%
Dravida Munnetra Kazhagam (DMK)	22	1.82%
Telugu Desam (TDP)	16	1.98%
Janata Dal (United) (JD(U))	12	1.25%
Shiv Sena – Uddhav Balasaheb Thackrey	9	1.48%
Nationalist Congress Party – Sharadchandra Pawar (NCPSP)	8	0.92%
Shiv Sena – Shinde	7	1.15%
Independents (IND)	7	2.78%
All India Majlis-E-Ittehadul Muslimeen (AIMIM)	1	0.22%
All Jharkhand Students Union Party (AJSUP)	1	0.07%
Apna Dal (Soneylal) (ADAL)	1	0.13%
Aazad Samaj Party (Kanshi Ram) (ASPKR)	1	0.10%
Marumalarchi Dravida Munnetra Kazhagam (MDMK)	1	0.08%
Lok Janshakti Party – Ram Vilas	5	0.44%
Yuvajana Sramika Rythu Congress Party (YSRCP)	4	2.06%
Rashtriya Janata Dal (RJD)	4	1.57%
Communist Party of India (Marxist) (CPI(M))	4	1.76%
Indian Union Muslim League (IUML)	3	0.27%
Aam Aadmi Party (AAP)	3	1.10%
Jharkhand Mukti Morcha (JMM)	3	0.41%
Janasena Party (JnP)	2	0.23%
Communist Party of India (Marxist-Leninist) (Liberation) CPI(ML)(L)	2	0.27%
Janata Dal (Secular) (JD(S))	2	0.34%
Viduthalai Chiruthaigal Katchi (VCK)	2	0.15%
Communist Party of India (CPI)	2	0.49%
Rashtriya Lok Dal (RLD)	2	0.13%
Jammu & Kashmir National Conference (JKN)	2	0.17%
Sikkim Krantikari Morcha (SKM)	1	0.03%
Bharat Adivasi Party (BHRTADVSIP)	1	0.57%
Rashtriya Loktantrik Party (RLTP)	1	0.09%
Shiromani Akali Dal (SAD)	1	0.28%
Zoram People's Movement (ZPM)	1	0.03%
Voice of the People Party (VOTPP)	1	0.09%
Nationalist Congress Party (NCP)	1	0.32%
Revolutionary Socialist Party (RSP)	1	0.09%
Kerala Congress (KEC)	1	0.05%
Hindustani Awam Morcha (Secular) (HAMC)	1	0.05%
Asom Gana Parishad (AGP)	1	0.20%
United People's Party, Liberal (UPPL)	1	0.20%
NOTA		0.99%

Source: the Election Commission of India

Win by highest margin

Shankar Lalwani of the BJP won from Indore parliamentary constituency by 11.72 lakh votes, which is the highest ever victory margin in Indian parliamentary polls.

Narendra Modi | Nitish Kumar | Chandrababu Naidu

India saw a coalition government again after 2009. The National Democratic Alliance (NDA), led by the Bharatiya Janata Party (BJP), formed a coalition government based on the support of chiefly two allies – the Janata Dal (United) or JD (U) and the Telugu Desam Party (TDP). Narendra Modi became the prime minister for the third time in a row and equalled the record of J. L. Nehru.

The 2024 general election saw the rise of a new alliance led by the Congress: Indian National Developmnt Inclusive Alliance (I.N.D.I.A). Replacing the previous United Progressive Alliance (UPA), the new alliance of 37 parties plus independent candidates has Mallikarjun Kharge, president of the Indian National Congress, as its chairman. Rahul Gandhi of I.N.D.I.A. has become the Leader of Opposition.

In order to boost inclusivity, the ECI introduced the 'other' gender category in voter registration forms. But the transgender voter turnout for the 2024 Lok Sabha election across states and Union Territories was a mere 27.08 per cent, indicating a significantly low participation rate, as per the version of a section of analysts. However, it was a far better figure compared to their percentage in the 2019 parliamentary polls, when the overall turnout for transgender voters was 14.58 per cent. One can argue that the participation of transgender community in 2024 polls indicates a more inclusive political environment. Nevertheless, only three transgender candidates contested the 2024 general election and all have lost their security deposits. They are Sunaina Kinnar from Dhanbad (Jharkhand), Rajan Singh from South Delhi, and Durga Mausi from Damoh (Madhya Pradesh).

I.N.D.I. Alliance

Only booth with 100% turnout

A polling booth was set up deep inside the Gir Forest of Gujarat, the last surviving natural habitat of Asiatic lions, to ensure that the solitary voter of the booth could cast his vote without facing any hassle. Though political parties did not carry out campaigns there for the fear of lions and other wild animals, a polling team of 10 people traversed through the forest and to set up a booth for the one and only voter – Haridas Udasin. Udasin, a Hindu monk, cast his vote on 7 May 2024. The polling station was set up adjacent to the Hindu temple Mahant Haridas Udasin is in charge of. Thus Udasin, being the single registered voter, ensured a 100 per cent turnout at the polling booth.

This special section on the 2024 Lok Sabha election has been created with inputs from Surbek Biswas.

Voter-verifiable paper audit trail in all constituencies for the first time

The Election Commission of India set up the voter-verifiable paper audit trail or VVPAT system in all constituencies in 2019. The VVPAT prints a slip with the serial number, name, and symbol of the candidate for whom the vote was cast.

PRESIDENTS AND VICE PRESIDENTS

First presidential election

The first presidential election in the country was held in 1952 when Dr Rajendra Prasad (1884–1963) became president of India.

First vice president

Dr S. Radhakrishnan (1888–1975) was vice president of India during 1952–62. He also had the longest tenure as vice president, that of 10 years, a record he shares with Hamid Ansari, who was in office from 11 August 2007 to 11 August 2017.

Dr S. Radhakrishnan: first vice president

Oldest vice president to assume office

Bhairon Singh Shekhawat (1923–2010) became vice president on 19 August 2002, when he was 79 years of age.

Oldest to become president

K.R. Narayanan (1920-2005) became India's oldest president when he assumed the office on 25 July 1997. He was 76 years and 271 days old.

First woman president

Pratibha Patil (b. 19 December 1934) became the first woman to be appointed president of India. Earlier, Pratibha Patil had held the office of governor of Rajasthan during 2004–07. She was affiliated with the Indian National Congress. Pratibha Patil started the Shram Sadhana Trust. The trust runs hostels for working women in New Delhi, Mumbai, and Pune.

Most presidents from a state

With three presidents to date, Tamil Nadu is the state that has given the country the most number of presidents. They are S. Radhakrishnan, R. Venkataraman, and A.P.J. Abdul Kalam. Dr S. Radhakrishnan, the first vice president and second president of India, held the position of president from 1962 to 1967. R. Venkataraman, the eighth president of India, held office from 1987 to 1992. A.P.J. Abdul Kalam, the 11th president of India, held the presidential office from 2002 to 2007.

UNION GOVERNMENT

First non-Congress government

The Janata Party, led by Jayaprakash Narayan, overthrew the Indira Gandhi government in the 1977 general election to form the first non-Congress government in the history of independent India. Morarji Desai was appointed prime minister of the government formed by the Janata Party.

First regional party to be the main opposition in Parliament

The Telugu Desam Party, founded by Nandamuri Tarak Rama Rao in 1982, is the first ever regional party to become the main opposition party in the Parliament when it won 30 seats in the 1984 Lok Sabha election, the second highest tally for that year.

First woman full-time finance minister

Nirmala Sitharaman (b. 18 August 1959) became the first woman to be a full-time finance minister of India on 31 May 2019. She is the second woman finance minister after former prime minister Indira Gandhi, who held the finance ministerial office for some time while she was prime minister during 1970–71. Sitharaman was also the first woman minister with defence as her sole portfolio from 2014 to 2019.

First Union minister to resign

Dr Shyama Prasad Mookerjee (1901–53) resigned from the Union cabinet on 19 April 1950. After leaving the Nehru government and the Congress party, he founded the Bharatiya Jana Sangh in 1951.

First Union minister to die in harness

Sardar Vallabhbhai Patel (1875–1950), India's first home minister and first deputy prime minister, who died on 15 December 1950, was the first Union minister to die while in office.

First woman cabinet minister

Vijaya Lakshmi Pandit (1900–90) was elected to the provincial legislature of the United Provinces as minister for local government and health in 1937, making her the first woman cabinet minister. Later, she was president of the United Nations General Assembly from September 1953 to September 1954.

Vijaya Lakshmi Pandit: first woman cabinet minister

First cabinet minister to be assassinated

Lalit Narayan Mishra (2 February 1923–3 January 1975), former minister of Railways, was making a speech at Samastipur railway station in Bihar, when a bomb was hurled on the dais. He died the next day.

Longest serving cabinet minister

Babu Jagjivan Ram (1908–86) was a Union minister for over 28 years from 15 August 1947 to 25 July 1979 with a break from 31 August 1963 to 24 January 1966. Some of the portfolios held by him included the Ministry of Labour, the Ministry of Defence, and the Ministry of Transport and Communications.

PRIME MINISTERS

First prime minister

Jawaharlal Nehru (1889–1964) became the first prime minister of India on 15 August 1947. Previously, he headed the interim government as prime minister, starting 2 September 1946. He served as prime minister until he died on 27 May 1964.

Oldest to become prime minister

Morarji Ranchhodji Desai (1896–1995), a freedom fighter during India's struggle for independence, became prime minister at the age of 81 years and 24 days on 24 March 1977. Earlier he had held many offices, such as those of minister of home affairs, deputy prime minister, and finance minister. He was also the chief minister of undivided Bombay state from April 1952 to October 1956.

First prime ministers to die in harness

Jawaharlal Nehru, the first prime minister of India, passed away on 27 May 1964, after serving the office for 17 years. He was the first prime minister of India to die in harness.

Jawaharlal Nehru's successor, Lal Bahadur Shastri, died at Tashkent, Uzbekistan, on 11 January 1966. He was the first prime minister of India to die in harness abroad.

Only woman prime minister

Indira Gandhi (1917–84), the first and only woman to become prime minister of India, was in office from 1966 until 1977. She was re-elected in 1980 and her second tenure lasted four years, until her assassination in 1984. She was the first prime minister to be assassinated.

First deputy prime minister

Sardar Vallabhbhai Patel was sworn in as the first deputy prime minister of India on 15 August 1947 in the first cabinet of independent India, which was headed by the then prime minister Jawaharlal Nehru.

Youngest to become prime minister

Rajiv Gandhi (1944–91) assumed office on 31 October 1984, when he was 40 years and 72 days, following the assassination of his mother, Prime Minister Indira Gandhi.

First prime minister born after Independence

Narendra Modi (b. 17 September 1950) is the first prime minister of India who was born after Independence.

First prime minister to resign

Morarji Ranchhodji Desai was the first prime minister of India to resign from the office. He assumed office on 24 March 1977 and resigned from his post on 28 July 1979, following a split in the Janata Party, which he was heading at the time.

Shortest tenure of a cabinet minister

Justice H.R. Khanna (1912–2008) was in office as the minister for law and justice in the Charan Singh ministry for five days from 30 July to 3 August 1979.

First use of Hindi at United Nations (UN)

Atal Bihari Vajpayee (1924–2018), former prime minister of India, gave a historic speech in Hindi at the United Nations General Assembly in 1977 as India's minister for external affairs. This was the first time when any Indian leader had given a speech in Hindi at any international platform. It was translated into English by an Indian diplomat. Vajpayee spoke again in Hindi in 1978.

THE STATES

State with the largest area

With an area of 3,42,239 sq km, Rajasthan is the largest state. It covers around 10.4 per cent of India's total area.

State with the smallest area

Goa is India's smallest state with a total area of 3,702 sq km.

State sharing borders with most states

Uttar Pradesh shares its borders with nine Indian states – Rajasthan, Haryana, Himachal Pradesh, Delhi, Uttarakhand, Bihar, Madhya Pradesh, Jharkhand, and Chhattisgarh.

Youngest chief minister

M.O. Hasan Farook Maricar, three-time chief minister of Pondicherry (now Puducherry), was the youngest chief minister when he came to power at 29 years in 1967. He died in office in 2012 as governor of Kerala. Pema Khandu, elected as chief minister of Arunachal Pradesh in 2016 at the age of 38 years, is the youngest serving chief minister of a state.

First woman chief minister

India's first woman chief minister was freedom fighter Sucheta Kripalani (1908–74). She was chief minister of Uttar Pradesh (1963 to 1967).

Youngest UTs

After abrogation of Article 370 on 5 August 2019, the former state of Jammu and Kashmir was bifurcated into two Union Territories: a) Jammu and Kashmir and b) Ladakh.

First 'film star' chief minister

M.G. Ramachandran (popularly known as 'MGR') was the first film star to become chief minister when he assumed office in Tamil Nadu on 4 July 1977. He was elected chief minister of Tamil Nadu while he was admitted in a New York hospital. His nomination papers for the Andipatti assembly constituency were flown in from the United States and he was elected in absentia. He was sworn in on 10 February 1985, forty-three days after the election. Thus, he was also the first chief minister of India who got elected while staying abroad.

M.G. Ramachandran: first 'film star' chief minister

State with the longest international border

West Bengal shares a 2,216.7 km long border with Bangladesh, making

State Firsts

First linguistic state (pre-1947)

The Orissa (now Odisha) province that was formed as a result of the division of the Bihar and Orissa province in 1936, was the first to be formed on a linguistic basis.

First linguistic state (post-1947)

The Telugu-speaking Andhra state was carved out of Madras state on 1 October 1953, with its capital at Kurnool. It was later merged with the Telugu-speaking areas of Hyderabad state to form Andhra Pradesh on 1 November 1956.

First modern Indian states/UTs

The Indian states of Bihar and Orissa were the first to be formed in British India. The Bihar and Orissa province of Bengal Presidency was carved out as a separate province on 1 April 1912, which included the present-day states of Bihar, Jharkhand, and parts of Odisha. On 1 April 1936, the then Bihar and Orissa province was divided into the separate provinces of Bihar and Orissa.

First state under president's rule

President's rule was imposed on Punjab from 20 July 1951 to 17 July 1952. The proclamation came after the resignation of the Congress ministry headed by Dr Gopichand Bhargava.

First elected communist government

On 5 April 1957, the Communist Party of India in Kerala formed the first communist government in the world to come to power by voting. It was led by E.M.S. Namboodiripad. It was dismissed by the Centre in 1959.

First state to implement a uniform civil code

Uttarakhand is the first state in India to enact a uniform civil code (UCC). It passed the bill on 7 February 2024, and on 13 March the president of India assented to the same. The UCC aims to create a uniform and equal set of rules on personal matters (marriage, divorce, succession, inheritance, and so on) for all citizens of the state without making any differences in terms of religion. The scheduled tribes of the state, however, have been kept out of the bill's purview.

it the state with the longest international border.

Youngest state
Telangana was formed on 2 June 2014, after its separation from the state of Andhra Pradesh.

Most chief ministers in a year
Haryana had four chief ministers in nine months from November 1989 to July 1990: Devi Lal (November 1989), Om Prakash Chautala (December 1989), Banarsi Das Gupta (May 1990), and Hukam Singh (July 1990).

Lowest suicide rate 
According to the Accidental Deaths and Suicides in India 2022 report of the National Crime Records Bureau (NCRB), Bihar has the lowest suicide rate in the country, which is 0.6 per 1,00,000 population.

Highest suicide rate 
Sikkim's suicide rate is the highest in the country – 43.1 per cent.

GOVERNANCE

First woman sarpanch
Chhavi Rajawat, the first woman sarpanch (head of the village panchayat) in India, looks after Soda, a village in Tonk District, Rajasthan. She assumed office in February 2010 at the age of 30 years. She is an alumna of Rishi Valley School, Madanapalle, Andhra Pradesh; Mayo College Girls' School, Ajmer, Rajasthan; and Lady Shri Ram College, New Delhi. She also holds an MBA degree from Balaji Institute of Modern Management, Pune, Maharashtra. She left her corporate job to work in rural India.

West Bengal and Bangladesh border–the longest international border

First Indian in the Imperial Civil Service
Satyendranath Tagore, elder brother of Rabindranath Tagore, was the first Indian to join the service in 1863. He was recruited into the Covenanted Civil Service (later named the Imperial Civil Service). His first posting was in the Bombay Presidency (which included parts of present-day Maharashtra, Gujarat, and Sindh).

First Indians in the Privy Council
In 1907, K.G. Puta and Syed Hussain Bilgrami were admitted to the Privy Council of India, the supreme appellate authority in British India, which advised the British monarchy.

First woman IAS officer
Anna Rajam George (b. 17 July 1927) from Calicut (now Kozhikode), Kerala, was the first woman to qualify for the Indian Administrative Service (IAS), in 1950. She was posted as a subdivisional officer in a small town in Tamil Nadu in 1951.

First municipalities
Municipal corporations for civic amenities were set up first between 1880 and 1884, when Lord Ripon was the viceroy of India.

First woman career diplomat
Chonira Belliappa Muthamma from Coorg (now Kodagu), Karnataka, qualified for the Indian Civil Service and joined the foreign service in 1949. She served in France, the UK, and Burma (now Myanmar), and later as ambassador to Hungary and Ghana.

First panchayats
Panchayats were first established in villages under the Panchayat Act in 1912, but with little success. It was in 1952 that a new Panchayat Act revived the system.

A panchayat office

First woman ambassador
Vijaya Lakshmi Pandit, the sister of India's first prime minister, Jawaharlal Nehru, was India's first woman ambassador, to the erstwhile USSR from 1947 to 1949. She also served as ambassador to the US and Mexico (1949–51) and Ireland (1955–61). She held a post in the cabinet in pre-Independence India, the first Indian woman to do so. Her longest tenure was in London, as high commissioner to the UK, serving from 1954 to 1961. Her last posting as ambassador was in Spain. She served as governor of Maharashtra from 1962 to 1964 and as member of the Lok Sabha from 1964 to 1968.

Youngest mayor
Arya Rajendran (b. 12 January 1999), the Left Democratic Front (LDF) councillor

from the Mudavanmugal ward, became the mayor of Thiruvananthapuram Corporation, Kerala, in December 2020 when she was 21 years old.

First woman mayor

Tara Cherian (1913–2000) was appointed mayor of Madras (now Chennai), Tamil Nadu, in 1957. She received the Padma Bhushan in 1967.

Youngest governor

Swaraj Kaushal (b. 12 July 1952) was appointed governor of Mizoram in February 1990 when he was 37 years and 7 months old.

Youngest sarpanch

Anant Parag Khadilkar, the youngest sarpanch in India, secured the post in Nagargao Sattari Village in Goa in 2017 when he was only 21 years old. He was then a graduate in commerce.

Anant Parag Khadilkar: youngest sarpanch

AADHAAR

State/UT with least Aadhaar coverage

Nagaland, with a low saturation percentage of 61.08 as on 31 May 2023, has the lowest Aadhaar saturation among all states and Union Territories in India, on the basis of total projected population for the year 2023.

State/UT with highest Aadhaar coverage

Delhi, with a saturation percentage of 106.43 as on 31 May 2023, has the highest Aadhaar coverage. The saturation percentage is calculated as the percentage of the number of Aadhaar cards assigned over the total projected population for the year.

Aadhaar Seva Kendra in Delhi

LAW AND ORDER

First Indian sheriff

Manackjee Rustomjee, a Parsi businessman and judge from Bombay (now Mumbai, Maharashtra), was appointed as the sheriff of Calcutta (now Kolkata, West Bengal) in 1873, the first Indian to be appointed to the position.

First Police Act

The Police Act of 1861 led to the creation of a police service. This Act introduced a uniform system applicable to entire British India.

First forensic science laboratory

In 1853, the Government Examiners' Laboratory was established in Calcutta followed by labs in Madras (now Chennai), Tamil Nadu, Bombay, Lahore (now in Pakistan), and Agra, Uttar Pradesh. At present, there are seven central forensic science labs in India, viz., Hyderabad, Kolkata, Chandigarh, New Delhi, Guwahati, Bhopal, and Pune.

First all-woman police station

The first all-woman police station in the country was started in October 1973 at Calicut (now Kozhikode) in Kerala. Sub-inspector Padmini was in charge of it.

First open prison

The first open prison in India, Durgapura Open Camp, was started in Rajasthan in 1956 by the then governor, Dr Sampurnanand, in the Government Agriculture and Research Centre campus at Jaipur. Prisoners who had spent six years behind bars could live with their families and go out in the day to earn.

First police dog squad

The Madras City Police Dog Squad, now called the Chennai City Police Dog

A police dog squad

Squad, was started in 1952 by a sub-inspector of police, Kanniah Naidu, in Chennai. It was the first police dog squad in India.

First Indian director of the Intelligence Bureau

T.G. Sanjeevi Pillai took over as the first Indian director of the Intelligence Bureau, Ministry of Home Affairs, from Sir N.P.A. Smith in April 1947 and held office till July 1950.

First fingerprint bureau

The first fingerprint bureau in the world was set up in Calcutta in June 1897. A murder case in 1898 in Jalpaiguri was the first to be solved on the basis of dactyloscopy, which is the science of fingerprint identification.

First woman IPS officer

Kiran Bedi (b. 9 June 1949) was the first woman to join the Indian Police Service (IPS) on 16 July 1972. She retired in 2007 and was later the lieutenant governor of Puducherry (May 2016–February 2021).

First transgender sub-inspector

India's first transgender sub-inspector, K. Prithika Yashini, joined the Tamil Nadu Police force on 2 April 2017. She was posted to Dharmapuri District in Tamil Nadu after a legal battle with the Madras High Court ruling in her favour.

K. Prithika Yashini: first transgender sub-inspector

Largest prison complex

Tihar Prisons, which started with the Central Jail in 1958, now includes nine central jails, apart from a district jail at Rohini, New Delhi, making it the largest prison complex in Asia. Its current capacity is of 5,200 prisoners.

Largest prison complex

LEGAL MATTERS

First Penal Code

The Indian Penal Code (IPC) and the Criminal Procedure Code (CrPC), which were introduced in Bengal in 1862, were drafted on the recommendations of the first Law Commission of India set up in 1834, chaired by British historian and politician Thomas Babington Macaulay.

High court with the most judges

Allahabad High Court has the largest sanctioned strength of 160 judges, but has never held its full complement. As on 21 March 2023, it had 82 permanent judges and 21 additional judges (total 103).

First British Indian Code

The East India Company's proposal for separate civil and criminal courts in districts of Calcutta on 15 August 1772 was the first British Indian Code.

First barrister-at-law

Gyanendramohan Tagore (1826–90) passed the barrister-at-law examination from Lincoln's Inn in England on 21 June 1862, becoming the first Indian to do so. In November 1865, he was enrolled into the Calcutta High Court in the then Bengal Presidency (now in Kolkata, West Bengal) as the first Indian barrister.

First woman advocate

Cornelia Sorabji (1866–1954) was the first woman to graduate in law in 1894. However, law being a male bastion then, she was enrolled in the Allahabad High Court Bar only in 1923.

First public prosecutor

S. Subramania Iyer (1842–1924), jurist and freedom fighter, was appointed public prosecutor in Madras, Tamil Nadu, in 1887.

First woman judge

Justice Anna Chandy (1905–1996) was the first ever woman judge of India, appointed in 1937. She was also the first female judge in any high court in India (appointed in Kerala High Court in 1959).

First chief justice of India

India's first chief justice was Justice Sir Harilal J. Kania (1890–1951), who held the position from 26 January 1950 to 6 November 1951.

First woman judge of the Supreme Court

Meera Sahib Fathima Beevi (b. April 1927) was appointed as a judge of the Supreme Court in October 1989, the first Indian woman to hold this post. She was also the second woman in the world to hold such a position.

First high court judge

Shambhunath Pandit, a Kashmiri domiciled in Calcutta was appointed judge at the Calcutta High Court on 2 February 1863. His tenure ended in 1867.

Shambhunath Pandit: first high court judge

First woman chief justice

Justice Leila Seth (1930–2017) was appointed the chief justice of Himachal Pradesh on 5 August 1991, becoming India's first woman chief justice of a high court. She was also the first woman to top the Bar exam of England and Wales (in 1958).

Justice Leila Seth: first woman chief justice

Youngest advocate general

Swaraj Kaushal (b. 12 July 1952) holds the record for the youngest advocate general of any state in India when he became advocate general of Mizoram in 1987.

First Indian judge of ITLOS

P. Chandrasekhara Rao (22 April 1936 – 11 October 2018) was a judge at the International Tribunal for the Law of the Sea (ITLOS) from 1996 to 2017. He was president of ITLOS from 1999 to 2002.

International Tribunal for the Law of the Sea (ITLOS)

First Indian woman judge of ITLOS

Neeru Chadha (b. 27 March 1955), an international law expert, became the first Indian woman to be appointed to the International Tribunal for the Law of the Sea (ITLOS), being elected to the UN body in June 2017. She was elected as a judge and has been its vice president since October 2023.

Oldest high court

The Calcutta High Court, established on 1 July 1862, under the Indian High Courts Act, 1861, is the oldest high court in India. It has jurisdiction over West Bengal, and the Union Territory of Andaman and Nicobar Islands. Its building was designed by British architect Walter Granville, who based it on the Cloth Hall at Ypres in Belgium. The seat of the high court is Kolkata. It also has a permanent circuit bench in Port Blair, the capital of the Andaman and Nicobar Islands. It has a sanctioned strength of 72 judges. T.S. Sivagnanam (b. 16 September 1963) is its current serving chief justice.

Oldest civic body

The Greater Chennai Corporation, Tamil Nadu, was inaugurated under a royal charter issued by King James II of England, on 29 September 1688, as the Corporation of Madras. It is the oldest civic body in the country and the

SDG Index 2023–24

NITI Aayog released India's fourth Sustainable Development Goal (SDG) Index, SDG India Index 2023–24, in July 2024. This is considered the country's principal tool for measuring national and subnational progress on SDGs. These goals were adopted by the United Nations and the 193 members of the United Nations General Assembly in 2015 aiming at ending poverty, protecting the planet, and ensuring peace and prosperity for all by 2030.

Overall SDG score for India in 2023–24 is 71, up from 66 in 2020–21. Among Indian states, Uttarakhand and Kerala have bagged the top spot together with a score of 79 each. Bihar lies at the bottom with 57.

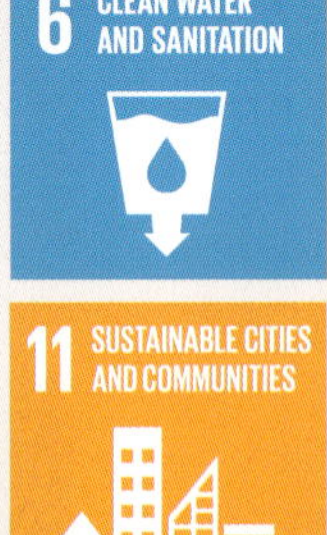

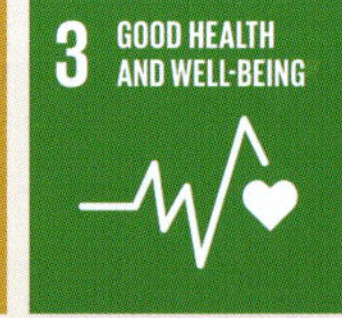

second oldest in the world. The first is in London, UK.

First Indian president of the International Court of Justice
Dr Nagendra Singh (1914–88) was the first Indian president of the International Court of Justice, serving from 1985 to 1988. He was also the first Indian to be a judge of the court. He received the Padma Vibhushan in 1973.

First citizen to have a 'no caste, no religion' certificate
M.A. Sneha Parthibaraja, a lawyer from Tirupattur, Tamil Nadu, became the first Indian citizen to win the right to not have a caste or religion, on 5 February 2021. She was granted the certificate after a nine-year-long court battle.

First transgender judge
Joyita Mondal Mahi, India's first transgender judge, was appointed as a judge in the Lok Adalat in West Bengal in 2017. She was 29 years old at the time.

First transgender lawyer
Sathyasri Sharmila, a lawyer in the Bar Council of Tamil Nadu and Puducherry, is the first transgender lawyer in India. Although she completed her education in 2007, she enrolled as an advocate after the National Legal services Authority of India (NALSA) judgment of 2014, which recognized the third gender. chief justice.

THE CENSUS*

First census
The first all-India census was conducted in 1872 in British India. However, the first regular census in the country was conducted in 1881, and then every 10 years. The last census was conducted in 2011. The Census due in 2021 was postponed because of Covid-19 and will start in 2025. The census is conducted by the registrar general and census commissioner under the Ministry of Home Affairs, Government of India.

Least populated state
Sikkim is India's least populated state, with 6,10,577 people.

Least populated UT
Lakshadweep, with a population of 64,473, is the least populated Union Territory.

Most densely populated state
Bihar has a population density of 1,106 persons per sq km, making it the most densely populated state in India.

Most densely populated Union Territory
Delhi, with a population density of 11,320 persons per sq km, is the most densely populated UT.

Most populated state
Uttar Pradesh is India's most populated state, with a population of 19,98,12,341.

Most populated Union Territory (UT)
Delhi is India's most populated Union Territory with a population of 1,67,87,941.

Least densely populated UT
Andaman and Nicobar Islands have a population density of 46 persons per sq km, making it the least densely populated UT.

Least densely populated state
Arunachal Pradesh, with a population density of 17 persons per sq km, is the least densely populated state in India.

Largest share of youth
The share of India's youth in the total population, the highest in the world, is 34.8 per cent (as per the 2011 census) or 42.2 crore (422 million). The National Youth Policy defines `youth' as persons between 15 and 29 years.

PARLIAMENT RECORDS

First session of Parliament
The first session of Parliament in free India was held on 13 May 1952 with Jawaharlal Nehru as prime minister and Dr Rajendra Prasad as president.

First Speaker of the Lok Sabha
Freedom fighter 'Dadasaheb' G.V. Mavalankar was the first Speaker of the Lok Sabha, holding the post from 15 May 1952 to 27 February 1956.

First woman secretary general of Rajya Sabha
V.S. Ramadevi was the first woman to be appointed as the Secretary General of the Rajya Sabha on 1 July 1993, for three years. She was also acting chief election commissioner for some time in 1990.

First deputy Speaker of the Lok Sabha
On 30 May 1952, Madabhushi Ananthasayanam Ayyangar was elected as deputy Speaker of the Lok Sabha.

First Lok Sabha dissolution
The fifth Lok Sabha was dissolved by Indira Gandhi in 1971, for the first time in the history of the Indian Parliament. The second Lok Sabha dissolution came in 1979 under Charan Singh, and the third was the ninth Lok Sabha on 6 March 1991 under Chandra Shekhar.

First representative in the British House of Commons
The 'Grand Old Man of India', Dadabhai Naoroji, was the first Indian-origin and non-white member of the British House of Commons, when he was elected as a Liberal Party member of Parliament in London from Central Finsbury in July 1892, by a bare majority of three votes. He held the position till 1895.

Dadabhai Naoroji: first representative in the British House of Commons

First visually impaired member of Parliament
Sadhan Chandra Gupta (1917–2015), an Indian lawyer and politician, became the first visually impaired member of Parliament (MP) in 1953. He later served as the advocate general of West Bengal. Gupta was elected to the Lok Sabha from the Calcutta South-east constituency in a 1953 by-election on a Communist Party of India (CPI) ticket.

First hung Parliament
A hung parliament is a situation where no single political party has an absolute

* Per Census 2011

majority of seats in the Parliament. For the first time in nine general elections, India's electorate did not give a decisive verdict in 1989. The Congress (I) was ousted in the north and the ruling regional parties were similarly ousted in the south.

First couple in Parliament

Joachim (21 January 1907–28 June 1979) and Violet Alva (24 April 1908–20 November 1969) from Karnataka were the first couple in Parliament. While Violet was elected to the Rajya Sabha in 1952, Joachim became a Lok Sabha member in the same year.

First woman legislator

Dr S. Muthulakshmi Reddy was a social worker, educationist, and physician, with many firsts to her credit. In 1926, she became the first woman legislator (Madras Legislative Council member) and in 1930, by way of the All India Women's Conference, pushed through the Child Marriage Restraint Act. She was also the first woman alderman of the Madras Corporation in 1937.

Youngest member of the Rajya Sabha

Anubhav Mohanty (b. 24 December 1981), the film star-turned-politician from Odisha, became a member of the Rajya Sabha on 13 June 2014. He was 32 years, 5 months, and 19 days old then. The youngest member's tenure at the upper house of Indian Parliament ended in 2019. Later he was elected to the Lok Sabha (2019 to 2024). He started his political career with the Biju Janata Dal (BJD) and switched to the Bharatiya Janata Party (BJP) in 2024.

Dr S. Muthulakshmi Reddy – second from the left (back)

Longest tenure as Rajya Sabha chairman

Dr S. Radhakrishnan, the second president and first vice president of India, had the longest tenure as chairman of the Rajya Sabha, from 1952 to 1962.

Shortest Lok Sabha term

The 12th Lok Sabha lasted from 10 March 1998 to 26 April 1999, a duration of around 13 months, due to the withdrawal of support by the All-India Anna Dravida Munnetra Kazhagam (AIADMK) from the National Democratic Alliance (NDA) government led by Atal Bihari Vajpayee.

Longest term as Speaker

Balram Jakhar served as Speaker from 1980 to 1989, for eight years and 329 days in two terms, becoming the Speaker with the longest tenure.

Shortest term as Speaker

Neelam Sanjiva Reddy was Lok Sabha Speaker from 26 March to 13 July 1977, thus serving the shortest term as Speaker. He was the sixth president of India, from 1977 to 1982.

Neelam Sanjiva Reddy: shortest term as Speaker

Most bills passed in a year

The Parliament passed 118 bills in 1976, which is the highest number of bills ever passed by it in a single year.

Lok Sabha with lowest average age

The 12th Lok Sabha (1998) had the lowest average age of 46.4 years.

Lok Sabha with highest average age

The average age of the elected MPs in the current 18th Lok Sabha is 56 years, making it the Lok Sabha with the highest average age in the history of the Indian Parliament.

Lok Sabha	Average Age (Years)
First (1951–52)	46.5
Second (1957)	46.7
Third (1962)	49.4
Fourth (1967)	48.7
Fifth (1971)	49.2
Sixth (1977)	52.1
Seventh (1980)	49.9
Eighth (1984–85)	51.4
Nineth (1989)	51.3
Tenth (1991)	51.4
Eleventh (1996)	52.8
Twelfth (1998)	46.4
Thirteenth (1999)	55.5
Fourteenth (2004)	52.63
Fifteenth (2009)	53.03
Sixteenth (2014)	55.64
Seventeenth (2019)	55
Eighteenth (2024)	56

State Legislature

First paperless assembly

Himachal Pradesh Legislative Assembly became India's first to use the e-Vidhan system and become completely paperless in 2014. This high-tech assembly was the first to implement the e-Governance solution called e-Vidhan with financial and technical help from the then Department of Electronics and Information Technology (DeitY), Government of India, in 2014.

First state legislative assembly

The maharaja of Travancore, Sree Moolam Thirunal Rama Varma, constituted an eight-member assembly in March 1888. A bicameral system was introduced on 28 October 1932 by King Chithira Thirunal Balarama Varma, who abolished the existing council and set up the Sree Moolam Assembly (Lower House) and the Sree Chitra State Council (Upper House).

Shortest session of state legislative assembly

There was a one-minute session of the Rajasthan Legislative Assembly from 11:00 a.m. to 11:01 a.m. on 14 August 1972, the shortest session of a legislative assembly on record.

Most legislative council elections won

Basavaraj Shivalingappa Horatti (b. 14 April 1946), currently chairman of Karnataka Legislative Council, scripted history in June 2022, when he got re-elected to the legislative council from the Karnataka West Teachers' Constituency for a record eighth time. He is the longest-serving member of a legislative council in India, a member since 1980.

Largest legislature

Uttar Pradesh Legislative Assembly is the largest state legislative assembly in India with 403 seats. Uttar Pradesh Legislative Council consists of 100 seats, which is also the highest in the country.

Dome of Vidhan Soudha

Largest legislative building

Vidhan Soudha, Bengaluru, Karnataka, is a rectangular building made with granite measuring 213.36 m (700 ft) north–south and 106.68 m (350 ft) east–west, with two inner open quadrangles on either side of the central wing measuring about 70.10 m (230 ft) by 70.10m (230 ft) each.

IN MEMORY OF
THOSE WHO SET OUT TO SERVE THE NATIONS CAL
AND DID NOT RETURN.
LADAKH 1947...

ARMY

PERSONNEL

First Indian commander-in-chief

General (later field marshal, in 1986) K.M. Cariappa (1899–1993) took over from the British commander-in-chief (C-in-C), General Sir Roy Bucher, on 15 January 1949 and held office till 14 January 1953. The only other C-in-C was General M. Rajendra Sinhji Jadeja, who took over as the first chief of army staff (CoAS) in April 1955, after which the post of C-in-C was abolished.

Field Marshal K.M. Cariappa

First chief of integrated defence staff

On 1 October 2001, Lieutenant General Pankaj Joshi was appointed the first chief of integrated defence staff (CIDS) in the country, reporting to General Sundararajan Padmanabhan, chairman of the Chief of Staff Committee at the time.

First chief of defence staff

On 31 December 2019, after demitting office as chief of army staff, General Bipin Rawat (1958–2021) took over as India's first chief of defence staff (CDS), serving as a tri-services chief and principal military adviser to the defence minister on all matters related to the army, navy, and air force. He also headed the Department of Military Affairs created within the Ministry of Defence.

General Bipin Rawat

First commissioned officer

Major General K. Bhagwati Singh (ID I-O-No. 1) was the first officer to be commissioned into the Indian Military Academy (IMA). He passed out of the

Medals and Honours

First Victoria Cross

The first Indian to be awarded the Victoria Cross was Sepoy (later Subedar) Khuda Dad Khan of the 129 Baluchis, on 31 October 1914, for gallantry at Hollebeke, Belgium, in the First World War.

Youngest to receive the Victoria Cross

At nineteen, Sepoy Kamal Ram of the Royal Indian Army was the youngest Indian to receive the Victoria Cross in 1944. Born in Bholupura Village of Karauli District, Rajasthan, he was with the 3rd Battalion of the 8th Punjab Regiment during the Second World War.

First prisoner of war and first Kirti Chakra recipient

Flying Officer Ulrich Anthony D'Cruz, whose aircraft was shot down by ground fire on 1 December 1947 in the 1947–48 Kashmir war, was taken prisoner by Pathan tribesmen and later by the Pakistan Army, and released after a year. He was awarded the Kirti Chakra in 1952 for bravery during captivity.

First George Cross

Havildar Nandlal Thapa of the Gurkha Rifles received the George Cross in 1935 for exceptional courage and devotion to duty. He was about 32 years old at the time and was serving in the 2nd Battalion of the 8th Gurkha Rifles.

First Param Vir Chakra

Major Somnath Sharma, heading a detachment of the Kumaon Regiment at Badgam, Jammu and Kashmir, laid down his life in the effort to save Srinagar city and airport from a Pakistani attack during the Kashmir operations in 1947. He was given the award posthumously in 1950.

First Ashok Chakra

Naik Nar Bahadur Thapa of 5 Gurkha Rifles was awarded the Ashok Chakra Class I (now known as the Ashok Chakra). On 15 September 1948, during the Hyderabad police action, as the No. 2 Platoon of the A Company came under fire on the banks of the Tungabhadra River, he dashed across the 100-yard open ground and single-handedly silenced the gun crew.

First Republic Day commander and first army officer to receive Padma Bhushan

The first Republic Day parade of independent India, which featured interservice contingents from the army, navy, air force, and police forces, was held on 26 January 1950, and was commanded by Brigadier (later Lieutenant General) Joginder Singh Dhillon, a Bengal Sapper. On 24 November 1965, as lieutenant general, he became the first Indian Army officer to receive the Padma Bhushan.

First Indian peacekeeper to win the United Nations Military Gender Advocate Award

Major Suman Gawani, an Indian Army officer, was awarded the UN (United Nations) Military Gender Advocate of the Year award on 29 May 2020 in a virtual ceremony, becoming the first Indian peacekeeper to receive the honour. She served as a peacekeeper in a UN mission in South Sudan (UNMISS) in 2019.

Most decorated regiment

The Sikh Regiment has to its credit the highest number of gallantry awards, viz.; 1,652. These include two Param Vir Chakras, eight Maha Vir Chakras, sixty-four Vir Chakras, and four Ashok Chakras among other decorations.

Indian Military Academy in 1934, with his batchmate (and later field marshal) Sam Manekshaw.

First women in the army

The first batch of 25 women outside the Army Medical Corps (AMC) was commissioned in the Indian Army on 6 March 1993 at the Officers Training Academy in Madras (now Chennai), Tamil Nadu. They were inducted into non-combat departments, such as supply, legal, education, and logistics.

First field marshal

S.H.F.J. (Sam) Manekshaw, the then general, became field marshal in 1973. He was honoured with the Padma Bhushan in 1968 and the Padma Vibhushan in 1972.

A stamp commemorating Field Marshal S.H.F.J. (Sam) Manekshaw

First woman lieutenant general

Dr Punita Arora from Saharanpur, Uttar Pradesh, was promoted to the rank of lieutenant general on 1 September 2004. She was the first woman in any of the four services (army, navy, air force, and coast guard) to reach a three-star rank.

Dr Punita Arora

First Woman DG Medical Services

On 1 August 2024, Lieutenant General Sadhna Saxena Nair assumed the office of Director General Medical Services (Army), becoming the first woman to be appointed to this prestigious position. Prior to this, she was the first woman to hold the post of DG Hospital Services (Armed Forces) on promotion to the rank of Air Marshal.

Lieutenant General Sadhana Saxena

First women in military police

On 25 April 2019, the Indian Army issued a formal notification inviting women applicants for the post of soldier – general duty. This was the first time that the army opened its ranks to women for personnel below officer rank (PBOR). The soldiers were to be inducted into the Corps of Military Police (CMP) to investigate offences such as theft, molestation, and rape. Their portfolio also included assisting civil police and the prevention of breach of regulations by army personnel.

First woman Subedar

On 28 January 2024, Havildar Preeti Rajak was promoted to the rank of Subedar, becoming the first woman to be promoted to this rank in the army. She is also a trap shooter and joined the army on 22 December 2022.

Subedar Preeti Rajak

UNITS

First artillery unit

On 15 January 1935, A Field Brigade (now 1 Field Regiment SP), with four batteries of horse-drawn guns, was raised at Bangalore (now Bengaluru), Karnataka. This date was adopted by the Regiment of Artillery as its raising day.

First artillery company

- The first artillery company was raised temporarily in 1748 in India under British rule with Indian troops, and was called the Gun Lascars.
- A company of Bombay Artillery, which still exists as 5 Bombay Mountain Battery, was raised on 28 September 1827, the date being celebrated as Gunners' Day.

First administrative unit

The Army Service Corps (ASC) was established in 1748 when Stringer Lawrence, commander-in-chief in India, appointed Robert Clive as commissary. It was formally set up in 1760 in the Bengal, Madras, and Bombay Presidencies, and became a formal Supply and Transport Corps in 1901. The ASC was the oldest administrative component of the East India Company and was then known as the Commissariat.

Insignia of Indian Army Service Corps

Oldest infantry unit

Raised on 4 August 1768, the 1 Maratha Light Infantry or Jangi Paltan is the only unit that does not hang captured enemy flags upside down in its mess. It is also the only unit that was in constant battle for 20 years after it was raised, and in this duration, it earned 18 battle honours and five theatre honours.

Oldest infantry brigade

In September 1933, 5 Mountain Brigade was raised. Deployed in the Along (now Aalo) sector of Arunachal Pradesh, its area of responsibility comprises a frontage of more than 460 km.

First cavalry unit

The first Indian cavalry unit was raised in 1787 as 5 Regiment of Madras Native Cavalry. It became 1 Regiment in 1788 under Major Tonyn. Renamed 26 Light Cavalry in 1903, it was amalgamated with 30 Lancers in 1922 and became the 8th Light Cavalry.

First cavalry regiment

The first cavalry regiment before India's independence, the Scinde Horse, was raised in 1838 as the Scinde Irregular Horse by Captain Ward in Hyderabad (in Sind, now in Pakistan) under the command of Captain John Jacob. It last paraded its horses in April 1938 at Rawalpindi (now in Pakistan).

First rifle regiment

The rifle regiment as a tactical unit was introduced in 1841 and the first such unit was the 4 Bombay Native Infantry, which till 1947 was 1 Battalion Rajputana Rifles, and is now 3 Guard. They were issued Enfield muzzle-loaders and 577 bullets.

A painting depicting members of the Rajputanta Rifles

First tri-services affiliation

Bengal Sappers has been affiliated with the Indian Navy and Indian Air Force since 2002. Originally known as the Bengal Sappers and Miners, and headquartered in Roorkee (now in Uttarakhand), it has won 80 battle honours and 11 theatre honours.

First Special Operations Division

India's first Special Operations Division was announced on 15 May 2019. At its peak, this tri-services division will have around 3,000 commandos from the Indian Army's special forces, the Indian Air Force's Garud force, and the Indian Navy's marcos commando units. The raising is the first step for counterterrorism operations. Major General A.K. Dhingra, from the 1 Para Special Forces Regiment, was the first chief of the division.

First and oldest extant armament checker

The Proof and Experimental Establishment in Chandipur in present-day Odisha, called the Proof Department, was set up on 7 November 1895. It has been associated with major armament developments. Included under the Defence Research and Development Organization (DRDO) in 1958, it had Lieutenant Colonel B.N. Mitra as its first Indian director.

EQUIPMENT

First gun foundry

The Board of Ordnance was constituted in April 1775, but it took 27 years to establish a factory at Cossipore in Calcutta (now Kolkata), West Bengal, on 18 March 1802 as the Gun Carriage Agency. In 1830, it was renamed the Gun Foundry and, in 1905, this name was changed to Gun and Shell Factory.

First rifle factory

A rifle factory, set up at Ichhapore, Bengal (now Ishapore, West Bengal), began production on 20 September 1904. It produced the .303-inch Bolt-action rifles in large quantities for the First and Second World Wars.

Earliest tanks

The first three tanks of the Indian Army were two varieties of Medium-D tanks brought in 1920 before Indian independence. Fifty Vickers MkII-B light tanks were acquired for use in India in 1933.

First flying spy

Unmanned aerial vehicles (UAVs) were used first in the Kargil conflict in 1999 to detect the movement of enemy troops and locate bunkers. UAVs were brought in to counter Pakistan's Gultari guns and the US-made AN/TPQ-36-37 gun-locating radars.

First indigenous tank

The first military tank that was made in India, named Vijayanta, rolled out of the assembly line on 12 December 1965 at the Heavy Vehicles Factory in Avadi in Madras (now Chennai), Tamil Nadu. It entered service on 29 December 1965.

Armament

Armament comes from the Latin word *armamentum*, coming from *armare* which means 'to arm'. The modern usage of the term means military equipments and weapons or the process of equipping armed forces with weapons. The archaic usage of the term was for a military force that was equipped for war.

First indigenous armoured personnel carrier

In 1987, the first BMP-2 infantry fighting vehicle, Sarath, was assembled at the ordnance factory at Shankarapally, Andhra Pradesh (now in Telangana), from Soviet-supplied components. Sarath was subsequently made indigenously in 1991.

Longest-range nuclear missile

On 26 December 2016, India successfully test-fired Agni-V, a surface-to-surface nuclear-capable missile with the longest range, from Abdul Kalam Island off the Odisha coast. Designed and developed by DRDO, this 17 m (55 ft 9 in.) long missile can carry a nuclear warhead of about 1.5 tonnes reportedly over 5,000–8,000 km. India is the sixth country after France, China, Russia, the US, and the UK to have a missile with a range of over 5,000 km.

Agni V being flight tested

First indigenous training simulator

On 20 February 2002, the Simulator Development Division, Secunderabad (now in Telangana), introduced the aiming-training simulator (ATS) for infantry combat vehicles.

First bulletproof helmets

In July 2017, the army obtained bulletproof helmets for the first time. The 1.2–1.4 kg lightweight helmets are being made in Kanpur, Uttar Pradesh, by MKU Systems, which is manufacturing them for the Indian Army for the first time. The company had earlier manufactured such helmets for the UN and the North Atlantic Treaty Organization (NATO) forces.

First indigenous revolver

In 2002, the research and development wing of the Ishapore Rifle Factory near in Barrackpore, West Bengal, after around two years of research, developed a low-cost and high-tech revolver, which weighs barely 380 g. The .22-in. automatic revolver has a range of 20 m (65 ft 7 in.).

First indigenously manufactured bulletproof vests

Shantanu Bhowmik, professor at the Department of Aerospace Engineering at the School of Engineering, Amrita University, Coimbatore, Tamil Nadu, designed the first indigenous bulletproof vest for the armed forces in 2017. The 20-layer vest, made with indigenous-ultra-modern lightweight thermoplastic technology, is being developed in collaboration with DRDO. The vest is effective up to a temperature of 57°C and weighs 1.5 kg while the earlier jacket weighed 15 kg.

Lightest towed artillery

On 18 May 2017, the Indian Army received the first batch of two M-777 A-2 ultralight howitzers (ULH) from the USA. These ULHs, with a maximum range of 30 km, manufactured by BAE Systems, were test-fired at Pokhran, Rajasthan. The 155 mm, 39-calibre guns are equipped to fire Indian ammunition.

First robot sentry

In 2017, the Indian Army built Robot Sentry, a mobile robot specifically meant for patrolling and surveillance applications in urban campuses of the army. Another robot, the Snake, has 14 active joints for lateral undulation, sidewinding, and rolling. These help the robot to navigate difficult passages.

First set of next-gen Armoured Engineer Reconnaissance Vehicle

Indian Army chief General Manoj Mukund Naravane flagged off and inducted the first set of indigenously developed next-generation Armoured Engineer Reconnaissance Vehicles (AERVs) at Bombay Engineering Group (BEG) on 21 December 2021. The AERV, which can match the speed of tanks, will upscale the existing engineer reconnaissance capabilities of the Indian Army significantly, keeping in view the possibility of future conflicts.

First indigenous sniper rifles

SSS Defence, based in Bengaluru, has developed the country's first indigenous sniper rifle prototypes with 7.62 mm x 51 mm calibre and .338 Lapua magnum platforms. The barrel length ranges from 20 to 24 in. (50.8 to 60.96 cm) based on use environments and specific missions.

OPERATIONS

First heli-lifted battalion

The First Guards (2 Punjab), raised in 1762 as 10 Battalion of the Coastal Sepoys and redesignated 18 times since, was heli-lifted during the counter-insurgency operations in Nagaland during 1969–70.

First heli-borne operations

In 1971, the Indian Army used helicopters to capture the 7,000-strong Sylhet garrison in East Pakistan (now Bangladesh). The 5 Gurkha Rifles (Frontier Force), which was led by Major M.M. Malik, landed with the first sortie of seven helicopters at Mirpara on the banks of the Surma River.

First para regiment in action

The 17 Para Field Regiment supported operations at Tangail in Bangladesh in 1971 by sending 49 Para Field Battery, a sub-unit of the regiment along with 2 Para.

First use of air cavalry

In May 2018, during Exercise Vijay Prahar carried out in the Mahajan Firing Range near Suratgarh, Rajasthan, Indian troops worked on the first use of the concept of air cavalry unleashed by the US Army in Vietnam during 1955–73. In these operations, weaponized attack helicopters carried out combined action against the 'enemy' in coordination with tanks and mechanized ground forces, while conventionally helicopters are called in only when ground forces cannot neutralize ground targets. This requires very precise coordination but speeds up the operation.

Highest tank battle in the world

On 1 November 1948, an Indian brigade group, supported by the 7th Cavalry (using Stuart Tanks), broke through the Himalayan range at Zoji La in Jammu and Kashmir at 3,528 m (11,575 ft) to drive out a group of invaders from Pakistan intermixed with Pakistan-occupied Kashmir (PoK) battalions and tribal groups.

Zoji La war memorial during a snowy day

High and Mighty Battles

Highest Battleground

Siachen is a 76.8 km glacier of ice abutted by knife-edged, fluted, serrated ridge lines, sometimes exceeding 6,400 m (20,997 ft and 4.5 in.), where temperatures dip to as low as −55°C. Army posts at altitudes from 4,572 m to 6,096 m (15,000 ft to 20,000 ft) face bitterly cold 200 km/hr blizzards.

SIACHEN

INDIAN DEFENCE HIGHLIGHTS 2024

JANUARY

- First all-girls Sainik School is inaugurated.
- Defence Research and Development Organization (DRDO) celebrates 66th Foundation day.
- Gallantry and Distinguished Services awards are given on Republic Day.

FEBRUARY

- Indian Navy declares 2024 as the year of 'Naval Civilians'.
- Indian Coast Guard celebrates 48th Raising day on 1 February.

MARCH

- Passing Out Parade for the third batch of Agniveers held at INS *Chilka*.

APRIL

- Army Medical Corps celebrates 260th Raising day.

MAY

- Army Dental Centre celebrates silver jubilee.
- Border Roads Organization (BRO) celebrates 65th Raising day.

JUNE

- Passing Out Parade for Naval Pilots is held at INS *Rajali*.

JULY

- *Triput*, constructed by Goa Shipyard Limited, is launched.

AUGUST

- Honorary ranks and Gallantry awards are given on Independence Day.

SEPTEMBER

- Directorate General of Aeronautical Quality Assurance celebrates 71st Raising day.

OCTOBER

- Indian Air Force celebrates its 92nd anniversary.
- Military Nursing Service celebrates 99th Raising day.
- Headquarters Integrated Defence Staff celebrates 24th Raising day.

NOVEMBER

- Ten years of 'One Rank One Pension' scheme is celebrated.

DECEMBER

- President's Colours are awarded to College of Defence Management, Secunderabad.

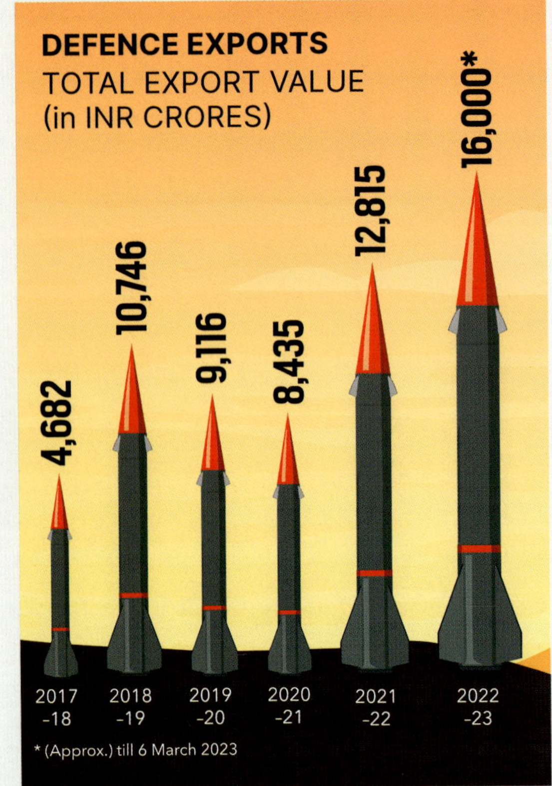

Source: 90 Years of Reforms, Ministry of Defence, August 2023

Source: 90 Years of Reforms, Ministry of Defence, August 2023

MISSION OLYMPICS WING

Medals won by Indian Army Sportspersons in 2022

Sport	National Events Gold	National Events Silver	National Events Bronze	International Events Gold	International Events Silver	International Events Bronze
Archery	8	14	13	2	0	0
Athletics	58	42	44	13	11	8
Boxing	26	17	5	7	1	10
Cycling	2	1	1	0	0	0
Diving	17	17	10	0	0	0
Equestrian	1	4	1	7	8	6
Fencing	10	12	17	1	2	2
Rowing	23	22	17	3	4	3
Sailing	11	13	11	1	0	2
Shooting	8	9	12	1	3	0
Swimming	13	11	9	0	0	1
Weight lifiting	15	17	12	3	0	0
Winter Games	17	13	15	0	0	0
Wrestling	27	31	61	7	3	13
Total	236	223	228	45	32	45

Source: Annual Report 2022–23, Ministry of Defence, Government of India

First army veterinary school

A veterinary school was started at Kirkee in Poona (now Pune) District, Maharashtra, in 1862, for officers and men of artillery, cavalry, and mounted police. Similar schools also came up in Hapur (Uttar Pradesh) in 1877, Lahore (now in Pakistan) in 1882, Ambala (now in Haryana) in 1889, and Simla (now Shimla, in Himachal Pradesh) in 1891.

Military Intelligence Training School and Depot, Pune

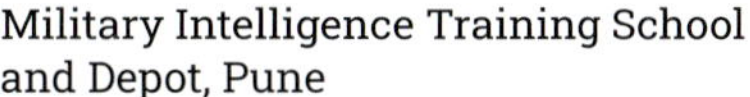

High Altitude Warfare School, Jammu and Kashmir

First military intelligence school

Opened in Karachi (now in Pakistan) on 20 January 1941, the first military intelligence school moved to Mhow (Dr Ambedkar Nagar) in Madhya Pradesh, and was renamed the Intelligence Corps Training School and Depot. It soon moved to its current location in Pune in 1952. On 29 February 1984, its name was changed to Military Intelligence Training School and Depot.

First counter-insurgency school

The Counter-Insurgency and Jungle Warfare School was established at Mynkre, Meghalaya, in 1967. It was relocated to Vairengte in Mizoram on 1 May 1970.

First military dog school

The War Dog Training School was opened in 1959 at the Indian Army Remount and Veterinary Corps Centre and School (now RVC Centre and School) in Meerut, Uttar Pradesh. Training for avalanche rescue operations began here in September 1976.

The War Dog Training School, Kolkata

First board of ordnance

The Board of Ordnance was set up in 1775 at Fort William, Calcutta. Currently, the Indian Ordnance Factories Organization – a set of 41 ordnance factories under the aegis of its corporate headquarters, the Ordnance Factory Board (OFB), Kolkata – has more than 200 years of experience in the development and marketing of a range of land, sea, and air defence systems. At present, the OFB has nine training institutes, three regional marketing centres, and four regional controllers of safety under it.

First drone show

For the first time ever a drone show was held during the Republic Day celebrations in the 75th year of Indian independence in 2022. The 10-minute show involved around 1,000 drones and they were conceptualized, designed, produced, and choreographed under the 'Make in India' initiative. It was organized by the start-up 'Botlab Dynamics' and supported by IIT Delhi and Department of Science and Technology, Government of India.

Longest bridge built during war

The Indo-Pakistan war in 1971, termed the Sappers War, saw the construction of a 421.8 m (1,384 ft) composite bridge across the River Madhumati in East Pakistan (now Bangladesh) in a matter of 34 hours. It was the longest 'war' bridge to be constructed by India after the Second World War and the longest operational bridge constructed during a war involving India.

First high altitude warfare school

Instituted as a formation ski school at Gulmarg, Jammu and Kashmir, the High Altitude Warfare School came into being on 8 April 1962. The courses at this institute include those on skiing and mountaineering.

First nuclear shelter

DRDO, the Pune-based research and development laboratory, introduced an integrated battlefield shelter for all three services in 2002 to withstand nuclear or chemical strikes for up to 96 hours. The portable shelter, 28 m (91 ft 10 in.) long and with a diameter of 2.5 m (8 ft 2 in.), has chemical toilets, water tanks, pumps for sewage disposal, and two power generators. It can accommodate 30 people and can be used as a command post, an observation post, and a communication centre.

First national war memorial

The armed forces first proposed a National War Memorial way back in 1960. On 25 February 2019, the memorial, designed by the Chennai-based WeBe Design Lab, led by Yogesh Chandrahasan, was inaugurated near India Gate, New Delhi. Covering over 40 acres (16.2 hectares), it has the names of Indian soldiers martyred in 1947–48 (Kashmir), 1961 (Goa), 1962 (China), 1965 and 1971 (Pakistan), 1987 (Siachen), 1987–88 (Sri Lanka), 1999 (Kargil) and other operations. It has concentric circles, with the Amar Chakra (Circle of Immortality) and an Eternal Flame in the centre. Around it are the Veerta Chakra (Circle of Bravery), a gallery depicting iconic battles and the Rakshak Chakra (Circle of Protection). The circles represent the *chakravyuh* or traditional Indian war formation. The Param Yodha Sthal has busts of 21 recipients of the Param Vir Chakra.

First Bactrian camels join the army

Since February 2017, the Bactrian camel was put through the paces at the Defence Institute of High Altitude Research (DIHAR), a DRDO laboratory in Leh, Ladakh. Bactrian camels are used to patrol the Line of Actual Control (LAC) in Ladakh and carry loads for the army.

First win at International Scout Masters Competition

Held in India for the first time, the host Indian Army team, trained by the Southern Command, won the Fifth Army International Scout Masters Competition (ISMC). Part of the International Army Games, it was held at Jaisalmer Military Station, Rajasthan, during 6–14 August 2019 and included five stages of competitions. Participants included teams from the armies of Armenia, Belarus, China, India, Kazakhstan, Russia, Sudan, and Uzbekistan.

First Indian dog breed in active duty

The Indian Army began to use dogs for active duty in 1959, the preferred breeds being the Labrador retriever, the Great Swiss Mountain dogs, and the German shepherd. In 2017, the Remount and Veterinary Corps introduced the first Indian breed, the Mudhol hound (or caravan hound), a sight hound used as a hunting hound first in Central Asia and later in the Deccan region, especially Karnataka. It is known for its courage, speed, and loyalty.

First all-girls Sainik School

On 1 January 2024, the Samvid Gurukulam Girls Sainik School at Vrindavan in Mathura, Uttar Pradesh, was inaugurated with a strength of approximately 870 students by Union minister of defence, Rajnath Singh.

Samvid Gurukulam Girls Sainik School, Mathura

NAVY

PERSONNEL

First naval pilot

Lieutenant Y.N. Singh of the Royal Indian Navy was deputed to England in 1941 for basic training and later to Canada where he obtained his wings in 1944 before serving in the escort carriers of the Royal Navy in the Second World War.

First four-star admiral

Admiral A.K. Chatterji (1914–2001) became a four-star admiral on 1 March 1968. He joined the Royal Indian Marines as a cadet in 1933 and became chief of naval staff in 1966.

Admiral A.K. Chatterji

First chief of naval staff

- Admiral Sir Mark Pizey was the first chief of naval staff in 1955.
- The first Indian chief of naval staff was Vice Admiral Ram Dass Katari in 1958.

Vice Admiral Ram Dass Katari

First commander-in-chief

- The first commander-in-chief of the Royal Indian Navy was Admiral Sir Edward Parry in August 1948.
- Rear Admiral I.T.S. Hall was the first post-Independence commander-in-chief of the Royal Indian Navy. The word 'Royal' was dropped on 26 January 1950.

First woman maritime reconnaissance pilot

Shubhangi Swaroop became the first woman pilot in the navy who was trained to fly maritime reconnaissance aircraft in 2017. Three other women cadets – Astha Segal, Roopa A., and Sakthi Maya S.– passed out with her in the first batch of women officers from the Indian Naval Academy, Ezhimala, Kerala, on 22 November 2017, and were inducted into the naval armament inspection (NAI) branch. The Indian Navy had inducted its first woman officer in 1991. Its aviation branch had women working as air traffic control officers and as observers in aircraft.

First woman pilot of naval aircraft

On 2 December 2019, 24-year-old sub-lieutenant Shivangi Singh graduated with two other trainee officers from the seventh Dornier Conversion Course (DOCC) at Kochi, Kerala. Originally from Muzaffarpur, Bihar, this Short Service Commission pilot entry scheme officer was commissioned into the Indian Navy in June 2018 and underwent a year of flying training at the Air Force Academy (AFA), Dundigal, Telangana, and Indian Naval

Air Squadron (INAS) 550 and INS *Garuda* in Kochi. During training, she flew aircraft such as Pilatus PC 7 Mk II, a basic trainer, at AFA before the Dornier Conversion Course.

First nuclear submarine

INS *Chakra*, the navy's first nuclear-powered submarine belonging to the Victor 1 SSN class had a speed of 32 knots and a dive displacement of 5,000 tonnes. It carried 90 sailors. On lease from the USSR, it was commissioned on 3 February 1988 and sent back in 1991.

INS *Chakra*

First woman officers as 'Observers'

Sub-lieutenant Kumudini Tyagi and Sub-lieutenant Riti Singh graduated as 'Observers' (airborne technicians) in the Indian Navy's stream of helicopters to be deployed on warships for short- or long-term missions. They were awarded their wings in a graduation ceremony held at INS *Garuda* on 21 September 2020.

Submarine

The term means something that functions underwater. Here, it specifically applies to naval vessels that can operate underwater. The earliest evidence of the term's usage was in 1626, in the writings of Francis Bacon, a famous politician and philosopher.

First woman naval helicopter pilot

At the passing out parade held at naval air station INS *Rajali*, Arakkonam, in Ranipet District, Tamil Nadu, on 7 June 2024, Sub-lieutenant Anamika B. Rajeev graduated as the first woman naval helicopter pilot.

UNITS

First navy air squadron

On 17 June 1959, the Fleet Requirement Unit was commissioned as the Indian Naval Air Squadron 550. INS *Vikrant*, formerly HMS *Hercules*, joined the Indian Navy on 16 February 1961 as the first aircraft carrier and saw action during the Goa liberation struggle in December 1961. It has flown 14 types of aircraft, starting with Sealands to the Dornier maritime reconnaissance aircraft flown currently.

Only training command

The Southern Naval Command is the only training command of the Indian Navy. It was augmented by INS *Magar*, which arrived at Kochi, Kerala, on 10 April 2018 to join the first Training Squadron for sea training of officers.

Insignia of the Southern Naval Command

First unmanned aerial vehicle squadron

The navy's first unmanned aerial vehicle (UAV) squadron, intended to patrol the seas, was commissioned on 6 January 2006, with 12 UAVs from Israel. The Intensive Flying and Training Units were based in Kochi, Kerala.

First exclusive naval base

INS *Kadamba*, inaugurated on 31 May 2005 near Karwar in Karnataka, is India's third operational naval base after Mumbai and Visakhapatnam, and the first under the sole control of the navy. Signifying another first, the inauguration speech was read out in Sanskrit. Sanctioned in 1985 as Project Seabird, its foundation stone was laid in 1986.

EQUIPMENT

First cruiser and flagship

HMS *Achilles*, a 7,030-tonne battleship, formerly of the Royal Navy, was commissioned as HMIS *Delhi* on 5 July 1948 in England, and became the first cruiser and flagship of the Indian Navy. It arrived at Bombay, on 15 September 1948. HMIS *Delhi* (renamed INS *Delhi*) was 169.1 m (554 ft 9 in.) long and 16.77 m (55 ft) across its beam, with a speed of 32 knots. Its armaments included six 152 mm guns, eight 102 mm guns, fifteen 40 mm guns, four anti-aircraft three-pounders, and eight torpedo tubes.

INS *Delhi*

First submarine depot ship

INS *Amba*, an ex-Soviet Ugra-class ship with a displacement of 6,750 tonnes, is a submarine tender and was commissioned on 28 December 1968. INS *Amba* has two cranes (6 tonnes and 10 tonnes) and it can accommodate 750 personnel.

ORGANIZATIONS OF THE MINISTRY OF DEFENCE, GOVERNMENT OF INDIA

MINISTRY OF DEFENCE

Department of Defence

- Border Roads Organization (BRO)
- Directorate General Defence Estates
- National Defence College
- National Cadet Corps (NCC)
- Institute for Defence Studies and Analyses
- School of Foreign Language
- Armed Forces Tribunal
- Armed Forces Medical College
- Military Engineering Services
- College of Defence Management
- Defence Services Staff College
- Indian Coast Guard (ICG)
- Services Sports Control Board
- Controller General of Defence Accounts

Department of Ex-Servicemen Welfare (DESW)

Department of Defence Research and Development

Department of Defence Production (DDP)

Department of Military Affairs (DMA)

- Indian Army
- Indian Navy
- Indian Air Force
- Headquarters Integrated Defence Staff (HQ IDS)

First missile boat

INS *Vinash*, a Soviet OSA (Russian word meaning 'wasp') 1 commissioned on 21 January 1971, was fitted with four SS-N-2A surface-to-surface missiles and four 30 mm guns. With a complement of 30 crew, it could reach speeds exceeding 35 knots.

First submarine base

On 19 May 1971, INS *Virbahu*, the Indian Navy's first submarine base, was commissioned near Visakhapatnam, Andhra Pradesh.

First indigenous patrol boat

Godavari-class frigate INS *Ajay*, commissioned on 21 September 1960, is a front-line warship equipped with missiles, guns, and anti-submarine equipment, as well as early warning navigation and electronic warfare systems. Built by Garden Reach Shipbuilders and Engineers (GRSE) Ltd, it could carry two Sea King helicopters.

First submarine rescue ship

INS *Nistar* was converted from a fleet minesweeper to a submarine rescue ship and commissioned on 29 March 1971. An ex-Soviet Valday-class ship, it features a diving bell, a recompression chamber, two rescue chambers, and a lift of 10 tonnes.

First indigenous nuclear-powered ballistic missile submarines

The Arihant-class submarines are India's first indigenously developed nuclear-powered ballistic missile submarines. The lead submarine of the class, INS *Arihant*, was commissioned in 2016. These submarines are designed to carry and launch nuclear ballistic missiles. It completed its first deterrence patrol on 5 November 2018.

Longest-serving warship/ aircraft carrier

INS *Viraat* – the second Centaur-class aircraft carrier in service – served India for 30 years after 27 years of service in the Royal Navy of the UK as HMS *Hermes*. The UK Royal Navy commissioned it in 1959, and it was later sold to the Indian Navy in 1986. It was decommissioned on 6 March 2017.

Largest aircraft carrier

INS *Viraat*, commissioned on 12 May

INS *Arihant*

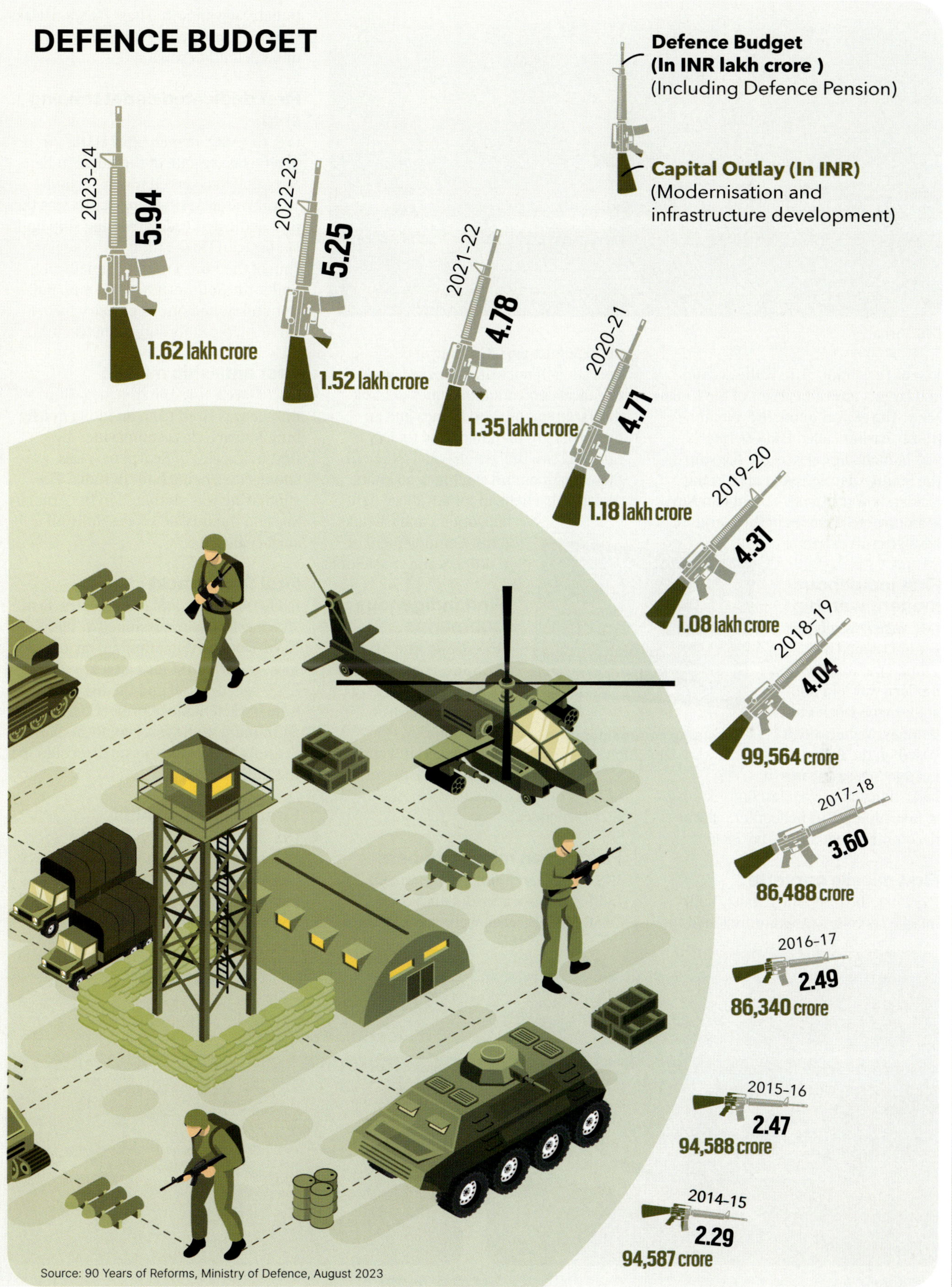
DEFENCE BUDGET
Defence Budget
(In INR lakh crore)
(Including Defence Pension)
Capital Outlay (In INR)
(Modernisation and
infrastructure development)
2023-24
5.94
1.62 lakh crore
2022-23
5.25
1.52 lakh crore
2021-22
4.78
1.35 lakh crore
2020-21
4.71
1.18 lakh crore
2019-20
4.31
1.08 lakh crore
2018-19
4.04
99,564 crore
2017-18
3.60
86,488 crore
2016-17
2.49
86,340 crore
2015-16
2.47
94,588 crore
2014-15
2.29
94,587 crore
Source: 90 Years of Reforms, Ministry of Defence, August 2023

INS *Viraat*

1987 at Devonport, UK, is the second and largest aircraft carrier of the Indian Navy. The 28,700 tonne INS *Viraat* (R-22), earlier called HMS *Hermes*, was launched in 1953 as the flagship of the South Atlantic Task Force in the Falklands War in 1982. The Indian Navy is among eight navies in the world to have aircraft carriers.

First indigenous modern warship

INS *Nilgiri*, which was commissioned on 3 June 1972, was the first modern warship built at Mazagon Dock Ltd, Bombay, Maharashtra. Based on the British Leander-class frigates, it had a hangar with a telescopic extension to take Alouette III helicopters. It was decommissioned on 31 May 1996.

A stamp commemorating INS *Nilgiri*

First missile corvette

INS *Kora*, the first indigenously built missile corvette, was commissioned on 10 August 1998. Capable of operating in nuclear, biological, and chemical confrontation zones, it has a displacement of 1,300 tonnes and an overall length of 91.16 m (299 ft). INS *Kora* has two indigenous, fuel-efficient diesel engines and can touch 26 knots. Along with a helipad for advanced light helicopters and Chetaks, it has a complement of 11 officers and 110 sailors.

First indigenous submarine

INS *Shalki*, the first of SSK Type-1500 submarines, built at Mazagon Dock Ltd, Bombay, was commissioned in February 1992. It has a displacement of 1,450 tonnes and carries 14 AEG SUT torpedoes.

First ocean minesweepers

INS *Pondicherry* and INS *Porbandar*, built at the Isora Yard, Leningrad, USSR (now Russia), were given to the Indian Navy in 1978. These Natya-1-class sweepers have steel hulls with active mine detection sonars.

First dedicated cadet training ship

INS *Tir* (A86), named after HMIS *Tir*, a River-class frigate of the Royal Indian Navy that had served in the Second World War as HMS *Bann* (K256), was the first dedicated cadet-training ship built at Mazagon Dock Ltd. It is the senior ship of the First Training Squadron under the Southern Naval Command. Commissioned on 21 February 1986, it carries 120 cadets and 20 instructors.

First anti-ship missile

On 2 March 2017, the first anti-ship missile was fired from an indigenously built Kalvari-class submarine, the first in a series of Scorpene-class submarines being built in India. The submarine was stationed in the Arabian Sea and the missile successfully hit a surface target.

First fast attacker

INFAC-T-80 (Indian Navy's extra-fast attack craft), commissioned at the Naval Dockyard in Mumbai, on 24 June 1998, was the first fast-attack, high-speed vessel and the first of an Indo-Israeli defence project. This aluminium-hull vessel could sustain 45 knots and it was the smallest ship in the Indian Navy.

First multi-warships

INS *Talwar* was launched in May 2000, INS *Trishul* in November 2000 and INS *Tabar* in May 2001. These Talwar-class guided missile frigates were designed and built by Russia.

INS *Kora*

INS *Talwar*

INS *Aditya*

First indigenous fleet replenishment tanker

INS *Aditya*, built by GRSE, Calcutta was commissioned at Visakhapatnam, Andhra Pradesh, on 3 April 2000. Manned by 16 officers and 140 sailors, the 172 m (564 ft) long fleet tanker has a deadweight tonnage of 1,700. It can touch a speed of 24 knots with an endurance of 10,000 nautical miles, and load six ships simultaneously on the high seas. It also carries a Sea King helicopter.

First Integrated Automatic Aviation Meteorological System

On 28 March 2017, the then chief of naval staff, Admiral Sunil Lanba, inaugurated the first Integrated Automatic Aviation Meteorological System (IAAMS) at INS *Rajali* (informally also known as the Arakkonam naval air station) in Tamil Nadu. The IAAMS has been established with the objective of modernizing the meteorological infrastructure and aviation safety of the nine naval air stations of the Indian Navy through automated monitoring of weather.

First 'green' ship

In February 2017, the survey vessel INS *Sarvekshak*, based at the Southern Naval Command in Kochi, became India's first naval ship to go green by installing a zero-maintenance solar power system that can generate 5.4 kW of electricity. It replaces the ship's emergency diesel alternator. The customized power-generating system has flexible, razor-thin solar panels on the canopy of the retractable helicopter deck, which use no-fume solid electrolyte batteries and are maintenance-free for 24 years. The solar-power-generating system can be used to run communication equipment and on-board lights, and charge batteries. With an annual carbon emission of 60,225 kg, it will replace about 22,995 litres of diesel.

INS *Sarvekshak*

First indigenous ammunition

The Indian Navy received its first made-in-India, 30 mm ammunition for AK-630 rotary cannons fitted on warships, as reported on 29 August 2022. The production of AK-630 guns was carried out by M/s Economic Explosives Ltd (EEL), Nagpur, Maharashtra, a subsidiary of Solar Industries India Ltd.

First indigenously developed naval anti-ship missile

The first indigenously developed naval anti-ship missile for the Indian Navy was test-fired on 18 May 2022. The missile was launched aboard a Sea King 42B Naval Helicopter from the Integrated Test Range (ITR) at Balasore in Odisha.

First pilotless drone

India's first passenger drone *Varuna* will be introduced in the navy. It is a pilotless drone with an ability to carry one person inside. Designed by the start-up Sagar Defence Engineering Company, this drone can cover a distance of 25 kilometres and can carry a payload of 130 kg. Its demonstration was held on 20 July 2022.

Varuna

GENERAL

First modern shipbuilder

In 1736, the East India Company invited Lowji Nusserwanji Wadia to build the first shipyard in Bombay (now Mumbai), Maharashtra. Since then, seven generations of the Wadias have built ships, including HMS *Minden* (the first constructed outside of Great Britain), HMS *Trincomalee* and HMS *Cornwallis*.

THE WADIA GROUP

Logo of the Wadia Group

First modern shipbuilding yard

Garden Reach Shipbuilders and Engineers (GRSE) Ltd, located on the eastern bank of the Hooghly River in present-day Kolkata, dates to 1884. The company's name was changed to Garden Reach Workshop in 1916 and on 1 April 1960, it was taken over by the Government of India. The name was changed back to Garden Reach Shipbuilders and Engineers on 1 January 1977. It builds a range of ships, including warships, sophisticated commercial vessels, harbour craft and fast, powerful patrol vessels for the Indian Navy and the Indian Coast Guard. It built INS *Ajay*, India's first indigenous patrol boat, in 1960.

First naval dockyard

The Naval Dockyard at Bombay started with the Bunder Pier in 1693. A tiny dry dock was constructed in 1750. The old Bombay Dock and the Duncan Dock were built in 1765 and 1810, respectively. A wet basin was constructed in 1892. The largest naval dockyard today, it is the premier maintenance facility for ships and submarines of the Indian Navy.

A stamp commemorating the Naval Dockyard Bombay

First naval academy

The first naval academy was established in Kochi, in January 1969. The first batch of cadets graduated in December 1970. Commander K. Ramdas was the first officer-in charge. Earlier, cadets used to be trained in England.

First naval school

The Signal School on INS *Venduruthy* was established at Bombay's Carnac Bunder in 1919 in Maharashtra. The next year, it was shifted to the Naval Dockyard, Bombay, and in 1941, to HMIS *Talwar*, also in Bombay. In 1946, it finally moved to Kochi.

First floating dry dock

The floating dry dock at Port Blair, Andaman and Nicobar Islands, commissioned in 1987, has a lifting capacity of 11,500 tonnes and can accommodate vessels that have a deadweight of up to 30,000 tonnes.

First indigenous floating dock

On 20 June 2017, FDN-2, the first indigenously designed and constructed floating dock of the Indian Navy was launched at the Larsen & Toubro Ltd shipyard at Kattupalli in Chennai, Tamil Nadu. The 185 m (607 ft) long and 40 m (131 ft 3 in.) wide platform has best-in-class machinery and control systems. It accommodates up to 8,000-tonne ships with draught up to 7 m (23 ft), including submarines.

First aircraft carrier dry dock

On 28 September 2019, the first aircraft carrier dry dock was inaugurated at the Naval Dockyard in Mumbai. The largest dry dock of the Indian Navy, it can accommodate INS *Vikramaditya* (IAC-I), the indigenous aircraft carrier under construction at Cochin Shipyard Ltd, and ships with a tonnage of up to 90,000 tonnes. Started in 2010, the completed dock is 281 m (921 ft 11 in.) long, 45 m (147 ft 8 in.) wide and 17 m (55 ft 9 in.) deep. Unlike most dry docks that are made by excavating land, this one is built into the sea, for which 38 caissons or watertight steel sections drained out seawater before construction could begin.

First unified theatre command

Vice Admiral Arun Prakash

Vice Admiral Arun Prakash took over as the first commander-in-chief of the Andaman and Nicobar Command in 2001, with operational control of all three services and the Indian Coast Guard in the Andaman and Nicobar theatre.

First helicopter training school

INS *Rajali* at Arakkonam, Tamil Nadu, houses the Indian Naval Air Station (INAS), which is a base for training helicopter pilots.

First deep-sea submarine rescue system

On 12 Dec 2018, the Indian Navy's first flyaway deep-sea submarine rescue system was inducted by Admiral Sunil Lanba at the Naval Dockyard, Mumbai. The system has a non-tethered Deep Submergence Rescue Vehicle (DSRV) and associated equipment, which give the navy the capability to search, locate, and rescue crew. The rescue system can be mobilized from the naval base at Mumbai, to the nearest mobilization port by air, land, or sea to expedite rescue. On 5 June 2019, an entirely Indian crew conducted its first full submarine rescue drill on the Kilo-class submarine, INS *Sindhudhvaj*, off the eastern coast of India.

First all-woman crew to circumnavigate the world

On 21 May 2018, a six-member all-woman crew completed circumnavigating the globe in 254 days on-board INSV *Tarini*, becoming the first Indian all-woman crew to do so. The journey ended at INS *Mandovi* jetty in Panaji, Goa, from where they had set sail on 10 September 2017. The crew included Lieutenant Commanders Vartika Joshi, Pratibha Jamwal, P. Swathi, and Lieutenants S. Vijaya Devi, B. Aishwarya, and Payal Gupta. The 17 m (56 ft) sailing vessel was captained by Lieutenant Commander Joshi. The crew was mentored by Commander

INSV *Tarini*

Dilip Donde, who became India's first solo circumnavigator in 2010.

First combat management system

A combat management system (CMS) for indigenous aircraft carriers has been developed by the Indian Navy along with the Tata Power Strategic Engineering Division (TPSED), in collaboration with the Weapon and Electronics System Engineering Establishment and MARS, Russia. On 28 March 2019, it was handed over to the navy. All tests and trials conducted on its hardware and software were successful. This is the first CMS developed by a private company for the Indian Navy.

Longest expedition with a mixed crew

INSV *Mhadei* and INSV *Tarini* set sail for the Bay of Bengal Offshore Sailing Expedition on 22 February 2020 from the Indian Naval Ocean Sailing Node in Goa. The crew comprised five naval officers, including two women officers in each boat, covering 6,100 nautical miles over 55 days. Captain Vipul Meherishi, the skipper of INSV *Tarini*, led the expedition. Captain Atool Sinha was the skipper of INSV *Mhadei*. The sailing vessels had scheduled halts at Colombo (Sri Lanka), Yangon (Myanmar), Chittagong (Bangladesh) and Phuket (Thailand).

INSV *Mhadei*

First virtual reality centre

On 12 April 2019, Admiral Sunil Lanba inaugurated the first virtual reality centre (VRC) at the Directorate of Naval Design (Surface Ship Group). This centre boosts the design of indigenous warships and collaborative design reviews between designers and end-users of warships. It has developed 19 warship designs.

AIR FORCE

PERSONNEL

First Indian pilots

• Lieutenant Indra Lal Roy from Calcutta, was the first Indian pilot with the Royal Flying Corps and later in the Royal Air Force during the First World War. He claimed 10 victories in air combat, all within two weeks, in July 1918. He was killed in action when only 19 years old and was posthumously awarded the Distinguished Flying Cross.

• The only other Indian pilots known to have flown in the First World War were Sardar Hardit Singh Malik, Lieutenant S.G. Welingkar, Lieutenant Errol Sharat Chandra Sen, and Lieutenant Naoroji.

Postal stamps commemorating Air Warriors: Indians in First World War

First air chiefs

Air Marshal Subroto Mukerjee became the first Indian chief of air staff when he succeeded Air Marshal Sir G.E. Gibbs on 1 April 1954. However, the IAF chief's rank was only equivalent to that of a lieutenant general of the Indian Army at the time. The IAF got its first air chief marshal only in 1966 when Air Marshal Arjan Singh was promoted to the post in recognition of the IAF's role in the 1965 war with Pakistan.

Air Marshal Subroto Mukerjee (saluting)

First Indian station commander

Wing Commander Subroto Mukerjee was given command of the airbase RAF

Combat

The term means 'fighting' or 'to be in a fight', especially in times of war. It originates from the mid 16th century, originally denoting a fight between two people or parties; It comes from the French word *combattre* (verb) and from a late Latin *combattere* (which combines *com*, 'together', with + *battere*, a variant of the Latin word *batuere* which means 'to fight').

Kohat (now in Pakistan), the first all-Indian station with only Indian Air Force (IAF) squadrons, in 1944.

First marshal
On 26 January 2002, former chief of the Indian Air Force, Air Chief Marshal Arjan Singh, was given the rank of marshal, equivalent to a field marshal.

Longest tenure as air chief
Air Marshal Subroto Mukerjee served the longest tenure as air chief, from 1 April 1954 to 8 November 1960.

First squadron commander
Flight Lieutenant Subroto Mukerjee took over command of 1 Squadron on 3 September 1939 – later becoming the first officer to command a flight, a squadron, a station and finally the IAF.

First woman air marshal
Air Marshal Padmavathy Bandopadhyay, AVSM, VSM, (b. 4 November 1944) took over as the director general of medical services (Air) on 1 October 2004. Having joined the IAF in 1968, she was also the first woman to reach the rank of air vice marshal in 2002.

First woman in the Defence Services Staff Course
Padmavathy Bandopadhyay (later air marshal) joined the Indian Air Force as a medical officer. Bandopadhyay was also the first woman to attend the prestigious Defence Services Staff Course (DSSC) in 1978, the first woman in Asia to specialize in aerospace medicine, and the first Indian woman to visit the North Pole (1989–90).

First woman flight commander
Wing Commander Shaliza Dhami was the first woman to become a flight commander in the IAF. She was commissioned to the position on 26 August 2019 and took command of a Chetak Helicopter Unit at Hindon Airbase, Ghaziabad, Uttar Pradesh. She is also the first woman to be granted a permanent commission and the first to be an authorized instructor for IAF helicopters.

First helicopter pilot
On 28 March 1954, Flight Lieutenant A. Neil Todd and his co-pilot Squadron Leader S.K. Majumdar flew the then prime minister, Jawaharlal Nehru, from Palam, Delhi, to Tilpat Range in Faridabad, Haryana, and back.

First commissioned woman pilot by order of merit
Squadron Leader Priya Nalgundwar (b. 28 November 1970) was commissioned in the Indian Air Force in the Flying Branch on 17 December 1994 as part of the first batch of seven women pilots and stood first in the order of merit in her batch. She received her wings from the then chief of air staff Air Chief Marshal S.K. Kaul.

First women combat pilots
In July 2016, for the first time, women combat pilots were inducted into the Indian Air Force with the then defence minister Manohar Parrikar commissioning Mohana Singh, Avani Chaturvedi, and Bhawana Kanth.

From left to right: Mohana Singh, Avani Chaturvedi, and Bhawana Kanth

S.K. Majumdar (*standing, centre*) with his family in earlier days

First chief of foreign air force
Air Commodore K. Jaswant Singh, who was on deputation to Ghana to plan and establish the Ghana Air Force, took charge on 25 March 1959 as its air chief.

First technical officer
Harjinder Singh, one of 19 Hawai Sepoys recruited to the IAF in 1931 (who later became air vice marshal), was promoted to the rank of warrant officer in 1941 and became a flying officer in 1942. He was 41 years old when he learned to fly, earned his wings, and became the air officer commander-in-chief of the then newly formed Maintenance Command in Kanpur, Uttar Pradesh, in 1955.

First woman medical officer
Dr Vijayalakshmi Ramanan (later, wing commander), an army doctor, was inducted into the IAF in 1955.

First woman pilot to lead the Republic Day fly-past
Flight Lieutenant Swati Rathore became the first woman pilot to lead the Republic Day fly-past on 26 January 2021. She flew an Mi-17 V5 with the IAF flag in a formation of four choppers. Flight Lieutenant Bhawana Kanth also participated in the Republic Day fly-past. A total of 38 IAF and four army aircraft were part of the parade.

Medals and Honours

First couple to be awarded the Vishisht Seva Medals

Flight Lieutenant (Dr) Sati Nath Bandopadhyay and his wife Flight Lieutenant Padmavathy Bandopadhyay were honoured with the Vishisht Seva Medal (VSM) at the same investiture ceremony by Air Chief Marshal O.P. Mehra for their service to the nation in the 1971 Bangladesh operations. They are the only Indian Air Force couple to be awarded such a commendation.

First woman to be awarded the Yudh Seva Medal

Squadron Leader Minty Aggarwal, a woman fighter controller who essayed a stellar role in intercepting retaliatory air attacks by the Pakistan Air Force after the Indian Air Force's Balakot air strikes in February 2019, was awarded the Yudh Seva Medal on 15 August 2019. Aggarwal thereby became the first woman in India's military history to be awarded the medal for distinguished service of a high order during war, conflict, or hostilities. Aggarwal was among seven fighter controllers on duty in an underground bunker at the Ambala airbase. She joined the air force in 2011.

First and only Sarvottam Yudh Seva Medal

On 15 August 1999, Air Marshal Vinod Patney was awarded the Sarvottam Yudh Seva Medal (SYSM) for his exemplary leadership during the Kargil conflict in 1999. The award is the highest wartime distinguished service decoration. The medal has been conferred thrice to date and he is the only IAF officer to receive it.

First Param Vir Chakra

Flying Officer N.J.S. Sekhon of 18 Squadron is the only Indian Air Force officer to have been decorated with the Param Vir Chakra, the highest gallantry award. It was given posthumously after he was killed in an air battle over Srinagar in Jammu and Kashmir on 14 December 1971.

UNITS

First transport squadron

The first transport squadron of the RIAF was raised with Spitfire fighter aircraft under the command of Squadron Leader S. Sajad Haider at Kohat (now in Pakistan). It moved to Bhopal, Madhya Pradesh, in 1946 and converted to Dakotas, which it flew till 1954, when it then converted to Packets, a twin-engine cargo aircraft.

First squadron

1 Squadron was formed on 1 April 1933 at Karachi's Drigh Road Airfield with Royal Indian Air Force (RAF) officer Flight Lieutenant C.A. Bouchier as the first commanding officer. The first six Indian officers commissioned into the IAF were: Subroto Mukerjee, H.C. Sirkar, A.B. Awan, Bhupendra Singh, Amarjeet Singh, and J.N. Tandon, along with 19 technicians who formed the complement. The six officers were pilots except Tandon, who was commissioned as first ground duty officer.

A stamp commemorating the No.1 Squadron of the IAF

First heavy-lift transport squadron

In 1961, 44 Squadron, known as 'Himalayan Geese', was raised and equipped with the An-12 four-engine turboprop transport aircraft. In the 1980s, it was renamed the 'Mighty Jets'.

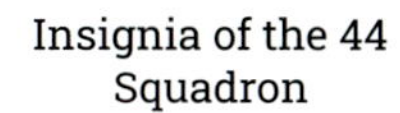

Insignia of the 44 Squadron

First squadron to have a jet bomber

106 SPR Squadron, though technically tasked with photo reconnaissance work, was the first unit to fly the famous English Electric Canberra in April 1957. The first squadron to have a jet bomber role again was No. 5 Squadron that took charge of the bomber variant of the Canberra in September 1957.

First attack helicopter squadron

On 1 November 1983, 125 Helicopter Squadron (also known as Gladiators), a fighter squadron, was formed with the Mil Mi-25 attack gunships. It was re-equipped with Mi-35 helicopters in April 1990. The squadron saw action in Sri Lanka during the operations of the Indian Peacekeeping Force (IPKF) between 1987 and 1990. It is currently based at the Pathankot air force station, Punjab.

First bomber squadron

The No. 5 Squadron (Tuskers) was raised on 2 November 1948 on the Consolidated B-24 Liberator bomber. It is now equipped with Jaguar IS and based in Ambala, Haryana.

EQUIPMENT

First aircraft

The biplane aircraft Westland Wapiti with a maximum speed of 362 km/hr was inducted into the IAF on 1 April 1933. Fitted with two machine guns, this aircraft could carry a load of 263 kg. Four Wapitis, which are believed to have been procured for 10 pounds sterling each, formed the A Flight of 1 Squadron, commanded by Flight Lieutenant C.A. Bouchier of the Royal Indian Air Force (RIAF).

Westland Wapiti

First jet bomber

The twin-engine English Electric Canberra, which is a long-range and reconnaissance air craft, was inducted into the Indian Air Force in 1957. Six IAF Canberras of 5 Squadron served with the UN forces on the Congo peacekeeping assignment in October 1961.

First supersonic aircraft

In February 1957, 1 Squadron (The Tigers) was equipped with the Dassault MD-452 Mystere Iva. The Mystere could break the sound barrier in a dive. However, the first squadron to fly a level-flight-capable supersonic aircraft was the 28 Squadron, raised in October 1963 on the MiG-21F. Aptly christened First Supersonics, 28 Squadron also has the honour of being the first squadron to fly a Mach 2-capable fighter.

First jet

The British single-seat Vampire was inducted in 1948, making India the first Asian country with jet fighters. In 1950, India entered into a licence agreement with de Havilland Aircraft Company Ltd, UK, and the first Vampire built by Hindustan Aeronautics Ltd (HAL) flew on 21 February 1952. Vampires were phased out in 1975.

First indigenous aircraft (trainer)

The HT-2-piston-engined elementary trainer was designed at HAL. It made its maiden flight on 5 August 1951 and was in operation from 1953 to 1990. It replaced the Tiger Moth and was used to train over 5,000 Indian and foreign pilots.

First indigenous light combat aircraft

Tejas is the first advanced fly-by-wire light combat aircraft (LCA) designed, developed, and manufactured indigenously by HAL, DRDO, NAL (National Aerospace Laboratories), and ADA (Aeronautical Development Agency). It is a lightweight single-seat multi-role jet fighter, and pegged as the world's smallest and lightest supersonic fighter. It is equipped with a satellite-aided inertial navigation system, a digital, computer-based attack system, and autopilot mode. Tejas can fire air-to-air missiles, and carry bombs and precision-guided ammunition with a reach of over 400 km. It is mainly for use in close air-to-ground operations.

HF-24 Mk I

First indigenous advanced light helicopter

The naval version of the advanced light helicopter (ALH), developed by HAL, took its first flight from INS *Viraat* on 8 March 1998. It had an integrated dynamic system, hinge-less main rotor and composite blades, bearing-less tail rotor, advanced cockpit, and high-power engines with electronic control. It could exceed a speed of 250 km/hr.

First indigenous fighter aircraft

The single-seat Mach-2 combat jet fighter HF (Hindustan Fighter)-24 Mk I (Marut Ground Attack Fighter), with two single-shaft turbojet engines, was designed at HAL, Bengaluru. It took its maiden flight on 17 June 1961.

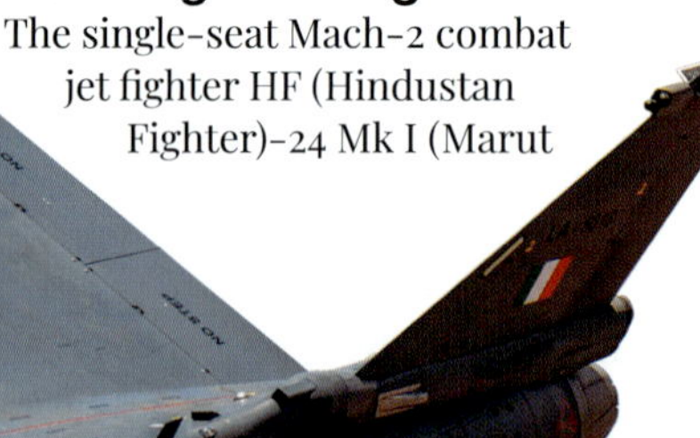
Tejas

First indigenous tandem-seat jet trainer

The intermediate jet trainer (IJT) was designed in India, with the fastest design-to-first-flight time, and flown officially by Squadron Leader Baldev Singh for 20 mins on 21 March 2003. With a 10 m (32 ft 10 in.) wingspan and an overall length of 11 m (36 ft), the 3,500 kg aircraft can touch 750 km/hr. However, the credit of being the first tandem-seat jet trainer used for intermediate flying training in the IAF goes to the Polish PZL TS-11 Iskra.

First indigenous AEW&C system class of aircraft

On 14 February 2017, the IAF was given its first indigenous Airborne Early Warning and Control (AEW&C) System class of aircraft in initial operational configuration (IOC) by DRDO, during Aero India 2017, a biennial air show and aviation exhibition, at the Yelahanka airbase in Bengaluru, Karnataka. It is built on an Emb-145 platform, and has an air-to-air refuelling capability to enhance surveillance time.

First AESA radar for IAF

The IAF gave the nod in July 2017 for the first Active Electronically Scanned Array (AESA) radar to be integrated with its aircraft. The radar is fitted on to the Jaguar fighter aircraft. In conventional radars, the antenna is moved manually to scan enemy targets. The AESA radar moves electronically and rapidly, tracking multiple and long-distance targets, while also jamming enemy communications and radars.

HAL Ajeet

First Gnat

The first Gnat or Ajeet, a single-seat, light, fighter bomber, about a third in size and half the weight of a conventional fighter, was inducted into the IAF in 1958. The first Gnat, made by HAL, flew on 18 November 1959. It helped Flying Officer Nirmal Jit Singh Sekhon win the IAF its only Param Vir Chakra, and was in front-line service for more than three decades.

First Apache helicopters

On 3 September 2019, eight Boeing-made Apache Guardian attack helicopters were inducted into service at the Pathankot air force station. The AH-64E (I) Apache helicopter has been built keeping in mind the high mountainous terrain that the IAF operates in. It can also carry out precision attacks. This helicopter can receive and transmit images from the ground to its weapon systems and likewise transmit images from its weapon systems to the ground. The air crew and ground crew were trained to operate the helicopter at the US Army base, Fort Rucker.

First S-400 air-defence system

The Indian Air Force deployed the first S-400 Triumf air-defence missile system in the Punjab sector near Pakistan border, as reported on 21 December 2021. The deployment was to take care of any aerial threat from either Pakistan or China, using its capability to shoot down enemy fighter aircraft and cruise missiles at a long range (400 km).

First indigenous anti-radiation missile

Rudram-1, a new-generation air-to-surface anti-radiation missile (NGARM), developed by DRDO for the Indian Air Force was test-fired on 9 October 2020 on a radiation target on Wheeler Island off the coast of Odisha. The missile Rudram-1 was fired from a Sukhoi-30 Mk I fighter aircraft, the potential launch source aircraft for the same. With its ability to detect radio sources from 100 km away, the missile can disarm enemy radars and target the range of emitters. Its strike range is between 100 and 250 km.

OPERATIONS

First active operation

In September 1937, 1 Squadron operated from Miranshah in North Waziristan (now in Pakistan) against hostile tribesmen. The IAF men lived inside a fort for safety and had to wheel in their aircraft into the fort every evening. Flying Officer (later Air Marshal) Aspy Merwan Engineer was the first officer to be Mentioned-in-Dispatches for the operations.

Rudram 1

Boeing Apache helicopter

First flight to the true North Pole

The IL-76 aircraft of the 44 Squadron, representing the IAF, flew over the true North Pole in Exercise Cope Thunder-03 in Alaska, USA, with 14 crew members. The mission was launched on 19 June 2003 at 8:15 p.m. IST from USA's Eielson air force base, south-east of Fairbanks, Alaska, and the crew flew over the true North Pole on 20 June 2003 at 00:16 a.m. IST. The aircraft returned to base on 20 June 2003 at 5:51 a.m. IST after a flight lasting 9 hrs 36 mins.

Biggest rapid airlift

On 18 December 2018, the Western Air Command of the IAF airlifted a record 463 tonnes from the Chandigarh airbase and dropped the load in Ladakh. The massive airlift was done in a single wave and proved the IAF's rapid airlift capability. The feat was completed by 16 fixed-wing transport aircraft including the C-17 Globemaster, the Ilyushin-76 Gajraj and the medium-lift tactical aircraft, Antonov-32. The airdrop was done in less than six hours.

First airlift of Indian troops

During the Kurdish uprising in April 1923, the Royal Air Force flew 280 Sikh troops from Kingarban to Kirkuk, Iraq. Covering the distance that would normally require a five-day march, the flight covered 120.7 km in 10 hours.

GENERAL

Only vintage flight

A vintage aircraft flight was raised in Palam, Delhi, in 1988 for heritage aircraft, such as the Howard, Tiger Moth and Dakota planes.

First forward surgical centre

During an IAF military exercise, Gaganshakti-2018, which was conducted from 8 to 22 April 2018, the IAF set up a Forward Surgical Centre (FSC) at Naliya air force station in Gujarat. An FSC can be used for life- and limb-saving surgeries as also to help stabilize a patient.

Hovercraft

A hovercraft is an amphibious vehicle that operates on water and land. It is also called an air-cushion vehicle (ACV) as they produce a current of air beneath it to support itself.

First private military aircraft plant

In October 2024, Tata Advanced Systems Limited partnered up with Airbus to open a private military aircraft plant in Vadodra, Gujarat. Inaugurated by Prime Minister Narendra Modi and President, Pedro Sánchez Pérez-Castejón of Spain, the facility will manufacture the Airbus C295 aircraft.

COAST GUARD

PERSONNEL

First director general of the Indian Coast Guard

Vice Admiral V.A. Kamath, PVSM, was the first director general of the Indian Coast Guard (ICG) from 19 August 1978 to 31 March 1980.

First and only Integral ICG contingent operating abroad

An ICG Dhruv helicopter – CG 853 – has been operating in Maldives along with an ICG contingent since 2019. Since its induction, the helicopter has aided in 168 medivac (medical evacuation) missions, saving 178 lives.

First woman hovercraft pilot

In 2017, Assistant Commandant Sneha Khatayak became the first woman hovercraft pilot in India.

First women combatants

In 2017, the Indian Coast Guard became the first Indian armed forces service to deploy women in combat roles on-board ships. Assistant Commandants Anuradha Shukla, Sneha Khatayak, Shirin Chandran, and Vasundhara Chouksey were trained at the Indian Coast Guard station at Mandapam, Tamil Nadu.

First woman pilot

Assistant Commandant Monica Seth joined the Indian Coast Guard on 5 June 1998. She flew a total of 1,500 hours during her tenure. She flew on missions during the Kargil conflict in Jammu and Kashmir in 1999 and also for earthquake relief in Gujarat in January 2001.

MEDALS AND HONOURS

First Yudh Seva Medal

Deputy Commandant S.P.S. Basra and Deputy Commandant B.A.S. Bhar were awarded the Yudh Seva Medal (YSM) on 26 January 1989. Commanding the Indian Coast Guard ships ICGS *Ahalya Bai* and ICGS *Tara Bai*, respectively, they prevented the infiltration of the Liberation Tigers of Tamil Eelam (LTTE) in the Palk Bay.

First to receive President's Tatrakshak Medal

Commandant A.K. Dey received the award for his efforts in firefighting during the construction of an Indian Coast Guard ship, and preventing an oil spill off the coast of Goa in June 1994.

EQUIPMENT

First indigenous offshore patrol vessel

On 21 February 2019, ICGS *Sachet*, the first indigenous offshore patrol

ICGS *Sachet*

Top: ICGS *Kuthar*
Above: ICGS *Kirpan*

vessel (OPV) of the Indian Coast Guard was launched at Goa Shipyard Ltd (GSL). This OPV is part of an indigenous project that was launched on 13 November 2016. Designed in-house, these OPVs will be used for protecting the Exclusive Economic Zone. The vessel weighs 2,400 tonnes and is equipped with features like quick-response boats for rescue and anti-piracy, gunnery simulators, and many more advanced features.

Latest training vessel

On 24 October 2018, ICGS *Varuna*, an indigenously designed training vessel built by Reliance Naval and Engineering Ltd (RNAVAL), was launched at the Pipavav Shipyard, Gujarat. ICGS *Varuna* is a 105 m (344 ft 6 in.) long vessel with a crew of 242 officers and sailors. It is powered by twin diesel engines and can reach a speed of 20 knots. It has ultra modern navigation and communication systems. This is the largest ship built yet for the Indian Coast Guard.

First vessels

ICGS *Kuthar* and ICGS *Kirpan* (formerly of the Indian Navy) were commissioned on 19 August 1978 under Commander N.S. Achreja and Commander V.K. Tuli, respectively.

OPERATIONS

First and longest deep-sea passage by hovercraft

On 13 January 2015, Indian Coast Guard Air Cushion Vehicle (ACV) H-198 undertook area deployment from New Mangaluru, Karnataka, to Androth Island in Lakshadweep, across the Arabian Sea. The ACV hovercraft, piloted by Commandant Amitabh Banerjee and Deputy Commandant Konark Sharma, covered 142.5 nautical miles (264 km) in five hours. The ACV H-198 is the only hovercraft in India to venture into the lagoon islands of Lakshadweep. The return run of 146 nautical miles (270.39 km) was made on 22 January 2015.

First underwater clean-up

On 5 June 2019, celebrated as World Environment Day, the Indian Coast Guard (Eastern Region) conducted an underwater debris clean-up exercise in the Bay of Bengal near the Chennai coast, in association with Dive India. The operation lasted two hours during which nearly 500 kg of trash was collected. This was the first underwater clean-up in India to remove debris, nets, and plastic from the ocean.

GENERAL

Youngest defence service

Insignia of the Indian Coast Guard

The Indian Coast Guard or Sea Police, was constituted under the Coast Guard Act on 18 August 1978, for the preservation and protection of the 2.01 million sq. km Exclusive Economic Zone. The force is under the direction and control of the director general, Indian Coast Guard.

First hovercraft berthing platform

In 2001, the first hovercraft berthing platform was built at Haldia, West Bengal, in eight months by the Military Engineering Services.

Largest integrated shipbuilding facility

Reliance Naval and Engineering Ltd (RNAVAL), known earlier as Reliance Defence and Engineering Ltd and Pipavav Shipyard Ltd, headquartered in Mumbai, Maharashtra, is one of the largest shipbuilding yards of its kind in the world. RNAVAL is the first private sector company in India to earn a licence and contract to construct warships. It has India's largest integrated shipbuilding facility with the shipyard located in Pipavav, Gujarat. Its dry dock measures 662 m x 65 m (2,172 ft x 213 ft). It has the only modular shipbuilding facility in India.

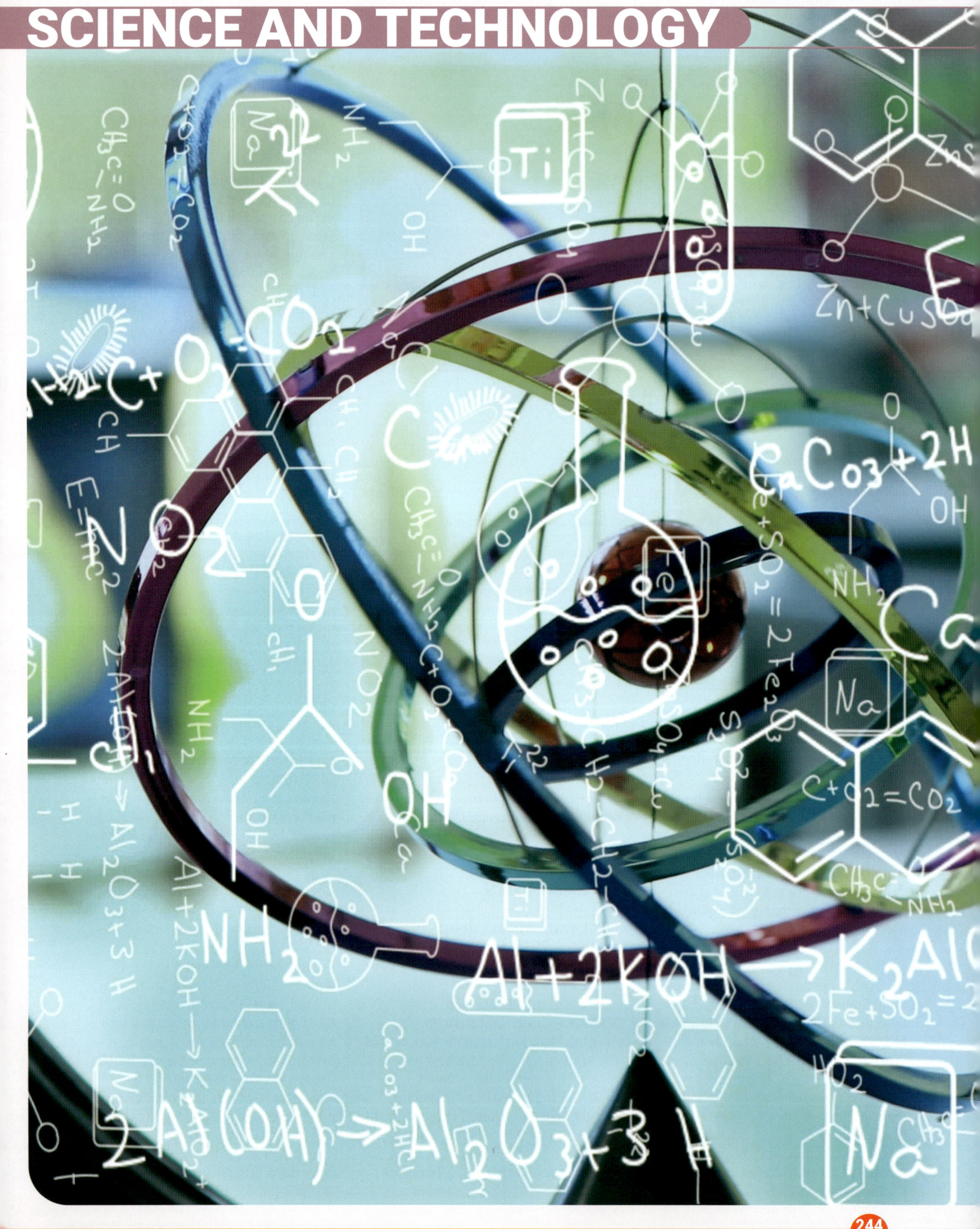
Ti
Na
C+O2=CO2
NH2
OH

Search...
CaCO3+2HCl
Al+2KOH
NaCl
NH3
H2O
H2SO4
Sn+O2→2HO
E=mc2
CH3COOH
H3PO4
ZnSO4
NO2
NH2
OH
Na
Ti

FORMAL SCIENCES

MATHEMATICS

Earliest mention of mathematical series

Arithmetic and geometric series were mentioned in Vedic literature as early as 2000 BCE in the *Taittiriya Samhita* and in the *Panchavimsa Brahmana*.

Earliest treatise on geometry

The *Shulba Sutras* are the earliest known treatises that are related to geometry. Dating to the Vedic period, these texts are focused on the measurement and the building of altars. Baudhayana, who lived around 800 BCE, wrote the first *Shulba Sutra*.

First application of geometry

In the first millennium BCE, Apastamba, the founder of a Vedic school, propounded practical geometry for the construction of sacrificial altars, which describes acute, obtuse, and right angles.

Earliest use of irrational numbers

The use of irrational numbers dates back to the *Shulba Sutras* (c. first millennium BCE).

Invention of algebra

Aryabhata (476–550 CE) from Kusumapura near Pataliputra (today's Patna) in Bihar is credited with the invention of algebra. He was also the first to approximate the value of π (pi) to 3.14159..., which is accepted today.

Earliest magic squares

The oldest magic square in India that can be dated occurs in polymath Varahamihira's encyclopaedic work the *Brihat Samhita* (c. 550 CE). Varahamihira used a modified 4 x 4 magic square to indicate combinations and quantities of ingredients for making perfumes.

Palm leaf manuscript of *Brihat Samhita*

Earliest use of the decimal system

A Gupta inscription from 448 CE found in Allahabad (now Prayagraj) District, Uttar Pradesh, indicates that the decimal system was known in India at the beginning of the fifth century CE.

Use of sines and cosines in place of chords

In a significant contribution to trigonometry, Indian mathematicians changed the use of chords to sines and cosines, making the system much more convenient and the various theorems on triangles much neater. Starting with the *Arya-siddhanta* (c. fifth and sixth centuries CE), Aryabhata used a simple table for sines. Varahamihira gave the first clear statements of $\sin^2 A$ and $\sin^2 A + \cos^2 A$.

Firsts to understand the idea of 'zero'

Brahmagupta (c. 598–668 CE) was the first mathematician to treat zero as a number and present its mathematical operations. Bhaskara I (c. 600–680 CE) was the first mathematician to understand the properties of both zero and infinity and to state that any number divided by zero equals infinity.

First study of infinite series

Founded in the 14th century by Madhava (c. 1340–1425 CE) of Sangamagrama, who is said to have been born in present-day Irinjalakuda in Thrissur District, Kerala; the Kerala school of astronomy and mathematics (or the Kerala school) was responsible for notable contributions to the study of infinite series, trigonometry, geometry, algebra, and calculus. The foundations for calculus laid by Madhava were further developed by his successors at the Kerala school, with many results that would later be repeated in Europe, including the infinite series for circular and trigonometric functions.

First textbook on arithmetic

Ganita Sara Sangraha, written by the great mathematician Mahavira in 850 CE, is the first known textbook on arithmetic. The subject matter and its arrangement is said to be practically the same as that in present-day textbooks. It only lacks a chapter on decimals.

Discovery of differential calculus

Bhaskara II (c. 1114–85 CE), said to have been born in Bijapur (now Vijayapura) in Karnataka, conducted mathematical operations that showed that he had invented calculus long before Isaac Newton and Gottfried Leibniz, who are considered its pioneers. Bhaskara II used calculus to determine the area and volume of a sphere and the daily motion of planets.

First to give the Gregory series

In 1502, Keḷallur Nilakantha Somayaji (1444–1545 CE) from Tirur in present-day Malappuram District, Kerala, devised the *Tantrasangraha* equation, which is employed to give the approximate value of π or pi (3.14159...). This is known today as the 'Gregory series' after it appeared in the works of later mathematicians James Gregory (1638–75) and Gottfried Leibniz (1646–1716).

Discovery of the Kaprekar Constant

D.R. Kaprekar (1905-81) discovered in 1946 what is known as the Kaprekar Constant in mathematics. Explained thus: Take a number, arrange its digits in descending order and in ascending order and calculate the difference. Arrange the digits of the result of the subtraction in the same way and find the difference. Keep repeating the process. For any four-digit number, this leads in a few steps to 6,174 and then it becomes a constant. This does not work for repetitive numbers like 1,111 and 2,222, which lead to a difference of zero in the first step itself. The numbers should have at least two different digits.

First mathematical society

The Indian Mathematical Society (IMS) was the oldest organization in India devoted to the promotion of the study of and research in mathematics. With its headquarters in Pune, Maharashtra, it was founded by V. Ramaswamy Aiyer in April 1907. The society's first president was Dr B. Hanumantha Rao.

Neelakantha Bhanu Prakash: first Indian to win MSO

First Indian to win MSO

Twenty-year old Neelakantha Bhanu Prakash (b. 13 October 1999) became the fastest human calculator in the world after winning the gold for India in the Mental Calculation World Championship at Mind Sports Olympiad (MSO) in September 2020.

Invention of the Mahalanobis distance

Pioneering statistician P.C. Mahalanobis (1893–1972) invented statistical tools such as the Mahalanobis distance and fractile graphical analysis in 1936. He was the first statistician to be elected a Fellow of the Royal Society, UK, in 1945.

First to propose a theory on infinite dimensional representations

Indian-born American mathematician-physicist Harish Chandra (1923–83) created a theory for infinite dimensional representations in 1947, which was used in quantum mechanics when it was necessary to analyse the effect of symmetries on the motions of particles and waves.

PHYSICAL SCIENCES

ASTRONOMY

Two firsts in astronomy

Lagadha, who lived around 900 BCE near Srinagar, Jammu and Kashmir, was the first to systematize astronomy, the first to complete a text – *Vedanga Jyotisha* or *Jyotishavedanga* – on astronomy, and the first to work out simple formulae to derive unknown quantities from known ones. Aryabhata was the first astronomer to deduce that the earth is round and that it rotates on its own axis, causing day and night.

First manual on the astrolabe

The astrolabe is an instrument for measuring the altitude of stars. Mahendra Suri (c. 1340–1400 CE), an astronomer, wrote a manual on the astrolabe in Sanskrit while under the patronage of ruler Firuz Shah Tughlaq of the Tughlaq dynasty.

Earliest extant astrolabe

The Yantraraja, which was 276 mm (10.87 in.) in diameter, was designed and built in Ahmedabad, Gujarat, in 1607 for astronomer Damodara during the reign of the Mughal ruler Jahangir.

Front of an Indian astrolabe now kept at the Royal Museum of Scotland at Edinburgh.

Observatory Records

First chain of observatories

WR

Sawai Jai Singh II (1686–1743), the maharaja of the kingdom of Amber in Rajasthan, was the first in the world to build a chain of astronomical observatories, in Mathura, Varanasi, Delhi, and Jaipur; from 1719 to 1737. It was about a century after European astronomers had verified Polish scientist Nicolaus Copernicus's theory that the sun (and not the earth) was at the centre of the universe.

First modern astronomical observatory

On 5 December 1786, William Petrie, an officer of the East India Company, made the first astronomical observations to calculate the latitude and longitude of the Masulipatnam Fort from his private observatory. This observatory on the terrace of his residence was fitted with an astronomical clock, a transit instrument, and two or three telescopes. The first modern astronomical observatory, the Nizamia Observatory, was set up more than a century later in Hyderabad (now in Telangana) in 1908 by the Nizam's government.

First university to teach astronomy

Osmania University, based in Hyderabad, was the first educational institution in the country to start teaching astronomy and astrophysics at postgraduate and research levels in 1959. The Astronomical Society of India was also registered in Hyderabad, in 1972.

Highest astronomical observatory

Established in 2001, the Indian Astronomical Observatory, under the aegis of the Indian Institute of Astrophysics, Bengaluru, is located in Hanle (at Digpa-Ratsa Ri, atop Mt Saraswati) in Ladakh. It has the world's second highest optical telescope at 4,17 m (14,819 ft 6.6 in.) above mean sea level.

M.P. Birla Planetarium in Kolkata: oldest planetarium

Oldest planetarium

The M.P. Birla Planetarium in Calcutta (now Kolkata), West Bengal, was established on 29 September 1962 by the Birla Education Trust. The planetarium coordinates the various activities of the Amateur Astronomers Association, which include telescope fabrication, astrophotography, and organizing skywatching sessions.

First modern catalogue of stars

The Madras or Taylor catalogue was made by T.G. Taylor, astronomer to the British East India Company, in 1844. The catalogue contained the positions of 11,015 stars, based on his observations of the night sky in Madras (now Chennai), Tamil Nadu.

Discovery of the Bappu–Wilson effect

Indian astronomer M.K.V. Bappu (1927–82), in collaboration with Colin C. Wilson at Mount Wilson and Palomar Observatories, USA, discovered a relationship between the luminosity of particular types of stars and their spectral characteristics. Known as the 'Bappu–Wilson effect', this helps determine the luminosity and distance of these types of stars. It was discovered in 1957.

WR First Liquid Mirror Telescope Only for Astronomical Observations

Aryabhatta Research Institute of Observational Sciences (ARIES), an autonomous institute under the Department of Science and Technology, now has the first liquid mirror telescope that is meant only for astronomical observations. It is called International Liquid Mirror Telescope (ILMT). This is also India's, as well as Asia's, largest. This telescope was inaugurated on 22 March 2023. It was designed and built by Advanced Mechanical and Optical Systems (AMOS) Corporation and the Centre Spatial de Lie'ge in Belgium. The telescope will generate 10–15 gigabytes of data, which in turn will allow application of big data and machine-learning algorithms that will be used for classifying the objects observed through the ILMT.

Discovery of the variability of stars

In 1958, astrophysicist K.D. Abhyankar (1928–2007), professor of astronomy at the Osmania University in Hyderabad, discovered the variability of two types of stars, called dwarf cepheid and the short period eclipsing binary.

First facility for ground-based, infrared observations of celestial objects

The Mount Abu Infrared Observatory in Mount Abu, Rajasthan, is the first Indian facility that offers ground-based infrared observations of celestial objects. This facility is operated by the Physical Research Laboratory and began its journey with a 1.2 m telescope. Currently it has five telescopes, a new 2.5-metre primary mirror telescope equipped with the PARAS-2 spectrograph being the most powerful.

The Mount Abu Infrared Observatory on Gurushikhara peak in Mount Abu

Discovery of solar radio burst

In 1958, Prof. Govind Swarup (b. 1929) and A. Maxwell discovered a burst, called 'type U solar radio burst'. A pioneer of radio astronomy, Swarup was behind the concept, design, and installation of the Ooty Radio Telescope near present-day Udhagamandalam, Tamil Nadu, and the Giant Metrewave Radio Telescope (GMRT) near Poona (now Pune) in Maharashtra.

First woman president of the Astronomical Society of India

In 2019, the Astronomical Society of India elected its first woman president, Dr G.C. Anupama, a senior professor and dean at the Indian Institute of Astrophysics in Bengaluru. She has projects such as the Himalayan Telescope at the Hanle Observatory in Ladakh to her credit and is a member of an international team setting up a 30 m (98 ft 5 in.) telescope (TMT) in Hawaii, USA.

WR Biggest sundial

The Samrat Yantra built by Sawai Jai Singh II, ruler of the kingdom of Amber in Rajasthan, in 1728 CE at Jaipur, Rajasthan, is the biggest sundial in the world. Its gnomon rises to 22.6 m (74 ft).

First robotic telescope

India's first robotic telescope became functional on the night of 12 June 2018 at Hanle, Ladakh. It is the first one designed to observe dynamic or transient events in the universe. GROWTH-India, the facility at Hanle, is part of a multi-country collaborative initiative, known as the 'Global Relay of Observatories Watching Transients Happen' (GROWTH), to observe transient events in the universe.

PHYSICS

Earliest atomistic theory

Kanada, an ancient Indian natural scientist and philosopher, who lived between the sixth and second centuries BCE, composed the *Vaisheshika Sutra*, a text in which he explored and presented the relationship between cause and effect for the first time in relation to physics and philosophy.

Celestial Records

First discovery of an asteroid

R. Rajamohan (b. 1944), associate professor at the Indian Institute of Astrophysics, Bangalore (now Bengaluru), and his team discovered an asteroid (No. 4130) in 1988, through the optical telescope at Kavalur, Tamil Nadu.

Earliest observation of the Pole Star

Ancient astronomers Ashwalayana and Patanjali recorded observing the Pole Star (or *Dhruvatara*) in c. 1300 BCE.

First to observe a nova

Radha Gobinda Chandra (1878–1975) from Jessore (now in Bangladesh) was the first Indian astronomer to observe a nova. A nova is a transient astronomical event that causes the sudden appearance of a bright and seemingly 'new' star that slowly fades over weeks or months. He sighted the nova in the Aquila constellation on 7 June 1918. A pioneer of observational astronomy in Bengal – now split into two parts, Bangladesh (a country) and West Bengal (an Indian state), Chandra was one of the first international members of the American Association of Variable Star Observers.

Rings of Uranus discovered

Prof. J.C. Bhattacharya and Sri Kuppuswamy from the Indian Institute of Astrophysics, Bangalore, Karnataka, discovered the rings of the planet Uranus in 1976 at the Vainu Bappu Observatory in Kavalur, Tamil Nadu. Around the same time, US astronomer James Elliot and his team, aboard the airborne Kuiper Observatory, discovered the same rings during an occultation of a star by the planet.

First double radio source

Mrinal Kumar Dasgupta from the Institute of Radio Physics and Electronics, Calcutta, West Bengal, discovered the first double radio source Cygnus A in 1953 in collaboration with R.C. Jennison at the Jodrell Bank Experimental Station in Cheshire, UK.

Trombay, the site of India's first atomic reactor (Aspara)

First solar heater

Prof. Shri Krishna Joshi from Almora, who lived in Allahabad (now Prayagraj), Uttar Pradesh, invented an apparatus for utilizing solar heat as a substitute for fire, named 'Bhanu Taap'. Also called the 'heliotherm', it was patented in 1900 and earned a gold medal at the Industrial Exhibition of Calcutta in 1901.

First optical fibre

Narinder Kalpany from the Imperial College, University of London, UK, invented optical fibre in 1955. This is a thin and long fibre of glass through which light can travel without hindrance, whether it is bent or not. Optical fibres have a wide variety of applications in a range of fields, including medicine, computers, communications, and the automotive industry.

First multicore fibre

STL Multiverse launched India's first multicore fibre and cable in October 2022. This development allows the fibre to carry multiple beams of light (separated within the body of the optic fibre cable) through it, making it more efficient than single-core fibre.

Optical fibres have a wide variety of applications (representative image)

First molecular distillation unit

Major General Sir Singh Sokhey of Haffkine Institute, in Bombay (now Mumbai), Maharashtra, installed the first molecular distillation unit in India to separate vitamin A from shark liver oil in the early 1940s. He was also the first Indian scientist to receive the Lenin Peace Prize in 1947.

First nuclear implosion

On 18 May 1974, India imploded its first nuclear device at Pokhran in Rajasthan. The test, code-named 'Smiling Buddha', was conducted at a depth of 107 m (351 ft). It yielded energy equivalent to 8–10 kilotonnes of TNT, and produced a 47 m (154 ft) wide and 10 m (33 ft) deep crater.

First semiconductor laser

The Bhabha Atomic Research Centre, Bombay, developed a semiconductor laser in 1965.

First nuclear reactor

Apsara was the first Asian research reactor to achieve criticality, when it became operational, at the Bhabha Atomic Research Centre (BARC) in Bombay in 1956. It was shut down in 2010.

First to measure ozone in the atmosphere

In 1985, M. Vivekananda and R.S. Arora from the Raman Research Institute, Bangalore, first measured the density and height distribution of ozone in the atmosphere over Bangalore by a simple ground-based technique using radio waves.

First prediction of hot superconductors

S.N. Ekbote and A.V. Narlikar from the National Physical Laboratory (NPL), New Delhi, were the first scientists to predict the presence of 'hot' superconductors based on their new theory of superconductivity formulated in 1981, which challenged the then accepted Nobel Prize–winning theory.

Discovery of the 'Krishnan effect'

In the 1930s, physicist Rappal Sangameswaran Krishnan (1911–99) from the Indian Institute of Science (IISc), Bangalore, discovered the 'Krishnan effect' – a new optical effect in the scattering of light. This led to the discovery of the presence of large clusters of molecules in liquid mixtures, glasses, and colloidal solutions. It also helps in assessing the size of the scattering particles.

First synchrotron radiation facility

The first synchrotron radiation facility in India was INDUS-1, set up in 2002. An advanced, indigenously built nuclear particle accelerator, it is part of the Centre for Advanced Technology at Indore, Madhya Pradesh.

Tata Institute of Fundamental Research in Mumbai

First Nobel Prize in physics

Sir Chandrasekhara Venkata Raman (1888–1970) from Tiruchirappalli, Madras Presidency (now Tamil Nadu), won the 1930 Nobel Prize in physics for his groundbreaking work in the field of the scattering of light, or the 'Raman effect'.

First advanced heavy water reactor

In 2016, the Bhabha Atomic Research Centre (BARC) in Mumbai designed an advanced heavy water reactor, which employed thorium instead of uranium as fuel. It was the centrepiece of India's nuclear power programme.

Left: Sir Chandrasekhara Venkata Raman
Right: Dr Homi J. Bhabha

Only nuclear safety institute

With the inauguration of the Safety Research Institute at Kalpakkam, Tamil Nadu, on 20 February 1999, India became the second country after France to have such a facility.

Discovery of quantum Zeno paradox

Indian theoretical physicists Baidyanath Misra and E.C.G. Sudarshan, then conducting research at the University of Texas at Austin, US, discovered the quantum Zeno effect (or paradox) in 1977. It is the quantum mechanical analogue of the proverbial adage 'a watched kettle never boils'. In 1989, the paradox was experimentally proven – under continuous measurement, an unstable atomic nucleus that normally decays was found not to decay.

Discovery of bosons

Satyendra Nath Bose

In the late 1920s, famous physicist and German Nobel Prize–winner Albert Einstein and Indian scientist Satyendra Nath Bose worked together on the Bose–Einstein equations, which pointed to a state of matter comprising particles, now known as 'bosons'. As researchers at the Joint Institute of Laboratory Astrophysics, Colorado, USA, they cooled thousands of atoms of rubidium to create the 'Bose–Einstein condensate'.

Discovery of helium isotope in cosmic rays

Dr K.M.V. Apparao (b. 1933), a scientist at the Tata Institute of Fundamental Research in Bombay discovered in 1961 an isotope of helium in cosmic rays, the energetic particles that fall down on earth like a continuous rain from outer space.

New method for thermal conductivity

Suresh Chand Jain (1926–2009), former director of the Solid State Physics Laboratory and Defence Research and Development Organization (DRDO), and his mentor R. S. Krishnan (1911–99) developed a new method known as the Jain–Krishnan method in 1952, which is now a standard method for measuring the thermal conductivity of solids at high temperatures.

Discovery of mesons

Indian nuclear physicist Dr Homi Jehangir Bhabha and German physicist Dr Walter Heinrich Heitler presented the 'Cascade Theory of Electron Showers', called the 'Bhabha–Heitler Cascade Theory' in 1937 in Cambridge, UK, which explains the process of electron showers in cosmic rays. Bhabha recognized heavy electron particles in cosmic rays, which he named 'mesons'.

First wireless demonstration

In 1894, scientist Jagadish Chandra Bose (1858–1937) at Presidency College, (now Presidency University) Calcutta, demonstrated the transmission of radio waves before Italian inventor Guglielmo Marconi did it in Europe, using very short radio waves or 'microwaves'.

Jagadish Chandra Bose also scientifically proved that plants have feelings. He wrote the first science fiction in Bengali.

CHEMISTRY

First heavy chemicals company

Behramji Sorabji Lalkaka (1880–1957) started the Pioneer Magnesia Works Ltd in 1915 at Kharagodha in the Little Rann of Kutch (now Run of Kachchh), Gujarat, for the manufacture of magnesium chloride, the import of which was stopped from Germany due to the First World War. Magnesium chloride is used in a variety of ways in the chemical industry.

First tokamak

The first Indian tokamak – essentially a magnetic bottle that can maintain conditions present inside the sun wherein enormous energy from nuclear fusion reactions is produced – named Aditya was set up at the Institute for Plasma Research, Gandhinagar, Gujarat, in 1986.

First Indian to receive the Chemical Landmark Plaque award

The Royal Society of Chemistry, UK, in 2011 honoured the life and work of Prafulla Chandra Ray with the first ever Chemical Landmark Plaque awarded to anyone from a country outside Europe.

Aditya: first tokamak

First observation of spontaneous fission

Prof. Shyamadas Chatterjee (1909–95) from the Indian Physical Society in Calcutta, West Bengal, first observed spontaneous fission – the splitting of a heavy nucleus on its own in uranium – in 1940, almost at the same time when scientists in Western countries reported its discovery.

Discovery of phosphocreatine

In 1927, Dr Yellapragada Subbarow (1895–1948) from Bhimavaram, Madras Presidency (now in Andhra Pradesh), and Cyrus H. Fiske discovered the function of adenosine triphosphate, an organic phosphorous compound, as an energysource in the human cell, connected with the chemical mechanism of muscle contraction.

PRODUCTION OF SELECTED MAJOR CHEMICALS (IN 000' MT)

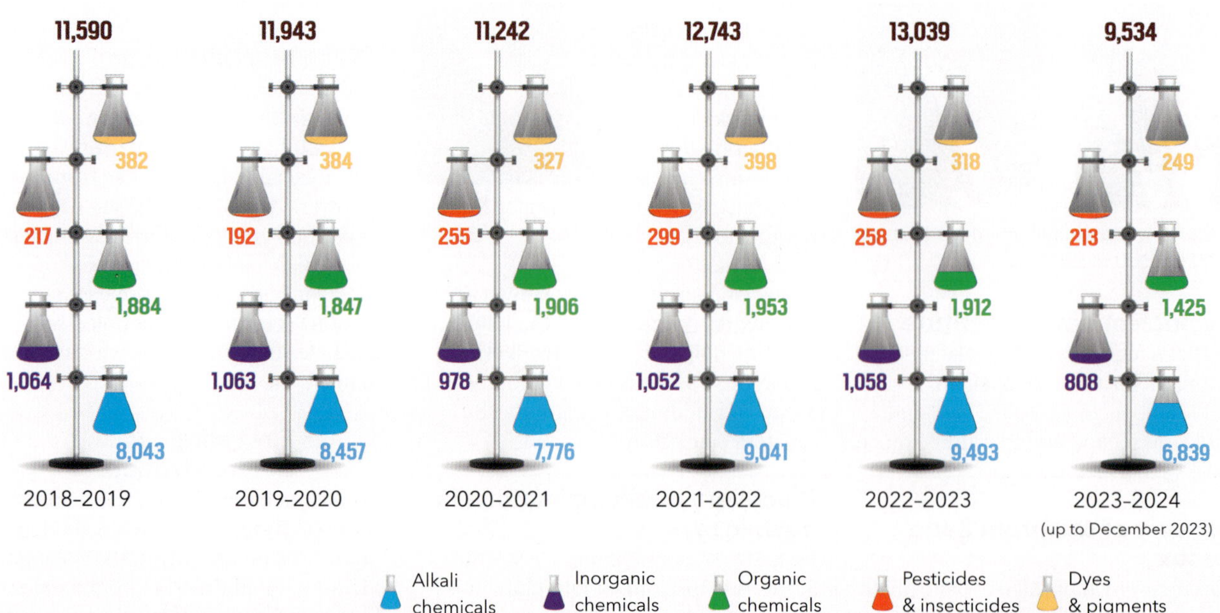

Source: https://chemicals.gov.in/sites/default/files/Reports/annual_report_english.pdf

He also discovered methotrexate (still used in chemotherapy) and diethylcarbamazine (DEC), which is used for effectively treating filariasis).

Discoveries in terpene chemistry

Dr Sukh Dev (b. 1923) from the Indian Institute of Technology, Delhi, discovered many new fundamental types of terpenoids, a class of naturally occurring organic compounds found in plants.

Prafulla Chandra Ray: founder of the first chemicals company

Dr Kalaiselvi N.: first woman director general of the CSIR

First chemicals company

In 1892, Prafulla Chandra Ray (1861–1944) set up Bengal Chemicals and Pharmaceutical Ltd at Calcutta, West Bengal, using locally available materials, which led to the production of many chemicals and medicines indigenously. He was also the first person to synthesize ammonium nitrite (NH_4NO_2) in its pure form.

Largest scientific and industrial research organization

The Council of Scientific and Industrial Research (CSIR), which was set up in 1942, is India's largest research and development organization for scientific and industrial research for economic and environmental development.

First woman director general of CSIR

Dr Kalaiselvi N. became India's first woman director general of the Council of Scientific and Industrial Research (CSIR), India's largest research organization. She primarily works on electrochemical power systems. She was appointed to the post in August 2022.

First chemistry department

Chemistry was first taught as a subject in 1872–73 at Presidency College (now Presidency University, Kolkata, West Bengal). Postgraduate courses were introduced in 1886. In 1889, chemist Prafulla Chandra Ray set up the first organized laboratory here for research.

Discovery of the isomerism of thiosulphuric acid

Prof. Priyada Ranjan Ray (1888–1982), director, Indian Association for the Cultivation of Science, Calcutta, established for the first time the isomerism (compounds that have the same molecular formulae but different molecular structures) of thiosulphuric acid.

Presidency College: first chemistry department

Discovery of tetracycline

Tetracycline, a life-saving drug, was discovered as a natural product and developed in 1948 by a research group headed by Dr Yellapragada Subbarow at the Lederle Laboratories in New York, US. An anti-plague drug, it helped save many lives in the 1994 plague epidemic in Surat, Gujarat.

First carbon dioxide laser

Chandra Kumar Naranbhai Patel (b. 1938), an Indian-origin scientist in the United States, invented the powerful carbon dioxide laser in 1963, which resulted in making lasers a valuable tool in scientific research.

GEOLOGY

First course in geology

Geology as a degree course leading to postgraduation was started at Presidency College, Calcutta, for the first time in the country in 1892.

First mention of seismological zones

Varahamihira, the ancient astronomer and scientist, was the first to mention seismological zones and the most earthquake-prone areas in his treatise *Brihat Samhita* (c. 550 CE).

First geologist

Dr Henry Wesley Voysey, a doctor by profession, became the first professional geologist in India under British rule in 1818.

First geomagnetic observatory

The Colaba Geomagnetic Observatory in Bombay was the first geomagnetic observatory to be set up in pre-Independence India. It was established in 1846 by the scientists of the East India Company to study the earth's magnetic field by using geomagnetic instruments.

First megafossil from the Himalayas

In 1984, R.N. Lakhanpal, a scientist at the Birbal Sahni Institute of Palaeosciences, Lucknow, Uttar Pradesh, and his team discovered a leaf of the temperate palm *Trachycarpus*, the first definite megafossil record of the Miocene period (23 million to 5.3 million years ago) in Ladakh in the Himalayas.

First underwater mining system

The National Institute of Ocean Technology, Chennai, Tamil Nadu, in collaboration with the University of Siegen, Germany, devised an underwater mining vehicle called the crawler, which extracts mineral-rich polymetallic nodules from the ocean floor. The mining system consists of a crawler, cutter, and slurry pump. Mounted on board the ship ORV *Sagar Kanya*, its first test was conducted successfully on 14 March 2000 near Tuticorin (now Thoothukudi), Tamil Nadu.

First president of the International Geological Congress

Dr D.N. Wadia (1883–1969), president of the 22nd International Geological Congress, which was held in New Delhi in 1964, was the first and only Indian to become president of the International Geological Congress.

First dinosaur fossils

The Geological Survey of India (GSI) discovered dinosaur bone fossils from the Lameta formation of the late Cretaceous age (145 to 66 million years ago) at Raiyoli near Balasinor in the Kheda District, Gujarat, in 1981. Dinosaur egg clutches were also found at the site in 1982. Both the eggs and bones are preserved at the Indian Museum in Kolkata.

Fossilized dinosaur eggs displayed at Indroda Dinosaur and Fossil Park, Gandhinagar

WR Periodicity of geomagnetic reversals

J.G. Negi and R.R. Tewari from the National Geophysical Research Institute, Hyderabad, put forward, in 1983, the theory that the flipping of the earth's magnetic field, i.e., the North Pole becoming the South Pole and vice versa, is related to variations in the gravitational force of the earth. They found that the frequency with which the earth's magnetic field flips is directly correlated to the periodicity of the orbit of the sun.

Largest mineral explorer

The Mineral Exploration Corporation Ltd, established in October 1972, is a public sector company under the Ministry of Mines, Government of India, with its corporate office at Nagpur, Maharashtra, and regional offices at Kolkata, Hyderabad, Ranchi, Jaipur, and Nagpur. Its functions include mineral targeting, deposit assessment, and mine development.

First geoscientific data centre

The Geological Survey of India (GSI) set up a geoscientific data centre at Calcutta on 3 November 1998. It is the largest repository of knowledge on earth sciences in Asia, Australia, and Africa.

First official Indian geologist

Pramatha Nath Bose is considered to be the first official Indian geologist. He joined the Geological Survey of India (GSI) as an officer in 1880. He is known to have mapped the Vindhya Range as well as the igneous rocks of Raipur and Balaghat areas of what was then the Central Province.

Pramatha Nath Bose: first official Indian geologist

Discovery of vanadium

Abani Kumar Dey and J.A. Dunn discovered a new vanadium-bearing mineral in the Singhbhum–Mayurbhanj area, which is in present-day Jharkhand and Odisha, in the 1930s and called this mineral coulsonite (composition FeV_2O_4), the main source of vanadium in India. It is of strategic importance for making special steels. Abani Dey was the recipient of the First National Mineral Award in 1968.

Discovery of iron ore deposits

Pramatha Nath Bose discovered the first iron ore deposit in Mayurbhanj region in present-day Odisha, in 1904, paving the way for the modern iron industry.

OCEAN STUDIES

First marine research institute

On 3 February 1947 the Central Marine Fisheries Research Institute was established in Chennai. Since 1971, it is headquartered in Kochi, Kerala.

Highest wave

Scientists on board the ship RV *Gaveshani* of the National Institute of Oceanography recorded a wave 13 m (42 ft 7.8 in.) high in the Arabian Sea off the coast of Goa in June 1979.

First oceanographic research vessel

RV *Gaveshani*, commissioned on 1 December 1975, was the first oceanographic research vessel. It carried teams of scientific personnel on various marine expeditions that could last from a few days to months.

First course in oceanography

The first postgraduate course in oceanography was introduced in 1948 at Andhra University in Visakhapatnam in Andhra Pradesh.

LIFE SCIENCES

BIOLOGY

Oldest biological fossils

Fossils of 3-billion-year-old photosynthetic blue-green algae of the Archaean era (4 billion to 2.5 billion years ago) were discovered at Kashia in Orissa (now Odisha) in 1998 by scientists of the Birbal Sahni

Andhra University in Visakhapatnam: first course in oceanography started here

First Antarctic expedition

Dr S.Z. Qasim, director, National Institute of Oceanography, Goa, reached Antarctica on 9 January 1982. The 21-member team left Mormugao Harbour, Goa, on 6 December 1981 on a Norwegian ship, MV *Polar Circle*, and returned on 21 February 1982. During the expedition, the team built Dakshin Gangotri, the first Indian scientific research base station in the Queen Maud Land area in Antarctica.

First women on Antarctica

Structural geologist Sudipta Sengupta and marine biologist and oceanographer Aditi Pant were the first Indian women to visit Antarctica, during the third Indian expedition to Antarctica from 3 December 1983 to 25 March 1984. The expeditions aimed to study atmospheric, biological, earth, chemical, and medical sciences in the region.

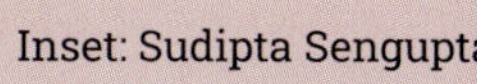

Inset: Sudipta Sengupta

Institute of Palaeosciences in Lucknow. The latest find includes 1.6-billion-year-old red algae fossils in the Chitrakoot region of central India.

First anther culture

S.C. Maheswari and Sipra Mukherjee from Delhi discovered the anther culture technique in 1967, in which anthers (part of a stamen that contains pollen, in a plant) were placed on a synthetic culture medium.

Discovery of earliest multicellular organisms

In October 1998, Pradip K. Bose, a professor at Jadavpur University, Calcutta, found a site close to Churhat town in Sidhi District, Madhya Pradesh, where multicellular organisms with body fluid existed around 1.1 billion years ago. He discovered tracks on sandstone rock left by wormlike creatures about half a centimetre thick, while burrowing through the sea floor ages ago. This was the first evidence of macroscopic animals in India.

First methane plant

Biomethane was first put to use in India in 1857, when a methane plant was installed in a colony near Bombay.

First national gene bank

R.S. Paroda, director general of the Indian Council of Agricultural Research, Delhi, established the first National Gene Bank in Delhi in 1985.

First to extract insulin from a plant

In the early 1980s, Pushpa Khanna, professor at the University of Rajasthan, Jaipur, was the first to extract an insulin-like substance from bitter gourd. That substance is an active ingredient called polypeptide-P, which lowers blood sugar in the body. Insulin is currently extracted from animal pancreas for the treatment of diabetes.

Bitter gourd: a source of polypeptide-P

First biocentre

The M.S. Swaminathan Foundation, Chennai, opened a biocentre in Pillayarkuppam Village in Pondicherry (now Puducherry) on 10 April 1999. This centre functions as a demonstration, training, information dissemination, and service unit for sustainable food security.

First to isolate insulin-blocking enzyme

In 2013, Indian-born Kanwal Gambhir

from Harvard University, US, and his co-workers isolated an insulin-blocking enzyme. As insulin controls sugar levels in blood, this discovery had far-reaching implications in the control of diabetes, cardiovascular diseases, and cancer.

First zoologist

Rama Brahma Sanyal (1850–1908) joined the Calcutta Zoological Gardens in Calcutta in 1876. He wrote scientific papers on birds and sea snakes and books on zoology.

Vintage ticket house of Calcutta Zoological Gardens

Discovery of gymnosperms

In 1948, Birbal Sahni (1891–1949), a pioneering palaeontologist, discovered Pentoxyleae (gymnosperms), a plant group belonging to the Jurassic period (208 to 145 million years ago).

First synthesis of a workable gene

Indian-born US resident Dr Har Gobind Khorana (1922–2011), using off-the-shelf chemicals, synthesized a total gene of the simple microbe *Escherichia coli* (which lives in the intestines of humans and animals) in 1976. He was awarded the Nobel Prize for physiology or medicine in 1968 for discovering the genetic code, which opened up the possibility of producing DNA in a laboratory. He shared the prize with US scientists Robert W. Holley and Marshall W. Nirenberg.

Dr Har Gobind Khorana

All India Institute of Medical Sciences (AIIMS), New Delhi

Discovery of the cholera exotoxin

S.C. Seal from the All India Institute of Hygiene and Public Health, Calcutta, discovered cholera exotoxin in the early 1940s. The vaccine based on this helped in the eradication of cholera epidemics in India.

Discovery of seminal plasmin

Pushpa M. Bhargava and E.S.R. Reddy from the Regional Research Laboratory, Hyderabad, discovered the protein seminal plasmin in the seminal fluid of a bull in 1979. This is a potent antimicrobial agent active on a wide range of micro-organisms, such as yeast.

First clone of hepatitis E virus

Dr S.K. Panda, professor of pathology, and his support team of scientists at the All India Institute of Medical Sciences (AIIMS), New Delhi, genetically engineered a clone of the hepatitis E virus in 1996.

First bamboo tissue culture

A.F. Mascarenhas, R.S. Nadgauda, and V.A. Parasharami from the National Chemical Laboratory in Pune worked to produce a tissue culture of bamboo in 1990.

First human organ regeneration

In 2001, Dr Balakrishna Ganpatrao Matapurkar from Maulana Azad Medical College, New Delhi, was granted US Patent No. 6227202 (from 1995) for enabling regeneration of mammalian organs in the body at the site of old and diseased organs. He used unique stem cells in the body to regenerate organs like the uterus, urethra, and ureters in animals and large tendons in the human abdomen.

First biologist to win the Linnean Medal

In 2018, Dr Kamaljit Bawa, president of the Ashoka Trust for Research in Ecology and the Environment (ATREE) and distinguished professor of biology at the University of Massachusetts, Boston, US, was awarded the Linnean Medal for his pioneering research in the field of conservation biology. He researched biodiversity, the evolution of tropical plants, deforestation, and non-timber forest products in Central America, the Western Ghats, and the Himalayas.

INTER-DISCIPLINARY AND APPLIED SCIENCES

COMPUTERS

First indigenous chip

The Graphics and Intelligence-based Script Technology (GIST), developed by the Centre for Development of Advanced Computing (C-DAC), hit the market in the 1990s. While it was designed especially for land records departments based in different climatic zones, where protection from dust and other vagaries is not always available, it was also used by industries and public information systems.

First human brain-like computing developed

A team of scientists led by Dheemahi Rao from the Jawaharlal Nehru Centre for Advanced Scientific Research

(JNCASR), Bengaluru, have developed brain-like computing using industry-compatible nitride semi-conductors on 25 January 2023. For this, the scientists have used scandium nitrite, a semiconductor with great stability. The human brain is an extraordinary biological computer that is smaller than a traditional man-made computer and is more efficient because of a synapse (the connection between two neurons) that plays the role of both the processor and the memory storage units. Traditional computers take enormous energy and time to transfer data between these units because they are physically partitioned. The invention of brain-like computation will take artificial intelligence to new heights.

First analogue computer

The first electrical analogue computing machine was developed by the Indian Statistical Institute (ISI) in 1953–54 by a team led by Samarendra Kumar Mitra (14 March 1916–26 September 1998). This invention eventually led to the building of an Electronic Computer Division at the ISI.

First digital computer

The British-built HEC-2M was installed at the Indian Statistical Institute in Calcutta in 1955. In 1964, the first indigenous computer, ISIJU-1, was developed by the Jadavpur University and the Indian Statistical Institute.

First indigenous palmtop computer

In 1995, a team of engineers working for Signals and Systems India Private Ltd, headquartered in Gurugram, Haryana, built the country's first indigenous palmtop computer suitable for a variety of industrial and field applications.

First powerful commercial computer

In 2001, Tata Consultancy Services (TCS) commissioned the 64-bit z-Series e-Server from IBM to become the first organization in South Asia to adopt the then latest technology being used in mainframe computing.

Top: Samarendra Kumar Mitra demonstrating India's first indigenous computer to the then prime minister of India, Pandit Jawaharlal Nehru
Bottom: Indian Statistical Institute, Kolkata

First supercomputer

On 25 March 1989, the Supercomputer Cray XMP-14 was installed as a key facility at the National Centre for Medium Range Weather Forecasting, New Delhi, to facilitate medium-range weather forecasting and agrometeorology programmes.

First indigenous supercomputer

Developed by C-DAC in Pune in 1991, PARAM 8000 was capable of one billion calculations per second. The then director of C-DAC, Dr Vijay P. Bhatkar, under whom this project was conducted, is considered to be the architect of India's national initiative in supercomputing.

First to invent a new and speedy algorithm

In 1984, Indian-born mathematician Dr Narendra Karmarkar from Bell Laboratories in New Jersey, USA, introduced a new algorithm, called 'Karmarkar's algorithm', which solved linear programming efficiently, and helped computers find solutions to simultaneous inequalities very quickly. It solved problems 50 to 100 times faster than the methods known at the time.

First Indian to obtain a PhD in computer science

Dr Raj Reddy (b. 13 June 1937), the dean of the School of Computer Science, Carnegie Mellon University, Pittsburgh, US, was the first Indian with a PhD in computer science, which he obtained in 1966 from Stanford University, US. He was also the first person of Asian origin to receive the Association for Computing Machinery (ACM) Turing Award, in 1994, then the highest award in computer

Dr Raj Reddy: first Indian to obtain a PhD in computer science

science, for his work in the field of artificial intelligence.

First Super Fab Lab

The first super fab lab (fabrication laboratory) of the country was inaugurated via remote control from the Government Polytechnic College, Palakkad, Kerala, on 25 January 2020. Located at the Integrated Startup Complex of the Kerala Start-up Mission (KSUM), Kalamassery, Kochi, the lab offers digital fabrication and computation and was launched in collaboration with MIT (Massachusetts Institute of Technology, US). The brainchild of Dr Neil Gershenfeld, director of the MIT Centre for Bits and Atoms, it aims to enable researchers, innovators, and developers to do things beyond the purview of the existing fab labs of the country.

First powerful indigenous supercomputer

PARAM 10000, also developed by C-DAC under Dr Vijay P. Bhatkar's directorship, in 1998, was the first powerful indigenous supercomputer, capable of 100 billion calculations per second. It is housed at the National PARAM Supercomputing Facility (NPSF) at C-DAC, Pune.

Fastest supercomputer

AIRAWAT-PSAI is currently India's fastest supercomputer, with a peak power of 13,170 teraflops (13.17 petaflops). The system is installed under the National Programme on AI by Government of India. It was manufactured by Natweb Technologies and is currently installed in C-DAC, Pune. It is currently ranked 75th among the top 500 supercomputers in the world. Earlier, in January 2018, India unveiled Pratyush and Mihir, an array of computers that are able to output a peak power of 6.8 petaflops. This was followed by PARAM Siddhi-AI, which was conceived by C-DAC, Pune, Maharashtra. Able to output a peak power of 6.5 petaflops, the supercomputer is used for research efforts in a wide range of areas, such as healthcare, agriculture, cybersecurity, and robotics. It was ranked 63rd among the top 500 most powerful supercomputers in the world in November 2020 (its current ranking is 131st).

Top: Integrated Startup Complex of the Kerala Startup Mission (KSUM)
Bottom: PARAM 10000: first powerful indigenous supercomputer

METALLURGY

Earliest copper kiln

A copper smelting kiln, 35 cm (13.8 in.) high with an 18 cm (7 in.) rim diameter and 10 cm (3.9 in.) base diameter, was discovered at the Harappan site of Lothal (2200–1500 BCE) in Gujarat. Lothal copper was found to be very pure.

Earliest use of iron

Around 1000 BCE, iron was used in eastern Punjab, western Uttar Pradesh, and Rajasthan. Excavations show that iron weapons such as arrowheads and spearheads were commonly used in western Uttar Pradesh from about 800 BCE. Iron is called *shyama* or *krishna ayas* (black/dark metal) in later Vedic texts.

First metallurgist to work with plutonium

Dr P.R. Roy, a scientist and director at the Bhabha Atomic Research Centre (BARC), Bombay, was the first Indian metallurgist to handle plutonium. He played a crucial role in India's first nuclear implosion at Pokhran, Rajasthan, in 1974.

New class of quasicrystals

In 1985, P. Ramachandra Rao and G.V.S. Sastry from the National Metallurgical Laboratory, Jamshedpur, now in Jharkhand, discovered a new class of quasicrystals composed of aluminium, manganese, and zinc metals.

Earliest iron furnace

An iron furnace was found at Pandu Rajar Dhibi in Burdwan (now Bardhaman District), West Bengal, and was dated to 1100–800 BCE.

Earliest zinc use

An artefact (No. 4189) containing 6.04 per cent zinc was found at the Harappan site of Lothal (dated to 2200–1500 BCE) in Gujarat. It indicated that the Harappan people could generate temperatures of above 1,000°C required for zinc metallurgy.

Lothal: the site of the first copper smelting kiln and the earliest known artefact containing zinc

First manufacture of steel

Indian smiths manufactured crucible steel, known as *wootz*, which was exported to many countries in medieval times. Indian craftsmen were known around the world at the time for their steel swords. After the British banned the production of weapons following the Indian Rebellion of 1857 wootz technology was lost.

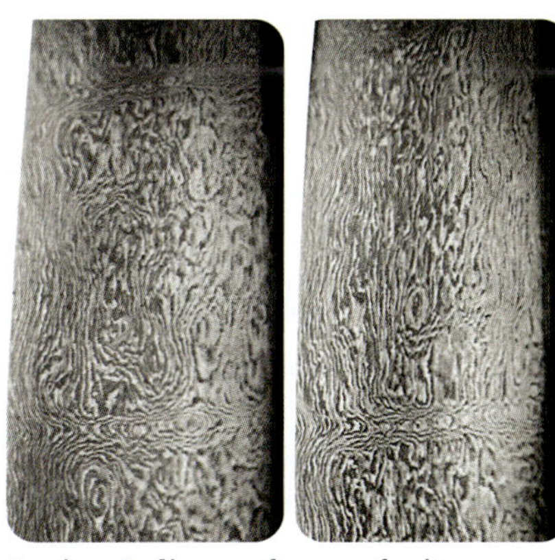

Ancient India was famous for its crucible steel called wootz, used to make swords

SPACE

First space venture

Launched from the base in Thumba near Trivandrum (now Thiruvananthapuram), Kerala, on 21 November 1963, a Nike-Apache rocket supplied by NASA kick-started the Indian space programme. Parts of this first sounding rocket launched by India were transported to the Thumba base on the carrier of a bicycle! St Mary Magdalene Church in Thumba is a preferred site for rocket launches because of its proximity to the magnetic equator. Quite fittingly, the church houses the Vikram Sarabhai Space Centre (VSSC) space museum.

First Indian space organization

Indian National Committee for Space Research (INCOSPAR) was India's first space research organization. It was formed in 1962 and helmed by Dr Vikram Sarabhai. When Indian Space Research Organization was formed in 1969, it superseded INCOSPAR.

First weather-cum-communications satellite

Indian National Satellite INSAT-1A, launched on 10 April 1982 on an American Delta-3920 launch vehicle, was India's first satellite employed for meteorological observations over India and the Indian Ocean, as well as for domestic telecommunications, including nationwide direct TV broadcasting, TV programme distribution, and meteorological data distribution.

First satellite centre

ISRO's Satellite Centre (ISAC), established in 1972, conducts research in satellite technology. Aryabhata, the first Indian satellite, Bhaskara I and II, and Rohini and APPLE satellites were all designed and built at ISAC. The spacecraft of the Indian Remote Sensing satellite series and the Stretched Rohini satellite series were also designed at ISAC.

First remote-sensing mission

IRS-1A, the first of a series of indigenous state-of-the-art remote-sensing satellites, was launched into a polar sun-synchronous orbit on 17 March 1988 from the then Soviet Cosmodrome at Baikonur. It carried two cameras, LISS-I and LISS-II, with a swathe width of 140 km during each pass over India.

First indigenous satellite series

Designed and built by ISRO, INSAT-2A was launched by the Ariane launch vehicle on 10 July 1992. INSAT-2B was also launched by Ariane on 23 July 1993. INSAT-2C, the third in this series of satellites, was launched on 7 December 1995 and put into operation in February 1996. All of these were launched from from Kourou, French Guiana.

First man in space

Squadron Leader Rakesh Sharma (b. 13 January 1949), then an Indian Air Force pilot, flew aboard spacecraft Soyuz T-11, launched on 2 April 1984, as part of the Intercosmos programme and spent over seven days orbiting the earth. He was the first Indian person to travel to space.

Highest-resolution imaging satellite

CARTOSAT-3, considered to be India's highest-resolution civilian satellite to date, was successfully launched into space along with 13 US nanosatellites by ISRO on 27 November 2019. Weighing 1,625 kg, the observation satellite lifted off from the Satish Dhawan Space Centre, Sriharikota High Altitude Range (SHAR), Sriharikota, Andhra Pradesh. It is an advanced imaging and mapping satellite with a mission life of five years and a panchromatic resolution of 0.25 m (9.8 in.).

India's first private rocket builder

Skyroot Aerospace, India's first private rocket builder, started operations in 2018. It is founded by a group of people that includes former ISRO scientists.

First privately developed launch vehicle

Skyroot Aerospace is credited with India's first privately developed rocket, Vikram-S, which was launched into space on 18 November 2022.

First ESCES 

India's first Experimental Satellite Communication Earth Station (ESCES) was operationalized in 1967

Use of PSLVs

Apart from PSLV, India has two other operaitonal launch vehicles: Geosynchronous Satellite Launch Vehicle (GSLV) and Geosynchronous Satellite Launch Vehicle Mk-III (LVM3). The development of Next Generation Launch Vehicle (NGLV) has been approved in September 2024 and is likely to be completed in eight years.

Smallest spacecraft launched

On 23 June 2017, the world's smallest spacecraft, Sprites, was launched by ISRO's PSLV rocket and placed in the low earth orbit. The 3.5 cm x 3.5 cm (1.38 in. x 1.38 in.) space probe weighs just 4 g and runs on sunlight.

First oceanographic satellite

IRS-P4 (OceanSat), the first satellite built for ocean applications, was launched into a polar sun-synchronous orbit, 720 km high, by the PSLV from SHAR, Sriharikota, Andhra Pradesh, on 26 May 1999. A 1,050 kg satellite measuring 2.8 m x 1.98 m x 2.57 m (9 ft 2 in. x 6 ft 6 in. x 8 ft 5 in.), the IRS-P4 orbited the earth in 99.31 mins. It completed its mission on 8 August 2010.

First interplanetary mission

On 5 November 2013, PSLV-C25, the 25th flight of PSLV launched Mangalyaan, the Mars Orbiter Mission (MOM) spacecraft, from SHAR, Sriharikota, Andhra Pradesh. Under the aegis of ISRO, the mission was conducted to observe the physical features of Mars and the Martian atmosphere.

First indigenous satellite launcher

The PSLV-D3, developed by ISRO, hoisted a 930 kg Indian remote-sensing satellite (IRS-P3) into an orbit of 807 km from the earth, 17 minutes after it shot into space on 21 March 1996.

First lunar probe

India's first lunar probe, Chandrayaan-1was launched by ISRO, using a PSLV-XL rocket, on 22 October 2008 from Satish Dhawan Space Centre (SDSC), SHAR, Sriharikota, Andhra Pradesh. It operated until August 2009.

The first commercial payload was an Italian satellite called Agile and was carried by PSLV-C8. For details, see the Business and Economics chapter.

in Ahmedabad. This also worked as a training centre for the Indian and international scientists and engineers.

First private satellite launched

Exseed SAT-1, built by Exseed Space Innovations Private Ltd, founded by scientists Kris Nair and Asshar Farhan, became the first private Indian satellite to be launched in space. The amateur (ham) radio satellite hitched a ride on the Elon Musk–led company SpaceX's Falcon 9 rocket on 4 December 2018.

First woman in space

Dr Kalpana Chawla (1962–2003), an American cosmonaut who was born in Karnal, Haryana, was the first woman of Indian origin in space. She zoomed into orbit aboard space shuttle Columbia on 19 November 1997 on a 16-day scientific mission, along with five fellow astronauts, and returned to Cape Canaveral on 5 December 1997. In 2003, Chawla was one of the seven crew members who died in the space shuttle Columbia disaster when it disintegrated during its re-entry into the earth's atmosphere.

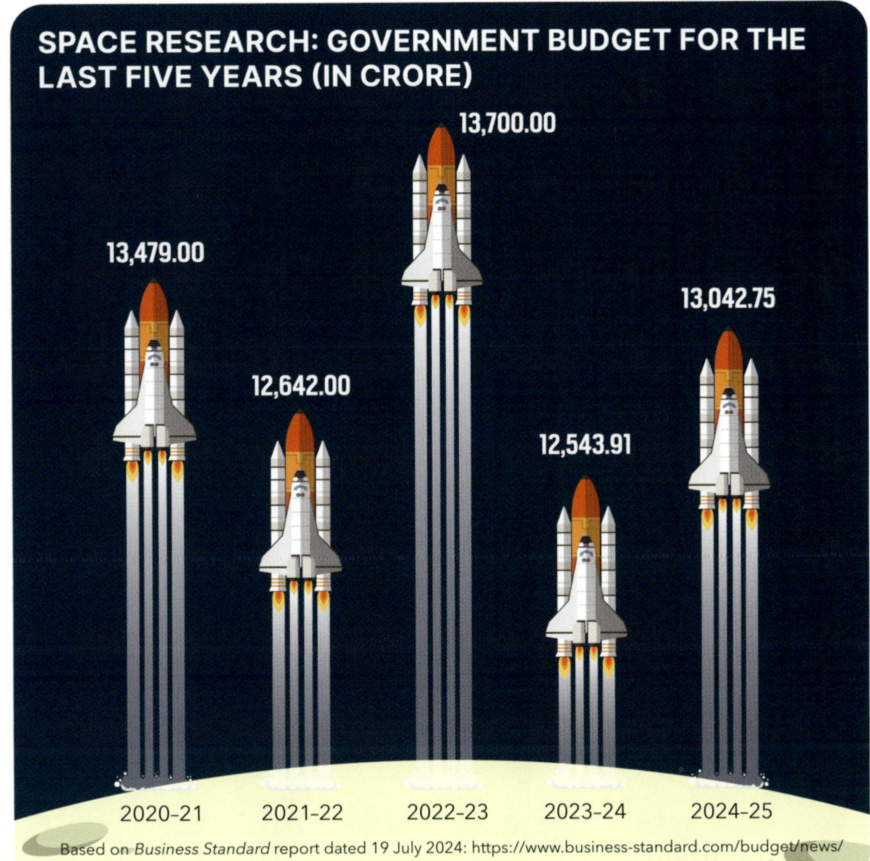

First space technology gallery

India's first space technology gallery came up on 28 November 2017 at the Visvesvaraya Industrial and Technological Museum, Bengaluru. It has been set up in an area of 7534.74 sq ft (700 sq m) on the second floor of the museum.

Heaviest satellite launched

GSAT-11, weighing 5,854 kg and laying claim to being the heaviest Indian satellite ever launched, was sent into space by ISRO on 5 December 2018 from the Ariane Launch Complex at Kourou in French Guiana. The satellite is expected to help boost communication services across India.

India's first solar mission

ADITYA-L1 is India's first satellite dedicated to studying the outer atmosphere of the sun. It has been indigenously developed by ISRO and launched on 2 September 2023.

Lightest satellite in orbit

Kalamsat-V2 was launched by ISRO on 24 January 2019 from the Satish Dhawan Space Centre, SHAR, Sriharikota. Weighing only 1.26 kg, it is said to be the world's lightest satellite to be put into orbit. It was made by students belonging to Space Kidz India, a Chennai-based aerospace start-up pioneering in design, fabrication, and launch of small satellites, spacecraft, and ground systems. The satellite will also serve as a communications device for ham radio transmission, which is a form of wireless communication used by amateurs for non-commercial activities. It took six days to make and cost around ₹12 lakh (1.2 million).

First polarimetry mission

XPoSat, X-ray Polarimeter Satellite, is the first dedicated scientific satellite launched by ISRO with the purpose of research in space-based polarization measurements of X-ray emission from celestial sources. It was launched on 1 January 2024.

Entrance to the Visvesvaraya Industrial and Technological Museum

MEDICAL SCIENCES

GENERAL

Earliest treatise on medicine

The Atharva Veda (1500–1200 BCE) is the earliest known treatise on human diseases and medicine.

First Persian text on medicine

Ma'dan-i-Shifa-i-Sikandar Shahi was the first Persian text on the Unani and Ayurvedic systems of medicine, authored by Hakim Bahwa bin Khwas Khan during 1512–13 CE. It was printed in 1987 by Naval Kishore Press in Lucknow, Uttar Pradesh.

Largest healthcare scheme

Ayushman Bharat Yojana, announced as a universal healthcare plan by the Government of India in February 2018, is the largest healthcare scheme in the world. Aimed at providing free healthcare access to around 50 crore (0.5 billion) people in the country, the Ayushman Bharat Pradhan Mantri Jan Arogya Yojana (AB-PMJAY) was launched in September 2018. A paperless and cashless scheme, it involves e-cards being issued to beneficiaries and health insurance coverage of up to ₹5,00,000 per family per year.

Pradhan Mantri Jan Arogya Yojana

WR Largest survey sample

India's Annual Health Survey (AHS) is the first nationwide survey initiative to provide district-level fertility and mortality statistics. Begun with a baseline study in 2010–11 and a sample size of 18.2 million people (3.6 million households), it is conducted in all 284 districts in eight Empowered Action Group (EAG) states, viz., Madhya Pradesh, Jharkhand, Bihar, Uttar Pradesh, Chhattisgarh, Uttarakhand, Odisha, and Rajasthan. It reports vital indicators such as crude birth and death rates, sex ratios (at birth, for 0–4 years, and for all ages) and mortality rates (maternal, infant, neonatal, and under-5), separated by urban/rural and male/female data.

Only state to legislate right to health

Rajasthan is the only state where all residents have the right to health. Everybody in the state can have free-of-cost emergency treatment at both government and private hospitals. The bill was passed in March 2023.

Only state to offer funding for treatment outside the state

Sikkim is the only Indian state where residents get government aid in getting treatment outside the state under the Chief Minister's Medical Assistance Scheme Rules, 2022.

First and only global outpost for traditional medicine

In 2022, WHO, with the support of the Indian government, established the Global Centre for Traditional Medicine (GCTM) in Gandhinagar, Gujarat, which is the first and the only global outpost for traditional medicine in the world. It is a collaborative project involving the Ministry of Ayush and WHO. It was established to provide leadership on matters related to traditional medicine as well as support to member countries in shaping various policies pertaining to public health and traditional medical research and practices. It had its first summit in August 2023.

FERTILITY, CHILDBIRTH, AND BABIES

Oldest IVF mother

On 12 October 2019, 75-year-old Prabha Devi became the oldest woman to give birth, after conceiving through in vitro fertilization (IVF). She delivered a baby girl, weighing 680 g, prematurely by Caesarean section performed at Kinker Hospital, Kota, Rajasthan.

First IVF baby

Baby Harsha was born to Mani and Shyami Chawda on 6 August 1986 by the in vitro fertilization and embryo transfer (IVF-ET) method. This technique was used after three years of research by Dr Indira Hinduja of King Edward Memorial Hospital and Seth Gordhandas Sunderdas Medical College, Bombay, Maharashtra.

IVF – under the microscope

First woman to give birth after a uterine transplant

Meenakshi Valand from Bharuch District, Gujarat, became the first Indian woman to deliver a baby after undergoing a uterine transplant on 19 October 2018 at Galaxy Care Hospital, Pune, Maharashtra.

First GIFT twins

The first twins, both male, were born through the gamete intra-fallopian transfer (GIFT) technology to Renuka and Vijay Thakkar on 5 September 1990 in Bombay (now Mumbai), Maharashtra.

GIFT

An assisted reproductive procedure for infertile couples, **Gamete Intra-Fallopian Transfer** (GIFT), is a laparoscopic technique that aims to achieve pregnancy by placing a mixture of eggs and sperm directly into the woman's fallopian tubes.

Heaviest baby at birth

On 26 May 2016, Nandini, a 20-year-old mother, gave birth to a baby girl by Caesarean section at a hospital in Hassan, Karnataka. The baby, whose birthweight was 6.8 kg, was reported to have been the heaviest one ever born in the country. The heaviest baby boy till then, who weighed 6.7 kg at birth, was recorded to have been born in November 2015.

Lightest baby

A premature baby girl, weighing 400 g and measuring 8.6 in. in length, was born by Caesarean section on 15 June 2017 at Jivanta Children's Hospital in Udaipur, Rajasthan. She was kept in the neonatal intensive care unit (NICU) at the hospital for 210 days under the care of Dr Sunil Janged, Dr Nikhilesh Nain, and trained nursing staff, and was discharged when she weighed close to 2.4 kg.

MEDICAL INSTITUTIONS AND LABORATORIES

First governmental family planning programme

India was the first country in the world to have government-sponsored family planning programmes in 1952. The first private family planning clinic was opened even earlier, in Mysore (now Mysuru), Karnataka, in 1930.

First hospital

The first modern hospital was established at Fort St George, Madras (now Chennai), Tamil Nadu, in 1664. Today, it exists as Rajiv Gandhi Government General Hospital.

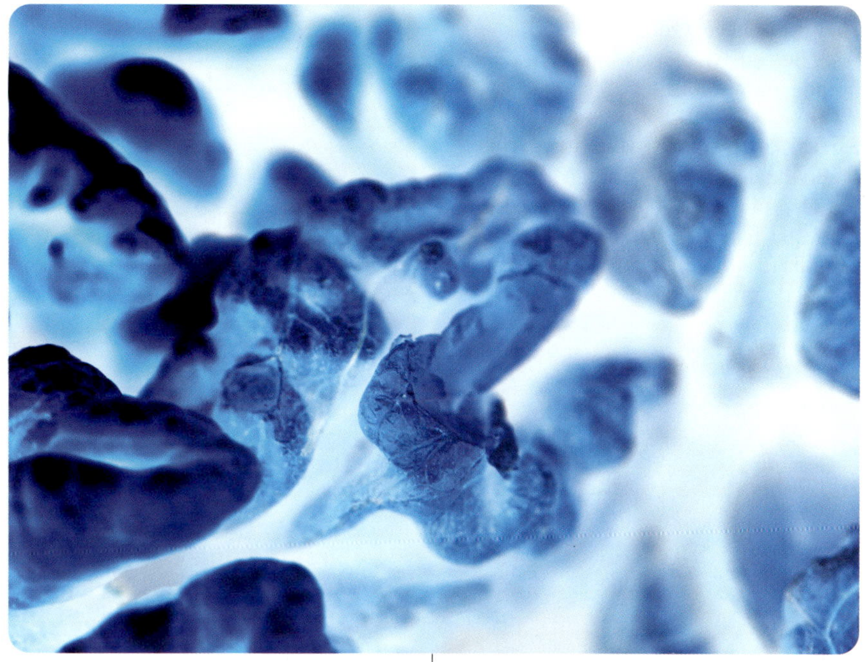

Microscopic image of cancer cells

First medical school to offer oncology degrees

The Adyar Cancer Institute in Chennai, Tamil Nadu, is a non-profit cancer treatment and research centre set up in 1954 under the leadership of Dr Muthulakshmi Reddy. It was the first medical school in India to offer degrees in various sub-specialities of oncology, recognized by the Medical Council of India.

First college of nursing

Christian Medical College and Hospital (CMCH), Vellore, Tamil Nadu, set up the first college of nursing in India in 1946.

First homoeopathic college

Dr L. Salzar from Austria began homoeopathic education in India in 1867. He influenced Dr P.C. Majumdar and Dr B.L. Bhaduri in Bengal, and in 1878, Dr Majumdar along with Dr D.N. Roy, Dr B.N. Banerjee, and Dr Younan set up the Calcutta Homoeopathic

Rajiv Gandhi Government General Hospital

Medical College, Calcutta (now Kolkata), West Bengal, which was India's first homoeopathic college.

First homoeopathic company

M. Bhattacharya and Company Pvt. Ltd in Calcutta was established in 1889 by Mahesh Chandra Bhattacharya from Comilla (now in Bangladesh), for making homoeopathic medicines.

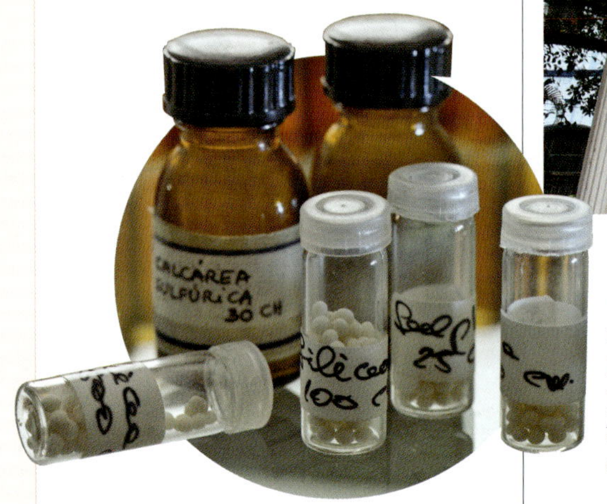

Homoeopathic medicine (representative image)

First organized medical service

The Indian Medical Service was the formal collective name for the top echelon of the East India Company's and British Indian Army's medical service from the early 19th century up to 1896. Its three divisions – Bengal Medical Service, Madras Medical Service, and Bombay Medical Service – were combined into a single service under government control in January 1897.

First dental college

Dr Rafiuddin Ahmed, the 'father of modern dentistry' in India, founded the Calcutta Dental College in Calcutta in 1920. By 1928, it was a well-known institution for scientific dental education in India.

Dr Rafiuddin Ahmed

First biotechnology department

Dr Indira Nath set up the first department of medical biotechnology at the All India Institute of Medical Sciences (AIIMS), New Delhi, in 1986, for teaching and research.

Dr Mukesh Batra

Calcutta Medical College

First medical college

Calcutta Medical College (now renamed Medical College and Hospital, Kolkata) set up on 28 January 1835 in Calcutta, was the first medical college to be established in India and Asia.

First centre for cancer rehabilitation

Dr Darab Jehangir Jussawala (1915–99) was a medical and surgical oncologist, medical writer, and director of the Lady Ratan Tata Memorial Centre in Bombay (now Mumbai), Maharashtra. Dr Jussawala was the co-founder of the Indian Cancer Society with Naval Tata in 1951 and established the Indian Cancer Rehabilitation Centre in Parel, Bombay, in 1956, which was the first such centre in India. He received the Padma Bhushan in 1975 from the Government of India.

First online clinic

Homoeopath Dr Mukesh Batra set up Dr Batra's Positive Health Clinic in Bombay in 1982, which now has 230 clinics across 122 cities in India, Bangladesh, Dubai, and the UK. He went online in 1997, which made him the first online medical consultant in the country.

First medical laser facility

India's first medical laser to destroy tumours with minimal blood loss was set up at the K.B. Bhabha Hospital in Bombay in October 1993.

First hospital with a stealth neuro-navigation system

The Sri Sathya Sai Institute of Higher Medical Sciences, Whitefield, Bangalore (now Bengaluru), Karnataka, set up in 2001, is the first in India and second in the world to acquire a stealth neuro-navigation system (for image-guided surgeries). It is one of the cutting-edge technologies in precision neurosurgery.

First hormone replacement therapy clinic

A hormone replacement therapy (HRT) clinic was started by Urvashi P. Jha in March 1993 at the P.D. Hinduja National Hospital in Mumbai, to deal with aspects of menopause.

First corporate hospital

Apollo Hospitals, founded by Dr Prathap C. Reddy in Madras, Tamil Nadu, in 1983, was the first corporate hospital in the country.

Apollo Hospital App

First low-vision rehabilitation centre

L.V. Prasad Eye Institute, Hyderabad (now in Telangana), opened the Meera and L.B. Deshpande Centre for Sight Enhancement on 18 February 1997, to provide complete low-vision rehabilitation for patients by restoring optimal physical, psychological and social functioning.

First institute of advanced virology

The first Institute of Advanced Virology was inaugurated in February 2019 at Thiruvananthapuram, Kerala. It is affiliated to the Global Virus Network, which has 45 centres of excellence in more than 29 countries.

First indigenously developed vaccine

Rotavac, a rotavirus vaccine, was India's first indigenously developed vaccine, launched in 2015. It was developed by Bharat Biotech India Limited and the Gates Foundation, and supported by the Government of India and National Institute of Health of the US Government. Rotavirus is the most common cause of serious (often fatal) diarrhoea in children.

First department of minimal access surgery

Dr Pradeep Kumar Chowbey from Sir Ganga Ram Hospital, New Delhi, set up the first dedicated department of minimal access surgery (MAS) in Asia in 1995 and has trained nearly 1,000 doctors in laparoscopy in India and abroad.

First hospital with a rooftop helipad

The eleven-storey Lakeshore Hospital and Research Centre, Kochi, Kerala, is the first super-speciality hospital in the country to have air, water, and road ambulance services at its doorstep. Inaugurated in January 2003, this hospital with its state-of-the-art medical services, has a helipad on its roof to facilitate heli-lifting of critically ill patients from airports in Kerala.

WR Largest vaccine company

The Serum Institute of India in Pune, Maharashtra, founded by Cyrus Poonawalla in 1966, is the world's largest vaccine-making company by the number of doses produced and sold globally, with 1.2 billion vaccine doses supplied yearly to 147 countries.

First liver clinic

The first liver clinic was opened at Sir Ganga Ram Hospital, New Delhi, in 2002 for treating patients with liver diseases.

Indian postal stamp commemorating Sir Ganga Ram and Ganga Ram Hospital

First rural medical college

Kasturba Health Society's Mahatma Gandhi Institute of Medical Sciences (MGIMS) in Sevagram, Wardha District, Maharashtra, was the country's first rural medical college. It was founded by Dr Sushila Nayar, a physician and politician, in 1969, and was affiliated to the Maharashtra University of Health Sciences.

First endoscopy lab

The first fully equipped endoscopy centre was established at the Bhatia General Hospital in Mumbai, in October 1994. An endoscopy is performed to examine the interior of a hollow organ.

AIIMS: A hub of medical firsts

The All India Institute of Medical Sciences (AIIMS) is a public hospital and medical endoscopy equipment research university based in New Delhi. Established in 1956, it operates autonomously under the Ministry of Health and Family Welfare. It was

- the first to start a medical toxicology lab in a medical college in 1986.
- the first to develop a DNA profiling lab in a medical college in 1990.
- the first Indian centre to perform a successful cardiac transplant in 1994.
- India's first minimally invasive surgery training centre.
- the first in the public sector to have an in vitro fertilization (IVF) facility, in February 2008.

All India Institute of Medical Sciences (AIIMS), New Delhi

Vaccine manufacturing facility, Serum Institute of India, Pune, Maharashtra

MEDICAL BANKS

First blood bank
Upendranath Brahmachari (1873–1946) set up a blood bank in Calcutta, in September 1939.

First sperm bank
Dr Aniruddha Malpani and Dr Anjali Malpani from Bombay opened a sperm bank in 1990 in Colaba, Bombay, to help infertile patients. It also had facilities for storing sperm of people who may be critically ill, for implantation at a later date.

First breast milk bank
Dr Armida Fernandez pioneered the establishment of Asia's first human milk bank at the Lokmanya Tilak Municipal General Hospital in Bombay, in November 1989.

PUBLICATIONS AND INNOVATION

First to win a Pulitzer Prize for a health/medicine-related publication
Indian-origin American oncologist Siddhartha Mukherjee won the Pulitzer Prize for General Non-Fiction in 2011 for *The Emperor of All Maladies: A Biography of Cancer*, published in 2010 by Scribner, New York, US. The book was acclaimed as one of the 100 most influential books of the last 100 years by *Time* magazine and one of the 100 best works of non-fiction by the *New York Times Magazine*.

Smallest medical robot
The smallest medical robot measuring 120 nm (one nanometre is one-billionth of a metre) was created by Soutik Betal, a doctoral research student from India, at the University of Texas, San Antonio, Texas, US, on 10 November 2016. Capable of being remotely controlled electromagnetically and of interacting with biological cells, these robots may be used to advance research in cell-based therapy and to provide direct medication to cells for treating cancers and Alzheimer's disease.

DOCTORS

First doctor of Western medicine
Pandit Madhusudan Gupta was the first Indian doctor to study Western medicine in India. Initially an Ayurvedic practitioner based in Calcutta in the nineteenth century, he was trained in Western medicine in 1835–36.

First dissection
Pandit Madhusudan Gupta, the first Indian doctor of western medicine, was also the first to perform human dissection in Asia in 1836.

Pandit Madhusudan Gupta

Most innovations by a medical professional
Dr Pankaj Garg (b. 27 December 1972), a colorectal surgeon from Panchkula, Haryana, has 16 innovations in the medical field to his name. Consisting of seven surgery procedures and nine treatment concepts, these have been published in national and international surgical journals from April 2015 to May 2019.

First psychosurgeon
M.S. Govindaswamy (1904–62) was the first psychiatrist to start psychosurgery in India. He combined psychological, medical, psychiatric, and nursing aspects for holistic treatment.

FIRST WOMEN IN MEDICINE

First doctor
Kadambini Ganguly (1861–1923) was the first South Asian female physician trained in Western medicine to graduate in 1888 from the Calcutta Medical College (now Medical College and Hospital, Kolkata, West Bengal).

Kadambini Ganguly

First surgeon general
Mary Poonen Lukose (1886–1976) from Kerala graduated from the University of Madras (now in Chennai), Tamil Nadu, in 1909, and studied medicine in the UK. She became the first woman surgeon general of India in 1938 and was awarded the Padma Shri in 1975.

First neurosurgeon
Dr Thanjavur Santhanakrishna Kanaka (1932–2018) was the first female neurosurgeon in Asia. She was also the first neurosurgeon in India to perform chronic electrode implants in the brain, having performed deep-brain stimulation as early as 1975.

First anaesthetist
Dr Rupa Bai Furdoonji was one of five female students to join the Hyderabad Medical School in 1885. She received her diploma in 1891. As a medical student, she achieved great proficiency in delivering chloroform anaesthesia. She went to Edinburgh in 1909 to gain greater knowledge in the field of anaesthesia. She is probably the first lady anaesthetist in the world who took on anaesthesiology as a full-time career.

First aerospace doctor
Dr Parvathi Gopal from Bengaluru, Karnataka, joined the Institute of Aerospace Medicine in the Department of High Altitude Physiology in 1992. Her field of work included research and treatment to determine whether a fighter pilot is medically and mentally fit to fly.

First nurse
Bai Kashibai Ganpat of Thane, Maharashtra, was the first Indian woman to undertake training to become a nurse at a hospital of Jamsetjee Jeejeebhoy Group in Bombay (now Mumbai), Maharashtra, in 1891.

Postgraduate Institute of Medical Education and Research (PGIMER), Chandigarh

First neurosurgeon

Dr Jacob Chandy (1910–2007) started the department of neurology and neurosurgery in 1949 at Christian Medical College and Hospital, Vellore, Tamil Nadu. He initiated the first training programmes in neurosurgery in 1958 and in neurology in 1962.

First cardiologist

Dr S. Srinivas from Bihar was the first cardiologist of India, who started his medical practice in 1950. He was trained by Dr Paul Dudley White and was also the first to bring ECG machine in India.

Discovery of a 'feeding' centre in the hypothalamus

Prof. Bal Krishan Anand (1917–2007) was a famous physiologist and pharmacologist, born in Lahore (now in Pakistan). He was credited with the discovery of the 'feeding' centre in the hypothalamus in 1951 and regarded as the founder of modern neurophysiology in India.

Hypothalamus

Hypothalamus is a minute region in the centre of the brain below the thalamus and acts as the coordinating centre for our body, regulating heart rate, body temperature, hunger, etc. The **lateral hypothalamus area is the feeding centre,** which induces hunger when stimulated.

First government-run department for disorders of sex development

The Postgraduate Institute of Medical Education and Research (PGIMER), Chandigarh, in July 2019, established the country's first government-run facility for children with disorders of sex development (DSD). The facility provides diagnosis of genetic and hormonal issues, surgical correction and psychological support for such children. Around 200 children per year can be treated here.

First doctor-to-doctor online session

A doctor-centric portal with the URL www.ranbaxyfordoctors.com hosted a discussion on 'Current trends in the management of cardiac arrhythmia' on 28 August 2000, where 69 doctors chatted online. It was moderated by Prof. (Dr) K.K. Sethi, director, interventional cardiology and cardiac arrhythmia services, Sir Ganga Ram Hospital, New Delhi.

MEDICINE AND SURGERY

Father of plastic surgery

Sushruta is considered the 'father of plastic surgery'. He is believed to have lived around the sixth century BCE and pioneered the advancement of medicine in ancient India. His teachings of anatomy, pathophysiology, and therapeutic strategies, featured in his *Sushruta Samhita*, were far ahead of his time.

Christian Medical College and Hospital's many firsts

Christian Medical College and Hospital (CMCH), Vellore, Tamil Nadu, is a private educational and research institute, which includes a network of primary, secondary, and tertiary care hospitals. Founded in 1900 by an American missionary, Dr Ida S. Scudder, CMCH has many firsts to its credit:

- First reconstructive surgery for leprosy in the world (1948)
- First department of neurological sciences (1948)
- First successful open-heart surgery in India (1961)
- First kidney transplant in India (1971)
- First virology department (1978)
- First bone marrow transplant (1986)
- First successful ABO incompatible (organ donated by a donor of a different blood type) kidney transplant (2009)

Christian Medical College and Hospital (CMCH), Vellore, Tamil Nadu

Statue of Sushruta

Earliest cataract surgery

Ancient Indian physician Sushruta (c. sixth century BCE) had diagnosed that cataract was a disease of the eye lens, characterized by its opacity resulting in impaired vision, and had prescribed surgery as the only remedy. It was performed with a curved needle used to loosen the lens and push the cataract out of the field of vision. The eye would later be soaked with warm butter and then bandaged.

First medical symposium

The Vedic sage Bharadwaja, who is believed to have founded the Indian Ayurvedic system of medicine, presided over the first-ever symposium on medicinal plants in the seventh century BCE, possibly in the Himalayan region.

First separation of conjoined twins

Dr J. Dalal, paediatrics and neonatology specialist, surgically separated a set of conjoined twins (also known as Siamese twins) born to one Mrs Kambli on 11 August 1962 at Bhatia Hospital, Bombay, Maharashtra.

First open-heart surgery

Dr Reeve H. Betts, an American missionary, founded the first department of thoracic and cardiovascular surgery in 1948 at the Christian Medical College and Hospital, Vellore, Tamil Nadu, with cardiac surgical work beginning in 1950. Along with Dr N. Gopinath, he performed the first successful open-heart surgery here on a 12-year-old patient, Beulah, in 1961.

First international homoeopathic congress

The first International Homoeopathic Congress in India was held in 1967. It was organized and presided over by the renowned homoeopathic doctor Diwan Harish Chand. All the earlier ones, commencing from 1876, had been held in Europe and North America.

First bloodless breast surgery

A team of doctors at the Dr B.R. Ambedkar Institute Rotary Cancer Hospital, AIIMS, New Delhi, carried out a major bloodless breast cancer surgery in September 1998, using ultrasonic waves.

First laser surgery on trachea

Dr Deepak Talwar, a leading pulmonologist, and his team at the Metro Hospital and Heart Institute, Noida, Uttar Pradesh, successfully opened up the lower part of a patient's windpipe, which had narrowed to 0.5 cm (0.2 in.) from the usual circumference of 2 cm (0.79 in.), in 1998. This was the first such surgery performed using laser technology.

First conference

The first medical conference, inaugurated by the then viceroy of colonial India, Lord Elgin, was held in Calcutta, Bengal, West Bengal, between 24 and 29 December 1894.

First craniopagus surgery

A team of 125 doctors and paramedical staff, led by Dr Deepak Kumar Gupta and Dr Ashok Kumar Mahapatra from the Department of Neurosurgery at the All India Institute of Medical Sciences (AIIMS), New Delhi, successfully separated 28-month-old twins Jagga and Kalia, who were joined at the cranium. The twins belong to Milipada Village of Kandhamal district in Odisha. The complex surgery was conducted in two stages, on 28 August 2017 (25 hrs long) and 25 October 2017 (20 hrs long).

First video-assisted heart surgery

Video-assisted thoracic surgery (VATS) was used for the first time in heart surgery at the B.M. Birla Heart Research Centre, Calcutta, on several children suffering from a congenital heart disease called patent ductus arteriosus (PDA), in August 1994.

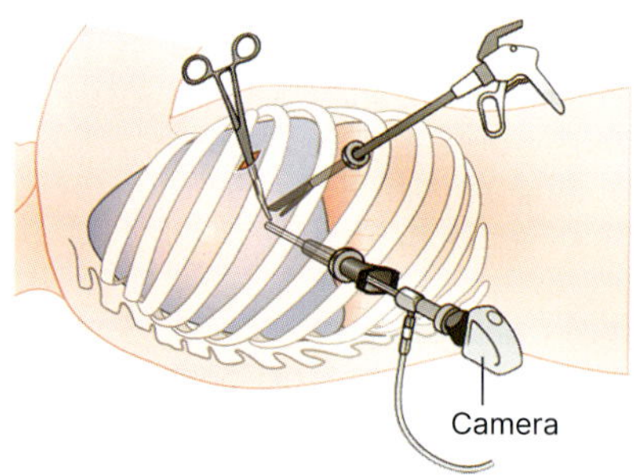

Diagram depicting Video-Assisted Thoracic Surgery (VATS)

First Maze III (atrial fibrillation) surgery

A heart surgery to cure arterial fibrillation (fast and irregular heartbeat) was performed for the first time in India by Dr Amit Banerjee, cardiothoracic surgeon, on 25-year-old Kiran Bir at the Govind Ballabh Pant Hospital, New Delhi, on 25 August 1994.

First global telecast of surgery

On 11 June 1998, a team of doctors, led by leading cardiovascular and cardiothoracic surgeon Dr Naresh Trehan, operated upon six patients with heart ailments at the Escorts Heart Institute and Research Centre, New Delhi. The procedure was beamed live to 200 cardiac specialists and 1,000 delegates in San Francisco, US. The back-end support was provided by the Medical Products Group at Hewlett-Packard.

First heart-shrink surgery

Dr Naresh Trehan (b. 12 August 1946), a cardiovascular and cardiothoracic surgeon, performed the first successful heart-shrink surgery in India, which was also the first in Asia, with his team of cardiac surgeons, on a 50-year-old patient, Mani Ram Gurera, at the Escorts Heart Institute and Research Centre, New Delhi, on 21 May 1996.

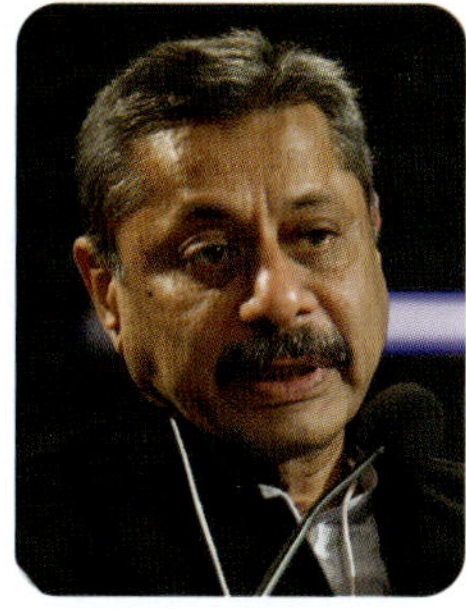
Dr Naresh Trehan

First bi-ventricular pacemaker
Prof. Kewal Kishan Talwar, cardiologist and former chairman of the Medical Council of India, New Delhi, and Dr T.S. Kler of Escorts Heart Institute and Research Centre, New Delhi, implanted bi-ventricular pacemakers on end-stage heart-disease patients on 8 May 2000 in two separate surgeries. This pacemaker ensures that all chambers of the heart contract and expand simultaneously.

Pioneering cataract removal
Cataract surgery was normally done through a 10–12 mm incision until 15 August 1998, when Dr Amar Agarwal pioneered the technique called Phakonit, in which a cataract was removed through a 0.9 mm incision at Dr Agarwal's Eye Hospital, Chennai, Tamil Nadu. This technique has now been adopted all over the world.

First cochlear implant
Dr Sandra Desa Souza was the first surgeon to perform a cochlear implant surgery in the human ear to treat complete deafness. The surgery was performed at Jaslok Hospital, Bombay, Maharashtra, in November 1987.

First coronary artery bypass surgery
Dr K.M. Cherian performed India's first successful coronary artery bypass surgery in 1975. He has pioneered several transplants at the Madras Medical Mission and Institute of Cardiovascular Diseases in Chennai, Tamil Nadu.

MEDICAL MARVELS

First double (liver and kidney) transplant
Ganesh Nehru became the first recipient of a liver from his maternal uncle Mohan Ram and a kidney from his mother Hemlata simultaneously. The double transplant lasted 18 hrs on 17 April 2007 and involved 50 doctors and paramedics, besides intricate coordination between three operating theatres at Sir Ganga Ram Hospital, New Delhi. Dr A.S. Soin was the transplant surgeon in charge of the case.

First scalp replantation
A completely avulsed scalp was replanted microsurgically on Gurkripal Singh by Dr Abraham Thomas and Dr Jaychandran of Christian Medical College and Hospital, Ludhiana, Punjab, in March 1985.

• A team of doctors at the Postgraduate Institute of Medical Education and Research (PGIMER), Chandigarh, performed a hip replacement surgery on a 110-year-old woman (age based on her Aadhaar card), Manjauki, on 8 January 2020. The team comprised Prof. Vijay G. Goni, Dr Tanvir Samra, Dr Deepak, Dr Karan, Dr Pradeep, and Dr Sumeet.

• Ram Lal, a 105-year-old patient, was the oldest to undergo a bipolar replacement of the right hip when he sustained a fracture around the hip joint. The surgery was carried out under Dr Sujoy Kumar Bhattacharjee, director, joint replacement surgery, at Metro Heart Institute with Multispeciality Hospital in Faridabad, Haryana, on 23 March 2018. The operation lasted 2 hrs 52 mins.

Oldest woman to deliver twins
Seventy-four-year-old Mangayamma Yaramati gave birth to a pair of twin girls on 5 September 2019 at the Ahalya Hospital, Guntur, Andhra Pradesh. Dr Sankayalla Uma Shankar delivered the babies by Caesarean section. Conceived through IVF, the babies were the first children of the couple.

Heaviest ovarian tumour removed
• The world's heaviest ovarian tumour, weighing 50 kg, was removed on 18 August 2020 at the Indraprastha Apollo Hospital, New Delhi, from a 52-year-old patient, by a team of surgeons led by Dr Arun Prasad. The surgery lasted for three-and-a half hours.

• *Malignant*: Kavita Khoiwal, assistant professor, Department of Obstetrics and Gynaecology, AIIMS, Rishikesh, Uttarakhand, along with her team of doctors, operated on a 24-year-old female patient on 21 August 2020 and removed the heaviest abdominopelvic mass. The weight of the cancerous ovarian mass was 41.1 kg, from which 36 litres of mucinous fluid was removed prior to removal and the remaining mass of 5.1 kg was removed subsequently. The size of the mass was 60 cm x 50 cm x 40 cm (23.62 in. x 19.68 in. x 15.75 in.) approximately.

Longest object removed from the brain
Dr Rahul Prakash Modgi, neurosurgeon, and Dr Rajendra Gawatre, anaesthesiologist, operated on Pallavi Vijay Shelke, 17, at Shri Saibaba Hospital, Shirdi, Maharashtra, on 29 December 2012. They removed a 12 cm (4.72 in.) long iron rod, weighing 47 g, from her right frontotemporo-parietal region.

Cochlear implant

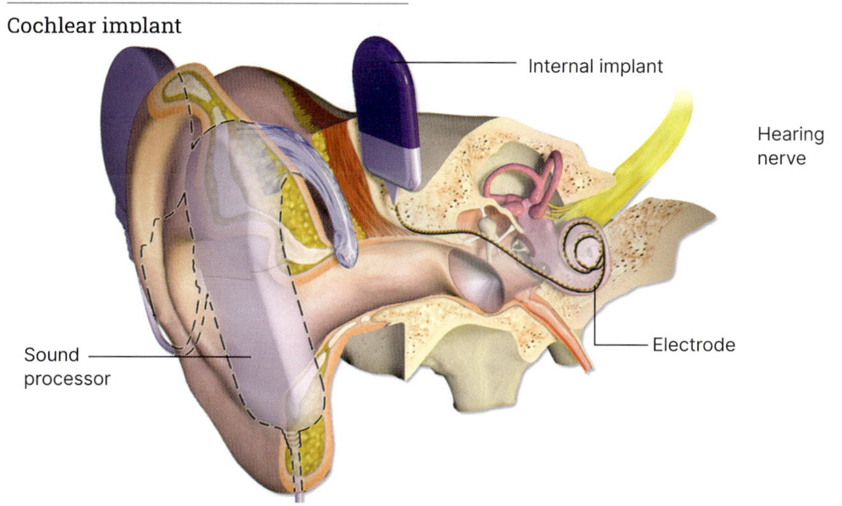

Saving Lives: Transplants

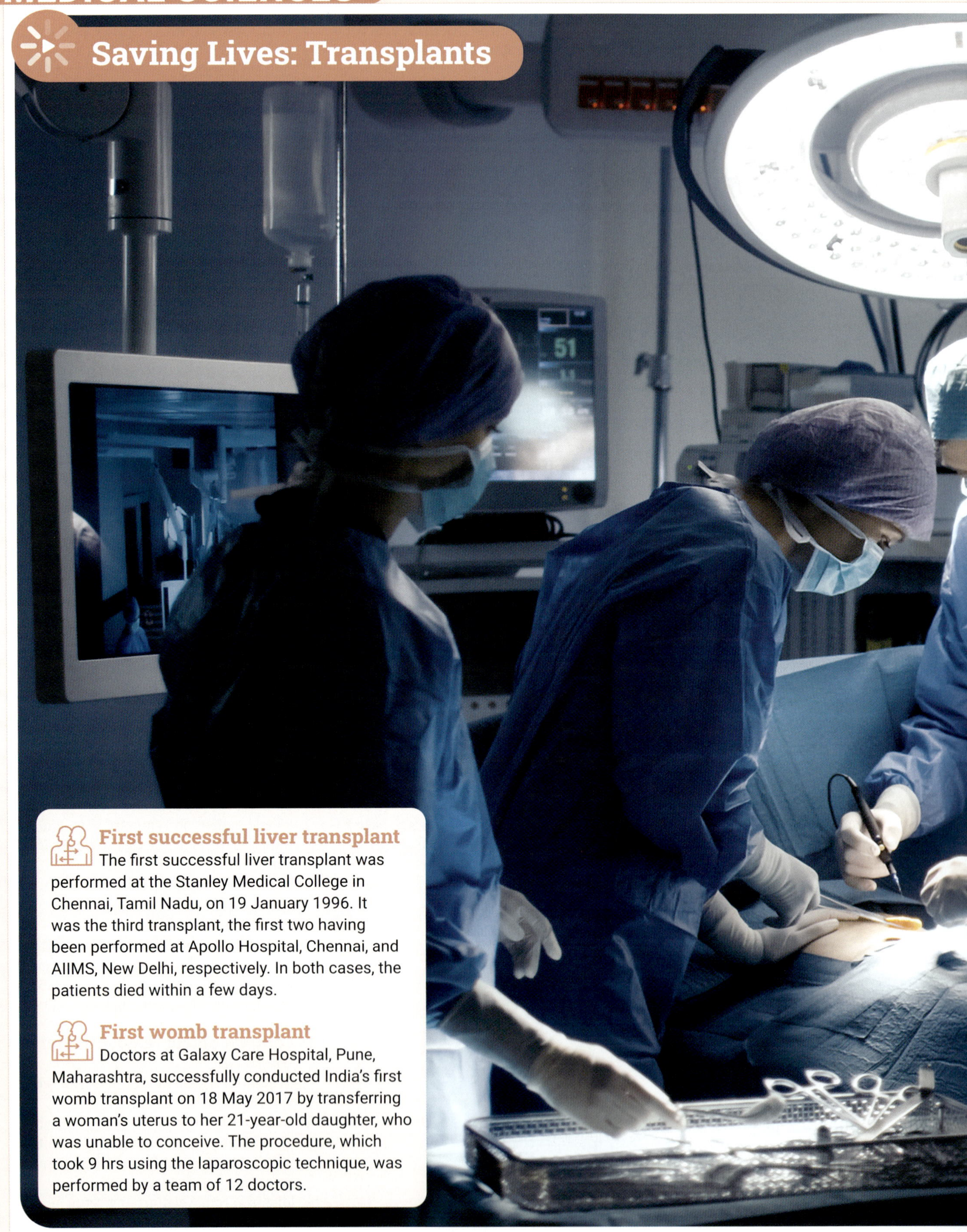

First successful liver transplant

The first successful liver transplant was performed at the Stanley Medical College in Chennai, Tamil Nadu, on 19 January 1996. It was the third transplant, the first two having been performed at Apollo Hospital, Chennai, and AIIMS, New Delhi, respectively. In both cases, the patients died within a few days.

First womb transplant

Doctors at Galaxy Care Hospital, Pune, Maharashtra, successfully conducted India's first womb transplant on 18 May 2017 by transferring a woman's uterus to her 21-year-old daughter, who was unable to conceive. The procedure, which took 9 hrs using the laparoscopic technique, was performed by a team of 12 doctors.

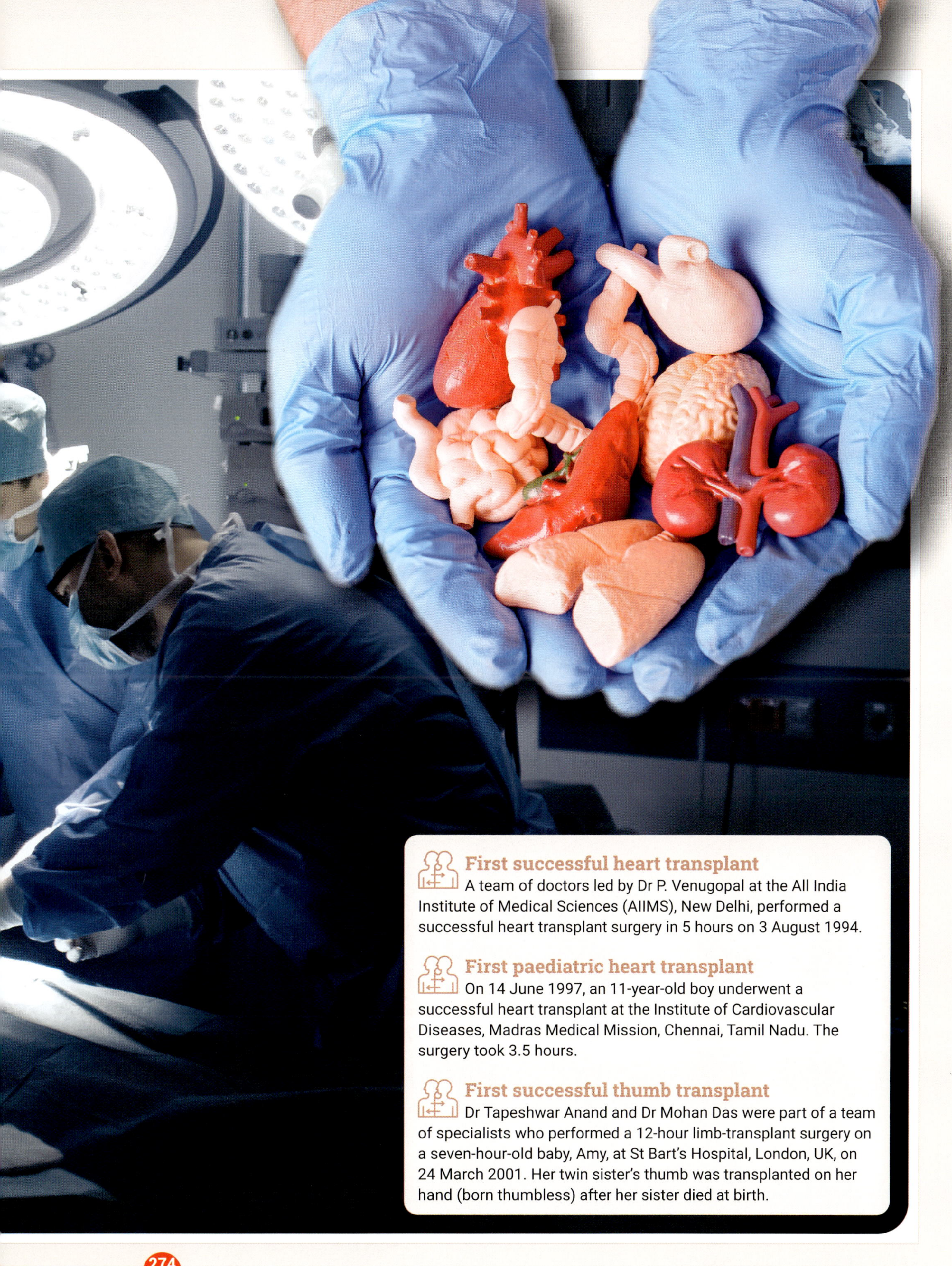

First successful heart transplant

A team of doctors led by Dr P. Venugopal at the All India Institute of Medical Sciences (AIIMS), New Delhi, performed a successful heart transplant surgery in 5 hours on 3 August 1994.

First paediatric heart transplant

On 14 June 1997, an 11-year-old boy underwent a successful heart transplant at the Institute of Cardiovascular Diseases, Madras Medical Mission, Chennai, Tamil Nadu. The surgery took 3.5 hours.

First successful thumb transplant

Dr Tapeshwar Anand and Dr Mohan Das were part of a team of specialists who performed a 12-hour limb-transplant surgery on a seven-hour-old baby, Amy, at St Bart's Hospital, London, UK, on 24 March 2001. Her twin sister's thumb was transplanted on her hand (born thumbless) after her sister died at birth.

BUDGETARY ALLOCATION FOR DEPARTMENT OF HEALTH RESEARCH

Value (in ₹ crore)

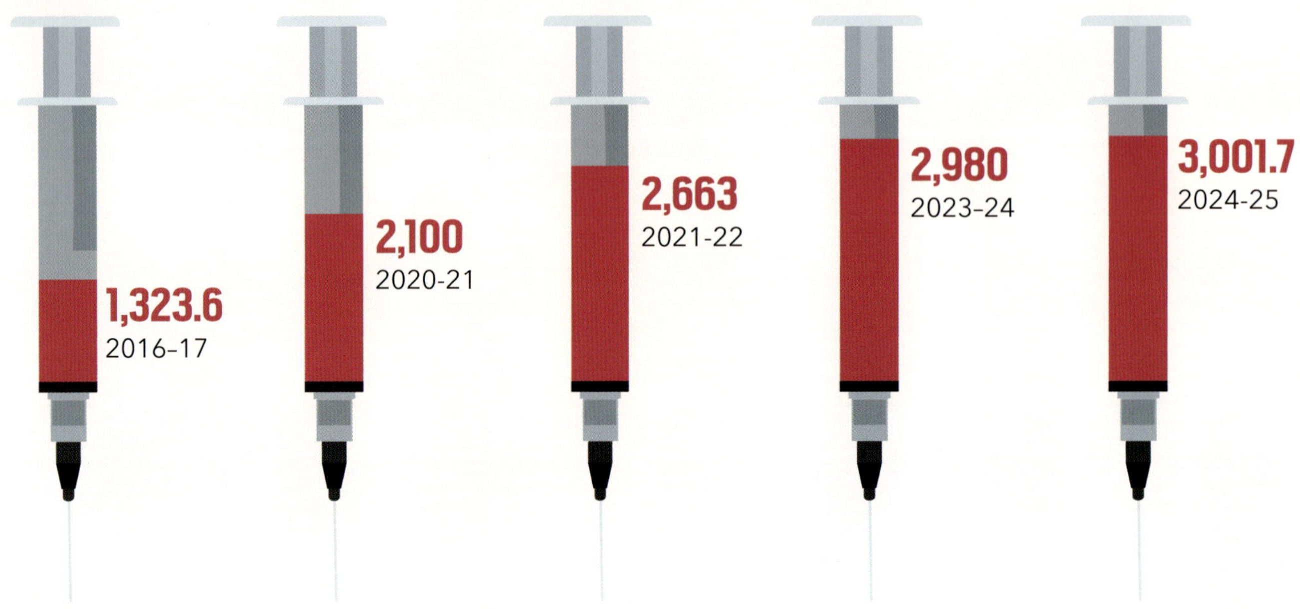

SOURCE: SDGs National Indicator Framework Progress Report 2024, MoSPI, GOI

NEONATAL MORTALITY RATE

(Per 1,000 live births)

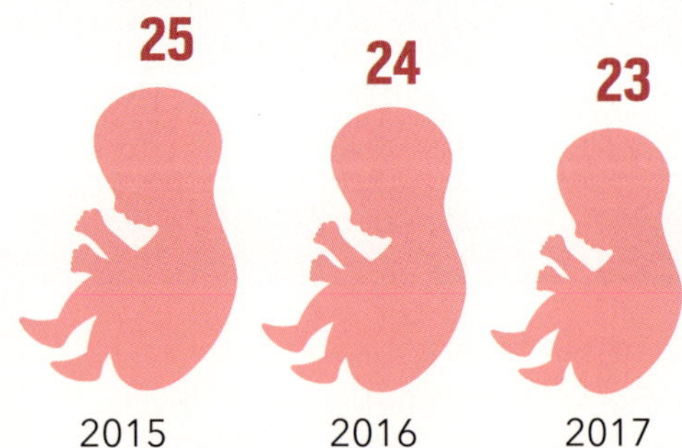

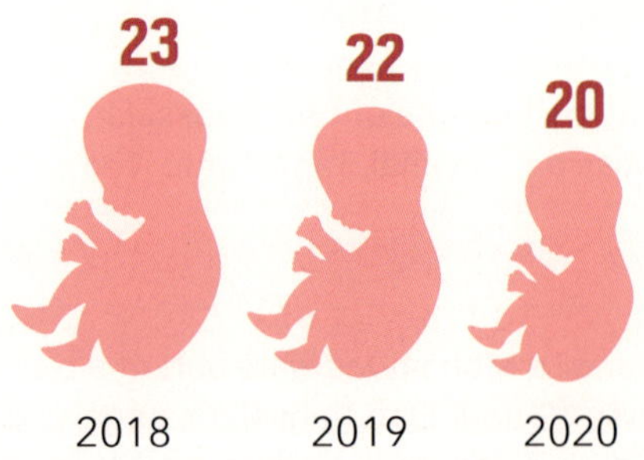

SOURCE: Office of the Registrar General & Census Commissioner, India, Ministry of Home Affairs

HEALTH PROFESSIONALS PER CAPITA, RELATIVE TO MAXIMUM THRESHOLDS FOR EACH CADRE IN 2021–22

Doctors
0.95
Per 1,000 population

Psychiatrists
1.2
Per 1,00,000 population

Surgeons
14.77
Per 1,00,000 population

SOURCE: SDGs National Indicator Framework Progress Report 2024, MoSPI, GOI

Heaviest kidney removed

Dr Puvvada Sandeep and three other doctors from his team at Ramaiah Medical College, Bengaluru, Karnataka, removed a kidney weighing 7.72 kg on 21 November 2019. Containing 3.12 litres of fluid, the kidney was removed from a 53-year-old patient suffering from bilateral adult polycystic kidney disease (APKD) and chronic kidney disease.

Heaviest brain tumour removed

Dr Saraj Kumar Singh, assistant professor, AIIMS, Patna, Bihar, and his assisting team removed a brain tumour weighing 2.280 kg (2,280 g) from a 50-year-old male patient on 22 November 2021 at the hospital. The surgery to excise the tumour began at 12:26 p.m. and ended at 3:42 p.m., lasting 3 hrs 16 mins. The tumour measured 24 cm x 24 cm x 14 cm (9.44 in. x 9.44 in. x 5.51 in.).

Longest foreign body removed

Dr Sanjay Kolte, urologist and kidney transplant surgeon at Sparsh Urology and Kidney Hospital, Dhantoli, Maharashtra, removed a 154 cm (5 ft 0.6 in.) long soft electric wire from the urinary bladder of a patient by percutaneous cystoscopy extraction of foreign body surgery on 28 August 2012.

Largest cystic tumour of the liver removed

Dr N. Bheerappa from the department of surgical gastroenterology at the Nizam's Institute of Medical Sciences, Hyderabad, Telangana, successfully removed the largest known cystic liver tumour (mucinous cystic neoplasm) in 2017. The 24-year-old female patient was operated on for a tumour measuring 40 cm x 28 cm x 15 cm (15.74 in. x 11.02 in. x 5.91 in.).

Largest kidney stone removed

Dr Hemendra Shah at R.G. Stone Urological Research Institute, Mumbai, Maharashtra, removed a 13 cm (5.12 in.) wide kidney stone from a patient on 18 February 2004.

Largest urethral calculus removed

Dr Neeraj Kumar Agrawal removed a 5.6 cm (2.2 in.) long stone from a patient at Neeraj Lifecare and Stone Centre, Bareilly, Uttar Pradesh, on 21 August 2019.

Largest thoracic tumour removed

On 13 September 2021, the largest thoracic tumour was successfully removed by Dr Anshuman Darbari of the cardiothoracic department, AIIMS Rishikesh, Uttarakhand. The tumour was removed from a 51-year-old female patient. The tumour measured 26 cm x 24 cm x 12 cm (10.23 in. x 9.44 in. x 4.72 in.).

Largest oral (head and neck) tumour removed – in one piece

Dr Saurabh Gupta, assistant professor and consultant, Surgical Oncology, Max Superspeciality Hospital, Shalimar Bagh, New Delhi, as operating surgeon, removed a head-and-neck tumour from a 38-year-old male patient in a left commando surgery. This, along with free alt flap reconstruction, took 11 hrs from 9:00 a.m. to 8:00 p.m. on 30 April 2020. The size of the tumour in this case of oral cancer was 18 cm x 12 cm x 8 cm (7.09 in. x 4.72 in. x 3.15 in.).

Largest urinary bladder stone removed

Dr D.C. Patel operated on Maheshbhai Patel, a 49-year-old suffering from blocked urine, at Shree Sainath Surgical and Maternity Hospital, Dharampur, Gujarat, on 6 April 2017. Dr Patel removed a bladder stone measuring 15 cm x 12 cm x 10 cm (5.90 in. x 4.72 in. x 3.94 in.) and weighing 1.365 kg. He was assisted by Dr Hemant Patel and Dr Nital Patel.

Largest bone tumour removed

On 9 June 2021, a team of doctors from the orthopaedics department of ACPM Medical Hospital, Dhule, Maharashtra, removed the largest tumour from the left femur of a 28-year-old patient. The team comprised Dr Yashwant Mahale, Dr James Kuris, Dr Ameya Thaware, and Dr Akash Metkar. The tumour measured 43.18 cm (17 in.) in length, 30.48 cm (12 in.) in breadth, and 25.4 cm (10 in.) in width. It had a circumference of 102 cm (40.16 in.). The surgery took a total of 3.5 hours.

Largest bone tumour removed

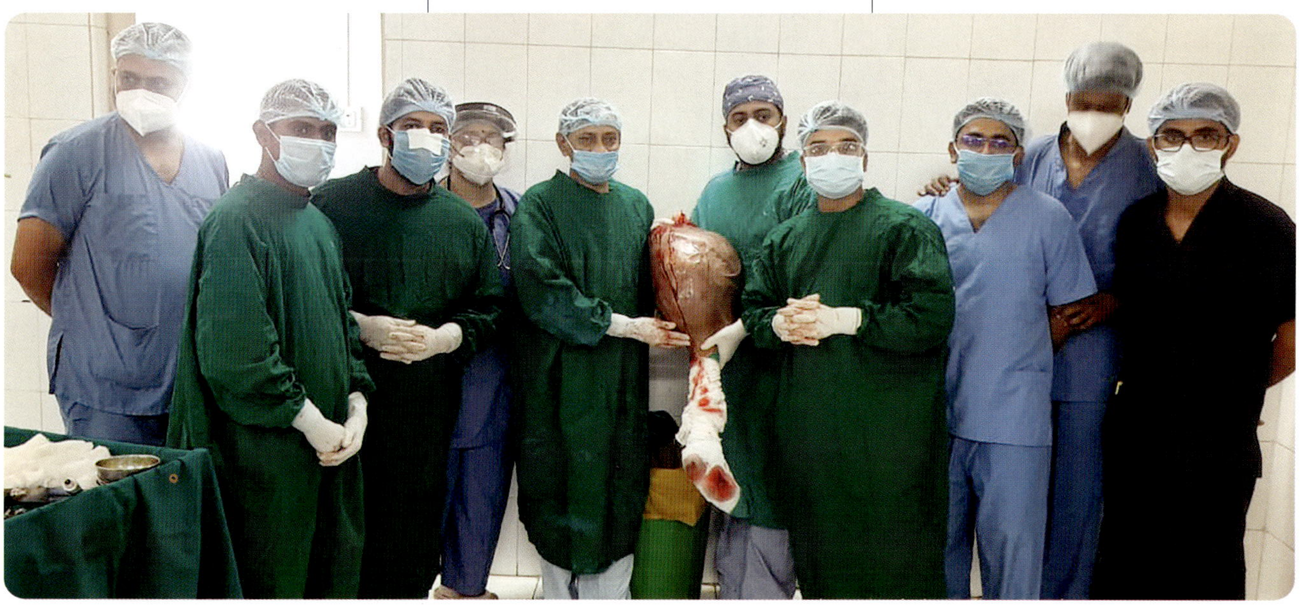

Longest fistula removed

A 110 cm (43.30 in.) long fistula was removed from a patient by Dr Ashwin Porwal at Healing Hands Clinic, Pune, Maharashtra, on 10 May 2019. The surgery was conducted from 3:00 p.m. to 7:00 p.m. using the distal laser proximal ligation (DLPL) technique.

Largest small-intestinal tumour removed

A tumour measuring 21 cm x 19 cm x 13 cm (8.26 in. x 7.48 in. x 5.12 in.) was removed from the small intestine of a patient by Dr Karthik Babu Perumalla at Ramesh Sanghamitra Hospital, Ongole, Andhra Pradesh. The surgery was conducted on 1 March 2019 from 11:00 a.m. to 4:00 p.m.

Largest adrenal cyst removed

On 24 January 2023, a team of urologists from ACE Hospital and Research Centre, Pune, Maharashtra, removed the largest adrenal cyst measuring 23 cm laparoscopically. The cyst was removed from a 58-yearold female patient. The team included Dr Suresh B. Patankar, Dr Gururaj R. Padasalagi, Dr Mayur M. Narkhede, and Dr Kashinath V. Thakare.

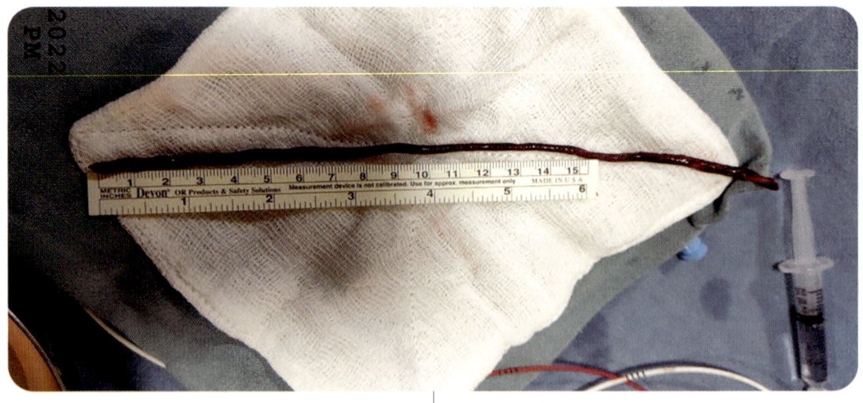

Longest blood clot removed

Longest blood clot removed

On 24 September 2022, Dr Anne Sai Pavan, a cardiothoracic surgeon at Aayush Hospitals, Vijayawada, performed a femoral artery embolectomy from 9:00 p.m. to 11:00 p.m. and removed the longest clot measuring 20 cm (7.87 in.).

Largest kidney operated on

- Dr A.K. Hemal, Dr S.N. Wadhwa, and their team from the Department of Urology, AIIMS, New Delhi, removed a non-functional kidney measuring 25 cm x 20 cm x 20 cm (9.84 in. x 7.88 in. x 7.88 in.), containing five litres of fluid, by laparoscopic nephrectomy in a unique operation with no incision, on 3 June 1996.
- A kidney measuring 40.5 cm x 22 cm x 12.5 cm (15.94 in. x 8.66 in. x 4.92 in.) and weighing 6.24 kg was removed by Dr Niket Kantilal Shah at Wanless Hospital, Miraj, Maharashtra, on 23 June 2017. It was removed from a 50-year-old patient suffering from adult polycystic kidney disease (APKD).

Largest breast tumour removed

The largest breast tumour recorded, which measured 41 cm x 39 cm x 37 cm (16.14 in. x 15.35 in. x 14.57 in.), was removed from a patient by Dr Vikas Jain at the B.J. Hospital, Gondia, Maharashtra. The surgery was conducted on 25 July 2019 from 3:30 p.m. to 6:00 p.m. The tumour weighed 5.6 kg after it was removed.

Largest adrenal cyst removed

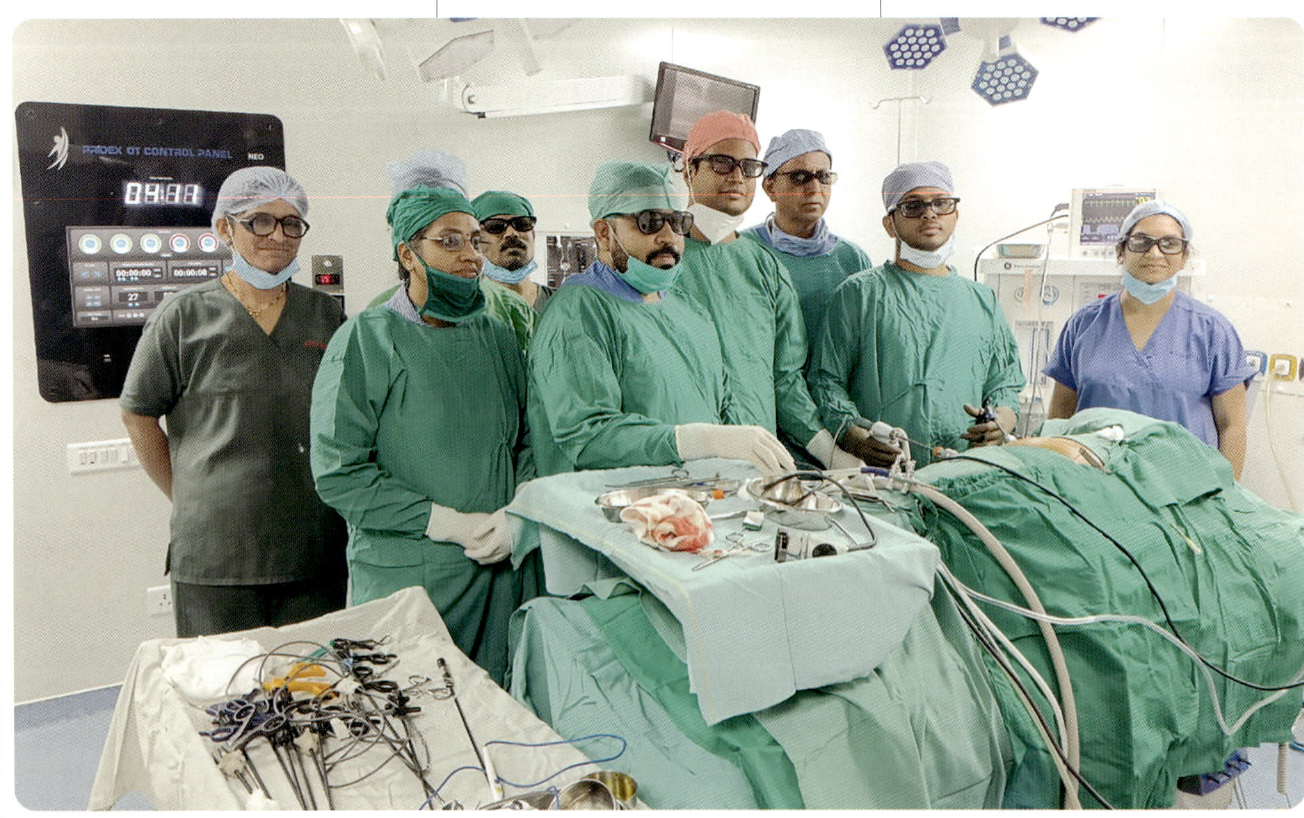

Most uterine fibroids removed

Dr Ravindra Keshavrao Shelmohkar removed 63 uterine fibroids from a 34-year-old female patient in an open abdominal myomectomy conducted on 14 April 2021 from 9:45 a.m. to 10:45 a.m. at Pune District Education Association's Ayurved Rugnalaya and Sterling Multispeciality Hospital in Nugdi, Pune, Maharashtra.

Surgery on the heaviest woman

Forty-two-year-old Amita Rajani, weighing 300 kg, underwent bariatric surgery performed by Dr Shashank Shah at his hospital in Pune, Maharashtra, in 2015. She was bedridden for eight years before the surgery and had multiple risk factors. She lost 214 kg as a result of the surgery.

Surgery on the world's heaviest teenager

Mihir Jain, then 14 years old, became the world's heaviest teenager to undergo bariatric surgery. He weighed 237 kg at the time, with a BMI of 92 kg/sq. m. The surgery was performed by Dr Pradeep Kumar Chowbey at Max Hospital, Saket, New Delhi, and a team of six doctors in 2 hrs 20 mins in July 2018.

Highest spectacle power corrected surgically

The highest spectacle power of –32.5 D was corrected surgically by Dr Rahil Chaudhary on 22 March 2021 at Eye7 Eye Hospital, Lajpat Nagar, New Delhi. Myopia of right eye –25.00 diopter and –32.50 diopter of left eye in a 24-year-old female patient was successfully corrected using a vision correction refractive eye surgery that employed Customized Implantable Contact Lens (ICL).

Highest spectacle power corrected through ICL surgery

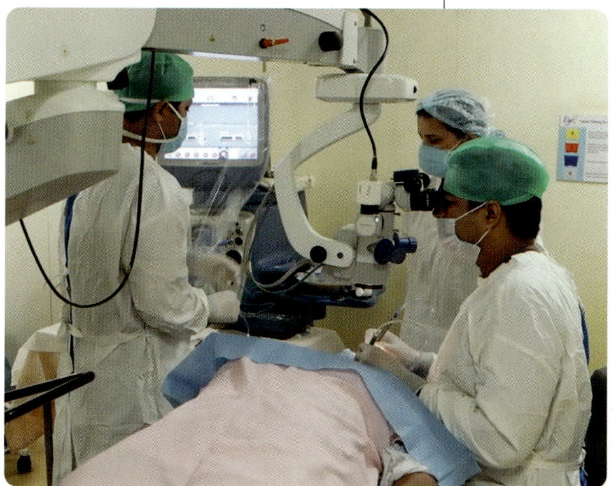

First homegrown CAR-T cell therapy

First home-grown anti-cancer CAR-T cell therapy

In April 2024, the President launched India's first home-grown anti-Cancer CAR-T cell therapy in Mumbai for cancer treatment, developed by IIT Bombay, Tata Memorial Centre and ImmunoACT. It is not only a first for India, but also deemed as the most affordable CAR-T therapy.

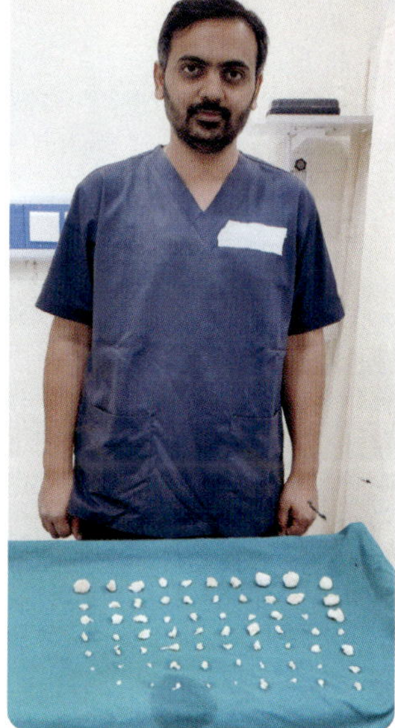

Most loose bodies removed from a joint

Largest ear tumour removed

Dr Saraj Kumar Singh surgically removed the largest ear tumour of size 10 cm x 10 cm x 04 cm and weighing 110 gms from the left ear of a 35-year-old male patient on 11 September 2023 at AIIMS, Patna.

Largest eye tumour removed

Dr Saraj Kumar Singh surgically removed the largest eye tumour of size 12 cm x 10 cm x 04 cm and weighing 180 gms from the left eye of a 14-year-old male patient on 28 August 2023 at AIIMS, Patna.

Most loose bodies removed from a joint

Dr Ajinkya Bhaskarrao Desale surgically removed 69 loose bodies (joint stones) from the left knee joint of a 54-year-old female patient on 20 July 2023 at Apex Wellness Hospital, Nashik, Maharashtra. Usually, 2–3 such loose bodies are encountered but 69 of such in a single knee joint was a unique occurrence.

Largest spinal disc removed

Dr Saraj Kumar Singh surgically removed the largest spinal disc of size 08 cm x 03 cm x 01 cm from a 55-year-old male patient on 25 September 2023 at AIIMS, Patna. The method employed for the surgery was endoscopic disectomy.

Largest nasal polyp removed

Dr Himanshu Jagdishchandra Thakkar surgically removed the largest nasal polyp of size 8 cm x 2.5 cm from the nose of a 55-year-old male patient on 16 September 2023 at Dr Thakkar's ENT and Dentala Hospital, Rajkot, Gujarat.

Search...

Himalayan Range

PHYSICAL FEATURES

Longest land mountain range

The Himalayan range is the loftiest and most rugged mountain barrier in Asia. Out of the 7,300 mountain peaks in the world, 96 are in the Himalaya–Karakoram range. The range stretches over 2,500 km and varies in width from around 500 km in Jammu and Kashmir to around 200 km in Arunachal Pradesh. Some of the higher ranges are composed of 600-million-year-old Precambrian rocks.

Largest glacier

Siachen Glacier, Ladakh, near the India–Pakistan border, is India's largest glacier. It is 75.6 km long and 2–8 km wide. It is also the second longest glacier outside the polar regions of the earth.

Largest brackish water lagoon

Chilika Lake in Odisha is the largest brackish-water lagoon and has an area of around 1,100 sq km.

Chilika Lake, Odisha

Longest river

The 2,525 km long Ganga River is the longest river in the country. Its source is in the western Himalayas in Uttarakhand, from where the river flows south and east through the Gangetic Plain and Bangladesh, finally merging into the Bay of Bengal.

Largest river system

Of the total river discharge in India, 65 per cent is from the Himalayan group of rivers. The Ganga, Indus, and Brahmaputra Rivers are part of this river system.

WR Largest delta

The triangular landmass formed by the Hooghly River, the Ganga, Padma, and Meghna Rivers combined, and the Bay of Bengal is called the Bengal Delta. It is the largest delta in the world. Two-thirds of this 57,000 sq km delta is in Bangladesh and the rest lies in West Bengal, India.

Largest catchment area

The Ganga–Brahmaputra–Meghna system is the biggest river system in the country, with a catchment area of 272 million acres (110 million hectares), which is more than 43 per cent of the catchment area of all the major rivers of the Indian subcontinent.

Largest desert

The Thar Desert is the largest desert in India that stretches over an area of about 200,000 sq km and spreads over four states: Punjab, Haryana, Gujarat, and Rajasthan. It is interspersed with hillocks, gravel plains, salt marshes, and lakes.

Thar Desert

Largest freshwater lake

Wular Lake, India's largest freshwater lake, has an area of 260 sq km. It is in Bandipora District, Jammu and Kashmir.

Largest cave

The Amarnath Cave, about 44 km from Pahalgam in Jammu and Kashmir, is the largest cave and a popular pilgrimage. It is a natural cave located at an altitude of 3,800 m (12,467 ft). The cave is 50 m (164 ft) wide and 25 m (82 ft) high. The Shivalinga worshipped in the cave is a remarkable example of a stalagmite.

Only cold desert

Ladakh, at an average altitude of 4,878 m (16,004 ft), is the only cold desert in India.

Largest crater

The Lonar meteorite crater in the Buldhana District of Maharashtra is India's largest meteorite crater. It measures 1,800 m (5,906 ft) across and is 170 m (558 ft) deep. It is estimated that it was formed 50,000 years ago by a meteorite that was around 100 m (328 ft) in diameter, weighed a million tonnes and was travelling at a speed of around 90,000 km per hour.

Highest peak

Kanchenjunga, with its base partly in India and partly in Nepal, is 8,586 m (28,169 ft) high. Yalung Kang (also on the India–Nepal border) is the second highest at 8,505 m (27,903 ft) and Nanda Devi comes in third at 7,817 m (25,646 ft).

Lonar crater, Maharashtra

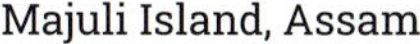

Majuli Island, Assam

Largest island – freshwater

The island of Majuli, with an area of 352 sq km in the Brahmaputra River in Assam, is the largest freshwater island in the world.

Largest island – ocean

The island of Middle Andaman (1,523 sq km) in the Andaman and Nicobar Islands is the largest ocean island in India.

Largest meteorite shower

On 14 July 1860, a heavy meteorite shower fell at Dharamshala (32°14′N, 76°28′E) in Kangra District, Himachal Pradesh. It consisted of many stones, the largest of which weighed 150 kg.

Highest waterfall

Kunchikal Falls in Nidagodu Village near Masthikatte in Shivamogga District, Karnataka, falls down a total height of 455 m (1,493 ft), making it the highest waterfall in India.

Mawsynram, Meghalaya

Maximum rainfall

Mawsynram, a village in the East Khasi Hills District, Meghalaya, about 65 km from Shillong, gets a mean annual rainfall of 11,873 mm (467 in.) in about 147 days. Earlier the record for the highest average rainfall was held by Cherrapunji (now Sohra) in the same district.

Minimum rainfall area

Jaisalmer in Rajasthan receives an average rainfall of only about 200 mm (around 7.87 in.) in a year.

Highest temperature

On 19 May 2016, India recorded its highest-ever temperature, 51°C, in Phalodi, a town in Jodhpur District, Rajasthan.

Lowest temperature

The lowest temperature recorded in Dras, Ladakh, was -60°C on 9 January 1995, making it the coldest inhabited place in India.

Highest surface salinity

The surface salinity in the Gulf of Kachchh, off the coast of Gujarat, varies from a maximum of 45.5 psu (practical salinity units) near the head of the gulf to 36.6 psu at the mouth. A practical salinity unit is equivalent to parts per thousand.

Lowest surface salinity

Salinity near the surface in the northern Bay of Bengal can be as low as 31 psu because the bay receives fresh water as rain as well as run-off from the Ganga, Brahmaputra, Irrawaddy, and other rivers.

WR Longest natural sandstone cave

Krem Puri, found in East Khasi Hills District, Meghalaya, is the world's longest sandstone cave with a length of about 24.58 km. It is also known for its dinosaur fossils from 66–76 million years ago. It is 6 km longer than the previous record holder – the 18.2 km long Cueva Del Saman sandstone cave in Edo Zulia, Venezuela.

Only active volcano

Barren Island, which lies 110 km north-east of Port Blair in the Andaman and Nicobar Islands, is India's only active volcano. On 10 April 1991, it blew up nearly two centuries after it erupted in 1803. It last erupted in 1995.

Barren Island, Andaman and Nicobar Islands

FOSSILS

Oldest dinosaur fossil discovery

The first dinosaur fossils in India were discovered by a British palaeontologist named William Henry Sleeman in 1828 in Jabalpur, Madhya Pradesh. The specimens were lost in 1877 and found in 2013 in the office of the Geological Survey of India, Kolkata, West Bengal.

W.H. Sleeman

Blue whale in the Indian Ocean

MAMMALS

Oldest living mammal

One of the oldest living mammals is the Indian one-horned rhinoceros (*Rhinoceros unicornis*). The Indian and Javan rhinoceroses first appeared in the fossil record of Asia 1.6–3.3 million years ago. The species may have diverged much earlier, around 11.7 million years ago.

Smallest mammal

- ***Land:*** The white-toothed pygmy shrew (*Suncus etruscus*), which has a head-and-body length of 3–5.5 cm (1.18–2.17 in.) and a tail length of 2.5–3.2 cm (0.98–1.26 in.), is the smallest Indian land mammal by weight. It weighs around 1.8 g. This shrew can be found across the Indian subcontinent, except in Jammu and Kashmir and arid areas of Gujarat and Rajasthan.
- ***Water:*** The smallest water mammal in the country is the finless porpoise (*Neophocaena phocaenoides*), which is only 1.2–2 cm (0.47–0.79 in.) long. It is found in the waters of peninsular India.

Largest land mammal

The adult Asian elephant found in India (*Elephas maximus indicus*) belongs to the species of the largest land mammal *Elephas maximus.* An adult bull elephant averages 2.74 m (9 ft) in height at the shoulder and weighs around 4.5 tonnes. The female elephant or cow measures 2.35 m (7 ft 8.5 in.) at the shoulder and weighs around 3 tonnes. Elephants are found in four clusters in the plains of north, south, east and central India and the north-east.

Fastest breeders

The Indian mole rat is the fastest-breeding mammal. The males mature in 58 days after birth and the females in 90–100 days. Females have an average count of 11.32 pregnancies a year with a total break of 32.3 days in between. The female may produce as many as 70 young ones a year.

Slowest breeders

The elephant's main breeding season is the summer and the beginning of monsoon. Only one calf is born at a time and at intervals of three years.

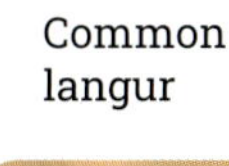

Asian elephant

Longest-living

- Humans (*Homo sapiens*) are the longest-living mammals, with the current average life expectancy of 72.5 years.
- The average lifespan of a blue whale (*Balaenoptera musculus*) is 80–90 years.
- The Indian elephant (*Elephas maximus indicus*) follows with an average lifespan of around 60 years, but they can live up to 80–90 years.

Largest litter

The Indian mole rat (*Bandicota bengalensis*), found in most plains and forests, is known to have litters of over 12 young ones at a time.

Longest gestation

The elephant has a gestation period of about 20 months.

Shortest gestation

Rodents have a gestation period averaging a month.

The only apes

The western hoolock gibbon (*Hoolock hoolock*) and the eastern hoolock gibbon (*Hoolock leuconedys*) are the only ape species found in India. They are the tallest gibbons, and the only ape species too. Their average height, standing on hind legs, is about 0.9 m (3 ft).

Primate with the longest tail

The tail of the common langur (*Semnopithecus entellus*) measures around 1 m (3 ft 3.4 in.) on average.

Common langur

Fastest and Slowest Mammals

Fastest Mammal – Land

The blackbuck (*Antilope cervicapra*), which is native to India, can run at a speed of up to 80 km per hour. It is found in regions ranging from Rajasthan to Punjab in the north, up to Odisha in the east, and Tamil Nadu in the south. The cheetah (*Acinonyx jubatus*), recently introduced in India, in Madhya Pradesh, can sprint at speeds of up to 120 km per hour.

Blackbuck in Gujarat

Slowest Mammal – Land

The Bengal slow loris (*Nycticebus bengalensis*), which measures 30–40 cm (11.8–15.7 in.), is the slowest land mammal in the country. It is found in Assam.

Fastest Mammal – Water

The 2–2.5 m (6 ft 6 in.–8 ft 2 in.) long-beaked common dolphin (*Delphinus capensis*), found off the coast of peninsular India, swims at 30 knots or 55.5 km per hour, and is the fastest mammal in water.

Slowest Mammal – Water

The slowest mammal in water is the 3.2 m (10 ft 6 in.) – long dugong or sea cow (*Dugong dugon*), found in the Gulf of Kachchh, off the Malabar Coast, and in the Andaman Islands.

Long-beaked common dolphin

Bengal slow loris on a branch

Dugong or sea cow

The only camels that swim

The Kharai camels from the Kachchh region in Gujarat are the only ones of their kind in the world that can swim. They live with nomadic camel herders, who are indigenous to the region. The camels have padded hooves that help them navigate wet and salty coastal land and they can swim up to 3 km.

Only herbivorous marine mammals

Dugongs and manatees (*Trichechus manatus latirostris/ Trichechus manatus manatus*) form the only group of herbivorous marine mammals. They are found in the Gulf of Mannar and Palk Bay, where seagrass meadows provide them with food. Highly endangered, dugongs are also found in the Gulf of Kachchh and near the Andaman Islands. They are 1 m to 3 m (3 ft 3 in. to 9 ft 10 in.) long and weigh around 400 kg.

Left: Manatee
Right: Rusty-spotted cat

Smallest feline

The world's smallest cat, about half to three fourths the size of a domestic cat, is the rusty-spotted cat (*Prionailurus rubiginosus*) found in southern and central India. The male has a head-and body length of 35–48 cm (14–19 in.) and the tail measures 15–30 cm (5.9–11.8 in.). Males weigh around 1.5–1.6 kg, while females weigh about 1.1–1.5 kg.

Largest/heaviest feline

Male tigers have a head-and-body length of 3.55–4.20 m (11 ft 7 in.– 13 ft 9 in.). Females have a head-and-body length of 2.40–2.65 m (7 ft 10 in. – 8 ft 8 in.). The height at shoulder is around 90–110 cm (35–43 in.). The

average weight of males is 175–260 kg and that of females is 100–160 kg.

Feline found at the highest altitude

The snow leopard (*Panthera uncia*) is found at around 3,650–3,960 m (12,000–13,000 ft) in the Himalayan mountains.

Rarest bat

Salim Ali's fruit bat (*Latidens salimalii*), found in southern India and named after the famous ornithologist Salim Ali, is the rarest bat in India, and one of the three rarest bats in the world.

Smallest bat

The Indian pygmy bat (*Pipistrellus tenuis*) has a head-and-body length of 3.3–4.5 cm (1.3–1.8 in.). Its tail is 3.5 cm (1.38 in.) and its forearm is 2.5–3 cm (1.0–1.2 in.) long.

Himalayan snow leopard

Largest bat

The large flying fox (*Pteropus vampyrus*) is the largest bat at 19.8–30 cm (7.8–11.8 in.) in the country and is found in the Himalayas and peninsular India.

BIRDS

Largest round nests

The nests made by the megapodes (*Megapodius nicobariensis*) reach a height of 1.5 m (4 ft 11 in.) and have a circumference of 10 m (32 ft 10 in.).

Smallest and lightest

The Nilgiri flowerpecker (*Dicaeum concolor*) is only 7 cm (2.7 in.) long and weighs around 4.5 g.

Flying fox

Smallest wingspan

The Nilgiri flowerpecker male has a wingspan of 43–48 mm (1.69–1.89 in.). The female has an even smaller wingspan of 42–45 mm (1.65–1.77 in.).

Largest wingspan

The bearded vulture (*Gypaetus barbatus*) or the lammergeier, found along the lower Himalayas in Jammu and Kashmir, Himachal Pradesh, Uttarakhand, Sikkim, Assam, and Arunachal Pradesh, has a wingspan of 2.31–2.83 m (7 ft 7 in.–9 ft 3 in.).

Longest claws

The hind claw of the bronze-winged jacana (*Metopidius indicus*) measures around 6.5–7 cm (2.5–2.7 in.) in length. Its leg (tarsus) is 6.5–6.8 cm (2.5–2.6 in.) long.

Smallest egg

The average size of the egg of the scarlet backed flowerpecker (*Dicaeum cruentatum*) is 14 mm x 10.3 mm (0.55 in. x 0.4 in.).

Largest egg

The average size of the sarus crane's egg is 10.4 cm x 6.4 cm (4 in. x 2.5 in.).

Longest beak

The beaks of the rosy pelican (*Pelecanus onocrotalus*) and the Dalmatian pelican (*Pelecanus crispus*) are 43–45 cm (1 ft 4.9 in.–1 ft 5.7 in.) long.

Slowest bird

The Eurasian woodcock (*Scolopax rusticola*) flies at a speed of around 8 km per hour.

First bird hospital

The Charity Birds' Hospital in Chandni Chowk, Delhi, which started in 1929, caters to about 20,000 birds a year and is the only exclusive hospital for birds in the country.

Most intricate nest

The weaver bird species, like the baya (*Ploceus philippinus*), makes the most intricate nests. Shaped like the pipe of a snake charmer, the nests have many chambers.

Shortest legs

The crested tree swift (*Hemiprocne coronata*) has around 7–9 mm (0.27 – 0.35 in.) long legs.

Peregrine falcon

Swiftest/ fastest dive

The peregrine falcon (*Falco peregrinus*) reaches speeds of over 320 km per hour. It can dive at a speed of up to 360 km per hour – faster than a moving racing car.

Only breeding ground for flamingos

The only known breeding ground in India for the lesser and greater flamingos is the Rann of Kachchh in Gujarat. Thousands of flamingos nest every year in the seasonal marshes of both the Great Rann and the Little Rann of Kachchh.

Flamingo

Longest legs

The legs (tarsus) of the sarus crane (*Grus antigone*) measure 31–35 cm (12–13 in.), making them the longest among birds.

WR Tallest flying bird

The sarus crane (*Grus antigone*) is the world's tallest bird, standing 1.52 m (5 ft) tall. This greyish crane with a red head is common around the *jheels* of northern and central India. Of the 14–15 species of cranes in the world, six are found in India.

Sarus crane

BUTTERFLIES

Smallest butterfly

The grass jewel butterfly (*Freyeria trochylus*) has a wingspan of only 1.5 cm (0.6 in.).

Biggest butterfly

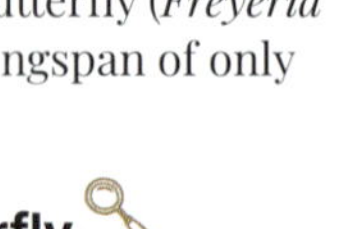

The female golden birdwing (*Troides aeacus*) has a wingspan of 19.4 cm (7.6 in.) and was seen in Didihat, Uttarakhand. The male is much smaller with a wingspan of 10.6 cm (4.2 in.).

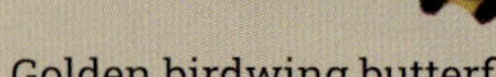
Golden birdwing butterfly

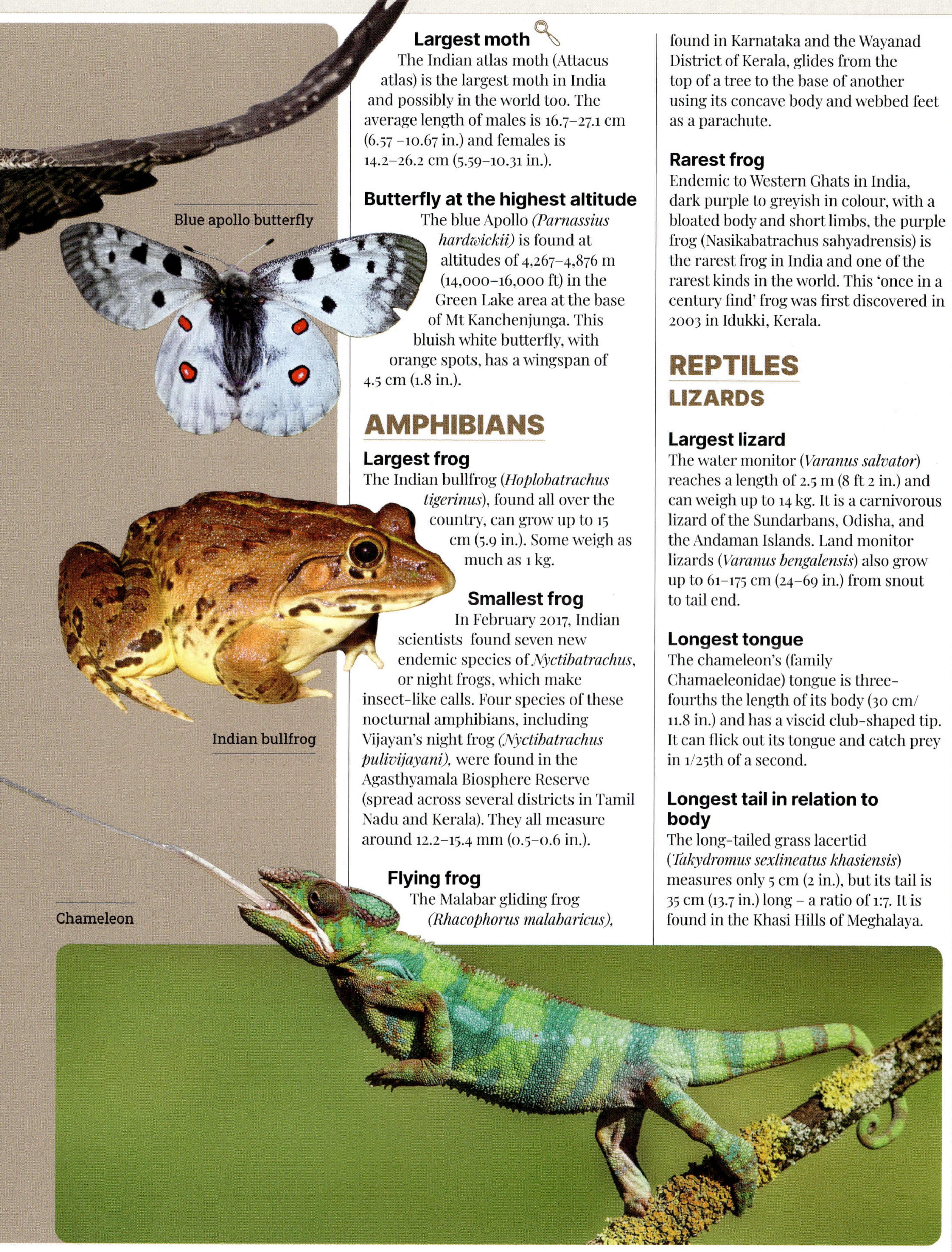

Blue apollo butterfly

Indian bullfrog

Chameleon

Largest moth

The Indian atlas moth (Attacus atlas) is the largest moth in India and possibly in the world too. The average length of males is 16.7–27.1 cm (6.57 –10.67 in.) and females is 14.2–26.2 cm (5.59–10.31 in.).

Butterfly at the highest altitude

The blue Apollo *(Parnassius hardwickii)* is found at altitudes of 4,267–4,876 m (14,000–16,000 ft) in the Green Lake area at the base of Mt Kanchenjunga. This bluish white butterfly, with orange spots, has a wingspan of 4.5 cm (1.8 in.).

AMPHIBIANS

Largest frog

The Indian bullfrog (*Hoplobatrachus tigerinus*), found all over the country, can grow up to 15 cm (5.9 in.). Some weigh as much as 1 kg.

Smallest frog

In February 2017, Indian scientists found seven new endemic species of *Nyctibatrachus*, or night frogs, which make insect-like calls. Four species of these nocturnal amphibians, including Vijayan's night frog *(Nyctibatrachus pulivijayani),* were found in the Agasthyamala Biosphere Reserve (spread across several districts in Tamil Nadu and Kerala). They all measure around 12.2–15.4 mm (0.5–0.6 in.).

Flying frog

The Malabar gliding frog *(Rhacophorus malabaricus),* found in Karnataka and the Wayanad District of Kerala, glides from the top of a tree to the base of another using its concave body and webbed feet as a parachute.

Rarest frog

Endemic to Western Ghats in India, dark purple to greyish in colour, with a bloated body and short limbs, the purple frog (Nasikabatrachus sahyadrensis) is the rarest frog in India and one of the rarest kinds in the world. This 'once in a century find' frog was first discovered in 2003 in Idukki, Kerala.

REPTILES

LIZARDS

Largest lizard

The water monitor (*Varanus salvator*) reaches a length of 2.5 m (8 ft 2 in.) and can weigh up to 14 kg. It is a carnivorous lizard of the Sundarbans, Odisha, and the Andaman Islands. Land monitor lizards (*Varanus bengalensis*) also grow up to 61–175 cm (24–69 in.) from snout to tail end.

Longest tongue

The chameleon's (family Chamaeleonidae) tongue is three-fourths the length of its body (30 cm/ 11.8 in.) and has a viscid club-shaped tip. It can flick out its tongue and catch prey in 1/25th of a second.

Longest tail in relation to body

The long-tailed grass lacertid (*Takydromus sexlineatus khasiensis*) measures only 5 cm (2 in.), but its tail is 35 cm (13.7 in.) long – a ratio of 1:7. It is found in the Khasi Hills of Meghalaya.

Only flying lizards
Norvill's flying lizard (*Draco norvillii*), found in north-east India, and the Indian flying lizard (*Draco dussumieri*) in the Western Ghats and south India are endemic to India. Their average length is 23 cm (9 in.) and they can glide through the air for around 17 m (55 ft 9 in.).

Only legless lizard
The Asian glass lizard or Burmese glass lizard (*Ophisaurus gracilis*) is found at altitudes of 820–1,500 m (2,690–4,920 ft) in Darjeeling, West Bengal, and the Khasi Hills, Meghalaya. It crawls and uses its tongue in a snake-like fashion.

GECKOS

'Flying' gecko
The gliding gecko (*Ptychozoon kuhli*), found in the Nicobar Islands and north-east India, can glide over 13 m (43 ft). It has skin flaps on the side of its head, body, and tail, which help it glide when the animal launches into the air.

Gliding gecko

Smallest gecko
A 4 cm (1.6 in.) Persian sand dwarf gecko (*Tropiocolotes persicus*), or the dwarf or pygmy gecko, was recorded in Rajasthan in 2011.

Largest gecko
The *Hemidactylus frenatus* or the common house gecko, found in Bihar, Bengal, and north-east India, grows to around 34 cm (13.4 in.) in length. It feeds on insects, rats, birds, and small snakes.

Rarest gecko
The golden hill gecko (*Calodactylodes avreus*), found in the Tirumala Hills of Andhra Pradesh, is a very rare species. Its body is golden yellow with brown spots.

CROCODILES

Shortest crocodile 
The mugger crocodile (*Crocodylus palustris*), found in streams, is only 3 m (9 ft 10 in.) long. It is found almost all over India except at higher altitudes such as in the Himalayan mountains.

Heaviest crocodile
The estuarine or saltwater crocodile (*Crocodylus porosus*) is the heaviest reptile in the country. The adult male crocodile may weigh around 200–1,300 kg while the adult female weighs around 76–100 kg.

Longest crocodile
The estuarine or saltwater crocodile grows to a recorded length of 7 m (23 ft). It is found in tidal estuaries, marine swamps, and coastal waters in and around the Sundarbans, Odisha, and the Andaman and Nicobar Islands.

First known white crocodile
Gori, an albino white crocodile, was artificially hatched at the Bhitarkanika Dangamal Crocodile Research Centre in Odisha on 26 June 1975.

Rarest crocodile
The rarest of the three crocodile species found in India, the gharial (*Gavialus gangeticus*) grows to 6.25 m (20 ft 6 in.) and is the only living member of the family Gavialidae in India. The surviving population is found in some of the tributaries and sub-tributaries of the Ganga River like the Girwa (Uttar

Mugger crocodile

Pradesh), Son (Madhya Pradesh), Ramganga (Uttarakhand), Gandak (Bihar), Chambal (Uttar Pradesh, Madhya Pradesh, and Rajasthan) and the Mahanadi River (Odisha). It is classified as critically endangered by the International Union for the Conservation of Nature (IUCN).

First/largest crocodile bank
The Madras Crocodile Bank Trust and Centre for Herpetology, 40 km from Madras (now Chennai), Tamil Nadu, was founded in 1976 by the naturalist Romulus Whitaker and had over 8,000 crocodiles of 10 different species.

SNAKES

WR Longest snake
The reticulated python (*Python reticulatus*) is the longest snake in the world. It is found in the Nicobar Islands. The average length is between 3 and 6 m (10 and 20 ft). While the reticulated python prefers small mammals, it can take larger animals up to the size of a full-grown wild boar.

Fastest snake
Rat snakes and bronze-back tree snakes can reach a speed of 10 km per hour.

Longest sea snake
The yellow sea snake (*Hydrophis spiralis*) grows 1.8 m (6 ft) long. Specimens up to 3 m (10 ft) long are not uncommon. It is found both in the Bay of Bengal and the Arabian Sea.

« More than 600 plant species and more than 950 animal species in India are classified as critically endangered, endangered, or vulnerable by the IUCN Red List as of January 2024. »

Loudest hiss
Russell's viper (*Daboia russelii*) hisses the loudest among all Indian snakes – nearly as loud as the hiss of a pressure cooker.

Only snake with heat sensors
The pit viper (subfamily Crotalinae), found in the hilly parts of India, is able to locate warm-blooded prey using two heat sensors between its nostrils and eyes.

Reticulated python

Only snake that builds a nest
The female king cobra (*Ophiophagus hannah*) is the only snake that builds a nest and is found in the Western Ghats, parts of north India, eastern India, the north-east and the Andaman Islands. It builds a 30 cm (11.8 in.) nest by scraping leaves, weeds, and loose vegetation together.

Snake at the highest altitude
No other species of snake has been found at an altitude higher than the Himalayan pit viper (*Gloydius himalayanus*), which can be found at altitudes

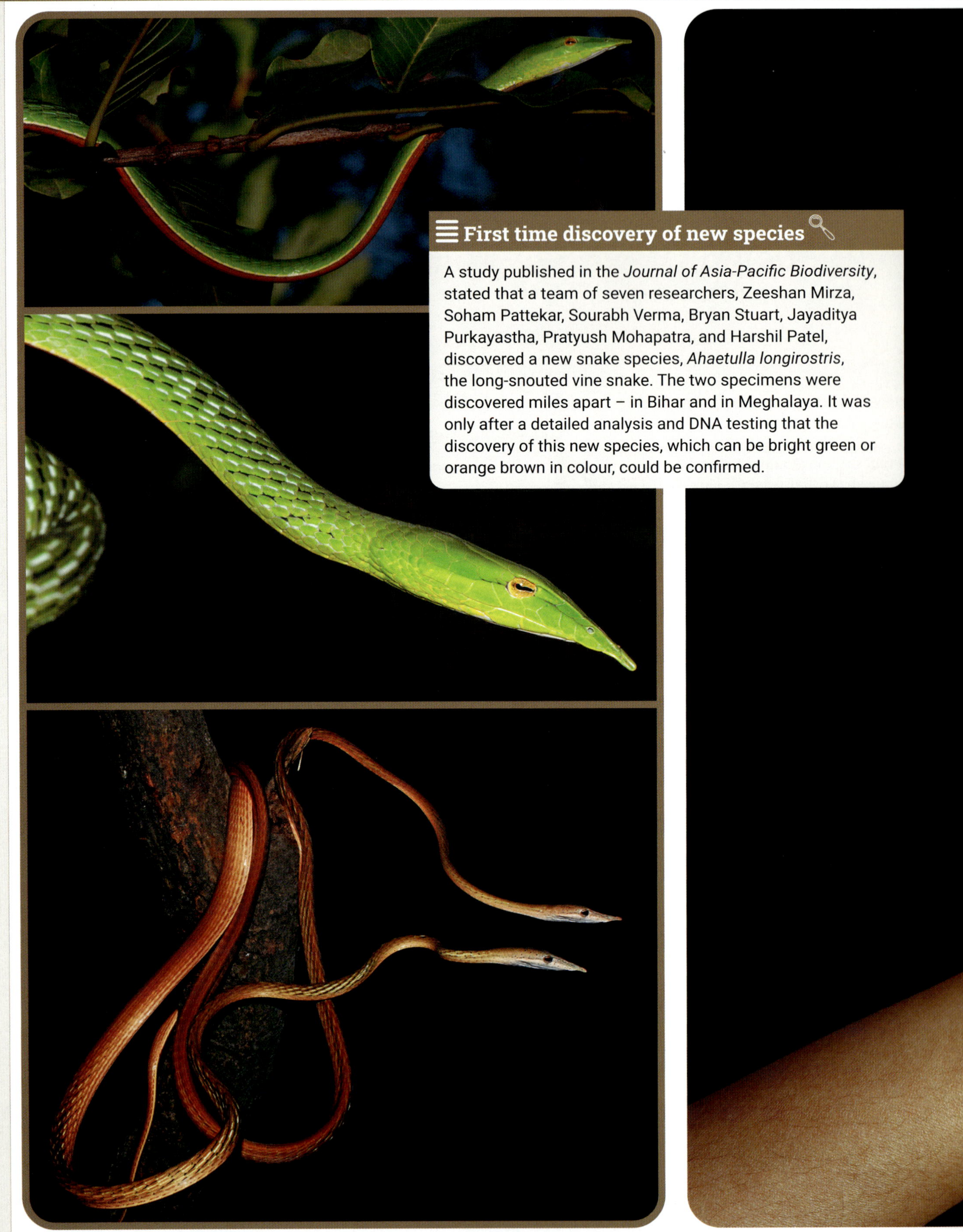

First time discovery of new species

A study published in the *Journal of Asia-Pacific Biodiversity*, stated that a team of seven researchers, Zeeshan Mirza, Soham Pattekar, Sourabh Verma, Bryan Stuart, Jayaditya Purkayastha, Pratyush Mohapatra, and Harshil Patel, discovered a new snake species, *Ahaetulla longirostris*, the long-snouted vine snake. The two specimens were discovered miles apart – in Bihar and in Meghalaya. It was only after a detailed analysis and DNA testing that the discovery of this new species, which can be bright green or orange brown in colour, could be confirmed.

Largest climate clock

India's largest climate clock was installed and activated by Council of Scientific & Industrial Research (CSIR), at the CSIR Headquarters Building at Rafi Marg, New Delhi, as a part of the Earth Day Celebrations on 23 April 2024. The aim was to spread awareness about climate change and its ill effects.

Tortoises and Turtles

Largest rookery
The 12 km long sandy beach in the Gahirmatha region of Odisha is one of the largest rookeries for marine sea turtles. During February and March, olive ridley turtles (*Lepidochelys olivacea*) come out here in hundreds of thousands to mate and nest. The olive ridley is one of the seven endangered species of turtles in the world due to disturbance and destruction of their habitat.

Largest turtle
The leatherback sea turtle (*Dermochelys coriacea*) has a shell length averaging 2.5 m (8 ft) and weighs 700 kg. It feeds mainly on jellyfish.

Largest terrapin
The Batagur terrapin (*Batagur baska*), found in the river estuaries of the Sundarbans, West Bengal, is the largest terrapin and a critically endangered species. The carapace of this terrapin is 59 cm (23 in.) long.

Rarest freshwater turtle
India's rarest freshwater turtle is possibly the Assam leaf turtle (*Cyclemys dentata*), found in the hill streams of Assam. It grows to a length of around 24 cm (9.4 in.).

Indian star tortoise

Smallest carapace
The Cochin cane forest turtle (*Vijayachelys silvatica*) has a carapace that is 13 cm (5.1 in.) long.

Smallest tortoise
The Indian star tortoise (*Geochelone elegans*) grows to a length of around 15 cm (5.9 in.).

Most turtles mass nesting
Between 23 February and 2 March 2023, Odisha's Ganjam District saw the arrival of a record 6.37 lakh Olive Ridley turtles for mass nesting. This huge number was attributed to the emergence of new beaches that remained unaffected by extreme weather conditions. These turtles, labelled as vulnerable by the IUCN, dig holes in the sand using their flippers, lay eggs, and cover them before returning to the sea. The eggs hatch after 40–60 days and the hatchlings make their way back into the sea. The Gahirmatha Beach in the Kendrapara District of Odisha also sees the arrival of turtles and is known as the world's largest rookery.

Newly hatched olive ridley turtles in Ganjam, Odisha

up to 4,900 m (16,072 ft). Herpetologist Frank Wall (1868– 1950), who lived in Sri Lanka and India, claimed to have seen one at an altitude of 3,658 m (12,000 ft) in Kashmir and one was captured at the foot of the glacier at Dharamshala at an altitude of 4,877 m (16,000 ft).

Only 'flying' snake
The ornate flying snake (*Chrysopelea ornata*) is capable of gliding by launching itself from a height. An instance of this species gliding for a distance of 50 m (164 ft) has been recorded. This snake inhabits the hilly forests of the southwest and the north-east, besides the Andaman Islands.

FISH AND MOLLUSCS

Oldest freshwater fish
Fossil remains of the Dipnoi subclass of fish or lungfish (*Ceratodus agassiz*) were found in the Maleri beds of the Godavari Valley in the late Triassic Period (237–201.3 million years ago). The genus *Ceratodus* evolved in the northern hemisphere in the early Triassic Period (251–247 million years ago).

Only fish with suction plates
The remora or suckerfish (family Echeneidae) can swim but is usually found attached to sharks, turtles, dolphins, and even ships. The first dorsal fin is modified into a suction apparatus, and the erection of the plate where the fish joins its host creates a vacuum, enabling the fish to stay attached.

Heaviest fish
The whale shark *(Rhincodon typus)* is the heaviest fish in India, weighing up to 60 tonnes.

Only fish without a bony skeleton
Sharks (and their relatives the guitarfish and swordfish) do not have a bony skeleton. They have cartilage or gristle. They are predominantly marine fish with a few freshwater representatives.

Only anadromous fish
Hilsa (*Tenualosa ilisha*) is India's only anadromous fish, which migrates from the sea or estuarine waters up rivers for breeding. This fish is found mostly in the Gangetic estuary.

Dwarf pygmy goby fish

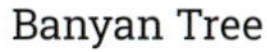

Banyan Tree

Lightest/smallest fish

The dwarf pygmy goby (*Pandaka pygmaea*) is 1 cm (0.39 in.) long and weighs 4–5 mg.

Largest recorded ocean fish

The whale shark (Rhincodon typus) is the largest fish in India and the world. Found in the Indian Ocean, including off the coast of Gujarat, the average size of an adult whale shark is 9.8 m (32.15 ft), but the largest ever recorded was 12.19 m (40 ft) long.

Shortest-living fish

Small fish such as the *Pandaka pygmaea* and those from the families Oreichthys and Gambusia (such as mosquito fish) live hardly for a year.

Longest-living fish

The common carp, a freshwater fish that is found in ponds, lakes, and large rivers, is said to live for over 50 years if left alone.

Largest recorded cave fish

Inside a secluded cave in the Jaintia Hills of Meghalaya, the largest species of cave fish in the world – growing to a length of about 40 cm, or around one and a half feet, was discovered. In February 2019, a group of researchers from India and around the world discovered the fish, which is linked to the Golden Mahseer. It has no eyes and is white because it lacks melanin pigmentation. It is the largest troglobitic fish recorded so far.

Largest clam

The giant clam (*Tridacna gigas*) grows to a length of 1 m (3 ft 3.4 in.) and weighs over 100 kg. This clam has been exploited throughout its Asia-Pacific range, but is fortunately plentiful in the coral reefs of the Andaman and Nicobar Islands.

A seahorse

Only male fish producing young

Seahorses (Genus *Hippocampus*) are predominantly marine. The male fish carries a kangaroo-like pouch in its belly. The female passes her eggs into this pouch where the father incubates them. The young are thus born from the father.

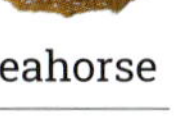

Troglobites

Troglobites are the species of animals that are strictly bound to underground habitats like caves.

PLANTS

Longest-living tree species

The banyan tree (*Ficus benghalensis*), found in most parts of India, is known to have lived for more than 250 years.

Oldest plant fossils

Fossils, which are 1.6 billion years old and appear to contain red algae, were found embedded in mats of cyanobacteria in phosphate-rich sedimentary rocks in Chitrakoot in central India, in May 2017. Until this discovery, the oldest known red algae were 1.2 billion years old.

Fastest-maturing trees

The eucalyptus and the subabul (*Leucaena leucocephala*) trees mature very fast and are both ready for cutting in 6–7 years.

Tallest trees

The fir (*Abies pindrow*) and deodar (*Cedrus deodara*) grow to an average height of 76.2 m (250 ft).

Largest hollow tree

A baobab or monkey-bread tree (*Adansonia digitata*), which is a species of African origin, stands amid the ruins of the eastern part of the historic Golconda Fort near Hyderabad, Telangana. Reportedly, its 3.3 sq m (35.5 sq ft) hollow trunk can comfortably accommodate 10–12 people.

Largest tree canopy

A banyan tree identified in Anantapur District of Andhra Pradesh in 1988, by freelance photographers 'Regret Iyer' and K.S. Ramakrishna from Bangalore

A flowering talipot palm tree

(now Bengaluru), Karnataka, was reported to have a canopy covering 2.1 hectares (5.19 acres) and was believed to be over 600 years old.

Biggest tree trunk

The deodar (*Cedrus deodara*) found in Jammu and Kashmir, Himachal Pradesh, and Uttarakhand have trunks with a circumference of around 12 m (39 ft 4 in.) or more.

Plants at the highest altitude

- The *Ermania himalayensis* grows at 6,000 m (19,685 ft) in the Himalayas.
- *Christolea himalayensis*, a herb usually about 10–15 cm (3.9–5.9 in.) tall, is found at 5,000–6,000 m (16,404–19,685 ft).

Rare flowering

Found in southern and eastern India, the talipot palm (*Corypha umbraculifera*) flowers once in 25–80 years and then dies.

Longest creeper

The elephant creeper (*Argyreia nervosa*) grows to a length of 1.5 km, making it the longest creeper in the country and one of the longest in the world.

Largest family of plants

The Family Poaceae is the largest plant family in the country, and is represented by as many as 263 genera and 1,291 species. Poaceae or Gramineae is a ubiquitous family of monocotyledonous flowering plants known as grass. The Poaceae family includes cereal grass, bamboo, and grasses of natural grasslands as well as the grasses of cultivated lawns and pastures.

Largest leaf

The leaf of the water lily (*Victoria amazonica*) may measure up to 1.5 m (5 ft) in diameter.

Lightest wood

Balsa (*Ochroma lagopus*) has a specific gravity of 0.12 to 0.15.

Heaviest fruit

The jackfruit tree (*Artocarpus heterophyllus*) is planted (but also grows wild) in the Western Ghats and elsewhere in India. The tree bears fruit of enormous size – weighing up to 40 kg.

Heaviest wood

Anjan (*Hardwickia binata*) wood is the heaviest, with a specific gravity of 0.61–0.73.

Tallest bamboo/grass

The tallest bamboo (*Dendrocalamus giganteus*), known as dragon bamboo, is found in Assam and West Bengal. It grows up to 40 m (130 ft) with a diameter of around 20–25 cm (8–10 in.).

CONSERVING NATURE AND WILDLIFE

Oldest botanical garden

The Acharya Jagadish Chandra Bose Indian Botanic Garden was established in 1787 in Shibpur, Howrah, near Kolkata in West Bengal. It has about 12,000 living plants and 2.5 million dried plant specimens in the herbarium, from all over the world. The garden covers 276.75 acres (112 hectares) in 25 sections.

Oldest zoos

- Raja Rajendra Mallick Bahadur started the Marble Palace Aviary and Zoo in Calcutta (now Kolkata), West Bengal, in 1854 specifically for the education and entertainment of the public.
- The Thiruvananthapuram Zoological Gardens in Kerala is said to have been set up by Maharaja Swathi Thirunal in

1859. Spread over 30 acres (12 hectares), it is the oldest extant zoo.

First conservation organization

The Indian Board for Wildlife (IBWL), with S. Dharmakumar Sinhji as its vice chairman, was set up in 1952 by the Government of India. It was replaced by the National Board for Wildlife (NBWL) in September 2003.

First marine reserve

The Marine National Park and Sanctuary in Jamnagar District, Gujarat, forms the first marine reserve in India. Including Pirotan Island and other islands, it was given the status of a national park in 1980. It is rich in corals, octopuses, giant snails, sponges, crabs, lobsters, and fish.

First virtual herbarium

Since February 2017, a virtual digital herbarium of specimens preserved in the Kerala Forest Research Institute at Peechi in Thrissur District, Kerala, can be accessed at the URL http://kfriherbarium.in.

Tallest flower

- The gigantic Himalayan rhubarb (*Rheum nobile*) grows 0.9–1.2 m (3–4 ft) long and is the tallest native species. It is found even at 4,268 m (14,000 ft) in the Himalayan ranges.
- The corpse flower (*Amorphophallus titanum*) or 'titan arum', though not a native species, is the tallest flower (2.4 m/7 ft 10 in.) in India, and the largest by diameter (more than 1 m/3 ft 3.3 in.).

The gigantic Himalayan rhubarb

Oldest NGO to be engaged in conservation and biodiversity research

On 15 September 1883, eight men established the Bombay Natural History Society at the then Victoria and Albert Museum (now Dr Bhau Daji Lad Museum) in Bombay (now Mumbai), Maharashtra. It was established to exchange information on natural history and exhibit interesting specimens. They were E.H. Aitken, Dr G.A. Maconochie, Dr D. MacDonald, J. C. Anderson, Colonel C. Swinhoe, J. Johnston, Dr Atmaram Pandurang, and Dr Sakharam Arjun, along with H.M. Phipson.

First wildlife magazine

Indian Wildlife was published by Jim Corbett in the 1930s.

Highest national park

The Kanchenjunga Biosphere Reserve or the Khangchendzonga National Park in Sikkim is the highest national park at 8,585 m (28,166 ft) above mean sea level.

Largest zoological park

Arignar Anna Zoological Park at Vandalur, near Chennai, Tamil Nadu, is the largest zoological park in South Asia. Spread over 602 hectares (1,487.57 acres), it has more than 100 species of birds, 50 species of mammals, and 20 species of reptiles.

Arignar Anna Zoological Park, Vandalur

Largest camera trap tiger census

India's tiger census of 2018 became the largest camera trap wildlife survey in the world. Camera traps (outdoor photographic devices fitted with motion sensors that start recording when an animal passes by) were placed in 26,838 locations across 141 different sites and surveyed an effective area of 1,21,337 sq km as part of the survey. Individual tigers (excluding cubs numbering 2,461) were identified using the stripe pattern recognition software from the photographs clicked by camera traps.

State and UT with the most wildlife sanctuaries

Andaman and Nicobar Islands have 96 wildlife sanctuaries (389.39 sq km) and Maharashtra has 46 (7,592.3 sq km).

State and UT with most national parks

Madhya Pradesh leads with 10 national parks, covering an area of 3,65,725 sq km. Andaman and Nicobar Islands follow with nine national parks covering an area of 1,15,394 sq km.

Largest collection of bamboo species

Prashant Atmaram Date, a bamboo farmer and entrepreneur from Lakhalgaon Village, Nashik Taluk and District, Maharashtra, has the largest collection of bamboo species in the country. He has a total of 94 species of 22 genera in one place called 'Date

Bambusetum', where they are placed in flowerpots. Different species have been collected from bamboo-growing states for conservation away from their place of origin.

Tallest bougainvillea

Prof. Dr Ramesh Babu (b. 12 February 1957) has grown a 10.33 m (33 ft 11 in.) tall *Bougainvillea spectabilis* in his garden in Bengaluru, Karnataka. The over 16-year-old bougainvillea with white blossoms had a spread of 6.09 m (20 ft) and a base girth of 0.2 m (7.8 in.) as on 29 January 2020. Normally, bougainvillea grows to an average height of 6.09 m (20 ft).

Biggest lemon

K. Mohanchandran from Kothanur, Bengaluru, Karnataka, grew a lemon measuring 28 cm x 14 cm (11 in. x 5.5 in.) in his garden. The lemon had a circumference of 49 cm (19.2 in.) and weighed 2.365 kg on 22 February 2020.

Longest mango leaf

A mango tree with a leaf measuring 61 cm (2 ft) was found at the primary school of Budapur in Varanasi, Uttar Pradesh, by Dr Bhola Vishwakarma, one of the school teachers, on 30 October 2018.

First national park

Jim Corbett National Park (earlier Hailey National Park and then Ramganga National Park), established in 1936, stretches over 521 sq km across the two hill districts of Pauri Garhwal and Nainital, Uttarakhand. It is home to around 110 tree species, 50 species of mammals, 580 bird species, and 25 species of reptiles. It was the first to come under the Project Tiger initiative. The elevation of the park ranges from 400 m to 1,200 m (1,300 ft to 4,000 ft).

Largest taro leaf

A taro (*Colocasia esculenta*) leaf measuring 76.0 cm x 64.5 cm (2 ft 5.9 in. x 2 ft 1.39 in.) was cultivated in Boudhgarh, Boudh District, Odisha, by Jayaram Rana on 7 January 2020.

GARDENING

Tallest rose plant

Arunsinh Solanki grew a rose plant 11.88 m (39 ft) tall at his home in Godhra in Gujarat, as recorded on 13 May 2019.

Tallest prickly amaranth plant

In August 2017, T. Damodar and his wife Shobha T. Damodar from Belagavi, Karnataka, grew the tallest prickly amaranth plant (*Amaranthus spinosus*), which measured 4.03 m (13 ft 3 in.) in height. Normally this plant grows to a height of 0.3 m to 2.43 m (1–8 ft).

Tallest coriander plant

Dalbir Maan (b. 1 June 1982) grew a 2.28 m (7 ft 6 in.) tall coriander plant at his home in Melbourne, Australia, as recorded on 18 November 2020.

Longest tapioca plant

Satheesha Nayak (b. 16 July 1969), an anatomy professor at the Manipal Academy of Higher Education, Udupi, Karnataka, has grown the longest tapioca (cassava) plant, measuring 16.76 m (55 ft 10 in.), as on 30 January 2022, in his kitchen garden. The plant was then about three years old and was provided support on an adjoining mango tree.

Tallest drumstick tree

Prof. Dr Ramesh Babu from Bengaluru, Karnataka, has the tallest drumstick tree (*Moringa oleifera*) growing in his residential garden. On 20 June 2019, the 11-year-old tree was 8.2 m (26 ft 11 in.) tall with a spread of 3.66 m (12 ft) and a base girth of 47.6 cm (1 ft 6.74 in.). The average height of a drumstick tree is 6.1 m (20 ft).

Tallest musk mallow plant

A.K. Narayanan from Thrissur, Kerala, had, in his garden, a three-year-old musk mallow plant, 2.74 m (9 ft) tall as in June 2016.

Tallest jamun tree

Prof. Dr Ramesh Babu from Bengaluru, Karnataka, has the tallest *jamun* tree (*Syzygium cumini*) in his garden. On 20 June 2019, the 15-year-old tree was 11.9 m (39 ft) tall with a spread of 6 m (20 ft) and a base girth of 1.04 m (41 in.). The average height of a jamun tree is 9.1–10.6 m (30–35 ft).

Panorama of the Kosi River in Jim Corbett National Park

RENEWABLE ENERGY SHARE IN THE TOTAL INSTALLED ELECTRICITY GENERATION
ELECTRICITY GENERATION (IN %)

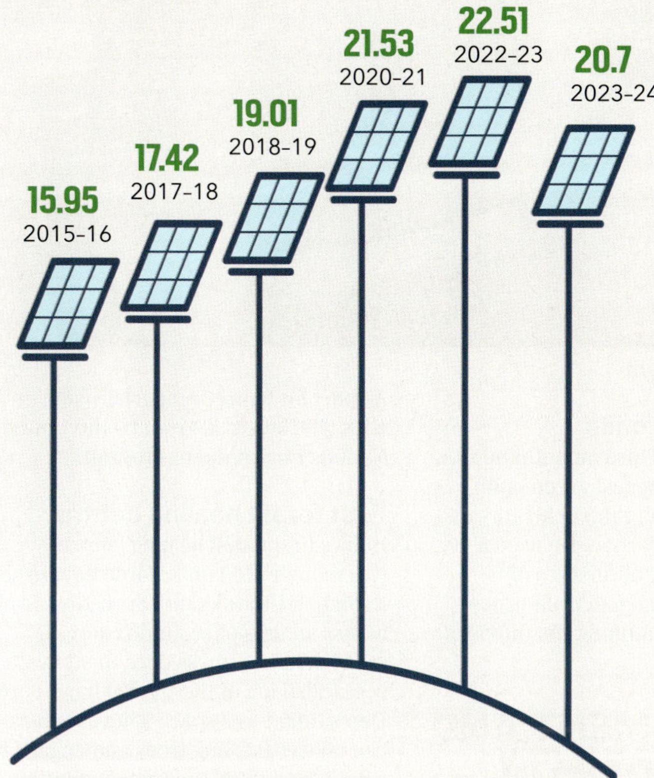

SOURCE: SDGs (Sustainable Development Goals) National Indicator Framework Progress Report 2024, MoSPI, GOI

PERCENTAGE OF GOVERNMENT SPENDING ON ENVIRONMENTAL PROTECTION TO TOTAL GOVERNMENT EXPENDITURE (IN %)

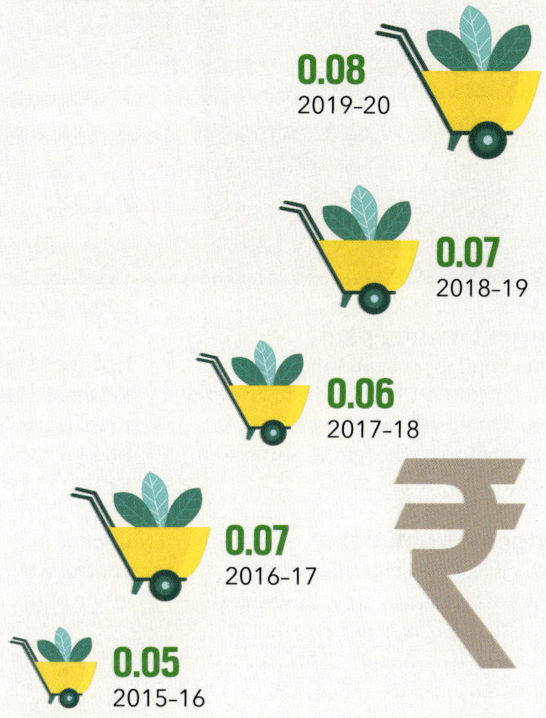

SOURCE: SDGs National Indicator Framework Progress Report 2024, MoSPI, GOI

AREA OF RAMSAR SITES TO TOTAL WETLAND AREA
AREA (PERCENTAGE OF TOTAL WETLAND AREA)

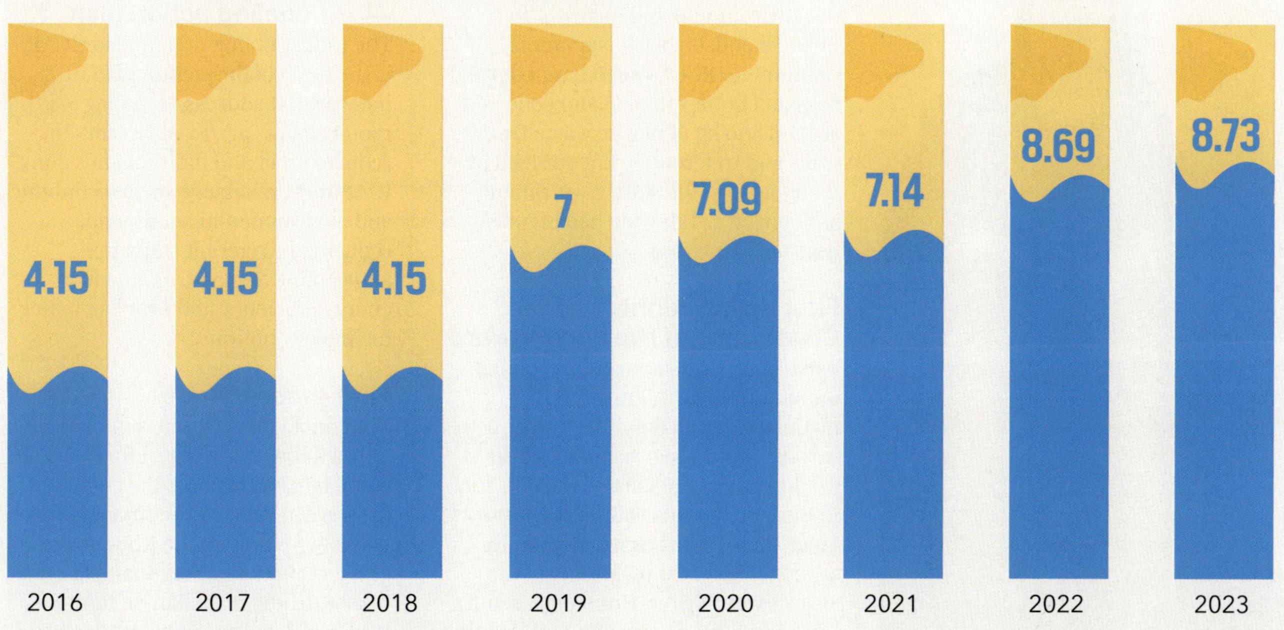

SOURCE: SDGs National Indicator Framework Progress Report 2024, MoSPI, GOI

Longest money plant

Longest money plant

Sapna Popli (b. 13 September 1982) from Lucknow, Uttar Pradesh, grew the longest money plant in her home. As on 21 April 2023, the length of the stem measured 11.7 m (38.4 ft).

Longest Drumstick

Rekha K.N. (b. 6 September 1973) from Kochi, Kerala, grew the longest drumstick (*Moringa oleifera*) on her drumstick tree. As on 17 April 2023, the drumstick measured 116.84 cm (46 in.).

Longest drumstick

Longest green chilli

Krishnalal L.S. of Thiruvananthapuram, Kerala, grew the longest green chilli, measuring 31 cm (12.1 in.) in his terrace garden in February 2020. He used a home-made nutrient mixture of organic and natural material for pest control while maintaining the nutrient grade of the soil.

ENVIRONMENT AND SUSTAINABILITY

First state/UT to place a ban on plastic bags

Sikkim became the first state to ban plastic bags in 1998. Local communities in Yuksom Village were upset by the harmful impact of plastics on the environment and formed the Khangchendzonga Conservation Committee (KCC), which banned plastic bags and bottles in 1996 and collected around 800 kg of plastic waste from trails and trek routes. Encouraged by their success, the state government announced a statewide ban on plastic bags on 4 June 1998.

First Indian winners of the Champions of the Earth Award

Tulsi Tanti, chairman and managing director of the wind turbine manufacturer Suzlon Energy Ltd, was the first Indian recipient of the Champions of the Earth Award in 2009 in the 'entrepreneurial vision' category. Since then, India has won five more awards. The latest recipients of the awards were Prime Minister Narendra Modi for policy leadership and the fully solar-powered Cochin International Airport for 'entrepreneurial vision' in 2018. The award is given by the United Nations Environment Programme.

First forest healing centre

India's first forest healing centre was inaugurated on 7 March 2021 in Ranikhet, Uttarakhand. Spread across an area of around 13 acres (5.26 hectares), it was developed by the research wing of the Uttarakhand Forest Department as a space where visitors can take walks, hug trees and engage in calming activities such as meditation and sky-gazing. The centre draws inspiration from the Japanese therapy of forest bathing (*shinrinyoku*) and ancient Indian traditions.

WR First country to have a cooling action plan

The India Cooling Action Plan (ICAP) is the first cooling action plan in the world. It addresses cooling requirements across all sectors to reduce direct and indirect emissions. ICAP aims to balance socio-economic and environmental needs while reducing refrigerant transition and cooling demand, enhancing energy efficiency and evolving better technology options.

First green village

Khonoma Village, located in the Sechu-Zubza Subdivision of Kohima District, Nagaland, has become the country's first 'green village'. The first steps were taken by setting up the Khonoma Nature Conservation and Tragopan Sanctuary in 1998, leading to a ban on hunting in a 20 sq km area. Ecological studies suggest that the village has

Khonoma village, Nagaland

250 plant species, 204 species of trees, 45 varieties of orchids, and 19 varieties of bamboo. The fauna includes 25 varieties of snakes, kinds of lizards, 11 types of amphibians, and 196 bird species, including the Blyth's tragopan, which is categorized as vulnerable on the IUCN Red List.

First green energy archaeological site

The Shore Temple in Mahabalipuram (also known as Mamallapuram), Tamil Nadu, is a seventh century UNESCO World Heritage site that became India's first green energy archaeological site in September 2023. This means that the temple will be illuminated with clean and sustainable solar power completely. The change was possible after the successful implementation of Green Heritage Project, a collaborative initiative between the Renault Nissan Technology & Business Centre India (Renault Nissan Tech) and Hand in Hand India (HiH). As part of the project, three solar plants of 10 kW capacity each have been set up in the region to harness solar energy and reduce carbon footprint in the area. The project promotes sustainable ecotourism with minimal ecological footprint. Other highlights of the Green Heritage Project

Shore Temple in Mahabalipuram

Towards a Greener Tomorrow...

Most trees planted – 15 mins

Under the supervision of the National Service Scheme (NSS) Programme Officer Shyam Sunder of the Government Dungar College, Bikaner, Rajasthan, a total of 1,05,000 saplings were planted at three locations in Gajsukhdesar Village in 3 mins 50 secs by a team of 15,000 participants comprising NSS volunteers, schoolchildren, and villagers on 4 August 2008. The total land covered under the plantation was 1,200 bighas (300 hectares).

Most trees planted – 1 hour

As part of the Green India Challenge, an initiative by J. Santhosh Kumar, a member of Parliament (Rajya Sabha) from Telangana, 3,54,900 trees were planted in 1 hr on 4 July 2021 in Durga Nagar, Adilabad, Telangana. The 16,900 people involved in the plantation drive planted 21 trees each.

Most trees planted – single day

The Department of Forests and Wildlife, Uttar Pradesh, planted 25,87,47,661 saplings in a day on 5 July 2020, with the participation of various departments of the state as well as the general public. Starting at 5:55 a.m., the plantation work at selected plantation sites in all 75 districts concluded at 6:00 p.m. This was part of their larger campaign for tree plantation.

Most trees planted – in a quarter

The Maharashtra Forest Department, with the support of individual volunteers, planted 35,13,76,361 seedlings across the state between 1 July and 30 September 2019. The plantation work was done by 9,51,963.5 million people at 23,986.8 million plantation sites. To integrate the work of the forest department, the government hosted a Plantation Monitoring Information System (PMIS) and captured the plantation data of forest and non-forest agencies.

Most saplings distributed – single day

The Department of Environment, Forest, and Climate Change and the Department of Tourism, Government of Uttar Pradesh, along with the Prayagraj District Administration, Uttar Pradesh, distributed 76,824 saplings on 9 August 2019. This was part of their larger campaign for tree plantation.

at the temple include women-operated electric buggies, solar-operated reverse osmosis plant that provides clean drinking water, dedicated parking shed with three charging units for electric vehicles, among others.

Most waste collected – beach clean-up – single day

The Maharashtra Navnirman Paryavaran Sena, headquartered in Matunga, Mumbai, Maharashtra, set three records in waste collection on 11 December 2021, based on data available from 16 local governmental bodies:

- ***Most waste collected – multiple venues***: A group of 13,194 registered volunteers, among others, collected 59.2 tonnes of waste from 37 locations in seven districts of Maharashtra.
- ***Most waste collected – single venue***: Volunteers collected 27 tonnes of waste from a single location – Uttan Beach, Bhavander, Thane District, Maharashtra.
- ***Most participants in a waste collection campaign – multiple venues***: The clean-up campaign saw the participation of 13,194 registered volunteers across 37 locations in seven districts of Maharashtra.

First solar-heated tent

Considered to be the first in the world, a 10-seater portable tent that can be heated using solar panels was built by engineer and innovator Sonam Wangchuk along with the Himalayan Institute of Alternatives of Ladakh (HIAL) for the Indian Army. Built in four weeks at a cost of ₹5 lakh (0.5 million), the tent weighs less than 30 kg and was specifically developed for Indian soldiers and army personnel serving in areas with very low temperatures.

Eiffel Tower replica, Waste to Wonder Park, New Delhi

Tallest scrap-metal structure – solo

Sandeep Pisalkar from Vadodara, Gujarat, created a replica of the iconic Eiffel Tower, measuring 21.33 m (70 ft) in height, with 40 tonnes (40,000 kg) of automobile scrap. The three levels of the structure were created separately and then assembled with the help of a crane. The material used included petrol tanks from trucks, C-channels, angles, and clutch plates. It was exhibited at the Waste to Wonder Park, New Delhi, in February 2019.

Tallest scrap-metal structure – group

A group of 120 students, training to be fitters, welders, electricians, plumbers, and painters at the Government ITI in Berhampur, Ganjam District, Odisha, created the tallest scrap-metal structure, a 21.33 m (70 ft) tall guitar, over a period of three months from 17 July 2019. The 'Best out of waste' mission sought to integrate skill development with waste management in an eco-friendly manner. The guitar was exhibited at the open-air Scrap Sculpture Museum of the ITI, along with 10 other smaller sculptures, which were also created from waste.

Plog run with most participants

The biggest plog run (combining jogging with picking up litter – from Swedish *plockaupp*) was organized on Gandhi Jayanti on 2 October 2018 from 55 locations of Bengaluru, Karnataka. Plastic waste weighing 6.5 tonnes (6,500 kg), including bottles and litter, was collected by 6,518 participants in four hours from 7:00 a.m. to 11:00 a.m. The participants, representing five organizations – BBMP (Bruhat Bengaluru Mahanagara Palike), Go Native, Namma Nimma Cycle Foundation, Let's Be the Change, United Way Bengaluru – and an individual, Ramakrishna Ganesh, created awareness on urban cleanliness by proper disposal of waste, especially plastic.

Largest single rooftop solar plant – by area

On 17 May 2016, a rooftop solar power plant was inaugurated at the Dera Baba Jaimal Singh (Radha Soami sect) premises at Beas, Amritsar District, Punjab. Spread over 42 acres (17 ha), the plant is the largest single rooftop facility and can generate 11.5 MW of electricity. The solar panels are laid over 82 acres (33.18 hectares) on eight rooftops and the project is planned to cater to 8,000 households.

First railway station with Green Building Certification

Kevadia railway station in Gujarat, from whose third, level platform one can view the Statue of Unity, is India's first railway station with a Green Building Certification by the Indian Green Building Council (IGBC). The railway station features LED lights and star-rated, branded electrical appliances to

save electricity; water management through rainwater harvesting; a sewage treatment plant; waterless eco-urinals; and drip irrigation. Additionally, the segregated green waste will be reused to produce fertilizers.

Largest biogas plant – by capacity

As a step towards clean and green energy, Asia's largest compressed biogas (CBG) plant with a total capacity of 33.23 tonnes CBG per day was commissioned on 12 August 2022 at Bhuttal Kalan village in Sangrur District, Punjab.

Widest scrap-metal structure – group

The Home Designers, an organization from Jodhpur, Rajasthan, created the widest replica of a blue whale, measuring 104 ft (31.7 m) in width from scrap metal. The team comprised 100 people who began work on the structure on 6 January 2023. It took 10 days to complete the structure.

Biogas plant

A facility that offers oxygen-free conditions for anaerobic digestion is known as a biogas plant. Simply, it is an artificial system that allows biodegradable trash to be converted into environmentally beneficial fertilizers and sustainable energy.

CLEANEST IN INDIA!

Cleanest cities

The Swachh Survekshan Awards 2023 ranked Indore in Madhya Pradesh as the cleanest city of the country for the seventh time in a row. Surat in Gujarat joined Indore to share the award for the first time. Navi Mumbai in Maharashtra was ranked third in the same category. Among the country's smaller cities with a population less than 1 lakh, Saswad in Maharashtra ranked first.

Cleanest states

The Swachh Survekshan Awards 2023, central government's annual cleanliness survey to promote urban sanitation standards, ranked Maharashtra, Madhya Pradesh, and Chhattisgarh, as the cleanest states in India with first, second, and third ranks respectively.

Aerial view of Indore, Madhya Pradesh

Search...
वंदे भारत
EXPRESS

AIR

First flight

On 18 February 1911, Henri Pequet flew a Humber-Sommer biplane carrying mail from Allahabad (now Prayagraj), Uttar Pradesh, to Naini Junction. It flew a distance of 10 km. However, proper and official civil aviation began on 15 October 1932, when aviator and industrialist J.R.D. Tata flew 2,092 km on the aircraft D.H. *Puss Moth*. The flight took place under the aegis of Tata Air Services. It delivered mail from the Drigh Road Aerodrome in Karachi (now in Pakistan) to Juhu Aerodrome in Bombay (now Mumbai), Maharashtra, and then continued to Madras (now Chennai).

First pilot licence

J.R.D. Tata; an aviator, entrepreneur, and chairman of Tata Group; became the first licensed pilot in India when he received his pilot licence No. 1 in 1929.

First airline

Tata Airlines, set up by J.R.D. Tata soon after he piloted India's maiden civil flight in 1932, was later converted into a public company in 1946 under the name Air India Ltd, with him as its chairman. In March 1953, it was raised to be a public corporation and became Air India. The state-run carrier was privatized to the Tata Group in 2021.

First airfield

The grass aerodrome at Juhu in Mumbai opened in 1932. It was the base for Tata Airlines.

First aircraft designer

S.V. Setty, an assistant engineer with the Public Works Department, Mysore, Karnataka, in 1911–12, designed, piloted and helped manufacture planes at Avro (a British company). With an eight cylinder engine, the Avro biplane had a 9.76 m (32 ft) span and weighed 362.8 kg without a pilot or passenger. The plane touched a speed of around 72–80 km/hr.

« Federation Aeronautique Internationale (FAI) is a non-profit organization that is the governing body in the world for recognized aero sports. It is based in Lausanne, Switzerland, and has 86 members under it. The Aero Club of India (ACI) is India's National Airsport Control and it has been a member of the FAI since 1950. »

First flying club

The Aero Club was established in Mumbai by industrial magnate Sir Victor Sassoon in 1928. In September 1929, the club was affiliated to the Royal Aero Club, UK. It was recognized by the Government of India as the coordinating body for flying clubs in India. In 1948, the club was affiliated to the Federation Aeronautique Internationale.

Left: D.H. *Puss Moth*
Right: Havilland DH-89 Dragon Rapide

First helicopter school

Hindustan Aeronautics Ltd (HAL), based in Bangalore (now Bengaluru), Karnataka, established a training school on 1 May 2000 for potential aviators to obtain commercial as well as private helicopter pilot licences.

First aeronautical society

On 17 December 1948, the Aeronautical Society of India was inaugurated at Bengaluru to promote advancement in the field of aeronautics and dissemination of knowledge about aeronautical science and aircraft engineering to the public.

First radio plane

The twin-engine aeroplane called de Havilland DH-89 Dragon Rapide, which was on the Karachi– Bombay– Colombo route, was equipped with wireless transmission facilities on 1 December 1937.

First international flight

The *Malabar Princess*, an Air India passenger flight, with Captain K.R. Guzder in command, flew from Bombay to London, UK, via Cairo (Egypt), and Geneva (Switzerland), on 8 June 1948, carrying 35 passengers.

First crash

On 17 July 1950, a DC-3 aircraft was recorded to have crashed near Pathankot, Punjab, tragically killing all 22 passengers.

First cargo service

An air cargo service started on 21 May 1927 between Calcutta (now Kolkata), West Bengal, and Bagdogra in Darjeeling District of West Bengal by West Bengal Air Transport, which operated for only a week.

First air ticket booking office

The first air ticket booking office was opened in 1939 in a building in the Churchgate Reclamation area in Bombay. The space now houses the Asiatic Department Store.

First air freight service

Air Freight Pvt. Ltd was set up in 1945 as handling agents for Tata Airlines and Air India International. It was also the first air cargo clearing agent.

First indigenously assembled plane

The first HS-748 was assembled at the Aircraft Manufacturing Depot, Kanpur, Uttar Pradesh, and delivered to Indian Airlines on 27 June 1967.

First all-jet carrier

In 1962, Air India became the world's first all-jet carrier when it replaced Super Constellation planes with a fleet of Boeing 707.

First Boeing 737-900 aircraft

Jet Airways acquired the first Boeing 737-900 aircraft in May 2003. The aircraft can seat up to 190 passengers and is the longest among the Boeing 737 family. It has a maximum flight range of 5,084 km. In 2018, Jet Airways took the delivery of the first 150 Boeing 737 MAX aeroplanes, becoming the first Indian carrier to fly the new variant.

First indigenous aircraft

The Hindustan Trainer-2, built by Hindustan Aeronautics Ltd (HAL), Bangalore, made its maiden flight in August 1951. Meant for military use, it was also used by flying schools.

Largest IT Outage at Airports

In July 2024 the American cybersecurity company CrowdStrike distributed a faulty update that caused an issue with Microsoft Windows computers running the software. As a result of this, nearly 8.5 million systems crashed and were unable to restart properly. This was considered the largest outage in the history of information technology. This outage disturbed the airport industry the most. It caused chaos all over the world at the same time. The systems in airports are optimized for efficiency and profit, and when it failed, the entire industry grinded to a halt. The Kempegowda International Airport in Bengaluru checked in passengers with handwritten tickets and urged fliers to show up well before take-off time. Nearly 4,000 flights were cancelled globally.

Hindustan Trainer 2

First indigenous helicopter

The advanced light helicopter (ALH) was built at HAL, Bangalore, in 1992. The ALH was used both in defence and civil operations.

First jet

Air India entered the jet age on 20 April 1960, when its Boeing 707 *Gauri Shankar* flew to London. Soon after, on 14 May 1960, it flew to New York. With this, India became the first Asian country to operate a transatlantic flight. The aircraft was written off after a landing accident at Bombay on 22 June 1982.

First air taxi

India's first air taxi service started at Chandigarh Airport on 14 January 2021 under the UDAN RCS (Regional Connectivity Scheme) of the Central government. With the capacity to seat a pilot and three passengers, the daily flight was of 45-minute duration and it plied on the Chandigarh–Hisar route at a cost of ₹1,755 per seat. This service was discontinued in August 2021, seven months after its launch.

First air traffic control system

A state-of-the-art Air Traffic Control (ATC) system, supported by Raytheon flight data and equipped with radar-processing hardware, was installed at the Indira Gandhi International Airport (IGIA), New Delhi, on 14 January 1999. It provided three-dimensional radial, bearing, and height information regarding the location and situation of any aircraft within a range of 250 nautical miles.

Boeing 707 *Gauri Shankar*

First air varsity

The Central Training Establishment in Hyderabad (now in Telangana), an independent training centre of Indian Airlines Ltd, was upgraded to a deemed university in 1997. The centre is equipped with infrastructure and training facilities for courses in civil aviation.

First heliport

India's first heliport was inaugurated at Rohini, Delhi, on 28 February 2017. Built by Pawan Hans Ltd, it is spread over an area of 25 acres (10.12 hectares) and has four hangars, nine parking bays, and a terminal building that has a capacity of 150 passengers. The first such facility in South Asia, it helps in offshore transport, emergency medical services, promoting heli-tourism, and reducing the congestion on the IGIA, Delhi.

First airport to install full-body scanner

The first full-body scanner system was installed on a trial basis at Terminal 1D of the Indira Gandhi International Airport, New Delhi, on 10 April 2010. Initially the system was used only on volunteering passengers and the scanning process took less than a minute. The scanning system, called SmartCheck, was built by American Science and Engineering (AS&E). The system works on the X-ray backscatter technology.

Highest commercial airport

Kushok Bakula Rimpochee Airport (or Leh airport) in Leh, Ladakh, is the highest commercial airport at 3,256 m (10,682 ft) above mean sea level. The airport is named after Kushok Bakula Rinpoche, whose Spituk Monastery is very close to the airfield. The Indian Air Force handed over the airport to the Airport Authority of India in 2016.

First airport to install waste recycling machines

The Rajiv Gandhi International Airport (RGIA) in Hyderabad, Telangana, became the first airport in the country to install waste recycling machines. It was launched as a pilot project in October 2017. Operated by the GMR Hyderabad International Airport Ltd (GHIAL), the airport has equipment to crush and recycle plastic PET (polyethylene terephthalate) bottles, steel or aluminium cans, and plastic bags into reusable raw material. These 'Swachh Bharat Recycling Machines' were designed and created by Mumbai-based company Wild West Media, and can be used to manufacture upcycled goods like bags, wallets, and denim. Passengers may make a donation or claim discount coupons in return for submitting their waste and plastic products. The RGIA is also the first airport to have its own composting plant, which processes the food waste generated at the airport.

Largest passenger airport terminal

On 3 July 2010, Terminal 3 of the Indira Gandhi International Airport, New Delhi, became India's and South Asia's largest aviation hub, with the capacity to handle more than 40 million (four crore) passengers a year. The airport handled over 73.6 million (7.36 crore) passengers in 2023-24.

Kushok Bakula Rimpochee Airport

Highest airfield

The Daulat Beg Oldi airstrip in Ladakh is the highest airfield in the world. It is situated at an altitude of 5,065 m (16,617 ft). The Indian Air Force landed a C-130J Super Hercules aircraft at this airfield, reactivating it in 2013.

Oldest fleet

Founded in 1932 as Tata Airlines and renamed in 1946 as Air India Ltd, this airline has a fleet size of 125 aircrafts (excluding subsidiaries), making it the oldest fleet in India. The airline has its headquarters in New Delhi.

Oldest to obtain a commercial pilot's licence

Captain Rajagopal Nagarajan (b. 25 April 1962) from Coimbatore, Tamil Nadu, joined the commercial pilot's course after retiring from the Indian Air Force. He obtained the commercial pilot's licence (CPL) from the Civil Aviation Authority, Philippines, at 48 years on 11 December 2009.

First woman commercial pilot

The first woman commercial pilot was Prem Mathur for Deccan Airways in 1951.

Most air freight traffic

Indira Gandhi International Airport, New Delhi, handled over 65,00,000 tonnes of freight traffic by the end of 2023.

First fully solar-powered airport

The Cochin International Airport in Kochi, Kerala, became the first airport in the world to run completely on solar power on 18 August 2015. The solar plant installed at the airport has 46,000 solar panels and can produce 50,000 to 60,000 units of electricity every day. The airport won the Champion of Earth Prize, awarded by the United Nations, in 2018.

Cochin International Airport

First dual-way elevated taxiway

On 14 July 2023, the country's first dual-way elevated taxiway was inaugurated at the Indira Gandhi International Airport, New Delhi. The elevated taxiway reduces taxi distance for aircraft by 7 km and annual carbon dioxide emissions by 53,000 tonnes. The Eastern Cross Taxiway is 2.1 km long and 44 m wide to allow safe passage for two big aircrafts.

Highest number of women pilots

In a report released by Air Line Pilots Association, International (ALPA), in 2018, India led the charts in the number of female pilots among all countries. Around 13 per cent of the pilots in the country are women whereas the global average is only 5 per cent. This means that out of every eight flights in India, one is flown by a woman. Airlines such as IndiGo, SpiceJet, and Air India have the highest recruitment numbers for women pilots.

First woman Airbus commander

Captain Indraani Singh, who joined Indian Airlines in April 1986, was the first Indian and Asian woman to fly the Airbus A320, in 1989, and became the world's first woman commander of the wide-bodied Airbus A300 in August 1996.

First woman chief executive officer of an airline

Harpreet A. De Singh was appointed chief executive officer (CEO) of Alliance Air, a regional subsidiary of Air India, on 30 October 2020. Previously executive director for flight safety in Air India, she became the first woman CEO of an airline. She was also the first woman pilot to be selected by Air India in 1988.

First woman chairperson of the International Civil Aviation Organization (ICAO) Aviation Security Committee

Shefali Juneja was elected chairperson of the ICAO Aviation Security Committee on 17 September 2021. A specialized agency of the UN, ICAO was formed to support and help nations with diplomacy and cooperation in air transport. India held the position 12 years ago. Shefali was also appointed as the representative in the council of ICAO in 2019.

> The government has clarified that in-flight passengers will be able to use internet services through Wi-Fi only when electronic devices are permitted to be used in aircraft even after it attains altitude of 3,000 metres in Indian airspace. The newly modified rule will be called Flight and Maritime Connectivity (Amendment) Rules, 2024.

First woman airbus pilot

On 14 May 1987, Durba Banerjee became the first woman to co-pilot a flight – Airbus A300 – on the Calcutta–New Delhi–Calcutta route.

First woman to obtain a pilot's licence

Urmila K. Parekh became the first woman to obtain a pilot's licence, in 1930.

Longest direct-route flight with an all-woman cockpit crew

Air India's flight AI-176 made history on 11 January 2021 when an all-woman cockpit crew flew a distance of 16,000 km from San Francisco, California, to Bengaluru, Karnataka. The flight departed on 9 January 2021 and was flown by four pilots – Captain Zoya Aggarwal, Captain Papagari Thanmai, Captain Shivani Manhas, and Captain Akansha Sonaware. The longest commercial flight to be operated by an Indian airline and longest flight entering India, its flying time was 17 hours and its route remarkably included flying over the North Pole.

First to offer free in-flight Wi-Fi on international flights

Vistara airlines has announced that passengers will now receive 20 minutes of complimentary Wi-Fi on international flights. This service will be available on Vistara's Boeing 787-9 Dreamliner and Airbus A321 neo aircraft.

First woman offshore captain

Captain Mayuri V. Deshmukh (b. 11 November 1982) with Commercial Helicopter Pilot Licence 991 became the first woman offshore captain in the country when she flew from Juhu to Mumbai High, Mumbai, Maharashtra, as captain from 11:07 a.m. to 1:25 p.m. on 8 March 2022. She was working for Pawan Hans Ltd (PHL) at the time. She has complied with the syllabus laid down by the Directorate General of Civil Aviation (DGCA) and validated by Oil and Natural Gas Company Ltd.

International Civil Aviation Organization (ICAO) headquarters

IndiGo's three-point disembarkation system

First three-point disembarkation system

IndiGo, a leading Indian airline with its headquarters at Gurugram, Haryana, introduced a three-point disembarkation system in a global first on 4 August 2022. To mark its 16th anniversary, the airline introduced a disembarkation process that was carried out from two forward and one rear exit ramp.

Longest length of runways

The Indira Gandhi International Airport, New Delhi, has the longest stretch of airport runways in the country, with a length of 4,430 m (14,534 ft).

Largest passenger airline

IndiGo, with its headquarters at Gurugram, is the largest passenger airline in India by passengers carried and fleet size. Since its inception in August 2006, it has grown from one plane to a fleet of 269 aircraft. It is also the largest individual Asian low-cost carrier in terms of jet fleet size. It has a destination count of 100 with 74 domestic destinations and 26 international ones.

RAIL AND METRO

First passenger train

India's first passenger train chugged away from Bori Bunder (later renamed Victoria Terminus, and then Chhatrapati Shivaji Maharaj Terminus) station in Mumbai to Thane, Maharashtra, on 16 April 1853. It was pulled by three locomotives named *Sindh*, *Sultan,* and *Sahib*, and carried 400 passengers in 14 railway carriages. This historic journey, which was of about 1 hr 15 mins duration, was flagged off with a 21-gun salute.

First rail construction company

R.M. Stephenson, a British railway engineer, formed the East Indian Railway (EIR) Company in 1844 for the construction of railways. In a contract signed on 17 August 1849, the EIR and the Great Indian Peninsula (GIP) Railway Company, England, were authorized to construct and operate railway lines in Kolkata, and Mumbai, Maharashtra.

First indigenous railway carriages

The first railway coaches made in India were built by two coach-building firms in Kolkata, Steward and Company, and Seton and Company John Hodgson was the chief engineer of the East Indian Railway Company then, and the coaches were employed for the first train journey from Howrah to Hooghly in West Bengal on 15 August 1854.

East Indian Railway plaque

First double-decker coaches

The Bombay, Baroda and Central India (BB&CI) Railway Company in Mumbai, introduced the first double-decker coaches in 1862.

First tramway company

The Calcutta Tramway Company was registered in London, in 1880. The Government of West Bengal nationalized it in 1976.

Victoria Terminus: first passenger train

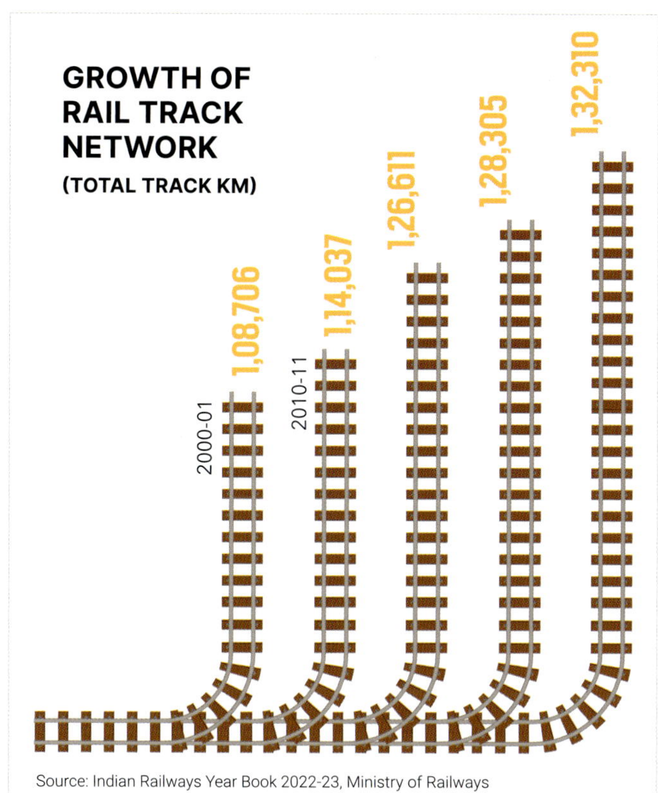

Source: Indian Railways Year Book 2022-23, Ministry of Railways

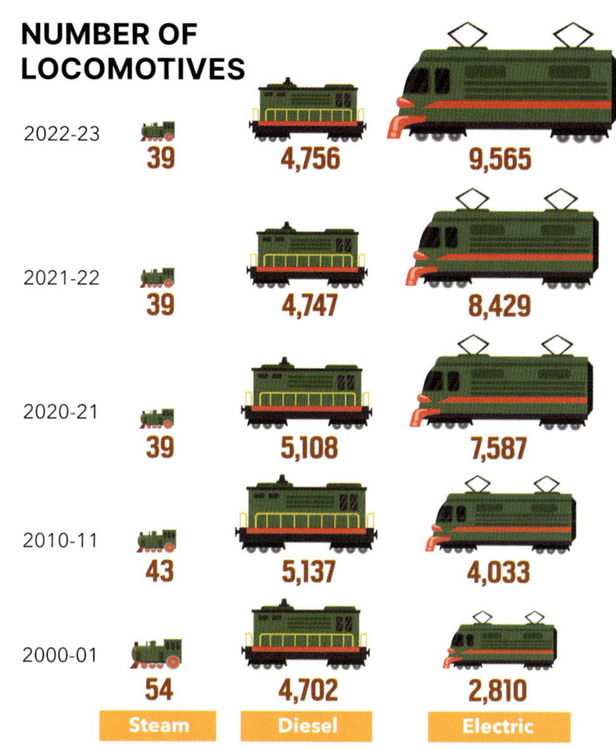

Source: Indian Railways Year Book 2022-23, Ministry of Railways

NUMBER OF TRAINS RUNNING DAILY

Electric Multiple Unit (EMU)

Mail/Express

Ordinary Passenger and Mixed trains

Source: Indian Railways Year Book 2022-23, Ministry of Railways

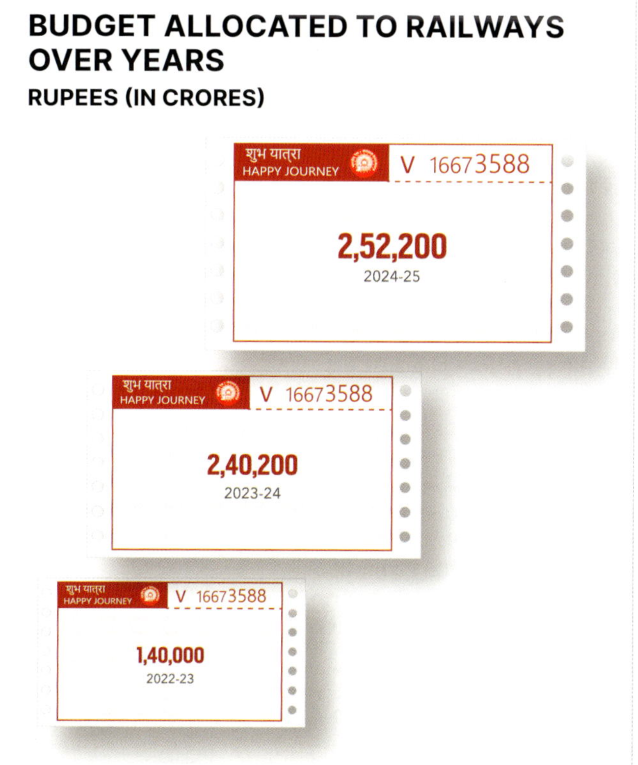

Source: Data collected from PIB press releases

> The whereabouts of *Sahib* and *Sultan* are unknown. The two engines vanished. However *Sindh* was seen at the Byculla office of GIPR (Great Indian Peninsula Railway) in Mumbai. Later it was brought to Delhi, but no one knows what happened to it after that.

Fastest train
The fastest train in India is the Vande Bharat Express or Train 18, which reached a top speed of 180 km/hr during test runs. Its current operating speed is 130 km/hr. As of October 2024, 66 Vande Bharat trains are in service which includes 17 sixteen-car services, 4 twenty-car service, and 45 eight-car services.

First double-decker train
India's first double-decker train was the *Flying Ranee*, a superfast train that runs between Mumbai Central and Surat station. It began operating in 1906, was halted in 1939 due to the Second World War, and resumed in 1950 as a daily service train.

Flying Ranee promotional poster

First locomotive factory
The first locomotive factory in India was set up at Chittaranjan in Paschim Bardhaman District, West Bengal, in 1950. The first diesel locomotive, with an imported engine, was manufactured at the Varanasi Diesel Locomotive Works, Varanasi, Uttar Pradesh, on 4 January 1964.

First deluxe train
The first deluxe train, the *Deccan Queen*, started operating between Victoria Terminus, Bombay and Poona (now Pune), Maharashtra, on 1 June 1930. It had 61 first class, 156 second-class, and 19 attendants' seats.

First air-conditioned train
Before 1936, some coaches on the Bombay, Baroda, and Central India (BB&CI) Railway Company, Mumbai, had double walls lined with lead–zinc sheets filled with ice. The Frontier Mail (now renamed the Golden Temple Mail), which runs between Mumbai and Amritsar, was the first train to get air-conditioned (AC) coaches, in 1934.

First tramcars
A horse-drawn tramcar ran on a 3.8 km route between Sealdah and Armenian Ghat Street in Calcutta on 24 February 1873.

First electric train
The first electric train operated on the Harbour branch of the Great Indian Peninsula Railway from Victoria Terminus to Kurla in Mumbai over 16 km, on 3 February 1925.

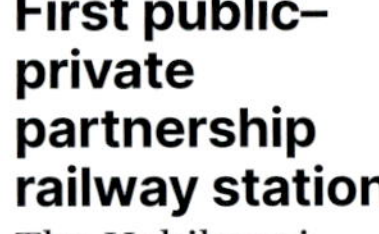

First public–private partnership railway station
The Habibganj railway station in Bhopal, Madhya Pradesh, is the first railway station to be built under a public–private partnership and on par with international standards. The redevelopment work began in partnership with the Bansal Group on 9 June 2017. It lies on the main Jhansi–Bhopal–Itarsi route. The plan includes airport-like facilities, such as shopping complexes, forex kiosks, and eateries, making it the first of its kind in the country.

Habibganj railway station

First Vistadome trains
A special seven-coach Vistadome passenger train was introduced on the Visakhapatnam–Araku route in Andhra Pradesh on 16 April 2017 by the Indian Railways. It has features such as see-through glass on all sides, glass roofs, LED lights, a GPS-based information system, and an observation lounge that offers panoramic views throughout the journey.

First green corridor
The Manamadurai–Rameswaram stretch of the Southern Railway was inaugurated as India's first green corridor in July 2016, by installing bio-toilets in 150 coaches of 13 pairs of express and passenger trains on the 114 km long train route. Developed by Indian Railways and the Defence Research and Development Organization (DRDO), the toilets have no discharge of human waste.

WR Most coaches produced in a year
The Integral Coach Factory, which is located at Perambur in Chennai, Tamil Nadu, manufactured 4,166 railway passenger coaches in 2019–20.

Longest rail tunnel
The Pir Panjal railway tunnel, or the Banihal railway tunnel, is 11.215 km long. It is located in the Pir Panjal range of the Himalayas in Jammu and Kashmir, and it opened in 2013.

First stations
Bori Bunder, Byculla, Sion, and Thane stations on the Bori Bunder–Thane line in Maharashtra were the first railway stations built at the time of the inaugural run of the first passenger train from Bori Bunder to Thane in 1853.

The End of a Journey

Kolkata's tram system is set to come to an end. The West Bengal government has decided to discontinue service due to traffic challenges in the city, but still maintaining that one route will remain operational. The operational route is between Esplanade and Maidan. The tram journey in Kolkata has lasted for 151 years and has stopped in October 2024.

Station with most platforms

Howrah Junction, West Bengal, serves around one million passengers every day. It has 23 platforms, making it the station with the most platforms in India.

Busiest railway station

Kanpur Central station, Uttar Pradesh, is the busiest railway station in the country in terms of the number of trains that pass through it every day. As many as 230 trains pass through the station daily. This railway station also has the world's largest interlocking route system.

Most locomotives produced in a year

The Chittaranjan Locomotive Works in Paschim Bardhaman District, West Bengal, produced 486 locomotives in the financial year 2021–22. It surpassed the Railway Board's production target for the period.

First woman train driver

Surekha Yadav Bhosale was the first woman to drive an Indian Railways train in 1988. She drove the first 'Ladies Special' local train, which started in April 2000 in Mumbai, Maharashtra. She was the first woman to join the Indian Railways as a trainee assistant driver in 1986. In 2011 she became the world's first Asian woman to drive the Deccan Queen from Pune to Chhatrapati Shivaji Maharaj Terminus.

Station with the longest platform

Shri Siddharoodha Swamiji railway station in Hubballi, Karnataka, has completed the construction of the 1,505 m (4,937 ft 7.97 in.) long Platform No. 1, thus becoming the station with the world's longest railway platform. The platform was inaugurated by Prime Minister Narendra Modi on 12 March 2023.

Longest rails manufactured

The Bhilai Steel Plant, the largest plant of the Steel Authority of India Ltd (SAIL), became the only rail maker in the world capable of producing 260 m (853 ft) long rails, on 23 February 2005. It first manufactures 65 m (213 ft) long rails, which are welded together to form the 260 m tracks for high-speed trains.

Kanpur Central railway station

Oldest steam engine

The *Fairy Queen*, officially called the East Indian Railway Nr. 22, has the world's oldest working steam engine. This train started running in 1855 but was stopped in 1908. It was restored in 1997 by Perambur Loco Works in Perambur in Chennai, Tamil Nadu. In July 1997, this heritage train resumed its route between Delhi and Alwar, Rajasthan, and it still runs occasionally.

Fairy Queen: Oldest steam locomotive

Only railway station listed as a UNESCO World Heritage Site

The first train in the country was flagged off on 16 April 1853 from Bori Bunder (now Chhatrapati Shivaji Maharaj Terminus) in Mumbai. The historic station is one of the busiest railway stations in India and the only one declared as a UNESCO World Heritage Site. The building, featuring a Victorian Gothic style of architecture, was designed and constructed by draughtsman Axel Herman and architect Frederick William Stevens in 1888.

Longest double decker viaduct

The longest double decker viaduct in India was built by Maharashtra Metro Rail Corporation Limited on Wardha Road, Nagpur. It has a length of 3.14 km. The double decker viaduct carries a highway flyover at the first level and a metro rail at the second level. Along with the already existing highway at ground level this viaduct is a three-tier transportation system.

First corporatized train

The Indian Railways launched the Tejas Express, India's first corporatized train, on 4 October 2019. The infrastructure is owned and run by the Indian Railway Catering and Tourism Corporation (IRCTC), a subsidiary of the Indian Railways, while the services on board are outsourced to private contractors. They include catering, housekeeping, ticketing and refund, among others. The train shuttles between Lucknow and New Delhi, and has only two halts in between – Kanpur and Ghaziabad. Running all week, except Tuesdays, it is contracted under the public– private partnership model.

Tejas Express: first corporatized train

Longest train route

The Dibrugarh–Kaniyakumari Vivek Express has the longest train route on the Indian Railways network, and the ninth longest in the world. It joins Dibrugarh in Assam to Kaniyakumari in Tamil Nadu, covering 4,286 km, while halting at 56 stations along the route. It starts at 11:05 p.m. and reaches at 9:50 a.m. on the fifth day, with a scheduled journey time of 82 hrs 45 mins.

Guwahati railway station

First fully solar-powered railway station

The Guwahati railway station in Assam is India's first fully solar-powered station. Commissioned in 2017, the project has 2,352 solar panels on the roof. This solar project aims to make the railways environmentally responsible and reduce their carbon footprint. The panels have an average power generation capacity of 2,048 kWh per day.

Underwater metro

First underwater metro

The East-West corridor project, India's first underwater metro service under the Kolkata Metro Rail Corporation was completed by June 2023. The metro line connects Salt Lake to Howrah via Kolkata with a 520 m (1,706 ft) stretch below the Hooghly River. It successfully completed a trial journey from Howrah Maidan to Esplanade and vice versa.

Most people at a public-service event – multiple venues

Ministry of Railways organized an event on 26 February 2024 which was attended by 40,19,516 people at 2,140 venues. The event was organized for the inauguration of road over / road under railway bridges and for laying the foundation stones of railway stations by Prime Minister Narendra Modi.

First metro

A 16.3 km underground mass rapid transit system in the country was inaugurated on 24 October 1984 in Kolkata, between Dum Dum and Tollygunge. The carrying capacity of this metro was 1.73 million passengers a day. The trains for the metro system were manufactured at the Integral Coach Factory, Perambur, Madras (now Chennai), Tamil Nadu, during 1981–82.

Deepest metro station

The Hauz Khas station on the Magenta Line and the Yellow Line of the Delhi Metro is the deepest metro station, located at a depth of 32 m (105 ft).

Most metro stations on a double-decker viaduct

The double-decker viaduct on Wardha Road has three metro stations along the length of 3.14 km. Each station has a length of 77.5 m. The three stations are Ujjwal Nagar, Jaiprakash Nagar, and Chhatrapati Square.

Largest metro network*

The Delhi Metro, set up by the Delhi Metro Rail Corporation (DMRC), spread across 391 km, is the largest metro rail network in India in terms of both route length and ridership. It has 12 lines and 286 metro stations.

Deepest metro tunnel

Delhi Metro Rail Corporation (DMRC) completed a metro tunnel at a depth of 45 m (147 ft 7 in.) on 30 April 2009. The 1,556 m (5,105 ft) long tunnel below the underground Rajiv Chowk metro station in New Delhi is part of the 22.7 km long Airport Express Line.

First driverless metro

The Magenta Line in the Delhi Metro became the first 'driverless' metro line in India. The 12.64 km long line started operating on 25 December 2017, and connected Kalkaji Mandir, New Delhi, to Botanical Garden, Noida, while halting at nine stations. The line was extended by 24.34 km to Janakpuri West in May 2018. Initially, it was run by an operator, with high levels of automation based on the Communications-based Train Control technology, and has begun driverless operations in 2020.

ROAD

First highway

Lord William Bentinck, the then Governor General of India (1828–35), began metalling work on the 2,400 km long historic Grand Trunk Road from Calcutta to Peshawar (now in Pakistan) and beyond. During his tenure, the initial steps were taken to build a metalled road from Calcutta to Delhi.

First state transport system

In June 1932, the Nizam's State Railways Transport Department (NSRTD), Hyderabad (now in Telangana), set up a road transport service on a 24 km route, with 27 buses operating through three depots. Each bus could seat as many as 25 passengers.

An NSR bus

First regular public transport

The first regular long-distance public road transport was introduced between Aligarh and Kanpur in Uttar Pradesh in November 1841.

First traffic police

The Traffic Department of Calcutta Police in Calcutta came into force in 1874 with 17 sepoys in its ranks.

First trolley bus

Twelve trolley buses were imported to replace tramcars on the Gowalia Tank–Mazagon route in Bombay on 11 June 1962. They were withdrawn in March 1971 in favour of buses.

Earliest route

In 1926, the Brihanmumbai (then Bombay) Electric Supply & Transport Undertaking (BEST) purchased motor buses, choosing two points to try them out. The route covered present-day Afghan Church to Crawford Market through Dadar tram terminus, King's Circle, Opera House, Lal Bagh and Arthur Road in Mumbai, Maharashtra.

First zero-emission electric car
REVAi, the environment-friendly electric car, is manufactured by the Reva Electric Car Company, Bengaluru, Karnataka, a joint venture formed by Amerigon Inc. of California, USA, and the Maini Group of Industries based in Bengaluru. This eco-friendly car was first flagged off from New Delhi in March 1998 and sold in 26 countries by 2011. It was acquired by the Indian conglomerate Mahindra & Mahindra in May 2010, and the company launched the electric hatchback e20 in 2013.

REVAi car

First motor bus
The motor bus was introduced in Mumbai on the Afghan Church–Crawford Market route on 15 July 1926. With a cruising speed of 20 km/hr, it carried 24 passengers, with 2–3 standing ones. Twenty-six buses were bought for ₹12,000 each.

First car
The first motor car was reportedly imported in 1892 by the then maharaja of Patiala in Punjab. It was a De Dion Bouton car.

De Dion Bouton

First stainless-steel bus
The first bus with a stainless steel body was built at the Maharashtra State Road Transport Corporation workshop in Aurangabad, Maharashtra. It was inaugurated on the Bombay–Ratnagiri route, Maharashtra, on 12 February 1988.

First Indian car manufacturers
Hindustan Motors Ltd, registered in 1942 to manufacture vehicles, was followed by Premier Automobiles (1944) and Standard Motor Products of India Ltd (1948). The first Indian-built car, Hindustan 10, not fully indigenous but identical to the series M10 HP Morris, rolled out of the factory located in Hooghly District, West Bengal, in 1946.

First CNG autos
Bajaj Auto Ltd launched the first of its Compressed Natural Gas (CNG) autorickshaws in Delhi on 29 May 2000. With a 3-kg CNG tank and a standby 3-litre petrol tank, it is powered by a 175 cc, four-stroke, overhead camshaft engine, which gives 50 km per kg of CNG and meets the Bharat-II emission norms.

First satellite navigation system
Sanjay, a navigation system using a Global Positioning System (GPS) receiver and mapping software, was launched on 15 February 1999 in New Delhi. Once installed in the vehicle, the user could access Delhi's road map and get audio information about routes. It also tracks the vehicle from elsewhere. Developed indigenously at the I.B. Saxena Design Lab in New Delhi, it uses 24 satellites.

First indigenous payment eco-system for transport
The National Common Mobility Card (NCMC) based on the 'One Nation, One Card' model was launched in Ahmedabad, Gujarat, on 4 March 2019, by the Ministry of Housing and Urban Affairs, Government of India. It allows users to make payments across multiple transportation platforms such as metros, toll taxes, buses, and parking across India.

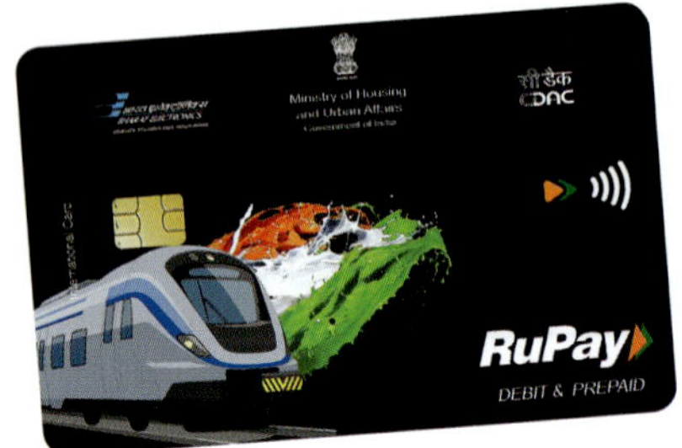

NCMC card

First battery-bus fleet
In 1987, for the first time, the Delhi administration introduced 76 battery operated buses on 11 routes in Delhi, through the Delhi Energy Development Agency. Each bus had a laden weight of 3,800 kg, a cruising speed of 40 km/hr, and a maximum speed of 60 km/hr.

First electric buses
- The first electric bus service in India is reported to have commenced in Himachal Pradesh for Rohtang Pass, near Manali, at an altitude of 3,962.4 m (13,000 ft). The bus has been developed by Goldstone Infratech and the Automobile Research Association of India. It had the capacity to carry 30 passengers and can run 200 km on fully charged batteries.
- India's first electric double-decker bus was launched at Y.B. Centre in south Mumbai, Maharashtra, on 19 August 2022. The bus – the 'Switch EiV 22' – are be run by the Mumbai civic transport body. Two new electric buses, including the first air-conditioned double-decker bus in the country, joined the fleet of the Brihanmumbai Electric Supply & Transport Undertaking (BEST).

First Advanced Traffic Control system
The Delhi Police installed the first Advanced Traffic Control system at 47 intersections of the capital city in April 2000. The intelligent sensors

Kona Electric

in this high-tech system are equipped to assess the volume of traffic at each intersection and control the traffic light system accordingly.

First fully electrical SUV

Hyundai launched India's first fully electric SUV, the Kona Electric, on 9 July 2019. The eco-friendly vehicle can cover approximately 452 km on a single charge and was introduced with four drive modes: Eco, Eco+, Comfort, and Sport.

First electric cabs

Nagpur in Maharashtra is India's first city to have an electric mass mobility system. It has a fleet of 200 electric vehicles including taxis, buses, e-rickshaws and autorickshaws, owned by cab aggregator Ola. This multimodal electric vehicle project, the first of its kind in India, was inaugurated on 26 May 2017.

Highest filling station

The Indian Oil Corporation Ltd operates a filling station at Kaza, Spiti Valley, Himachal Pradesh, at an elevation of about 3,740 m (12,270 ft) above mean sea level.

Shortest national highway

National Highway 327 B, located in West Bengal, is the shortest national highway in India. Only 1.2 km long, it starts from its junction with NH-327 near Panitanki in Darjeeling District, connecting Mechi Bridge and terminating at the Indo-Nepal border.

Highest national highway

The 490 km long Manali–Leh national highway has an average elevation of over 4,000 m (13,123 ft). Its highest elevation is 5,328 m (17,480 ft) at Tanglang La in Ladakh.

Longest highway construction in a single day

National Highway Authority of India (NHAI) has broken a world record by laying 75 km highway in under five days. The highway was laid as a single-layer of bituminous concrete in a single lane between Amaravati and Akola.

Longest highway tunnel

Atal Tunnel, a 9.2 km long tunnel on the Manali–Leh highway, was inaugurated on 3 October 2020. It cuts down the distance between Manali and Leh by 46 km and reduces travel time by four hours. Equipped with CCTVs and fire hydrants, the tunnel is the only one in India to have an emergency exit tunnel inside.

Largest automotive company

Tata Motors Ltd (earlier Tata Engineering and Locomotive Company), founded in 1945 and headquartered in Mumbai, Maharashtra, is the largest automotive company with a portfolio of cars, sports vehicles, buses, trucks, and defence vehicles. The company's consolidated net revenue for the fiscal year 2021-22 was ₹2,78,454 crore (₹2,784.54 billion) with 10,86,734 vehicles sold.

Most bituminous concrete poured – single day

Travelling over an approximate linear distance of 18,701 km, Hyderabad-based IJM (India) Infrastructure Ltd (IJMIL) poured 15,656 tonnes (6,068.217 cu.m) of bituminous concrete in 20 hrs 40 mins on 25 February 2021. The laying of the 26.82 km Solapur–Bijapur single lane of the four-lane NH-13 between Maharashtra and Karnataka was implemented under the National Highway Authority of India.

State/UT with the largest fleet of buses

Tamil Nadu State Transport Corporation (TNSTC) has a fleet of 22,000 buses. It is the largest government-owned bus transport corporation in the country (2019).

Tanglang La: Highest national highway

The Inland Waterways of India

India has about 14,500 km of navigable waterways comprising rivers, canals, backwaters, creeks, etc. Large quantities of cargo are annually transported by Indland water transport. It is a fuel efficient and environment-friendly mode of transport. The Inland Waterways Authority of India (IWAI) has been instituted for the development and regulation of inland waterways for shipping and navigation.

Out of the many waterways available in India there are five that have been declared as the national waterways of India as per the constitution. These are:

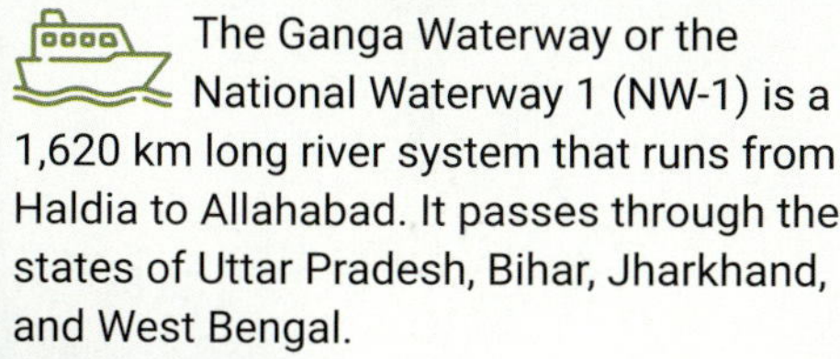

The Ganga Waterway or the National Waterway 1 (NW-1) is a 1,620 km long river system that runs from Haldia to Allahabad. It passes through the states of Uttar Pradesh, Bihar, Jharkhand, and West Bengal.

Brahmaputra river which is also known as **National Waterway 2 (NW-2)** is a 891 km stretch from Dhubri to Sadiya.

The **West Coast Canal** from Kottappuram to Kollam or the **National Waterway 3 (NW-3)** has a navigable length of 205 km. It includes the Champakara and Udyogmandal canals. It has been extended to Kozhikode by the National Waterways Act, 2016.

The **Kakinada–Puducherry canal** stretch along with the Godavari and Krishna rivers is considered as **National Waterway 4 (NW-4)**. It connects the states of Andhra Pradesh, Telangana, Tamil Nadu, and Puducherry. It has a total length of 1,095 km.

The **East Coast Canal** stretch along with Brahmani and Mahanadi delta river system is the National Waterway 5 (NW-5). It has a total length of 623 km.

Mahanadi delta river

WATER

Earliest compass

According to the *Bombay Gazetteer*, Vol. XIII, Part II, Appendix A, a crude forerunner of the modern magnetic compass, Matsya Yantra was used around the fifth century CE. It featured an iron fish that floated in a vessel of oil, and pointed north.

Oldest ships

- HMS *Foudroyant (Trincomalee)*, used for training, was built in Mumbai in 1817 and is now a museum ship in Hartlepool, UK. The *Trincomalee* carried 46 guns and displaced 1,065 tonnes.

HMS *Trincomalee*

- MV *Safeena* of Ellon Hinengo Ltd, Port Blair, Andaman and Nicobar Islands, built at the government dockyard in Rangoon (now Yangon), Myanmar, in 1942, is the oldest passenger ship.

Earliest representation of ships

A rectangular seal portraying a vessel with a sharply upturned prow and stem was unearthed in an excavation at Mohenjo-Daro (now in Pakistan). It was dated to 3000 BCE.

WR Longest river cruise

The MV *Ganga Vilas* is a vessel made in India that was flagged off on its journey from Varanasi on 13 January 2023 by Prime Minister Narendra Modi. The cruise covered a distance of 3,200 km in over 46 days. It reached Dibrugarh on 28 February 2023. It covered 27 river systems in India and Bangladesh.

Oldest operating port and largest riverine port

Calcutta Port, Bengal (later called Kolkata Port, and now renamed Syama Prasad Mookerjee Port, West Bengal), built by the East India Company and operating since 1870, is the oldest operating port in India. It is also the only major riverine port and the largest riverine port in the country.

MV *Ganga Vilas*

Reshma Nilofer guides ships in and out of Haldia Port

Largest covered dock

Hindustan Shipyard houses the largest covered dock at Visakhapatnam in Andhra Pradesh. The dock measures 240 m x 53 m x 11.25 m (787 ft x 174 ft x 37 ft) with an intermediate twin gate and undocking draft of 8 m (26 ft). It can accommodate ships of up to 80,000 deadweight tonnage.

First roll-on–roll-off ferry service

A roll-on–roll-off ferry service began on 22 October 2017 between Ghogha Port and Dahej in Gujarat. The 31 km service reduces the travel time between the two towns from 7–8 hours to just over an hour. It can carry 1,000 passengers and 150 vehicles.

First private sector port

Pipavav Port in Gujarat, which was inaugurated in November 1996, has three dry cargo berths built as a single-length jetty of 725 m (2,379 ft), and a liquid cargo berth.

First superfast catamaran service

A superfast catamaran service between Mumbai, Maharashtra, and Goa became operational from 14 November 1994. The 40 m long, 400-seater, twin-hull luxury catamaran was imported by Damania Shipping Ltd from Norway. It moved at 40 knots, covering 225 nautical miles (417 km) in 6 hrs 30 mins.

The Firsts of Water

First steamboat

The steamboat *Diana* was built in India in 1819 by Jessop & Co. Ltd in Calcutta, and launched on 12 July 1823.

First ship to sail from India

The first ship carrying the flag of an Indian Shipping Company, SS *Loyalty* of the Scindia Steam Navigation Company, sailed with a full complement of passengers from Bombay to the British Isles. A hospital ship, *Loyalty,* was bought on 17 February 1919 and converted to a passenger vessel. National Maritime Day is observed on 5 April, the day on which the ship started this voyage in 1919.

First woman marine pilot

Reshma Nilofer Naha (b. 4 February 1989) is the first and only Indian woman marine pilot in the country. She joined the Kolkata Port Trust in 2011 and became a trained marine pilot in January 2018. As a river pilot, she guides ships in and out of Sagar, to and from ports at Haldia and Kolkata ports through the Hooghly River.

First shipping company

Freedom fighter V.O. Chidambaram Pillai set up the Swadeshi Shipping Company at Tuticorin (now Thoothukudi), Tamil Nadu, in 1906.

First diesel engine ship

MV *Dwarka,* a modern D-class passenger and cargo ship of the British India Steam Navigation Company, entered service in 1947. Weighing 4,851 gross tonnes, it was 1,21.6 m (399 ft) long and 16.8 m (55 ft) wide. It had a service speed of 13.5 knots.

First hovercraft ferry

A diesel hovercraft service began between Surat and Ghogha Port in Gujarat on 10 December 1992, linking the two ports, 55 nautical miles (101.85 km) apart, in two hours.

First overseas cargo service

On 3 February 1948, a continental line for an overseas cargo service between India and European countries was inaugurated by the Scindia Steam Navigation Company, with the sailing of the cargo steamship SS *Jalabala* from present-day Mumbai, Maharashtra.

First solar ferry boat

The first solar-powered boat was launched in the country in December 2017. Named *Aditya*, the boat is 21.18 m (69 ft 7 in.) long and 7.0 m (22 ft 11 inc.) wide. Constructed by the NavAlt Solar and Electric Boats Pvt. Ltd, it accommodates 78 rooftop solar panels and sails at a maximum speed of 7.5 knots. The boat seats 75 passengers and operates on the 2.5 km Vaikom–Thavanakadavu route in Kerala.

First corporatized port

Ennore Port (now Kamarajar Port Ltd) on the Coromandel Coast, Chennai, Tamil Nadu, was the first Indian port that was a public company, and later became a corporatized port in 1999.

First indigenous hovercraft

A twin-engine, air-cushioned hovercraft, made in 1987 by the Scientific Instrument Co. Ltd, Allahabad, had a 55 HP thrust engine for propulsion and an 8 HP engine for lift, with a payload capacity of 500 kg and a speed of 45 km/hr.

Search...

PLANNING

First national economic planning

Prasanta Chandra Mahalanobis (1893–1972), an Indian scientist and applied statistician, laid down the framework for modern formal economic planning in India. A member of the first Planning Commission of independent India, Mahalanobis was the first to use statistical tools to forecast, plan, analyse, and evaluate social and economic welfare policies and implementation in India.

Left: Prasanta Chandra Mahalanobis
Right: R.K. Shanmukham Chetty

First budget

The first Indian budget was presented by James Wilson on 18 February 1860 in colonial India. Wilson, who founded *The Economist* magazine, was a finance member of the Council of India, which advised the Indian viceroy at the time.

First Union budget

The first Union budget of independent India was presented by then finance minister R.K. Shanmukham Chetty, on 26 November 1947. This was an economic review without any new taxes levied, as the Union budget for 1948–49 was only 95 days away. After this, a budget for a short period began to be called an 'interim' budget.

First interim budget

An interim budget, to enable government expenditures to continue until the regular budget, was presented first in 1957 by the then finance minister T.T. Krishnamachari.

First book on political economy

Written in Sanskrit by Chanakya in the 4th century BCE, the *Arthashastra* is an ancient Indian treatise on statecraft, economic policy, and military strategy. It was influential till the 12th century, after which it disappeared. A copy of it was rediscovered in 1905 by R. Shamasastry, a Sanskrit scholar, who published it in 1909. Its first English translation was published in 1915. The *Arthashastra* places the knowledge of economics at the heart of a king's education. Its discussion on taxation and expenditure gives expression to three traditional Indian principles: the taxing power of the state is limited, taxation should not be felt to be heavy or exclusive or discriminatory, and tax increases should be graduated.

Arthashastra: First book on political economy

Longest budget speech

- Dr Manmohan Singh holds the record for the longest budget speech in India. His 1991 budget speech consisted of 18,650 words.
- Longest budget speech in terms of duration is held by Nirmala Sitharaman. Her 2020 budget speech went on for 162 minutes.

Shortest budget speech

The shortest budget speech record is held by Hirubhai Mulljibhai Patel. His budget speech in 1977 had only 800 words.

First Union budget papers in Hindi

While introducing the budget for 1955–56, then finance minister Sir C.D. Deshmukh circulated the Hindi version of the budget speech for the first time. Hindi versions of the Annual Financial Statement and the Explanatory Memorandum were also circulated from then on.

First paperless budget

The Union budget for 2021 was presented on a 'Made-in-India' tablet on 1 February 2021 by Finance Minister Nirmala Sitharaman, doing away with the long-standing tradition of printing the budget papers and also the convention of carrying them in a briefcase. The budget, presented amid the COVID-19 pandemic, was distributed electronically to members of Parliament (MPs).

Only tax-free state in India

The only state in India where residents don't have to pay income tax is Sikkim. Since 1975, when Sikkim became part of India, the north-eastern state had its own tax laws, according to which Sikkimese people did not have to pay tax to the central government. In 2008,

Left: Dr Manmohan Singh
Right: Nirmala Sitharaman

Sir C.D. Deshmukh: former finance minister

the Government of India repealed the existing tax laws, but the new law also exempted this north-eastern state's residents from tax (under Section 10(26AAA) of the Income Tax Act). Also the Securities and Exchange Board of India has exempted Sikkimese people from the requirement of have a permanent account number (PAN) for investing in Indian securities market and mutual funds.

State GST collection from a single state

In FY 23-24, Maharashtra has contributed ₹3,02,317 crore from Goods and Services Tax (GST) collection—highest ever for any state since GST was introduced.

GST Bhavan, Mumbai

First winner of the Nobel Prize in Economics

Dr Amartya Kumar Sen (b. 3 November 1933) received the Nobel Prize in economic sciences in 1998, becoming the first Indian and Asian to do so. Born in Santiniketan, West Bengal, he is considered to be a pioneer of welfare economics.

WORKFORCE AND HUMAN RESOURCES

Oldest trade union

The Madras Labour Union, the first organized trade union, was formed in 1918–19 by labour veterans Annie Besant, B.P. Wadia, Thiruvarur Viruttachala Kalyanasundaram, Sakkarai Chettiar, G. Ramanujalu, and G. Selvapathy Chetty.

Earliest public association

The earliest public association in modern India was the Landholders' Society, an association of the landlords of Bengal (now West Bengal), Bihar and Orissa (now Odisha), founded in 1837. It was established to look after the interests of landlords, or zamindars.

Workers on board

Delhi Cloth Mills (DCM) was the first company to recognize labour rights by inducting a workers' representative into its board in 1938.

Oldest banking employees' trade union

The All-India Bank Employees Association (AIBEA) was founded on 20 April 1946. This is the oldest and largest trade union of bank employees.

Oldest insurance trade union

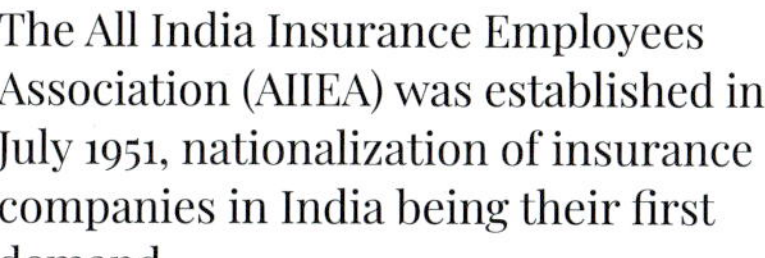

The All India Insurance Employees Association (AIIEA) was established in July 1951, nationalization of insurance companies in India being their first demand.

First labour strike

The first labour strike in India was that of the palanquin bearers of Calcutta (now Kolkata), West Bengal, in 1827 in pre-Independence India. They refused to wear badges and demanded fare on the basis of the distance they covered instead of time.

First Labour Day

The International Workers' Day celebrations were first organized by communist leader Singaravelar, or Malayapuram Singaravelu Chettiar, (1860–1946) in Madras (now Chennai), Tamil Nadu on 1 May 1923.

First industrial association

The Industrial Association of Western India was formed in 1890 at the annual conference held at Poona (now Pune), Maharashtra.

First organized strike

In 1877, labourers struck work at the Empress Mills in Nagpur, Maharashtra, following a wage cut. In 1884, as many as 5,000 textile workers of Bombay (now Mumbai), Maharashtra, submitted a petition asking for regular payment of wages, a weekly holiday, and a midday recess.

First all-India farmers' organization

The All-India Kisan Sabha was formed in 1936 in British India. It was the first pan-India organization of farmers.

First LGBTQIA+ job fair

The RISE (Reimagining Inclusion for Social Equity) job fair organized by the Pride Circle on 12 July 2019 in

Largest employers

- The record for the largest employer in India belongs to the country's government-controlled sector – Indian Railways. On 1 July 2023 the number of gazetted and non-gazetted employees of the Indian Railways stood at 12,18,221.

Rail Bhawan, New Delhi

- In the private sector, Tata Consultancy Services continues to be the largest employer with 6,01,546 employees in March 2024 — a significant drop from 6,15,316 in June 2023.

Bengaluru, Karnataka, was the first job fair exclusively for the LGBTQIA+ community. The fair attracted 450 candidates competing for 250 job opportunities in 35 companies. The employers included Goldman Sachs, Uber, Accenture, and Intel.

First labour legislation

- The Industrial Employment (Standing Orders) Act of 1946 was followed by protective regulations, such as the Factories Act and the Minimum Wages Act in 1948.
- The first effort to protect unorganized labour was the Coal Mines Provident Fund and Bonus Schemes Bill introduced in 1948, which became an Act in the same year.

Highest Forex Reserves

India's foreign exchange reserves increased by $8.895 billion to touch an all-time high of US $666.85 billion on 12 July 2014, according to Reserve Bank of India (RBI) data.

Largest strike

On 26 November 2020, over 250 million (25 crore) workers struck work for 24 hours in a nationwide general strike organized by a joint platform of 10 trade unions.

Highest FDI in a year

India recorded the highest ever annual foreign direct investment (FDI) inflow of US $83.57 billion in the financial year (FY) 2021–22.

Longest-serving chairperson

Jehangir Ratanji Dadabhoy Tata, a recipient of the Bharat Ratna in 1992, held the post of chairman of Tata Sons for 53 years (1938–91).

J.R.D. Tata: longest-serving chairperson

COINS AND CURRENCY

Earliest gold coins

The Kushanas (130 BCE–185 CE) issued the earliest gold coins in India. They weighed 121 or 123.1 grains (1 grain = 0.068 g approx.) and appear to be based on the auric standard (122.9 grains) of the Romans with whom the Kushanas had regular trade.

Kushana gold coins

First lead coins

The first lead coins were found in the Deccan, dating back to the reign of Sri Satai (c. 150 BCE).

First coins for the visually impaired

On 7 June 2019, in New Delhi, Prime Minister Narendra Modi released a new series of coins, specially conceived to help visually impaired people to identify them. Designed by the National Institute of Design in Ahmedabad, Gujarat, the series has coins in denominations of ₹1, ₹2, ₹5, ₹10, and ₹20. These coins are characterized by increasing size and weight from lower to higher denominations. The newly included coin of ₹20 was designed as a 12-sided coin with no serrations. The other denominations are circular.

First coins for the visually impaired

Earliest coinage

Ingots of silver, with only three dots as a mark, probably represent the earliest form of coinage on the Indian subcontinent (in circulation as early as 600 BCE).

Earliest known use of cowries as currency

Cowries were used as legal tender in the Bengal kingdom of Lakhnauti during the reign of Ghiyasuddin Bahadur Shah I (r. 1322–24 CE).

Oldest surviving gold coins

The oldest surviving gold coins are from the reign of Kushana emperor Vima Kadphises (c. 45–78 CE) and they were struck in three denominations – the double stater, the stater or dinara, and the quarter stater. On the obverse of these appears either the king's head or bust, or the king seated cross-legged on a couch, or sitting in a chariot drawn by two horses.

Coins of Vima Kadphises

Highest denomination rupee notes

The highest-denomination note ever printed by the Reserve Bank of India was the ten-thousand rupee note issued in 1938. This was demonetized in January 1946. The ten-thousand rupee note was re-introduced in 1954, only to be demonetized again in 1978.

First 200-rupee note

The RBI issued the first-ever currency notes in the denomination of ₹200 on 25 August 2017.

First mint

The East India Company started the first mint in India in 1640 at Fort St George, Madras. In 1671, the first English mint was installed in Bombay through a letter of patent issued by King Charles II of England, but the first coin was minted there only a few years later in 1678.

BANKING

First automated teller machine facility

The Hong Kong and Shanghai Banking Corporation (HSBC) started 24-hour banking facilities by installing automated teller machines (ATMs) at its main office in Bombay on 4 September 1987.

First credit card issued by an Indian bank

The Central Bank of India introduced the Central Card in 1980.

First floating ATM

The State Bank of India launched a floating ATM installed on a jhankar (ferry) plying between Ernakulam and Vypin (one among a group of islands forming part of Kovhi) in Kerala on 9 February 2004. The ship was owned by the Kerala Shipping and Inland Navigation Corporation.

First ATMs on wheels

In December 2002, the Industrial Credit and Investment Corporation of India (ICICI) Bank introduced an ATM on wheels using vans equipped with ATM machines and parked at four locations in Mumbai suburbs – Vile Parle (East), Juhu, Andheri (West), and Kandivali – for fixed hours. The mobile ATM was connected to the central database of the bank through GPRS (General Packet Radio Service) technology for a fixed number of hours every day.

First Banks

First bank

The Bank of Hindostan was established in 1770 by Alexander and Co. of Calcutta and survived three economic crises before shutting down in the 1830s.

First government banking agency

The Imperial Bank of India, formed in 1921 by merging the Presidency Banks of Bengal, Bombay, and Madras, became the State Bank of India (SBI) on 1 July 1955.

Oldest private bank

The Punjab National Bank Ltd, the first private bank wholly owned and run by Indians, opened in 1895.

First regional rural banks

The first regional rural banks (RRB) in India were opened in Moradabad and Gorakhpur in Uttar Pradesh, Bhiwani in Haryana, Jaipur in Rajasthan, and Malda in West Bengal on 2 October 1975.

First foreign bank

The Chartered Bank, established in 1853 in Madras, was the earliest foreign bank in India. In 1969, it merged with the Standard Bank in London, UK, and was incorporated as the Standard Chartered Bank.

First bank for housing development

The National Housing Bank (NHB), a subsidiary of the Reserve Bank of India, was established on 9 July 1988.

First Indian bank to open a branch overseas

The Bank of India was the first Indian bank to open a branch outside India, in London, UK, in 1946, and also the first to open a branch in Paris, France, in 1974.

First cooperative bank

The Greater Bombay Cooperative Bank Ltd was registered on 5 November 1952 under the Bombay State Cooperative Act, with 50 members and an initial capital of ₹21,000.

Most branches

In June 2024, the State Bank of India (SBI) had over 22,500 branches – most for any Indian bank.

First institution for agri-loans

On 12 July 1982, the National Bank for Agriculture and Rural Development (NABARD) was established, with its headquarters in Bombay, to implement the National Bank for Agricultural and Rural Development Act, 1981. The agricultural credit functions of RBI and refinance functions of the then Agricultural Refinance and Development Cooperation (ARDC) were transferred to NABARD.

NABARD: first institution for agri-loans

Digital Payments

NPCI

Founded in December 2008, National Payments Corporation of India (NPCI) is a Section 8 company under the Indian Companies Act, 2013, and has been set up by the Reserve Bank of India and Indian Banks' Association. The Certificate of Commencement of Business was issued in April 2009. Its products and services include retail, retail payment services like unified payments interface (UPI), and cheque truncation (electronic image of the cheque is transmitted to the drawee bank by NPCI along with relevant other information). It also acts as the national automated clearing house.

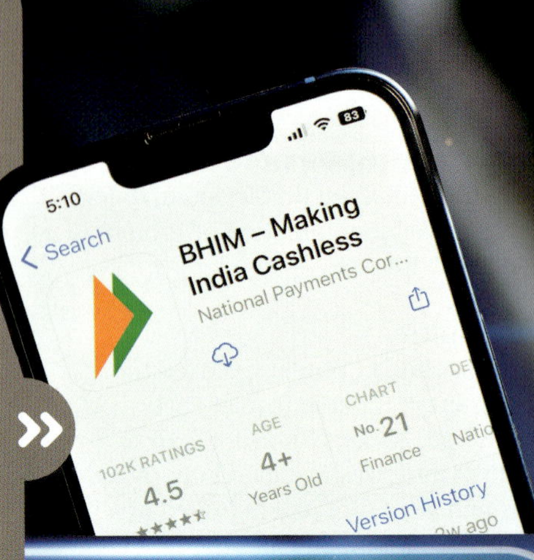

As part of the financial inclusion drive, the entire UPI ecology was planned to take the banking system to the doorstep of the citizens of India even in the remotest part of the country. Owned and operated by the National Payments Corporation of India (NPCI) and introduced in 2016, it facilitates inter-bank transactions. A single app helps access multiple bank accounts of the owner. It supports both collect and pay requests. From 8 June 2022, the Reserve Bank of India allowed linking RuPay credit cards to UPI as well.

UPI is being actively marketed through a subsidiary of NPCI called NPCI International Payments Limited (NIPL) in other countries as well. And now it is accepted in the following seven countries: 1. Bhutan, 2. France (e-commerce), 3. Mauritius, 4. Nepal, 5. Singapore 6. Sri Lanka, 7. UAE

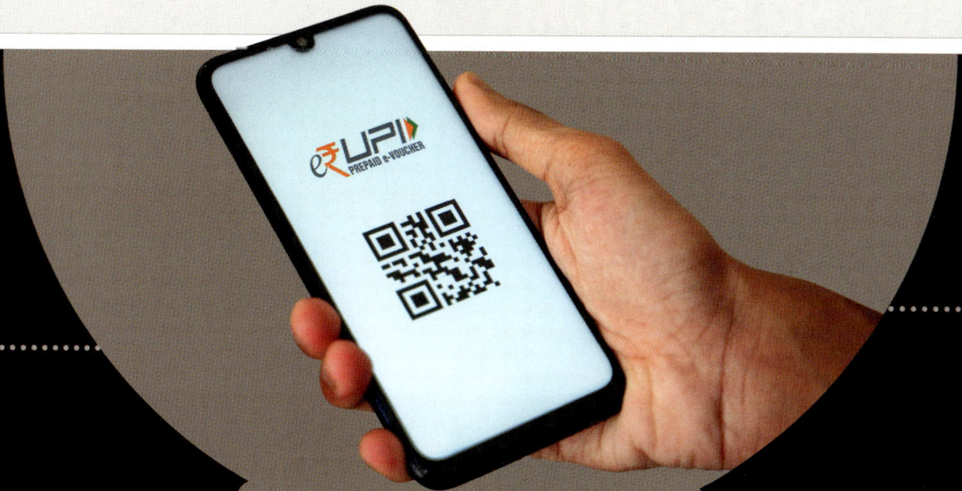

World's most popular payment platform

- According to the global payments hub Paysecure, India's unified payments interface processed 3,729.1 transactions per second during the April–July 2024 period.

- UPI processed nearly Rs 81 lakh crore transactions in the April–July 2024 period, thus leading all other global digital payment platforms.

- More than 40 per cent of all payments in India are done through UPI, per the Press Information Bureau, 30 October 2023.

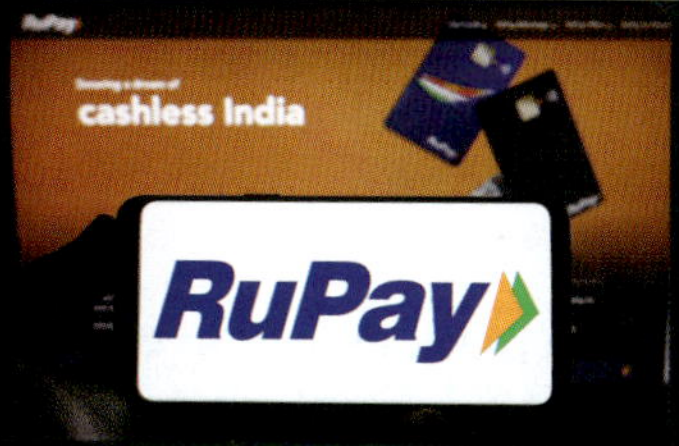

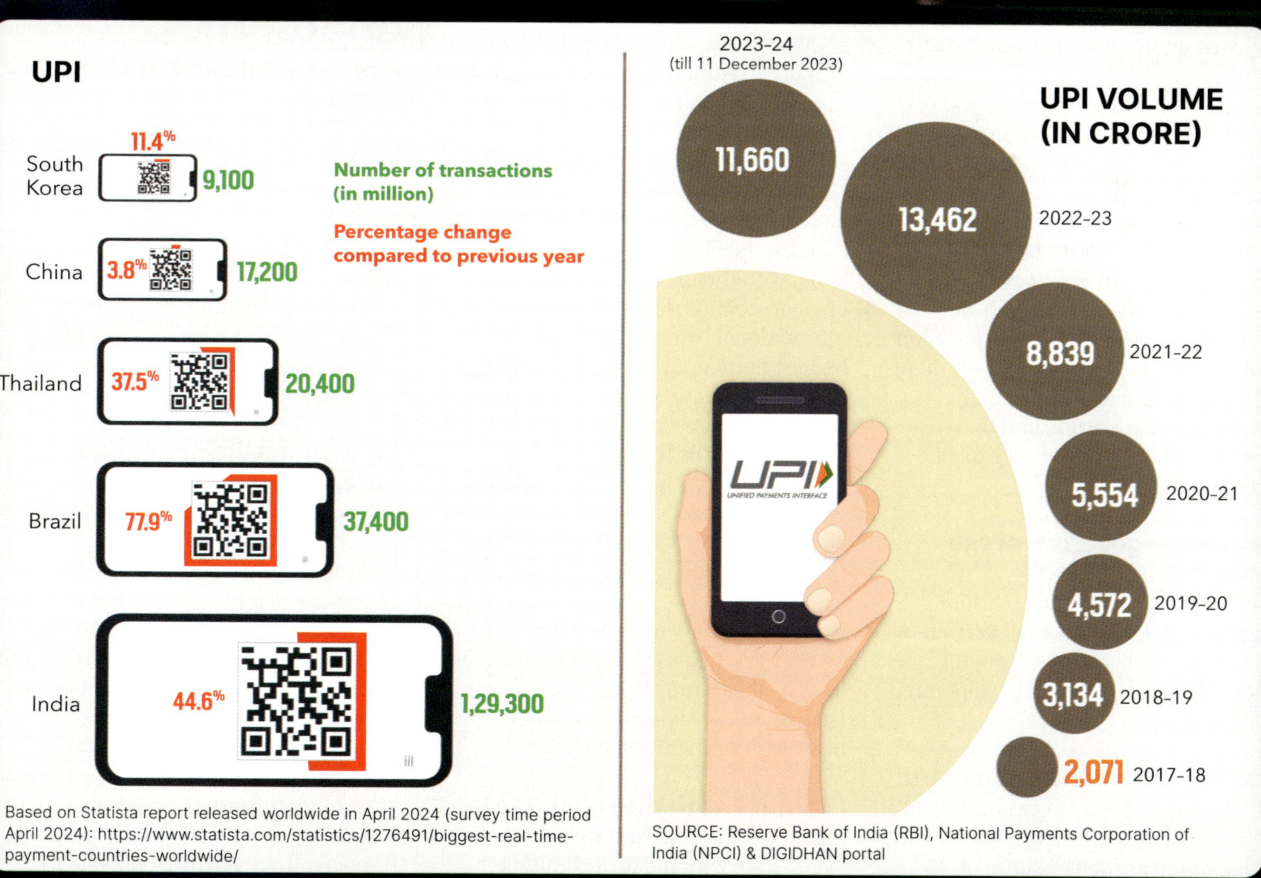

State Bank of India: King Street branch, London

Bank with most foreign offices

The State Bank of India has 241 offices in 29 foreign countries to service the bank's foreign customers, in addition to retail operations (as in July 2024). The focus of these offices is India-related business.

First Indian bank listed on the New York Stock Exchange

On 22 September 1999, ICICI Bank was listed on the New York Stock Exchange (NYSE), with its American Depository Shares priced at US $9.80. After the Bank of Tokyo-Mitsubishi, it was the second Asian bank to be listed on the NYSE.

First export–import bank

The Government of India set up the Export–Import Bank of India (EXIM Bank) in 1982 as a statutory corporation wholly owned by the Union government to provide financial assistance to exporters and importers and to coordinate the operations of export–import institutions.

First Indian governor of the Reserve Bank of India

Sir Chintaman Dwarkanath Deshmukh, a member of the Indian Civil Service, was the first Indian governor of the Reserve Bank of India (RBI) – appointed governor in 1943.

First indigenous payment card

The National Payments Corporation of India (NPCI) introduced the RuPay debit card in Mumbai, Maharashtra, on 26 March 2012.

The bank with the largest network

The India Post Payments Bank (IPPB), launched in 2018, currently has 1,58,988 access points (one controlling branch, 649 banking outlets – one in every district – as well as 1,36,078 post offices and 22,251 head and sub post offices both in both urban and rural areas, which also work as IPPB's access points). This makes it the largest banking network in the country. It also has more than 2,00,000 postmen or *gramin dak sevaks* who provide doorstep services.

International bank with most branches in India

As reported by the Reserve Bank of India, the Standard Chartered Bank, with the UK as its country of incorporation, leads the list of international banks in India with the highest number of branches, totalling 100 till July 2024.

Biggest bank fraud

On 14 February 2018, Punjab National Bank (PNB), India's second-largest government-owned lender at the time, declared the largest ever bank fraud in India's financial history. It involved fraudulent letters of undertaking worth around ₹11,400 crore (114 billion) issued by PNB at its Brady House branch in Fort, Mumbai, Maharashtra, to overseas branches of other Indian banks.

State/UT with the most ATMs

Maharashtra ranks first in the country as the state with the highest number of ATMs and WLAs (White Label ATMs) deployed, with 29,392 ATMs as reported in September 2022. Tamil Nadu, with 23,524 ATMs, comes second in the list.

First Indian bank with a merchant banking subsidiary

The State Bank of India was the first bank to set up a wholly owned merchant banking subsidiary when it set up SBI Capital Markets Ltd in April 1986.

First demonetization

In 1946, currency notes of ₹1,000 and ₹10,000 denominations were removed from circulation in the first instance of demonetization. Both notes were then reintroduced in 1954, with the introduction of ₹5,000 and ₹500 notes.

First bank with a satellite network

The State Bank of India installed the first satellite network in September 1988, connecting 134 offices in 64 cities. This network facilitated communication by voice, facsimile, and message switching via digital electronic exchanges.

INSURANCE

First general insurance company

Triton Insurance Company Ltd, set up by the British in 1850, was the first general insurance company in India.

First life insurance company in India

The Oriental Insurance Company, the first life insurance company in India, started in Calcutta in 1818, but served only the Europeans in India then.

First Indian life insurance company

The Bombay Mutual Life Assurance Society was the first Indian life insurance company. It started in 1870.

Largest insurance company

The Life Insurance Corporation of India (LIC) was founded on 1 September 1956. It grew into what is now the biggest public sector insurance company in the country and leads in the insurance sector. Apart from its corporate office in Mumbai, it has 2,048 fully computerized branch offices, 113 divisional offices, 8 zonal offices, and 1,381 satellite offices.

Life Insurance Corporation of India: largest insurance company

FINANCIAL INSTRUMENTS

First bank to establish a mutual fund

The State Bank of India launched the SBI Mutual Fund in July 1987. Managed by its subsidiary, SBI Capital Markets Ltd, it was established under the amended Banking Regulations Act, 1949, to attract funds from small investors in rural and semi-urban areas.

First domestic mutual fund

The Unit Trust of India's (UTI) scheme launched in 1964 was the first domestic mutual fund in the country.

First private sector mutual fund

Shyam Kothari, head of the H.C. Kothari group of companies, floated the Kothari Pioneer Bluechip Fund in November 1993.

India's first depository

The National Securities Depository Limited (NSDL) was jointly promoted by the Industrial Development Bank of India (IDBI), UTI, and the National Stock Exchange (NSE). It started operations in August 1996. C.B. Bhave was the first managing director of the NSDL. In September 2016, when the depository completed 20 years of operations, it had 15 million demat accounts.

Largest mutual fund

HDFC Asset Management Company Ltd is the largest mutual fund company in India, with quarterly average assets worth ₹6,12,900crore (6,129 billion) under its management for the quarter ended 31 March 2024.

First offshore mutual fund

Unit Trust of India (UTI) and Merrill Lynch promoted the ₹75 million India Fund in 1986.

Highest price for stock exchange membership

A broking card for the Bombay Stock Exchange was auctioned for ₹4.1 crore (41 million) to Jardine Fleming Asia, which later shut down. Before that, Baring Securities India Ltd had paid ₹3 crore (30 million) for one in 1995.

First rating agency

Crisil, formed in 1988, was the first rating agency in India. It was set up jointly by the LIC, ICICI, GIC, and various banks.

First secured promissory notes

Tata Iron and Steel Company Ltd (TISCO), now Tata Steel Ltd, issued secured promissory notes in June 1992.

First global depository receipts issue

Reliance Industries Ltd issued global depository receipts worth US $150 million in March 1992.

First PSU to go public

Indian Petrochemicals Corporation Ltd (IPCL) went public on 16 November 1992, with a ₹320 crore (3.2 billion) equity issue.

First sectoral fund

The first sectoral mutual fund by the name of CanExpo was offered by Canara Bank in February–March 1994 as the first emerging industry fund.

POWER AND ENERGY

First builder of the steam engine

Golak Chandra, who was a blacksmith in Titigur (now Titagarh), near Barrackpore in West Bengal, indigenously built a steam engine to pump groundwater, without any European help, in 1828.

First commercial use of electricity

Electricity was first introduced commercially on 10 November 1897 at Sidrapong Hydroelectric Power Station in Darjeeling, West Bengal.

First electrification

Calcutta was the first city in India to go electric when it received current in 1899 with the commissioning of Calcutta Electric Supply Corporation's (CESC's) first generating station at Emambagh Lane the same year.

Tata Iron and Steel Company Ltd: company that issued first secured promissory notes

Women Power

First woman president of a stock exchange

Forty-five-year-old Omana Abraham became the first woman president of a stock exchange in India when she was nominated president of the Cochin Stock Exchange in Kochi, Kerala, in 1991.

First all-woman bank

Bharatiya Mahila Bank (BMB) is India's first bank only for women. This government-owned bank was set up with the vision of economic empowerment of women, and it opened its first branch at Nariman Point in Mumbai, Maharashtra, on 19 November 2013. It was incorporated on 5 August 2013 and received a banking licence from the RBI on 25 September 2013. It was merged with the State Bank of India in April 2017.

First woman to head a foreign bank in India

Naina Lal Kidwai was the first Indian woman to lead a foreign bank (ANZ Grindlays, where she worked from 1982 to 1994) in India. She was also the first Indian woman to graduate from Harvard Business School (1982). Her contribution in the areas of trade and industry earned her the Padma Shri in 2007.

First woman bank manager

Shanta Kumari became the manager of the Syndicate Bank, Seshadripura, Bangalore (now Bengaluru), Karnataka, in 1962.

First woman managing director and chief financial officer of World Bank Group

Anshula Kant, born in Roorkee (now in Uttarakhand), was appointed managing director (MD) and chief financial officer (CFO) of the World Bank on 12 July 2019. Kant is responsible for managing the International Development Association (which offers concessional loans and grants to the world's poorest developing countries), finance, and risk management of the group. Previously a financial officer of the State Bank of India, Kant became the first woman to become MD and CFO of the international financial institution.

First heavy water plant

The first heavy water plant was set up at Nangal in the Rupnagar District of Punjab in 1962. Heavy water or deuterium oxide was the basic fuel used by first-generation nuclear power plants.

Largest private sector thermal power station

The 4,620 MW Mundra Thermal Power Station at Mundra in the Kachchh District of Gujarat is the largest privately operating thermal power plant in India, with nine generating units. It is a coal-based power plant, owned and operated by Adani Power.

First private sector power company

Tata Power Company Ltd (TPCL) was the first private sector power company to start operations, in 1910 in Bombay.

First steam-powered plant

The Calcutta Electric Supply Company (CESC) set up a steam-powered plant in 1899 at Emambagh Lane near Prinsep Ghat in Calcutta, marking the start of thermal power generation in India.

First nuclear power plant

The Tarapur Atomic Power Station (TAPP) in Palghar, Maharashtra, with an installed capacity of 380 MW, was commissioned in 1969. It started with two boiling-water reactor units with an initial generating capacity of 210 MW each (de-rated to 160 MW), fuelled by enriched uranium. It was built by Bechtel Corporation and General Electric Company, US, under an agreement between the Government of India, the United States, and the International Atomic Energy Agency.

First indigenous atomic power plant

Madras Atomic Power Station (MAPS) at Kalpakkam near Chennai, Tamil Nadu, was India's first fully indigenously built nuclear power station under the Indira Gandhi Centre for Atomic Research (IGCAR). Each of its two units generates 220 MW of electricity. The first indigenous 40 MW Fast Breeder Test Reactor (FBTR) was commissioned in August 1985 here.

First state electricity board

On 1 May 1955, the West Bengal State Electricity Board was the first electricity board in the country to become operational.

First hydropower station

Sidrapong Hydroelectric Power Station in the foothills of Arya Tea Estate near Darjeeling, West Bengal, is the oldest hydroelectric power plant in India. It was commissioned on 10 November 1897 with a capacity of 2 x 65 kW. This was increased in phases to meet the rising demands and reached 1,000 kW (1 MW) by 1916.

First solar-powered thermal plant

The country's first 50 MW solar-powered thermal power plant, developed by Chhattisgarh-based Godawari Green Energy Ltd (GGEL) in Nokh Village in Jaisalmer District, Rajasthan, went operational in 2013.

Largest grid-connected rooftop solar plant

The country's largest grid-connected rooftop solar plant, with a capacity of 7.52 MW, started operations in May 2016 at Dera Beas in Amritsar District, Punjab.

Largest power supplier

The National Thermal Power Corporation (NTPC) Ltd, set up in 1975, is the country's largest power company. As of April 2024, it has an installed capacity of 76,294MW (including joint ventures). NTPC's own stations include 27 coal-based, 7 gas-based, 1 hydroelectric, 1 small hydro, and 16 renewable energy-based stations. Under joint ventures, the company has 9 coal-based, 4 gas-based, 8 hydroelectric, 1 small hydro, and 20 renewable energy projects.

Tarapur Atomic Power Project, Palghar, Maharashtra: first nuclear power plant

National Thermal Power Corporation: largest power supplier

Financial Institutions

Oldest stock exchange

The Bombay Stock Exchange (BSE) was born under the shade of a giant banyan tree way back on 9 July 1875 by Premchand Roychand, a cotton merchant. Educated in Elphinstone College, Bombay (now Mumbai), he was the first Indian broker able to write, read, and speak in English. Indian brokers doing business in stocks and shares decided to form an association in Bombay to protect the interests of Indian share brokers and stockbrokers. It was also Asia's first stock exchange and tenth oldest in the world.

Stock exchange with most listed companies

As of 24 January 2024, the Bombay Stock Exchange (BSE) had 5,309 listed companies with a market capitalization of about ₹3,76,36,886.

First stock exchange to cross the 80,000 mark

On 4 July 2024 the 30-stock BSE share Index crossed the historic 80,000 mark.

Bombay Stock Exchange

Premchand Roychand legacy

1. Premchand Roychand started the Native Share & Stock Brokers, Association, which is today's Bombay Stock Exchange.
2. Premchand Roychand Gallery was created in 2002 at the Chhatrapati Shivaji Maharaj Vastu Sangrahalaya, Mumbai.
3. The Premchand Roychand studentship – one of the most prestigious scholarship awards in India given by the University of Calcutta – was started by Premchand Roychand in 1866.
4. The Rajabai Clock Tower at the University of Bombay was named after Premchand Roychand Jain's mother. He donated ₹2,00,000 for its creation during 1869–1878.

National Stock Exchange

Highest single-day transactions

On 5 June 2024, the NSE traded 1,971 crore (19.71 billion) orders and 28.55 crore (280.55 million) trades in 6 hours and 15 minutes.

First to cross the 100 billion mark in monthly turnover

The National Stock Exchange is the stock exchange with the highest turnover. In August 2024, GIFT Nifty set an all-time high monthly turnover of US $100.13 billion (about ₹8,40,000 crore) for the month of May 2024.

Stock exchange with highest average daily turnover

The National Stock Exchange holds the record for the highest daily turnover with $81,721 crore (₹817.21 billion) in 2023–24.

State/UT with the highest contribution to equity trading

Maharashtra leads among states in its contribution to equity trading, with 3,35,99,064 registered investors as in June 2024 (18.61 per cent contribution as a state).

Shares of most companies held by an individual

Rajiv Maheshwari (b. 10 April 1961) held shares of 5,348 companies in dematerialized form in National Securities Depository Ltd (NSDL) and Central Depository Services (India) Ltd (CDSL) depository accounts as on 12 June 2023.

First automatic exchange and screen-based trading

The automated Over the Counter Exchange of India (OTCEI), set up in 1992 in Bombay, Maharashtra, was the ideal avenue for small- and medium-sized companies with an issued capital ranging from ₹30 lakh (3 million) to ₹25 crore (250 million). This exchange failed to live up to its promise and the National Stock Exchange (NSE) came into being in November 1994. The NSE started the first screen-based trading system, in which a network of computers is linked to a central computer located in the stock exchange.

Vindhyachal Super Thermal Power Station: largest thermal power plant

Largest thermal power plant
Vindhyachal Super Thermal Power Station in Singrauli District, Madhya Pradesh, with an installed capacity of 4,760 MW, is ranked as the biggest thermal power plant in the country. It is a coal-based power plant, owned and operated by NTPC Ltd.

Longest underwater hydrocarbon pipeline
India's longest underwater hydrocarbon pipeline was completed in April 2023. It stretches 1,656 km, from the river island Majuli in Assam to Jorhat in Upper Assam. The pipeline runs under the Brahmaputra River. Its diameter is 24 inches, and it cost ₹9,265 crore.

First oil well
- Oil was first located at Borbil (later Digboi) in Assam in 1890, but systematic drilling for oil had begun in Upper Assam in 1866 and oil was struck at Makum near Margherita at a depth of 36 m (118 ft) on 26 March 1867.
- The first offshore well was sunk in the Bombay High oilfield in 1974.

First pipeline
The Guwahati–Siliguri petroleum product pipeline (between Assam and West Bengal) was commissioned by the Indian Oil Corporation in 1965.

First refinery
The Assam Railways and Trading Co. built a small refinery at Margherita in present-day Tinsukia District, Assam, in 1893 to refine oil from Makum and Digboi areas.

First public sector oil refinery
Guwahati Refinery, Assam, built with Romanian collaboration started operations on 1 Jan 1962. It belongs to Indian Oil Corporation.

WR Oldest running refinery
The Digboi Refinery, under the Indian Oil Corporation since 1981, was commissioned in 1901 in Assam. It is the world's oldest running refinery. Earlier it was owned by Assam Oil Company Limited under Burmah Oil Company.

First refinery to produce lead-free products
Mangalore Refineries and Petrochemicals, commissioned on 25 March 1996, has been jointly promoted by the A.V. Birla Group and Hindustan Petrochemicals Ltd. It has an oil processing capacity of 3 million tonnes per annum and is the first refinery to manufacture lead-free products.

Largest refinery
The Jamnagar Refinery is a private sector crude oil refinery owned by Reliance Industries in Jamnagar, Gujarat. The refinery was commissioned on 14 July 1999 with an installed capacity of 6,68,000 barrels per day. It's current capacity is 12,40,000 barrels per day, and it is the largest single-site refinery in the world.

First private branded LPG
Reliance Gas was launched in 1998 by Reliance Petroleum Ltd in collaboration with the local LPG bottlers for the packaging of the product.

Highest-ever crude throughput and distillate yield
Numaligarh Refinery Limited (NRL) recorded its highest-ever crude throughput of 3.093 million tonnes (MT) against its nameplate capacity of 3.0 MT in the FY 2022–23. The company has also announced a distillate yield of 87.6 per cent, which is its highest since inception. NRL has kept its capital

Digboi Refinery: oldest running refinery

Reliance Gas: first private branded LPG

Bharat Petroleum Corporation Ltd: first company to market LPG

expenditure at ₹6,615 crore (66.15 billion) in FY 2022–23, which is the highest ever to date, surpassing its earlier record of ₹3,605 crore (36.05 billion) in the FY 2021–22.

State with highest installed capacity of renewable power

As on 31 December 2023 Rajasthan's total installed renewable capacity stood at 24,531.05 MW – the highest in India. A close second is Gujarat with 23,967.01 MW.

First company to market LPG

The first company to market liquefied petroleum gas (LPG) in India was Bharat Petroleum Corporation Ltd (BPCL) in 1955. Now BPCL reaches more than 8.5 crore (85 million) households with over 6,500 LPG distributors across the country.

MINING

Largest coal-producing company

Coal India Limited (CIL), a government-owned coal-mining company headquartered in Kolkata came into being in November 1975, when the Government of India took over private coal mines. It is now the single largest coal producer in the world. Operating through 84 mining areas, it has seven wholly owned coal-producing subsidiaries as well as a mine planning and consultancy company, across eight states in India. CIL produced an all-time high of 773.65 MT in FY 2023–24 and coal offtake of 753.59 MT.

First lithium resource

Geological Survey of India has found lithium for the first time. They discovered 5.9 million tonnes of inferred reserves of lithium in Salal-Haimana area of Reasi District, Jammu and Kashmir, in February 2023.

First coal mining

The first tonne of coal was struck in Raniganj Coalfield in 1775 by Suetonius Grant Heatly, the then collector of the East India Company for Palamu and Hazaribagh, in present-day Jharkhand. Records show that John Summer and Grant Heatly jointly obtained a licence from the then British Governor General Warren Hastings in 1774 to exploit what they then called 'Panchet coal'. They were later joined by another Englishman called Redfern.

State/UT with the most mines

There are 1,319 reporting mines (excluding minor, fuel, and atomic minerals) in the country as recorded in

Coal India Limited: largest coal-producing company

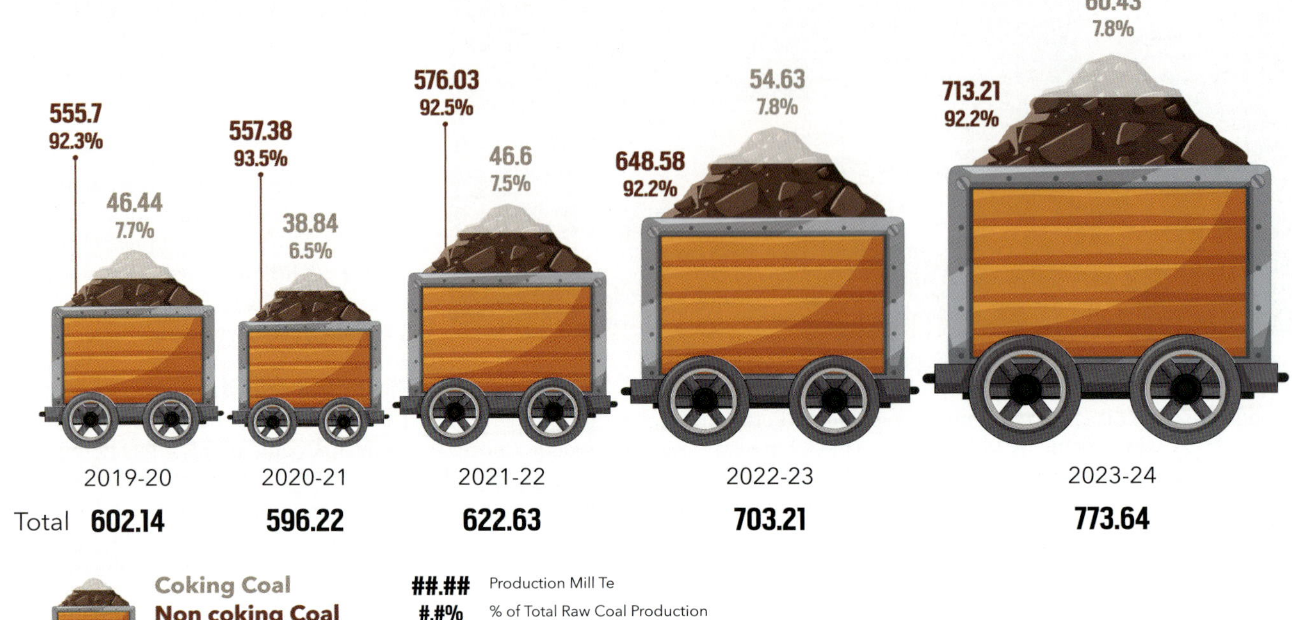

SOURCE: https://www.coalindia.in/departments/production/

2021–22. Among these, Madhya Pradesh tops the chart with 263 mines, followed by Gujarat (147), Karnataka (132), Odisha (128), Chhattisgarh (114), Andhra Pradesh (108), Telangana (92), Rajasthan (84), and Maharashtra (67). In terms of the value of mineral production, Odisha leads with ₹32,841 crore (328.41 billion), followed by Rajasthan (₹22,776 crore/ 227.76 billion), and Andhra Pradesh (₹17,906 crore/ 179.06 billion).

Oldest gold mine

India's oldest gold mine was located in Kolar, Karnataka. The production here in the mid-1970s was 3,000 kg a year, but was on a decline ever since, and the mines were closed in 2001.

Gold from a mine (representative image)

Only diamond mines

India's only diamond mines are at Panna in Madhya Pradesh and are administered by the government owned National Mineral Development Corporation (NMDC).

India's first international Bullion Exchange

The India International Bullion Exchange (IIBX), India's first international bullion exchange, is located at Gujarat's GIFT (Gujarat International Finance Tec-City) in Gandhinagar. It was inaugurated on 29 July 2022. This exchange is the third such exchange in the world. India's first bullion exchange will sell physical gold and silver. The jewellers registered as trading partners with the exchange, with a minimum net worth of ₹25 crore as a prerequisite, will be able to buy and sell gold and silver in the exchange. Jewellers abroad will also be able to do the same, following certain conditions, after registering with the International Financial Services Centre Association (IFSCA).

INDUSTRIES AND COMPANIES

First factory

The first factory in India, which was a dye-manufacturing unit, was set up by the East India Company with the permission of the then Mughal emperor Jahangir in Surat in 1609, marking the beginning of colonialism.

First commercial production of iron and steel

- In 1830, a unit was set up at Porto Novo (now Parangipettai) in Cuddalore District, Tamil Nadu, to produce iron, but it failed.
- In 1853, the East India Iron Company set up two blast furnaces in South Arcot and Coimbatore Districts, Tamil Nadu. These closed in 1858.
- In 1875, the Barakar Iron Works, Kulti, Bengal, produced pig iron.
- Steel production began in 1892 at the Metal and Steel Factory at Cossipore (now Kashipur, West Bengal), moving to Ichapore (now Ishapur, West Bengal) in 1905.

First ice-cream company

Joy Ice Creams Pvt. Ltd, which was

Registered office of Imperial Tobacco Company on J. L. Nehru Road, Kolkata

founded by L.C. Java, was the first company to manufacture and market ice cream. In 1948, Java bought a homogenizer and pasteurizer, and set up a small business that became India's first ice-cream company.

First cotton textile mill

Though the British had established a cotton textile mill in 1817, the first truly Indian textile mill was set up in July 1854 in Bombay by Cawasji N. Davar. It was called the Bombay Spinning and Weaving Company.

Oldest jute mill

Wellington Jute Mill in Rishra, near Serampore (now Srirampur), West Bengal, was established by George Auckland in 1855 as the Rishra Twine and Yarn Mills Ltd, with machinery bought from John Kerr of the Douglas Foundry, the leading manufacturers of flax and manufacturing machines in Dundee, Scotland. The mill had an output of eight tonnes a day. It shut down in 1868 and resumed as Calcutta Jute Mills, which later became Wellington Jute Mills. It is now under AI Champdany Industries Ltd.

First cigarette company

Imperial Tobacco Company (ITC) was established in Calcutta in 1910.

First rubber estate and company

The first rubber company, called Malankara Rubber and Produce Company, was started in 1910 by P. John on a 70-acre (28.3-hectare) estate in Thodupuzha, Idukki District, Kerala.

First tea company

Tea seeds were first imported into India from China in 1774. In 1837, the East India Company set up the first tea estate at Chabua, Dibrugarh District, Assam. The Alubari Tea Company, established in 1856 in Darjeeling (now in West Bengal) under the Kurseong and Darjeeling Tea Company, was the first to commercialize tea.

First car factory

In 1928, General Motors had commenced the assembly of cars and trucks in Bombay using imported components. The first indigenous car manufacturing company was the Birlas' Hindustan Motors, which was established at Uttarpara near Calcutta. The first Indian car, 'Hindustan 10', rolled off the assembly line in 1948.

First foreign collaboration

Carr, Tagore and Company was the first Indo-British collaboration under the Charter Act of 1833. There were four partners: W. Carr, Dwarakanath Tagore, D.M. Gordon, and William Prinsep. It closed in 1847.

First car to be exported

Hindustan Motors Ltd's Ambassador was the first car to be exported in 1975–76 to Guyana in South America.

India leads in the export of measles vaccines

Ninety per cent of measles vaccines in the world are supplied by India, which also supplies 65 per cent of DPT and BCG vaccines in the world.

First retail chain for computers

Computer Point launched the country's first retail chain for computers and computer accessories by establishing the first showroom in Bombay on 31 December 1984. It

Jessop Building on N. S. Road, Kolkata: old head office of Jessop & Company

also had stores in other cities, like New Delhi.

Oldest engineering company

Jessop & Company Ltd, the oldest engineering company in the country, was established in 1788 by two engineers from Britain – Henry and George Jessop.

First champagne manufacturer

In 1987, its very first year, Shyam Chougule's Champagne India, a subsidiary of Indage in Narayangaon, Pune District, Maharashtra, with a 42-acre (17-hectare) vineyard, entered the export market. Champagne Indage Ltd, as it was renamed after being restructured, was the market leader in wines then, with a production of about 1,00,000 cases a year.

Wine case

A wine case usually contains 12 bottles of wine, and a standard wine bottle contains 750 ml of wine. Thus a case consists of 9 litres of wine.

First tyre company

The Dunlop Rubber Company (India) Ltd was established on 19 August 1926, with its registered office in Bombay and an authorized share capital of ₹50 lakh (5 million). Dunlop opened its first tyre factory in India at Sahagunj, Hooghly District, West Bengal, in 1936.

First five-star hotel

The Taj Mahal Hotel in Mumbai, Maharashtra, said to have been built back to front, was founded by Jamshetji Nusserwanji Tata in 1904. The story goes that in those days there were very few hotels that permitted entry to Indians and Tata himself had been denied admission to Pyrke's Apollo Hotel, close to the present-day Taj Mahal Hotel. This motivated Tata to build the hotel.

First batch of microchips

The first microchips rolled out of Semiconductor Ltd, located in Chandigarh, in March 1984.

A microchip (representative image)

First scooter manufacturing company

Lambretta, the first scooter introduced by Automobile Products of India (API), was manufactured in 1956.

First plastic factories

A plastic factory was established in 1926 at Jessore, now in Bangladesh. It manufactured combs, soapboxes, ashtrays and other articles. It started with machinery that was imported from Germany. The first thermosetting plastic produced in India, starting in 1946, was phenol formaldehyde.

First hosiery company

The Oriental Hosiery Company Ltd, the first hosiery company of India, was started in Calcutta in 1893 by Ananda Mohan Mukherjee.

First power loom

The first power loom for jute cloth was started in 1958 by Henderson and Company, agents of Borneo Jute Company, in present-day Baranagar, Kolkata, in West Bengal. On becoming a limited company, it was named the Baranagore Jute Manufacturing Company and had 512 looms at its peak.

First private sector space launches

On 24 June 2022, the Indian Space Promotion and Authorization Centre (IN-SPACe) authorized Dhruva Space Pvt. Ltd, Hyderabad, Telangana, and

Digantara Research and Technologies Pvt. Ltd, Bengaluru, Karnataka, to launch their payloads. This marked the beginning of private sector space launches in India. Dhruva Space's Dhruva Space Satellite Orbital Deployer (DSOD 1U), a technology payload, along with Digantara's ROBust Integrating Proton Fluence Meter (ROBI), a proton dosimeter payload, were carried onboard the PSLV Orbital Experimental Module (POEM).

First commercial payload

India launched its first full commercial payload on 23 April 2007 from Sriharikota in Andhra Pradesh. The payload was an Italian satellite called Agile and was carried by PSLV-C8. The Polar Satellite Launch Vehicle or PSLV has been fully developed by the Indian Space Research Organisation (ISRO). It is an expendable medium lift launch vehicle and has capabilities of launching small size satellites into geostationary orbit. The commercial space service to launch such satellites is called ride-share services as a single such launch can carry multiple payloads. With the launch India acquired its own independent commercial payload launch capabilities into the space and breaks into the league of five nations (the United States of America, Russia, France, China and Japan) in commercial satellite launching market.

First infrastructural index

The Government of India launched a City Liveability Index on 23 June 2017 to measure the quality of life in 116 major cities, based on a set of 79 parameters, such as the availability of roads, education, healthcare, mobility, employment opportunities, emergency response, grievance redressal, pollution, availability of open and green spaces, cultural and entertainment opportunities, and so on.

RETAIL

First virtual mall

The Digital Mall of Asia is a virtual e-commerce platform, an amalgamation of digital space and real estate, making it the first virtual mall in the country. The mall is open in Delhi, Noida, Pune, Ahmedabad, Bengaluru, Chennai, Gurugram, Hyderabad, Jaipur, Lucknow, and Mumbai. Each location has a different digital interface and e-shops can be bought or acquired on rent. The mall works 24 hours a day, 7 days a week.

Highest number of stores opened in a single day

On 29 October 2018, the Chinese electronics company Xiaomi opened 500 retail stores, called Mi Stores, in rural regions of India, thereby setting a record for the most number of stores opened in a single day. These stores are on the lines of the larger 'Mi Home' stores in metropolitan cities.

Biggest business deal

In August 2018, Walmart Inc., a US multinational retail corporation, announced the deal agreements that

Largest exporter of spice

India is the largest exporter of spice in the world. FY 2023–24 saw the export of spices / spice products from the country shoot up to 15,39,692 tons. This is valued at ₹36,958.80 crore ($4,464.17 million).

Khari Baoli, Asia's largest spice market located near the Red Fort in Delhi, is operating since the 17th century.

made it the largest shareholder in the Flipkart Group, an e-commerce company founded by Sachin Bansal and Binny Bansal in 2007 and based in Bengaluru, Karnataka. Walmart bought roughly 77 per cent stake in the e-retailer for around US $16 billion (approx. ₹1,000 billion then). This was India's largest acquisition and also the world's biggest purchase of an e-commerce company.

ADVERTISING

First known advertisements

Advertising in India began with the first printed newspaper, called *Hicky's Bengal Gazette*, and printed from the 1780s onwards in Calcutta. The advertisements consisted of a series of simple messages 'classified' into different categories for easy reference of readers, or they were lists of the latest merchandise from England.

First ad association

On 21 September 1945, the Advertising Agencies Association of India (AAAI) was registered as a society in Calcutta. In 1961, its headquarters moved to Bombay.

First patented brand

Horlicks, the first patented brand in the country, was launched in the last decade of the 19th century. In the 1940s, Hindustan Thompson Associates (HTA), an advertising agency, which is now J. Walter Thompson India (JWT), coined the 'Balanced Nourishment' concept for the malt-based beverage to make Horlicks more relevant to India.

First multinational advertising agencies

- Alliance Advertising was set up during the First World War (1914–18), and other foreign (American) agencies such as L.A. Stronach and D.J. Keymer followed later.
- The first fully multinational agency in the country was Hindustan Thompson Associates (now JWT) in 1926.

First full-service Indian advertising agency

In 1934, Venkatrao Sista opened Sista Advertising and Publicity Services in Bombay as the first Indian agency offering creative work and space selling in the media. Sista, who came to the financial capital of India as a stenographer of the Great Indian Peninsular Railway, will always be associated with Khatau Voiles, popularized by his agency's campaign.

First Indianized foreign brand

Lux toilet soap, sold as the 'favourite beauty soap of film stars', signed on Hindi cinema actor Leela Chitnis as its first Indian model in 1941, in order to Indianize the brand.

First ads on TV

The first product to be advertised on TV was Gwalior Suitings in an advertisement that appeared in January 1976.

Horlicks: first patented brand

First ad agency abroad

Interads, a Delhi-based ad agency, was the first Indian advertising agency to open a foreign branch in Moscow, Russia, in 1962.

Most awards at the Cannes Lions

In 2022, India won 47 medals including five Grand Prix awards. Dentsu Creative won three Grand Prix awards, the highest by a single agency. It also became the agency of the year.

The Lion trophy

Firsts at the Cannes Lions

In 1996, the advertising fraternity bagged three awards at the International Advertising Festival in Cannes, France.

First commercials on radio

The first commercial came on Vividh Bharati in 1967.

First colour TV ad

An advertisement made for Bombay Dyeing was the first colour TV ad in 1982, the year that colour TV came to India.

Largest LED display screen – on water (aboard a ship/ boat/vessel)

On 21 March 2021, Zen Media Ltd LLP, a digital-first Make-in-India start-up, launched Broadcoasters, LED screens on waters in India, used as an advertising platform on a ship. The vessel *My Blue Papillon*, in the waters near the Bandra–Worli Sea Link, carried a screen measuring 20 m (65.61 ft) x 5 m (16.40 ft) – with a total area of 100 sq m (1076.39 sq ft). The LED screen was powered with a display of 10,000 NITs (Network Interface Taps) and auto-sensors to adjust picture brightness as per daylight.

India hosts G20 summit for the first time

The Group of Twenty (G20) is the premier intergovernmental forum for international economic cooperation. The forum plays an important role in shaping and strengthening global architecture and governance on all major international economic issues.

India held the presidency of the G20 from 1 December 2022 to 30 November 2023. The theme of India's G20 Presidency was Vasudhaiva Kutumbakam, or 'One Earth. One Family. One Future.'

G20 Members

The Group of Twenty (G20) comprises 19 countries (Argentina, Australia, Brazil, Canada, China, France, Germany, India, Indonesia, Italy, Japan, Republic of Korea, Mexico, Russia, Saudi Arabia, South Africa, Türkiye, the United Kingdom, and the United States) as well as the European Union. The G20 members represent around 85 per cent of the global GDP, over 75 per cent of the global trade, and about two-thirds of the world population.

Vasudhaiva Kutumbakam

The phrase *Vasudhaiva Kutumbakam* literally means 'the whole world is my family'.

How G20 Works

- The G20 presidency steers the G20 agenda for one year and hosts the summit. The G20 consists of two parallel tracks: the Finance Track and the Sherpa Track. Finance ministers and central bank governors lead the Finance Track while Sherpas lead the Sherpa Track.
- The G20 process from the Sherpa side is coordinated by the Sherpas of member countries, who are personal emissaries of the leaders. Finance Track is led by the finance ministers and central bank governors of the member countries. Within the two tracks, there are thematically oriented working groups in which representatives from the relevant ministries of the members as well as from invited/guest countries and various international organizations participate.
- The Finance Track is mainly led by the Ministry of Finance. These working groups meet regularly throughout the term of each presidency. The Sherpas oversee negotiations over the course of the year, discussing agenda items for the summit and coordinating the substantive work of the G20.
- In addition, there are Engagement Groups which bring together civil societies, parliamentarians, think tanks, women, youth, labour, businesses, and researchers of the G20 countries.
- The Group does not have a permanent secretariat. The presidency is supported by the troika: previous, current, and incoming presidency. During India's presidency, the troika comprised Indonesia, India, and Brazil.

AERO SPORTS

First jump from a microlight
Wing Commander U.K. Palat skydived from a powered hang-glider piloted by Captain K.A. Vasan from 8,000 ft at 7:40 a.m. on 18 October 1999 in Bangalore (now Bengaluru), Karnataka.

First international paramotor medallist
Appasaheb Bhimraj Dhus (b. 26 December 1970) from Maharashtra is the first Indian to win international medals in paramotor games. He won a gold medal in the Pure Economy Task category of the World Paramotor Championship Test Event at Lopburi, Thailand, held from 28 April to 7 May 2017. In the same event, Captain Prafulla Raj Singh won a silver medal in the Pure Navigation Task category.

First Indian woman to skydive over seven continents
Shital Mahajan (b. 19 September 1982) from Pune, Maharashtra, completed 705 skydives across seven continents during 2017–18, adding to her skydive at Skydiver Empuriabrava in Spain (Europe) in 2014. She skydived at Skydive Go Fly in Boituva, Brazil (South America); Skydive Utti in Sky Dance Skydiving Center, US (North America); Sydney Skydivers in Sydney (Australia); Patriot Hill (Antarctica); Skydive Pretoria, Johannesburg, South Africa (Africa); and Skydive Pattaya, Thailand (Asia), taking the total to seven continents.

First aerial world circumnavigation in a single-engine plane
Ravinder K. Bansal (b. 26 February 1949) from Clarence, New York, US, undertook an aerial circumnavigation in a Cessna 400 and flew solo, covering 36 cities over 20,959 nautical miles. He started from Buffalo, New York, US, on 4 July 2017 and returned on 20 August 2017. The expedition was undertaken to raise funds for the Rotary Ambala Cancer and General Hospital.

Rachel Thomas: first woman skydiver

First woman skydiver
Rachel Thomas (b. 9 August 1955) from Chittaranjan, West Bengal, was the first Indian woman to skydive from 2,133.6 m (7,000 ft) over the North Pole. She achieved this feat on 20 April 2022 to commemorate 150 years of the Indian Railways. An employee of the Indian Railways, Thomas was also the first woman to represent the country in a skydiving competition in 1987. She was honoured with the Padma Shri in 2005.

First paraglide from a high cliff
Anand Munje (b. 7 November 1956) from Kitty Hawk Ground School, Pune, Maharashtra, launched a flight from the 1,646 m (5,400 ft) high Kalsubai Peak, part of the Western Ghats in Maharashtra, on 25 February 1997. The flight covered 4 km in 11 mins.

Highest bungee jump – woman
Sudhalakshmi Thanigai Arasu (b. 2 July 1965) performed a 220 m (721 ft 9 in.) high bungee jump on 13 August 2010 at Diga Verzasca, Switzerland.

First balloon bungee jump
Major M.K. Yadav jumped from a hot-air balloon, which was at a height of 3,310.73 m (10,862 ft) on 18 August 1995 over Leh, Ladakh.

Ravinder Bansal

First at the Mantar Paragliding XC Open Championship
Prakash Chand Thakur won the first prize at the Mantar Paragliding XC Open Championship, organized from 18 to 24 July 2017 by the Asian Continental Paragliding Association in Mantar, Indonesia.

First BASE jump
- *Men*: Lieutenant Colonel Satyendra Verma (b. 24 August 1969), then an officer of the Indian Army from the Corps of Signals, carried out a BASE (Building, Antenna, Span, and Earth) jump from the 137.16 m (450 ft) high deck of the Pitampura TV Tower, New Delhi, on 29 October 2010. This feat was part of the centenary celebrations of the Corps of Signals and the silver jubilee of the Army Adventure Wing.
- *Women*: Archana Sardana (b. 1 April 1972) from Visakhapatnam, Andhra Pradesh, is India's first female BASE jumper. She performed 25 BASE jumps off a 122 m (400 ft) high bridge above a canyon in Utah, US, on 13 July 2010.

BASE jump: representative image

First to complete a BASE jump during day and night
Mayank Nagpal (b. 21 September 1983) from New Delhi became the first Indian to complete a BASE jump from all four platforms, during both day and night. For the day BASE number, he jumped

BASE jump

BASE jumping is an extreme sport where participants jump from fixed objects, such as buildings, antennas, spans (bridges), and Earth (cliffs), using a parachute to land safely. It is considered highly dangerous due to the low altitudes and short time for parachute deployment.

from Perrine Bridge, US (5 September 2014), a cliff called Crooked Stick in Idaho, US (11 September 2014), a mobile antenna in Gua Damai Xtreme Park, Malaysia (6 October 2015), and an under-construction building in Delhi, India (31 December 2016). For the Night BASE number he jumped from Perrine Bridge, US (7 September 2014), an antenna in Idaho, US (on 8 September 2014), an under-construction building in Delhi (26 June 2017) and Gua Damai Cliff, Malaysia (28 September 2018).

Highest BASE jump

Mayank Nagpal (b. 21 September 1983) from New Delhi erformed the highest BASE jump from the 3,080 m (10,105 ft) high point of Eiger Mountain in the Bernese Alps, Switzerland, on 24 July 2019.

Lowest BASE jump

Lieutenant Commander Mahesh V. Birajdar from the Indian Navy performed the lowest BASE jump from a 116 m (380 ft 6 in.) high span over a river in the Solang Valley, Himachal Pradesh, on 30 January 2011.

Highest hot-air balloon take-off

Indradhanush, the hot-air balloon of the Ballooning Club of India, piloted by the then club president Vishwa Bandhu Gupta along with pilot R.K. Wason, took off from the Kushok Bakula Rimpochee Airport (3,310.7 m/ 10,862 ft) in Leh, Ladakh, on 29 September 1988.

Highest and longest wingsuit flight

Lieutenant Colonel Satyendra Verma (b. 24 August 1969), a retired Indian Army officer, on 31 March 2018, jumped from 5,913.12 m (19,400 ft) using a hot-air balloon platform at Phalodi, Rajasthan. He flew in his wingsuit for 4 mins, covering 10 km across the Jodhpur desert.

Highest flight

Megha Jain (b. 21 September 1988) from New Delhi made the highest flight in an MiG-29 fighter jet, touching 18,400 m (60,367 ft 5 in.) at a top speed of 1,850 km/hr over Sokol Airbase in Nizhny Novgorod, Russia, on 16 February 2017.

MiG-29 fighter jet

Most microlight expeditions

Mountain Eagles, the Indian Army microlight formation flying team, based at Army Adventure Nodal Centre (Microlight and powered Hang-gliding), Mhow, Madhya Pradesh, conducted three expeditions in 13 months from February 2015. The first, with seven aircraft, covered 1,800 km in 10 flying days between 13 and 26 February 2015.

Parade of Corps of Signals

In the second one, commemorating the golden jubilee of the India–Pakistan war 1965, three microlights covered 3,050 km in 10 flying days from 5 to 14 September 2015. The third one, at the 15th reunion of the Corps of Signals, was from 9 to 17 February 2016, with six aircrafts covering 1,500 km in nine flying days. The core team remained the same in all three expeditions.

Highest skydive landing

Warrant Officer Anshu Kumar Tiwari (b. 3 February 1978) and Wing Commander Gajendra Yadava from the Indian Air Force jumped off an aircraft and landed at Khardung La, 5,481 m (17,982 ft) above mean sea level, on 8 October 2020.

Longest motor glider flight

Captain Surendra Prasad Sinha (b. 26 July 1968), director, Flying Operations, Civil Aviation Department, Government of Jharkhand, flew a Sinus 912 VT-GEE two-seater aircraft for 1,098.24 km for eight flying hours, making it the longest motor glider flight in the country. Along with his co-pilot Captain Anil Gill, he took off from Karnal, Haryana, on 13 March 2014 and reached Ranchi, Jharkhand, the next day.

Longest cross-country microlight expedition

The Cross India Air Expedition 2011, organized by the Indian Air Force, covered 7,600 km in 80 hrs 15 mins over 20 days. Wing Commander Akhilesh Chauhan piloted the two-seater microlight, while Squadron Leader Asha Vashisht, Squadron Leader N.D. Gholba, and Sergeant M.P. Singh joined him as co-pilots at different stages of the journey. The flight took off from the air force station at Hindon, Ghaziabad, Uttar Pradesh, on 8 February 2011, proceeded to Udhampur, Jammu and Kashmir, and traversed the length of the country, flying over Delhi, Jodhpur (Rajasthan), Vadodara (Gujarat), Pune (Maharashtra), Bangalore (now Bengaluru, Karnataka), Sulur (Tamil Nadu), and Thiruvananthapuram (Kerala). It returned to Hindon by the same route on 27 February 2011.

Longest paramotor expedition

The Indian Air Force paramotor team, with Wing Commander M.P.S. Solanki as leader, conducted a circumnavigation-of-India expedition called 'Pradakshina', covering 10,041.7 km in 53 days from 3 February to 26 March 2016. Flagged off from the air force station at Kalaikunda, West Bengal, the team flew along the periphery of the country before returning to Kalaikunda. They followed a clockwise route along the eastern and western coasts and the north-western and eastern regions, covering an average of 218.3 km per day.

First Asian triple amputee to complete a bungee jump

Tinkesh Kaushik (b. 21 June 1993) from Jhajjar, Haryana, became the first Asian triple amputee to perform a bungee jump from the world's highest canyon swing. He performed the jump from a height of 160 m (525 ft) on 25 November 2018 at The Last Resort, Kathmandu, Nepal.

Highest zipline by a disabled person

Vijay Kumar Devarkhyani (b. 13 March 1989) from Delhi zipped across Tower 1 and Tower 3 at a height of 473 ft for a distance of 250 ft at 9:58 p.m. on 19 May 2013 at the 40th level of Crown Regency Hotel and Tower, Philippines.

Vijay Kumar Devarkhyani: highest zipline by a disabled person

First visually impaired person to paraglide

Divyanshu Ganatra, who lost his eyesight due to glaucoma at 19 years, performed a solo paraglider flight over Kamshet near Pune, Maharashtra, on 30 April 2014. The flight up to 213.36 m (700 ft) lasted 1 min 30 seconds.

First to paraglide with a prosthetic leg

Lieutenant Colonel Dharam Dutt Goel (b. 14 August 1976) from Pune, Maharashtra, successfully performed solo paragliding on 19 October 2013 at Al-Hilal, Himachal Pradesh, thereby becoming the first Indian with a prosthetic leg to paraglide. He performed the paraglider flight from an altitude of 2,400 m (7,874 ft) for 25 mins.

First disabled skydiver in Asia

Major Devender Pal Singh (b. 13 September 1973) from Gurugram, Haryana, is the first disabled skydiver in Asia. A war-injured amputee veteran, Major Singh skydived from an altitude of 2,743.2 m (9,000 ft)on 28 March 2019 at the military cantonment in Nashik, Maharashtra.

Major DP Singh: first disabled skydiver in Asia

Most podium finishes in FAI F3M Championship

Harshil Virendra Mane (b. 3 March 1999) from Pune, Maharashtra, has six international podium finishes in the FAI F3M category championship of aeromodelling, the highest number by an Indian. He is also the first aeromodeller representing India in international championships including the World Cups conducted by the Federation Aeronautique Internationale (FAI).

Longest-harness hang-glider flight

Havildar Sanjeev Kumar from the Indian Army Hang-Gliding Team completed the longest-harness hang-glider flight from Suratgarh to Barmer, Rajasthan, on 12 December 2018. He covered 465.33 km on Fox hang-gliders powered by a Mosquito NRG harness. He covered the distance in 8 hrs 43 mins.

Most skydiving jumps

Rajkumar Balakrishnan (b. 1 April 1977) from Theni, Tamil Nadu, started performing skydiving jumps in February 2006 and completed his 10,000th jump on 23 March 2018.

Most hours logged in free fall

Rajkumar Balakrishnan (b. 1 April 1977) from Theni, Tamil Nadu, has logged a total of 84 hours in free fall while skydiving, up to 6 July 2018.

Microlight aircraft flight

- *First:* Flying at a cruising speed of 56 km/hr on a 90 kg tricycle-shaped aircraft, Lieutenant Anil Kumar Yadav covered 3,000 km from Jaisalmer, Rajasthan, to Calcutta (now Kolkata), West Bengal, in 31 days starting 21 September 1994.
- *Fastest:* Squadron Leader B.K. Das flew a microlight aircraft from Jaisalmer, Rajasthan, to Dibrugarh, Assam, covering 3,250 km during 1 - 23 February 1999.

Oldest woman skydiver

Usha Arun Mahajan (b. 20 November 1945) from Pune, Maharashtra, successfully performed a tandem skydive from an altitude of 4,114.8 m (13,500 ft) on 1 October 2017 in Pennsylvania, US, at the age of 71 years 10 months 11 days.

Representative image of tandem skydiving

Daring dives

Wing Commander Gajanand Yadava of the Indian Air Force (IAF) created four national records in the field of wingsuit skydive jumping in 2019 in Agra, Uttar Pradesh:

1. First wingsuit skydive jump from a high-speed aircraft (An-32),
2. Highest wingsuit jump from an altitude of 7,437.12 m (24,400 ft),
3. First to do a night-time wingsuit jump from 2,438.40 m (8,000 ft),
4. The only jumper to undertake a high-altitude night-time wingsuit jump from 3,657.60 m (12,000 ft), where he opened the chute at 914.40 m (3,000 ft) after doing wingsuit flying for 2,743.2 m (9,000 ft) Part of the IAF's skydiving team Akashganga and a parachute jump instructor, Wing Commander Yadava has taken more than 2,900 jumps to date and was awarded the Tenzing Norgay National Adventure Award 2019 in the air adventure category.

Skydiving from the highest altitude

Jithin Vijayan skydived from an altitude of 12,933 mt (42,431 ft) at Whiteville, Tennesse, US on 1 July 2023.

ROAD EXPEDITIONS

FOUR-WHEELER

Fastest East–West India expedition – group

Apurba Kumar Deka (b. 27 March 1975), Animesh Deka (b. 15 January 1982), and Md Zillur Rahman (b. 2 December 1975) from Guwahati, Assam, completed the fastest East–West India expedition from Tezu, Arunachal Pradesh, to Koteshwar, Gujarat, covering 3,771.4 km in 70 hrs 52 mins. The team drove a Renault Duster car, starting their journey on 27 October 2015 and ending the expedition on 30 October 2015.

Longest journey within a country – solo

Shashi Kapila (b. 3 November 1942) from New Delhi completed the longest journey in a Honda Mobilio car, covering 8,227 km in 105 hrs 15 mins. He started from Delhi at 6:00 a.m. on 12 November 2016 and reached back at 12:28 p.m. on 22 November 2016. The farthest location he travelled to was Kanniyakumari.

Eric Paul: fastest East–West India expedition by a disabled person – solo

Fastest East–West India expedition by a disabled person – solo

Eric Paul (b. 14 January 1988), a wheelchair-bound paraplegic from Rohini, New Delhi, completed the East–West India solo expedition in a hand-controlled Maruti Swift, covering 3,697 km in 4 days 18 hrs 55 mins. He started from Tezu, Arunachal Pradesh, on 30 November 2017 at 4:13 a.m., reaching Koteshwar, Gujarat, at 11:43 p.m. on 4 December 2017.

Fastest Four Corners of India expedition – solo

Suresh Joseph (b. 14 May 1958) from Tamil Nadu successfully completed the four corners of India tour (Kanniyakumari, Tamil Nadu; Koteshwar, Gujarat; Leh, Ladakh; and Tezu, Arunachal Pradesh), covering 13,214 km in 403 hrs. Driving a Mahindra XUV500, he started his expedition on 7 May 2015 and ended it on 12 June 2015.

Fastest GQ expedition – group – women

Sukraty Saxena, Rupam Devedi, Swaranjali Saxena, and Apala Rajvanshi completed the Golden Quadrilateral (GQ) expedition, covering a distance of 6,263 km in 6 days 14 hrs 5 mins. They started their expedition at 1:35 a.m. on 10 May 2023 from India Gate, New Delhi, and concluded it at 4:30 p.m. on 16 May 2023 at Subroto Park Air Force Station, New Delhi.

Fastest GQ expedition – group – women

Fastest North–South expedition – group

Sameer A.S. (b. 14 December 1986), Noufal K.N. (b. 30 May 1985), and Bibin Krishnan (b. 20 April 1984) from Kerala set a record for the fastest North–South India group expedition, covering 3,870 km in 49 hrs 34 mins. The trio started from Leh, Ladakh, at 7:05 a.m. on 1 September 2021, reaching Kanniyakumari, Tamil Nadu, at 8:39 a.m. on 3 September 2021.

Fastest East–West India expedition – group

Apurba Kumar Deka (b. 27 March 1975), Animesh Deka (b. 15 January 1982), and Md Zillur Rahman (b. 2 December 1975) from Guwahati, Assam, completed the fastest East–West India expedition from Tezu, Arunachal Pradesh, to Koteshwar, Gujarat, covering 3,771.4 km in 70 hrs 52 mins. The team drove a Renault Duster car, starting their journey on 27 October 2015 and ending the expedition on 30 October 2015.

Trailblazing Firsts

First All-India expedition – group

Arun Kumar Basra and Kamaljit Singh Virdi from Rapid Action India completed an all-India car expedition in their Fiat Padmini, covering 15,179 km in 19 days 19 hrs 5 mins. They were flagged off from Delhi on 5 January 1998 and returned on 25 January 1998.

First Four Corners of India expedition – solo

Dr S.S. Chaudhari (b. 7 March 1962) from Jalgaon, Maharashtra, completed a solo drive connecting the four corners of India, covering 13,834 km in 26 days 22 hrs 15 mins. Driving a Maruti SX4 car, he set out from Kanniyakumari, Tamil Nadu, on 30 October 2014. He reached Tezu, Lohit District, Arunachal Pradesh, on 8 November 2014; Leh, Ladakh, on 16 November 2014; Koteshwar, Kachchh District, Gujarat, on 22 November 2014; and concluded the expedition at Kanniyakumari on 26 November 2014.

First South-North India round expedition – solo

Suresh Joseph (b. 14 May 1958) from Tamil Nadu is the first person to complete the trailblazing North–South India round expedition trip in 2012 and, in the process, breaking the record of the fastest North–South solo expedition. He started his expedition from Kanniyakumari, Tamil Nadu, on 2 July 2012 and reached Leh, Ladakh, on 7 July 2012, covering 3,811 km in 129 hrs 30 mins. Four days later, he was back on the trip, taking off from Leh on 11 July 2012. He reached Kanniyakumari on 15 July 2012. He drove a Maruti Swift car for the journey.

First Trans-Himalayan expedition – solo

Suresh Joseph (b. 14 May 1958) from Tamil Nadu set out in a Ford Endeavour to create a new record for a Trans-Himalayan solo trip, which he accomplished in 18 days 13 hrs 15 mins. Starting his journey from Jammu in Jammu and Kashmir on 21 August 2015, he reached Tezu in Arunachal Pradesh on 8 September 2015. Joseph covered 5,845 km across nine Indian states, Nepal and Bhutan, and crossed altitudes of up to 2,554.2 m (8,380 ft).

First disabled person to reach Umling La – solo

Eric Paul (b. 14 January 1988) from Delhi was the first disabled person to reach Umling La, Ladakh on 6 July 2022 at 2:57 p.m. He started on 1 July 2022 from Delhi and covered a distance of 1,260 km in 126 hrs 27 mins. He is paralysed from below the chest and drove his hand-controlled car to this high altitude.

First West–East India round expedition – solo

Daljit Singh Matharoo (b. 29 September 1986) completed a solo West–East–West India expedition, covering 7,715 km in 217 hrs 25 mins. He broke the record for the fastest solo East–West India expedition by covering 3,832 km in 94 hrs 44 mins. He started in his Maruti Zen car from Koteshwar, Kachchh District, Gujarat, on 27 April 2018, and reached Tezu, Arunachal Pradesh, on 1 May 2018. He started back on 1 May 2018 and reached Koteshwar on 6 May 2018.

Daljit Singh Matharoo

Sagar Thakar and Kanak Barsadia

Longest journey within a country – group

Sagar Thakar (b. 30 June 1982) and Kanak Barsadia (b. 14 February 1984) from Surat, Gujarat, completed the longest journey in a Maruti Swift Dzire car, covering 60,830 km in 82 days. They set off from Bardoli, Gujarat, on 20 March 2017 and reached back on 12 June 2017.

Longest distance travelled across countries – solo

Hitendra Sharma (b. 11 January 1978) from Gwalior, Madhya Pradesh, successfully undertook a solo expedition by road, covering 30,195 km across 11 Asian countries in a Honda Amaze car in 92 days. Starting from Gwalior in Madhya Pradesh, India, on 10 February 2017, he reached Bangladesh, driving through India, Myanmar, Thailand, Laos, Vietnam, Cambodia, Malaysia, Singapore, Bhutan, and Nepal, and returned to India on 21 May 2017.

Hitendra Sharma: longest distance travelled across countries – solo

Fastest North–South expedition – solo

Dhruveer Singh Gandhi (b. 6 March 1985) from Mumbai, Maharashtra, completed the North–South expedition, covering a distance of 3,819.17 km in 56 hrs 20 mins. He started his expedition at 4:45 a.m. on 10 September 2021 from the office of the deputy commissioner GST Division, Srinagar, and concluded it at 1:05 p.m. on 12 September 2021 at the deputy superintendent of police's office at Kanniyakumari.

TWO-WHEELER (MOTORCYCLE)

UP TO 150 CC

First Trans-Himalayan expedition – solo

Rajeev Kumar Mondal from Burdwan, West Bengal, successfully completed a solo two-wheeler expedition along the Trans-Himalayan route covering 7,120 km in 303 hrs 58 mins of travel time. Kick-starting the expedition on a 150 cc Hero Honda Achiever from Guwahati, Assam, on 5 May 2013, he first went to Arunachal Pradesh and then, passing through Bhutan, West Bengal, Nepal, Uttarakhand, and Himachal Pradesh, reached Srinagar in Jammu and Kashmir on 12 July 2013. He crossed 22 passes including Khardung La at 5,602 m (18,380 ft).

151–450 CC

First North–South India round expedition by a disabled person – solo

Vadivel Baluchamy (b. 14 June 1990), a disabled person from Madurai, Tamil Nadu, completed the first North–South solo round expedition by a disabled person, covering 9,136 km in 576 hrs 23 mins. He started on a Royal Enfield Classic 350 bike from Kanniyakumari on 30 August 2018 at 4:25 p.m. and travelled to Leh, Ladakh. He returned to Kanniyakumari on 22 September at 8:18 p.m.

Fastest East–West India expedition – solo

Dr S.T. Thomas (b. 8 January 1987) from Tamil Nadu covered 3,729 km from Tezu, Arunachal Pradesh, to Koteshwar, Gujarat, in 68 hrs 18 mins to set a new record in the East–West India two-wheeler expedition category. He started his journey on his Honda CBR 250R bike on 20 March 2016 and concluded the expedition on 23 March 2016.

Fastest All-India expedition – solo

Srinath K.A. from Chennai has completed the all-India expedition on 31 March 2024 on his TVS Apache RR310 covering a distance of 16,433 km in 25 days. He began his journey on 7 March 2024 and completed it on 31 March 2024 travelling through 28 states and 8 union territories.

Fastest Four Corners of India expedition – solo

Vishvesh Dhirendrakumar Mehta (b. 10 June 1980) from Jamnagar, Gujarat, completed the fastest solo expedition connecting the four corners of India, covering 11,217 km in 313 hrs 51 mins. Riding a Royal Enfield Classic 350, he set out from Koteshwar, Gujarat, on 21 May 2019 and returned to Koteshwar

Khardung La

Khardung La, at an altitude of 5,359 mt (17,582 ft), is one of the highest motorable mountain passes in the world, located in the Ladakh region of India. It serves as a gateway to the Nubra Valley and offers stunning panoramic views of the surrounding Himalayan peaks. Going on an expedition to Khardung La is a challenging yet exhilarating experience due to the high altitude and unpredictable weather conditions. The trail passes through rugged terrain, barren landscapes, and snow-clad mountains, testing both physical endurance and mental stamina. Trekkers need to be well acclimatized to the altitude, as the thin air can make breathing difficult. Despite the challenges, reaching the pass is highly rewarding, offering an unmatched sense of achievement and breathtaking vistas of Ladakh's stark beauty.

Vishvesh Dhirendrakumar Mehta

after covering Kanniyakumari, Tamil Nadu; Leh, Ladakh; and Tezu, Arunachal Pradesh, on 8 June 2019. His break time was 113 hrs.

Fastest GQ expedition by a disabled person – solo

Vadivel Baluchamy (b. 14 June 1990), completed the fastest Golden Quadrilateral (GQ) expedition by a disabled person, covering 6,723 km in 14 days 9 hrs 30 mins. He started on a Royal Enfield Classic 350 bike from Chennai, Tamil Nadu, on 25 September 2017 and travelled to Kolkata, Delhi, and Mumbai, returning to Chennai on 9 October 2017.

Longest journey within the country – solo

Krishanu Kona (b. 27 September 1991) from Delhi travelled 50,338 km on his motorcycle in 224 days to set the record for the longest motorcycle journey in India. He started on a Bajaj Pulsar NS200 bike on 30 August 2015 from Delhi and returned on 9 April 2016.

Longest distance covered within the country by a disabled person – solo

Mahinder Singh Raghuwanshi (b. 2 October 1987), who has 70 per cent disability and a prosthetic limb, covered 5,331.5 km on an Enfield Bullet 350 bike in 17 days. He started from his hometown Mhow, Madhya Pradesh, on 3 June 2016 and went up to Khardung La (5,359 m/17,582 ft) in Leh, Ladakh, returning to Mhow on 19 June 2016.

OVER 450 CC

Fastest All-India expedition – solo

Prashant Kumar (b. 14 July 1987) from Bengaluru, Karnataka, completed the all-India expedition on 7 November 2019 on his Triumph Tiger XCA 800 bike, covering 16,305 km in 23 days 9 hrs

Prashant Kumar

Pallavi Fauzdar

46 mins. He started from Hyderabad, Telangana, on 15 October 2019 and returned on 7 November 2019, travelling through the then 29 states and five Union Territories.

Fastest GQ expedition – solo

Shraiyans Mittal from Noida, Uttar Pradesh completed the GQ solo motorcycling expedition, covering a distance of 6116.6 km in 87 hrs 13 mins on a Royal Enfieldn Interceptor 650 between 18 March 2022 and 21 March 2022.

GENERAL

First to cross Umling La – solo

Pallavi Fauzdar (b. 20 December 1979) from Delhi was the first to cross Umling La pass on 4 August 2017 at 3:16 p.m. It is the highest motorable pass in the world, situated at an altitude of 5,882.64 m (19,300 ft) above sea level. On her expedition, she even named the Bonni La, situated at an altitude of 5,083 m (16,677 ft), which was unnamed before.

Largest rally (less than 100 km) by women riders – multiple venues

The largest two-wheeler rally by only women riders was organized by the Akhil Bharatiya Terapanth Mahila Mandal on 8 March 2020, International Women's Day. As many as 6,205 women rode distances ranging from 1.5 to 10 km at locations like Udaipur, Ahmedabad, Balotra, Surat, and Delhi. The rally was held as part of their 'I Respect' campaign to emphasize the need for women to respect one another for their choices.

Akhil Bharatiya Terapanth Mahila Mandal

Longest ride while standing anywhere on the bike – solo

Vishwajeet Bhatia (b. 22 January 1983) of the Border Security Force (BSF) successfully covered 95.42 km while standing on the side footrest of the Royal Enfield 350. He completed the ride in 2 hrs 36 mins on 28 December 2022 at 25 Battalion, BSF, R.K. Wadhwa parade ground, Chhawla, New Delhi. He performed this stunt without any belts, harnesses, or supporting equipment.

Longest ride while standing on a structure – solo – woman

Satabdi Dhar (b. 23 December 1990) of the Border Security Force performed a continuous ride on a 2.49 m (8 ft 2.4 in) ladder fitted on a Royal Enfield 350 for 2 hr 30 mins on 26 December 2022. She covered a distance of 76 km at 25 Battalion, BSF, R.K. Wadhwa parade ground, Chhawla, New Delhi. She performed this stunt without any belts, harnesses, or supporting equipment.

Satabdi Dhar

Longest ride while standing on a structure – group

Inspector Awadhesh Kumar Singh (b. 19 April 1980) and Constable Sudhakar (b. 8 July 1987) of the Border Security Force performed a continuous ride on a 3.35 m (11 ft) ladder fitted on a Royal Enfield 350 for 2.5 hrs. They covered a distance of 75 km at 25 Battalion, BSF, R.K. Wadhwa parade ground, Chhawla, New Delhi. They performed this stunt without any belts, harnesses, or supporting equipment.

Longest ride on a structure facing backwards – solo

Inspector Awadhesh Kumar Singh (b. 19 April 1980) of the Border Security Force performed a continuous ride on a 3.42 m (11 ft 3.6 in) pole fitted on a Royal Enfield 350 for 4 hrs 37 mins while facing backwards. He covered a distance of 169 km at 25 Battalion, BSF, R.K. Wadhwa parade ground, Chhawla, New Delhi. He performed this stunt without any belts, harnesses, or supporting equipment.

Longest ride while standing anywhere on the bike – solo – woman

Inspector Himanshu Sirohi (b. 4 May 1988) of the Border Security Force successfully covered 178 km while standing on the side bracket of a Royal Enfield 350. She completed the ride in 6 hrs 2 mins on 24 December 2022 at 25 Battalion, BSF, R.K. Wadhwa parade ground, Chhawla, New Delhi. She performed this stunt without any belts, harnesses, or supporting equipment.

Himanshu Sirohi

Longest ride while sitting on a bike facing backwards – solo – woman

Constable Rajwinder Kaur (b. 1 May 1986) of the Border Security Force performed a continuous ride while sitting facing backwards on a Royal Enfield 350. She covered a distance of 32 km in 1 hr on 28 December 2022 at 25 Battalion, BSF, R.K. Wadhwa parade ground, Chhawla, New Delhi. She performed this stunt without any belts, harnesses, or supporting equipment.

TWO-WHEELER (BICYCLE)

GEARED

Fastest East–West expedition – solo

Naresh Kumar Rajendran (b. 3 June 1992) from Vellore, Tamil Nadu, completed the fastest East–West solo expedition on a geared bicycle by covering 3,613 km in 10 days 8 hrs 57 mins. He started from Tezu, Arunachal Pradesh, at 4:00 a.m. on 5 December 2018 and ended at Koteshwar, Gujarat, at 12:57 p.m. on 15 December 2018.

Fastest GQ expedition – solo

Bharat Pannu (b. 8 May 1983) from Bengaluru, Karnataka, completed the Golden Quadrilateral (GQ) solo expedition, covering a distance of 5,938.2 km in 14 days 23 hrs 52 mins on his geared bicycle. He started his expedition at 12:08 a.m. on 16 October 2020 from India Gate, New Delhi, and concluded it at 12:20 a.m. on 31 October 2020.

Fastest North–South expedition – solo

Nimesh Mansukhbhai Jivrajani (b. 11 February 1980) from Bhavnagar, Gujarat, completed a solo North–South India expedition on a geared bicycle, covering 3,400 km in 14 days 16 hrs 20 mins. He started from Jammu, Jammu and Kashmir, at 5:40 a.m. on 24 December 2018 and reached Kanniyakumari, Tamil Nadu, at 10:00 p.m. on 7 January 2019.

Longest distance covered within the country – solo

Karan Singh Jagawat (b. 1 March 1948) covered a distance of 20,948 km on his geared cycle in 178 days. He started his journey on 23 April 2017 from Jaipur, Rajasthan, and returned to Jaipur on 18 October 2017. He travelled through Koteshwar, Gujarat; Tezu, Arunachal Pradesh; Khardung La, Ladakh; and Kanniyakumari, Tamil Nadu.

GEARLESS

Fastest North–South expedition – group

Ashwani Kumar Singh (b. 14 August 1995) from Deoria, Uttar Pradesh, and Akash Yadav (b. 1 February 1990) from Azamgarh, Uttar Pradesh, completed the

Largest moving human pyramid – women

On 27 December 2022, the female team of 38 women led by Inspector Himanshu Sirohi of the Border Security Force formed a human pyramid on nine Royal Enfield 350 bikes. They covered more than 1 km in 2 mins 10 secs at Kartavya Path between Vijay Chowk and India Gate, New Delhi. They performed this stunt without any belts, harnesses, or supporting equipment.

B S F
B S F
B S F
B S F

fastest North–South India expedition by cycle, covering 4,197 km in 14 days 15 hrs 37 mins. The duo started from Leh, Ladakh, on 13 June 2016 and reached Kanniyakumari, Tamil Nadu, on 27 June 2016.

Fastest North–South expedition – solo

Saurabh Bharat Zagade (b. 28 October 1996) from Pune, Maharashtra, completed a solo North–South India expedition on a gearless bicycle, covering a distance of 3,440 km in 14 days 7 hrs. He started the expedition from Dharmal, Jammu and Kashmir, at 6:25 a.m. on 15 April 2019 and reached Kanniyakumari, Tamil Nadu, at 1:25 p.m. on 29 April 2019.

Oldest Super Randonneuse

Ela Ghose (b. 8 April 1961) successfully completed four brevets organized by Noida Randonneurs and Delhi Randonneurs (a part of Audax India Randonneurs) under the aegis of Audax Club Parisien of France, and earned the title of Super Randonneuse in the 2018–19 season. A randonneuring event is called a randonnée or brevet, and a rider who has completed a 200 km event is called a randonneur. The Super Randonneur/Randonneuse title is awarded on the completion of a series of four brevets within a single (cycling) year, say, November 2018–October 2019. The four brevets cover 200 km (completed within 13 hrs 30 mins), 300 km (completed within 20 hrs), 400 km (completed within 27 hrs) and 600 km (completed within 40 hrs).

Ela Ghose: oldest Super Randonneuse

Randonneuse

A randonneuse is a long-distance touring bike designed for endurance rides, offering comfort and stability over extended distances. It features a durable frame, wider tires, and mounts for carrying gear, ideal for randonneuring events.

Saurabh Bharat Zagade: fastest North–South expedition – gearless – solo

GENERAL

Largest bicycling marathon

Organized by Vodafone India, the second edition of the Vodafone Cycling Marathon held in Bengaluru, Karnataka, on 1 March 2015, attracted 6,123 cyclists. The event was held under four different categories: Champion Race (60 km), Passion Race (40 km), Green Ride (20 km) and Fashion Ride (5 km). It was conducted under the aegis of the Cycle Federation of India, supported by Bengaluru City Traffic Police. Around 5,000 cyclists took part in the first edition of this marathon.

Longest tandem bicycling – women

Sheetal Bambulkar (b. 27 October 1978) from Mumbai, Maharashtra, and Dr Meera Velankar (b. 11 December 1975) from Bengaluru, Karnataka, completed a tandem cycling brevet ride of 206 km in 12 hrs 27 mins in Vadodara, Gujarat, on 20 December 2015.

First tandem bicycling

Ashok N. Bhanushali (b. 21 May 1974) from Mumbai, Maharashtra, and Dr Meera Velankar (b. 11 December 1975) from Bengaluru, Karnataka, completed India's first 300 km brevet ride on a tandem bicycle. The feat was part of an event organized by Surat Randonneurs on 10 July 2016. The duo started the ride from M.T.B. College, Surat, Gujarat, and covered a distance of 309 km in 17 hrs 36 mins.

Fastest Asian to cycle across the world

Vedangi Kulkarni (b. 1998) from Pune, Maharashtra, became the fastest Asian to cycle across the world. She started her expedition from Perth, Australia, in July 2018 and reached Kolkata, West Bengal, on 23 December 2018. She crossed 29,000 km in 159 days, pedalling up to 300 km every day.She covered 14 countries including New Zealand, Canada, Iceland, Portugal, Spain, France, Belgium, Germany, Denmark, Sweden, Finland, and Russia, and endured temperatures ranging between –20°C and 37°C.

Most consecutive cycling expeditions – 100 km

Gurpreet Singh (b. 28 June 1972) from Jalandhar, Punjab, cycled at least 100 kms per day consecutively for 300 days from 19 May 2020 to 14 March 2021 with geared Merida Sculptura 400 and Trek FX2 bicycles in Jalandhar, Punjab.

All-India tour on a mono-wheeler

Subrata Chakraborty (b. 5 November 1976) from Kolkata, West Bengal, completed an all-India solo expedition on a monocycle, covering 10,500 km in 256 days. He started his journey from Raj Bhavan, Kolkata, on 8 September 2000 and returned to Kolkata on 21 May 2001. He passed through 17 states of the country, viz., West Bengal, Odisha, Andhra Pradesh, Tamil Nadu, Kerala, Karnataka, Goa, Maharashtra, Gujarat, Rajasthan, Haryana, Delhi, Uttar Pradesh, Madhya Pradesh, Bihar, Assam, and Arunachal Pradesh.

Monocycle: representative image

« **Sappers** are military engineers specialized in tasks like fortifications, demolitions, and clearing obstacles, crucial for battlefield logistics and mobility. They also construct bridges, roads, and tunnels, enabling safe passage for troops. »

WATER SPORTS

First circumnavigation of the globe – group

On 28 September 1985, ten sappers, led by Colonel T.P.S. Chowdhury, set off on INS *Trishna*, for a 55,000 km sail in an 11.3 m (37 ft) long, 10.5 tonne fibreglass yacht. They sailed from Mumbai, Maharashtra, to Maldives and Mauritius, and then to St Helena Island. Crossing the Equator for the second time, they sailed into the Port of Belem in Brazil, then through the Panama Canal towards the Galapagos Islands, the Polynesian Islands and Bali, reaching Mumbai on 10 January 1987.

First sailing expedition on the Brahmaputra River and longest on any Indian river

Sixty NCC cadets of Assam undertook a 220 km long sailing expedition on the capricious Brahmaputra River in three whaler boats of the NCC naval units, with safety and support vessels provided by the Indian Army Eastern Command. This maiden expedition named 'Lachit-1' was flagged off at Biswanath Chariali, Assam, and flagged in at Pandu Port, Guwahati, on 16 October 2019.

First to sail down the Ganga River

Captain P.P. Sabharwal and Captain S.N. Dubey performed the first sail down the Ganga River in a racing craft from Chandi Ghat at Haridwar, Uttarakhand, to Kolkata, West Bengal, from 26 to 28 July 1960. The total distance they covered was 1,931.23 km.

First circumnavigation – man – solo

Commander Dilip Donde of the Indian Navy completed a solo circumnavigation of the globe in 276 days. He covered 21,600 nautical miles sailing on INSV *Mhadei*, a 17 m (56 ft) long sailing boat fitted with high-tech navigation and communication equipment. He embarked on the voyage on 19 August 2009. On return, his boat touched base at Sunk Rock Lighthouse at Mumbai harbour on 22 May 2010. The expedition was part of the Indian Navy's 'Sagar Parikrama' project.

INS *Trishna*

First circumnavigation of the globe by a disabled sailor

Major Ashok Kumar Singh, a permanent member of the INS *Trishna* crew and winner of the National Adventure Award in 1994, went around the globe in 1985. It was the longest journey undertaken by a disabled person.

First circumnavigation – woman – solo

On 15 October 1988, Ujwala Rai became not only the first Indian woman, but also the first Asian one, to sail around the world after a 17-month voyage in *Jaykus III*, a 9.75 m (32 ft) Vancouver-class sailboat.

First expedition on the Beas River

A team of 13 people from Atal Bihari Vajpayee Institute of Mountaineering and Allied Sports (ABVIMAS), Manali, Himachal Pradesh, was the first to raft

Representative image of the Beas

across the length of the Beas River from 23 to 26 October 2019. Led by Colonel Neeraj Rana, the director of ABVIMAS, the 230 km long rafting expedition was undertaken with two rafts and three kayaks from Manali to Dehra Gopipur Bridge at Pong Dam.

First catamaran sailing expedition

A team of sailors from the Artillery Water Sports Association, Hyderabad, Telangana, completed the Sarvatra Sailing Expedition, a 1,364 km long marine voyage along the eastern coast of India. The longest such expedition in the country, it was launched from Marina Beach, Chennai, Tamil Nadu, on 18 December 2011 and culminated at Gopalpur, Odisha, on 3 January 2012. They also set records of sailing 153 km non-stop in a day on 21 December 2011 and of 15 hours of non-stop sailing on 31 December 2011.

First sailing expedition around the Indian peninsula

Alok Kumar Yadav (b. 20 June 1984) from EME Sailing Association completed the first sailing expedition around the Indian peninsula. He started from Haldia, West Bengal on 21 October 2018 and reached Porbandar, Gujarat on 1 December 2018. He covered a distance of 4,597 nautical miles in 41 days.

First rafting event in the country

The Indo-US Upper Ganga Rafting Expedition in 1984 was the first rafting expedition in India led by American Ken Warren and Avinash Kohli. The expedition rafted sections of the Bhagirathi and Alaknanda Rivers till Devprayag, and the Ganga River from Devprayag to Rishikesh in Uttarakhand.

Youngest in the world to complete the Oceans Seven Challenge

Prabhat Koli (b. 27 July 1999) from Navi Mumbai, Maharashtra, became the youngest person in the world, at the age of 23, to complete the Ocean Seven Challenge on 1 March 2023. He completed the challenge in 8 hrs 41 mins, crossing the Cook Strait between New Zealand's North and South Islands amid bad weather. He is also the recipient of Tenzing Norgay National Adventure Award.

First Asian woman to swim across the seven seas

Bula Chowdhury (b. 2 January 1970) from West Bengal was the first Asian woman to swim across the seven seas: the Arctic Ocean, the North Atlantic Ocean, the South Atlantic Ocean, the Indian Ocean, the North Pacific Ocean, the South Pacific Ocean, and the Antarctic Ocean. She crossed the English Channel twice in 1989 and 1999, and in 2005 she became the first woman to swim across sea channels off five continents. She received the Arjuna Award in 1990 and the Padma Shri in 2008.

First to complete the Ocean Seven Challenge

Rohan Dattatrey More (b. 30 October 1985) from Pune, Maharashtra, became the first Asian swimmer at the age of 32, to complete the Ocean Seven challenge on 9 February 2018 when he swam across the Cook Strait between North and South Islands of New Zealand in 8 hrs 37 mins. He became the ninth swimmer in the world to complete the difficult open-water swimming challenge that includes the English Channel, the North Channel, the Molokai Channel, the Catalina Channel, the Tsugaru Channel, the Strait of Gibraltar, and the Cook Strait.

First and youngest Asian woman to swim in Antarctic waters

Bhakti Sharma (b. 30 November 1989) from Udaipur, Rajasthan, is the first Asian woman and the youngest in the world to set a record in open swimming in Antarctic waters. She swam 2.3 km in 41 hrs 14 mins, in temperatures of around 1°C, breaking the record of L. Cox (US) and L. Pugh (Britain). She was awarded the Tenzing Norgay National Adventure Award in 2010.

First saturation dive

Commodore Vimal Kumar of the Indian Navy conducted the first saturation dive in May 1985 in a decompression chamber, using a mix of helium and oxygen, on INHS *Ashvini* in Mumbai. Pratap Singh and T. Vinod Rao were pressurized to a depth of 67 m (219 ft 10 in.) on 16 May 1985 and stayed in saturation for six days.

Fastest Asian swimmer to cross the Gibraltar Strait

Shubham Dhananjay Vanmali (b. 20 December 1995) from Mumbai became the fastest Asian swimmer to cross the Strait of Gibraltar, completing 16.7 km from Isla de Tarifa in Spain to Point Cires in Morocco in 3 hrs 16 mins on 14 August 2014. Earlier, Vanmali had also

Rohan Dattatrey More

The Gibraltar Strait

swum the English Channel (England to France), crossing the channel in 12 hrs 42 mins on 4 August 2014, and the 35 km long stretch from Dharamtar in Raigad district, Maharashtra, to the Gateway of India in Mumbai in 8 hrs 1 min 17 secs on 21 January 2014.

First deep-bounce dive

Commodore Vimal Kumar of the Indian Navy was the first person to dive to a depth of 160 m in a diving bell in the Black Sea in 1970. He explored the bottom of the sea for about 10 mins. After surfacing, he underwent a decompression schedule for 10 hrs.

First canoeing expedition

Sheo Shankar Gope and Ravindra Kumar Bhuyan were team leaders of a canoeing expedition that started from Kolkata on 6 July 1991. They paddled upstream on the Ganga and sailed a distance of 2,000 km, touching Bhagalpur, Mokama, Patna, Allahabad (now Prayagraj), and Etawah, reaching Delhi on 25 September 1991.

First backstroke swimming across the Strait of Gibraltar without neoprene

Tejesh Vishnu Parsekar (b. 30 May 1990) from Mumbai, Maharashtra, became the first Indian and second in the world (since 1928) to successfully complete backstroke swimming across the Strait of Gibraltar from Isla de Tarifa, Spain, to Perejil Island near Morocco on 16 August 2010. He was the first in the world to complete it without neoprene (protective suit). He covered 19. 4 km in 5 hrs 21 mins.

First to swim from mainland to Anacapa Island

Prabhat Raju Koli (b. 27 July 1999) from Navi Mumbai, successfully swam from Hollywood Beach, Oxnard, to Anacapa Island in 6 hrs 22 mins 17 secs on 10 July 2019. The route was 20 km long in open sea.

First woman to cross the English Channel – solo

Arati Saha (b. 24 September 1940) from West Bengal became the first Indian woman to cross the English Channel on 29 September 1959. She swam from Cape Gris Nez, France, to Sandgate, England, in 16 hrs 20 mins.

First to swim the English Channel thrice – solo

- *Men*: Taranath Narayan Shenoy (b. 1958) from Maharashtra became the first person to cross the English Channel three times by 1985. Deaf and nearly blind, he had previously swum across the channel in 1983 and 1984.
- *Women*: Rashmi Sharma (b. 1988) from Kolkata became the first woman to cross the English Channel three times by 2009. She had previously swum across the channel in 2006 and 2007.

King of Gibraltar

B. R. Ghadge of Mumbai Police, Maharashtra, crossed the shark-infested and freezing Strait of Gibraltar (Spain–Morocco) four times. He was conferred the title 'King of Gibraltar' by the Gibraltar Strait Association in August 2002 as he completed the fourth feat in 6 hrs 10 mins on 2 August 2002. He was also the first Indian to cross the

Representative image of the Ganga River

26 km long Toroneos Gulf, Greece, in 10 hrs 43 mins on 20 July 2002.

First to complete the Round-Trip Angel Island marathon

Shubham Dhananjay Vanmali (b. 20 December 1995) from Mumbai, Maharashtra, was the first Indian to complete the Round-Trip Angel Island marathon swimming. He completed the 16.1 km marathon swim in 10 hrs in San Francisco, California, US, on 24 May 2018. He is also the youngest male swimmer and 12th in the world to complete this challenging bay-water swim marathon.

First woman to swim the Gibraltar Strait

Aarti Pradhan from Maharashtra became the first Indian woman to swim the Strait of Gibraltar in 1988. She covered the distance of 22.2 km in 7 hrs 17 mins from Isla de Tarifa, Spain, to Morocco. She received the Arjuna Award in 1988.

Most stand-up paddle-boarding

Kumaran M. (b. 2 March 1981) from Chennai had completed standup paddle-boarding on 19 different waterbodies, including 17 in India and one each in Sri Lanka and Malaysia, as on 30 June 2016.

First surfing and stand-up paddle competition

The Surfing Federation of India, with the Kerala Tourism Department, organized Spice Coast Open, India's first official national surfing and stand-up paddle (SUP) competition at Kovalam Beach, Kerala, from 3 to 5 May 2013. The three-day event had more than one hundred participants in surfing contests under five categories and SUP races under two.

First to complete the Triple Crown

Taranath Narayan Shenoy (b. 1958) from Maharashtra became the world's second swimmer and the first Indian to complete the Triple Crown of Open Water Swimming when he crossed the 32.2 km long Catalina Channel (or San Pedro Channel), separating Santa Catalina Island from the southern Californian mainland, US), on 25 August 1987. Deaf and nearly blind, he had previously swum the 20 Bridges Swim (a 45.9 km circumnavigation of Manhattan Island, New York City, US) on 9 August 1987 and the English Channel on 18 August 1983.

Longest stand-up paddle-boarding – group

Sri Krishnan (b. 31 July 1991) and Siddharth C. (b. 6 July 1992) from Chennai, Tamil Nadu, accomplished the longest stand-up paddle-boarding in the open sea, covering 31 km in the Bay of Bengal on 15 April 2016. They started at Kovalam Beach, Kerala, and paddled to reach Marina Beach, Tamil Nadu, covering the distance in 6 hrs 27 mins.

Most rivers rafted in a month

National Institute of Mountaineering and Allied Sports (NIMAS), Dirang, Arunachal Pradesh, conducted an expedition with seven members, namely, Colonel Sarfaraz Singh, Naib Subedar Jadhav Laxman Vishnu, Havaldar Loushambam Labango Singh, Havaldar Darshan Singh, Lance Naik Patil Suraj Ravindra, Lance Naik Himmat Singh, and Mr Tosap Rime, and rafted seven rivers in one month. They rafted on Kameng, Dibang, Noa Dihing, Lohit, Subansiri, Siyom, and Siang in Arunachal Pradesh from 23 November 2020 to 23 December 2020, covering a total distance of 720.21 km.

Longest social campaign through an adventure sport

The National Mission for Clean Ganga, operated under the Department of Water Resources, River Development, and Ganga Rejuvenation, Ministry of Jal Shakti, Government of India, organized the Ganga Aamantran Abhiyaan – a river-rafting and kayaking expedition on the Ganga River, conducted between 10 October and 12 November 2019 with a team of nine members. The expedition started from Devprayag and culminated at Ganga Sagar after covering 2,500 km. They spread the message of water conservation and river rejuvenation.

Longest kayaking – solo

Kaustubh Kisan Khade (b. 17 January 1987) from Mumbai completed the west coast expedition from Dwarka, Gujarat, to Kanniyakumari, Tamil Nadu, from 17 November 2016 to 7 February 2017. He paddled 1,845 km in 83 days.

Longest kayaking – group

Tarun K. Roy and Brij Mohan Bisht from New Delhi completed the Himalaya-to-Ocean Ganga Expedition from Rishikesh, Uttarakhand, to Ganga Sagar Island in the Bay of Bengal from 5 January to 19 March 2003. They paddled 2,443 km in 74 days.

Representative image of stand-up paddle-boarding

Representative image of Kayaking

Fastest to swim across the English Channel

Anita Sood from Maharashtra remains the fastest Indian to swim the Great English Channel. She swam in the year 1987 and took 8 hrs 15 mins (England to France).

Longest open-sea swimming by a paraplegic

M.S.A. Shaikh (b. 17 July 1986) from Mumbai, a paraplegic with 100 per cent disability due to a spinal cord injury, participated in open-sea swimming from Sinquerim to Baga and back to Candolim Beach, Goa, on 8 April 2017 at the UMOJA #BeachFest 2017. He completed the 8 km swim in 4 hrs 4 mins.

Long-distance swimming by a paraplegic woman

Deepa Malik (b. 30 September 1970) is an Indian athlete from New Delhi. She swam against the current in the Yamuna River at Allahabad (now Prayagraj), Uttar Pradesh, covering a distance of 1 km in 35 mins 36 secs on 15 June 2008. She received the Khel Ratna award in 2019.

Deepa Malik: Long-distance swimming by a paraplegic woman

Longest white-water rafting expedition

Aqua Scullers, the nine-member rafting team of the Indian Air Force, completed the longest white-water rafting expedition on the Ganga River, covering over 3,000 km from Gangotri in Uttarakhand to Ganga Sagar in West Bengal in 16 days from 19 October to 4 November 2013. The first such expedition undertaken by the Indian Air Force, it included the Himalayan portion of the river from Gangotri (3,049 m/ 10,003 ft) to Haridwar (295 m/ 968 ft), a very challenging white-water stretch with Grade IV–V rapids.

Marathon windsurfing

Rahul Rastogi from Hyderabad, Telangana, was the first Asian to windsurf 400 km from Kavaratti, Lakshadweep, to Kozhikode, Kerala. He started on 22 April 1988 and completed the marathon three days later. His average windsurfing timing was 14 hrs a day.

Representative image of windsurfing

Non-stop rafting expedition

Eight members of the Bihar Adventure Foundation, led by Sanjay Kumar Dutta, set off on a non-stop rafting expedition on the Ganga River. They began from Haridwar, Uttarakhand, on 29 October 1991 and covered 2,400 km in 621 hrs, ending at Calcutta (now Kolkata), West Bengal, on 24 November 1991.

Swimming at the highest altitude

Petty officer R.L. Sharma and leading seaman Dhani Ram swam a distance of 4,746 m (15,571 ft) across the breadth of Kedartal, a glacial lake at an altitude of 4,750 m (15,584 ft) in Uttarakhand, on 25 September 1995.

Oldest to complete the Triple Crown

Srikaanth Viswanathan (b. 15 July 1972) from Bengaluru, Karnataka, at the age of 47, completed the 20 Bridges Swim in New York City, US, in 8 hrs 7 mins on 31 August 2019, becoming the oldest Indian to complete the Triple Crown of Open Water Swimming. He had previously swum across the English Channel (14 hrs 7 mins) on 21 July 2018 and the Catalina Channel (13 hrs 4 mins) on 16 August 2019.

Oldest to cross English Channel

Srikaanth Viswanathan (b. 15 July 1972) from Bengaluru, crossed the English Channel on 21 July 2018, at the age of 46, becoming the oldest Indian to do so. He started swimming at 5:00 a.m. and completed the crossing at 7:07 p.m., crossing the channel in 14 hrs 7 mins.

Yachting at the highest altitude

Captain Gautama Dutta from Mumbai, carted his laser boat to an altitude of 5,460m (17,913 ft) at Devtal Lake, Uttarakhand, and yachted there on 18 September 1993.

Deepest underwater cycling – ocean – solo

Nishant K. Patel (b. 15 February 1982) from Mumbai, successfully attempted underwater cycling at a depth of 32.7 m (107 ft 3 in.) on 25 October 2016. He covered a distance of 100 m in 6 mins 47 secs in the Bay of Bengal off Puducherry coast. He used a Firefox Vortex 20 cycle and tied weights of 5 kg in the front and 2 kg at the back of the cycle to avoid floating. He had a 12-litre (200 bar) air tank attached for breathing support.

Fastest to complete Cape2Rio race

Indian Navy's Captain Atool Sinha (b. 1 August 1968) from Pune, Maharashtra, skippered INSV *Mhadei* in the Transatlantic Intercontinental Cape2Rio Race 2017 and completed the race in a record time of 20 days 19 hrs 27 minutes. The crew began the race on 1 January 2017 at 12:00 noon and finished the race on 22 January 2017 at 7:27 a.m., covering a distance of 3,800 nautical miles (7,038 km). The boat had six crew members including the skipper.

Women Who Outran Expectations

First to complete Grand-to-Grand Ultramarathon

Arpita Maitra (b. 31 October 1978) from Kolkata, became the first Indian to successfully complete the Grand-to-Grand Ultra (G2G) marathon, a gruelling week-long foot race from the Grand Canyon to the Grand Staircase in the US, in which she covered the 273 km route in 76 hrs 21 mins 43 secs in six stages from 22 to 28 September 2013.

First to complete the GQ run

Michelle Kakade (b. 9 October 1968), a long-distance runner from Pune, became the first person to cover the Golden Quadrilateral (GQ) on foot. The GQ is a highway network connecting Mumbai, Delhi, Kolkata, and Chennai. She covered 5,968.4 km in 193 days, 1 hr 9 mins from 21 October 2015 to 1 May 2016.

MARATHONS

First 4 Deserts Grand Slam winner

Atul Patki (b. 8 November 1965), a US citizen of Indian origin, completed the 4 Deserts Ultramarathons Series on 8 November 2014. He became the first Indian to complete all four 250 km events in one calendar year.

WR First to complete all six World Marathons

Siddhartha Ghosh (b. 21 February 1975) from Kolkata, was the first person to complete all Six World Marathons in one calendar year during 2013. He is also the first recipient of the six Star World Marathon certificate and has received the same five times consecutively from 2012 to 2016. The World Marathon Majors consist of six races annually across cities and are accredited by the International Association of Athletics Federations.

Siddhartha Ghosh: first to complete all six world marathons

First to complete the 7 Emirates Run

M.A. Shaikh (b. 29 September 1974) from Mumbai, became the first Indian to successfully complete the 7 Emirates Run, an ultramarathon across all seven emirates of the United Arab Emirates (UAE). He covered a distance of 575 km in 12 days from 21 November to 2 December 2014.

First Ultraman triathlete

Arunaabh Shah (b. 11 August 1990) from Delhi completed the Ultraman Triathlon (a 10 km swim, 421.1 km of cycling and an 84.3 km run) in Australia on 16 May 2016. He is the first Indian to do so in Ultraman's 33-year-long history.

First to complete the World Marathon Challenge – full marathon

Aditya Raj (b. 22 June 1983) from Gurugram, Haryana, became the first Indian to complete the World Marathon Challenge, in 2020, in which runners travel across the globe, completing seven marathons (each 42.2 km) in seven days on seven continents. Starting on 6 February 2020 in Novo, Antarctica, Raj travelled to Cape Town in Africa, Perth in Australia, Dubai in Asia, Madrid in Europe, and Brazil in South America, finishing his seventh marathon in Miami, North America, on 12 February 2020. His total running time was 36 hrs 47 mins 36 secs.

First Ironman triathlon

The first Indian Ironman triathlon was held in Goa with over 1,000 participants on 20 October 2019. Considered the most prestigious endurance triathlon event worldwide, the race included 1.9 km of swimming, 90 km of cycling, and 21.1 km of running, which were all done sequentially in a single day. Bishworjit Singh Saikhom from Pune, completed the triathlon in 4 hrs 42 mins 44 seconds, securing the first place.

First to finish the Ultraman World Championship

Gaurav Makkar (b. 26 November 1979) from Gurugram, became the first Indian to finish the Ultraman World Championship. The championship is a three-day, 515 km multi-sport race held annually in Hawaii, US. He completed a 10 km swim (in 4 hrs 24 mins), a 421 km bicycle ride (in 16 hrs 20 mins),

Gaurav Makkar

and an 84 km run (in 8 hrs 56 mins) during 23–25 November 2018. He also completed the Ultraman Florida 2018 during 16–18 February 2018, thereby completing two Ultraman races, the most by an individual in a year.

Most half-marathons organized in a single day – multiple venues

The Indian Air Force organized half-marathons simultaneously across 100 air force stations as part of the centenary celebrations of the marshal of the Indian Air Force, Arjan Singh on 14 April 2019. The marathon began at 5:30 a.m. and concluded at 9:30 a.m., and saw the participation of 12,600 air force officers. The marathon distance was 21 km and it was conducted in three age categories: below 35 years; between 35 and 45 years; and above 45 years. Marshal of the Indian Air Force, Arjan Singh, was the first and only officer of the Indian Air Force to hold a five-star rank.

Most triathlons completed in a year

Adil S. Nargolwala (b. 31 August 1969) from Gurugram, Haryana, completed the most triathlon races in a year in 2019. He completed the Triathlon Sprint at the Delhi International Triathlon 2019, the Triathlon Olympics at the New Delhi Triathlon Championship, the Ironman (70.3 miles/113 km) in Kazakhstan, the Ironman in Sweden, and the Ultraman India Race conducted in Delhi-NCR.

Adil Nargolwalal

Longest relay race

As part of its golden jubilee celebrations, while also paying tribute to former president A.P.J. Abdul Kalam, the Border Security Force (BSF) Sector Headquarters in West Bengal organized the BSF Golden Jubilee Baton Relay Race 2015. The event saw 1,785 BSF jawans in commando uniform cover a distance of 174.2 km in relay format in 8 hrs 55 mins 36 secs on 24 August 2015.

Longest distance covered while running – single day

Ullas Narayana from Bengaluru, ran 250.3 km in 24 hours on 1 December 2018, becoming the first to cover this distance in a day. He completed the non-stop run at the 2018 International Association of Ultra Running (IAU) 24-Hour Asia and Oceania Championships in Taipei, Taiwan.

Most half-marathons in a year

Vijay Boddupalli (b. 1 September 1988) from Chennai, completed 17 half-marathons, the most by an individual in a year, from 1 June 2017 to 31 May 2018. The 17th half-marathon was completed at the H2O Run on 22 April 2018. The half-marathons were conducted across seven states in India.

Fauja Singh

Most half-marathons by an individual

B. Srinivasan from Chennai, Tamil Nadu has completed 301 half-marathons, the most by an individual, beating the previous record of 164. These marathons were conducted at different venues in India including Gurgaon, Haryana and Madurai, Tamil Nadu. He has run a total distance of 7037.77 km.

Most full marathons in a year

Sivabalan Pandian (b. 21 September 1958) from Mumbai, completed 114 full marathons, the most by an individual in a year, from 6 January to 31 December 2019. These full marathons were conducted at venues both within India and abroad. The count also includes 14 ultramarathons.

Most ultramarathons in a year

Sivabalan Pandian (b. 21 September 1958) from Mumbai, has run and completed 18 ultramarathons in a year from 16 June 2018 to 23 December 2018.

Most consecutive half-marathon distance runs

Abhishek Singh Pandher (b. 27 September 1977) from Ahmedabad, Gujarat, completed 685 half-marathon distance (21.1 km) runs in 685 days from 15 July 2020 to 30 May 2022. The runs were conducted in Gujarat and Madhya Pradesh.

WR Oldest marathoner

Fauja Singh (b. 1 April 1911) of Indian origin, residing in the UK, is the world's oldest marathon runner. He completed the London Marathon, covering a distance of 42.2 km in 6 hrs 2 mins on 22 April 2012. His marathon record, for age 90-plus, was 5 hrs 40 mins at the Toronto Waterfront Marathon held in Canada in 2013.

Only Asian to complete Ironman triathlons in six continents

Kaustubh Radkar has completed the Ironman triathlon in six continents between March 2014 and November 2016, and is the only Asian to do so. He has completed 25 Ironman triathlons since he ran his first triathlon in 2008.

Fastest at Badwater Ultramarathon

Brij Mohan Sharma (b. 1 January 1974) of the Indian Navy, from Mumbai, is the fastest Indian at the Badwater Ultramarathon, one of the world's toughest foot races, held in California, US, from 18 to 20 July 2016. He completed the 217 km run in 40 hrs 47 mins.

Brij Mohan Sharma

Longest cross-country run

Long-distance runner Raj Vadgama (b. 18 June 1967) from Mumbai, successfully undertook 'Bharathon 10,000', a unique run across 70 cities in 17 states of India to spread the message of unity. He covered a distance of 9,902 km from 15 August 2014 to 26 January 2015, making it the first and longest such self-supported cross-country run. He ran about 60 km a day on an average for 165 days.

Praveen Kumar

First disabled Ironman

Praveen Kumar (b. 17 July 1985) from New Delhi became India's first disabled Ironman on 17 November 2018 in the Ironman event organized in Langkawi, Malaysia. He completed a 3.86 km long swim in 1 hr 36 mins 7 secs, 180 km of cycling in 7 hrs 49 mins 50 secs, and a 42 km long run in 5 hrs 40 mins 55 secs. Kumar is a battle-casualty soldier who was injured during the terrorist attack in Mumbai, in November 2008.

Most visually impaired athletes completing marathons

Six visually impaired athletes – Nandeesh J., Sunita N.D., Renuka Rajput, Kavya Ramesh, and Ajay and Mala Kolkar – ran a full marathon in 7 hrs 21 mins on 21 October 2018 at Sree Kanteerava Outdoor Stadium, Bengaluru, Karnataka. Helped by guide runners, the students, who were from the Samarthanam Trust for the Disabled, Bengaluru, were led by their coach, Bhumika Patel.

MOUNTAIN ADVENTURES

First club

The Himalayan Club was founded in February 1928 in the room of Field Marshal Sir William Birdwood, then commander-in-chief of the British Indian Army.

First mountaineering expedition

In 1951, Gurdial Guru Singh from Dehradun, Uttarakhand, led an expedition to the 7,120 m (23,360 ft) high Trishul 1 Peak in the Garhwal Himalayas, Uttarakhand.

First to summit the Volcanic Seven and youngest to climb both the Seven Summits and Volcanic Seven summits

At 34 years, Satyarup Siddhanta (b. 29 April 1983) from Bengaluru, completed the Volcanic Seven Summits (Messner list) on 15 December 2017 becoming the first Indian to do so. The Volcanic Seven Summits include Mt Kilimanjaro (5,895 m/19,341 ft – Africa), Mt Ojos del Salado (6,893 m/22,615 ft – South America), Mt Elbrus (5,642 m/18,510 ft – Europe), Mt Damavand (5,628 m/18,465 ft – Asia), Mt Giluwe (4,367 m/14,327 ft Australasia), Mt Pico de Orizaba (5,610 m/18,406 ft – North America), and Mt Sidley (4,181–4,285 m/13,717– 14,058 ft – Antarctica). He also completed the Seven Summits challenge on 15 January 2019, becoming the youngest Indian to climb both the Volcanic Seven Summits and Seven Summits.

First to walk the Siachen Glacier

Siachen Glacier, lying along India's border with China, is about 700 sq km in area and situated at an altitude touching 5,753 m (18,875 ft) above mean sea level. Under Indian Army protection since 1984, it is the highest battlefield in the world. In 1984, Captain (now Colonel) Ashok Pratap Tanwar became the first person to cover the entire glacier on foot. Appointed as the official photographer of a military formation, he walked the length and breadth of the 76 km long and 3–5 km broad glacier.

First to complete the Seven Summit challenge

Mastan Babu Malli (3 September 1974–24 March 2015) was an Indian mountaineer best known for his 2006 world-record-setting feat of climbing each continent's highest peak in the shortest period at the time – a total of 172 days – with the first climb on 19 January 2006 and the seventh on 10 July 2006. This feat made him the fastest Seven Summiteer in the world by 2006, and the first Indian and South Asian to climb the Seven Summits.

Satyarup Siddhanta

Most Himalayan summits

Sange Sherpa from Darjeeling, West Bengal, has six summits to his credit, which include Mt Everest three times, Aqtash in 1993, Jaloni in 1994, and Nanda Devi in 2000. He is the only person in the world to climb Mt Everest from three faces: from South Col in 1992, North Col in 1996, and Kangshung face in 1999. He received the National Adventure Award in 1998.

First mountaineering institute

The Himalayan Mountaineering Institute at Darjeeling, West Bengal, the first in India, was formed in 1954 by the then Prime Minister Jawaharlal Nehru, along with Major Nandu Jayal of the Corps of Engineers of the Indian Army, who was its first director.

Oldest to climb the Seven Summits

Ankur Bahl (b. 25 January 1961) from Haryana, became the oldest, at 57 years, to complete the Messner list of the Seven Summit challenge in 2018, which involves the summiting of the highest mountains in each continent. These include Mt Kilimanjaro (5,895 m/ 19,341 ft – Africa), Mt Elbrus (5,642 m/18,510 ft – Europe), Mt Denali/McKinley (6,190 m/ 20,310 ft – North America), Mt Aconcagua (6,961 m/22,838 ft – South America), Mt Everest (8,848.86 m/ 29,031 ft 8 in. – Asia), Mt Kosciuszko (2,228 m/7,310 ft – Australia), and Mt Vinson (4,892 m/ 16,050 ft– Antarctica).

Ankur Bahl

First Indian to summit the three highest peaks of South America

Vikas Shukla (b. 6 December 1989) from Bhusawal, Maharashtra, is the first Indian to summit the three highest peaks of South America. He scaled Mt Aconcagua (6,961 m/ 22,838 ft) on 16 February 2019; Mt Pissis (6,793 m/ 22,287 ft) on 24 February 2019; and Mt Ojos del Salado (6,893 m/ 22,615 ft) on 1 March 2019.

First woman to scale Mt Everest

Bachendri Pal (b. 24 May 1954) became the first Indian woman to reach the summit of Mt Everest in 1984.

First to summit four unscaled peaks above 6,000 m

A team of eight mountaineers from the Nehru Institute of Mountaineering, Uttarkashi in collaboration with Uttarakhand Tourism Development Board, summited four unscaled and unnamed peaks in the Gangotri region of the Garhwal Himalayas in eight days between 9 October and 16 October 2018. The team, led by Colonel Amit Bisht, SM, scaled peaks 6,566 m (21,542 ft), 6,557 m (21,512 ft), 6,126 m (20,098 ft), and 6,086 m (19,967 ft) high.

Bachendri Pal

First to summit Mt Everest without supplemental oxygen

Phu Dorjee was the first to summit Mt Everest (then measured at 8,848 mt/29,028 ft) without supplemental oxygen on 9 May 1984 through the south-east ridge route. He was part of the third Everest expedition led by Captain M.S. Kohli in 1965. Dorjee died in 1987 on the Kangchenjunga Expedition of the Assam Rifles.

Oldest to scale Mt Everest

- *Men*: S.C. Negi (b. 8 March 1950), additional deputy inspector general of the Border Security Force, became the oldest to scale Mt Everest on 24 May 2006 at the age of 56 years.
- *Women*: Sangeeta Sindhi (b. 9 February 1965) from Gurugram, became the oldest Indian woman to summit Mt Everest on 19 May 2018 at the age of 53 years.

Fastest scaling of Mt Everest

Kazi Sherpa climbed Mt Everest in 20 hrs 24 mins in 1998, breaking the earlier record of 22 hrs 29 mins.

TREKKING

First women's team to complete Snowman Trek

A team of 11 women led by iconic Indian mountaineer Bachendri Pal successfully completed the Snowman Trek in Bhutan, considered one of the toughest in the world. Starting at Paro Valley on 4 June 2011, the trek was completed at Sephu Village on 27 June 2011. It involved

Snowman trek route

crossing 11 high mountain passes and other difficult terrain. This expedition was sponsored by the Tata Steel Adventure Foundation in Jamshedpur, Jharkhand.

Fastest to scale most 8,000 m peaks

Baljeet Kaur became the first Indian to summit four out of the 14 peaks at altitudes of 8,000 metres or more in less than a month. The 27-year-old from Solan, Himachal Pradesh, started her journey by summitting Mt Annapurna I (8,091 m) on 28 April 2022 and Mt Kanchenjunga (8,586 m) on 12 May 2022, and became the first Indian woman to summit these peaks in less than two weeks. She continued her journey two weeks later and summitted Mt Everest (8,849 m) on 21 May 2022 and Mt Lhotse (8,517 m) on 22 May 2022, the first and fourth highest mountains in the world, respectively.

Oldest trekker

Gopal Vasudev Lele (b. 8 March 1932) from Pune, then 81 years of age, made a week-long trek to Rupin Pass (4,680 m/15,354 ft) in Himachal Pradesh from 21 to 28 September 2013. He completed a 70-degree climb. Lele had completed 20 treks since 1972.

Longest desert trek – group

The 22nd battalion of the Mahar Regiment, part of the Golden Katar Division of the Indian Army, successfully completed the 'Golden Katar Desert Trek 2017–18'. A ten-member team of soldiers trekked 700 km through the Thar Desert, Rajasthan, in 21 days from 22 December 2017 to 12 January 2018. The arduous journey on foot through the Great Indian Desert began from Bakhasar, Barmer District, and concluded in Gajjewala, Bikaner District, Rajasthan.

Fastest Everest Base Camp trek by a disabled person

Mahinder Singh Raghuwanshi (b. 2 October 1987) completed the longest trekking in Nepal, with a prosthetic leg, to the Everest Base Camp from an altitude of 2,859.9 m to 5,642.7 m (9,383 ft to 18,513 ft). He started his trek on 28 April 2018 and ended it on 11 May 2018, covering 150 km in 14 days. He started his trek from Lukla, Nepal, and covered Kala Patthar (5,550 m/ 18,209 ft), Cho La (5,368 m/ 17,612 ft), Gokyo (4,790 m/15,715 ft), Renjo La (5,360 m/ 17,585 ft), and Everest Base Camp (5,364 m/17,598 ft). He was accompanied by a friend and a guide.

THE POLES

First at the Arctic

Sharat Kumar Roy (1897–1962) was the first to reach the Arctic as a member of the Rawson–Macmillan Arctic Expedition in 1927.

First to reach North Pole by surface

Dr M.R. Shetty from Bangalore (now Bengaluru), Karnataka, reached the North Pole by surface on 5 August 2001 with a 100-strong team, by *Yamal*, a nuclear-powered ice-breaking ship, starting from Longyearbyen, Svalbard's administrative centre in Norway, on 1 August 2001.

First at Antarctica

Meher Moos (b. 1944) from Maharashtra was the first woman to set foot on the icy continent of Antarctica way back in 1976, long before any of the scientific expeditions went there.

First route recce to the South Pole

Major Anand Swaroop and Captain R.R. Bhat of the Corps of Engineers of the Indian Army were the first to recce the route from the Maitri base, Antarctica, to the Polar/Antarctic Plateau in 2000.

First at the Geographic South Pole

On 17 January 1989, Colonel J.K. Bajaj became the first Indian to reach the Geographic South Pole at 22:15 hrs (GMT). He was the only Indian in this 11-member international expedition that skied over 1,200 km in 50 days to the Geographic South Pole. The five-nation expedition was organized by Mountain Travel, US, and the International Adventure Network, Canada.

First organization to reach 'three' poles

Indian Navy teams have been to three poles: Mt Everest, the vertical pole, in 2004; the Geographic South Pole in 2006; and the Geographic North Pole in 2008. Commander Satyabrata Dam and two POMAs (petty officer medical assistants) Vikas Kumar and Rakesh Kumar were the first to reach all three poles.

Longest stay in Antarctica

Shaik Mastan (b. 12 February 1968) from Gudavalli Village, Guntur District, Andhra Pradesh, had the longest uninterrupted stay of 490 days in Antarctica at the Indian Antarctic research station, Bharati, from 16 November 2011 to 19 March 2013. He was a member of the 35th Indian expedition to Antarctica.

First to ski to the North Pole

Ajeet Bajaj is the first Indian to ski to the North Pole and complete the polar trilogy, which entails skiing to the North Pole and South Pole and crossing the Greenland Ice Sheet. He started his ski expedition to the North Pole from the Russian Arctic Polar Research Station called Barneo and reached the North Pole on 26 April 2006, along with three other skiers.

Deeya Bajaj (*left*) and Ajeet Bajaj at the summit of Mt Vinson, Antarctica (2019)

SPORTS

GENERAL

First Indian president of the International Cricket Council
Jagmohan Dalmiya became the first Indian president of the International Cricket Council (ICC) in 1997. He served till 2000.

First Indian chairman of the ICC
N. Srinivasan was the first ICC chairman from India (2014–15).

First Indian independent chairman of the ICC
Shashank Manohar was the first independent chairman of the International Cricket Council in 2016, and he was re-elected for another two years.

First Indian president of the World Squash Federation
Indian squash administrator Narayana Ramachandran was president of the World Squash Federation (WSF) for two terms from 2008 to 2016.

First Indian president of the International Kabaddi Federation
Sports administrator Janardan Singh Gehlot was the founder president of the International Kabaddi Federation from 1985 to 2013. He became the life president from May 2013.

First Indian on the Federation Internationale de Football Association (FIFA) executive panel
Praful Patel was the first Indian to be elected to the FIFA Executive Council in April 2019. He was also the president of All India Football Federation and was the senior vice president of the Asian Football Confederation.

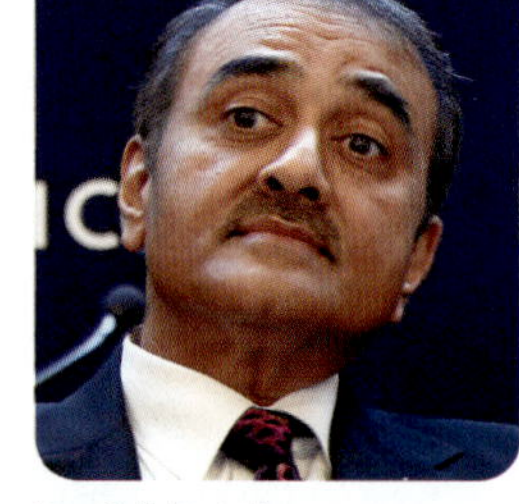
Praful Patel

First Indian to become a FIFA World Cup match commissioner
Former All India Football Federation president Priya Ranjan Dasmunsi was the match commissioner in a FIFA World Cup 2006 game. It was a group stage match between Australia and Croatia.

Priya Ranjan Dasmunsi

First Indian woman to be a member of International Olympic Committee's (IOC) Athletes' Commission
Badminton player Saina Nehwal was appointed a member of the IOC's Athletes' Commission in October 2016.

First sportsman to be nominated to the Rajya Sabha
Wrestler Dara Singh was the first sportsman to be nominated to the Rajya Sabha, the Upper House of the Indian Parliament, in 2003.

Dara Singh

First sportsperson to be awarded the Padma Shri
Triple Olympian gold medallist Balbir Singh Sr. (1924–2020) became the first sports-person to be awarded the Padma Shri in 1957. The versatile centre forward played a key role in India's victories in the Olympics in 1948 in London, in 1952 in Helsinki, and in 1956 in Melbourne.

Balbir Singh Sr

First woman sportsperson to receive the Padma Vibhushan
Boxer M.C. Mary Kom was honoured with the Padma Vibhushan in 2020.

First sportsperson to receive the Padma Vibhushan
In 2008, the Padma Vibhushan was first awarded to sports-persons and the first to receive the award was the chess wizard Viswanathan Anand. The two other recipients of the award are mountaineer Edmund Hillary (posthumous) and cricket icon Sachin Tendulkar, who also received it in 2008.

First sportsperson to receive an honorary doctorate degree
Man: Raja Randhir Singh, former shooter, was conferred with a honorary doctorate degree in literature by the Lakshmibai Institute of Physical Education, Gwalior, Madhya Pradesh on 8 September 2000. He had represented India in six Olympic Games: Tokyo (1964), Mexico City (1968), Munich (1972), Montreal (1976), Moscow (1980), and Los Angeles (1984).
Woman: P.T. Usha was conferred with an honorary doctorate degree by Kannur University, Kerala, on 1 November 2000 for her contribution to athletics. She represented India in four Olympic Games, five Asian Games, and five Asian Championships. She also won the most medals ever by an Indian athlete at the Jakarta Asian Championships in 1985, with five gold medals and a bronze medal.

First sportsman and coach to receive an honorary doctorate degree
Pullela Gopichand, former badminton sports star and chief Indian coach, was bestowed an honorary doctorate degree by The Indian Institute of Technology, Kanpur, Uttar Pradesh, on 28 June 2019 in recognition of his contribution to badminton. Gopichand was the second Indian to win the All England Open Badminton Championships in 2001. In 2008, he switched to coaching and launched his academy in Hyderabad, Telangana.

First sweep in the Asian Para Games
At the 2018 Asian Para Games, Indian para-athletes occupied all three positions in high jump when Sharad Kumar (1.90 m), Varun Bhati (1.82 m), and Thangavelu Mariyappa (1.67 m) got the gold, silver, and bronze medals respectively, in the T-42/63 category (lower limb deficiency, leg length difference, impaired muscle power, and impaired range of movement).

First woman to head a state cricket association

Rupa Gurunath became the first woman president of the Tamil Nadu Cricket Association (TNCA), a State Association of the Board of Conduct for Cricket in India (BCCI), on 27 September 2019.

First sports magazine

Bengal Sporting was first published in 1837. It was edited by British journalist Joachim Hayward Stocqueler.

First Indian woman to participate in the World Transplant Games

Reena Raju (b. 4 December 1982) from Bengaluru, Karnataka, was the flag bearer in the opening ceremony at the World Transplant Games 2017 in Malaga, Spain. She represented India in the 100 m sprint and badminton mixed doubles. She was the first Indian to undergo a repeat heart transplant on 22 October 2017 at Frontier Lifeline Hospital, Chennai, for cardiac allograft vasculopathy.

Olympic Order

First recipient of the Olympic Order (Gold)

The Olympic Order (Gold), the highest award of the Olympic movement, is given for distinguished contribution to the movement. Former Indian prime minister Indira Gandhi was its first recipient in 1983. The Olympic Order is also awarded in silver and bronze categories.

First international rugby 15s win

The Indian women's rugby team scripted history by clinching their first ever international 15s victory against a higher ranked Singapore for a bronze medal in the Asian women's Division 1 Rugby 15s Championship 2019.

Fencing

Fencing, a combat sport, involves two athletes who use swords to attack and defend against each other. The goal is to strike the opponent in order to score points. Modern fencing is divided into three disciplines: épée, sabre (sometimes known as saber), and foil. Each discipline has its own set of regulations and employs a distinct type of blade, albeit they all have the same name.

First to win a world title in motorsport

Aishwarya Pissay from Bengaluru, Karnataka, became the first Indian to win a world title in motorsport. She won the Federation Internationale de Motocyclisme (FIM) Bajas World Cup (women's category) with 65 points on 13 August 2019 in Varpalota, Hungary. She won the first round in Dubai, UAE, was placed third in Portugal, fifth in Spain, and fourth in Hungary.

Best performance in the Olympic Games

India capped off its best-ever performance in the 2020 Tokyo Olympics with a haul of seven medals, including a gold, two silver, and four bronze medals.

First fencer to qualify for the Olympics

C.A. Bhavani Devi became the first Indian fencer to qualify for the 2020 Tokyo Olympics on 14 March 2021 at the Women's Sabre World Cup in Budapest, Hungary. Chennai-based Devi secured her slot through the Asia/ Oceania Zone of the Adjusted Official Ranking (AOR).

First Indian fencer to win a medal at the Asian Fencing Championships

C.A. Bhavani Devi became the first Indian fencer to win a medal at the Asian Fencing Championships by winning the bronze medal in 2023. She defeated Misaki Emura with a remarkable score of 15-10 in the quarter-finals but in the semi-finals she had to settle for a bronze because she lost 14-15 to Uzbekistan's Zaynab Dayibekova.

C.A. Bhavani Devi

Best performance in the Asian Para Games

Indian para-athletes won 72 medals in the 2018 Asian Para Games in Jakarta, Indonesia, bagging 15 golds, 24 silvers, and 33 bronzes.

Best performance in the Asian Games

India participated in the 2018 Asian Games in Jakarta and Palembang, Indonesia (from 18 August to 2 September), and had the best ever haul with 69 medals, including 15 gold, 24 silver, and 30 bronze medals from 465 events. After 67 years, since the inaugural edition of the Games in Delhi in 1951, India matched its best haul of 15 golds.

Best performance in the Commonwealth Games

India's best performance was in the 2010 CWG held in New Delhi, when India won 101 medals in all.

Indian postal stamp commemorating Commonwealth Games 2010

India's Olympic Medal History

India's Olympic Medal Count by Sport

SPORT	GOLD	SILVER	BRONZE	TOTAL
Field hockey	8	1	4	13
Athletics	1	3	0	4
Shooting	1	2	4	7
Wrestling	0	2	6	8
Badminton	0	1	2	3
Weightlifting	0	1	1	2
Boxing	0	0	3	3
Tennis	0	0	1	1

India's Olympic Medal Performance – British India Era

YEAR	CITY	GOLD	SILVER	BRONZE	TOTAL	RANK
1896	Athens	0	0	0	0	-
1900	Paris	1	0	0	1	19
1904	St. Louis	0	0	0	0	-
1908	London	0	0	0	0	-
1912	Stockholm	0	0	0	0	-
1920	Antwerp	0	0	0	0	-
1924	Paris	0	0	0	0	-
1928	Amsterdam	1	0	0	1	23
1932	Los Angeles	1	0	0	1	19
1936	Berlin	1	0	0	1	20

India's Olympic Medal Performance – Post-Independence Era

YEAR	CITY	GOLD	SILVER	BRONZE	TOTAL	RANK
1948	London	1	0	0	1	22
1952	Helsinki	1	0	1	2	26
1956	Melbourne	1	0	0	1	24
1960	Rome	0	1	0	1	32
1964	Tokyo	1	0	0	1	24
1968	Mexico City	0	0	1	1	42
1972	Munich	0	0	1	1	43
1976	Montreal	0	0	0	0	-
1980	Moscow	1	0	0	1	23
1984	Los Angeles	0	0	0	0	-
1988	Seoul	0	0	0	0	-
1992	Barcelona	0	0	0	0	-
1996	Atlanta	0	0	1	1	71
2000	Sydney	0	0	1	1	71
2004	Athens	0	1	0	1	65
2008	Beijing	1	0	2	3	50
2012	London	0	2	4	6	55
2016	Rio de Janeiro	0	1	1	2	67
2020	Tokyo	1	2	4	7	48
2024	Paris	1	1	5	7	71

Indians Who Have Won Multiple Individual Medals in the Olympics

ATHLETE	MEDALS	SPORT
Neeraj Chopra	2024 Silver, 2020 Gold	Athletics
Norman Pritchard	1900 (both silver medals in the same edition)	Athletics
Manu Bhaker	2024 (both bronze medals in the same edition)	Shooting
Sushil Kumar	2008 Bronze, 2012 Silver	Wrestling
P. V. Sindhu	2016 Silver, 2020 Bronze	Badminton

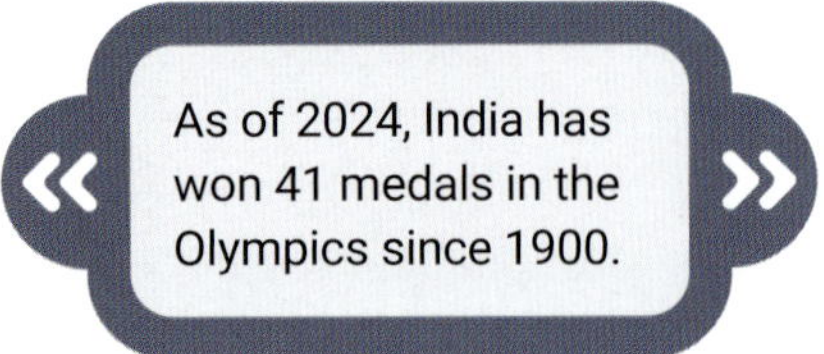

Best performance in the South Asian Games

India bagged 174 gold, 93 silver, and 45 bronze medals in the 13th South Asian Games 2019 in Kathmandu, Nepal.

Most national awards

Woman: M.C. Mary Kom, six-time world champion, was the recipient of the Arjuna Award in 2003, the Rajiv Gandhi Khel Ratna Award in 2008–09, the Padma Shri in 2006, the Padma Bhushan in 2013, and the Padma Vibhushan in 2020.

M.C. Mary Kom

Man: Pullela Gopichand, the second Indian to win All England Open Badminton Championships in 2001, was the recipient of the Arjuna Award in 1999, the Rajiv Gandhi Khel Ratna Award in 2000–01, the Dronacharya Award in 2009, the Padma Shri in 2005, and the Padma Bhushan in 2014.

Pullela Gopichand

Youngest Commonwealth Games captain

Seventeen-year-old Prachi Tehlan was the youngest captain representing India in netball at the 2010 Commonwealth Games, New Delhi.

Youngest to receive the Padma Bhushan

Badminton player P.V. Sindhu, at 24 years, became the youngest sportsperson to receive the Padma Bhushan in 2020. Sindhu is the third badminton player to be awarded the honour after Pullela Gopichand received it in 2014 and Saina Nehwal in 2016.

ARCHERY

GENERAL

First to win back-to-back titles

Deepika Kumari became the first Indian archer to win titles back-to-back when she won the cadet individual recurve title in 2009 at Ogden in Utah, USA, and the junior individual recurve gold in 2011 at Legnica, Poland.

Deepika Kumari

First Indian compound archery women's team to be ranked world no. 1

The Indian compound archery women's team of Jyothi Surekha Vennam, P. Lily Chanu, Trisha Deb, Muskan Kirar, Divya Dhayal and Madhumita was the first ever team from India to be ranked world no. 1 in 2018.

First Indian to win World Archery Award

Sheetal Devi became the first Indian to win a World Archery Award, clinching the para women's category in 2023. She is also the first female para-athlete without arms to compete internationally. Additionally, Aditi Swami won the Breakthrough Archer of the Year Award, making her the first able-bodied Indian recipient.

Sheetal Devi

First compound para medal

Indian compound mixed pair of Shyam Sundar Swami and Jyoti Bullyan made history with a silver at the World Archery Para Championships 2022 in Dubai.

First Indian archer to get World Games Athlete of the Year Award nomination

Aditi Swami became the first Indian archer nominated for the 2023 World Games' Athlete of the Year Award. The 17-year-old made history as India's youngest individual World Archery Champion, securing multiple titles, including team golds at the World Championships and Asian Games. Hockey stalwarts Rani Rampal (2019) and P.R. Sreejesh (2021) have won the award in the past.

ASIAN CHAMPIONSHIP

First medal in the Asian Championships – men

Limba Ram became the first Indian archer to win an Asian Archery Championships medal in 1988.

Most medals in the Asian Championship

Indian recurve archers won one gold, four silver, and two bronze medals at the 2021 Asian Archery Championships in Dhaka (Bangladesh). In the Asian Championships in 2019 too, in Bangkok, Thailand, during 22–28 November 2019, India had won seven medals: one gold, two silver, and four bronze medals.

Hat-trick of bronzes – men

Atanu Das bagged three bronze medals in the 2019 Asian Archery Championships in Bangkok, Thailand. He clinched the men's recurve individual bronze, the recurve mixed team bronze (with Deepika Kumari), and the third bronze with Tarundeep Rai and Jayanta Talukdar in the team recurve event.

ASIAN PARA GAMES

First gold medal in the Asian Para Games

Harvinder Singh won India's maiden archery gold in the Asian Para Games 2018 in the men's individual recurve. He outplayed China's Zhao Lixue 6–0 in the W2/ST category.

Harvinder Singh

COMMONWEALTH GAMES

Most medals in the Commonwealth Games

The Indian team won three gold, a silver, and four bronze medals in archery at the 2010 Commonwealth Games in Delhi.

INTERNATIONAL

First Junior World Championships title – men

Palton Hansda won the World Junior Archery Championships (compound – men's) in 2006 at Merida in Mexico.

First individual international medal

Shyam Lal won a bronze in the 50 m event at the fifth Asia Cup Championship in Calcutta (now Kolkata), West Bengal, in January 1988. He represented India in the 1988 Seoul Olympics in South Korea.

First Archery World Cup team gold – women

Rimil Buriuly, Bombayla Devi Laishram, and Deepika Kumari toppled Olympic champions South Korea 219–215 to win the first back-to-back World Cup titles at the Archery World Cup (stage 4) at Wroclaw, Poland, on 25 August 2013, after winning the first medal at the World Cup (stage 3) in Medellin, Colombia, in July.

First international gold

In October 1989, India took the gold in the team event at the Asian Archery Championships in Beijing, China, with 1,850 points, while reigning Olympic champion South Korea stood second with 1,842 points. The Indian team comprised Limba Ram, Shyam Lal, and Skalzang Dorje.

Abhishek Verma

First Olympics representation – men

The Indian national archery team, with Shyam Lal, Limba Ram, and Sanjeeva Singh, participated in the individual and team archery events at the Olympics in 1988 at Seoul, South Korea.

First international gold – individual

Jayanta Talukdar won an individual gold medal at the Federation Internationale de Tir a l'Arc (FITA) Meteksan World Cup, in 2006 in Merida, Mexico.

Jayanta Talukdar

First international gold – women

Dola Banerjee outclassed Tatyana Dorkhova of Ukraine 102-96 in the women's recurve final at the 18th Golden Arrow Grand Prix Championship 2005 at Antalya, Turkey.

First Olympics representation – women

Dola Banerjee, Reena Kumari, and Sumangala Sharma were the first women to represent India in archery at the 2004 Olympic Games in Athens, Greece.

First gold medal in a World Cup

Dola Banerjee from West Bengal is the only Indian archer to win gold in a World Cup final, in the women's individual recurve event at the World Cup in Dubai, UAE, in November 2007.

First World Cup compound title – men – individual

Abhishek Verma won an archery World Cup (stage 3) event at Wroclaw, Poland, on 15 August 2015.

First World Cup compound title – men – team

The men's compound archery team of Abhishek Verma, Chinna Raju Srither, and Amarjeet Singh bagged the World Cup (stage 1) on 20 May 2017 in Shanghai, China, scoring 226–221 against Colombia.

First World Championship medal

The Indian men's archery team won a silver medal, behind Korea, at the 43rd World Outdoor Target Archery Championship 2005 in Madrid, Spain. The recurve team comprised Tarundeep Rai, Gautam Singh Sardar, Jayanta Talukdar, and Robin Hansda.

First silver at the Youth Olympics

Fifteen-year-old Akash Malik from Haryana became India's first archery silver medallist at the Youth Olympic Games 2018 in Buenos Aires, Argentina, on 17 October 2018.

Most medals in the World Championship

India won a silver and two bronzes in the World Archery Championships during 10–15 June 2019 at 's-Hertogenbosch, Netherlands. The men's team of Tarundeep Rai, Atanu Das, and Pravin Yadav won silver. The women's compound team of Jyothi Surekha Vennam, Muskan Kaur, and Raj Kaur won the bronzes.

Most gold medals at the World Cup by an individual

India won three gold medals in the

Archery World Cup (stage 3) 2021 in Paris, France: the individual gold – Deepika Kumari; the mixed team event – Deepika Kumari with her husband Atanu Das; and the women's team event trio of Deepika Kumari, Komalika Bari, and Ankita Bhakat.

Most medals in a World Cup

India won one gold, two silver, and two bronze medals in the Archery World Cup (stage 4) at Wroclaw, Poland, in August 2014. The team of Deepika Kumari, Bombayla Devi Laishram and Laxmirani Majhi won the gold in the women's recurve team event. The men's recurve team, with Tarundeep Rai, Jayanta Talukdar, and Atanu Das, won a silver medal. Abhishek Verma and Purvasha Shende clinched the silver in the compound mixed pair event. Deepika Kumari bagged two bronze medals in the women's recurve individual event and in the mixed team event with partner Jayanta Talukdar.

Dola Banerjee

Only siblings to represent India in archery at the Olympics

Archers Dola Banerjee and Rahul Banerjee are the only brother-and-sister pair to represent India at the Olympics.

Rahul Banerjee

Only Indian couple to represent India at the Olympic Games

Atanu Das and Deepika Kumari are the only Indian archer couple to represent India at the Olympic Games 2020. They married in June 2019 amid the pandemic.

Three gold medals in the World Cup

Deepika Kumari won three gold medals in the World Cup (stage 3) in Paris in 2021. India took the top honour in the women's team, mixed team, and women's individual events.

Two medals in World Cup Stage 3

Jyothi Surekha Vennam claimed two medals in the World Cup (Stage 3) in Paris in June 2022. When she was four years old, she crossed the Krishna River in 3 hrs, 20 mins, 6 secs to cover 5 km three times across, entering the *Limca Book of Records*.* Starting with two bronze medals in the World Youth Archery Championships in 2013, she went on to win 10 medals in the Asian Archery Championships, nine medals in the World Cup and six medals in the World Archery Championships. She has nearly 100 medals in national and international competitions.

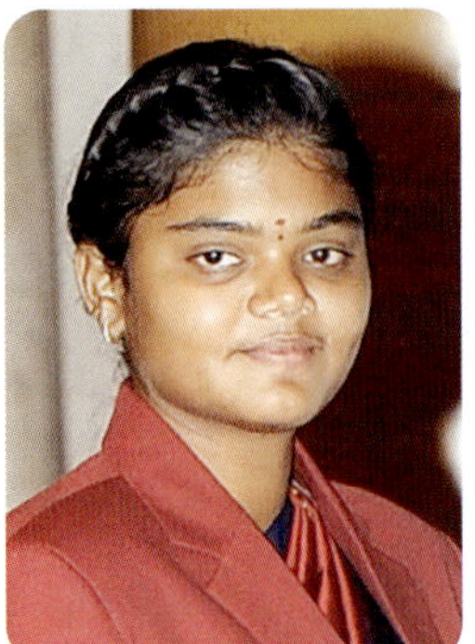

Jyothi Surekha Vennam

First to equal women's compound archery world record of qualification round

Indian archer Jyothi Surekha Vennam equalled the world record in the women's compound qualification at the 2023 Archery World Cup in Antalya, Türkiye, scoring 713 out of 720 points. Her performance matched Sara Lopez's 2015 record and broke the Asian record of 709 set by Korea's So Chaewon in 2017.

Three individual gold medals in World Cup

Compound archer Abhishek Verma won three individual gold medals at the World Cup with his latest coming at the World Cup Stage III 2023 in Medellin. He earlier won gold medals in Paris 2021 and Wroclaw, Poland, in 2015.

Aditi Gopichand breaks U-18 world record

Aditi Gopichand broke the U-18 world record with 711 points out of possible 720 (72 arrows) during the qualification round of the World Cup Stage III in Medellin. The 16-year-old broke the previous age group record of 705 held by Riko Arreola of the USA.

First Indian to win Youth World Champion in recurve – men

Parth Salunke became the first Indian male archer to win recurve under-21 men's individual champion during the World Archery Youth Championships 2023 in Limerick. The 19-year-old archer defeated Korea's Song In Jun in the gold medal match.

Best medal show at Archery World Cup

India's archery team achieved a historic milestone of eight medals at the 2024 Archery World Cup Stage 1 in Shanghai, securing their highest-ever medal tally at a single edition. The Indian contingent took home five golds, two silvers, and one bronze. Notably, the men's recurve team of Tarundeep Rai, Pravin Jadhav, and Dhiraj Bommadevara captured gold, while Deepika Kumari claimed silver in the women's individual recurve event. The mixed team, comprising Ankita Bhakat and Dhiraj, added a bronze. This stellar performance was driven by the compound archers (non-Olympic event) who secured four golds.

PARALYMPICS

First archery medal in Paralympics

Harvinder Singh clinched India's first-ever archery at the 2020 Paralympics. He won the bronze medal in the men's singles recurve archery at the 2020 Summer Paralympics in Tokyo, Japan.

World's first armless archer to reach World Championship final

Sheetal Devi became the first female armless archer to make a World Championship final as she won the silver medal in the compound women individual category in Pilsen. She lost the gold medal match to Turkey's Oznur Cure after defeating compatriot Sarita in the semis.

First World Archery Para Championship gold

Sarita and Rakesh Kumar set world record in the Compound Mixed Team Open category with a score of 1398 out of possible 1440 in the qualification round. The duo went on to win the gold medal as well by beating Brazil in the final, winning India's first para archers to win gold medal in World Archery Para Championships.

World record in Women's Team

Sarita and Sheetal Devi set a new world record in the Compound Women Team Open category with a score of 1386/1440 in the qualification round. The duo also won the bronze medal, defeating Iran.

ATHLETICS

ASIAN ATHLETICS CHAMPIONSHIPS

Triple excellence in shot put

Former shot putter Bahadur Singh Chouhan is the only Indian to receive the Arjuna Award, the Dronacharya Award as well as the Padma Shri. Between 1973 and 1985 he won three gold, two silver, and three bronze medals at the Asian Games and Asian Championships.

Best performance in the Asian Athletics Championships

India clinched five gold, one silver, and three bronze medals in the 2017 Asian Athletics Championships in Bhubaneswar, Odisha, to top the medal tally for the first time in the championships.

Biggest point-haul in pentathlon – women

Swapna Barman set the pentathlon record with a point haul of 4119 points (out of 5000) while clinching the Asian Indoor Championships silver medal. She broke the old record held by Purnima Hembram of 4062 points (in 2017).

First to win gold at Asian Athletics Championships – women

Jyothi Yarraji won the first gold for India in the women's 100m hurdles at the Asian Athletics Championships held in Bangkok in July 2023. She clocked in 13.09 seconds.

Joint – highest medal tally at Asian Athletics Championships

India won 27 medals (six gold, 12 silver and nine bronze medals) at the Asian Athletics Championships, equalling the joint-highest tally of medals at the event as the nation did in 2017 at Bhubaneswar.

ASIAN GAMES

First double gold at the Asian Games

Lavy Pinto won the first double gold at Asian Games in the 100 m and 200 m races in Delhi, 1951. Six other athletes have won at least two golds each in a single Asian Games event.

First Asian Games medals – women

In the 1951 Asian Games in Delhi, Roshan Mistry won the silver in the 100 m race, while Mary D'Souza (200 m) won a bronze. The women's 4 x 100 m relay team of Nilima Ghose, Stephie D'Souza, Mary D'Souza, and Roshan Mistry also won a silver.

First Asian Games gold – men – individual

Ranjit Singh won a gold in the 800 m marathon on 8 March 1951 at Delhi, clocking 1 hr 59 mins 3 secs. Indian men won 10 golds in this edition of the Asian Games.

First Asian Games gold – women – individual

Kamaljeet Sandhu won the 400 m race in 57.3 secs at the sixth Asian Games held in Bangkok, Thailand, in 1970.

Only Asian Games gold medal in marathon

Chhota Singh won a gold in the men's marathon in 1951 in Delhi with a timing of 2 hrs 42 mins 58 secs 6 microseconds.

First gold medal – women – team

Christine Brown, Stephie D'Souza, Violet Peters, and Mary D'Souza won the gold in the 4 x 100 m relay, clocking 49.5 secs at the second Asian Games held in Manila, Philippines, in 1954.

First to win three golds successively in the Asian Games

Manjeet Kaur was the first Indian to win three consecutive gold medals in the women's 4 x 400 m relay race in the Asian Games (2002, 2006, and 2010).

Milkha Singh

P.T. Usha

Most individual golds in the Asian Games

Two sportspersons have won four gold medals each at the Asian Games:

- Milkha Singh won four golds in two Asian Games in 1958 and 1962.
- P.T. Usha won four golds in the 1986 Asian Games at Seoul, South Korea, in the 200 m, 400 m, 400 m hurdles, and the 4 x 400 m relay.

Longest career – women

- P.T. Usha represented India from 1980 to 1998 in four Olympic Games, five Asian Games and five Asian Track and Field (ATF) meets.
- Shiny Wilson represented India 72 times in international meets from 1981 to 1995. She won the 800 m in her last major meet – the ATF meet in 1995 in Jakarta, Indonesia.

Longest career – men

Bahadur Singh Chouhan, who represented India in the inaugural ATF meet in 1971, also participated in the ninth one at Delhi in 1989. He won gold medals in shot put in the Asian Games in 1978 and 1982, and a silver medal in 1974.

ASIAN YOUTH ATHLETICS CHAMPIONSHIPS

Best performance in the Asian Youth Athletics Championships

India clinched six gold, eleven silver, and three bronze medals in the 2022 Asian Youth Athletics Championships, held in Kuwait between 13 and 16 October 2022, topping the medal tally.

COMMONWEALTH GAMES

First gold medal in throws at the Commonwealth Games – men – individual

This feat was achieved by the 6 ft 9 in. tall Vikas Gowda in discus throw. Gowda won this event in 2014 in Glasgow, Scotland, with a throw of 63.64 m.

Anju Bobby George

First medal in the Commonwealth Games – women

Anju Bobby George won the bronze medal in long jump with a best of 6.49 m at the 2002 Commonwealth Games in Manchester, UK, followed by Neelam J. Singh, who won a silver in the women's discus throw.

First Commonwealth Games gold medal – women

The first Commonwealth Games gold medal for women came when Krishna Poonia won the discus throw (61.51 m), while the quartet of Sini Jose, Mandeep Kaur, Manjeet Kaur, and Ashwini Chidananda Akkunji won the women's 4 x 400 m relay (3 mins 27.77 secs) at the 2010 New Delhi Games.

First to win a gold medal in triple jump in the Commonwealth Games

Eldhose Paul became the first Indian to win a gold medal in the men's triple jump at the Commonwealth Games 2022, recording a massive 17.03 m.

First medal in race walk – women

Priyanka Goswami is the first Indian woman to win the silver medal in the women's 10,000 m race walk at the 2022 Commonwealth Games. It is India's second medal in the race walk at the Commonwealth Games after Harminder Singh's bronze in the 20 km event in the 2010 Commonwealth Games.

First high jump medal in the Commonwealth Games

Tejaswin Shankar, the 2015 Commonwealth Youth Games gold medallist in high jump, became the first Indian to win a medal – a bronze – in high jump with a jump of 2.22 m at the 2022 Commonwealth Games.

First javelin throw medal in the Commonwealth Games – women

Annu Rani, a javelin thrower, is the first Indian woman to win a medal, a bronze, in the 2022 Commonwealth Games in Birmingham, UK.

Best Commonwealth performance

India won 12 medals – two golds, three silvers, and seven bronzes – during the 19th Commonwealth Games in New Delhi in 2010.

First title in the Commonwealth Fencing Championships

Chennai-born fencer C.A. Bhavani Devi made history in November 2018 by becoming the first Indian to win the gold medal at the Commonwealth Championship. The 42nd ranked Indian fencer and the first-ever Indian fencer to have qualified for an Olympics (Tokyo 2020), Bhavani Devi, defeated second-seeded Australian Veronika Vasleva 15-10 in the senior women's sabre individual category final in London, UK, in the Commonwealth Championships in August 2022.

COMMONWEALTH AND ASIAN GAMES

Gold medal in Commonwealth and Asian Games

Milkha Singh won gold in the 440 yards (the quarter-mile dash) race at the 1958 British Empire and Commonwealth Games in Cardiff, Wales, with a timing of 46.6 secs. He also won the 400 m races back-to-back in the Asian Games in Tokyo, Japan (1958), in 47.0 secs, and Jakarta, Indonesia (1962), in 46.9 secs. He was the first Indian to win individual gold medals in both the Asian Games and the Commonwealth Games. He was also the first Indian athlete to win a gold medal in the Commonwealth Games.

INTERNATIONAL

First Indian elected to the International Association of Athletics Federations (IAAF) Council

Adille J. Sumariwalla was elected to the IAAF (now World Athletics) Council at the IAAF Congress in 2015.

First international medal in a marathon – women

Asha Agarwal won the Hong Kong Marathon on 27 January 1985. She later won the Asian track and field gold at Jakarta, Indonesia, in 1985, and the Trinidad Marathon in 1986.

First individual gold medal in track events at the IAAF World U-20 Championships

Hima Das won the gold in the 400 m race in the IAAF (now World Athletics) World U-20 Championships in Tampere, Finland, on 12 July 2018 with a timing of 51.46 secs. She holds the current Indian national record in 400 m with a timing of 50.79 secs set at the 2018 Asian Games in Jakarta, Indonesia.

Hima Das

India at World Athletics Championships 2023

India broke the world Asian record for the men's 4x400 m relay at the World Athletics Championships in Budapest, Hungary. It qualified for the finals. After the first run Muhammed Anas Yahiya came in the sixth place. But the run by Amoj Jacob put India in the second place. Muhammed Ajmal Variyathodi and Rajesh Ramesh broke the Asian record clocking in at 2:59.05 seconds. The earlier Asian record of 2:59.51s was held by Japan.

First clean sweep in a major international meet

Krishna Poonia, Harwant Kaur, and Seema Antil bagged the gold, silver, and bronze medals respectively in the women's discus throw in the 2010 Commonwealth Games in New Delhi.

First athlete to win a medal at the IAAF Continental Cup

Arpinder Singh, the 2018 Asian Games gold medallist in triple jump, was the first Indian to win a medal in the IAAF Continental Cup. He won a bronze medal in triple jump with a distance of 16.59 m.

First Indian to win gold at the IAAF World U-20 Championships

Neeraj Chopra, by clinching the gold on 23 July 2016 at the IAAF (now World Athletics) World U-20 Championships in Bydgoszcz, Poland, with a winning javelin throw of 86.48 m, became the first Indian to win a gold medal at any event in the championships and the first Indian to set a junior world record in athletics. In 2018, he became the second Indian after the legendary runner Milkha Singh to win both Commonwealth Games and Asian Games gold medals in the same year, breaking the national record on both occasions. At 20 years, he was the youngest ever flag-bearer of the Indian contingent at the 2018 Jakarta Asian Games.

First to receive IAAF Veteran Pin

Indian track and field legend P.T. Usha was presented the Veteran Pin by the World Athletics governing body – IAAF (now World Athletics), on 24 September 2019.

First World U-20 Athletics Championships twin medals

Quarter-miler Rupal Chaudhary is the first Indian to win twin medals in a single edition of the 2022 World U-20 Athletics Championships. She won silver in 4x400 m relay silver and a bronze medal in the women's 400 m.

First to finish among podium places at Diamond League

Murali Sreeshankar became the first long jumper to finish among the podium places of a Diamond League as he finished third in the Paris Diamond League 2023 with an attempt of 8.09 m. He is overall the third Indian to finish in top three of Diamond Leagues after discus thrower Vikash Gowda (2015) and Neeraj Chopra (2022).

MARATHONS

Most appearances in marathons

Sunita Godara has completed 85 half- and 69 full marathons in 24 different countries. Starting with the Rath Marathon in 1984, she finished first in 25 marathons, second in 12, and third in 14 of them. She has won 25 gold medals in half-marathons.

OLYMPICS

First Olympic marathoner

Phadeppa Dareppa Chaugule represented India in the 1920 Antwerp Olympic Games. He finished 19th in 2 hrs 50 mins 45.2 secs.

Neeraj Chopra

First women at the Olympics

Mary D'Souza and Nilima Ghose participated in the 1952 Helsinki Olympics. They were both eliminated in the heats of the 100 m and 200 m races, and 80 m and 100 m hurdles respectively.

First woman captain

Shiny Wilson captained the Indian athletes' contingent at the 1992 Olympic Games in Barcelona, Spain.

Shiny Wilson

Best performances in the Olympics

Milkha Singh and P.T. Usha finished fourth in the 400 m and the 400 m hurdles in the 1960 Rome and the 1984 Los Angeles Olympic Games, respectively.

WORLD ATHLETICS

First gold at World Athletics final

In the World Athletics Championships held in Monte Carlo in September 2005, Anju Bobby George from India came second in long jump. The gold medallist, Tatyana Kotova, from Russia, was later disqualified following a failed retest for doping, and Anju Bobby George was upgraded to gold medallist, India's first, in January 2014.

First Indian to win gold at World Athletics Championships

Neeraj Chopra wrote history when he became the first Indian to win a gold medal at the World Athletics Championships. He had a big throw of 88.17 m in the men's javelin final.

WORLD CHAMPIONSHIPS

First World Championship medal

Anju Bobby George won a bronze in long jump at the 2003 World Championships in Paris, France, in August, with a leap of 6.70 m. She surpassed this at the 2004 Olympics in Athens, Greece, finishing sixth with 6.83 m.

WORLD UNIVERSIADE

First gold at the World Universiade

Dutee Chand, the current national champion in the women's 100 m race, became the first Indian to win the gold at the World Universiade, Naples, Italy, in the 100 m race with a timing of 11.32 secs on 10 July 2019. She is also the first Indian to win a gold in the 100 m race at a global championship. She also won a silver in the 100 m race at the 2018 Asian Games in Jakarta.

Dutee Chand

Deepa Malik

PARA ATHLETICS

First participation in the Paralympics

In 1968, India made its Paralympics debut at the Tel Aviv Games. India did not participate in the first two Games, in 1960 and 1964. India completed again in 1972 and then consistently from the 1984 New York Games in the United States to Tokyo 2020 in Japan.

First triple medal in the Paralympics

India's Joginder Singh Bedi had won three medals – a silver each in javelin and shot put, and a bronze in the discus throw – at the 1984 Paralympics in Stoke Mandeville and New York, USA.

First gold in javelin

Sumit Antil won the gold medal in the men's javelin throw F64 category at the 2020 Summer Paralympics in Tokyo, Japan. He holds the current world record, having thrown 68.55 m in the Paralympics final.

First bronze medal at the World Para Athletics Championships

Varun Kumar Bhati won the bronze medal in the men's T-42 category high jump and Karan Jyoti Dalal settled for bronze in the discus throw F-55 at the World Para Athletics Championships in London in 2017.

Best performance in the World Para Athletics Championships

India won two gold, two silver, and five bronze medals (a total of nine) at the World Para Athletics Championships 2019 held in Dubai.

Best throw – discus F-36 (para-athletics) – men

Yogesh Kathuniya smashed the world record in men's discus F-36, when he threw 45.18 m to win the gold medal in the World Para Athletics Grand Prix in Berlin, Germany, on 1 July 2018.

First Paralympics gold – women

Deepa Malik became the first Indian woman to win a medal at the Paralympics by bagging a silver medal in shot put in the 2016 Paralympic Games. She also won gold in the F-53/54 javelin event at the Para Athletics Grand Prix held in Dubai in 2018.

First para athlete to get the Rajiv Gandhi Khel Ratna Award – women

Deepa Malik was the first woman para-athlete to receive the Rajiv Gandhi Khel Ratna Award in 2019.

Best javelin throw – men

Sumit Antil's world record javelin throw of 68.55 m in the F64 category came at the 2020 Tokyo Olympics. He threw the spear to a record distance of 68.62 m in the Open National Para Athletics Championships.

First ever IAS officer to win a silver medal

Suhas Yathiraj, a 2007 Indian Administrative Services (IAS) officer of Uttar Pradesh cadre bagged the silver medal in the men's SL4 category at the Tokyo 2020 Paralympics.

T20 400m world record – women

Deepthi Jeevanji clinched India's first gold at the 2024 World Para Athletics Championships by winning the women's T20 400m event in a world-record time of 55.07 seconds on 20 May. She broke Breanna Clark's previous record of 55.12 seconds. Earlier In the qualifying rounds, Deepthi set a new Asian record of 56.18 seconds and secured a Paris 2024 Paralympics quota.

Best javelin throw F64 – men

Sumit Antil won gold in the Hangzhou Asian Para Games javelin throw F64 event with a world record of 73.29m, surpassing his previous record of 70.83m set at the 2024 World Para Athletics Championships. He also set a world record with a 68.55m throw at the Tokyo Paralympics.

Best javelin throw F46 – men

Sundar Singh Gurjar set a new world record with a 68.60m throw in the men's javelin throw F46 event, winning gold at the Asian Para Games in Hangzhou on 25 October 2023. He broke the previous world record of 67.79m held by Sri Lanka's Dinesh Priyantha.

NATIONAL GAMES

Fastest 100 m hurdles – women

In the women's-only 100 m hurdles, Jyothi Yarraji became the first Indian woman to finish the race with a sub-13 timing, as she clocked 12.82 seconds at the 61st National Open Athletics Championships in Bengaluru on October 2022.

Fastest 3000 m steeplechase – men

Avinash Sable improved his national record in the 3000 m steeplechase at the Paris Diamond League on 7 July. Sable clocked 8:09.91 to finish sixth while shaving over a second off his earlier personal best of 8:11.20. Sable has been re setting the national record several times since 2019 when he clocked 8:28.94 at the Federation Cup in Patiala.

Avinash Sable

Fastest 400 m – U-18 – women

Neeru Pathak clocked 52.85 seconds to break the under-18 national record in the girls' 400 m at the 19th National Youth Athletics Championships in Bilaspur on J16 June. The 17-year-old quarter-miler from Delhi surpassed Rezoana Mallick Heena's previous record of 52.98 seconds and qualified for the U-20 World Championships.

Fastest 5,000 m and 10,000 m – men

Gulveer Singh set two new national records in 2024. On 10 June, he broke the men's 5,000 m record with a time of 13:18.92 at the Portland Track Festival, surpassing Avinash Sable's previous mark. Later, at The Ten in California, Gulveer shattered a 16-year-old men's 10,000 m record, clocking 27:41.81 and beating Surendra Singh's 2008 record by over 20 seconds.

Fastest 110 m hurdles – men

Tejas Shirse set a new national record in the men's 110 m hurdles at the World Athletics Continental Tour meeting in Jyvaskyla, Finland, on 22 May. Shirse clocked 13.41 seconds to win the final, surpassing the previous record of 13.48 seconds held by Siddhanth Thingalaya since 2017.

Fastest 4×400 m mixed relay – team

The Indian 4 x 400 m mixed relay team, consisting of Muhammad Ajmal, Jyothika Sri, Amoj Jacob, and Subha Venkatesan, set a new national record at the 2024 Asian Relay Championships on 20 May. They secured gold with a time of 3:14.12, breaking the previous record of 3:14.34 set at the 2023 Asian Games, in which Ajmal and Subha also participated.

Fastest 1,500 m – women

K.M. Deeksha set a new national record in the women's 1,500 m at the Sound Running Track Fest in Los Angeles on 11 May, surpassing Harmilan Bains' three-year-old mark. The 25-year-old distance runner from Madhya Pradesh clocked 4:04.78, improving her personal best by over a second. Deeksha had previously won gold at the Interstate Nationals by defeating Harmilan.

Highest pole vault

Women: At the 36th National Games Rosy Meena Paulraj cleared a height of 4.20 m to break the eight-year-old record of 4.15 m held by V. S. Surekha in the women's pole vault in the National Games 2022. A week later, she bettered her own record by vaulting 4.21 m on 15 October 2022 at the National Open Athletics Championships 2022 in Bengaluru.

Men: At the 36th National Games, held between 29 September and 12 October 2022, Siva Subramani (5.31 m) eclipsed his own record of 5.30 m in the men's pole vault, set four years back.

Fastest race walk

Ram Baboo clocked 2.36.34 to break the previous national record in the men's 35 km race walk (2.40.16) by nearly four minutes in the 36th National Games in 2022.

Oldest gold medallist

Rambai, at 105 years, won gold in the 100 m race at the National Open Masters Athletics Championships on 21 June 2022 in Vadodara, Gujarat.

Longest triple jump – women

On 13 June 2022, Aishwarya Babu made a record in the triple jump women at the 2022 National Inter-State Athletics Championships in Chennai, Tamil Nadu, leaping 14.14 m and breaking the national record of 14.11 m set by Mayookha Johny set at the Asian Championships in Japan in 2011.

Youngest athletics champion

Henry Rebello won the triple jump at Bangalore (now Bengaluru), Karnataka, in 1946 when he was only 17 years old. He set a record of 50 ft 2 in. at the 1948 National Games, which was surpassed only after a gap of 23 years by Mohinder Singh in 1971.

Longest shot put – women

Abha Khatua set a new women's shot put national record with a throw of 18.41 m at the Federation Cup 2024 on 13 May, breaking Manpreet Kaur's previous record of 18.06 m. The 28-year-old shot putter from Maharashtra achieved this mark on her fifth attempt, surpassing her previous joint national record of 18.06m set at the 2023 Asian Athletics Championships.

INDOOR ATHLETICS

Fastest 60 m indoor hurdles – women

India's Jyothi Yarraji set a new National Record of 8.12 seconds to win gold in the women's 60 m hurdles at the Asian Indoor Athletics Championships in Tehran on 17 February 2024.

BADMINTON

INTERNATIONAL

First doubles pair to reach World No. 1

Indian men's doubles pair Satwiksairaj Rankireddy and Chirag Shetty achieved the world No. 1 ranking in the BWF rankings for the first time in their careers after winning gold in the men's doubles at the 2023 Asian Games in Hangzhou. Satwik-Chirag, popularly known as 'Sat-Chi', have also set new record as the longest-reigning world No. 1 Indian badminton players, holding the top spot in men's doubles for 11 weeks after regaining top spot on 23 January 2024. They surpassed Saina Nehwal, who held the world No. 1 rank for nine weeks in 2015.

OLYMPIC GAMES

First medallist

Saina Nehwal became the first Indian medallist, winning a bronze medal in London, UK, in 2012.

P.V. Sindhu

First silver medallist

P.V. Sindhu finished runner-up in Rio de Janeiro, Brazil, in 2016.

First two-time medallist

P.V. Sindhu remains the only two-time medallist with the silver medal in Rio de Janeiro, Brazil (2016), and the bronze medal in Tokyo, Japan (2020).

WORLD CHAMPIONSHIP

First individual medallist – men – singles

Prakash Padukone claimed the men's singles bronze medal in Copenhagen, Denmark, in 1983.

First individual medallist – women – singles

P.V. Sindhu received the women's singles bronze medal in Guangzhou, China, in 2013.

First doubles medallists – women

Jwala Gutta and Ashwini Ponnappa became the first Indian bronze medallists in women's doubles in London, UK, in 2011.

Jwala Gutta and Ashwini Ponnappa

First doubles medallists – men

Satwiksairaj Rankireddy and Chirag Shetty finished with a bronze in the men's doubles in Tokyo, Japan, in 2022.

First silver medallist – men – singles

K. Srikanth finished runner-up in the men's singles in the 2021 edition at Huelva, Spain.

First silver medallist – women – singles

Saina Nehwal finished runner-up in the women's singles in Jakarta in 2015.

First two-time silver medallist – women - singles

P.V. Sindhu finished runner-up in women's singles in Glasgow, Scotland (2017), and Nanjing, China (2019).

Saina Nehwal

First world champion

P.V. Sindhu claimed the honour by winning the women's singles in 2019.

Highest number of medals

P.V. Sindhu has five medals – a gold, two silver and two bronze medals – from the premier championship.

> The 2023 India Open badminton tournament was the first India Open to have a Super 750 status.

Two medals from one edition – women

P.V. Sindhu, with the silver medal, and Saina Nehwal, with the bronze, were on the podium of the women's singles at Glasgow in 2017.

K. Srikanth

Two medals from one edition – men

K. Srikanth, with the silver medal, and Lakshya Sen, with the bronze, made it to the podium in Huelva, Spain, in 2021.

ASIAN GAMES

First gold medal at Asian Games

The Indian men's doubles badminton duo of Satwiksairaj Rankireddy and Chirag Shetty made history on 7 October 2023 by securing India's first-ever gold medal in badminton at the Asian Games.

The dynamic pair emerged victorious after defeating the formidable Korean duo with a scoreline of 21–18, 21–16 in the final match.

First medal – men – team

The men's team comprising Prakash Padukone, Dinesh Khanna, Davinder Ahuja, Partho Ganguli, and Raman

P.V. Sindhu

Sindhu was in the Forbes' list of highest paid female athletes in 2018, 2019, 2021, and 2022. She is a recipient of the highest of sports honours such as Arjuna Award and Rajiv Gandhi Khel Ratna, and also civilian awards such as Padma Shri and Padma Bhushan. She entered the international circuit at a young age of 14 in the year 2009. In February 2023 she was part of the Indian team that won a bronze medal at the Badminton Asia Mixed Team Championships.

Ghosh won a bronze medal in Tehran in 1974.

First medal – women – team

The women's team comprising Ami Ghia, Madhumita Goswami, Amita Kulkarni, Hufrish Nariman, Kanwal Thakur Singh and Vandana Chiplunkar claimed a bronze medal in New Delhi in 1982.

First to win a medal – men – singles

Syed Modi claimed a bronze in New Delhi in 1982.

First to win a medal – women – singles

Saina Nehwal received a women's singles bronze in Jakarta - Palembang in 2018.

First to win a medal – mixed – doubles

Leroy D'Sa and Kanwal Thakur Singh received a bronze medal in New Delhi in 1982.

First to win a medal – men – doubles

Leroy D'Sa and Pradeep Gandhe claimed a bronze medal in New Delhi in 1982.

Multiple medal – winner in a single edition

Leroy D'Sa received three bronze medals – for the men's team, the doubles and the mixed doubles – in New Delhi in 1982.

Two medallists in a single event

P.V. Sindhu (silver) and Saina Nehwal (bronze) made it to the podium in the women's singles in Jakarta - Palembang in 2018.

COMMONWEALTH GAMES

First medallist – men – singles

Dinesh Khanna claimed a bronze medal in 1966 in the British Empire and Commonwealth Games. (In 1978, these Games were rechristened as the Commonwealth Games.)

Dinesh Khanna

First medallist – women – singles

Aparna Popat received a bronze medal in women's singles in Manchester in 2002.

First medallists – men – team

The team comprising P. Gopichand, Abhinn Shyam Gupta, George Thomas, Jaseel P. Ismail, Marcos Bristow, Nikhil Kanetkar, and Vincent Lobo claimed a silver medal in Kuala Lumpur in 1998.

First medallist – women – doubles

Ami Ghia and Kanwal Thakur Singh, claimed a bronze in Edmonton in 1978.

First medallists – women – team

The team comprising Manjusha Kanwar, P.V.V. Lakshmi, Madhumita Bisht, Aparna Popat, Archana Deodhar, K. Neelima Chowdhary, and C. Deepthi won a bronze medal in Kuala Lumpur in 1998.

First gold medallist – mixed – team

The team comprising K. Srikanth, Saina Nehwal, P.V. Sindhu, H. S. Prannoy, Ashwini Ponnappa, Sikki Reddy, Ruthvika Shivani, Chirag Shetty, Satwiksairaj Rankireddy and Pranav Chopra won the title in Gold Coast in 2018.

First silver medallist – mixed – team

The team comprising Saina Nehwal, P. Kashyap, Jwala Gutta, Ashwini Ponnappa, Chetan Anand, Aditi Mutatkar, Sanave Thomas, Rupesh Kumar, Aparna Balans and V. Diju finished runner-up in Delhi in 2010.

First bronze medallist – mixed – team

The team comprising Anup Sridhar, Aparna Popat, Chetan Anand, Jwala Gutta, Shruti Kurien, Saina Nehwal, Trupti Murgunde, V. Diju, Sanave Thomas, and Rupesh Kumar claimed the bronze in Melbourne in 2006.

Prakash Padukone

First gold medallist – men – singles

Prakash Padukone won the men's singles title in Edmonton in 1978.

First gold medallist – women - singles

Saina Nehwal won in New Delhi in 2010.

First gold medallists – women – doubles

Jwala Gutta and Ashwini Ponnappa won gold in Delhi in 2010.

First gold medallists – men – doubles

Chirag Shetty and Satwiksairaj Rankireddy won the title in Birmingham in 2022.

Most gold medals from one edition

India won three gold medals – from men's singles (Lakshya Sen), women's singles (P.V. Sindhu) and men's doubles (Chirag Shetty and Satwiksairaj Rankireddy) – in Birmingham, UK, in 2022.

Most medals from one edition

India won six medals – women's singles gold (Saina Nehwal), mixed team gold, men's singles silver (K. Srikanth), women's singles silver (P.V. Sindhu), men's doubles silver (Chirag Shetty and Satwiksairaj Rankireddy) and women's doubles bronze (Ashwini Ponnappa and N. Sikki Reddy) – in Gold Coast, Australia, in 2018.

ASIAN CHAMPIONSHIPS

First gold medal at Badminton Asia Team Championships

India's women's badminton team won their first-ever gold medal at the Badminton Asia Team Championships 2024 in Shah Alam, Malaysia. This historic victory marks the first time India's women made the podium, with the men's team previously earning two bronze medals in 2016 and 2020. The winning team members were PV Sindhu, Anmol Kharb, Ashmita Chaliha, Gayatri Gopichand-Treesa Jolly (doubles), and Tanisha Crasto-Ashwini Ponnappa (doubles). The Indian men's team had previously won two bronze medals in 2016 and 2020 while the women's team reached podium first time.

First gold medal from Asian Championships

Dinesh Khanna won the men's singles gold medal in Lucknow in 1965.

First bronze medal – men – singles

Suresh Goel claimed a men's singles bronze in Lucknow in 1965.

First medal – women – singles

Meena Shah claimed a women's singles bronze in Lucknow in 1965.

First medal – men – doubles

Dipu Ghosh and Raman Ghosh received a bronze at Jakarta in 1971.

First silver medal – men – doubles

Prakash Padukone and Syed Modi received the silver medal in Peking (now Beijing) in 1978.

First medal – mixed – doubles

Owen Roncon-Sarojini Apte and A.I. Sheikh-Achala Karnik received bronze medals in Lucknow in 1965.

First medal – women – doubles

Jwala Gutta and Ashwini Ponnappa received a bronze medal in Gimcheon, South Korea, in 2014.

WORLD JUNIOR CHAMPIONSHIP

First medallist – girls – singles

Saina Nehwal received a silver medal in the girls' singles in Incheon, South Korea, in 2006.

First gold medallist – girls – singles

Saina Nehwal won the girls' singles in Pune in 2008.

First medallist – boys – singles

R.M.V. Gurusaidutt claimed a bronze medal in the boys' singles in Pune in 2008.

First silver medallist – boys – singles

Siril Verma received a silver medal in the boys' singles in Lima, Peru, in 2015.

BWF SUPER SERIES MASTERS FINALS/BWF WORLD TOUR FINALS

First medallist – women – singles

Saina Nehwal received a bronze in Kota Kinabalu, Sabah, Malaysia, in 2008.

First medallist – men – singles

K. Srikanth received a bronze medal in Dubai in 2014.

First gold medallist – women – singles

P.V. Sindhu won the title in Guangzhou, China, in 2018 when the event was rechristened as BWF World Tour Finals.

First silver medallists – mixed – doubles

V. Diju and Jwala Gutta finished runners up in the mixed doubles in Johor Bahru, Malaysia, in 2009.

First silver medallist – women – singles

Saina Nehwal received a silver in Liuzhou, China, in 2011.

Highest world ranking – women – singles

Saina Nehwal became the world no. 1 in the women's singles in April 2015.

Highest world rankings – mixed – doubles

Jwala Gutta and V. Diju were ranked world no. 6 in August 2010.

Highest world ranking – men – singles

K. Srikanth became the world no. 1 in the men's singles in April 2018.

Highest world ranking – women – doubles

Jwala Gutta and Ashwini Ponnappa were ranked world no. 10 in August 2015.

Highest world ranking – men – doubles

Chirag Shetty and Satwiksairaj Rankireddy were ranked world no. 7 in November 2019.

OTHER INTERNATIONAL COMPETITIONS

First medal in the Thomas Cup – men – team championship

Indonesian postal stamp commemorating Thomas Cup

India defeated 14-time champion Indonesia at the Thomas Cup 3-0 to win the prestigious title in 2022 for the first time ever, with World Championships medallist Lakshya Sen, K. Srikanth, and the current world no. 8 doubles duo of Chirag Shetty and Satwiksairaj Rankireddy.

First duo to win Super 1,000 title

Satwiksairaj Rankireddy and Chirag Shetty became the first Indian pair to win Super 1000 title as they won the men's doubles final at Indonesian Open 2023. They are also the first Indian pair to win a BWF World Tour Title at all levels.

First winner of the World Cup – men – singles

Prakash Padukone won in Kuala Lumpur, Malaysia, in 1981.

First winner at the All England Championship

Prakash Padukone won in London in 1980.

First finalist at the All England Championship – men – singles

Prakash Nath reached the men's singles final in 1947 in London.

Two semi-finalists at the All England Championship

Prakash Nath and Davinder Mohan reached the men's singles semi-finals in 1947. Interestingly, the two players chose not to play each other. They tossed a coin, Prakash Nath called it right and advanced to the final.

First medal in the Uber Cup – women's – team

India claimed its first bronze medal in New Delhi in 2014.

Most titles – women
Saina Nehwal won 10 titles in the BWF Superseries from 15 appearances in the final.

Most titles – men
K. Srikanth won six titles in the BWF Superseries in seven appearances in the final.

PARALYMPICS

First gold medallist – men – singles
Pramod Bhagat became the first gold medallist after winning the men's singles in the SL3 category in the 2020 Tokyo Paralympics.

First silver medallist – men – singles
Suhas Yathiraj became the first silver medallist in men's singles in the SL4 category in Tokyo in 2020.

First bronze medallist – men – singles
Manoj Sarkar became the first bronze medallist in the men's singles SL3 category in Tokyo in 2020.

DOMESTIC: NATIONALS

First National champions
Vijay Madgavkar (men's singles in 1934); T. P. Boland (women's singles in 1935); D. Minas–V. Minas (men's doubles in 1934); T. P. Boland–Cameron (women's doubles in 1935); and N. Knight–I. Brydges (mixed doubles in 1936).

Aparna Popat

DRIBBLE AND SWISH: BASKETBALL

First appearance in the Asian Games
India took part in the first Asian Games at New Delhi in 1951, under the captaincy of Ranbir Chand. In its best performance at the Games to date, the team came fourth.

Satnam Singh Bhamara

First Indian-born player in the NBA
Satnam Singh Bhamara set a milestone in the history of Indian basketball when he was drafted into the National Basketball Association (NBA), the premier professional basketball league in the USA, in June 2015. Selected by the Dallas Mavericks, he played his Summer League debut match against the New Orleans Pelicans, scoring four points for his team, on 11 July 2015.

First and only sisters representing the country
Prashanti, Pratima, Priyanka, and Divya Singh – four sisters from Varanasi, Uttar Pradesh – have all played basketball for India.

Longest sequence of Nationals titles
- Services won the men's national title 26 years in a row from 1957 to 1982.
- Railways won the women's title 17 years in a row from 1986 to 2002.

Most appearances in the Asian Games – women
Prashanti Singh is the only woman basketball player to represent the Indian team in two Asian Games, in 2010 and 2014. She also represented the national team in the 2006 CWG. She has won 22 medals in national championships and federation events.

Prashanti Singh

Best win
Indian basketball's biggest win was at the 2014 FIBA Asia Cup, held in Wuhan, Hubei, China, winning against home favourites and against the most successful Asian team, China, by 7 points.

Most titles – men – singles
Prakash Padukone holds a unique record of winning all his nine singles titles in a row from 1971 to 1979.

Most titles – women – singles
Aparna Popat matched Prakash's record by winning her nine singles titles on the trot from 1997 to 2005.

Most titles – men – doubles
Rupesh Kumar was part of the men's doubles title-winning pair for nine successive years between 2002 and 2010. Rupesh partnered Markose Bristow in 2002 and 2003, and thereafter joined hands with Sanave Thomas.

Most titles – women – doubles
Jwala Gutta formed part of the title-winning combination 10 times between 2000 and 2013. She won with Shruti Kurien in 2000 and again from 2002 to 2008. She paired with Ashwini Ponnappa in 2009 and 2013.

Most titles – mixed – doubles
Madhumita Goswami-Bisht won the mixed doubles title 12 times with five different partners. She won in 1981, 1986–88 (with Sanat Mishra); in 1989–1990 (with Harjeet Singh); in 1994–97 (with Vinod Kumar); in 2000

India at World Athletics Championships 2023

Chirag Shetty and Satwiksairaj Rankireddy ranked number one in the Badminton World Federation (BWF) men's doubles rankings, as of 21 May 2024.

(with Vincent Lobo); and 2001 (with Markose Bristow).

Most versatile and successful player in the Nationals

Madhumita Goswami-Bisht, in an international career spanning almost a quarter of a century from 1978, won eight national women singles, nine women's doubles and 12 mixed doubles titles.

First badminton gold – Paralympics

Pramod Bhagat of Odisha won India's first ever Paralympics gold in badminton. (Badminton made its debut at the 2020 Tokyo Olympics). He clinched gold in men's singles badminton (SLB) event.

BOXING

Most golds in an international meet

India won 10 gold and two silver medals at the 1995 South Asian Games (SAG; formerly SAF) in Chennai, Tamil Nadu. This achievement is second only to South Korea's haul of all 12 gold medals in the 1986 Seoul Asian Games.

Most successive professional wins

Vijender Singh demolished former Commonwealth champion Charles Adamu to claim his 12th straight win in November 2019. The winning streak ended when he was defeated by Russian opponent, Artysh Lopsan, in Goa in March 2021.

Best Youth Boxer – men

Sachin Siwach was named Asian Boxing Confederation's Best Youth Boxer of 2017.

Oldest existing boxing association

The Maharashtra Amateur Boxing Association was formed in 1924.

AIBA

First boxer in the AIBA athletes' commission

In November 2019, veteran Indian boxer Laishram Sarita Devi was elected unopposed to the AIBA's first-ever athletes commission to represent the Asian bloc. She is an eight-time Asian Championship medallist, with five being gold medals.

AIBA LEGENDS

First Indian woman boxer to receive AIBA Legends Award

M.C. Mary Kom received the AIBA Legends Award at AIBA's 70th anniversary gala in Montreux, Switzerland, in 2016.

First male boxer to win the APB Best Boxing trophy

Asian Games gold medallist Vikas Krishan was awarded the APB Best Boxing trophy at AIBA's 70th anniversary in Montreux, Switzerland, 2016.

World no. 1

- In 2009, AIBA announced Vijender Singh as the top-ranked boxer in the annual middleweight category.
- In January 2019, M.C. Mary Kom (48 kg category) was the top-ranked boxer in the AIBA World Ranking (women).

Vijendra Singh

ASIAN CHAMPIONSHIPS

Most medals in the Asian Championship – women

M.C. Mary Kom (46 kg), L. Sarita Devi (54 kg), Jenny R. Lalremliani (63 kg), and Jyotsna (80 kg and 86 kg) won two golds each at the 2003 and the 2005 Asian Women's Boxing Championship, in Hisar, Haryana, and Kaohsiung, Taiwan, respectively.

Best performance at the Asian Championship

Indian boxers won two gold, four silver, and seven bronze medals in Bangkok, Thailand, in April 2019 to finish at the third position with 13 medals. Pooja Rani (81 kg) and Amit Panghal (52 kg) won gold medals; Deepak Singh (49 kg), Kavinder Singh Bisht (56 kg), Ashish Kumar (75 kg), and Simranjit Kaur (64 kg) won silvers; Nikhat Zareen (51 kg), Manisha Moun (54 kg), Sonia Chahal (57 kg), L. Sarita Devi (60 kg), Shiva Thapa (60 kg), Ashish (69 kg), and Satish Kumar (91 kg) won bronze medals.

First Asian Schoolgirl Champion

Young boxer Deepali Thapa made history as the first Asian Schoolgirl Champion as India secured seven women's titles at the Asian Championships in Al Ain, UAE, on 8 September.

ASIAN GAMES

First Asian Games medal – men

Hari Singh won the silver in the middleweight category at the 1958 Manila Games in the Philippines. Sunder Rao and Ranganathan won the bronze in the lightweight and the welterweight categories respectively.

First Asian Games gold – men

Padam Bahadur Mal won the gold medal in the lightweight category in 1962 in the Asian Games held in Jakarta, Indonesia.

Most Asian Games golds

Hawa Singh (heavyweight) won two golds at the 1966 and 1970 Asian Games, both held in Bangkok, Thailand.

Best performance in the Asian Games

India won two gold, three silver, and four bronze medals in the 2010 Asian Games, its best haul at an Asian Games. The gold medallists were Vikas Krishan (60 kg) and Vijender Singh (75 kg). Silver medals were won by V. Santosh Kumar (64 kg), Dinesh Kumar (81 kg), and Manpreet Singh (91 kg). The bronze went to Suranjoy Singh (52 kg), Paramjeet Samota (+91 kg), M.C. Mary Kom (51 kg), and Kavita Goyal (75 kg).

Best performance in Asian Games – gold – women

India won a gold and two bronze medals at the 2014 Incheon Asian Games in South Korea. M.C. Mary Kom won the gold in the women's flyweight (51 kg) event. L. Sarita Devi (lightweight, 60 kg) and Pooja Rani (middleweight, 75 kg) won bronze medals.

India's best-ever medal haul at Asian Games – total – women

The Indian women boxers delivered an impressive performance at the Huangzhou Asian Games 2023, securing their best-ever haul of four medals (one silver and three bronze) along with four Paris 2024 Olympic quota spots. In terms of gold medal, India's beast show remains one gold and two bronze medals at 2014 Incheon.

Amit Panghal

Amandeep Singh

COMMONWEALTH CHAMPIONSHIPS

Most Commonwealth Championship gold medals

India won six gold medals and the overall title at the Commonwealth Championship in New Delhi in March 2010. Amandeep Singh (49 kg), Suranjoy Singh (52 kg), Jai Bhagwan (60 kg), Vijender Singh (75 kg), Dinesh Kumar (81 kg), and Paramjeet Samota (+91 kg) won a gold medal each.

COMMONWEALTH GAMES

First Commonwealth Games gold

Mohammed Ali Qamar won the gold medal in the lightweight category, defeating Darren Langley 27–25 at the Commonwealth Games in Manchester, UK, in 2002.

Best performance at the Commonwealth Games

At the 2018 CWG in Gold Coast, Australia, India won three gold, three silver, and three bronze medals. M.C. Mary Kom in women's lightweight (48 kg), Gaurav Solanki in flyweight (52 kg), and Vikas Krishan in middleweight (75 kg) won gold medals. Amit Panghal in light flyweight (49 kg), Manish Kaushik in lightweight (60 kg) and Satish Kumar in superweight (+91 kg) won silver medals. Mohammed Hussamuddin in bantamweight (56 kg), Manoj Kumar in welterweight (69 kg), and Naman Talwar in heavyweight (91 kg) won bronze medals.

INTERNATIONAL

Most international titles

- Heavyweight boxer Kaur Singh won gold at four major international events: the 1980 Asian Boxing Championship (Bombay, now Mumbai, Maharashtra) and 1982 (Seoul, South Korea), the 1982 Delhi Asian Games and the 1982 King's Cup in Bangkok, Thailand.
- Super heavyweight boxer Rajkumar Sangwan also won four golds: at the 1991 Asian Invitational Championship in Bangkok, Thailand; the 1993 China Invitational Championship in Beijing, China; the 1993 South Asian Federation (SAF) Games at Dhaka, Bangladesh; and the 1994 Asian Boxing Championship at Tehran, Iran.

NATIONALS

First National Championship

The very first National Boxing Championship in the country, organized by the Indian Amateur Boxing Federation, was held in Bombay (now Mumbai), Maharashtra, from 18 to 22 March 1950.

OLYMPICS

First Olympic appearance

India entered a boxing team in seven divisions for the first time at the 1948 London Olympics but could not reach the quarter-finals.

First Olympic medal – men

Vijender Singh won a bronze medal (middleweight) in the 2008 Beijing Olympics.

First Olympic medal – women

Six-time women's world champion M.C. Mary Kom won a bronze medal (51 kg) in the 2012 London Olympics. Lovlina Borgohain (69 kg) became the second Indian woman to win a bronze medal at Tokyo 2020 after losing to Turkey's Busenaz Surmeneli 0–5 in the semi-finals.

WORLD BOXING CHAMPIONSHIP

First medal in the World Boxing Championships – men

- Amit Panghal was the first Indian male boxer to win a silver medal in the World Boxing Championship 2019. Seven Indians have won World Championships medals until now: Amit Panghal (2019, silver), Vijender Singh (2009, bronze), Vikas Krishan (2011, bronze), Shiv Thapa (2015, bronze), Gaurav (2017, bronze), Manish Kaushik (2019, bronze), and Akash Kumar (2021, bronze)
- Parveen Kumar won a bronze medal in the lightweight category in the World Junior Championship in Budapest, Hungary, in November 2000.

First World Boxing Championships medal – women

- M.C. Mary Kom from Manipur bagged a silver medal in the 48 kg category in the United States in December 2001.
- Manju Rani became the second Indian to enter the World Boxing Championships final and won the silver at Ulan-Ude, Russia, in 2019.

Most medals in the World Boxing Championships

In October 2019, M.C. Mary Kom became the first boxer in the world (male or female) to win eight World Championship medals (six gold, a silver and a bronze).

Best performance in the World Boxing Championships – women

India won four gold, one silver and three bronze medals in the fourth World Women's Boxing Championship 2006 in New Delhi. M.C. Mary Kom (46 kg), L. Sarita Devi (52 kg), Jenny R. Lalremliani (63 kg), and Lekha K.C. (75 kg) won gold medals. N. Usha (57 kg) won a silver. The bronze winners were Chhotu Loura (50 kg), Aruna Mishra (60 kg), and Renu (82 kg).

WORLD CHAMPIONSHIP

First medal in the World Championship – senior – men

Vijender Singh won a bronze medal in the 2009 Milan World Cup in Italy.

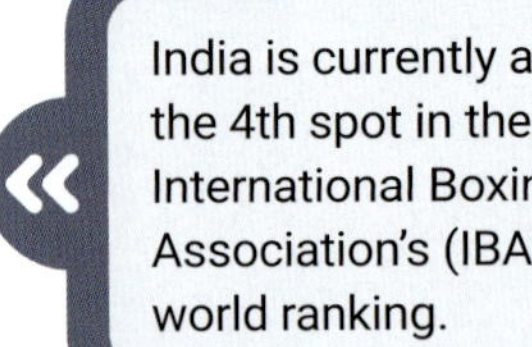

Most World Championship titles – women

M.C. Mary Kom is the first female pugilist to win the World Championship crown six times (2002, 2005, 2006, 2008, 2010, and 2018). She also won the most world titles (five) in a row between 2002 and 2010. Others to have won gold medals in the World Championships are Sarita Devi (2006), Jenny R. Lalremliani (2006), Lakha K.C. (2006), and Nikhat Zareen (2022).

WORLD CUP

First medal at the World Cup – men

Zoramthanga defeated teammate Dharmender Yadav 17–4 on points to win the light flyweight bronze on 17 November 1990 in Bombay (now Mumbai), Maharashtra.

Most medals in the World Cup – men

The Indian team won a silver, and a bronze medal, and the sixth position overall, in the AIBA Boxing World Cup in October 2019 in Yekaterinburg, Russia.

YOUTH BOXING CHAMPIONSHIP

Best performance in the World Youth Women's Boxing Championship

Seven Indian women boxers clinched gold medals in their respective weight categories in the AIBA Youth World Boxing Championships in Kielce, Poland, in August 2021. They were Gitika (48 kg), Naorem Babyrojisana Chanu (51 kg), Poonam (57 kg), Vinka (60 kg), Arundhati Choudhary (69 kg), T. Sanamacha Chanu (75 kg) and Alfiya Pathan (+81 kg).

Postal stamp from USSR commemorating AIBA Championship

Most medals at the Youth Boxing Championships

The Indian team won five gold, two silver, and five bronze medals at the Youth Boxing Championship in November 2019 in Ulaanbaatar, Mongolia.

CHESS

GENERAL

Most times world champion

Viswanathan Anand has won the World Chess Championship five times (2000, 2007, 2008, 2010, and 2012).

Most successful Commonwealth champion

Abhijeet Gupta is the only player to win the title five times, including three times in a row from 2015 to 2017.

Board Prize with a perfect score

Viswanathan Anand scored seven points from seven rounds to win the top Board Prize in the Asian Team Championship in 1989.

Viswanathan Anand

Longest reign as top-ranked Indian in the world

Viswanathan Anand remained India's top-ranked player in the world for 37 successive years. His supreme reign ended when D. Gukesh overtook him in the World rating list released on 1 September 2023.

Grand Slam victories

In chess, the tournaments in Wijk Aan Zee (the Netherlands), Linares (Spain), and Dortmund (Germany) were considered the equivalent of the Grand Slam in golf. Anand won at Wijk

Aan Zee five times, and at Linares and Dortmund, both three times.

First GM norm
Pravin Thipsay was the first to achieve GM norm in the 1985 Commonwealth championship in London.

Pravin Thipsay

First GM norm in National Championship
P. Konguvel was the first Indian to date to gain a nine-game norm from the National 'A' Championship in New Delhi in June 2001.

First Grandmaster (GM)
Viswanathan Anand became India's first GM on 28 December 1987 at the Sakthi Finance Grandmaster tournament in Coimbatore.

First International Master (IM) – men
Manuel Aaron of Tamil Nadu became an International Master in 1961.

First International Master (IM) – women
S. Vijayalakshmi got the International Master's title in Sept 2000.

First Olympiad golden sweep
India became only the third nation - after Russia and China to make a sweep of team titles in the 2024 edition, Budapest, Hungary. Seeded two, India won the Open title with a stupendous tally of 21 match points (out of a maximum of 22) in the 11-round competition for its maiden gold in the games' most prestigious team championship, involving 197 nations/federations. The team members were D. Gukesh, R. Praggnanandhaa, Arjun Erigaisi, Vidit Gujrathi and P. Harikrishna. Coach: N. Srinath. Top-seeded Indian women scored 19 points to justify its ranking in a field of 183 nations/federations. The team comprised D. Harika, R. Vaishali, Divya Deshmukh, Vantika Agrawal, and Tania Sachdev with Coach: Abhjiit Kunte.

Most individual gold medallists in a single edition of Olympiad
Five Indians won gold medals for their individual performance in Budapest, 2024. D. Gukesh (Open, Board 1), Arjun Erigaisi (Board 3), Divya Deshmukh (Women, Board 3) and Vantika Agrawal (Women, Board 4) played stellar roles in India's historic twin-triumphs.

FIRSTS

First Olympiad gold
Dibyendu Barua won the gold on the second board of the Olympiad in Novi Sad (erstwhile Yugoslavia) in 1990.

First Olympiad gold on top board
D. Gukesh won the gold on top board in Mahabalipuram in 2022. He retained it in 2024 to set a unique record.

First Olympiad medal
Rafiq Khan, a carpenter from Bhopal, won a silver medal in the 1980 Olympiad.

First time when India won medals in both sections of Olympiad
India won bronze medals in Open and women sections of the Olympiad in Mahabalipuram in 2022.

First sweep of titles in Grand Swiss
Vidit Gujrathi and R. Vaishali won the Open and women titles in the premier Grand Swiss Chess in 2023 and qualified for their prestigious Candidates Tournaments.

First medal in the Chess Olympiad
India won its maiden medal from the Tromso Chess Olympiad in 2014 in Norway. In the open section, India was represented by Parimarjan Negi, K, Sasikiran, S.P. Sethuraman, B. Adhiban, and M.R. Lalith Babu. They claimed the bronze medal, ahead of traditional powerhouses like Russia, Armenia and Ukraine.

First medal in Asian Games
K Humpy won the gold in the Doha Asian Games in 2006.

First international recognition
Mir Sultan Khan, born in 1905 in village Mittha, Punjab, received international recognition at a time when there was no system of Elo ratings. In 1928, he won the all-India title scoring 8.5 out of 9 points at the British Championship. He won again in 1932 and 1933. He also defeated world champion Jose Casablanca of Cuba at the Hastings tournament. Considered among the 10 best players in the world then, he returned to India in 1933 but played little chess. He died in Sargodha, Pakistan, on 25 May 1966.

First team medal in Asian Games
The trio of K. Sasikiran, P. Harikrishna, and K. Humpy won the mixed team gold in Doha in 2006.

First to win the Asian Junior girls' title thrice
Mary Ann Gomes won the title in 2006 (New Delhi), 2007 (Mumbai), and 2008 (Chennai).

First WGM norm
Bhagyashree Thipsay, 21, was the first to achieve a Woman Grand Master (WGM) norm in 1986 in the Lloyds Bank Master's tournament.

First WIM
Jayshree Khadilkar became a WIM (Woman International Master) in 1978.

First woman to lead a team in the open section
K. Humpy led India 'B' in the open section of the Asian Team Championship at Jodhpur in 2003.

Two World Cups
Viswanathan Anand is the first person in the world to successfully defend the men's World Cup title. He did so at Hyderabad in October 2002.

First World Sub-junior medal
Viswanathan Anand claimed a bronze after sharing the second place in the 1984.

First World Junior title
Viswanathan Anand was 17 years 225 days when he won the title on 2 August 1987

at Baguio City in the Philippines. P. Harikrishna (2004) and Abhijeet Gupta (2008) are the other junior title winners.

First country to win both World Junior titles in a single edition

India became the first country to win both the World Junior titles in a single edition in 2008 when Abhijeet Gupta and D. Harika won the open and girls' sections respectively in the World Junior Chess Championship in Gaziantep, Türkiye. Parimarjan Negi claimed the silver to give India a rare 1-2 finish in the open section.

MOSTS

Youngest winner of the Candidates Tournament

D. Gukesh, 17, became the youngest winner of the prestigious Candidates Tournament in Toronto in April 2024. The title earned him the right to challenge reigning World champion China's Ding Liren for the world crown, in Singapore, in November-December 2024.

D. Gukesh

Highest cheque

Viswanathan Anand won €1.20 million for retaining the World Chess title in Sofia, Bulgaria, in May 2010.

Most International age group titles (in a single year)

Tejas Bakre won three gold medals in eight months in 1998: the Asian Junior at Rasht (Iran) in May, the World Youth Games championship in Moscow in July, and the Asian Sub-Junior in Mumbai in December.

Most Indians in World Cup quarter - finals

Four Indians – R. Praggnanandhaa, Vidit Gujrathi, D. Gukesh, and Arjun Erigaisi – qualified for the World Cup quarter-finals in Baku, Azerbaijan, in 2023.

Most medals

Indians won 21 medals – seven gold, seven silver, and seven bronze – in the Asian Youth Championship held in New Delhi in 2005. This was the biggest haul by India in a continental competition.

World Champions

So far, 36 Indians have won 55 world titles. They are Viswanathan Anand (World 2000, 2007, 2008, 2010, 2012, and Junior, 1987); P. Harikrishna (U-10, 1996 and Junior, 2004); K. Humpy (girls' U-10, 1997, girls' U-12, 1998, girls' U-14, 2000 and junior 2001); Aarthie Ramaswamy (U-18, 1999); Deep Sengupta (U-12, 2000); D. Harika (girls' U-14, 2004, girls' U-18, 2006, and Junior girls', 2008); N. Srinath (U-12, 2005); Sahaj Grover (U-10, 2005); Girish A. Koushik (U-8, 2006); Ivana Furtado (girls' U-8, 2006 and 2007); C.H. Mohineesh (U-10, 2006); Ch. Sahajasri (U-10, 2006); Abhijeet Gupta (Junior, 2008); Sayantan Das (U-12, 2008); Vidit Gujarathi (U-14, 2008); Padmini Rout (girls' U-14, 2008); B. Adhiban (U-16, 2008); Sowmya Swaminathan (Junior girls', 2009); M. Karthikeyan (U-12, 2011, U-16, 2013); M. Mahalakshmi (girls' U-14, 2012, and girls' U-18, 2015); R. Vaishali (girls' U-12, 2012, and girls' U-14, 2015); N. Priyanka (U-10, 2012); Saina Salonika (girls' U-10, 2013); R. Praggnanandhaa (U-8, 2013, and U-10, 2015); Divya Deshmukh (girls' U-10, 2014, and girls' U-14, 2017); Nihal Sarin (U-10, 2014, and U-18 online, 2020); Bharath Subramanium (U-8, 2015); Rakshitta Ravi (girls' U-10, 2015); Aakanksha Hagawane (girls' U-16, 2016); D. Jishitha (girls U-14, 2017); D. Gukesh (U-12, 2019, and U-14 online, 2020); B. Savitha Shri (girls' U-12, 2019); A. Charvi (girls' U-8, 2022), Shubhi Gupta (girls' U-12, 2022); A. R. Ilamparthi (U-14, 2022); and Pranav Anand (U-18, 2022).

Oldest to regain the world rapid title

Viswanathan Anand, at 48, became the oldest world champion in the rapid format (25-minute time format) in Riyadh in December 2017. He regained the title won in 2003. Two days later, he also became the oldest medallist in the blitz format (five-minute time format) by claiming the bronze medal.

Commonwealth champions

Twelve Indians have won the Commonwealth title. They are Pravin Thipsay (1985), D.V. Prasad (1986), P. Mithrakanth (1996), Atanu Lahiri (1999), K. Sasikiran (2000), P. Harikrishna (2001), Dibyendu Barua (2003), R.B. Ramesh (2007), R.R. Laxman (2010), M.R. Lalith Babu (2012), Abhijeet Gupta (2013, 2015, 2016, 2017 and 2019), and P. Karthikeyan (2018).

Asian champions – men

Six Grandmasters – K. Sasikiran (2003), Surya Shekhar Ganguly (2009), P. Harikrishna (2011), Parimarjan Negi (2012), S.P. Sethuraman (2016), and R. Praggnanandhaa (2022) – have been crowned champions.

Asian champions – women

Ten Indians have won the title on 12 occasions – Rohini Khadilkar (1981 and 1983), Anupama Gokhale (1985 and 1987), Bhagyashree Thipsay (1991), K. Humpy (2003), Tania Sachdev (2007), D. Harika (2011), Bhakti Kulkarni (2016), Padmini Rout (2018), P. V. Nandhidhaa (2022), and Divya Deshmukh (2023).

Asian junior champions – boys

V. Ravi Kumar (1978); Viswanathan Anand (1984 and 1985); Abhijit Kunte (1997); Tejas Bakre (1998); K. Sasikiran (1999); P. Harikrishna (2000); Deepan Chakravarthy (2002); P. Magesh Chandran (2003); S. Arun Prasad (2004); P. Karthikeyan (2007); Aswin Jayaram (2008 and 2009); M. Shyam Sundar (2010 and 2011); N. Srinath (2012, 2013, and 2014); and Aravindh Chithambaram (2016).

Asian junior champions – girls

Anupama Abhyankar (1985); Saheli Dhar (1993); K. Humpy (2000); M. Kasturi (2001); Tania Sachdev (2002); Y. Pratibha (2003); Mary Ann Gomes

Most Indians in Candidates Tournament

For the first time, five Indians – R. Praggnanandhaa, Vidit Gujrathi, D. Gukesh, R. Vaishali and K. Humpy – qualified for their respective Candidates Tournaments, in Toronto, in April 2024.

Most National titles (in a season)

P. Harikrishna won five National titles in 1997–98 season – the 1997 National Sub-juniors held in January 1998 at Aurangabad, the U-12 in Ahmedabad, the U-18 in Bikaner, the U-14 rapid chess title in Guntur and the 1998 National Sub-junior at Aurangabad.

Most National titles

- *Men*: Manuel Aaron won nine National titles, five of them in a row from 1969–74.
- *Women*: S. Vijayalakshmi has claimed the National title six times, including five times in a row from May 2002.

City to host most Commonwealth Championships

New Delhi hosted the Commonwealth Championship six times between 2007 and 2019.

Most titles in a year

Viswanathan Anand won a string of eight titles in the year 2000. Starting with the World Blitz Cup, he won the Wydra International at Haifa, Israel, the Advanced Chess title in Leon, Spain, the Giants Classic in Frankfurt, the Dortmund International (joint winner), Germany, the World Cup in Shenyang, China, and the Corsica Masters in France, finishing with the World Championship title in December 2000.

Most participants in an International Open

As many as 2,810 entries were received across three sections of the 17th Delhi International Open held in January 2019.

Most prize money offered in an International Open

The 2019 Delhi International Open offered ₹1.01 crore as prize money across three sections.

FASTEST

Fastest to achieve norms

P. Harikrishna achieved three International Master norms – in the Asian Championship in Udaipur, the Goodricke tournament in Kolkata, and the Commonwealth Championship in Sangli – in less than two months in 2000.

YOUNGEST

Youngest to achieve an IM norm

R. Praggnanandhaa became the youngest Indian to make an IM norm. At 10 years, 6 months, he gained the distinction in Cannes (France) in February 2016.

(2006, 2007, 2008); Padmini Rout (2009); Bhakti Kulkarni (2011); and Ivana Furtado (2012 and 2017).

Domination in Advanced Chess

Viswanathan Anand won a hat-trick of titles in 1999, 2000, and 2001 in Leon, Spain. In 2000 and 2001 he beat Alexei Shirov of Spain in the final to win the tournament. In Advanced Chess, players have the benefit of using database searches on their computers before making a move.

Four successive Asian Junior titles

Indians twice won the title for four years in a row. The Indian boys won from 1997 to 2000 and again from 2007 to 2010.

Golden sweep – Asian Youth Championship

India won 18 medals, including all eight gold medals at stake, in the Asian Youth Championship in 2006. Sweety Patel (girls' U-8), Sahajasri (Girls U-10), Padmini Rout (girls' U-12), Bhakti Kulkarni (girls' U-14), Prince Bajaj (boys' U-8), G.V. Sai Krishna (boys' U-10), Vidit Gujarati (boys' U-12) and S. Nitin (boys' U-14) were the gold medal winners.

Grandmasters of India

The list of Indian grandmasters now stands at 84. They are 1. Viswanathan Anand (1987); 2. Dibyendu Barua (1991); 3. Pravin Thipsay (1997); 4. Abhijit Kunte (2000); 5. K. Sasikiran (2000); 6. P. Harikrishna (2001); 7. Koneru Humpy (2001); 8. Surya Shekhar Ganguly (2002); 9. Sandipan Chanda (2003); 10. R.B. Ramesh (2004); 11. Tejas Bakre (2004); 12. P. Magesh Chandran (2006); 13. Neelotpal Das (2006); 14. Deepan Chakravarthy (2006); 15. Parimarjan Negi (2006); 16. G.N. Gopal (2007); 17. Abhijeet Gupta (2008); 18. S. Arun Prasad (2008); 19. S. Kidambi (2009); 20. R.R. Laxman (2009); 21. Sriram Jha (2010); 22. Deep Sengupta (2010); 23. B. Adhiban (2010); 24. S.P. Sethuraman (2011); 25. D. Harika (2011); 26. M.R. Lalith Babu (2012); 27. Vaibhav Suri (2012); 28. M.R. Venkatesh (2012); 29. Sahaj Grover (2012); 30. Vidit Gujrathi (2012); 31. M. Shyam Sundar (2012); 32. Akshayraj Kore (2013); 33. Vishnu Prasanna (2013); 34. Saptarshi Roy Choudhury (2013); 35. Debashis Das (2013); 36. Ankit Rajpara (2014); 37. Aravindh Chithambaram (2015); 38. Murali Karthikeyan (2015); 39. Ashwin Jayaram (2015); 40. Swapnil Dhopade (2015); 41. S.L. Narayanan (2015); 42. Shardul Gagare (2015); 43. Diptayan Ghosh (2016); 44. K. Priyadarshan (2016); 45. Aryan Chopra (2016); 46. N. Srinath (2017); 47. Himanshu Sharma (2017); 48. Anurag Mhamal (2017); 49. Abhimanyu Puranik (2017); 50. M.S. Thej Kumar (2017); 51. Saptarshi Roy (2018); 52. R. Praggnanandhaa (2018); 53. Nihal Sarin (2018); 54. Arjun Erigaisi (2018); 55. Karthik Venkatraman (2018); 56. Harsha Bharathakoti (2018); 57. P. Karthikeyan (2018); 58. G.A. Stany (2018); 59. N.R. Vishakh (2019); 60. D. Gukesh (2019); 61. P. Iniyan (2019); 62. Swayams Mishra (2019); 63. Girish Koushik (2019); 64. Prithu Gupta (2019); 65. Raunak Sadhwani (2019); 66. G. Akash (2020); 67. Leon Mendonca (2021); 68. Arjun Kalyan (2021); 69. Harshit Raja (2021); 70. Raja Rithvik (2021); 71. Sankalp Gupta (2021); 72. Mithrabha Guha (2021); 73. Bharath Subramaniyam (2022); 74. Rahul Srivatshav (2022); 75. V. Pranav (2022); 76. Pranav Anand (2022); 77. Aditya Mittla (2022); 78. Koustav Chatterjee (2022); 79. M. Pranesh (2023); 80. N. R. Vignesh (2023); 81. Sayantan Das (2023); 82. V. Praneeth (2023); 83. Aditya Samanth (2023); 84. R. Vaishali (2023); 85. P. Shyaamnikhil (2024).

Youngest International Master
R. Praggnanandhaa, at the age of 10 years and 9 months, became the youngest International Master in chess history in May 2017 by making his third and final IM norm at Bhubaneswar. His earlier two norms had come in Cannes and Moscow.

R. Praggnanandhaa

Youngest Grandmaster
D. Gukesh became the country's youngest and the world's second youngest Grandmaster in January 2019 at the age of 12 years, 7 months, and 17 days.

K. Humpy

Youngest Grandmaster – female
K. Humpy is the youngest female to become a GM at 15 years 58 days.

Youngest to beat a GM
Hetul Shah (9) defeated Kazakh Nurlan Ibrayev in the first round of the Parsvnath International Open chess tournament in New Delhi on 11 January 2009, to become the youngest Indian to beat a Grandmaster. He broke the record of Parimarjan Negi who had achieved the feat at the age of eleven.

Youngest to qualify for the National Championship
• Dibyendu Barua, then 12, remains the youngest to qualify for the National championship in 1978.
• D. Harika holds the unique record of being the youngest girl to qualify for the men's National championship in 2004 as well as for the women's National championship in 2001.

Youngest finalist of World Cup
R. Praggnanandhaa became the youngest finalist of World Cup in Baku, Azerbaijan, in 2023.

Youngest National Junior – champion
Abhijeet Gupta of Bhilwara became the youngest National Junior champion at Nagpur in 2002. He won the U-19 event at the age of 13 years 10 days.

Youngest Indian in the World Cup and the Chess Olympiad
D. Harika played in the World Cup at 11 years and 9 months in Hyderabad 2002. She also became the youngest to play for India in the Chess Olympiad after her undefeated performance in Mallorca, Spain, in 2004.

Youngest international title winners
Sanskruti Wankhede and Vallabh Kavi were the winners of the Asian Schools' chess (U-5) girls' and boys' titles, respectively, in New Delhi in 2011.

Youngest National champion
Sixteen-year-old G. Akash became the youngest National champion in 2012.

Youngest to win the Commonwealth title
P. Harikrishna, then 15, won the gold in London in 2001 after a three-way tie with two British players.

First woman to win World Rapid Chess title twice
K. Humpy regained the title after a gap of five years in December 2024 after defeating Indonesia's Irene Sukandar. She finished with 8.5 points after 11 rounds to finally clinch the title. She became only the second woman after China's Ju Wenjun to achieve the feat.

Youngest WIM
K. Humpy became the youngest Woman International Master (WIM) in Asia at 12 years, 3 months, 4 days.

Youngest winner of Asian Junior (U-20) title
M. Kasturi, then 14 years old, won the Asian Junior title in Teheran in 2001.

Youngest rated player
At 3 years, 8 months and 19 days, Anish Sarkar became the youngest rated player in the world. Born on 26 January, 2021, this prodigy entered the World list with a rating of 1,555 in November 2024.

Youngest world champion in any sport
Ivana Furtado claimed the World Girls' U-8 crown at the age of 7 years and 226 days at Batumi, Georgia, on 29 October 2006.

BEST

Best achievement
• *Men*: Viswanathan Anand's rating of 2,817 in March 2011 is the highest recorded by an Indian.
• *Women*: Among women, Koneru Humpy's rating of 2,623 in July 2009 is the highest.

Best performance (Category 21)
Viswanathan Anand beat a field of seven super Grandmasters at Madrid between Feb 21 and 10 March 1998. The Category 21 tournament attracted seven of the top nine GMs of the world. Anand beat Alexey Shirov, Peter Svidler, Vassily Ivanchuk, Vaselin Topalov 1.5–0.5; lost to Gary Kasparov 0.5–1.5 and drew 1-1 with Vladimir Kramnik.

Best performance in Candidates Tournament (women)
K. Humpy finished runner-up after topping a three-way tie, including compatriot R. Vaishali, for the second spot in the 2024 edition held in Toronto.

Best performance in Asian Team Championship
Indian men won three gold and women claimed five silver medals in the continental championships.

Youngest to win World Junior (under-20) title
K. Humpy, 14, won the prestigious title in 2001.

ONLY

Only Asian to win at Wijk Aan Zee
Viswanathan Anand is the only Asian to win the Hoogovens Chess Tournament (Corus tournament since 2000) at Wijk Aan Zee in 1989, though jointly with three others. He won the title again in 1998, jointly with Vladimir Kramnik, and outright in 2003, 2004, and 2006.

First/only winner of Asian Junior and Sub-junior titles

Tejas Bakre won the Asian Junior and Asian Sub-junior titles at the same time, in 1998.

Only Indian to win against computers

Viswanathan Anand simultaneously played six computers and won 4-2, in the Aegon Man versus Computer Chess Event in 1997.

Only Indian to win rapid/ blindfold event

Viswanathan Anand won the first-of-its-kind Melody Amber Blindfold and Rapid chess event in 1994, 1997, 2003, and jointly in 2006.

Only Chess Oscar award winner

Viswanathan Anand is the only Indian to receive the Chess Oscar (founded in 1967) by the Russian chess magazine *64 - Chess Review*. He has claimed the Chess Oscar six times (in 1997, 1998, 2003, 2004, 2007 and 2008).

Only girl to win the National U-12 – open section

K. Humpy won the U-12 title in Ahmedabad in 1999.

Only Indian with three World Championship bronze medals

D. Harika claimed three successive bronze medals from the Women's World Championship in 2012, 2015, and 2017.

D. Harika

CRICKET

WOMEN'S CRICKET

GENERAL

Youngest to debut across all formats

Shafali Verma became the youngest Indian cricketer to make her debut across all three formats of the game when she played her first One-Day International (ODI) on 27 June 2021, against England in the UK, when she was 17 years and 150 days old. She made her Test debut on 16 June 2021 in Bristol, UK, against England. Her T20I debut came at the age of 15 against South Africa in September 2019 in Surat, Gujarat. She is also the youngest woman ever to play an ODI, and the first Indian and fourth woman to score a half-century in both innings on a Test debut.

Shafali Verma

Most career runs in women's international cricket

Mithali Raj has scored 10,868 runs in her international career, with 669 runs in Tests, 7,805 in ODIs and 2,364 in T20Is.

Longest career

Mithali Raj's cricketing career spans more than 23 years.

Most career wickets across formats

Jhulan Goswami, with 355 wickets in 284 matches, has the most wickets across formats.

TESTS

 Highest-ever total in Test

India Women set a new record for the highest-ever team total in Test cricket, scoring 603/6 declared during their match against South Africa Women in Chennai on 29 June 2024. This total surpassed the previous record of 575/9 declared, held by Australia Women, which was set in February against South Africa in Sydney. India women also set a new record for the most runs scored by any team in a single day's play in Test history, accumulating a total of 515 runs on the opening day of the same Chennai Test. This achievement surpassed the previous record of 509 for 9 by the Sri Lankan men's team on the second day of the 2002 Colombo Test against Bangladesh.

Fastest Double Hundred in Test Cricket

Shafali Varma set a new record for the fastest double century in Women's Test cricket during the match against South Africa in Chennai on 28 June 2023. The 20-year-old batter reached her double hundred in just 194 balls, marking her maiden international century in the longest format. She broke the previous record held by Australia's Annabel Sutherland, who scored 210 runs off 256 balls against South Africa in Sydney in February 2024.

Biggest win in women's Test history (by margin)

India recorded the biggest win in women's Test history by defeating England by a massive 347-run margin in Navi Mumbai on 16 December 2023. This victory surpassed Sri Lanka's previous record of a 309-run win over Pakistan set in 1998, setting a new benchmark for the largest win by runs in women's Test cricket.

Most career dismissals by a wicketkeeper

Anju Jain has the most career dismissals by a wicketkeeper with 23 dismissals from 1995 to 2003, including 15 caught and 8 stumped.

Biggest victory margin

India won by an innings and 34 runs while playing against South Africa in Mysuru, Karnataka, on 16 November 2014.

Narrowest victory margin

India won by 5 wickets against West Indies in Patna, Bihar, on 17 November 1976, and then against England at Taunton, UK, on 1 September 2006.

Lowest total

The lowest total ever was 65 runs for 10 wickets in 46 overs against the West Indies at Jammu, Jammu and Kashmir, on 29 November 1976.

Highest total
The highest total by the women's Test cricket team is 467 in 177.1 overs versus England at Taunton, UK, on 17 August 2002.

First and only double century
Mithali Raj scored 214 runs in 407 balls, against England at Taunton, UK, on 16 August 2002. She also has the best batting average of 51.00 in 10 matches.

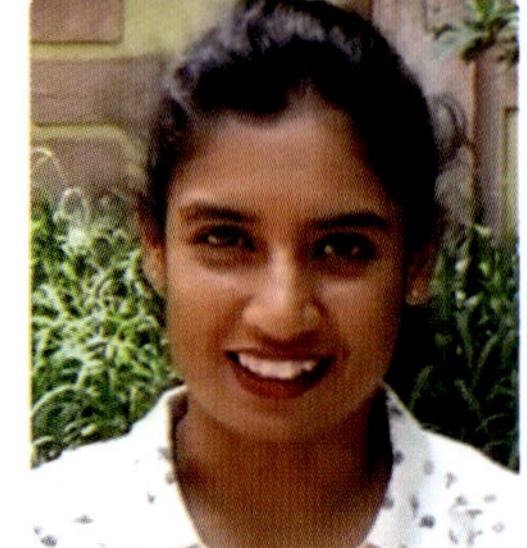
Mithali Raj

Most runs
Sandhya Agarwal has 1,110 runs in 13 matches. She also holds the record for the most centuries, with four in 13 Tests and 23 innings.

WR Most balls delivered
Former Indian player and left-arm spinner Diana Edulji is the only woman to deliver more than 5,000 balls (5,248) in Test matches.

Best bowling average
Jhulan Goswami, with an average of 17.36 with 44 wickets in 12 matches, has an unmatched bowling average in women's Test cricket in India.

Jhulan Goswami

Most wickets in a Test
Right-arm pacer Jhulan Goswami took 10 wickets in the match against England at Taunton, UK, on 1 September 2006.

Most career wickets in Tests
The record for most wickets in a Test career belongs to Diana Edulji, with 63 wickets taken from 1976 to 1991.

WR Best bowling – innings
Neetu David's 8 wickets for 53 runs in the India versus England match at Jamshedpur, Jharkhand, on 27 November 1995, makes her the only bowler in women's Test cricket to have claimed eight wickets in an innings.

Most career catches by a fielder
Sudha Shah has taken 21 catches in as many matches, an Indian record for a fielding position.

ONE-DAY INTERNATIONALS

WR Highest partnership
Deepti Sharma and Poonam Raut made a 320-run stand for the first wicket at the India versus Ireland match at Potchefstroom, South Africa, on 15 May 2017.

Highest individual score
Deepti Sharma was 188 not out at the India versus Ireland match at Potchefstroom, South Africa, on 15 May 2017.

Best bowling average – minimum 50 wickets
Neetu David holds the record with an average of 16.34 (141 wickets in 97 matches).

First Indian to score consecutive centuries in ODI
Smriti Mandhana became the first Indian woman to score consecutive centuries in ODIs, achieving this milestone during the first two matches of the India-South Africa series in June 2024. She came close to securing a third consecutive century but fell just 10 runs short in the third ODI.

Smriti Mandhana

Clean sweep victories in a bilateral series
The Indian team won all five matches in a bilateral series twice – against England in January 2002, and then against West Indies during February–March 2004.

Century on debut
Mithali Raj scored a century on her debut with 114 runs (not out) versus Ireland at Milton Keynes, UK, on 26 June 1999.

WR Most runs scored
Mithali Raj has scored 7,805 runs in 232 matches. She is the only woman cricketer to score more than 7,000 runs.

Most career dismissals by a wicketkeeper
Anju Jain has 81 dismissals to her credit, including 30 caught and 51 stumped.

Most career catches by a fielder
Jhulan Goswami has notched up 69 catches in 204 matches.

Most career stumpings by a wicketkeeper
Anju Jain holds a world record with 51 stumpings across her career.

T20 INTERNATIONALS

Oldest Indian player to debut in T20I
Asha Sobhana Joy made her international debut for India at the age of 33 years and 51 days during the T20I series against Bangladesh in Sylhet on May 6. By doing so, she became the oldest Indian player to debut in the T20I format.

Women's IPL
The Women's Indian Premier League (WPL) is a significant milestone in the evolution of women's cricket in India. Launched in 2019, the Women's IPL, also known as the Women's T20 Challenge, has had a run of two successful seasons so far, in 2023 and 2024. The tournament aims to provide a platform for women cricketers to showcase their skills and gain exposure on a global stage. Similar to the IPL format, it has garnered attention due to the participation of international and Indian women cricketers. Players like Harmanpreet Kaur, Smriti Mandhana, and Mithali Raj have been instrumental in promoting the tournament. Shakti, a tigress wearing a sky blue cricket uniform, is the league's mascot.

Largest victory margin

- The largest victory margin in terms of runs is 142 runs versus Malaysia on 3 June 2018 at the Kinrara Academy Oval, Kuala Lumpur, Malaysia.
- In terms of wickets, the largest victory margin has been by 10 wickets against the Australian team on 29 January 2016 at Melbourne, Australia.

Highest partnership

Shafali Verma and Smriti Mandhana put on a 143-run stand for the first wicket versus West Indies at the Darren Sammy National Cricket Stadium, Saint Lucia, on 9 November 2019.

Narrowest margin of victory

- By runs, the narrowest margin was 3 runs on two occasions. The first was against the West Indies at North Sound, Antigua, on 19 February 2012, and the second was against New Zealand in Melbourne, Australia, on 27 February 2020.
- By wickets, India's narrowest margin has been against New Zealand, of 3 wickets at Aldershot, England, on 27 June 2011.

Harmanpreet Kaur

Most career runs

Harmanpreet Kaur has scored 2,694 in 137 matches with a batting average of 27.48.

Highest team total

India's highest team total was 198 for 4 wickets in the third match versus England at Brabourne Stadium in Mumbai, Maharashtra, in the Tri-Nation Women's T20I Series in March 2018.

Lowest team total

India scored only 62 runs in 18.2 overs versus Australia at Billericay, Essex, UK, on 23 June 2011.

Most career wickets

Poonam Yadav has notched up 98 wickets in 72 matches.

Best bowling average (minimum qualification of 30 matches)

Poonam Raut has a record bowling average of 9.66.

Best bowling

Jhulan Goswami took 5 wickets for 11 runs in a T20I match against Australia at Visakhapatnam, Andhra Pradesh, on 23 March 2012.

Most career dismissals by a wicketkeeper

Tania Bhatia has 67 dismissals (23 caught and 44 stumped) in 50 matches.

Most career catches by a fielder

Harmanpreet Kaur holds the record of 53 catches in 137 matches, the highest number of career catches.

MEN'S CRICKET

GENERAL

Player with the most IPL titles

Rohit Sharma has earned the most IPL titles, totalling six: one with the Deccan Chargers, Hyderabad (2009), and five with the Mumbai Indians (2013, 2015, 2017, 2019, and 2020).

First cricketer to hit 50 ODI centuries - World Record

Virat Kohli made history by becoming the first cricketer to score 50 ODI centuries. He achieved this milestone during the 2023 ODI World Cup semi-final against New Zealand on 15 November, surpassing his idol, Sachin Tendulkar.

TESTS

First victory

India, captained by Vijay Hazare, defeated England by an innings and 8 runs on 10 February 1952 at Madras (now Chennai), Tamil Nadu. The victory came in the fifth match of a five-match series and India managed to draw the series 1–1.

Sunil Gavaskar

First to reach 10,000 runs

Indian cricket legend Sunil Gavaskar first went past the 10,000 mark in 125 matches, reaching 10,122 Test runs in his last series against Pakistan in 1987.

Highest team innings score

The highest innings score was 759 runs for 7 wickets against England at Chennai, Tamil Nadu, in 2016.

Highest score on debut (series)

Legendary batsman Sunil Gavaskar scored 774 runs in his very first Test series against West Indies in 1971, a record that remains unbroken.

Most consecutive wins at home (series)

India recorded their 15th consecutive Test series wins at home when they beat Sri Lanka in a two-match series in March 2022, beating Australia to the top spot in the longest winning streak by any team.

Most career runs

Sachin Tendulkar's total of 15,921 runs is an unbroken world record for the most career runs in men's Test cricket.

Most individual centuries

Sachin Tendulkar scored 51 centuries – 3 versus West Indies in 19 Tests, 11 versus Australia in 35 Tests, 2 versus Pakistan in 18 Tests, 7 versus England in 28 Tests, 4 in 22 Tests versus New Zealand, 9 in 25 Tests versus Sri Lanka, 7 in 25 Tests versus South Africa, 5 in seven Tests versus Bangladesh and 3 in 9 Tests versus Zimbabwe.

Most runs in an over

Jasprit Bumrah scored 35 runs (not out) in an over off England Stuart Broad at Edgbaston, Birmingham, in May 2022. He hit two fours off the first two deliveries, followed by a wide ball, then a six, followed by a no ball, and the next three balls were hit for fours. The penultimate ball went for a six and he scored a single off the last ball.

The Blue Army: T20 World Cup 2024

First to get out for a duck in T20 World Cup Final

Rishabh Pant made history as the first Indian batter to be dismissed for a duck in a T20 World Cup final. He was out for 0 off 2 deliveries against South Africa in the 2024 T20 World Cup final at Kensington Oval, Bridgetown, Barbados on 29 June.

Most dismissals by a wicketkeeper in a single edition

Rishabh Pant set the record for the most dismissals by a wicketkeeper in a men's T20 World Cup, with a total of 14 dismissals. He took 13 catches and executed one stumping. No other wicketkeeper—or player—has recorded even ten dismissals in a single men's T20 World Cup.

First team to win T20 World Cup unbeaten

India became the first team in history to win the men's T20 World Cup without losing a single game. They secured victory in all eight matches they played, with one group-stage game against Canada being abandoned without a toss.

Most wickets in a single T20 World Cup

Arshdeep Singh matched the record for the most wickets in a single T20 World Cup, claiming 17 wickets in the tournament. This achievement tied him with Afghanistan's Fazalhaq Farooqi in the same edition. Both bowlers surpassed the previous record of 16 wickets set by Wanindu Hasaranga in 2021.

First Indian to win T20 World Cup as player and then as captain

Rohit Sharma made history as the first Indian to win the men's T20 World Cup both as a player in 2007 and as a captain in 2024.

Best bowling figure by an Indian in T20 World Cup

Left-arm pacer Arshdeep Singh (4-0-9-4) recorded the best bowling figure by an Indian in T20 World Cup history during a match against the USA in New York. Spinner R. Ashwin held the previous record at 4/11 against Australia in Mirpur, Bangladesh, in 2014 edition.

Most career wickets

Anil Kumble holds the record with 619 wickets in his Test career spanning from 1990 to 2008.

Most wickets in a debut series

In the India–England Test series from 5 February to 8 March 2021, Axar Patel took 27 wickets in the four-match series. He holds the record jointly with Dilip Doshi, who took the same number of wickets during a six-match home series against Australia in 1979.

Most sixes in a series

Rohit Sharma scored 17 sixes in the Test series against South Africa on 20 October 2019 in Ranchi, Jharkhand.

Highest run chase

India's run chase of 406 runs for 4 wickets against West Indies in Port-of-Spain, Trinidad, in 1976 is its highest successful chase to date.

Highest individual score in a day

Virender Sehwag, in his knock of 293 against Sri Lanka in Mumbai, Maharashtra, during 2009–10, made 284 runs on the second day of the Test match – the highest individual score in a single day to date.

Virender Sehwag

Highest individual innings

Virender Sehwag's 319 against South Africa in Chennai, Tamil Nadu, in 2008 is the highest individual score in a Test match.

Fastest Indian opener to score 1,000 runs

Right-handed batsman Rohit Sharma achieved this landmark in his 17th innings as the Indian opener against England on 5 March 2021.

Lowest team innings score

India recorded an all-time low of 36 runs against Australia in Adelaide in December 2020. It is the fifth lowest in the world.

Most 1,000+ runs in a calendar year

Sachin Tendulkar has scored more than 1,000 runs in a calendar year on six occasions. He made 1,000 runs in 12 Tests in 1997; 1,088 runs in 10 Tests in 1999; 1,003 runs in 10 Tests in 2001; 1,392 runs in 16 Tests in 2002; 1,063 runs in 13 Tests in 2008; and 1,562 runs in 11 Tests in 2010.

Highest run aggregate

Sachin Tendulkar's score of 15,921 runs from 1989 to 2013 in 200 Tests is a world record. This score, from 329 innings, amounts to an average of 53.78.

Wicket off first ball on debut

Nilesh Kulkarni is the first and only Indian, and the 15th in the world, to capture a wicket off the very first ball on debut, when he bowled out Marvan Atapattu of Sri Lanka in Colombo, Sri Lanka, in 1997.

Wicket off first ball in a match

Syed Abid Ali took the wicket of Roy Fredricks off the very first ball in Port-of- Spain, Trinidad, against the West Indies in 1971. Kapil Dev emulated him twice by dismissing Mohsin Khan at Jalandhar, Punjab, against Pakistan during 1983–84, and Jimmy Cook at Durban versus South Africa in 1992–93.

Best bowling figures on Test debut

Narendra Hirwani took 16 wickets for 136 runs against West Indies at Madras (now Chennai), Tamil Nadu, during 1987–88.

Best bowling in an innings

Anil Kumble took 10 wickets for 74 runs against Pakistan at Delhi in one innings during 1998–99. He became the second bowler after England's Jim Laker to do so, and is now joined by Ajaz Patel of New Zealand.

Best bowling in a match

Narendra Hirwani took 16 wickets for 136 runs versus West Indies at Madras (now Chennai), Tamil Nadu, during 1987–88.

Most catches in an innings

The world record of five catches is held by four individuals (along with eight foreign players): Yajurvindra Singh (versus England at Bengaluru, Karnataka, in 1977); Mohammad Azharuddin (versus Pakistan at Karachi, Pakistan, in 1989); K. Srikkanth (versus Australia at Perth, Australia, in 1992); and Ajinkya Rahane (versus Sri Lanka at Galle, Sri Lanka, in 2015).

Most career dismissals by a wicketkeeper

M.S. Dhoni has dismissed 294 batsmen (caught 256 and stumped 38) in 90 Tests.

Most dismissals by a wicketkeeper in an innings

The record for most dismissals is six, shared by four players: Syed Kirmani, who caught five and stumped one against New Zealand at Christchurch, New Zealand, in 1975–76; M.S. Dhoni, who caught six against New Zealand at Wellington, New Zealand, in 2008–09; Wriddhiman Saha, with five caught and one stumped against West Indies at North Sound, Antigua, in 2016; and Rishabh Pant, with six caught in Adelaide, Australia, in December 2018 versus Australia.

Anil Kumble

Dismissing all 11 batsmen in a match

S. Venkataraghavan dismissed all 11 batsmen in the Delhi Test against New Zealand in 1964–65. His final tally was 12 for 152. He became the second bowler after England's Jim Laker and one among only six bowlers in the world to do this.

Most dismissals by a wicketkeeper in a match

Rishabh Pant shares the world record with England's Jack Russell (versus South Africa, 1995) and South Africa's A.B. de Villiers (versus Pakistan, 2013), with 11 dismissals in Adelaide, versus Australia, in December 2018.

Most catches in a match

With eight catches in the match against Sri Lanka at Galle, Sri Lanka, in 2015 (three in the first innings and five in the second), Ajinkya Rahane holds the world record for most catches in a match.

Most dismissals by a wicketkeeper in a series

N.S. Tamhane holds the record with 19 dismissals in five Tests against Pakistan in the 1954–55 series.

Wicketkeeper with the fastest 100 dismissals

Risabh Pant reached the milestone of 100 dismissals in only 26 matches, with 92 catches and 8 stumpings. He achieved it in the first Test against South Africa at SuperSport Park, Centurion, in December 2021.,

Highest score and fastest 100 on debut

Shikhar Dhawan scored 187 runs in 174 balls (33 fours, 2 sixes) in his Test debut against Australia at Mohali, Punjab, in 2013. Dhawan reached his 100 in just 85 balls – the fastest by a debutant (where full figures are available).

Most player of the series awards

In the India–England Test series during February–March 2021, R. Ashwin became the first Indian with more than 30 (he took 32) wickets and a century in a four-match Test series, and only the fifth player in the world to do so. He also became the first Indian to take 30 or more wickets in a Test series twice. Ashwin's nine Player of the Series awards in Test cricket are the most won by an Indian, just behind Sri Lankan player Muttiah Muralitharan (11) in this format.

Highest century partnerships

Rahul Dravid has been part of the most three-figure partnerships, on 88 occasions; 3 times for the first wicket, 34 times for the second, 26 times for the third, 8 times for the fourth, 12 times for the fifth, 3 times for the sixth and 2 times for the eighth wicket. He partnered with Sachin Tendulkar in 100-plus stands in a world record 20 times and with V.V.S. Laxman 12 times. Dravid's highest stand was with Virender Sehwag in a 410-run stand against Pakistan at Lahore in 2006. Dravid and Tendulkar have added 6,920 partnership runs, the most by any pair in history.

Rahul Dravid

Most career catches

Rahul Dravid holds the record for most career catches, with 210 catches in 164 matches (including one catch for the ICC World XI): 47 versus Australia, 30 versus England, 26 versus West Indies, 21 versus South Africa, 21 versus Zimbabwe; 19 versus Pakistan; 17 versus New Zealand; 16 versus Sri Lanka; and 13 versus Bangladesh.

ONE-DAY INTERNATIONALS

First bowler to take more than three wickets on debut

Prasidh Krishna is the only bowler to take four wickets in an ODI debut. He finished 4/54 in his debut ODI on 23 March 2021, against England, at the Maharashtra Cricket Association Stadium in Pune.

Highest team total

The Indian men's cricket team scored 418 runs for 5 wickets in 50 overs against West Indies at Indore, Madhya Pradesh, on 9 December 2011.

First to score 100 centuries in international cricket

Sachin Tendulkar was the first to score 100 international centuries (51 Test and 49 ODI hundreds). He scored his 100th century at the fourth ODI of the Asia Cup versus Bangladesh on 16 March 2012.

Sachin Tendulkar

Most centuries scored in a decade

Virat Kohli is the batsman who has notched up the most centuries in a decade (2010–20) with 42 centuries.

Highest score on debut

K.L. Rahul scored an unbeaten 100 against Zimbabwe at Harare, Zimbabwe, on 11 June 2016 – the only Indian to make an ODI century on debut.

Fastest 50 runs on debut

Krunal Pandya became the fastest-scoring debutant to post a half-century in an ODI match in just 26 balls, finishing at 58 not out in 31 balls on 23 March 2021 at the Maharashtra Cricket Association Stadium in Pune, Maharashtra, against England. He became the 15th Indian to score over 50 runs on an ODI debut.

Lowest team total

India scored only 54 runs in 26.3 overs against Sri Lanka at Sharjah, UAE, on 29 October 2000.

Most ODI century partnerships

Sourav Ganguly and Sachin Tendulkar have 26 century-plus stands as a pair.

Most runs in all World Cups

Sachin Tendulkar scored 2,278 runs in 45 World Cup matches from 1992 to 2011. He also holds the world record for the most centuries in World Cups, with six in 45 World Cup matches; this was equalled by Rohit Sharma in 17 matches.

Most centuries

Sachin Tendulkar has scored 49 centuries in 463 ODI matches.

Most career Man of the Match awards

Sachin Tendulkar has won 62 Man of the Match awards in his career. He won the first Man of the Match award in the 1992 World Cup against Pakistan.

Most total career runs

Sachin Tendulkar has made a total of 18,426 runs (including 49 centuries) in his ODI career spanning 463 matches.

Most career wickets

Anil Kumble holds the record with 337 wickets.

Highest individual innings

Rohit Sharma's 264 runs versus Sri

Lanka on 13 November 2014 at Kolkata, West Bengal.

Most career catches
Mohammad Azharuddin took 156 catches in ODIs.

Most sixes in an innings
Rohit Sharma hit 16 sixes in his total of 209 runs against Australia in Bengaluru, Karnataka, on 2 November 2013. This record, at the world level, was broken by England's Eoin Morgan who hit 17 sixes against Afghanistan during the 2019 World Cup.

Best strike rate
Hardik Pandya has achieved a record strike rate of 115.59 across 66 matches.

Yuvraj Singh

Best bowling
Stuart Binny took 6 wickets for 4 runs against Bangladesh at Mirpur, Bangladesh, on 17 June 2014.

Most consecutive ODI Man of the Match awards
Sourav Ganguly is the only player to have won four consecutive Man of the Match awards in ODIs, a record made against Pakistan at Toronto, Canada, in 1997.

Most centuries in a single World Cup
Rohit Sharma notched up five centuries in the 2019 World Cup, breaking Kumara Sangakkara's previous record.

First wins in the World Cup and ICC World Twenty20
India won its first World Cup under the captaincy of Kapil Dev in 1983 and its second World Cup under the leadership of M.S. Dhoni in 2011, thus becoming the third nation after West Indies and Australia to win the World Cup more than once. Dhoni also led India to its first ICC World Twenty20 win in its inaugural 2007 edition.

Unique 100
Shikhar Dhawan scored a century in his 100th ODI, a first-of-a-kind feat in Indian cricket.

Virat Kohli

T20 INTERNATIONALS

Highest team total
The highest team total is 260 for 5, for India versus Sri Lanka in Indore, Madhya Pradesh, on 22 December 2017.

Lowest team total
India scored 74 runs in 17.3 overs against Australia at Melbourne on 1 February 2008.

Fastest to 50
Yuvraj Singh's 50 runs in 12 balls against England in Durban, South Africa, on 19 September 2007, is the fastest half-century in T20Is.

Highest run chase
The Indian team made 211 runs for 4 wickets on 12 December 2009, chasing Sri Lanka's 206 runs for 7 wickets, at Mohali, Punjab.

Most career wickets
Bhuvneshwar Kumar has the most T20I career wickets with 90 in 86 matches.

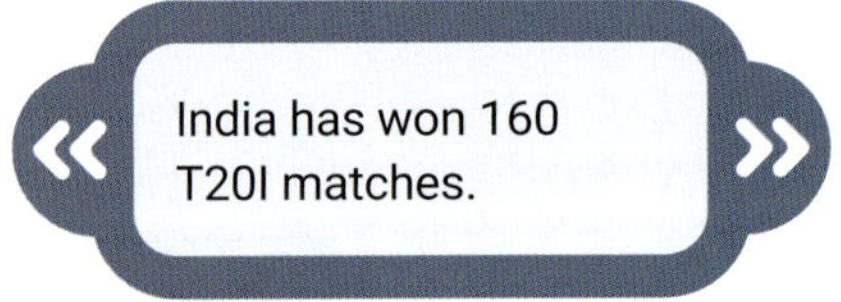

Best bowling average (minimum 10 wickets)
L. Balaji's bowling average of 12.10 is the best on record for T20I matches.

Best batting average (minimum 50 matches)
Virat Kohli has the best batting average of 52.73 in 115 matches.

Most runs in T20
Virat Kohli has 4,008 runs in 115 matches.

Best individual bowling
Deepak Chahar took 6 wickets for 7 runs while playing against Bangladesh at Nagpur, Maharashtra, on 10 November 2019.

Most career dismissals as a wicketkeeper
M.S. Dhoni holds the record of most career dismissals, with 91 dismissals in 98 matches, including 57 caught and 34 stumped.

Only captain to win all three ICC trophies
M.S. Dhoni is the only captain to lead his team to victory in all the three major ICC tournaments: the World T20 in 2007, the Cricket World Cup in 2011 and the Champions Trophy in 2013.

M.S. Dhoni

CUE SPORTS

DOMESTIC

First National Championship – billiards
The first National Championship was held in 1931 in Calcutta (now Kolkata), West Bengal, with only eight entries. M.M. Beg won the title.

First National Championship – snooker
The first National Snooker Championship was held in 1939 in Calcutta (now Kolkata, West Bengal). P.K. Deb won the title.

First billiards and snooker hat-trick
Geet Sethi achieved a hat-trick of three consecutive National Championship titles in billiards and snooker from 1985 to 1987. He also won the national titles for both sports in 1988.

Most national titles – billiards and snooker
Pankaj Advani has won the national titles for both billiards and snooker a record 32 times.

Highest break – snooker
Geet Sethi had the maximum possible break of 147 against Latif Nazarali at the 54th National

Snooker was invented in 1875 in the city of Jabalpur in Madhya Pradesh.

Pankaj Advani

Championship in Guntur, Andhra Pradesh, in 1988.

INTERNATIONAL

First world snooker champion

Om B. Agarwal won the IBSF World Snooker Championship at Dublin, Ireland, in 1984.

First world billiards team title

India 'B' won a gold while India 'A' bagged a silver in the inaugural World Billiards Team Championship in Glasgow, Scotland, in August 2014. The winning team, with Pankaj Advani, Rupesh Shah, Devender Joshi, and Ashok Shandilya, beat India 'A' 5–4.

First world champion on debut

Geet Sethi became world champion on debut when he beat legendary billiards player Bob Marshall, fifty years his senior, to win the 25th World Amateur Billiards Championship in 1985 in Delhi. He was also the first unseeded player to become world champion.

First World Games snooker title

Aditya Mehta won the Quadrennial World Games snooker gold at Cali, Colombia, in July 2013.

First win at the World Ladies Billiards and Snooker Championship

Chitra Magimairaj and Varsha Sanjeev won the senior gold medal and the U-21 gold medal respectively, at the World Ladies Billiards and Snooker (WLBS) Championship in Leeds, UK, in April 2016.

President Giani Zail Singh presenting the World Billiards Championship Cup to Geet Sethi

Cue sports

Historically, cue sports have been referred to as billiards, while in other countries, the term 'billiards' refers to the English Billiards specifically. It is a broad phrase used to describe a wide range of sports in which players move around a pool table while hitting or striking a billiard ball with a cue stick. It is believed that outdoor stick and ball lawn games gave birth to the present-day cue sports.

First snooker team World Cup title

Pankaj Advani and Manan Chandra won the inaugural International Billiards and Snooker Federation (IBSF) Snooker Team World Cup in 2018 in Doha, Qatar.

First Asian Games title

Billiards was introduced at the 1998 Bangkok Asian Games. India won two golds, a silver and a bronze. Ashok Shandilya won the gold, beating the world champion Geet Sethi 5–4. In the doubles, Ashok Shandilya and Geet Sethi won a gold, beating Devendra Joshi and Balachandra Bhaskar, who won the bronze.

R. Umadevi

First World Ladies Billiards and Snooker Association title

R. Umadevi won her maiden, and India's first, World Ladies Billiards and Snooker Association title, beating the then world no. 13, Eva Palmius, 2–0 in the final at Cambridge, England, in April 2012.

First Asian snooker title

Yasin Merchant beat Udon Khaimuk of Thailand by eight frames in New Delhi on 15 July 1989 to win the Asian Confederation of Billiard Sports (ACBS) Championship.

Most billiards gold medals in the Asian Games

Pankaj Advani won two gold medals in the 2006 Doha Asian Games and in the 2010 Asian Games at Guangzhou, China.

Best performance in the Asian Games – snooker

At the 2010 Asian Games held in Guangzhou, China, the Indian team won a silver, while Aditya Mehta (individual) and Alok Kumar (8-ball pool) won bronze medals.

Most world titles – billiards and snooker

Pankaj Advani has the world champion titles for both billiards as well as

Aditya Mehta

snooker a record 24 times. He claimed at least one International Billiard and Snooker Federation world title every calendar year.

Best performance at the Asian Billiards Sports Championship

India won a gold, a silver, and three bronze medals in the inaugural Asian Billiards Sports Championship at Al Fujairah, UAE, held from 24 September to 2 October 2016. Siddharth Parikh (billiards 100-up) won the gold medal and Vidya Pillai won the silver (6-red, women). The bronze medallists were Sourav Kothari (billiards 100-up), Kamal Chawla (6-red, men), Amee Kamani and Arantxa Sanchis (6-red, women), Manan Chandra, Sundeep Gulati and Ishpreet Singh Chadha (team snooker).

Highest break in the World Billiards Championship

Geet Sethi had a break of 1,276 over two sessions in 80 mins against Bob Close of England in the quarter-final of the World Professional Championship in Mumbai, Maharashtra, on 1 October 1992.

Highest break under three-pot rule – billiards

Michael Ferreira scored 630 against S.B. Agrawal at the World Championship in Delhi in 1981, a world record for the highest break under the three-pot rule.

Most billiards grand doubles

Pankaj Advani has won four world doubles in billiards (time and points format) in 2005, 2008, 2014, and 2018.

World 6-red title

Laxman Rawat won the 6-red title versus Muhammad Asif of Pakistan in Mandalay, Myanmar, on 20 September 2019.

Most competitive 147 breaks in snooker

Aditya Mehta became the first Indian to make 147 maximum breaks in 2014 at the Paul Hunter Classic snooker tournament.

Most Asian titles

Pankaj Advani – 24-time snooker and billiards world champion – retained the Asian snooker title by defeating former champion Amir Sarkhosh of Iran at the 2021 Asian Snooker Championship. Advani had won the title in 2019 before the 2020 edition got scrapped due to COVID-19. Advani's tally of Asian titles across both snooker and billiards stand at 13, including two Asian Games gold medals in 2006 and 2010.

Youngest world champion – snooker

Pankaj Advani was 18 years old when he won the amateur World Snooker Championship title in October 2003.

Youngest to win the World Professional title

Pankaj Advani was 24 years old when he won the World Professional Billiards title at the Northern Snooker Centre, Leeds, England, on 6 September 2009. He outclassed 41-year-old Mike Russell, who has won the World Professional Billiards title a record nine times.

Oldest woman champion – billiards

Kamala Devi Chandrababu from Tamil Nadu beat Judy Walia from Karnataka 109–63, 65–112, 53–76, 98–72, 95–74 in the 1995 National Championship at Bangalore (now Bengaluru), Karnataka. At 63 years, it was her fourth championship and the second national title after 1991.

Two titles in 6-red snooker

Pankaj Advani was the world's first player to hold both world and continental titles in 6-red snooker at the same time. He is also the only player to win world titles in both 15-red and 6-red snooker.

FOOTBALL

GENERAL

Oldest football tournament

The Durand Football Tournament is the third oldest tournament in the world and the oldest in Asia and India. Started by British diplomat and civil servant Sir Henry Mortimer Durand in 1888 for the British troops in India, it was held in Simla (now Shimla, Himachal Pradesh). In 1940, the tournament was moved to New Delhi. The latest edition, the 131st in the history of the tournament, was held from 16 August to 18 September 2022, with Bengaluru FC winning the tournament.

First Indian team to win the Durand Cup

Mohammedan Sporting won the Durand Cup in 1940 when it was first moved to Delhi and the final played at Irwin Amphitheatre (now Dhyan Chand National Stadium). Mohammedan Sporting beat Royal Warwickshire Regiment 2–1 in the final.

Most wins at the Durand Cup

Mohun Bagan has won the Durand Cup 16 times and finished runner-up 11 times. East Bengal has won 16 times and been runner-up 10 times.

Most clean sheets

The men's national team created a new record of eight consecutive clean sheets between 22 March 2023 and to 24 June 2023. It surpassed the previous record of six clean sheets kept during 1952–53.

Most individual goals at the Durand Cup

Mohammed Habib scored 12 goals for East Bengal in seven matches (both the semi-finals and the final were replayed) in the 1972 Durand tournament.

First football academy

The Tata Football Academy (TFA) was started at Jamshedpur, Jharkhand, in 1986 with Mohammed Habib and Ranjan

Mohun Bagan was founded in 1889. It is the oldest football club of India and one of the oldest in Asia. Bhupendra Nath Bose was the first president of Mohun Bagan.

Chowdhury as coaches, and Subimal 'Chuni' Goswami as technical director. It has produced over 100 junior and senior international players for India. It was followed by the Williamson Magor Football Academy in Assam and the Chandigarh Football Academy that started in the 1990s.

First Indian to be national coach of a foreign country

Syed Nayeemuddin was appointed national coach of Bangladesh in July 2007. He was also the first Indian to coach a club side abroad – the Brothers Union of Bangladesh in 2004. In India, he won 33 trophies with Mohammedan Sporting, East Bengal, and Mohun Bagan. As national coach, he led India to victory in the 1987 South Asian Federation (SAF) Games in Calcutta (now Kolkata), West Bengal, the 1997 Kathmandu South Asian Football Federation (SAFF) Championship in Nepal, and the 2005 Karachi SAFF Championship in Pakistan.

Syed Nayeemuddin

First Olympic referee

Komaleeswaran Sankar became an Olympic referee when he was selected for the football tournament of the 2000 Sydney Olympics, one among the four match officials chosen from Asia. Sankar, who became a referee in 1988 and a national referee in 1994, retired in 2007 at the age of forty-five, as mandated by FIFA rules.

First World Cup referee

Komaleeswaran Sankar was the first World Cup referee from India when he was chosen to officiate at the 2002 World Cup in South Korea and Japan. His first match was a Group G league match between Mexico and Croatia on 3 June 2002. He officiated in three matches.

First international tournament win by a club

- Mohammedan Sporting won the Aga Khan Gold Cup in Dhaka (then Pakistan, now Bangladesh) on 11 October 1960, defeating Makassar XI, Indonesia 4–1 in the final.
- East Bengal, coached by Subhas Bhowmick, won the LG ASEAN Club Cup Championship on 26 July 2003 in Jakarta, Indonesia, beating BEC Tero Sasana of Thailand in the final 3–1.

First Indian club to enter the Asian Football Confederation Cup final

- Bengaluru FC was the first Indian club to enter the final of Asia's prestigious club competition, the Asian Football Confederation (AFC) Cup, in October 2016. They lost the final match against Iraq Air Force 0–1 in Doha, Qatar, on 5 November 2016.
- Dempo SC (Goa) was the first club to enter the semi-finals of the Cup in September 2008.

First professional coach

Amal Dutta, India's first professional coach, started his career in 1963, coaching East Bengal. He also coached the other two big Kolkata clubs: Mohun Bagan and Mohammedan Sporting (Dhaka).

First hat-trick in Mohun Bagan versus East Bengal match

On 13 July 1997, Bhaichung Bhutia scored a hat-trick for East Bengal versus Mohun Bagan in the KBL Federation Cup semi-final, in which East Bengal won 4-1.

First foreign coach

English professional footballer Harry Wright was appointed coach of the Indian football team in 1963. He held the position till 1964, leading India to one of its best performances – a runner-up position at the 1964 Asian Football Confederation (AFC) Cup.

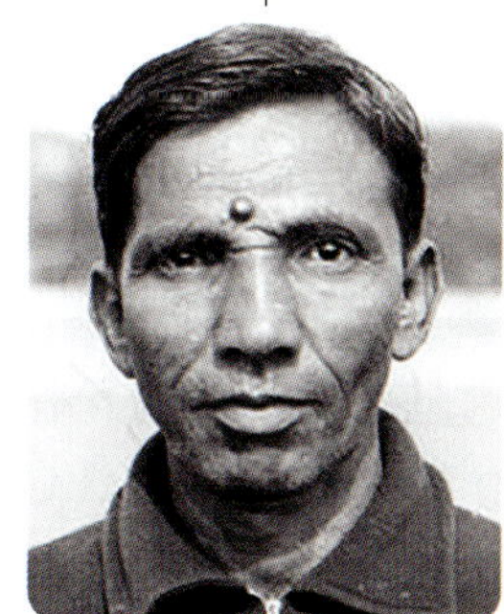

S.A. Rahim

Most appearances as coach in the Olympics

Syed Abdul Rahim (1909–63) from Hyderabad (then in Andhra Pradesh) was the coach of the Indian football team in three consecutive Olympic Games in 1952 (Helsinki), 1956 (Melbourne), and 1960 (Rome).

Most appearances as coach in the Nehru Cup

Syed Nayeemuddin coached the Indian team in the Nehru Cup on four occasions – in 1987 at Kozhikode, Kerala; in 1988 at Siliguri, West Bengal; in 1989 at Margao, Goa; and in 1997 at Kochi, Kerala.

First Indian club to win a major trophy

The first win in a major domestic tournament was by Mohun Bagan of Calcutta (now Kolkata, West Bengal), who beat East Yorkshire Regiment of Ghaziabad 2–1 in the Indian Football Association (IFA) Shield tournament final at the Calcutta Football Club ground on 29 July 1911.

Bhaichung Bhutia

Most individual goals in an international club match

Bhaichung Bhutia scored six goals, a double hat-trick, for East Bengal against Army FC of the Philippines in the LG ASEAN Cup in Jakarta, Indonesia, on 16 July 2003.

Bidding Adieu to the Indian Football Star: Sunil Chhetri

Sunil Chhetri retired from international football at the age of 39, leaving behind an unparalleled legacy in Indian football. Known for his remarkable goal-scoring prowess, Chhetri netted 94 goals in 151 appearances for the national team, placing him as the fourth highest goal-scorer in international football, only behind legends Cristiano Ronaldo, Ali Daei, and Lionel Messi. Throughout his 20-year career, Chhetri led India to multiple titles including three Nehru Cups, three SAFF Championships, and qualification to the 2011 AFC Asian Cup. His leadership, consistency, and unmatched records cement his status as one of India's greatest footballers.

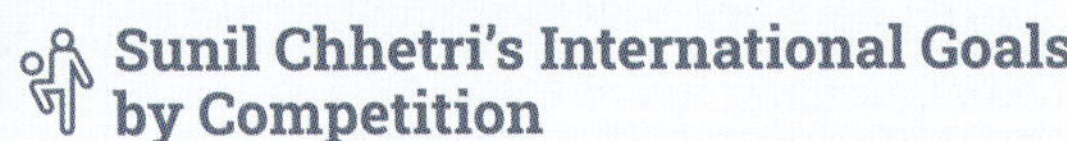

Sunil Chhetri's International Goals by Competition

COMPETITION	GOALS	MATCHES
SAFF Championship	23	27
FIFA World Cup qualifiers	10	24
Nehru Cup	9	14
AFC Asian Cup qualifiers	8	12
AFC Challenge Cup	4	8
Intercontinental Cup	13	11
AFC Challenge Cup qualifiers	3	6
AFC Asian Cup	4	8
King's Cup	1	1
Merdeka Cup	1	1
International friendlies	18	39

Sunil Chhetri's Total Goal Tally (Club and International)

LEVEL	GOALS	MATCHES
International (India)	94	151
Club Level	163	372
Total	257	523

Clubs Sunil Chhetri Played For

YEAR	CLUB
2002–2005	Mohun Bagan
2005–2008	JCT
2008–2009	East Bengal
2009–2010	Dempo
2010	Kansas City Wizards (USA)
2011	Chirag United
2011–2012	Mohun Bagan
2012–2013	Sporting CP B (Portugal)
2013	Churchill Brothers
2013–2015	Bengaluru FC
2015–2016	Mumbai City FC
2016–Present	Bengaluru FC

Most Hat-Tricks for Indian Football Team

PLAYER	HAT-TRICKS
Sunil Chhetri	4 (still active)
K. Appalaraju	2
R. Lumsden	1
Sheoo Mewalal	1
Neville D'Souza	1
Puran Bahadur Thapa	1
Marto Gracias	1
Subhash Bhowmick	1
Magan Singh Rajvi	1
Shabbir Ali	1
I.M. Vijayan	1

Highest Goal-Scorer in Indian Football

PLAYER	GOALS
Sunil Chhetri	94
Bhaichung Bhutia	42
I.M. Vijayan	39
Shabbir Ali	30
P.K. Banerjee	26
Jeje Lalpekhlua	23
Magan Singh	20
Inder Singh	15
Chuni Goswami	14
Neville D'Souza	13

Most Appearances by a Player for Indian Football Team

PLAYER	APPEARANCES
Sunil Chhetri	151
Bhaichung Bhutia	107
I.M. Vijayan	88
Shabbir Ali	81
Mahesh Gawali	79
Climax Lawrence	78
Gouramangi Singh	73
Sudip Chatterjee	67
Subrata Paul	67
Rennedy Singh	66

First in English professional club

• Mohammed Salim from Calcutta (now Kolkata, West Bengal) was the first from the Indian subcontinent to play for a European club, Celtic FC, in 1936.
• Bhaichung Bhutia was the first Indian footballer to join an English club when he signed a contract to represent second division outfit, Bury FC, from 1999 to 2002.
• Aditi Chauhan was the first Indian woman to play in the English league football on 16 August 2015, as a goalkeeper for West Ham United. She attended Loughborough University, completing an MSc in sports management and represented their football team from 2014-15. Chauhan joined Gokulam Kerala FC for the 2019–20 Indian women's league.

First hat-trick in Indian football

Norman Pritchard scored a hat-trick for St Xavier's College, Calcutta (now Kolkata), West Bengal, against Sovabazar Club in the 1889 Trades Cup.

First tiebreaker

• The first tiebreaker in a final came when Mohammedan Sporting won the tie 3-1 against Mohun Bagan at the 1983 Peerless Trophy final at Calcutta.
• The first tiebreaker match occurred in a third round match of the Durand Tournament played on 17 February 1972 at Delhi. Mohun Bagan beat Indian Navy 5-3.

First woman player to sign a contract with a foreign club

Ngangom Bala Devi made history when she signed a contract with Scottish Giant Rangers FC, a professional football club in Glasgow, UK. She donned a no. 10 jersey for the club and created yet another record on 6 December 2020 when she scored the final goal against Motherwell Women in the Scottish Women's Premier League, becoming the first Indian woman to score for a professional European Club.

Most matches officiated

S.S. Hakim officiated in 33 international matches and was a referee in the final of every major domestic tournament including three Nehru Cups. He represented India in the 1960 Rome Olympics and was the team's assistant coach for the 1982 Delhi Asiad. He is the only individual to have played football, coached the national team, and functioned as an international referee.

Most successful coach at the Asian Games

• S.A. Rahim led as coach on five successful occasions – twice at the Asian Games (1951 and 1962), and thrice at the Quadrangular Tournament (1953, 1954, and 1955).
• The foreign coach with the best record is Bob Houghton of the UK with three trophies: the Nehru Cup (2007 and 2009) and the AFC Challenge Cup (2008).

Most successful Indian coaches in domestic tournaments

P.K. Banerjee led domestic teams to 53 trophies, Amal Dutta to 35 and Syed Nayeemuddin to 33 of them.

Longest sequence of wins

Mohun Bagan won 42 consecutive matches in the 1994 season till they lost to Dempo SC (Goa) in the Scissors Cup final in November 1994.

Inder Singh

Longest unbeaten-streak at home

Indian football team is currently on a 17-match unbeaten streak under head coach Igor Stimac, starting since. The streak began with a draw against Bangladesh back in 2019.

Only Indian coach to gain success with a foreign club

In his eight-year stint in Bangladesh, Syed Nayeemuddin helped his club, Brothers Union of Bangladesh, win three trophies.

Best record against foreign clubs

East Bengal has the best record against foreign clubs: played 239 matches (both exhibition and tournaments), won 97, drawn 40 and lost 102. They scored 343 goals and conceded 348

Fastest goal

Midfielder Dipankar Roy scored a goal in 9.33 seconds after kick-off for Bengal versus Karnataka in the 2000 Santosh Trophy held in Thrissur, Kerala.

SANTOSH TROPHY RECORDS

Most wins in Santosh Trophy

The National interstate championships for the Santosh Trophy started in 1941. The football trophy was instituted in the name of maharaja of Santosh, the former president of IFA, the parent body of Bengal football. Bengal won the title 32 times and finished runners-up on 14 occasions. Punjab have won eight times, Kerala seven times, Services six times and Goa five times. Bengal hold the record of winning the trophy six times in a row from 1993-98 and five times in a row from 1975 to 1979.

Most individual goals in the final match

Playing for Bengal, Mohammed Habib scored five goals in the 6-1 win over Services in Nowgong in 1969.

Most individual goals in a single edition

Playing for Punjab, Inder Singh scored 23 goals in the 1974 edition in Jalandhar.

Highest number of goals by an individual in a single match

Burma (now Myanmar) striker Fred Pagsley, while playing for Bengal, scored seven goals against Rajputana in Mumbai in 1945. Punjab's Inder Singh scored seven goals against Gujarat in Jalandhar in 1974.

Biggest margin of victory

Bengal beat Tripura 18-0 in Jalandhar in 1974; Punjab beat Gujarat 17-0 in Jalandhar in 1974; Kerala beat Andaman and Nicobar Islands 17-0 in Siliguri in 2014.

All-time top scorers

Inder Singh (Punjab) has 45 goals. Mohmmed Habib and Shyam Thapa (both Bengal) have 34 and 31 goals to their credit.

Only to win Santosh Trophy for three teams

Peter Thangaraj won the Santosh Trophy for three different teams – Services (1960), Bengal (1962), and Railways (1966).

INDIAN SUPER LEAGUE (ISL)

Maximum titles

ATK (now ATK Mohun Bagan) has won three titles in 2014, 2016, and 2019–20 seasons.

Biggest margin of victory

FC Goa defeated Mumbai City FC 7–0 in Margao, Goa, in 2015.

Most goals scored in a match

A total of 11 goals were scored when Odisha FC defeated SC East Bengal 6–5 in the 2020–21 season.

Most goals scored by a team

FC Goa has scored 267 goals, followed by Chennaiyin FC's 199 goals.

Left: Bartholomew Ogbeche; *Right*: Ferran Corominas

Most individual goals by a foreign footballer

Punjab's Nigerian footballer Bartholomew Ogbeche has played four seasons in ISL for NorthEast United, Kerala Blasters, Mumbai City FC, and Hyderabad FC, scoring a total of 53 goals. FC Goa's former Spanish striker Ferran Corominas has a record of 48 goals to his credit for one club.

Most wins by a team

FC Goa have won 70 matches, followed by Mumbai City FC, who have won 92 matches.

Most individual goals by an Indian footballer

- Sunil Chhetri has played in all editions of the Indian Super League since 2014, scoring 51 goals. He played for Mumbai City FC and Bengaluru FC.
- Jeje Lalpekhlua, while playing for Chennaiyin FC and SC East Bengal, has 24 goals.

Hat-trick records

A total of 31 hat-tricks have been scored. Brazilian Andre Mortiz, while playing for Mumbai City FC against FC Pune City, scored the competition's first hat-trick in October 2014. Canadian Iain Hume (ATK and Kerala Blasters) and Nigerian Bartholomew Ogbeche have scored 3 hat-tricks each in the ISL. Sunil Chhetri (Mumbai City FC and Bengaluru FC) has two hat-tricks to his credit.

DOMESTIC EVENTS

First to win three National Football League titles

Mohun Bagan has won three National Football League (NFL) titles: in 1997–98, 1999– 2000, and 2001–02. East Bengal emulated this when they won their third NFL crown in 2003–04. Their earlier wins were in 2000–01 and 2002–03.

Most individual goals in a match in NFL

- Bhaichung Bhutia scored the most goals in an NFL match when he scored five goals playing for JCT against Mahindra in the first NFL in 1997. JCT won the match 6–1.
- In the fourth NFL, Francis Silveira of Churchill Brothers scored four goals in a match against Dempo SC (Goa) for a 5–0 win.

Most goals by a club in the NFL/ Indian League (I-League)

East Bengal has scored 690 goals in 460 matches. Other teams to score are Churchill Brothers with 664 goals in 406 matches and Mohun Bagan with 619 goals in 446 matches.

Most individual hat-tricks in the NFL and I-League

Nigerian striker Odafa Onyeka Okolie has scored 14 hat-tricks: nine for Churchill Brothers; four for Mohun Bagan; and one for Sporting Clube de Goa.

> « India first sent a football team to the Olympics in the year 1948. »

Most individual goals in a match in the I-League

The most goals by a player in an I-League match are seven by Ranti Martins for Dempo SC (Goa) in their 14–0 win versus Air India in Margao, Goa, on 30 May 2011.

INTERNATIONAL EVENTS

First International match

With seven barefoot players, India entered the 1948 Olympics under captain Talimeren Ao from Bengal but lost to France 1–2. Sarangapani Raman scored the lone goal. Since then, India has played eight matches in four Olympic Games – 1948, 1952, 1956 and 1960 – won one, drawn one, lost six; scored 10 and conceded 27 goals. After 1960, India has been eliminated in the pre-Olympic stage.

Only win in Olympics

On 1 December 1956, India beat hosts Australia 4–2 to register their only win in Olympics.

Best performance at the Olympics

India became the first Asian nation to reach the semi-finals of an Olympic football event, beating Australia 4–2 at the 1956 Melbourne Games. India took the lead against Yugoslavia but lost 1–4. In the play-off for the bronze, India lost 0–3 to Bulgaria, ending at fourth position. Samar 'Badru' Banerjee was India's captain and S.A. Rahim was the coach.

Biggest margin of victory

In the 1963 pre-Olympics, India won 7–0 against Ceylon (now Sri Lanka) at Bangalore (now Bengaluru), Karnataka, and later 7–0 against Bangladesh in the Aga Khan Tournament at Dhaka, Bangladesh, in 1977.

Best performance at pre–World Cup

With 3 wins, 2 draws, and 1 defeat (0–1 versus UAE in an away match in Al Ain), India's performance in the 2001

World Cup qualifiers has been the best yet. It is also the only series of matches where the Indian team scored more goals (11) than they conceded (5).

Biggest margin of victory at the Asian Games

India beat Hong Kong 5–2 at the 1958 Asiad in Tokyo, Japan, in its biggest margin of victory at the Asian Games. Mohammad Rahmatullah scored two goals while Subimal 'Chuni' Goswami, D. Damodaran, and T. Balaram scored a goal each. India scored three goals in extra time, the first time India played extra time in an international match.

Subimal 'Chuni' Goswami

Biggest defeat at the Asian Games

India lost 1–7 to China in 1974 at Tehran in Iran. Magan Singh scored the lone goal.

Biggest margin of victory at pre–World Cup

India beat Brunei 5–0 at Bangalore (now Bengaluru, Karnataka) in a Group 8 qualifier on 20 May 2001. Jules Alberto, I.M. Vijayan, Bhaichung Bhutia, Jo Paul Ancheri, and Abdul Hakeem scored for India.

Worst defeat at pre–World Cup

India lost 0–7 to South Korea at Seoul, South Korea, in the 1993 World Cup qualifiers.

India's longest unbeaten run in a year

In 2017, India remained unbeaten in nine matches, three away games and six at home:

- 1–0 versus Myanmar; 1–0 versus the Kyrgyz Republic; 2–0 versus Macau; 4–1 versus Macau; and 2–2 versus Myanmar (all Asian Cup qualifiers).
- 3–2 versus Cambodia; 2–0 versus Nepal; 2–1 versus Mauritius; and 1–1 versus St Kitts and Nevis (all friendly matches).

Worst defeats

In international tournaments, India's worst defeats have been 1–10 to Yugoslavia at the 1952 Helsinki Olympics and 1–9 to Burma (now Myanmar) in the 1971 Merdeka Tournament in Kuala Lumpur, Malaysia.

Most successful team in Intercontinental Cup (AIFF)

India became the most successful team in the AIFF's Intercontinental Cup with their second title. India defeated Lebanon 2–0 in the final of the 2023's edition in Bhubaneswar. North Korea are the only other winners as the competition has been played thrice since 2018.

Most wins by a team

Mumbai City have won 76 matches, followed by FC Goa, who have won 70 matches.

INDIVIDUAL RECORDS

Maximum caps earned (top five)

Sunil Chhetri (131 matches), Bhaichung Bhutia (107), I.M. Vijayan (88), Shabbir Ali (81), and Mahesh Gawli (79) have played the maximum number of matches for India.

Maximum goals scored (top five)

Sunil Chhetri (92), Bhaichung Bhutia (42), I.M. Vijayan (39), Shabbir Ali (30) and P.K. Banerjee (26) have scored the maximum goals for India.

Fastest international goal

I.M. Vijayan scored against Bhutan within 12 seconds after kick off in a Group A league match played on 28 September 1999 at the SAF Games at Kathmandu, Nepal.

Back-to-back hat-tricks

K. Appalaraju and I.M. Vijayan scored back-to-back hat-tricks in international matches. Appalaraju scored against Ceylon (now Sri Lanka) on 22 December 1963 in the pre-Olympics in Colombo and against Ceylon on 29 December 1963 in the pre-Olympics in Bengaluru. I.M. Vijayan scored against Pakistan in Kathmandu on 26 September 1999 in the SAF Games and against Bhutan on 28 September 1999 in the same SAF Games in Kathmandu.

Only player to score hat-trick in Olympics

Neville D'Souza is the only Indian to score a hat-trick in Olympics. He scored three goals in India's 4-2 win over Australia on 1 December 1956.

P.K. Banerjee

Most goals in the Asian Games

P.K. Banerjee scored the highest number of individual goals for India in the Asian Games, He scored six goals – one in 1958, four in 1962, and one in 1966.

Hat-trick on debut

K. Appalaraju scored a hat-trick in his first international appearance against Ceylon (now Sri Lanka) on 22 December 1963 in the pre-Olympics.

Most hat-tricks

Sunil Chhetri is the only Indian to score three hat-tricks in international matches. Chhetri's three hat-tricks came against Tajikistan (13 August 2008, AFC Challenge Cup, New Delhi), against Vietnam (10 October 2010, Friendly, Pune), and against Chinese Taipei (1 June 2018) in the Hero International Cup, Mumbai).

Most successful captain

Bhaichung Bhutia has five tournament wins to his credit as captain: the LG Cup in Vietnam (2002), the SAFF Cup in Karachi, Pakistan (2005), the Nehru Cup in Delhi (2007 and 2009), and the AFC Challenge Cup in Hyderabad and Delhi in 2008. He is also the second highest international scorer, with 42 goals in 107 matches.

Youngest match winner at the Nehru Cup

Bhaichung Bhutia was 19 years old when he scored a goal to beat Uzbekistan 1-0 in 1995 in Calcutta (now Kolkata), West Bengal.

GOLF

GENERAL

Sponsorship bonanza

Golf offered the most prize money in any individual event on the domestic circuit. The prize fund offered in 2010 was ₹8.80 crore, spread over 29 tournaments.

Indian Open winners

Nine Indians have won this prestigious title spread over 13 times. They are P.G. Sethi, Kolkata, 1965; Ali Sher, Delhi, 1991 and 1993; Feroze Ali, Kolkata, 1998; Arjun Atwal, Kolkata, 1999; Jyoti Randhawa, Gurugram, 2000; Vijay Kumar, Delhi, 2002; Jyothi Randhawa, Delhi, 2006 and 2007; C. Muniyappa, Gurugram, 2009; Anirban Lahiri, Delhi, 2015; S.S.P. Chawrasia, Delhi, 2016 and Gurugram, 2017.

Indian men winning international tournaments

So far, 25 Indians have won 88 international titles on various tours. Jeev Milkha Singh heads the list with 13 victories, followed by Gaganjeet Bhullar (11), Arjun Atwal (10), and Jyoti Randhawa (9).

Most Indian tournaments on the Asian Tour

In 2002, for the first time, three tournaments – the Royal Challenge Indian Open, the Hero Honda Masters, and the Honda-SIEL tournament figured on the Asian Professional Golf Association Tour.

Jyoti Randhawa

Indian Open record

Jyoti Randhawa won the Indian Open in October 2007 at the Delhi Golf Club course for the third time and equalled the record of Australia's Peter Thomson.

Indians at the Majors

So far, eight Indians – Anirban Lahiri (17 times); Jeev Milkha Singh (14 times); Jyoti Randhawa, Arjun Atwal, Shiv Kapur, and Shubhankar Sharma (5 each); Gaganjeet Bhullar and Gaurav Ghei (1 each) – have made 52 appearances at the Majors.

Indians topping the Asian Tour Order of Merit

Jeev Milkha Singh won the Asian Tour Order of Merit in 2006 and 2008. Jyoti Randhawa (2002), Arjun Atwal (2003), Anirban Lahiri (2015), and Shubhankar Sharma (2018) are the other Indians to top the Order of Merit.

S. Chikkarangappa

'Rookie' on a rampage

The Rookie Golfer of the Year award was introduced in 1997–98 on the domestic tour. To date, S. Chikkarangappa remains the most successful 'rookie' on the Tour. He won ₹32,65,313 and finished second to Rashid Khan on the 2013 Order of Merit.

FIRST

First international recognition

India was invited to the 1969 World Cup qualifying event at Singapore. Ruda Valji and Shadi Lal represented India.

First Olympians

Anirban Lahiri, S.S.P. Chawrasia, and Aditi Ashok represented the country in the 2016 Rio Olympics in Brazil.

First to win all three National titles

Arjuna Award-winner Amit Luthra is the first Indian to have won all three National titles: the Junior National (1979), men's National (1993, 1994) and Senior Nationals (2015, 2016).

First victory in Nomura Cup

India's first major victory in an international team event came in the 1973 Nomura Cup at Jakarta where the squad of Raj Kumar Pitamber, P.G. Sethi, Vikramjit Singh, and Lakshman Singh was crowned Asia-Pacific Golf champions.

First sweep of gold medals in the Asian Games

Golf was introduced in the Asian Games in 1982. Besides the team gold, India won the individual gold and silver medals through champion Lakshman Singh and runner-up Rajiv Mohta. Two other members of the gold-winning team were Amit Luthra and Rishi Narain.

First to gain qualification for the PGA Tour

Arjun Atwal became the first Indian to gain qualification for the full US Tour after making it through the Q-school for the year 2004.

First to qualify for the British Open

Gaurav Ghei was the first Indian to qualify for the premier event in 1997.

First to play in the US Open

Jeev Milkha Singh was the first to play the US Open in 2002.

First to play the Masters at Augusta

Jeev Milkha Singh was the first to play the Masters at Augusta in 2007.

First to play the PGA Championship

Arjun Atwal was the first to play the PGA Championship in 2005.

First European–Asian Tour win

Arjun Atwal is the first Asian to win two co-sanctioned titles on the Tour. He won the Caltex Singapore Open in February 2002 and the Carlsberg Malaysian Open in February 2003. Both these events enjoy joint sanction of the European and Asian PGA Tours.

Jeev Milkha Singh

Jeev Milkha Singh is the first Indian golfer to have played in the Masters Tournament and the Ryder Cup. Jeev's career boasts multiple victories on the European Tour and the Asian Tour, showcasing his skill and consistency across diverse golfing landscapes. His triumphs include wins at prestigious events like the Scottish Open and the Volvo Masters. Beyond his achievements on the course, Jeev's sportsmanship and dedication have earned him respect among fellow players and fans alike. He has paved the way for Indian golfers to shine on the global stage and continues to inspire the next generation of talent in the country.

First participation in World Cup

Arjun Atwal and Jyoti Randhawa formed the first Indian team to take part in the World Cup in 2005.

First to play in three WGC events in a year

Jyoti Randhawa became the first Indian to play in three events in the World Golf Championship (WGC) series in 2005.

First to play in a Major

Jeev Milkha Singh became the first Indian to qualify for a Major when he made it to the 2002 US Open in July.

First to gain a full 'card' on PGA Tour

Arjun Atwal became the first Indian to gain a full card (exemption from playing qualifying rounds) after his stupendous showing in the 2005 season.

Arjun Atwal

First to qualify for European PGA Tour

Jeev Milkha Singh was the first to qualify for the European Tour for the 1998 season.

First to win on the Japanese PGA Tour

Jyoti Randhawa won the Suntory Open in 2003.

First win on PGA Tour

Arjun Atwal won the 2010 Wyndham Championship.

First to make the 'cut' in a Major

Jeev Milkha Singh became the first Indian to make the 'cut' of a Major championship playing all four rounds of the 2002 US Open.

First win on the European Tour

Arjun Atwal won the 2002 Singapore Masters.

First win on the European Tour in Europe

Jeev Milkha Singh won the Volvo Masters in Spain in October 2006.

Rashid Khan

First team to qualify for World championship

The Indian team of Gaurav Ghei and Digvijay Singh qualified for the 2003 World Golf Championship held at Kiawah Island, USA, after finishing joint second in the Nations Cup.

MOSTS

Highest prize money (women)

Aditi Ashok collected US $60,000 in becoming the first to win the Ladies Indian Open title in November 2016.

Tournament with highest prize money

The ₹1.50 crore McLeod Russel Tour Championship in 2014 became the first domestic tournament to offer such high prize money in any individual domestic sport.

Most birdies

Jyoti Randhawa broke the course record at Shanghai with a seven-under par 65 that included eight birdies at the Volvo China Open Golf tournament in 2000. He finished in a tied fourth place.

Most lucrative season

During the 2017–18 PGAI Tour, 97 golfers earned over ₹1 lakh, including 79 over ₹2 lakh, 67 over ₹3 lakh, 51 over ₹5 lakh, 29 over ₹10 lakh, 19 over ₹15 lakh, 13 over ₹20 lakh and six players over ₹25 lakh during the season.

Highest prize money earner in a domestic season

Rashid Khan won two events from 14 tournament appearances in the 2019 season and collected ₹66,27,650 as prize money.

Most international titles

Jeev Milkha Singh has won 14 tour titles spread over three tours – four on the European Tour, six on the Asian Tour and four on the Japanese Tour.

Most titles in an Indian Tour season

Mukesh Kumar won six titles during the 2004-05 season.

Most career prize money from the domestic Professional Golf Tour of India (PGTI)

Shamim Khan has earned ₹4,38,03,143 from 265 tournament appearances.

Quickest to reach the million mark in prize money

Ashok Kumar won ₹1,00,10,334 in the 2004-05 season of the Indian Tour after just nine events.

Five titles in a season twice on the Indian Tour

Ashok Kumar won five titles in 2004 and repeated the feat in 2007.

Tee-rific Golfer: Aditi Ashok

First to win the Ladies Indian Open
She became the first to win the Ladies Indian Open in November 2016.

First to represent the country in four multi-discipline Games
She has participated in the 2013 Asian Youth Games, the 2014 Youth Olympic Games, the 2014 Asian Games, and the 2016 and 2020 Olympic Games.

First to secure her card (playing rights) winner on the Ladies European Tour
By winning the Lalla Aicha Tour School, Aditi Ashok secured the Ladies European Tour card for 2016 season. She also became the youngest to win the title.

First to win LET title outside India
She won the 2016 Qatar Ladies Open.

Best finish on the LET Order of Merit
She finished second on the 2016 LET Order of Merit and also won the Rookie of the Year award.

First woman to qualify for the Olympic Games
She is the first woman to qualify in golf for the Olympic Games in Rio in 2016. She attained her best finish – fourth – in the 2020 Tokyo Olympics.

First to qualify for the Ladies PGA Tour
She gained the playing rights for the 2017 LPGA Tour via the LPGA Final Qualifying School.

First to win on the Ladies European Tour (LET)
She is the first to win a title on the Ladies European Tour by claiming the 2016 Ladies Indian Open.

Most titles on the Asian Tour

Jyoti Randhawa has won eight titles: the 1998 Hero Honda Masters, the 1999 Hero Honda Masters, the 2000 Indian Open, the 2000 Singapore Open, the 2004 Volvo Masters of Asia, the 2006 Indian Open, the 2007 Indian Open, and the 2009 Thailand Open.

BEST

Best finish in a Major

Anirban Lahiri finished tied fifth in the 2016 PGA Championship.

Best finish in the European Tour Order of Merit

Jeev Milkha Singh finished 12th on the 2008 European Tour Order of Merit.

Anirban Lahiri

Best Indian performance on the PGA Tour

In the 2022 season, Anirban Lahiri had already earned $3,084,598 when the season was ongoing – the highest by an Indian on the PGA Tour – from 24 events. His best came in the Players Championship where he finished runner-up, earning a $2.18 million pay cheque.

Best world ranking

Jeev Milkha Singh was placed 28th in the World ranking list in 2009.

Best performance based on prize money received

Arjun Atwal became the first Indian to win a title on the PGA Tour by claiming the honours in the Wyndham Championship in August 2010. The first qualifier to win the title in 24 years on the PGA Tour, Atwal collected $918,000 – the highest ever by an Indian golfer.

Kapil Dev

LOWEST

Lowest winning score on the European Tour

Arjun Atwal scored title-winning 24-under 260 in the Carlsberg Malaysian Open in February 2003.

Least putts on the European Tour

Jeev Milkha Singh needed just 94 putts for four rounds of the 2001 Desert Classic. Jeev fell one short of the world record of 93, which stands in the name of Kenny Knox from the USA since 1990.

Lowest winning score on the Asian Tour

Jeev Milkha Singh scored 26-under par in the Philip Morris Championship in Seoul, when he won the four-round tournament on the Asian Tour. This is the lowest score by an Indian in winning an international title.

Lowest winning score on the Indian Tour

Mukesh Kumar fired 30-under 250 to win the DDA Open tournament at the Qutub Golf Course in New Delhi in April 2005.

Lowest round on the Indian Tour

Mukesh Kumar carded 11- under 59 in the third round of the DDA Open tournament at the Qutub Golf Course, New Delhi, in April 2005.

S.S.P. Chawrasia

ONLY

Only team title in the USA

Former Test cricketer Kapil Dev led India to the TAG Heuer Invitational Golf title in Boston in September 2004. The team comprising Kapil Dev, Rakesh Rao, Nikhil Dewan, and Rohit Duggal shot seven 65-under to win ahead of China, Indonesia, South Africa, and two teams from North America, among others.

Only Indian to win four titles on Japanese Tour

Jeev Milkha Singh has won four titles on the Japanese Tour: the 2006 Casio World Open, the 2006 Golf Nippon Series JT Cup, the 2008 Nagashima Shigeo Invitational Sega Sammy Cup, and the 2008 Golf Nippon Series JT Cup.

Only Indian to win two European Tour titles in a year

Anirban Lahiri won the Malaysian Open and the Indian Open – both co-sanctioned events on the European Tour – in 2015.

Quickest to win two European Tour titles

Shubhankar Sharma won two European Tour titles in the space of 55 days. He won the Joburg Open in December 2017 and Maybank Championship in February 2018.

Only Indian to win four European Tour events in India

S.S.P. Chawrasia's all four European Tour titles have come in India: the 2008 Emaar MGF Indian Masters, New Delhi; the 2011 Avantha Masters, Gurugram; the 2016 Indian Open, New Delhi; and the 2017 Indian Open, Gurugram.

GENERAL

Oldest club

The Royal Kolkata Golf Club founded in 1829 is the oldest club outside Britain. The Kolkata Ladies Golf Club was established in 1891.

Highest golf course

The Yak Golf Club is located at an altitude of 3,970 m (13,025 ft) at Kupup, Sikkim.

First international success in the U-10 category

Tanya Wadhwa of Delhi finished third in an U-10 International Golf tournament in San Diego, USA, in July 2001.

YOUNGEST

Youngest hole-in-one

Viraat Badhwar was all of 6 years 11 months and 19 days when he scored a hole-in-one at the sixth hole (par 3 at 155 yards) using a 3 wood at the Peacock Course, Delhi Golf Club on 17 August 2002.

Youngest to win two back-to-back international titles

Shubham Juglan won the IMG Academy golf championship in San Deigo and the International Golf Academy titles in Vegas – both for children aged 9–10 years – in successive weeks in 2015.

Youngest to win European Tour title

Shubhankar Sharma, at 21 years and 4 months, won the Joburg Open to become the youngest Indian winner on the European Tour.

Youngest to win Asian Tour Order of Merit

Shubhankar Sharma became the youngest to win the Asian Tour Order of Merit in December 2018.

Shubhankar Sharma

Youngest winner on the domestic PGTI Tour

Playing only his second pro event, amateur Karandeep Kochar became the youngest winner on the PGTI Tour by beating the field in the 2016 Players Championship in Kolkata. Kochar, at 17 years and 5 months, broke Shubhankar Sharma's record of 17 years and 8 months set in 2014.

Oldest to get hole-in-one

Lt Gen. Ajit Singh at the grand old age of 90 achieved his first hole-in-one on 18 October 2005 at the Delhi Golf Club on the 9th hole (par 3 at 160 yards).

Longest hole-in-one

Amit Luthra scored a hole-in-one at the second hole of Delhi Golf Club (par 4 at 258 yards) using a 5-iron on 16 March 1998.

« India currently has 196 registered golf courses. »

GYMNASTICS

DOMESTIC

First National Rhythmic Gymnastics event – women

The first National Rhythmic Gymnastics Championships held in 1989 at Kottayam, Kerala, had an event for women, where Neelamjit Kaur won the rhythmic gymnastics title. She won it again in 1990 at Udaipur, Rajasthan, and in 1991 in Delhi.

Most individual titles in the Nationals

- Kalpana Debnath from Madhya Pradesh won the all-round individual title four years in a row from 1976–77 to 1979–80.
- Rajesh Kumar from Chandigarh won the all-round individual title four times in a row between 1990–91 and 1994–95.

First National Championship

The first National Gymnastics Championship was held in 1952 in Madras (now Chennai), Tamil Nadu, where Khushi Ram emerged as the all-round individual champion and Punjab won the team championship.

Most successive titles – team

Services won the team National Championship six times in a row between 1954–55 and 1961–62. They won it again six times in a row between 1963–64 and 1971–72. (The tournament was not held for some years in between.)

INTERNATIONAL

First Olympic appearance

Khushi Ram and Vir Singh were the first gymnasts to represent India at the Olympics, in 1952 at Helsinki.

First World Cup medal

Aruna Reddy, then 22 years old, from Hyderabad, Telangana, became the first Indian gymnast to win a medal at the Gymnastics World Cup when she won a bronze in vault in Melbourne, Australia, with a score of 13.649 points on 24 February 2018.

First appearance in the World Championship

Daljit Inder Singh, Manjit Singh, and Vithal Karande participated in the 1970 World Championship held at Ljubljana (in present-day Slovenia).

First appearance in the Commonwealth Games

Manjit Singh, B.S. Nandi, and N.B. Bhosle represented India at the 1978 Edmonton Commonwealth Games in Canada.

First medal in the Commonwealth Games – men

Ashish Kumar won the first-ever medals (and a rare two at that) in gymnastics: a bronze in the individual floor exercise (score: 14.475) and a silver in the vault (with 15.312 points) at the 2010 Commonwealth Games, New Delhi.

First medal in the Asian Games – men

With a score of 14.925, Ashish Kumar won a bronze in the floor exercise at the 2010 Guangzhou Asian Games in China, which was India's first and only medal in gymnastics at the Asian Games.

First medal in the Asian Championship

Ashish Kumar won a bronze medal in the floor exercise at the third Senior Asian Gymnastics Championship at Pandit Deen Dayal Upadhyay Indoor Stadium, Surat, Gujarat, on 2 August 2006.

First Asian Champion

Dipa Karmakar made history by clinching the gold medal in the women's vault apparatus at the 2024 Asian Gymnastics Championship in Tashkent, Uzbekistan on 26 May 2024. This remarkable achievement marks the first time an Indian gymnast has secured a gold medal at the Asian Championships. Prior

Dipa Karmakar

to this, Indian gymnasts had earned four bronze medals at the continental event, with Karmakar herself claiming one in the women's vault back in 2015.

Most Olympic representations

Anantram Dogra is the only gymnast who has represented India in two Olympic Games – in Melbourne in 1956 and in Tokyo in 1964. He was also selected for the 1960 Rome Olympic Games, but the Indian Army team was called back due to an emergency.

Dilip Tirkey

HOCKEY

GENERAL

First Indian to head the International Hockey Federation

Dr Narinder Dhruv Batra was the first non-European president of the FIH. He was elected twice to the prestigious post, first in 2016 and re-elected in 2022.

First Olympian to head Indian hockey

Dilip Tirkey from Odisha, who had participated in three Olympic Games (in 1996 in Atlanta, USA; in 2000 in Sydney, Australia; and in 2004 in Athens, Greece), was unanimously elected president of Hockey India on 23 September 2022.

Most Arjuna Awards for any sport in a year

Normally, two or three hockey players (both men and women collectively) used to get the Government of India's top sporting award. However, with the success of Indian men's team at the Tokyo Olympics, all the 16 members (except the duo of goalkeeper P.R. Sreejesh and captain Manpreet Singh, who have already received the award earlier) were awarded the honour. P.R. Sreejesh and Manpreet Singh were given the Khel Ratna award.

Most FIH Hockey Star Awards

Indian players and coaches swept all the annual FIH Hockey Star Awards in 2021. The winners include Player of the Year: Harmanpreet Singh (men) and Gurjit Kaur (women); Best Goalkeeper: P.R. Sreejesh (men) and Savita Punia (women); Best Rising Star: Vivek Sagar Prasad (men) and Sharmila Devi (women); Best Coach: Graham Reid (national men's team coach) and Sjoerd Marijne (national women's team coach).

Most appearances in the Olympics

Five Indian players played Olympics four times: Leslie Claudius (1948 to 1960, Udham Singh (1952 to 1964), Dhanraj Pillay (1992 to 2004), PR Sreejesh (2012 to 2024) , and Manpreet Singh (2012 to 2024).

WR First nation to start commercial league for men (where players were auctioned)

India became the first nation to start a commercial league for men with Hockey India League 2023.

Unique Records: Goalkeeper Parattu Raveendran Sreejesh

Only goalkeeper to captain India (2016), only goalkeeper to play in four Olympics, only goalkeeper to play in four World Cups.

Most Olympics by an Indian goalkeeper

P.R. Sreejesh playing in four Olympics (2012 to 2024), surpassed Shankar Laxman's three (1956 to 1964).

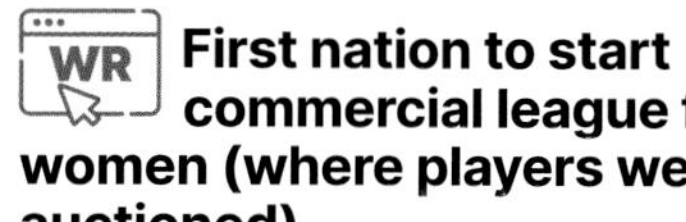

First nation to start commercial league for women (where players were auctioned)

India became the first nation to start commercial league for women with Hockey India League 2024-2025 where four teams together bought 96 women hockey players (64 Indian, 32 foreign).

Successive Olympic bronze

India won successive bronze only twice, first in the 1972 Olympics when it beat Netherlands 2-1 and then in 2024 with a victory over Spain (2-1) on 8th Oct.

Successive Olympic bronze medallists

1968 and 1972: Three, Ajit Pal Singh, Harbinder Singh, P. Krishnamurthy. 2020 and 2024: Eleven. P.R. Sreejesh, Manpreet Singh, Hardik Singh, Gurjant Singh, Mandeep Singh, Harmanpreet Singh, Lalit Kumar Upadhyay, Sumit, Shamsher Singh, Amit Rohidas, and Vivek Sagar Prasad.

DOMESTIC

Oldest tournament – men

The Beighton Cup was started in Calcutta (now Kolkata), West Bengal, in 1895 and is considered to be the oldest tournament. Presented by T.D. Beighton, the legal remembrancer of the then Government of Bengal, the Cup was held initially in the form of local matches, evolving into a regular tournament. Its latest edition was held in December 2016, with Indian Oil defeating Bharat Petroleum 5–3.

Oldest tournament – women

First National Championship held in 1947 in the then Bombay is the oldest domestic tournament for women.

First National Championship – men

The first National Championship, then known as the Inter-Provincial Championship, was staged in 1928 at Kolkata (then Calcutta). India became a member of the International Hockey Federation in 1927 and thus became eligible to participate in the 1928 Olympics. The Calcutta edition was held to select the team for participation in the 1928 Olympic Games in Amsterdam.

Women's Hockey

Women's hockey in India has a storied history marked by moments of triumph and determination. The Indian women's national hockey team earned its first international gold medal in 1982 Asian Games, New Delhi. In recent times, led by iconic players like Rani Rampal, Salima Tete, etc., the team has made significant strides on the international stage. Their consistent performances have resulted in podium finishes in various tournaments, including the Asian Games and the Asian Champions Trophy.

First Domestic League – women

The Khelo India Women Hockey League for U-21 (2021)

First National Championship – women

Various attempts were made to start a National Championship. However, these efforts did not bear any results, after an edition was initially held. Subsequently, when the Bombay Inter-Provincial Hockey Association started in 1947. It got the much elusive consensus of all the states and thus a legacy was born.

Most wins in the National Championship – men

Indian Railways has won 25 times.

Most wins in the National Championship – women

Indian Railways has won 30 times.

INTERNATIONAL

First international appearance – men

In 1926, the Indian Army team went to New Zealand to play 21 matches. They won 18, drew 2, and lost 1 match. They scored 192 and conceded 24 goals.

First medal and most successful team in the Olympics

The Indian hockey team won its first Olympic medal in 1928, under the captaincy of Jaipal Singh Munda. From 1928 to 1956, the team was unbeaten, winning six gold medals. Since then, India has been adding medals to its Olympic tally, and currently, with a total of 8 gold, 1 silver, and 2 bronze medals, it is the single most successful team at the Olympic Games.

First major success by a foreign coach

Australian Terry Walsh was India's coach at the time of the gold medal win at the 2014 Incheon Asian Games in South Korea. In the final, India drew with Pakistan 1–1 but won 4–2 in the penalty shoot-out.

First women professional players

Penalty corner expert Jasjeet Kaur Handa and Subhadra Pradhan played for HC Den Bosch club in the Dutch League in 2007.

First foreign coach

- *Men*: Gerard Rach from Germany, India's first foreign coach, was with the team at the 2004 Athens Olympics, and till January 2005.
- *Women*: Herman Kruis from the Netherlands was the first foreign coach for the women's hockey team, and was in charge of the Asia Cup in Hong Kong in September 2007.

First Commonwealth Games success – women

At the 2002 Commonwealth Games in Manchester, UK, the Indian women's hockey team won the gold medal, defeating England 3–2. The team was led by Suraj Lata Devi.

First Asia Cup win – women

Coached by M.K. Kaushik, the Indian women's hockey team won the Asia Cup for the first time, beating Japan 1–0 in the final at the National Stadium (now Dhyan Chand National Stadium), New Delhi, in February 2004.

First Junior Asia Cup win
India won the fifth Junior Asia Cup in Karachi, Pakistan, in March 2004, beating the hosts 5–2. Tushar Khandekar scored a memorable hat-trick in the final.

Inaugural FIH Hockey 5s Championship win
The International Hockey Federation (FIH) introduced a new tournament in 2022. India, led by Gurinder Singh, won, by defeating Poland (4–3) in the final on 7 June 2022 in Geneva, Switzerland.

First Asian Men's Hockey Champions Trophy win - Men
India won the inaugural edition of the tournament held in Ordos City, China, during August–September 2011, by defeating Pakistan 4–2 in the final via penalty strokes.

First Asian Women's Hockey Champions Trophy win - Women
India, led by Deepika Thakur, won the Asian Women's Champions trophy held in Singapore in 2016, beating China in the final on shoot-out.

Biggest Asian Games final victory
India won 5-1 against Japan at Hangzhou Asian Games on 6th October 2023.

Most Olympic goals – individual
Dhyan Chand scored 33 goals in three Olympics – 10 in 1928, 12 in 1932, and 11 in 1936.

Most goals in the Olympics – team
India scored 43 goals in six matches at Moscow in 1980, a record for the most goals in an Olympics. In the 1936 Berlin and 1956 Melbourne Olympics, India notched up 38 goals in five matches. It did not concede a single goal in 1928 and 1956.

Most medals in the Olympics
The world record for the most medals in hockey at the Olympics is held by Leslie Claudius and Udham Singh, who were in four medal-winning teams – with three golds and one silver. Claudius was in the teams that won the gold in 1948, 1952, and 1956, and silver in 1960, while Singh played for the gold-winning team in 1952, 1956, and 1964, and the silver-winning team in 1960.

Most capped player
Dilip Tirkey is the most capped player in India (412).

Most Junior Asia Cups — men
India under-21 hockey team lifted the Men's Hockey Junior Asia Cup 2023 after defeating Pakistan 2-1 in the final played in Salalah, Oman. This was India's record fourth Asian title at the age group ahead of Pakistan's three. India previously won in 2004, 2008, and 2015.

Most international caps — women
Vandana Katariya became the first Indian woman player to play 250 matches in national colours in January 2022. At 31, the forward has played 287 matches for India. Savita Punia and Deep Grace Ekka are the other two current players with 250 or more matches.

Most appearance in the Women's World Cup
Deepika Thakur is the only Indian woman hockey player to appear in three World Cups (2006, 2010, 2018). India did not qualify for the 2014 edition.

Dhyan Chand

Most appearances in the World Cup
Three players have the record of figuring in four World Cups. They are Ashok Kumar (1971, 1973, 1975, 1978), Dhanraj Pillay (1994, 1998, 2002, 2006), and P.R. Sreejesh (2010 to 2023) played in four World Cups.

Most goals in a World Cup
In the fifth World Cup in Bombay (now Mumbai), Maharashtra, during 1981–82, India scored 29 goals in seven matches, winning five and losing two.

Biggest victory margin in the Olympics
India created a world record for the biggest victory margin at the Olympics when they beat the USA 24–1 on 11 August 1932 at Los Angeles, USA.

Playing for teams with most Olympic golds
The record for playing for teams winning the most Olympic golds – three each – is held by seven Indians: Richard Allen and Dhyan Chand (1928–36); Balbir Singh, R.S. Gentle, Leslie Claudius, and R. Francis (1948–56); and Udham Singh (1952, 1956, 1964).

Best performance in the World Cup – men
India, led by Ajitpal Singh, beat Pakistan 2–1 in the final of the third World Cup at Kuala Lumpur, Malaysia, in 1975, displaying its best performance at the World Cup.

Best performance in the World Cup – women
India, led by Ajinder Kaur, finished fourth in 1974.

Best performance in the Commonwealth Games
Hockey was first introduced in the Commonwealth Games in 1998. India's best performances at the Commonwealth Games include three silver medals (in 2010 in New Delhi, in 2014 in Glasgow, and in 2022 in Birmingham).

Best performance on a foreign tour
Dhyan Chand, who led the team to New Zealand in 1935, played 48 matches and won them all. India scored 584 goals and conceded 40 goals. Dhyan Chand alone scored 201 goals, his brother Roop Singh scored 187, and F.C. Wells scored 112 goals.

Best performances in the Champions Trophy
India reached the final in the 2016 Champions Trophy in London, UK, and the 2018 Champions Trophy in Breda, Netherlands. In both, India lost 1–3 to Australia in the penalty shoot-out. The traditional tournament is not being held after 2018.

Best recovery in the Men's Hockey Champions Trophy
- The Indian team rallied from 0–3 at Amstelveen, Netherlands, to beat Pakistan 5–4 in 1982.
- India trailed West Germany 1–5 in 1985 at Perth, but in the last seven minutes levelled at 5–5. Centre half

Joaquim Carvalho scored an equalizing penalty stroke.

Biggest victory margin in the Asian Games – men

India's biggest victory margin at the Asian Games was 26–0 versus Hong Kong in the League phase of the 2018 Jakarta Asian Games in Indonesia.

Biggest victory margin in the Asian Games – women

India's biggest victory margin at the Asian Games came in the League phase of the 2018 Bangkok Asian Games when it beat Kazakhstan 21–0 on 21 August.

Biggest win in the Asia Cup finals

India beat South Korea 7–2 in the final of the 2007 Asia Cup in Chennai, Tamil Nadu, on 19 September 2007.

Highest goal scorer in the Asia Cup

Centre forward Sheikh Mohammed Nayeem scored 11 goals in the second Asia Cup in Dhaka, Bangladesh, in 1985.

Highest goal scorer and double hat-trick in the Youth Asia Cup

Defender Jugraj Singh scored 14 goals, including a double hat-trick, in the Youth Asia Cup in Malaysia in June 2001.

Best goalkeeping in the Olympics

Richard J. Allen did not concede a single goal in the five matches in the 1928 Olympics. He let in only two goals in 1932 and one in five games in 1936, conceding only three goals in three successive Olympics – a rare feat.

Highest goal scorer at the World Cup

Defender Rajender Singh, who played a solitary World Cup, scored all 12 goals in the 1981–82 tournament in Bombay (now Mumbai), Maharashtra, making him the highest goal scorer at the World Cup.

Fastest goal

Ajit Singh scored within 15 seconds of the start of the League match against Argentina in the 1976 Montreal Olympics – the fastest goal on artificial turf.

Only captain in successive Olympics

Pargat Singh was the captain first at Barcelona in 1992 and then in 1996 at the Atlanta Olympics in the USA, but India did not win a medal at either Games.

Only goalkeeper in three finals

Goalkeeper Shankar Laxman played in three Olympic finals – in 1956 in Melbourne, in 1960 in Rome, and in 1964 in Tokyo.

Only double hat-trick in the Olympics

Mohammed Shahid scored seven goals, including a double hat-trick, against Thailand (11–0) on 24 September 1986 in the Seoul Olympics in South Korea.

Only hat-trick in succession

At the 1952 Helsinki Olympics, centre forward Balbir Singh scored three goals in the semi-final against Great Britain and netted five, including a hat-trick, against the Netherlands in the final.

Youngest to win a gold in the Olympics

Cinnadorai Desamuthu was the youngest player to be in a gold-winning team, aged 19 years and 272 days, when India won in the 1952 Helsinki Olympics.

Vandana Katariya

Only hat-trick in the Olympics – women

Vandana Katariya scored a hat-trick against South Africa on 31 July 2021 in the 2020 Tokyo Olympics in Japan.

Oldest players in the Olympics

Udham Singh (b. 1928) was 36 when he played in the 1964 Tokyo Olympics. Prithipal Singh (b.1932) was also 36 when he was joint captain of 1968 Mexico Olympics. Goalkeeper P.R. Sreejesh (b.1988) was also 36 when he played in the 2024 Paris Olympics.

KABADDI

First Nationals

- The first kabaddi Nationals for men were held in 1951 in Maharashtra. The host state won the title.
- The first Nationals in kabaddi for women were held in 1955 in Calcutta (now Kolkata), West Bengal. Maharashtra won here too.
- The first championships for junior boys and girls were held in 1974 and 1976 respectively at Asansol, West Bengal.

First demonstration in the Olympics

Kabaddi and other indigenous games were the demonstration games in the 1936 Olympic Games held in Berlin, Germany.

First appearance of kabaddi in the Asian Games

Kabaddi was played for the first time in the 11th Asian Games in 1990 in Beijing, China. Pakistan, Japan, China, Nepal, Bangladesh, and India participated, with India winning the gold medal.

First Asian Championship

The first Asian Championship for men was held in Calcutta (now Kolkata), West

Richard J. Allen (standing extreme left)

Bengal, in 1980, in which teams from Bangladesh, Nepal, and India played. India won the gold medal.

First demonstration at the Asian Games

Kabaddi was an exhibition sport at the 1982 Asian Games held in New Delhi.

Pro Kabaddi League

Women's Kabaddi

The Indian women's kabaddi team has emerged as a dominant force in the world of kabaddi. Since the inception of the Women's Kabaddi World Cup in 2012, India has consistently showcased their prowess, securing gold medals in all editions until 2019. Led by exceptional players like Payel Chowdhury and Priyanka Negi, the team's performances have captivated fans with their remarkable agility, strategy, and teamwork. Women's kabaddi has gained popularity across the country due to their achievements, motivating more women to participate in sports and fostering a sense of empowerment.

First Pro Kabaddi League

The first Pro Kabaddi League was held in 2014, with eight teams participating. Sixty games were played, with the Jaipur Pink Panthers winning the inaugural title, defeating U-Mamba 35–24.

First team to win three consecutive Pro Kabaddi titles

Patna Pirates won three consecutive Pro Kabaddi League titles in 2016–17.

First participation in the Asian Junior Championship

The championship was held for the first time at Faridabad, Haryana, in January 2000, with teams from Bangladesh, Nepal, Sri Lanka, and Thailand. India won the gold.

Most World Cup wins – men

The Indian team won all three Kabaddi World Cups, organized by the International Kabaddi Federation, in 2004, 2007, and 2016, beating Iran in the finals of all three.

Most Asian Games titles – men

Kabaddi was introduced in the Asian Games in 1990 in Beijing, China, and was open only to men at that time. The Indian team has since won the Asian Games gold seven times – in 1990, 1994, 1998, 2002, 2006, 2010, and 2014.

Most Asian titles – men and women

India won their record eighth Asian Kabaddi Championship title after defeating Iran in the final 42-32 in Busan, South Korea, in July. India, under captain Pawan Sehrawat, remained unbeaten in all six games played in the campaign. This was eighth title in nine editions for India with Iran a one-time champion.

Most Asian Games titles – women

Kabaddi first made an appearance as a competitive sport for women in the 2010 Guangzhou Asian Games in China, 20 years after it was introduced for men. The Indian team won gold in 2010 and 2014, but got a silver in the 2018 Asian Games in Jakarta, Indonesia, losing to Iran in the final.

Most World and Asian Championship medals – women

Sarala Shetty of Bank Sports Board is the only Indian to win the Asian Kabaddi Championship eight times. Captain of the Indian team on eight occasions, she has also won three World Championship medals.

Most expensive non-cricket player

Raider Monu Goyat from Haryana became India's most expensive non-cricket sportsperson when Haryana Steelers bought him at ₹1.51 crore (15.1 million) for season 6 of the Pro Kabaddi League 2018.

Most expensive player in Pro Kabaddi League (PKL)

Pawan Sehrawat set a new record as the most expensive player in Pro Kabaddi history after being purchased by Telugu Titans for ₹2.605 crores at the 2023 auction. This breaks his own previous record when he was acquired by Tamil Thalaivas for ₹2.26 crores in the 2022 auction.

Most expensive foreign player at PKL

Iran's Mohammadreza Chiyaneh became the most expensive foreign player at the 2023 PKL auction as he was bought for Rs 2.35 crore by Puneri Paltans. He surpassed his compatriot Fazel Atrachali's previous record of ₹1.38 crore at the 2022 auction.

LUGE

Youngest luge Olympian

India's single representative in luge in the Winter Olympics, Shiva Keshavan from Manali, Himachal Pradesh, was the youngest luge Olympian in history, when he participated in the 1998 Nagano Olympics in Japan at the age of 16 years. Keshavan holds the record of participating in six winter Olympics: 1998 Nagano, Japan; 2002 Salt Lake City,

Pawan Sehrawat receiving the Arjuna Award from President Draupadi Murmu

Luge

Luge, a winter Olympic sport, is a timed competition in which competitors slide through a predetermined ice track while lying on their backs and their feet stretched out in the front on a sled.

USA; 2006 Turin, Italy; 2010 Vancouver, Canada; 2014 Sochi, Russia; and 2018 Pyeongchang, South Korea. He won the Asian Luge Championships in 2011, 2012, 2016, and 2017. He set a new Asian speed record of 134.3 kmph in 2011.

Shiva Keshavan

MARTIAL ARTS

WUSHU

First world wushu champion – men

Praveen Kumar of the Indian Army became the first Indian to win the gold medal on 23 October 2019 in the Sanda 48 kg category of the 15th World Wushu Championship.

First world wushu champion – women

In 2017, Pooja Kadian became the first Indian to be crowned World Champion in the women's 75 kg Sanda category.

Pooja Kadian

JUDO

First National Championship

The first National Championship was held in Hyderabad in 1965. Till 1981, it was held every two years.

First international medal

India, represented by Sandeep Bayala (below 65 kg), Cawas Billimoria (below 95 kg), Shyam Singh Gurjar (+95 kg), and Bannu Singh (open), won four bronze medals in the 1986 Asian Games in Seoul.

Youngest champion

Sandeep Bayala was 15 years old when he won the Nationals at Srinagar in 1982.

Most wins in the Nationals

Sandeep Bayala of Delhi Police has won 11 titles successively during 1982–93.

First judoka to win a world title

Sixteen-year-old Linthoi Chanambam clinched a historic gold medal at the World Cadet Championship on 22 August 2022. She won the title across age groups.

First medal in the Asian Games – women

Poonam Chopra won a silver medal in the 56 kg weight category at the 1994 Hiroshima Games in Japan.

First medal in the Asian Championship – women

Poonam Chopra won a bronze medal in 56 kg weight category at the Asian Championship in 1993 in Macau, China.

Oldest competitor

Banu Singh was 39 years old when he represented India at the Seoul Games in 1986. He won a bronze in the open category.

Best performance in the Commonwealth Games

India won two silver and two bronze medals in 2018 at Gold Coast in Australia.

The 1986 Asian Games was the first international event in which an Indian team participated.

Most silver medals in the Commonwealth Games – women

Judoka Shushila Devi Likmabam won two silver medals in the women's 48 kg category, the first in Glasgow in 2014 and the second in Birmingham in 2022.

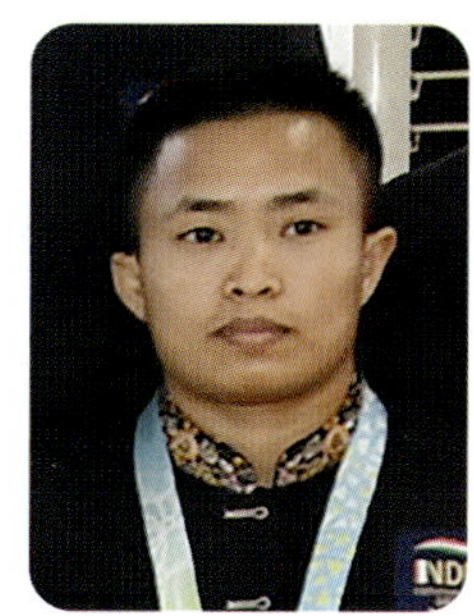
Sushila Devi

POWERLIFTING

Most medals in one edition of the Asian Championship

V.S.N.L. Renuka won four golds in the 48 kg category in squat, bench, deadlift, and overall lift of 310 kg at the Asian Powerlifting Championship in Zarafshan, Uzbekistan, in 2000.

Most Commonwealth Championship golds – individual

Sampa Guha won four gold medals in the first Commonwealth Championship in Newcastle, UK, in September 2005.

Most medals in Asian Championship

In the biggest haul at the Asian Championship to date, Indian powerlifters won 49 medals (22 gold, 19 silver and 8 bronze medals), besides the Women's Team Championship and overall medals (men and women), at the 18th Asian Senior, Junior, Sub-junior, and Masters (men and women) Championship 2006 at Taebaek City, Korea.

Best performance in the World Championship

India won all three medals in the World Championship in Akita, Japan, in November 2000. N. Anbu (52 kg) won gold in the deadlift and an overall silver, while Jentry Francis (56 kg) won the bronze medal.

Best performance in the Asian Junior Championship

At the Asian Junior Championship, Indian boys won the team trophy with 4 gold, 4 silver, and 2 bronze medals in New Delhi in May 2001. In the same championship, Indian girls also won the team trophy with 3 gold medals, 2 silver medals, and 2 bronze medals.

Best performance in the Commonwealth Championship – men

India bagged a total of 5 gold, 3 silver, and 4 bronze medals, and were declared runner-up in the team event in the second Commonwealth Championship in Christchurch, New Zealand, held from 6 to 9 December 2007.

Best performance in the Asian Sub-junior Championship

The Indian boys' team won the team trophy with five gold and two silver medals at the inaugural Asian Sub-junior Championship held in New Delhi in May 2001. In the same championship, the Indian girls' team bagged four gold and two silver medals.

Back-to-back Olympia Pro-Powerlifting wins

Mukesh Singh Gehlot from Delhi is the only Indian to win an individual medal in successive IPL (International Powerlifting League) Olympia Pro Powerlifting. He won the gold on his debut in IPL Olympia Pro Powerlifting 2017 in the 100 kg open category and a bronze in Las Vegas, USA, in 2018.

First medal in powerlifting in the Asian Para Games

Farman Basha won India's first medal – a bronze – in the 48 kg category at the inaugural Asian Para Games held in Guangzhou, China, in December 2010.

Farman Basha

First medal in the Commonwealth Games in para powerlifting

Sakina Khatun won the bronze medal in the lightweight category at the 2014 Commonwealth Para Games held in Glasgow, UK.

First gold in para powerlifting

Sudhir Lath claimed the gold medal in the men's heavyweight para powerlifting event at the 2022 Commonwealth Games in Birmingham. The 27-year-old, who has an impairment due to polio, lifted 212 kg.

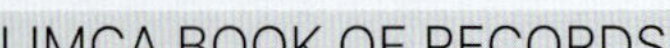

SHOOTING

World champion with a world record

Rudrankksh Patil became the world champion in men's air rifle in the World Championship in Cairo, Egypt, in October 2022. He had shot a world record 633.9 in the first stage of qualification. 18-year-old Rudrankksh beat Danilo Dennis Solazzo of Italy 17–13 for the gold. He beat two Chinese shooters, including the reigning world and Olympic champion Yang Haoran. He became the second Indian to become world champion in air rifle after Abhinav Bindra in 2006. Rudrankksh also led the Indian team to the gold later, along with Arjun Babuta and Kiran Jadhav, as the trio beat China 16–10.

Abhinav Bindra

First Asian Games medals

- *Men:* India's Asian Games medal haul started with Dr Karni Singh winning silver in the trap event in 1974 in Tehran, Iran.
- *Women:* Soma Dutta won a silver in the individual rifle 3-position event and a bronze medal in air rifle at the 1986 Seoul Games, South Korea.

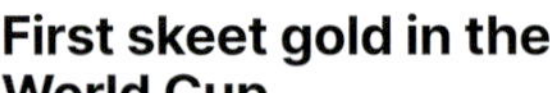

First Olympic finalist

Anjali Vedpathak-Bhagwat of the Central Industrial Security Force (CISF), Mumbai, Maharashtra, reached the air rifle final in the 2000 Sydney Olympics. She finished eighth with 493.1 points.

First skeet gold in the World Cup

Olympian Mairaj Ahmad Khan became the first Indian to win a skeet gold in a World Cup in Changwon, Korea, in July 2022. The 46-year-old Mairaj beat Kin Minsu of Korea 37–36 for the gold. Khan shot 119 in qualification and had to win a shoot-off with four others for the last two slots in the second stage. Mairaj had lost the shoot-off for the gold in the World Cup in Rio de Janeiro in 2016, and won the silver.

Mairaj Ahmad Khan

First World Championship medal

India's first World Championship medal came when Dr Karni Singh from Bikaner, Rajasthan, won a silver medal in the trap event in Cairo, Egypt, in 1962. The gold medal in the event was bagged by Vladimir Zimenko of the USSR.

First ever individual Olympic gold medal

Abhinav Bindra won India's first individual Olympic gold medal by claiming the honour in the men's air rifle event on 11 August 2008 in Beijing, China.

First World Championship gold

- Ace shooter Abhinav Bindra won India's first gold medal in the World Championship in air rifle in Zagreb, Croatia, on 24 July 2006.
- Manavjit Singh Sandhu won the first shotgun gold medal in the World Championship by beating 124 shooters to the title in the trap event in Zagreb, Croatia, two days after Bindra's effort.

First Asian Games gold

- Randhir Singh won gold in the trap event in the 1978 Games in Bangkok, Thailand, and a bronze in 1982.
- Jaspal Rana won the men's individual 25 m centre-fire pistol event in the 1994 Hiroshima Asian Games with 588 points, a new Asian record then. It was the only individual gold medal for India that year and the first Asian Games gold in that event.

First Commonwealth Games gold

- *Men:* Ashok Pandit won the gold in the free pistol event in Auckland, New Zealand, in 1990.
- *Women:* Roopa Unnikrishnan clinched the gold in the rifle prone event in the 1998 Commonwealth Games in Kuala Lumpur, Malaysia. In the 1994 Games in Victoria, Australia, Unnikrishnan won two medals – a silver

in the small-bore rifle 3-position and a bronze in the pairs with Kuheli Ganguly.

First World Cup silver and gold medals

Anjali Vedpathak-Bhagwat won the gold in the air rifle event in the World Cup in Milan, Italy, in 2003. She had earlier won the silver in Munich, Germany, in 2002.

Rahi Sarnobat receiving the Arjuna Award in 2018

First woman to win a gold in the Asian Games

Rahi Sarnobat became the first Indian woman to win a gold in the Asian Games (25 m pistol event) in 2018 at Jakarta, Indonesia.

First World Cup pistol medal

Sonia Rai from Himachal Pradesh won the bronze in the women's air pistol in the World Cup at Resende, Brazil, on 28 April 2006. She shot a 482.2, after 384/400 in the qualification phase.

Gold in the World Cup

Saurabh Chaudhary won the gold medal in the 10 m air pistol event in the World Cup in Munich, Germany, in May 2019. He shot a 246.3 to break his own world record of 245.5 set in the World Championship. He won gold medals in the 2018 Youth Olympics in Buenos Aires, Argentina, and in the 2018 Asian Games in Jakarta, Indonesia.

First gold in the Asian Championship

Dr Karni Singh won an individual gold in the trap event in 1971 in Seoul, South Korea. This was India's first gold in the Asian Championship.

> Out of the 41 Olympic medals that India has, 7 are for shooting.

First medal haul in the Asian Championship

India won 2 gold, 1 silver, and 2 bronze medals in Jakarta, Indonesia, in 1983, in its first haul in the Asian Championship. Ashok Pandit and Mohinder Lal won the gold in the centre-fire pistol team event with a world record.

First mixed air pistol gold medal in the World Cup – team

Heena Sidhu and Jitu Rai won the gold in the mixed air pistol team event in the World Cup in Delhi in 2017, when it was officially made a medal event.

First Nationals

The first shooting national tournament was held in Delhi from 9 to 16 November in 1952.

World record in skeet in the Asian Championship

Angad Vir Singh Bajwa shot a perfect 60 out of 60 to win the gold medal in the men's skeet final in the Asian Championship held in Kuwait in November 2018.

First team gold in the Asian Clay Championship

Mansher Singh, Moraad Ali Khan, and Manavjit Singh won India's first team gold at the Asian Clay Shooting Championship at Chengdu, China, in July 1995 with a tally of 357/375, equalling Kuwait's Asian record at the 1994 Hiroshima Asian Games in Japan.

First ever Olympic medal in shooting

Rajyavardhan Singh Rathore won the silver medal in double-trap shooting, behind Ahmed Al Maktoum of the UAE, in the 2004 Athens Olympics in Greece. Rathore made his maiden Olympic appearance in the 2004 Olympic Games in Athens, Greece, merely about six years after he had taken up the sport. A year before, he had won the gold medal in the 2003 World Cup in Sydney, Australia.

Rajyavardhan Singh Rathore

First to win two golds in a World Cup

Manu Bhaker, then 16 years old, from Jhajjar, Haryana, won the 10 m air pistol gold medal and partnered with Om Prakash Mitharval for the 10 m air pistol mixed team gold in the 2018 World Cup in Mexico.

Most individual medals in the Asian Shooting Championship

Ronak Pandit won seven gold medals and a silver medal in the junior pistol events of the Asian Championship in Kuala Lumpur, Malaysia, in 2004.

World record at the Asian Championship

Suma Shirur shot a perfect 400 out of 400 to win the gold medal in the women's air rifle in the Asian Championship in Kuala Lumpur, Malaysia, in February 2004. She shares the record with 8 others.

Most career golds at the South Asian Games

Jaspal Rana won 23 golds and a silver in three editions of the SAF Games (now South Asian Games). He won 8 golds each in Madras (now Chennai), Tamil Nadu, in 1995; and in Kathmandu, Nepal, in 1999; and seven golds and a silver in Islamabad, Pakistan, in 2004.

Jaspal Rana

Best haul in the World Championship

- The Indian team won 34 medals including 12 gold medals in the World Championship for rifle and pistol in Cairo, Egypt, in 2022. It is the best ever performance by India in a World Championship and India finished second in the medals table behind China.
- In 2018, India had won

27 medals in the World Championship in Changwon, Korea, finishing third behind China and Korea.

Best haul in the World Cup

The Indian team topped the medals table with a record total of 22 medals in the World Cup in Delhi in March 2021, with 10 gold, 8 silver, and 4 bronze medals. The USA came a distant second with 4 gold, 3 silver, and a bronze medal. Yashaswini Singh Deswal (women's air pistol), Aishwary Pratap Singh Tomar (men's rifle 3-position), and Chinki Yadav (women's sports pistol) won the individual gold medals.

Back-to-back gold medals in the Junior World Cups

Elavenil Valarivan (b. 2 August 1999) won gold medals in air rifle in the 2018 Junior World Cups in Sydney, Australia, and Suhl, Germany. She also won the mixed air rifle team gold with Divyansh Singh Panwar in the Junior World Cup in Suhl, with a junior world record of 498.6 in the final.

Best Asian Games haul

Indian shooters won three gold, five silver, and six bronze medals in the Asian Games at Doha, Qatar, in 2006, for their best haul of 14 medals in an edition of the Asian Games. India had won only 17 medals in all the previous editions put together.

Best performance at the World Cup on debut

Shahzar Rizvi created a world record at the ISSF World Cup when he scored 242.3 points in the final of the 10 m air pistol event on 3 March 2018 in Guadalajara, Mexico. In his debut performance at the World Cup, Rizvi won the gold medal beating the reigning Olympic champion Christian Reitz of Germany.

Best haul in the Junior World Championship

The Indian juniors topped the medal standings in the Junior World Championship in Lima, Peru, in October 2021, with a total of 31 medals, including 12 gold and 13 silver medals. Manu Bhaker (women's air pistol), Naamya Kapoor (women's sports pistol), Aishwary Pratap Singh Tomar (men's rifle 3-position), Vijayveer Sidhu (men's standard pistol), Rhythm Sangwan (women's standard pistol) and Arjun Singh Cheema (men's free pistol) won the individual gold medals.

Best haul in the Commonwealth Games

Indian shooters bagged 27 medals in the 2006 Commonwealth Games in Melbourne, Australia, with 16 gold, 7 silver, and 4 bronze medals. Gagan Narang bagged 4 gold medals (a feat he repeated in the 2010 Commonwealth Games, New Delhi), while Vijay Kumar and Omkar Singh bagged three gold medals each.

Ronjan Sodhi

Double world record

- Ronjan Sodhi gained the unique distinction of equalling both the qualifying and final world records in double trap while winning the gold in the World Cup in Belgrade, Serbia, in 2008. He shot 147 in the qualifying phase and ended with 194.

What a Calibre! – Champions of Shooting

Best Olympics in terms of number of medals

Indian shooting enjoyed its best fare in the 2024 Paris Olympics, with three bronze medals in Paris. After having drawn a blank in the earlier two Olympics in Rio and Tokyo, it was a memorable outing for the Indian shooters. Manu Bhaker stood out with the individual bronze medal in air pistol, and the mixed air pistol bronze with Sarabjot Singh. She also finished fourth in the 25-metre sports pistol. She missed a better medal in air pistol by 0.1 point. Swapnil Kusale won the men's 50-metre rifle 3-position bronze. It was the first time that India was winning an Olympic medal in the event. He missed a better medal by 0.5 point.

First woman to win an Olympic medal in shooting

Manu Bhaker, 22, was the first Indian woman shooter to win an Olympic medal. She became the first Indian to win two medals in the same Olympics. She joined Rajyavardhan Singh Rathore (Athens 2004, silver), Abhinav Bindra (Beijing 2008, gold), Vijay Kumar (London 2012, silver), and Gagan Narang (London 2012, bronze) among the league of Olympic-medal winning Indian shooters.

Best haul in World University shooting championship

As the host of the World University shooting championship at Dr Karni Singh Shooting Range in Tughlakabad, New Delhi, in November 2024, India had the distinction of topping the medals table with ten gold, nine silver, and seven bronze medals. The Czech Republic was the second best with eight gold and a silver. Italy was third with three gold, a silver, and four bronze.

Bhavtegh Singh Gill won the men's skeet gold, and Abhay Singh Sekhon won the bronze in the same event. Smit Moradiya missed the men's air rifle gold by 0.1 point to Jiri Privratsky of the Czech Republic. Aishwary Pratap Singh Tomar and Sanjeeta Das won the mixed air rifle gold, after trailing 2-12 at one stage in the race to 16 points against the Koreans. Aishwary also won the silver in the rifle 3-position event. Palak Gulia and Samrat Rana won the mixed air pistol gold. In women's trap, Neeru won the silver, and Kirti Gupta, bronze. Yashasvi Rathore won the women's skeet bronze in her maiden international competition. Simranpreet Kaur Brar won the bronze in women's sports pistol.

World Cup Finals in Delhi

As the host, India got to field a record number of 24 shooters, two each in the 12 Olympic events, in the season-ending World Cup Final at the Dr Karni Singh Shooting Range in Tughlakabad, New Delhi. With the Olympic medallists still enjoying the celebrations, the onus of winning medals for India was fulfilled with the silver medals by Vivaan Kapoor in men's trap, Sonam Maskar in women's air rifle, apart from the bronze by Anantjeet Singh Naruka in men's skeet and Akhil Sheoran in men's 50-metre rifle 3-position

• Gagan Narang won the World Cup final gold medal in men's air rifle with two world records in Bangkok, Thailand, in November 2008.

Best haul in the Olympics

India's win of two medals in the 2012 London Olympics was the best in terms of numbers. Gagan Narang won the bronze medal in the air rifle and Vijay Kumar won the silver in the rapid fire pistol.

Gagan Narang

Youngest to win a Junior World Championship gold – men

In 2017, Anish Bhanwala (b. 26 September 2002) became the youngest Indian shooter to win a Junior World Championship gold medal in standard pistol.

Youngest to win a World Cup gold – women

At Guadalajara, Mexico, in March 2018, Manu Bhaker (b. 18 February 2002) was the youngest to win a gold medal in the women's air pistol, and the air pistol mixed gold with Om Prakash Mitharval. She also clinched the gold medals in the Junior World Cups in Sydney, Australia, and Suhl, Germany, in 2018. She also won the air pistol gold, ahead of compatriot and former world record holder Heena Sidhu, in the 2018 Commonwealth Games in Gold Coast, Australia.

Most medals in a Junior World Cup

India topped the medals table in the

events. As in the Olympics, China was dominating the elite field with five gold and three bronze medals in topping the table, in the competition meant for the season's best performers. Italy, Germany, France, Hungary, Denmark, San Marino, and the USA won a gold medal each, sharing the rest of the seven golds, which gave a hint about the intensity of competition.

Akhil Sheoran at ISSF World Cup Finals, New Delhi

Record haul in Junior World Championship

India topped the table with thirteen gold, three silver, and eight bronze medals in the Junior World Championship in Lima, Peru, in September-October 2024. It won 13 individual medals including five gold through Parth Mane (air rifle men), Mukesh Nelavalli (men's sports pistol), Sura Sharma (men's standard pistol), and Divanshi (two gold medals in 25-metre pistol events).

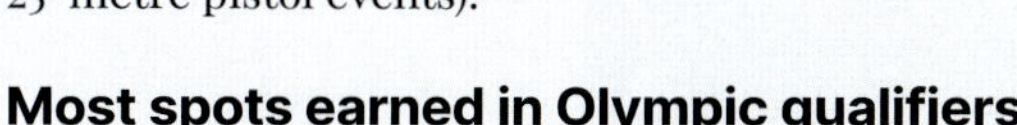

Most spots earned in Olympic qualifiers

Maheshwari Chauhan sparkled with the women's skeet silver medal in the last shotgun Olympic qualifier in Doha, Qatar. After being tied on 54 with Francisca Corvetto Chadid of Chile in the final, Maheshwari was beaten 4-3 in the shoot-off. The silver helped India to take its Olympic qualifiers to a record 22. India was able to field a shooter in every one of the 15 shooting events in the Paris Games. In fact, with Manu Bhaker shooting both the air pistol and sports pistol events, the Olympic quota won by Palak Gulia in air pistol was exchanged for the women's trap quota for Shreyasi Singh. So, except for men's trap and skeet, in each of which only one shooter qualified, India earned the right to field the maximum possible two shooters in 10 of the 12 individual events. It was a remarkable progress from the Sydney Games in 2000, when India earned only one Olympic qualification through Anwer Sultan in men's trap, while the air rifle spots in men's and women's events were presented to Abhinav Bindra and Anjali Bhagwat by the international federation ISSF, as 'hardship quota', meant for countries unable to win Olympic quota places in shooting but had meritorious shooters.

India tops World Cup for air pistol and rifle events

India topped the medals table with four gold, three silver and three bronze in the World Cup for air events in Granada, Spain, in February 2024. Except for Manu Bhaker winning the women's air pistol bronze, the rest of the medals were won by Indian juniors. Isha Takasale (junior women's air rifle), Umamahesh Maddineni (junior men's air rifle), and Devanshi Dhama (junior women's air pistol) won the individual gold medals. Isha and Umamahesh also combined to win the mixed junior air rifle gold.

2018 Suhl World Cup in Germany with 26 medals: 15 gold, 2 silver, and 9 bronze medals. This bettered the country's share of 22 out of 66 medals in the 2017 Sydney World Cup in Australia, when it won nine gold, five silver, and eight bronze medals, to be placed second behind China (25).

Most medals in a World Cup

India topped the medals table in the 2019 World Cup in Rio de Janeiro, Brazil, with five gold, two silver, and two bronze medals.

Most medals in four consecutive World Cups

India has topped the medals table in four consecutive World Cups in rifle and pistol events. India topped the table in the 2018 Munich World Cup (with five gold medals and one silver medal), the 2019 New Delhi World Cup (with three golds), the 2019 Beijing World Cup (with three golds and a silver), and the 2019 Rio de Janeiro World Cup (with five gold, two silver, and two bronze medals).

SQUASH

First professionals

In the early 1990s, the first pros were Arjun Singh (men) and Misha Grewal. The latter became a professional in 1993, and played the women's professional circuit in Asia, Europe, and the USA. Her best rankings were second in Asia and 27th in the world.

First champion

Rajkumar Narpat Singh won the first squash Nationals in 1953 and made a hat-trick, holding the title for two more years.

First junior and senior Nationals title

Anil Nayyar won both the junior and senior titles in the Nationals in 1964, when he was 18 years old.

First junior world no. 1

Saurav Ghosal was the first Indian to be ranked junior world no. 1 when he won the British Junior Open in 2004.

First to win world ranking titles

In August 2003, Ritwik Bhattacharya became the first Indian to win back-to-back international Professional Squash Association (PSA) world ranking tournaments in New Zealand when he won the North Island Championship and the Royal Oak Open titles. In 2005, he annexed two more titles – the Esportiu Rocafort Squash Open in Barcelona, Spain, and the Rochester ProAm Squash Championship in New York, USA. He has won four international squash titles.

First individual medals in the Asian Championships

- Bhuvaneshwari Kumari won the bronze in the 1990 and 1992 Asian Championships.
- Misha Grewal won a silver in the Asian Championship in 1996 in Amman, Jordan.

First silver in the Asian Junior Championship

The Indian girls' squad bagged a silver medal in the Asian Junior Championship in Chennai, Tamil Nadu, in February 2003. They lost 0–3 to Malaysia in the final.

First international success – women

Joshna Chinappa became the first Indian woman to claim a Women's International Squash Players Association (WISPA) title, defeating Malaysia's Low Wee Wern 11–8, 11–5, 11–3 in the NSC Super Satellite (no. 3) Squash Tournament final at National Squash Centre, Kuala Lumpur, Malaysia, in November 2008.

First Commonwealth Games gold

India bagged its first gold medal when Dipika Pallikal and Joshna Chinappa defeated Laura Massaro and Jenny Duncalf of England 11–6, 11–8 to win the women's doubles event in the Commonwealth Games in Glasgow, UK, in 2014.

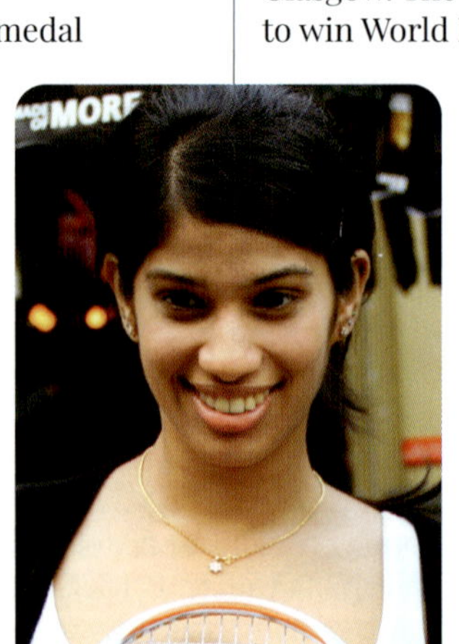

Joshna Chinappa

First to win the Asian junior title – girls

Joshna Chinappa was the first to win the Asian junior title (U-19) in 2003. Later, Dipika Pallikal also won the title in July 2010.

Dipika Pallikal

First Indians to win World Doubles titles

Dipika Pallikal became the first Indian to win two gold medals at the World Doubles Squash Championships winning the gold in women's and mixed finals. Dipika partnered Joshna Chinappa in the women's final and teamed up with Saurav Ghosal in the mixed doubles in the 2022 edition in Glasgow. The trio are the first Indians to win World Doubles title since the inception of the tournament in 1981.

First doubles champions in the Nationals

In the first National Doubles Squash Championship held in Chennai, Tamil Nadu, in 2004 Joshna Chinappa and Dipika Pallikal, representing Tamil Nadu, won the women's title and Saurav Ghosal and Harinder Pal Singh Sandhu, also representing Tamil Nadu, won the men's title.

First Indians to win Asian Mixed Doubles Championship

Dipika Pallikal Karthik and Harinderpal Singh Sandhu won the inaugural Asian Mixed Doubles Squash Championship 2023 in Huangzhou, China. The duo defeated the Malaysian pair of Rachel Arnold and Ivan Yuen 11-10, 11-8 in the final.

Saurav Ghosal

Best performance in the World Championships

Saurav Ghosal was the first Indian to reach the quarter-finals of the World Championships in Manchester, UK, in October 2013. Though he lost to world no. 1 Ramy Ashour in the match, this is India's best performance to date at the World Championships.

Best in the Asian Games

For the first time, India won the men's team event gold medal in the 2014 Incheon Asian Games in South Korea, beating Malaysia 2–0. Saurav Ghosal, Harinder Pal Singh Sandhu and Mahesh Mangaonkar represented India in this event. The women's team of Dipika Pallikal, Joshna Chinappa, and Anaka Alankamony won the silver medal, losing to Malaysia 0–2 in the 2014 Asian Games team event final.

Most titles in a row in the Nationals – women

Bhuvaneshwari Kumari was the women's national champion 16 times in a row from 1977 to 1992, a record that remains unbeaten.

Bhuvaneshwari Kumari's first national triumph was in 1977 at 16 years.

Most National titles won

Joshna Chinappa won 18 national titles, the most yet by an Indian.

Most titles in a row in the Nationals – men

Major K.S. Jain and Brigadier R.K. Manchanda hold the men's record for the highest number of titles won in the Nationals, with six wins each in a row. Jain won the title from 1958 to 1963, while Manchanda was the champion from 1978 to 1983.

Best performance in the World Team Championships

The Indian men's team, led by Saurav Ghosal, made a second successive appearance among the top eight in the World Team Championships in June 2013. The women's team also reached the quarter-finals in 2012. This is India's best performance in the World Team Championships.

Youngest to represent India

Saurav Ghosal and Joshna Chinappa were the youngest to represent India in an international event. Ghosal was 16 years old and Chinappa was 15 when they played for India in the 2002 Asian Games in Busan, South Korea.

Best performance in the Asian Juniors

Anaka Alankamony from Chennai, Tamil Nadu, became the youngest winner of the Asian Junior title (U-19) at 16 years when she beat Tsz-Wing Tong of Hong Kong 6–11, 11–8, 10–12, 11–7, 11–7 at Amman, Jordan, in June 2011. India enjoyed triple success in this event: Ramit Tandon (U-19 boys' and Saumya Karki (U-17 girls') won silver medals in India's largest haul at the event.

Youngest national champion – women

Joshna Chinappa became the youngest national women's champion at 14 years in 2001.

Oldest national champion

Brigadier R.K. Manchanda was 37 years old when he won the Nationals title in 1983, thus becoming the oldest national champion in squash. He also became the oldest finalist in 1987 when he was 41 years old. He reached the final in the Nationals a record 11 times, as did Anil Nayyar. Manchanda won 6 of the 11 finals in which he competed.

Youngest national champion – men

Adrian Ezra and Ritwik Bhattacharya were both 17 when they won the senior national singles title in 1989 and 1997 respectively, making them the youngest national squash champions to date.

Highest rankings

- Saurav Ghosal is the first Indian to break into the top 10 in the Professional Squash Association (PSA) world rankings. He was ranked 10th with 6,455 points in April 2019.
- Joshna Chinappa is the highest ranked Indian woman in the 27th position with 2,345 points (*at the time of going to press*).
- In 2012, Dipika Pallikal and, in 2016, Chinappa were placed 10th in the world rankings.

SWIMMING

First woman to participate in the Asian Games

Kumari Rima Dutta participated in the fifth Asian Games in Bangkok, Thailand, in 1966.

First swimmer in the Olympics

D.D. Mulji of Bengal was the first Indian swimmer in the Olympics, taking part in the 1928 Amsterdam Olympics. Indian women participated in the Olympics for the first time at the 1952 Helsinki Olympics, with Dolly Nazir and Arati Saha representing India.

First swimmers in the Asian Games

Nine Indian swimmers participated in the inaugural Asian Games in 1951: Sachin Nag, Bimal Chandra, Issar Mansoor, Santosh Bhattacharjee, Kanti Shaw, Protip Mitra, Shambu Shaw, J.J. Naigamwalla, and Bhubaneswar Pandey. The first Indian woman to participate in Asian Games was Kumari Rima Dutta in the fifth Asian Games held at Bangkok in 1966.

First water polo team in the Asian Games

- In 1951, the Indian water polo team first participated in the inaugural Asian Games and won a gold medal. The team members were Ganesh Dass (captain), G. Rattansey, D. Daver, Isaac Mansoor, Jhair Ahir, Rober Dean, and Kanti Shaw.
- The Indian water polo team participated in Asian Games in 1970 in Bangkok and won the silver medal. The team included Pijus Mitra (Captain), Samir Kapadia, Tarun Goswami, Abdul Mutlib, Ashok Biswas, Bharat Merchant, Chand Ram, Umed Singh, Avinash Sarang, Pattabhi Raman, and Deep Narayan Singh.

First diver in the Asian Games

Three Indian divers participated in the first Asian Games in 1951: K.P. Thakkar, Ashu Dutta, and T.T. Dand. Thakkar of Maharashtra won gold medals in the high-board and springboard events, while Dand won a bronze in high-board diving.

First Asian Games gold

India won its first Asian Games gold when Sachin Nag clocked 1 min 4.7 secs to win the 100 m freestyle in the 1951 Asian Games in Delhi. In the same Asian Games he won two bronze medals as well. He represented India in two Olympics: in 1948 in London and in 1952 in Helsinki.

First to participate in the Commonwealth Games

- Divers Dum Bahadur and Vasant Gadge were the first to represent India in the aquatics events at the 1978 Commonwealth Games in Edmonton, Canada.
- In 1982, for the first time, Indian swimmers participated in the Commonwealth Games at Brisbane, Australia. The team members were Wilson Cherian, Khazan Singh Tokas, T. Thoiba Singh, Sanjeev Chakraborty, Persis Madaan, Geeta Anand, and Giselle Bharucha.

First to qualify for two Olympic events

Shikha Tandon of Bengaluru, Karnataka, qualified for the 50 m and 100 m freestyle events in the 2004 Athens Olympics, but did not win.

Shikha Tandon

First to reach a Commonwealth Games final

During the 2010 Commonwealth Games in New Delhi, two Indian men – Virdhawal Khade and Sandeep Sejwal – reached the finals in their best events. Khade was placed seventh in the 50 m butterfly, while Sejwal came eighth in the 50 m breaststroke.

First relay team in the Commonwealth Games final

The quartet of Virdhawal Khade, Anshul Kothari, Arjun Jayaprakash, and Aaron D'Souza qualified for the 4 x 100 m freestyle relay final at the 2010 Commonwealth Games in New Delhi. They clocked 3 mins 27.14 secs to better their qualifying timing, but only finished sixth.

Virdhawal Khade

First 100 m freestyle – under 1 min.

- The first Indian swimmer to swim under 1 min. in the 100 m freestyle category was Basakha Singh, clocking 59.75 secs in 1971.
- The best performance is by Virdhawal Khade, who clocked 49.47 secs in October 2008. Among women, Shikha Tandon of Karnataka holds the record, with 58.91 secs in 2003.

First National Championship

The first National Championship was held in Mumbai, Maharashtra, in 1945.

First para swimmer to win bronze at the Commonwealth Games

Prasanta Karmakar was the first Indian para swimmer to claim a bronze medal in the 50 m freestyle in the S-9 category at the 2010 Commonwealth Games in New Delhi.

First to win a medal in the Asian Indoor Games

Shikha Tandon won a bronze in the 100 m backstroke event at the Asian Indoor Games in Bangkok, Thailand, in November 2005.

First visually impaired swimmer to win a gold

Kanchanmala Pande won gold in the 200 m medley event in the S-11 category on 8 December 2017 at the World Para Swimming Championship in Berlin.

First Indian para swimmer to win gold in the Para Asian Games

Jadhav Suyash Narayan won the gold medal in men's 50 m butterfly S7 (6 –7) category at the Para Asian Games held in Jakarta, Indonesia, in 2018. He clocked 32.71 secs.

First 200 m freestyle – under 2 mins

Virdhawal Khade of Maharashtra, who clocked 1 min. 49.86 secs, holds the record.

First Indian para swimmer to qualify for the Paralympic Games

Sharath Gayakwad was the first Indian para swimmer to qualify for the 2012 London Paralympic Games. He secured the ninth position. He also has a bronze at the 2010 Asian Para Games.

First swimmer to make Olympic 'A' cut – 100 m backstroke – men

Srihari Nataraj became the second Indian swimmer to qualify for the 2020 Tokyo Olympics after FINA approved his 'A' standard qualification time in men's 100 m backstroke time trial at the Sette Colli Trophy in Rome. He clocked 53.77 secs in time trial.

First swimmer to make Olympic 'A' cut 200 m butterfly – men

On 26 June 2021, Sajan Prakash became the first-ever Indian swimmer to breach the 'A' Olympic qualification time by clocking 1:56:38 secs in the men's 200 m butterfly event at the Sette Colli Trophy in Rome. He made the Tokyo Games 'A' standard, set at 1:56:48 secs, by 0.10 seconds at the FINA-accredited Olympic qualifier. Earlier, he was the only Indian male swimmer who represented India in the 2016 Rio Olympics and was the only one to qualify with, B, timings for Rio.

Sajan Prakash

Participation in two consecutive Olympic Games

Sachin Nag represented India in the 1948 London Olympics and the 1952 Helsinki Olympics. Sajan Prakash represented India at Rio in 2016 and the 2020 Tokyo Olympics (in 2021).

Participation in two consecutive Paralympics

Suyash Narayan Jadhav represented the country at Rio in 2016 and the 2020 Tokyo Paralympics (in 2021).

Women's 400 m freestyle national record

Hashika Ramachandra set a new national record in the Women's 400m Freestyle event at the 77th Senior National Aquatic Championships 2024 in Mangaluru, on 10 September. The Karnataka swimmer broke the 13-year-old record of 4:25.76, previously held by Jharkhand's Richa Mishra, with an impressive time of 4:24.70.

Men's 4×200 m freestyle relay national record

Swimmers Aryan Nehra, Aneesh Gowda, Sajan Prakash, and Srihari Nataraj set the national record in the 4x200 m freestyle relay, securing a gold medal at the Asian Group Aquatics Championships in the Philippines. The Indian quartet clocked an impressive 7:26.64, surpassing the previous best of 7:29.04 secs achieved by Aryan, Aneesh, Kushagra Rawat, and Tanish George Mathew at the Hangzhou Asian Games last year.

TABLE TENNIS
GENERAL

Most National singles titles in a row

A. Sharath Kamal among men and Indu Puri among women have won most National singles titles in a row. Kamal won the title five times between 2006 and 2010. Indu was champion six times between 1980 and 1985.

Junior/ Senior titles in a year

Four girls have won both titles in one calendar year – Rinku Gupta Acharya (Madhya Pradesh) in 1988; Mantu Ghosh (Bengal) in 1991; Kasturi Chakraborty (Bengal) in 1998, and Poulomi Ghatak (Bengal) in 1998-99.

No games conceded

Farokh Khodaiji was the first to achieve this feat, winning the men's singles title in 1967 in Guwahati, followed by Kaity Chargeman in the women's singles in Kolkata in 1970 and Chetan Baboor in the men's singles in 1999.

FIRST

First gold medallist in the Asian Championship

Gool Nasikwala won the singles, doubles, and mixed doubles gold medals in the 1952 Asian Championship in Singapore.

First Indian to reach World Championship quarter-finals

Krishna Nagaraj reached the men's singles quarter-finals in the 1956 World Championship in Tokyo, Japan.

First doubles pair in World championship quarter-finals

Mouma Das and Manika Batra became the first to reach the women doubles quarter-finals in the 2017 World Table Tennis Championship.

First woman to play in two Olympics

Mouma Das became the first woman player to qualify for two Olympic Games (2004, Athens, and 2016, Rio).

Youngest to qualify for the Olympic Games

Manika Batra became the youngest to play Olympic Games in Rio (2016) at the age of 21 years and 2 months.

First to be a medallist in five successive Commonwealth Games

A. Sharath Kamal is the only player to win Commonwealth Games medals in five successive editions – 2006, Melbourne; 2010, New Delhi; 2014, Glasgow; 2018, Gold Coast; and 2022, Birmingham.

First Commonwealth Games winner – women – singles

Manika Batra won the women's singles gold at Gold Coast in 2018.

First Commonwealth Games winner – men – singles

A. Sharath Kamal won the men's singles

A total of 44 international medals have been won by Indian paddlers in major tournaments as of October 2024.

gold at Melbourne in 2006. He regained the medal in Birmingham in 2022.

First Commonwealth Games gold – men – team

The Indian men's team won the first Commonwealth Games table tennis gold medal in Melbourne in 2006.

First to regain Commonwealth Games gold – men – team

A. Sharath Kamal was the only member of the Indian team that won the men's team gold in 2006 and again in 2022.

First Commonwealth Games gold – women – team

India's women team won the first Commonwealth Games team gold medal in Gold Coast in 2018.

First Commonwealth Games gold medal – mixed doubles

A. Sharath Kamal and Sreeja Akula won the mixed doubles gold in Birmingham in 2022.

First Commonwealth Championship team title – men

India won the Commonwealth men's team title in Kuala Lumpur in 2004.

First time when six Indian men and three women broke into the top 100 in world rankings

G. Sathiyan (ranked 49th), Sharath Kamal (51st), Soumyajit Ghosh (58th), Harmeet Desai (60th), Sanil Shetty (68th) and A. Amalraj (87th) were in the top 100 of world rankings in January 2018. At the same time, Manika Batra (62nd), Mouma Das (74th), and Madhurika Patkar (81st) also made the grade.

First Commonwealth Games gold – men – doubles

A. Sharath Kamal and Subhajit Saha won the men's doubles gold in New Delhi in October 2010.

First Commonwealth Games medal – women – doubles

Poulomi Ghatak and Mouma Das claimed the bronze in the women's doubles in New Delhi in October 2010.

First ITTF Pro-Tour title

A. Sharath Kamal won the Egypt Open to become the first Indian to win an ITTF Pro-Tour event in July 2010.

A. Sharath Kamal

A. Sharath Kamal, born on 12 July 1982, is a prominent Indian table tennis player who has made significant contributions to the sport. With a career spanning several decades, Sharath Kamal is recognized as one of India's top table tennis players. He has represented the country in multiple Olympic Games and Commonwealth Games, showcasing his skill and consistency on the international stage. Sharath Kamal has secured several national championships and international titles, cementing his status as a seasoned professional. Notably, he became the first Indian paddler to break into the top 30 of the International Table Tennis Federation (ITTF) world rankings.

First pair to win WTT Contender title

Manika Batra and G. Sathiyan became the first Indian pair to win WTT Contender title after beating Hungary's Nandor Ecseki and Dora Madarasz 3-1 (11-9, 9-11, 12-10, 11-6) in the final in Budapest in 2021.

First Indian to be ranked world no. 1 in U-18

Manav Thakkar became the first Indian to be ranked world no. 1 in the boys' U-18 category in February 2018.

First team medal in the World Junior Championship

The Indian boys' team, comprising Soumyajit Ghosh, Harmeet Desai, and G. Sathiyan, won India's first-ever bronze medal in the 2011 Junior Championship held in Bahrain.

First medal in Asian juniors

India won the bronze medal in the 2006 Asian Junior Championship at Kitakyushu, Japan, by reaching the semi-finals of the girls' event.

First title-triumph in the ITTF Junior tour

Harmeet Desai defeated Soumyajit Ghosh in the 2011 Austrian Open junior boys' final to become the first Indian to win a title on the ITTF (International Table Tennis Federation) Junior Tour.

First national champion

- M. Ayub won the men's singles title in Calcutta (now Kolkata) in 1938.
- P. Lima won the women's singles in Bombay (now Mumbai) in 1939.

First international league

The first edition of the Ultimate Table Tennis (UTT) was held in July 2017 in Chennai, New Delhi, and Mumbai. Six teams took part in the event and Falcons Club won the title by beating Shaze Challengers 14-9 in the final.

First professional

Chetan Baboor played as a professional with Enig Club in Kalmar, Sweden, from 1998.

Harmeet Desai

First Indian in the ITTF's Umpires and Referees Committee

Neelakanta Ganeshan was the first Indian inducted as a member of the International Table Tennis Federation's Umpires and Referees Committee (URC) in June 2017.

Manika Batra

First to win Asian Cup medal – women

Manika Batra became the first Indian woman to win a medal at the Asian Cup in 2022 as she defeated Japan's World No. 6 Hina Hayata in the bronze medal match. She also became the first Indian woman paddler to reach the semis of the continent.

First pair to win Asian Junior Championship in mixed doubles

Payas Jain and Yashaswini Ghorpade became India's first mixed doubles pair to win Asian Junior Table Tennis Championship in 2022 as the duo defeated China's Han Xinyuan and Qin Yuxuan in the final.

MOST

Most Commonwealth Games medals won by an individual player in a single edition

- *Men*: A. Sharath Kamal won four medals in the 2022 Commonwealth Games in Birmingham, UK.
- *Women*: Manika Batra won four medals in the 2018 Commonwealth Games in Gold Coast, Australia.

Most medals from Commonwealth-level competitions

Mouma Das has claimed 19 medals in both team and individual events of the Commonwealth Games and Commonwealth Championships between 2001 and 2018.

Most medals from the Commonwealth Games

Indians won eight medals, including three golds, in the 2018 edition of the Games in Gold Coast. India claimed gold medals in the men's team, women's team, and women's singles (Manika Batra); silver medals in the men's doubles (A. Sharath Kamal and G. Sathiyan) and the women's doubles (Manika Batra and Mouma Das); and bronze medals in the men's singles (A. Sharath Kamal), men's doubles (Harmeet Desai and Sanil Shetty), and mixed doubles (Manika Batra and G. Sathiyan).

Longest mixed doubles reign

Farokh Khodaiji and Kaity Khodaiji of Mumbai won the Susan Barna Cup five years in a row during 1967–71. They had earlier won the title in 1965.

Most World Championship appearances

Mouma Das has played in 16 editions of World Championship since 1997.

Mouma Das

Most state representations at the Nationals

N. Ravichandran represented five different units, including four states in the National Championships: Tamil Nadu, Punjab, Goa, and Puducherry, apart from the Central Revenue Sports Board at National-level tournaments.

Most appearances in the National Championships

S. Ramaswamy, who first played the Nationals in Allahabad in 1976, appeared in 30 successive National Championships until February 2006.

Most gold medals in the South Asian Federation (SAF) Games

A. Sharath Kamal won four gold medals – men's team event, men's singles, doubles, and mixed doubles – in Colombo in August 2006.

Most team titles – men/women

Bombay won the team title for the Barna Bellack Cup 16 times. Maharashtra won the team title for the Corbillion Cup 14 times. The championship was first introduced in 1946 at Madras (now Chennai) where Bombay (now

Mumbai) won the title and remained unbeaten till 1952.

Most National titles – singles

- Sharath Kamal has won 10 National singles titles in the men's singles section. Sharath broke Kamlesh Mehta's record of eight singles titles in 2019.
- Indu Puri won the ladies singles title eight times – 1972, 1975, and from 1979–84.

Most participants in a tournament

An unprecedented 4,104 entries were received across 17 categories in the first Indian Table Tennis Marathon 2019 held between 1 and 5 May 2019 at the Table Tennis Federation TT Hall, Sant Sujan Singh Ji International School, Swaroop Nagar, New Delhi. A record 4,102 matches were played.

YOUNGEST

Youngest to win the National title

Mantu Ghosh was 16 when she won the title at Jaipur in 1990–91.

Highest world ranking

Men: G. Sathiyan attained his career-high world ranking of 24 as of 1 May 2019.
Women: Manika Batra reached her career-best world ranking of 38 as of 3 May 2022.

BEST

Best team performance in the World Championship

India finished 10th – its best finish till date – in the men's team events of the 1959 World Championship in Dortmund (Germany). In 2018, India produced its second-best performance and took the 13th place.

Best performances in the Commonwealth Games – doubles

A. Sharath Kamal holds the distinction of winning the men's doubles medal in four successive Commonwealth Games. He partnered Subhajit Saha to win the gold in the 2010 Commonwealth Games in New Delhi. In 2014, he joined hands with Anthony Amalraj to claim the silver in the men's doubles in Glasgow. In 2018, he and G. Sathiyan settled for a silver medal in Gold Coast and again in 2022 in Birmingham.

Best Indian performance (individual): beating three top 20 players in one event

A. Sharath Kamal defeated three players from the world's top 20 list in the Asian Cup held in Jaipur in March 2015. They included world no. 8 Chuang Chih-Yuan (Chinese Taipei), world no. 15 Gao Ning (Singapore), and world no. 16 Joo Sae Hyuk (Korea).

Best doubles performance in the Commonwealth Championship

Chetan Baboor and S. Raman won two successive Commonwealth Championship titles in 1997 and 2000.

Second division titles in World championship

Indian men and women won the second division titles in the 2016 World Championship in Kuala Lumpur on 5 March 2016. In the final, Indian men beat Brazil 3–2 and the women defeated Luxemburg 3–1.

TENNIS

GENERAL

Oldest World No. 1 in tennis – men

At 43 years and 331 days, Rohan Bopanna became the oldest world No. 1 in men's tennis. He joined an elite group of Indian tennis players, including Leander Paes, Mahesh Bhupathi, and Sania Mirza, who have reached the top of the tennis rankings during their careers.

Best women's singles result

Karman Kaur Thandi's singles title in the US $60,000 ITF women's tournament in Saguenay, Canada, with a 3-6, 6-4, 6-3 victory over Katherine Sebov (Canada) in the final in October 2022, was a big breakthrough for Indian women's tennis. It was the biggest singles title for an Indian woman since Sania Mirza won the $75,000 tournament in Dubai in 2010. The biggest title ever by an Indian woman was Mirza winning the US $140,000 WTA event in Hyderabad in 2005. The 24-year-old Karman became no. 1 in India with a rank of 217.

BILLIE JEAN KING (FEDERATION) CUP

First world play-offs qualifying team

Earlier known as the Fed Cup, the Billie Jean King Cup is a team event for women's tennis players who represent their country in singles and doubles matches. The Indian Fed Cup team created history by progressing to the play-offs for the first time ever in March 2020, defeating Indonesia in the Asia–Oceania Group I event in Dubai, and finishing second behind China. They lost the world group play-off tie against Latvia. The team comprised Ankita Raina, Rutuja Bhosale, Zeel Desai, Karman Kaur Thandi, and Sania Mirza.

ASIAN GAMES

First gold – men – doubles

Leander Paes and Gaurav Natekar won the gold medal in the Hiroshima

Karman Kaur Thandi

Asian Games, held in 1994 in Japan – making this the country's first doubles gold medal at the Asian Games. They won by defeating the South Korean duo of Chang Euijong and Kim Chi-wan.

Somdev Devvarman

First singles gold
Somdev Devvarman won the gold medal at the 2010 Guangzhou Asiad in China, defeating Denis Istomin of Uzbekistan 6–1, 6–2.

First gold medallist – doubles – mixed
India got its first mixed doubles gold at the Asian Games when the team, with Leander Paes and Sania Mirza, won the gold in the Doha Asian Games in Qatar in 2006. They defeated the Japanese pair of Satoshi Iwabuchi and Akiko Morigami 7–5, 5–7, 6–2.

DAVIS CUP

First appearance
India played in the Davis Cup for the first time in 1921 against France in Paris and won 4–1. The Indian team comprised S.M. Jacob, Mohammed Sleem, A.A. Fyzee, and L.S. Dean.

Most successful player – doubles
Leander Paes became the most successful doubles player in the history of the Davis Cup with a record 45th victory in March 2020, when he and his partner Rohan Bopanna won India's Davis Cup match against Croatia in the do-or-die round of the World Group Qualifiers.

Best Davis Cup record in Asia
Though India has not yet won the Davis Cup, they have managed to reach the finals three times (in 1966, 1974, and 1987). Japan is the only other Asian nation to have figured in the Davis Cup finals (once in 1921).

Most appearances
Leander Paes holds the record of playing the most Davis Cup matches – 128 in 58 ties (as of March 2020). His win/loss records are 48/22 in singles and 45/13 in doubles.

Junior Davis Cup regional champs
The Indian Under-16 team of Rushil Khosla, Bushan Haobam, and Debasis Sahoo under the captaincy of Sajid Lodi won the Asia–Oceania Junior Davis Cup title in Delhi, to make the World Group along with Japan and Australia in 2022. In the World Group played in Turkey, India, represented by Rushil Khosla, Kriish Tyagi, and Vansh Nandal, finished 14th among 16 countries.

GRAND SLAM TOURNAMENTS

WIMBLEDON

First to play at Wimbledon
Sardar Nihal Singh was the first Indian to play at Wimbledon in 1908. He lost

Leander Paes

in the first round to Briton Herbert Wilson Fox, who beat him 11–9, 6–2, 6–4.

First junior boys' title

Ramanathan Krishnan won the first junior boy's Wimbledon title in 1954, defeating Ashley Cooper of Australia 6–2, 7–5. Twenty-five years later, Ramanathan's son Ramesh Krishnan won the same title in 1979, creating a unique father-and-son record. Both were recipients of the Padma Shri in 1962 and 1998 respectively. Ramanathan Krishnan was also awarded the Padma Bhushan in 1967.

Leander Paes and Mahesh Bhupathi

First men's title – doubles

The dominant Indian tennis pair of Leander Paes and Mahesh Bhupathi, then popularly known as Lee-Hesh, won India's first men's doubles title

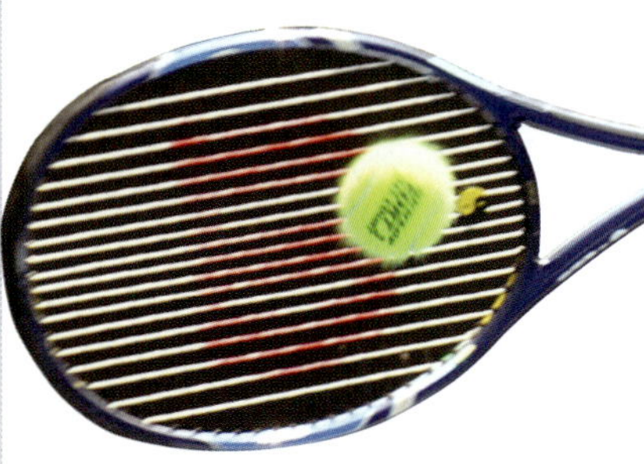

at Wimbledon in 1999, defeating Paul Haarhuis (the Netherlands) and Jared Palmer (USA) 6–7, 6–3, 6–4, 7–6.

First title – doubles – mixed

Leander Paes was the first Indian to win a mixed doubles title when he won it with Lisa Raymond (USA) in 1999. They defeated the pair of Anna Kournikova (Russia) and Jonas Björkman (Sweden) 6–4, 3–6, 6–3. Paes was awarded the Padma Shri in 2001.

First seeded at Wimbledon

Dilip Bose was the first seeded Indian player, at no. 15, in Wimbledon singles in 1950. He was a product of the Calcutta South Club (now in Kolkata, West Bengal), one of Asia's oldest tennis clubs.

First Indian woman at Wimbledon

Jenny Sandison was the first woman to represent India in tennis at Wimbledon, way back in 1929. However, she lost in the first round to French player Simone Barbier 6–2, 6–3.

First junior girls' title – doubles

Sania Mirza and her Russian partner Alisa Kleybanova won the junior girls' doubles title in 2003.

FRENCH OPEN

First title – doubles – mixed

Mahesh Bhupathi and his Japanese partner Rika Hiraki won the French Open title in 1997, defeating the American team of Lisa Raymond and Patrick Galbraith 6–4, 6–1. With this Bhupathi became the first Indian to win a Senior Grand Slam title.

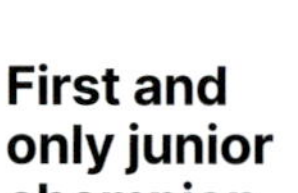

First and only junior champion

Ramesh Krishnan won the juniors title in 1979, the first and only Indian to achieve this feat, and was ranked the world's no. 1 junior player. He became India's Davis Cup captain in 2007.

First all-Indian title – mixed doubles

Mahesh Bhupathi and Sania Mirza won India's first ever all-Indian mixed doubles title in 2012, defeating Klaudia Jans-Ignacik (Poland) and Santiago González (Mexico) 7–6 (7–3), 6–1.

First all-Indian men's title – doubles

Leander Paes and Mahesh Bhupathi won India's first men's doubles title in 1999. The pair defeated Goran Ivanisevic (Croatia) and Jeff Tarango (USA) 6–2, 7–5.

US OPEN

First title – doubles – women

Sania Mirza was the first Indian to win a women's doubles title in 2015 at the US Open in New York, with Swiss player Martina Hingis. The pair defeated Casey Dellacqua (Australia) and Yaroslava Shvedova (Kazakhstan) 6–3, 6–3.

Sania Mirza

First and only junior boys' title

Leander Paes is the first and only Indian to win the junior boy's crown at the US Open in 1991. He beat Karim Alami (Morocco).

First title – doubles

Mahesh Bhupathi and his partner Max Mirnyi of Belarus won the US Open doubles title in 2002, defeating the Czech pair of Jiri Novak and Radek Stepanek 6–3, 3–6, 6–4.

First title – doubles – mixed

Mahesh Bhupathi, with his Japanese partner Ai Sugiyama, won the mixed doubles US Open title in 1999, the first Indian to win a mixed doubles title here. The pair defeated Kimberly Po and Donald Johnson of the USA 6–4, 6–4.

AUSTRALIAN OPEN

First men's title – doubles

Leander Paes became the first Indian to win a men's doubles title at the Australian Open, along with Radek Stepanek (Czech Republic) in 2012. They defeated Bob Bryan and Mike Bryan of the USA 7–6 (7–1), 6–2.

First title – doubles – mixed

Leander Paes, with Martina Navratilova of the USA, won the mixed doubles title in 2003, becoming the first Indian to do so. They defeated Eleni Daniilidou (Greece) and Todd Woodbridge (Australia) 6–4, 7–5.

First all-Indian title – doubles – mixed

Mahesh Bhupathi and Sania Mirza won India's first all-Indian mixed doubles Australian Open title in 2009, defeating the pair of Nathalie Dechy (France) and Andy Ram (Israel) 6–3, 6–1.

First junior boys' champion

Yuki Bhambri defeated Alexandros-Ferdinandos Georgoudas of Greece 6–3, 6–1 to win the Junior Boys' Championship in 2009.

ATP TOUR

First Indian to win 2 ATP Challengers singles titles in Europe

Sumit Nagal is the first Indian to win two ATP Challengers titles in Europe after he won the Tampere Open title in Finland in July 2023. He surpasses Somdev Devvarman, Rohan Bopanna and Harsh Mankad, who have won a title each. It was also his fourth ATP title overall and second of the season.

World's oldest player to win ATP Masters title – doubles

Rohan Bopanna at 43 became the oldest tennis player to win the ATP Masters 1000 title after he and Mathew Ebden won the Indian Wells in March 2023. Bopanna surpassed the record of Canada's Daniel Nestor, who won the Cincinnati Masters doubles title in 2015 at the age of 42.

Rohan Bopanna

First Indian to win ATP Challenger on European clay

Sumit Nagal became the first Indian to win ATP Challenger on European soil after winning the ATP Rome Challenger in April 2023. He defeated Jasper De Jong in the final 6-3, 6-2.

Yuki Bhambri

NATIONALS

First Nationals – grass court

The first tennis Nationals were held in 1946 at the Calcutta South Club lawns in Calcutta (now Kolkata), West Bengal. Sumant Misra beat Manmohan Lal in the final, becoming the first national champion. Khanum Singh (née Haji) was the first women's national champion.

Most Nationals titles

Ramanathan Krishnan won eight grass-court titles in 1953, 1956, 1958 to 1960, and 1962 to 1964.

WEIGHTLIFTING

First medals in the World Championships

Kunjarani Devi from Manipur bagged three silvers at Manchester, UK, in 1989 in India's debut performance at the World Championships. The Indian squad won seven medals in all at the event. Shyamala Shetty and Chhaya Adak won silver medals for individual lifts, while Lalita Polley claimed two bronze medals.

First gold in the Commonwealth Games – men

E. Karunakaran won gold in the flyweight class in the 1978 Edmonton Games in Canada.

First Junior weightlifting gold

Harshada Sharad Garud became the first Indian boy or girl to win a World Junior Weightlifting Championship by lifting a total of 153 kg (clean and jerk 83 kg + snatch 70 kg)

First Olympic-qualifying gold

Saikhom Mirabai Chanu won the gold medal in the women's 49 kg category at the EGAT Cup International Weightlifting Championship, an Olympic-qualifying event in Chiang Mai, Thailand, on 7 February 2019. She lifted 82 kg in snatch and 110 kg in clean and jerk to total 192 kg, and took gold on her return to international competition after a nine-month lay-off due to an injury. She had won the gold medal on her last appearance in 2018 at the Gold Coast Commonwealth Games in Australia.

First back-to-back gold medals

Khumukcham Sanjita Chanu made history for the second time when she bagged the gold medal in the women's 53 kg weightlifting event at the 2018 Commonwealth Games at Gold Coast, Australia. Her first gold was at the 2014 Commonwealth Games in the 48 kg category.

First silver medal at the Olympic Games

Saikhom Mirabai Chanu scripted a remarkable performance by winning a silver in the 2020 Olympic Games held in Tokyo, Japan, on day one. With an 87 kg lift in snatch and a 115 kg lift in the clean and jerk section, Chanu finished with a total of 202 kg.

Women's Weightlifting

Women's weightlifting in India has experienced a remarkable journey of growth and success. With the emergence of talents like Karnam Malleswari, who won India's first Olympic medal in weightlifting with a bronze at the Sydney 2000 Olympics, the sport gained national attention. Subsequently, athletes like Mirabai Chanu have continued to shine on the global stage, clinching medals at international events including the World Weightlifting Championships and the Commonwealth Games. The Indian women weightlifters have defied stereotypes and challenges, showcasing their strength and determination. Their achievements have not only bolstered the sport's popularity in the country but also motivated aspiring athletes, particularly women, to pursue weightlifting as a competitive endeavor.

Karnam Malleswari

Saikhom Mirabai Chanu

First Asian Games medals – women

Women's weightlifting was introduced in the 1990 Beijing Asian Games in China, where India won two silvers: Bharati Singh (82 kg category) and Jyotsna Dutta (+82 kg); and two bronzes: Kunjarani Devi (44 kg) and Chhaya Adak (52 kg).

First gold medal at the Youth Olympic Games

Jeremy Lalrinnunga became the first Indian to win a gold medal at the Youth Olympics Games 2018 held in Buenos Aires, Argentina.

Clean and jerk at the Asian Weightlifting Championships

Saikhom Mirabai Chanu set a new world record in the women's 49 kg clean and jerk with a lift of 119 kg on 17 April 2022 at the Asian Weightlifting Championships in Tashkent, Uzbekistan.

Jeremy Lalrinnunga

Yumnam Renu Bala Chanu

Most medals in the Commonwealth Games – women

Yumnam Renu Bala Chanu has won two golds in the Commonwealth Games. Her first came in the women's 58 kg category in Melbourne in 2006. She repeated this in the 2010 Delhi Commonwealth Games in the same category.

First Asian Games medal

Kamineni Eswara Rao won the silver in the 90 kg category in the 1951 Asian Games held in New Delhi. He was also adjudged the 'Strongest Man of India' at the 1954 Senior Nationals.

Most medals in world and Asian meets

Kunjarani Devi, who holds the record for the highest number of world and Asian meet medals, won 55 medals overall – 21 in six World Championships and the remaining in the Asian Games, and the Asian and Commonwealth Championships.

Most national titles

Balbir Singh Bhatia won 15 national and all-India titles.

Best performance at an Asian meet

India's weightlifters bagged five gold medals and a bronze in Busan, South Korea, in July 1995. Karnam Malleswari won three gold medals, and Kunjarani Devi claimed two gold medals and the overall title. Arun Murugesan won a bronze in snatch in the 54 kg category for men.

Most medals in the Commonwealth Games

India won five gold, two silver, and two bronze medals in the 2018 Gold Coast Commonwealth Games, the most at the Commonwealth Games in weightlifting. Saikhom Mirabai Chanu made a record-breaking performance in the clean and jerk event in the 48 kg category. Khumukcham Sanjita Chanu (53 kg) set a Commonwealth Games record in snatch, and Punam Yadav won a gold in the 69 kg category. In the men's section, Sathish Sivalingam (77 kg) and Ragala Venkat Rahul (85 kg) won gold medals too. P. Gururaja (56 kg) and Pradeep Singh (105 kg) won silvers, and Vikas Thakur (94 kg) and Deepak Lather (69 kg) won bronzes.

Most gold medals in World Championships

Karnam Malleswari won the gold in the World Championships twice – in 1994 (Istanbul, Turkey) and 1995 (Guangzhou, China).

Oldest National champion

Alok Nath Ghosh won the National Championship title in 1974 at 40 years. He had won the first national title in 1958 in Cuttack, Odisha. His first title was for Services and the last one was for the Railways.

Youngest Commonwealth Games medal winner

Eighteen-year-old Deepak Lather (69 kg) from Haryana became the youngest Indian weightlifter to win a medal at the 2018 Commonwealth Games in Glasgow, UK, by clinching a bronze medal.

Youngest National champion

P.K. Mahanand from Hyderabad won the All-India Championship in Calcutta (now Kolkata), West Bengal, in 1955 at the age of eighteen.

WRESTLING

First woman at the Olympics

Geeta Phogat from Bhiwani, Haryana, was the first Indian woman wrestler to compete at the Olympics during the 2012 London Games. However, she did not advance to the quarter-finals.

First at the Olympics

U. Zaw Weik (75 kg), the first to represent India at the Olympics, was placed 15th in the 1936 Olympics in Berlin, Germany.

First Olympics medal – men

Khashaba Dadasaheb Jadhav from Satara, Maharashtra, won a bronze in the bantamweight category (57 kg) in the 1952 Helsinki Olympics.

First winner of both Olympic and World Championship medals

Sushil Kumar is the first Indian to win medals at both the Olympics and the World Championships. He won a bronze at the 2008 Beijing Olympics in the 66 kg freestyle category and a silver medal in the same category at the 2012 London Olympics. He also won a gold in the same category in the Moscow World Championship in Russia in 2010.

First Olympic medal – women

Sakshi Malik created history as the first Indian woman to win an Olympic medal, a bronze, for wrestling, in the women's freestyle 58 kg category in the Rio Olympics in Brazil on 17 August 2016.

First medal at the World Championship – men

India's first medal in the World Championship was a bronze in the freestyle category (67 kg) won by Udey Chand from Hisar, Haryana, in the 1961 World Championship in Yokohama, Japan. He participated in three Olympics: in Rome, Italy, in 1960; at Tokyo, Japan, in 1964; and in Mexico City, Mexico, in 1968.

First medal at the World Championships – women

Alka Tomar of the Noida College of Physical Education won a bronze in the women's 59 kg class in the Senior World Wrestling Championship in Guangzhou, China, during September–October 2006. She was the first Indian woman wrestler to win a World

Championship medal after a gap of 39 years.

First Indian woman to win a silver medal at the World Championship
Anshu Malik (57 kg) became the first Indian female wrestler to win a silver medal at the 2021 World Championship in Oslo.

First woman triple winner – World Championships, Asian Games, and Commonwealth Games
Vinesh Phogat became the first Indian woman to win medals at the World Championships, Asian Games, and Commonwealth Games. While she won bronze at the 2019 World Championships in the 53 kg freestyle and a bronze at the 2014 Incheon Asian Games in the 48 kg category, she was also the first Indian woman to win a gold medal in the 2018 Asian Games in Jakarta and Palembang, Indonesia, in the 50 kg category. She won three consecutive Commonwealth crowns at Glasgow in 2014, Gold Coast in 2018, and Birmingham in 2022.

First World Championship gold medallist
Sushil Kumar from Delhi was the first Indian to win a World Championship gold medal in the 66 kg freestyle category in Moscow, Russia, in 2010.

First medal in the Commonwealth Games
- Rashid Anwar won a bronze medal at the 1934 Commonwealth Games held in London, UK, in the 74 kg category. This was the country's first medal won in the Commonwealth Games.
- Lila Ram won the first gold medal in the 1958 Games at Cardiff, Wales, in the heavyweight (100 kg) category.

First medal in the Asian Games
Vinesh Phogat, competing in the 50 kg freestyle category, fetched India its first gold medal in wrestling in the Asian Games in 2018 in Jakarta, Indonesia. She is the first Indian woman to win a gold medal in wrestling and to win back-to-back Asian Games medals, having won a bronze in 48 kg in Incheon, South Korea, in 2014.

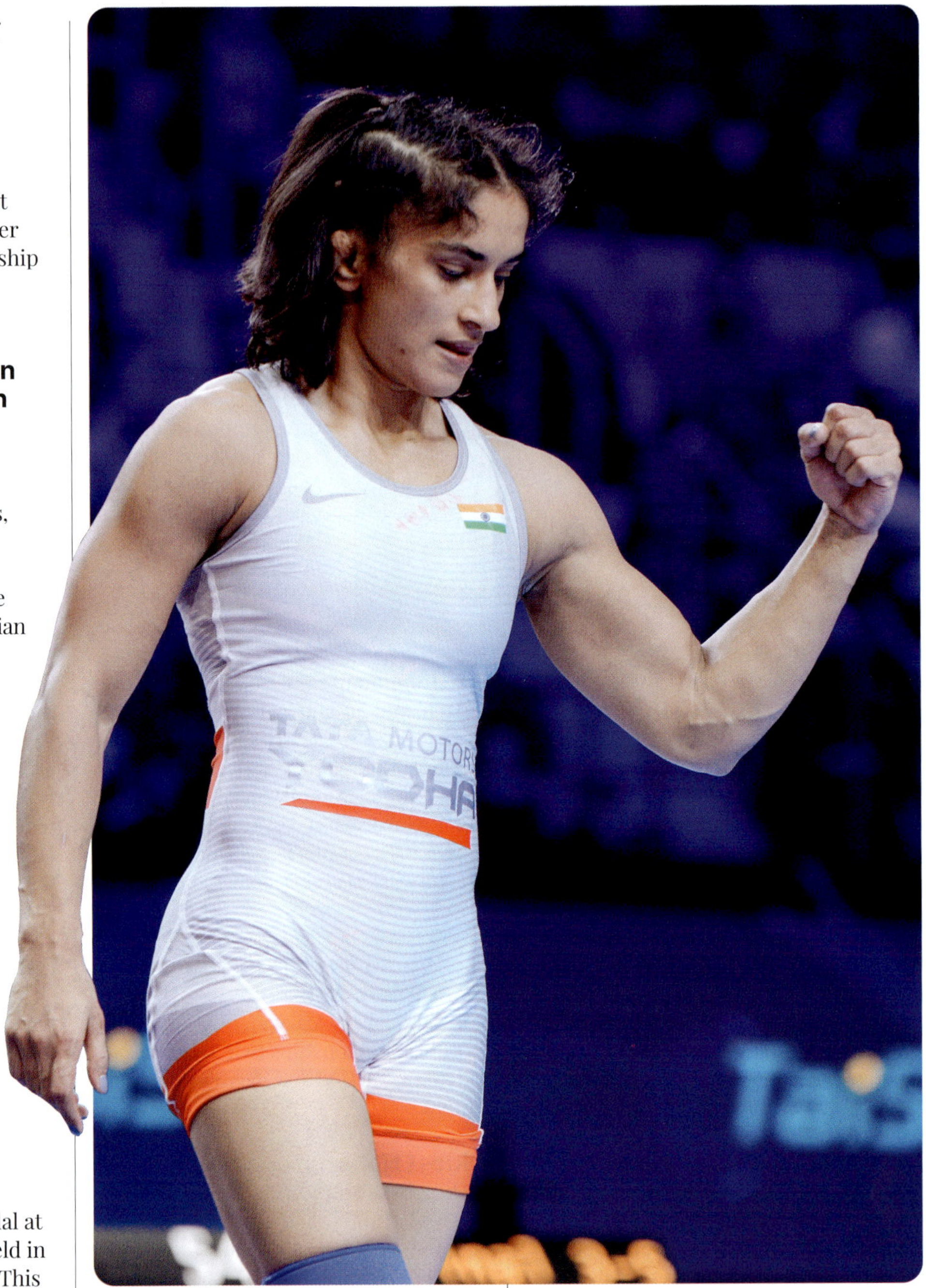

Vinesh Phogat

First Asian Games gold – men
Gold medals were won by Maruti Mane in 90 kg freestyle, Malwa Singh in 52 kg Greco-Roman, and Ganpat Andalkar in 100 kg Greco-Roman section at the 1962 Asian Games in Jakarta, Indonesia.

First and only Indian woman wrestler to win the Laureus World Sports Award
Vinesh Phogat is the first and only Indian wrestler to be awarded the Laureus World Sports Award, in 2019, in the comeback-of-the-year category. Phogat not only returned from her injury but also won the gold medal in both the 2018 Commonwealth Games at Gold Coast, Australia, and the 2018 Asian Games in Jakarta and Palembang, Indonesia.

> India has won a total of 23 medals in World Wrestling Championships so far.

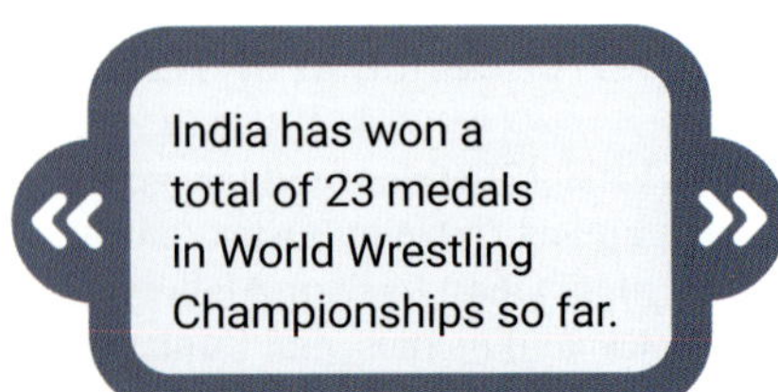

Bajrang Punia

First Asian Championships gold medal – women

Navjot Kaur from Punjab became the first Indian woman to win the gold at the Senior Asian Wrestling Championships on 2 March 2018 at Bishkek, Kyrgyzstan. She beat Japan's Miya Imai 9–1 to win in the women's 65 kg category.

First to win gold in U-20 World Championships – women

Antim Panghal became the first to win gold in the U-20 World Championships on 10 September 2022 in Sofia, Bulgaria.

First to be ranked as world no. 1

In March 2021, the UWW announced Bajrang Punia (65 kg) and Vinesh Phogat (53 kg) as top-ranked wrestlers.

First Junior World Champion

- The first gold medallists at the Junior World Championship were Ramesh Kumar (69 kg) and Palwinder Singh Cheema (130 kg) in 2001.
- Deepak Punia became India's junior world champion after 18 years, winning the gold medal in Tallinn, Estonia, on 14 August 2019. He defeated Russia's Alik Shebzukov in the 86 kg men's freestyle category.

First Junior Wrestler of the Year award

Deepak Punia (86 kg freestyle) became the first Indian wrestler to receive the Junior Wrestler of the Year title in 2019 from the UWW.

First Coach of the Year award

Late Yashvir Singh was the first Indian coach to be recognized as the Coach of the Year in 2010 by the Federation Internationale des Luttes Associées (FILA), the then apex body that governed wrestling.

First gold in Greco-Roman wrestling

- Pappu Yadav was the first grappler to win a gold medal in the 48 kg Greco-Roman category at the 1993 Asian Wrestling Championships held in Ulaanbaatar, Mongolia.
- On 19 February 2020, Sunil Kumar (87 kg) won a gold in Greco-Roman wrestling in the Asian Championships, which came 27 years after the first gold in 1993.

First Indian couple to win silver medals

Sakshi Malik (65 kg) and Satyawart Kadian (97 kg) became the first Indian wrestler couple to win silver medals in the 2020 Asian Championships in New Delhi.

First gold medal in the Asian Games

The first Indian to win a gold medal in the Asian Games was Kartar Singh in the 1986 Seoul Asiad in South Korea in the 100 kg category.

First medals in Greco-Roman Championships – Under-17

- Vinod Kumar (1980) and Pappu Yadav (1990) bagged the U-17 world title.
- Suraj Vashisht (55 kg) won it again after 32 years in July 2022 in Rome.

Back-to-back World Championship medals

Sajan Bhanwal became the first Indian to win back-to-back medals in the World Championship in the 77 kg category in the Greco-Roman style. He won a silver on 20 August 2019 in

Trnava, Slovakia, and a bronze at the Tampere World Championship, Finland, in 2017.

Best performance in the Asian Championship

India won a record haul of 20 medals (five gold, six silver, and nine bronze) across formats and genders in the 2020 Asian Championships. The gold medallists were Sunil Kumar (87 kg Greco-Roman [GR]); Pinki (55 kg women's freestyle [WFS]); Sarita Mor (59 kg WFS); Divya Kakran (68 kg WFS); and Ravi K. Dahiya (57 kg men's freestyle [MFS]). The silver medals were won by Nirmala Devi (50 kg WFS); Sakshi Malik (65 kg WFS); Bajrang Punia (65 kg MFS); Gourav Baliyan (79 kg MFS); Satyawart Kadian (97 kg MFS); and Jitender (74 kg MFS). The bronze went to Arjun Halakurki (57 kg GR); Ashu (67 kg GR); Aditya Kundu (72 kg GR); Hardeep (97 kg GR); Vinesh Phogat (53 kg WFS);Anshu Malik (67 kg WFS); Gursharan Preet Kaur (72 kg WFS); Rahul Aware (61 kg MFS); and Deepak Punia (86 kg MFS).

Best performance in the Greco-Roman event of the Asian Championships

India's best performance in the Greco-Roman category was at the 2020 Asian Championships in New Delhi where Indian grapplers won one gold and four bronze medals. Sunil Kumar (87 kg) won the gold medal while Arjun Halakurki (55 kg), Ashu (67 kg), Aditya Kundu (72 kg) and Hardeep (97 kg) won the bronzes.

Best performance at the Commonwealth Games – men

At the Commonwealth Games in 2010 in Delhi, the Indian men's team won seven gold, three silver, and three bronze medals in freestyle and the Greco-Roman style. The gold medals were won by Yogeshwar Dutt (60 kg); Sushil Kumar (66 kg); and Narsingh Panch Yadav (74 kg), all in freestyle wrestling; and Rajender Kumar (55 kg); Ravinder Singh (60 kg); Sanjay Kumar (74 kg); and Anil Kumar (96 kg), all in Greco-Roman wrestling. The silver medals were won by Anuj Kumar (84 kg) and Joginder Kumar (120 kg) in freestyle, and Manoj Kumar (84 kg) in the Greco-Roman style. The bronze medals were bagged by Anil Kumar (55 kg in freestyle); and Sunil Kumar (66 kg) and Dharmender Dalal (120 kg), both in the Greco-Roman style. These wrestlers made history by winning 13 medals (in both freestyle and Greco-Roman categories), the highest by any country in the Commonwealth Games.

Deepak Punia

Best performance at the World Championship

India has a record haul of five medals at the 2019 World Championship held at Nur-Sultan, Kazakhstan. Deepak Punia won a silver in the 86 kg category. Bronze medals were won by Bajrang Punia (65 kg), Rahul Aware (61 kg), Ravi Dahiya (61 kg), and Vinesh Phogat (women, 53 kg).

Best performance in the Commonwealth Games – women

Women's wrestling was introduced in the 2010 Delhi Commonwealth Games, where India bagged three gold medals, two silver medals, and one bronze medal in freestyle. Geeta Phogat (55 kg), Alka Tomar (59 kg), and Anita Sheoran (67 kg) won gold medals. The silver medals were won by Nirmala Devi (48 kg) and Babita Phogat (51 kg). Suman Kundu (63 kg) won the bronze medal.

Anita Sheoran

Most consecutive Commonwealth Games titles – women

Vinesh Phogat became the first to win three consecutive Commonwealth Games crowns at Glasgow, UK, in 2014; Gold Coast, Australia, in 2018; and Birmingham, UK, in 2022.

Most medals in the Asian Championship

Between 2013 and 2022, Bajrang Punia won a record eight medals in the 60 kg to 65 kg categories. He won bronze in 60 kg (2013, New Delhi), silver in 61 kg (2014, Astana, Kazakhstan), gold in 65 kg (2017, New Delhi), bronze in 65 kg (2018, Bishkek, Kyrgyzstan), gold in 65 kg (2019, Xian, China), and silver in 65 kg (2020, New Delhi; 2021, Almaty, Kazakhstan; 2022, Ulaanbaatar, Mongolia).

Most medals in the Commonwealth Championships

The Indian contingent, with 42 wrestlers, bagged 40 medals – 15 gold, 20 silver, and 5 bronze – in the 2011 Commonwealth Championships in Melbourne, Australia.

Most medals in the Asian Games – men

Kartar Singh won the gold at Bangkok, Thailand, in 1978, a silver in 1982 at Delhi, and another gold at the 1986 Seoul Asian Games in South Korea. He competed in the 90 kg category in 1978 and 1982, and in 100 kg in 1986 (all in freestyle).

Most individual medals in the Commonwealth Championships – men

Sushil Kumar won the title five times between 2003 and 2017. He won the gold medal in 2003 (London, UK), 2005 (Cape Town, South Africa), 2007 (London, UK), 2009 (Jalandhar, India), and 2017 (Johannesburg, South Africa).

Most individual medals in the World Championship

Bajrang Punia won the World Championship medal three times between 2013 and 2019. He won the bronze medal in the 60 kg category in

Sushil Kumar

2013, a silver in the 65 kg category in 2018, and a bronze in 2019.

Most gold medals in the Asian Championship

Sushil Kumar won the title in 2003, 2008 and 2010. Thereafter Ravi Kumar Dahiya won triple gold in Asian Championship titles in 2020, 2021 and 2022.

Most gold medals in the Commonwealth Games – men

Sushil Kumar of the Indian Railways and an alumnus of the Noida College of Physical Education, Noida, Uttar Pradesh, won India's first ever men's triple gold in the Commonwealth Games (2010, Delhi; 2014, Glasgow, UK; and 2018, Gold Coast, Australia).

Youngest gold medallist at the Commonwealth Games

Ved Prakash was 14 years old when he won the gold medal in the light flyweight class at the 1970 Commonwealth Games in Edinburgh, UK.

Youngest champion in the Asian Games

Malwa Singh won the gold medal in the Greco-Roman style in the light flyweight category at the 1962 Asian Games in Jakarta, Indonesia, at the age of 14 years, thus creating history by becoming the youngest wrestling champion from India.

Most medals at the Asian Girls Championship (U-15)

Indian girl wrestlers won seven medals in the Asian Girls Championships (U-15) in November 2018 in Fujimi, Japan. The gold medallists were Pooja Rani (33 kg), Komal (36 Kg), and Sweety (43 kg). Silver medals were won by Pinki (39 kg), Antim Panghal (46 kg), and Bhagyashree Fand (58 kg). Pratibha Janghu (54 kg) won the bronze.

The Chess Prodigy: Youngest World Champion

The chess world witnessed history as 18-year-old Indian prodigy D. Gukesh defeated defending champion Ding Liren in the final round of the 2024 World Chess Championship on 12 December in Singapore, becoming the youngest undisputed World Champion in history, surpassing the legendary Garry Kasparov. This remarkable achievement solidified Gukesh's place as a chess titan and a source of immense pride for India.

India @ Paris Olympics 2024

At the Paris Olympics 2024, the Indian contingent consisted of 117 athletes across 16 sports disciplines, including 70 men and 47 women. They competed in 69 events, vying for 95 medals. India secured a total of six medals at the Games, including three in shooting, one each in wrestling and athletics, and one in hockey. This was India's third-best outing at the summer games as they finished 71st.

PARIS 2024
PARIS 2024
ARIS 2024

Oldest Indian at Paris Olympics

Tennis Doubles World No. 1 Rohan Bopanna (44) was the oldest Indian at the Paris Olympics. He and partner Sriram Balaji made a first-round exit in the men's doubles event.

Youngest Indian at Paris Olympics

Swimmer Dhinidi Desinghu (14) was the youngest Indian at the Paris Olympics. She finished 23rd in heats of the women's 200 m freestyle event with a timing of 2:06.96.

Youngest Indian to win medal at Olympics

Aman Sehrawat became India's youngest-ever Olympic medallist by winning bronze in the men's freestyle 57kg wrestling event at the Paris 2024 Olympics. At 21 years and 24 days old, he surpassed P.V. Sindhu's record, set at the Rio 2016 Olympics, where she won silver at 21 years, one month, and 14 days old.

Aman Sehrawat

First Indian to win two medals at a single edition of Olympics

Manu Bhaker became the first athlete from independent India to win two medals at a single Olympic Games. She achieved this feat with a medal in the individual 10 m air pistol event and another in the 10 m air pistol mixed team event (with Sarabjot Singh). Norman Pritchard was the first Indian athlete to win two Olympic medals, securing silver in both the men's 200 m and 200 m hurdles at the 1900 Paris Olympics.

First India House at Olympics

For the first time, India had its own pavilion, the India House, at the 2024 Paris Olympics. Established by the Reliance Foundation and the Indian Olympic Association, it celebrated India's Olympic journey and culture. Located at Parc de la Villette, it served as a hub for fans, athletes, and cultural experiences.

India's first shooting team medal

Manu Bhaker and Sarabjot Singh became the first Indian shooting pair to win an Olympic team medal at Paris 2024, marking India's sixth Olympic medal in shooting. The duo secured the bronze by defeating the Republic of Korea's Oh Ye Jin and Wonho Lee 16-10. Notably, Oh Ye Jin had previously won gold in the women's 10 m air pistol event just days before the match.

Manu Bhaker and Sarabjot Singh

First Indian paddler to reach pre-quareter-finals in individual event

Manika Batra made history at Paris 2024 by becoming the first Indian table tennis player to reach the pre-quarter finals of the Olympic Games. Her campaign ended in the pre-quarter finals with a 4-1 loss to Japan's eighth-seeded Miu Hirano. Compatriot Sreeja Akula also reached pre-quarter finals right after in Paris.

Indian archers' best result at Olympics

Dhiraj Bommadevara and Ankita Bhakat achieved India's best-ever result in archery at the Olympics by finishing fourth in the mixed team event at Paris 2024. In the bronze medal match, they narrowly missed a historic podium finish, losing 6-2 to the USA's Brady Ellison and Casey Kaufhold.

First Indian shuttler to reach men's semifinals

Lakshya Sen made history as the first Indian shuttler to reach the semifinals in a men's badminton event at the Olympics. Competing in men's singles at Paris 2024, he topped his group, defeating players like Jonatan Christie of Indonesia. He went down to Denmark's two-time Olympic Champion Viktor Axelsen in the semifinal before losing to Malaysia's Lee Zii Jia.

First Indian to compete in dressage event of equestrian

Anush Agarwalla made history at the Paris Olympics as the first Indian ever to compete in the dressage event of equestrian. Agarwalla and his horse Sir Caramello Old did not advance to the medal round, finishing ninth in Group E with a score of 66.444%.

Indian men's hockey team's record-extending medal haul

The Indian men's hockey team clinched the bronze medal at the Paris 2024 Olympics, defeating Spain 2-1 after trailing by a goal. This win marked India's record-extending 13th Olympic hockey medal and the second consecutive bronze. It also marked the first time in 52 years that India secured back-to-back Olympic medals in hockey, following their success at the Munich 1972 Olympics.

Paris Olympics 2024 medal winners from India with PM Narendra Modi standing in the middle (left to right: Swapnil Kusale, Parattu Raveendran Sreejesh, Manu Bhaker, Sarabjot Singh, Aman Sehrawat, Harmanpreet Singh)

Indian Medal Winners at Paris 2024 Olympics

NO.	ATHLETE	EVENT	SPORT	MEDAL
1	Manu Bhaker	Women's 10 m air pistol	Shooting	Bronze
2	Manu Bhaker–Sarabjot Singh	Mixed team 10 m air pistol	Shooting	Bronze
3	Swapnil Kusale	Men's 50 m rifle 3 positions	Shooting	Bronze
4	Team India	Men's event	Hockey	Bronze
5	Neeraj Chopra	Men's javelin throw	Athletics	Silver
6	Aman Sehrawat	Men's freestyle 57kg	Wrestling	Bronze

India's Medals Tally by Sport

SPORT	GOLD	SILVER	BRONZE	TOTAL
Athletics	0	1	0	1
Hockey	0	0	1	1
Shooting	0	0	3	3
Wrestling	0	0	1	1
TOTAL	**0**	**1**	**5**	**6**

Paris 2024 Olympics Medals Table

RANK	COUNTRY	GOLD	SILVER	TOTAL
1	USA	40	44	42
2	China	40	27	24
3	Japan	20	12	13
4	Australia	18	19	16
6	France	16	26	22
71	India	0	1	5

India @ Paris Paralympics 2024

India's best-ever performance at Paralympics

India achieved its highest-ever medal tally at the Paralympic Games, winning a total of 29 medals, including seven gold, nine silver, and thirteen bronze. This performance surpassed the previous record of 19 medals won at the 2020 Paralympic Games.

First Indian man to successfully defend his title at Paralympics

Sumit Antil became first Indian to successfully defend his gold medal in the Men's Javelin Throw F64 category at the 2024 Paris Paralympics, achieving a throw of 70.59 metres and surpassing his own Paralympic Games record.

Youngest Indian Paralympian to win medal

At 17 years, 7 months, and 23 days, Sheetal Devi became the youngest Indian medallist in Paralympics history, winning bronze in the mixed team compound open archery event at Paris 2024.

Praveen Kumar sets new Asian record in Men's High Jump T64

Praveen Kumar claimed the gold medal in the men's high jump T64 event at the 2024 Paris Paralympics. He set a new Asian record with a personal best jump of 2.08 m, earning his second consecutive Paralympic medal. Praveen had previously won a silver at the Tokyo 2020 Paralympics, where he cleared 2.07m, which was his personal best at the time,

First medal in Men's Javelin Throw F41

Navdeep Singh secured a historic gold in the men's javelin throw F41 category at the 2024 Paris Paralympics, setting a new record with a throw of 47.32 m. This marked India's first-ever medal in this event. Navdeep's outstanding performance surpassed the previous Paralympic record of 47.13 m, set by China's Sun Pengxiang at the 2020 Tokyo Games.

Avani Lekhara

WR Mixed Compound Archery Qualification Round

The Indian mixed compound archery duo of Sheetal Devi and Rakesh Kumar set a new World and Paralympic Record of the qualification round at the Paris Games, achieving a remarkable combined score of 1399.

First Indian woman to successfully defend her title in Paralympics

Para shooter Avani Lekhara made history by becoming the first Indian woman to win two gold medals at the Paralympics. She initially secured her place in history during the women's 10 m air rifle standing SH1 event at the Tokyo 2020 Games and successfully retained her title in Paris. Avani claimed her second gold in spectacular fashion, setting a new Paralympic record of 249.7 points, surpassing her previous record of 249.6 set in Tokyo.

India's first-ever judo medal at Paralympics

Kapil Parmar made history by winning India's first-ever Paralympic medal in

Indian medal winners at Paris 2024 Paralympics

NO.	ATHLETE	SPORT	EVENT	MEDAL
1	Avani Lekhara	Shooting	Women's 10m air rifle standing SH1	Gold
2	Mona Agarwal	Shooting	Women's 10m air rifle standing SH1	Bronze
3	Preethi Pal	Athletics	Women's 100m T35	Bronze
4	Manish Narwal	Shooting	Men's 10m air pistol SH1	Silver
5	Rubina Francis	Shooting	Women's 10m Air Pistol SH1	Bronze
6	Preethi Pal	Athletics	Women's 200m T35	Bronze
7	Nishad Kumar	Athletics	Men's high jump T47	Silver
8	Yogesh Kathuniya	Athletics	Men's discus throw F56	Silver
9	Nitesh Kumar	Badminton	Men's singles SL3	Gold
10	Thulasimathi Murugesan	Badminton	Women's singles SU5	Silver
11	Manisha Ramadass	Badminton	Women's singles SU5	Bronze
12	Suhas Yathiraj	Badminton	Men's singles SL4	Silver
13	Rakesh Kumar / Sheetal Devi	Archery	Mixed team compound open	Bronze
14	Sumit Antil	Athletics	Javelin throw F64	Gold
15	Nithya Sre Sivan	Badminton	Women's singles SH6	Bronze
16	Deepthi Jeevanji	Athletics	Women's 400m T20	Bronze
17	Mariyappan Thangavelu	Athletics	Men's high jump T63	Bronze
18	Sharad Kumar	Athletics	Men's high jump T63	Silver
19	Ajeet Singh	Athletics	Men's javelin throw F46	Silver
20	Sundar Singh Gurjar	Athletics	Men's javelin throw F46	Bronze
21	Sachin Khilari	Athletics	Men's shot put F46	Silver
22	Harvinder Singh	Archery	Men's individual recurve open	Gold
23	Dharambir	Athletics	Men's club throw F51	Gold
24	Parnav Soorma	Athletics	Men's club throw F51	Silver
25	Kapil Parmar	Judo	Men's -60kg J1	Bronze
26	Praveen Kumar	Athletics	Men's high jump T64	Gold
27	Hokato Hotozhe Sema	Athletics	Men's shot put F57	Bronze
28	Simran	Athletics	Women's 200m T12	Bronze
29	Navdeep Singh	Athletics	Men's javelin throw F41	Gold

judo, securing a bronze in the men's 60 kg (J1) category. He achieved this milestone with a dominant victory over Brazil's Elielton de Oliveira in the final.

Dharambir sets Asian record in club throw – men

Dharambir set a new Asian record of 34.92m to win the men's club throw F51 event at the Paris Paralympics, securing India's fifth gold. His record-breaking throw also helped India equal its gold medal tally from the Tokyo Paralympics. Pranav Soorma clinched the silver medal in the same event for India's one-two finish.

India's first-ever gold medal in para archery

Harvinder Singh made history by winning India's first-ever gold medal in para archery at the Paris Paralympics. He secured the title with a dominant 6-0 victory over Poland's Lukasz Ciszek (28-24, 28-27, 29-25) in the men's individual recurve open final, earning his second consecutive Paralympic medal.

First Indian para-athlete to win medal at three consecutive Paralympics

Mariyappan Thangavelu became the first Indian para-athlete to win medals at three consecutive Paralympic Games with his bronze (1.85 m) at the Paris Games. He previously secured gold at Rio 2016 with a jump of 1.89 m and silver at Tokyo 2020 with a 1.86 m attempt.

First Indian women to win two medals at Paris Paralympics

Preethi Pal won bronze medals in both the women's 200 m T35 and the women's 100 m T35 events, making her the first Indian woman to win two medals at Paris Paralympics. Her 100m bronze also mader her India's first medallist in track events.

Paris 2024 Paralympics: India's medal tally by sport

SPORT	GOLD	SILVER	BRONZE	TOTAL
Archery	1	0	1	2
Athletics	4	6	7	17
Badminton	1	2	2	5
Judo	0	0	1	1
Shooting	1	1	2	4
TOTAL	**7**	**9**	**13**	**29**

Paris 2024 Paralympics medal table

RANK	COUNTRY	GOLD	SILVER	BRONZE
1	People's Republic of China	94	76	50
2	Great Britain	49	44	31
3	United States of America	36	42	27
4	Netherlands	27	17	12
5	Brazil	25	26	38

Paris Paralympics 2024 Indian contingent with PM Narendra Modi and other dignitaries

A

Aadhaar, state/UT with highest coverage, state/UT with least coverage 212
Académie des Beaux – Arts Photography Awards – William Klein, first winner 155
academy, first defence, first radio jockey training 109, first for visual arts 157
actor, first woman stunt 14, most pairings, oldest debut 144
Aditya-L1, India's first solar mission 263
admiral, first four-star 230
advertising, **agency**, first abroad, first full-service Indian, first multinational 344; **association**, first 344; **advertisements**, first known, first on colour TV, first on radio, first on TV, 344
aeronautical society, first 308
affiliation, first tri-services 222
agency, first rating 333
agriculture, first society, first university 87, first, theme park, society 86, research institute 88
agri-plane, first 99
AIFF Intercontinental Cup, most successful team 412
AIIMS, a hub of medical firsts 269
air, first taxi 309
aircraft, **airfield**, first 308, highest 310; **airline**, first, first designer 308, largest passenger 312, first 239, first Boeing 737-900, first indigenous 309, first free in-flight Wi-Fi services on international flights 311, first indigenous AEW&C class of, first indigenous fighter, first indigenous light combat, first indigenous (trainer), first supersonic 240, first private military plant 242, oldest fleet 310
air force, first forward surgical centre 242, first S-400 defence system 241, first technical officer 238
air freight, first service 308, most traffic 310
airlift, biggest rapid, first of Indian troops 242
Airline, largest collection of boarding passes 52
airmail, first 188, first 190
airport, **club**, first flying 308; first to install a body scanner, largest IT outage 309, first fully solar-powered, recycling machines, highest commercial, first to instal waste, largest passenger terminal 310
algebra, invention of 246
algorithm, first to invent new and speedy 259
alliance, first Indo-European 198
alumni association, first college 107
ammunition, first indigenous 235
amusement park, first, first indoor, first marine 79, first water 80
anaesthetist, first woman 270
Antarctic, first expedition, first women 257
anther culture, first 257
anthology, earliest known 162
apes, only 285
app, first Aadhaar-based payment 194
aquarium, largest underground 82
archaeological site, first green 301
archery, Aditi Gopichand breaks U-18 record 380; **Asian Championship**, first medal (men), most medals 378, hat-trick of bronze medals 379; **Asian Para Games**, first gold 379; **Commonwealth Games**, most medals won 379, first compound para medal, first compound team (women) ranked no.1, first to win back-to-back, 378; **Internationals**, First gold, first gold (women), first medal (individual) 379; **Olympics**, first representation (men), first representation (women) 379, only Indian couple to represent, only siblings to represent India 380; **Paralympics**, first armless archer to reach final, first ever medal 380; **World Championships**, first junior title (men), first medal, most medals, first compound title (men) (individual), first compound title (men) (team), first gold medal, first team gold (women), most gold medals won (individual) 379; **World Cup**, best medal show, most medals, three gold medals, three individual gold medals, two medals in stage 3 380; **Youth Olympics**, first silver 379; **Youth World Champion**, first Indian to win in recurve - men 380
architect, first 60
Arihant-class submarines 232
arithmetic, first textbook on 246
armament checker, first administrative unit 221, first and oldest extant, first special operations division 222
armoured personnel, first indigenous 222
army, **Ashok Chakra**, first 220; **Padma Bhushan**, first republic day commander and first to receive 220; **UN Military Gender Advocate award**, first Indian Peacekeeper to win the 220; first woman DG Medical Services 221; **George Cross**, first 220; **Param Vir Chakra**, first (Army) 220
art, **district**, first public; first bank, highest price for an Indian piece at an auction 157, first modern school, first summit 156, sand castle 159; **festival**, largest 125
artillery, first company; first unit 221; lightest towed 223
artworks, most leaf – solo 159
ash gourd, longest 92
Asian Games, India's best performance, 375
Asian Para Games, best performance 375
association, earliest public, first industrial 327

asteroid, discovery of 250
Asthana Nartaki, only 124
astrolabe, earliest extant, first manual on 247
astronomers, first 247
astronomy, first university to teach 247; **observatory**, first, first chain, highest 247; **society of India**, first woman president 249
athletics, Asian Athletics Championships, best performance, first to win gold - women, joint-highest medal tally, triple excellence in shot put 381; **Asian Games**, first double gold, first gold (men) (individual), first gold (women) (individual), first gold (women) (team), first medal (women), first to win three successive gold medals, most individual goals, only gold in marathon 381; **Asian Indoor Championships**, biggest point-haul in pentathlon – women 381; **Asian Youth Athletics Championships**, best performances, 381; **career**, longest (men), longest (women) 381; **Commonwealth Games**, first individual gold medal in discus throw (men) 381, best performance, first title in fencing, first gold (women), first medal in high jump, first medal in javelin throw (women), first medal in racewalk (women), first medal (women), first to win gold medal in triple jump, Gold medal in Commonwealth and Asian Games 382; **International**, first Indian to be elected into the IAAF council, first individual gold in track events in World U-20 championship, first medal in a marathon (women) 382, Diamond League, first clean sweep in a meet, first Indian to win gold in World U-20 championship, first to receive veteran pin by the IAAF, first win in IAAF continental cup, first world U-20 Athletics Championships twin medals, 383; **marathoner**, most appearances, 383; **nationals**, fastest 100 m hurdles – women, fastest 3000 m steeplechase – men 384, fastest 1,500 m – women, fastest 4x400 m mixed relay – team, Fastest 5,000 m and 10,000 m – men, fastest 110 m hurdles – men, Fastest 400 m – U-18 – women, fastest race walk 385, highest pole vault, longest shot put – women, longest triple jump – women 385, youngest athletics champion, oldest gold medallist, 385; **Olympics**, best performances, first marathoner, first woman captain, first women in 383; **para athlete**, best javelin throw (men), first gold (women), first IAS officer to win a silver medal, first to get Rajiv Gandhi Khel Ratna Award (woman) 384; **Paralympics**, best discus throw (men), First gold in javelin, first participation in, first triple medal 384; **World Athletics**, first gold 383; **World Championships**, first medal 383; **World Para athletic championship**, best performance, first bronze medal 384; **World Universiade**, first gold 383
ATM, first floating, first on wheels 329, state/UT with the most 332
atomistic, earliest theory 249
auditorium, largest 80
auto, first CNG 318
automated teller machine, first facility 329
automotive, largest company 319
AVGC, top 10 states with most educational institutions in India 150
awards, first to host Emmy 187, most national won (*see under each sport*) 378

B

baby, heaviest at birth 266, lightest 267
badminton, Asian Championship, first bronze medal (singles) (men) 388, first gold 387, first medal (doubles) (men), first medal (doubles) (mixed), first medal (doubles) (women), first medal (singles) (women), first silver medal (doubles) (men) 388; **Asian Games**, first individual medal (men), first individual medal (woman), first medal (men) (doubles), first medal (mixed doubles), first team medal (women), Multiple medal – winner in a single edition, two medallists (single event) 387; **BWF Super Series Masters Finals/BWF World Tour Finals**, first gold medallist (singles) (women), first medallist (singles) (men), first medallist (singles) (women), first silver medallist (doubles) (mixed), first silver medallist (singles) (women), 386, 388, highest world ranking (doubles) (men), highest world ranking (doubles) (mixed), highest world ranking (doubles) (women), Highest world ranking (singles) (men), highest world ranking (singles) (women), 388; **Commonwealth Games**, first bronze medallist (team) (mixed), first gold medallist (doubles) (men), first gold medallist (singles) (men), first gold medallist (singles) (women), first gold medallists (women) (doubles), first gold medallist (team) (mixed), first medallist (doubles) (women), first medallist (individual) (men), first medallist (individual) (women), first medallist (team) (men), first medallist (team) (women, first silver medallist (team) (mixed), most gold medals from one edition, Most medals from one edition 387; **International competitions**, first duo to win Super 1,000 title, First finalist at the All England – men – singles, first medal in Thomas Cup championship (team) (men), first medal in Uber Cup (team) (women), first winner at All England

Championship, first winner of the World Cup – men – singles, two semi-finalists at All England 388, most titles (men), most titles (women) 389; **National Competitions**, first champions, most titles (doubles) (men), most titles (doubles) (mixed), most titles (doubles) (women), most titles (singles) (men), most titles (singles) (women) 389, most versatile and successful player 390; **Olympics**, first medallist, first silver medallist, first two-time medallist 385; **Paralympics**, first bronze medallist (singles) (men), first gold medallist (singles) (men), First silver medallist – men – singles 389, first badminton gold 390; **World Championships**, first medal (individual) (men) 385, first doubles medallist (men), first doubles medallist (women), first medal (individual) (women), first silver medallist (individual) (men), first two-time silver medallist (individual) (women), first world champion, highest number of medals, two medals from one edition (men), two medals from one edition (women) 386; **World Junior Championship**, first gold medallist (singles) (girls), first medallist (singles) (boys), first medallist (singles) (girls), first silver medallist (singles) (boys) 388
Baha'i, first house of worship 68
balancing, longest time balancing a hockey stick on the little finger, longest time hockey stick on the middle finger 14
ball, cricket, longest duration of non-stop hitting a dangling 14
ballet, first film 123
balloon, hot-air, highest takeoff 349
ballot, first use of single paper and single box 200
bamboo, first tissue culture 258, grass, tallest 296 largest collection of species 297
band, first on MTV 131
bank, first, first cooperative, first credit card issued by an Indian oldest private, first foreign, first for housing development, first Indian to open a branch overseas, first regional rural 329, biggest fraud, first export-import, first listed on the New York Stock Exchange, first with a satellite network, largest international by number of branches, with most foreign offices, with the largest network 332, first to establish a mutual fund 333
banking, first government agency 329
Bappu-Wilson effect, discovery 249
barrage, largest 78
barrister-at-law, first 213
BASE jump, first to complete during day and night, highest, lowest 348, highest, lowest 349
basketball, longest shot 14; **Asian Games**, first appearance, most appearances (women), best win, first and only sisters representing the country 389; **Nationals**, longest sequence of titles 389; **NBA**, first Indian-born player in 389
bas-relief, largest 62
bat, largest, rarest, smallest 287
bathing, biggest tank 69
battle, ground, highest 224
Belur Math, smallest model 29
benches, most, donated – 1 year 31
Bhagavadgita, most translated work 163
Bharatanatyam, first campaign for revival 123, largest ensemble 124
bill, longest 45
bindi, largest collection of 52
biocentre, first 257
biocide, first neem-based 99
biocontrol agents, first 99
biogas plant, largest by capacity 305
biotechnology, first department 268
bird, egg, largest, smallest, first hospital, largest wingspan, longest beak, longest claws, nest, largest round, most intricat, shortest legs, slowest, smallest, smallest and lightest 287, longest legs, swiftest/fastest dive, tallest flying 288
blood, first bank 270, longest clot removed 278
boat, first indigenous patrol, first missile, first indigenous patrol 232
book, grammar text, oldest surviving 162, earliest extant English work, earliest known Gujarati work, earliest known Kannada works, earliest known Malayalam work, earliest known Marathi works, earliest known Tamil work, earliest known Telugu work, earliest original Odia work 163, audio, longest, largest, smallest, thickest 164, biggest retail chain - high street, fair, first, first comic convention 165, oldest shop 166, first known printed, first printed in local languages, first printed to use Bengali, first printed to use Bengali type, first village, largest book market, largest sales (Children's hardback), largest sales (fiction on release-hardback) 168, largest lifetime sales-hardback, most travel 170; **title**, top 5 front-list in 2023 169; **novel**, longest 164,
booking office, first air ticket 308
bosons, discovery 253
boxes, first 190
boxing, AIBA, first in athletes commission 390
AIBA legend, best performance, first Indian man to receive APB best boxing trophy, first Indian woman to receive award 390

Asian Championships, most medals (women) 390
Asian Games, best performance, best performance (women), first gold (men), first medal, most Golds 391, golden sweep in Youth Championship, junior champions (girls) 393; **association**, oldest existing, best youth boxer (men) 390; **Commonwealth Championship**, most golds 391; **Commonwealth Games**, best performance, first gold 391; **International**, most golds in an international meet, most successive professional wins 390, most titles 391; **Nationals**, first championship 391; **Olympics**, first appearance, first medal (men), first medal (woman) 391; **World Boxing Championship**, best performance (women), first medal (men), first medal (women), most medals, 392; **World Championship**, first medal (men), most World Championship titles – women 392; **World Cup**, most medals (men), world number one, first medal 392; **Youth Boxing Championship**, Best performance in the World Youth Women's Boxing Championships, most medals 392
brain, longest object removed from 273
branches, most 329
brand, first Indianized foreign, first patented 344
breakwater, longest 78
breast milk, first bank 270
bridge, first cable-stayed road, first iron, longest bailey, longest balanced, only bascule, widest double-decker steel 75, longest cable-stayed 76, busiest, cable-stayed rail, highest bailey, highest rail, longest cantilever, longest road-and-rail 77, longest built during war 229
British House of Commons, first representative in the 215
broadcasting, first, first controller of broadcasting, first private FM broadcaster, first service 180, first company 184
broiler, first chicken variety 97
browser, most popular 195
budget, first, first interim, first paperless, first papers in Hindi, first Union, longest speech, shortest speech 326
buffalo, first milk powder 96, first cloned, first female cloned by hand-guided technique, first cloned 97
building, first all-steel, first reinforced concrete 81
bull, first artificial insemination, first frozen semen bank 93, heaviest and highest-priced 96, most calves cloned from 97
Bullion Exchange, India's first international 340
bungee, first balloon jump, highest jump (woman) 348, first Asian triple amputee to complete a jump 350
burpees, most by a woman in 1 hr 17
bus, first trolley 317, first battery fleet, first electric, first motor, first stainless-steel 318, State/UT with largest fleet 319
bust, largest 73
butterfly, biggest, smallest 288, at the highest altitude 289

C

cab, first electric 319
cable link, first submarine 192
calculus, largest urethral removed 277
calf, first cloned from frozen semen 97
camels, the only that can swim 286
camera, largest collection of 154, largest museum 152
campaign, longest social through an adventure sport 364
canal, earliest system, longest 78
cancer, first centre for rehabilitation 268
candles, largest collection of 55
Cannes Lions, first at the, most awards at the 344
canoeing, first expedition 363
Cape2Rio, fastest to complete race 365
Capitals, fastest to identify of all the countries of the world 39
car, first, first Indian manufacturers, first zero-emission electric 318, SUV, first fully electrical 319
card, first indigenous payment 332
cardiologist, first 271
cargo, service, first English periodical on dance 122, first 308, first overseas 323
Carnatic music, first codifier of concert format 125, earliest treatise 128, first all-woman Hindustani-Carnatic music band 130, first whistling LP 131 marathon vocal performance 132
carrier, first all-jet 309
carrier, aircraft, largest 232, first dry 236
CAR-T cell therapy, first home grown 279
cartoon, gallery, first 157
Carvaan, first portable digital audio player 130
carving, smallest pencil-lead 159
castor, first hybrid 93
catalogue, first modern of stars 248
catamaran, first superfast service 323
cataract, pioneering removal 273
catchment area, largest 282
cavalry, first regiment, first unit 221, first use of air 223
cave, largest 283, longest natural sandstone 284
cave fish, largest recorded 295
CBFC Statistics 141
cellular service, first 194
censor, first boards 140

Census, first 215
Central Production Centre, first 184
certificate, first gender-neutral 110
chain, longest and largest human, longest paper 45
chairperson, longest-serving 328
Champions of the Earth Award, first Indian winners 300
chancellor, vice, first Indian 110, youngest 111
Chandra, Prakash 201
channel, first 24-hour news, first business, first high-definition, first infotainment, first private, first TV station to get to get a second 185
charcuterie, longest platter 45
Chemical Landmark Plaque, awarded to outside Europe 254
chemicals company, first heavy 254, first 255
chemistry, first department, terpene 255
chess, **Anand**, **Viswanathan**, Board Prize with a perfect score, domination in advanced chess 393, first grandmaster 394; **Asian**, champions (men), champions (women), four successive junior titles, junior champions (boys) 393, fastest to achieve norms, first junior title, first sub-junior champion, most participants in International Open, most prize money in International Open 395, first/only winner Asian junior and sub-junior, youngest winner of Asian junior U-20 396; **Asian Games**, first medal, first team medal, first to win Junior girls' title thrice 394, best achievement, best performance, best performance Asian Team 396, chess Oscar award 397; **Commonwealth**, most successful champion 393, first international recognition, first woman to lead a team in open section 394, city to host most championships 395, youngest to win title 396; **GM norm**, first, first in national championship 394; **Grandmaster**, youngest, youngest (female), youngest to beat 396; **Grand Slam**, victories 394, highest cheque 395; **International Master**, most times world champion 393, first (men), first (women) 394, most international age group titles, youngest, youngest to achieve norm, most medals 395; **National**, oldest to regain world rapid title 392, most titles, most titles in a year, most titles (season) 395, youngest champion, youngest junior, youngest to qualify for championship 396, only girl to win U-12 397; **Olympiad**, first gold, first gold on top board, first in both sections, first medal, first medal in chess 394, youngest in World Cup and Olympiad, only to win against computers 396, rapid/blindfold event 397; **WGM**, first norm 394; **Wijk Aan Zee**, only Asian 396; **WIM**, first 394, youngest 396; **World Cup**, two, 394, first country to win both world junior titles (single edition) 395, only Indian to reach final of World Championship, youngest international title winners, youngest to win the World Junior title, youngest world champion in any 396, only Indian with three World Championship medals, only semi-finalist of World Championship and World Cup 397
Chetak, first flight commander 238
Chhau, first woman to perform 123, only dance form varied in three states 124
Chhetri, Sunil, Indian footballer 408, 409, 411, 412
chief, first of foreign air force, longest tenure, first air 238
Chief Election Commissioner, first 199, longest tenure as, shortest tenure as 200
Chief Justice, first 213, first woman (*See also Woman*) 214
chief minister, longest tenure, shortest tenure 199, first 'film star', youngest 210, most in a year 211
chilli, hottest 93, longest green 300
chimney, tallest 80
chip, first indigenous 258
cholera exotoxin, discovery 258
Christian Medical College and Hospital, firsts 271
Christmas tree, tallest man-made 41
church, largest, tallest 72
church, oldest, largest, Se Cathedral, St Thomas Syro-Malabar Church 72
cinema, largest multiplex 80, first hall 140
circumnavigation, first aerial world in a single-engine plane 348, first by a man - solo, first by a woman - solo, first of the globe by a differently abled sailor 361
cities cleanest 305
citizen, first to have a 'no caste, no religion' certificate 215
civic body, oldest 214
clean-up, **beach**, most waste collected in a single day 304
climate clock, largest 293
clinic, first, hormone replacement therapy, online 268, liver 269
Clocks, largest collection of antique 52
club, first flying 308
coaches, double-decker, first 312, most produced in a year 314
Coast Guard, first and only Integral ICG contingent operating abroad, first director general, first and only Integral ICG contingent operating abroad, Tatrakshak Medal, first (Coast Guard) to receive President's, Tatrakshak Medal, first (Coast Guard) to receive President's 242

coconut, first hybrids, longest and biggest 92, largest producer 95
code, first British Indian, first penal 213
Coin, tallest stacked tower 41
coinage, earliest 328
coins, earliest gold, first for the visually impaired, first lead, oldest surviving gold 328
cold storage, State/UT with highest cold storage capacity 92
collage, largest (group) 157
collections, one-quarter British anna 38, credit cards 45, maps 46, Amitabh Bachchan memorabilia, Models of owls, Owl-shaped jewellery, playing cards 48, Autographs – national awardees, Autographs of Ajit Laxman Wadekar, Chitra Kathayen comics, Hair clips, napkins, Obituaries – from a single family, Seer, Stickers, ties, matchboxes featuring horses 49, aircraft models, Cinema press booklets – on a single personality, Soap covers – single brand, Nokia handsets 50, antique matchbox labels, Badges - political theme, lapel pins, lighters, Pradhan Mantri Yojana matchboxes, Toothpaste wrappers 52; **newspapers**, clippings featuring Lata Mangeshkar, clippings featuring Mahatma Gandhi, foreign-language newspapers 56, press clippings featuring Sridevi 55, largest collection from most countries 56, largest collection of clippings featuring Atal Bihari Vajpayee, largest collection of clippings featuring deities, largest collection of clippings on cinema, largest collection of same-day, largest collection of sequential same-day 55
college, first modern 104, first intermediate, oldest dental in South-east Asia 106, first of nursing, first science, for women 107, first for the hearing-challenged, first home science, first for physical education 109, first for sanitation workers 110
columns, most published in a year 180
command, only training 231
commander, first Indian station 237, first squadron 238
commander-in-chief, defence, first chief of integrated and staff, first chief of staff, first 220
commentary, longest-running 180
Commonwealth Games, best performance in 375, youngest captain 378
communist, first elected government in power 210
company, largest coal-producing 339, first ice-cream 340, first cigarette, first rubber estate, first tea 341, first scooter manufacturing, first tyre, oldest engineering 342
compass, earliest 322
computer, fastest, science, first to obtain PhD, first analogue, first digital, first indigenous palmtop, first powerful commercial, super, first, indigenous 259, powerful indigenous 260
computing, first human brain-like 258
concrete, most bituminous poured (single day) 319
conservation, first organization, oldest NGO to be engaged in conservation and biodiversity research 297
control system, first air traffic 309
conveyor, longest 80
cooking, **vessel**, largest 80
copper kiln, earliest 260
correspondence, first courses 110
cottages, first floating 81
cotton, earliest cultivation 87, first hybrid 92
counter-insurgency, first school 229
country, first to have a cooling action plan 300
course, first pharmacy education 106
cow, first cross-bred 96, first cloned, oldest 97
craft, most pieces made out of waste 32
crane, first hand-operated 79
crash, first air 308
crater, largest 283
creeper, longest 296
cricket, **association**, International Cricket Council, first Indian chairman, first Indian president, Indian independent chairman 374, first woman to head a state 375; **men's One Day Internationals**, fastest 50 runs on debut, first bowler to take more than three wickets on debut, first to score 100 centuries, highest individual innings, highest score on debut, highest team total, lowest team total, most career catches, most career Man of the Match awards, most career wickets, most centuries, most centuries partnerships, most centuries scored in a decade, most runs in all all World Cups, most total career runs 403, best bowling, best strike rate, first wins in the World Cup and World Twenty20, most centuries in a single World Cup, unique 100 404; **men's T20 International**, most sixes in an innings 403, best batting average (minimum 50 matches), best individual bowling performance, fastest to 50, best bowling average (minimum 10 wickets), highest run chase, highest team total, lowest team total, most career dismissals as a wicketkeeper, most career wickets, most runs in T20, only captain to win all three ICC trophies, 404; **men's Tests**, first to reach 10,000 runs, first victory, highest score on debut (series), highest team innings score, most career runs, most consecutive wins at home series, most individual centuries, 399, best bowling figures on debut, best

bowling in a match, best bowling innings, Fastest Indian opener to score 1,000 runs, highest century partnerships, highest individual score in a day, Highest run aggregate, highest run chase, lowest team innings score, most 1,000+ runs in a calendar year, most career dismissals by a wicketkeeper, most career wickets, most catches (innings), most runs in an over, player with the most IPL titles (men) 399, most sixes in a series, most wickets in a debut series, wicket off first ball (debut)/(match) 402, dismisses all 11 batsmen in a match, highest score on debut and fastest century on debut, most catches (match), most dismissals by a wicketkeeper (match), most dismissals by a wicketkeeper series, most player of the series awards, wicketkeeper with fastest 100 dismissals 403; **women's**, longest career, most career runs in international cricket (women's), most career wickets across formats, youngest to debut 397; **women's One Day Internationals**, best bowling average (minimum 50 wickets), century on debut, clean sweep victories in a bilateral series, highest individual score, highest partnership, most career catches by a fielder, most career dismissals by a wicketkeeper, most runs scored, most stumpings by a wicketkeeper 398; **women's T20 International**, best bowling, best bowling average, highest partnership, highest team total, largest victory margin, lowest team total, most career catches by a fielder, most career dismissals by a wicketkeeper, most career runs, most career wickets, narrowest, 399; **women's Tests**, biggest victory margin, narrowest victory margin , lowest total 397, best bowling average, best bowling (innings), first and only double century, highest total, most balls delivered, most career catches by a fielder, most career wickets, most runs, most wickets 398

crocodile, first known white, heaviest, longest, rarest, shortest 290, first/largest bank 291

crop, only genetically modified approved for commercial cultivation 92

cross-country longest run 369

cruiser and flagship, first 231

crunches, most, abdominal – 1 min, bicycle 18

cue sports, Asian billiards, best performance 406; **Asian Games**, best performance in snooker, first title, most billiards gold medals 405; **billiards and snooker**, most world titles, first snooker team World cup title, highest break under three-pot rule (billiards), World 6-red title 405, highest break under three-pot rule (billiards), most Asian title, World 6-red title 406; **Nationals**, first billiards championship, first snooker championship, highest break (snooker) 404, most competitive 147, breaks (snooker), most titles in snooker and billiards, oldest woman champion (billiards), two titles in 6-red snooker, most competitive 147, breaks (snooker), oldest woman champion (billiards) 406; **WLBS championship**, first title, first win 405; **World Billiards**, first team title 405, highest break in the championship 406; **world champion**, first on debut 405, youngest snooker 406; **World Games**, first snooker title, first world championship 405; **World Professional**, youngest to win 406

currency, earliest known use of cowries as 328; **largest**, collection of 7-digit notes, collection of high denomination notes, collection of notes with birth dates of presidents and prime ministers of India, collection of specimen notes 34, coins, collection of COVID-19 themed, Largest collection of star series currency notes 35, collection of FAO 37, largest collection of solid number currency notes 38

cycles, fastest assembling 45

cycling, deepest underwater – ocean – solo 365

cyst, largest adrenal removed 278

D

daguerreotype, first use 152

daily (newspaper), first financial, first with an international edition, largest - English 177, largest - Hindi/English, largest read regional-language daily, multi-edition with the largest readership 178

dairy, largest development programme 96

dam, earliest, highest earth-fill, largest river, oldest extant 78

dance, first known form, oldest surviving dance-drama form, dancer, earliest scriptural mention, earliest evidence of formalized, first classical to be revived, first national seminar, first schools 122, first revivalist school, first modern work on 123, competition, first celebrity, first to win an international, dance-drama, first dance theatre form recognised by UNESCO, only Persianized classical, only with an artificial foot, first Indian-European fusion, oldest recipient of President's award, only extant pre-Vedic 124

deal, biggest business 343

decimal system, earliest use 246

Defence Budget 233

delta, largest 282

demolition, India's biggest 82

demonetization, first 332

dental, first college 268
department, first government-run for disorders of sex development 271
depository, first, first global receipts issued 333
desert, largest 282, only cold 283
destination first live entertainment, theatre, and leisure 79
Devi, Bhavani C.A. 375, 382
Dhoni, M.S., 402, 404
D. Gukesh, 392, 393, 394, 395, 396, 443
Dice, largest collection of 55
dictionary, first official sign language 163, largest-selling bilingual dictionary 170
differential calculus, discovery of 246
disc, first compact 130
display, largest decorative using currency 24
dive, first deep bounce 363, first saturation 362
dives, daring 351
diyas, most lit – multiple venues – group – single day, most lit – single venue – group – single day 41
DJ, first differently abled 132
dock, first dockyard, first floating dry, first indigenous floating, first unified theatre 236, largest covered 323
doctor, first western medicine, first woman, first woman aerospace 270, first doctor-to-doctor online session 271
dome, largest corbelled cornice 61, pillar-less 82
Doordarshan, first director general of 185
drainage system, earliest extensive 60
drama, first modern (translations) 132, first club, first and only on Broadway and West End, first foreign translation of a Sanskrit, first Marathi musical, first protest, most stage plays performed in a day - solo, performed in most languages (single day) 133, earliest dramatic references 135; **plays**, earliest, earliest street, early political, most performances as a character - (mythological) stage, most performances as a personality - stage and screen, oldest extant 135; **playwright**, earliest, school, longest serving director of NSD 135
Dravid, Rahul, 403
Drone, first pilotless 235, first show 229
drum, first mention 128
drumstick, tallest tree 298, longest 300
DTH service, first 187

E

eco-hotel, first 83
editor, first letter to 178, longest letter to, longest spell as 179
education, first minister, first national council 102, first steps 104
effects, first 'trick' 142
egg, biggest of hen 98
eggs, most held in one hand – palm down 42, most held in one hand – palm up 43
election, candidate, youngest winning 201; **electorate**, first general 200, largest 202, state/UT with the largest, state/UT with the smallest 203, first presidential 208; **general elections**, fewest independent candidates elected, fewest women elected, highest voter turnout, Lowest voter turnout in the Lok Sabha general election, most independent candidates, most independent candidates elected, most women elected 201; **vote**, first app launched for vigil, first electronic machines, 200, first NOTA option, first 'others' category, first teenage, most IDs Distributed in 1 hr 201, verifiable paper audit trail in all constituencies for the first time 208
electricity, first commercial use 333, first state board 335
electrification, first 333
elevator, first 79
email, first free service 194
employer, largest 327
endoscopy, first lab 269
enzyme, first insulin blocking isolated 257
escalator, tallest 81
expedition, longest with a mixed crew 237; **four-wheeler**, fastest East-West India by a disabled person - solo, fastest East–West India – group, fastest Four Corners of India – solo, fastest GQ - group – women, longest journey within a country – solo, 352 fastest East-West India – group, fastest North–South – group, first all-India - group, first four corners of India - solo, first South-North India round – solo, first Trans-Himalayan – solo, first West–East India round – solo 353, fastest North-South expedition – solo, longest distance travelled across countries – solo, longest journey within a country – group 354; **two-wheeler, 151-450 cc**, fastest All-India – solo, fastest East-West – solo, fastest Four Corners of India – solo, first North-South round by a differently abled person - solo 354, fastest GQ by a disabled person - solo, longest distance covered within the country by a disabled person - solo, longest journey within the country - solo 355, first to cross Umling La – solo, 353, 356, human pyramid, largest moving – women 358; **over 450 cc**, fastest All-India – solo 355, fastest GQ expedition – solo 356; **rally**, largest by woman riders – under 100 km - multiple venues

356; **ride, longest**, while standing anywhere on the bike – solo, while standing on a structure – solo – woman, while standing on a structure – group, on a structure facing backwards – solo 356, on a structure facing backwards – solo, while sitting on a bike facing backwards – solo – woman, while standing anywhere on the bike – solo, while standing on a structure – solo – woman, while standing on a structure – group, on a structure facing backwards – solo – woman, while standing on a structure – group, while standing on a structure – solo – woman 357; **up to 150 cc**, first trans-Himalayan - solo 354; **expedition, two-wheeler (bicycle)**, fastest Asian across the world, first tandem 360, all-India tour on a mono-wheeler 361; **geared**, Fastest East–West – solo, fastest GQ – solo, fastest North–South – solo, longest distance covered within the country – solo 357; **gearless**, fastest North-South – group 357, fastest North-South – solo, largest marathon, longest tandem – women, most consecutive – 100 km, oldest super randonneuse 360

explorer, largest mineral 256

export, first car to be 341, India leads in measles vaccines 341

F

Facebook, largest user base 195

factory, first 340, first car 341, first plastic 342

FAI F3M Championship, most podium finishes 350

family planning, first governmental programme 267

famine commission, first 87

farm, Highest stud 96, largest average holdings in a state/UT 89, largest cattle 96, largest single 89, Only camel 96; **loan**, biggest waiver, first nationwide waiver 86, most sold equipment with largest market share 99, smallest average holdings in a state/UT 92

fax, first net service 193

FDI, highest in a year 328

Federation Aeronautique Internationale 308

feline, found at highest altitude 287, largest/heaviest, smallest 286

fencing, Asian Fencing Championships, first Indian fencer to win a medal at the 375; **Olympics**, first fencer to qualify for 375

ferry, first hovercraft, first roll-on-roll-off service, first solar boat 323

fertilizer, first factory 98, state/UT with highest use per hectare 99

festival, literary, largest 171

fibre, first multicore 252

fibre-optic link, first 192

fibroids, most uterine removed 279

filling station, highest 319

film, 70 mm 143, edited in most languages/dialects 138, evolution of the most expensive 148, first 3D 143, first adult 140, first advertisement 138, first animated 143, first cinemascope 143, first concern 138, first feature to be shot on indigenous camera 142, first Indian in English, first in multilingual versions, first one-actor, one-set, first review, first serial, first shot in India 138, first use of surround sound 143, fraternity MPs 147, largest archives 113 ,largest poster 146, longest footage 144, longest-running 152, most aspects handled 146, most episodic films in a single feature 144, most feature directed, most horror produced 152, most number of songs in a Hindi 144, most produced, tallest cut-out 146, the pan-India 138; **awards**, first academy, first academy for best documentary (short subject), first foreign 140; **box-office**, first hit 140; **Hollywood**, first to act in a film 140; **music**, most songs recorded in a day 144, studio, first 140; **film, footage**, longest use of reused archival 144

Films, Timeline of Technical Advances 142

fine arts, first exhibition 156

fingerprint, first bureau 213

First ESCES 261

First hosiery company 342

First polarimetry mission 263

First to cross the 100 billion mark 337

First voter of independent India 201

First woman judge 213

First women in medicine 270

fish, first marine aquarium for ornamental 98, first transgenic rohu 98, heaviest 294, largest clam, lightest/smallest, longest-living 295, oldest freshwater, only anadromous 294, only male producing young 295, only without a bony skeleton, only with suction plates 294, shortest-living 295

fisherwoman, first and only licensed 98

fishing station, first deep-sea 98

fission, first observation of spontaneous 254

fistula, longest removed 278

flag, largest of recycled material 27

flamingo, only breeding ground 288

fleet replenishment tanker, first indigenous 235

flight, first, first international 308, first to the true North Pole 242, highest, highest and longest wingsuit 349, longest direct-route with an all-woman cockpit crew 311, longest motor glider 349, only vintage 242

flower, tallest 297
flute, marathon performance 132
flying, **spy**, first 222
food, most, donated – single day – multiple venues, most packets, distributed among the poor 30
footage, longest use of reused archival 144
football, **academy**, first 406; **Asian Games**, biggest defeat, biggest margin of victory 412; **club**, best record against foreign, first hat-trick 410, first Indian to enter Asian Football Confederation Cup Final, first Indian to win a major trophy 407, first in English professional club 410, first international tournament win 407, first woman to sign a contract with a foreign 410, most goals in NFL/I-league 411; **coach**, first foreign, first professional, most appearance in Olympics, most appearances in Nehru Cup 407, most successful at the Asian Games, most successful in domestic tournaments, only Indian to gain success with a foreign club 410; **Durand Cup**, first team to win, most individual goals 406, most individual goals 411, most wins 406; **FIFA**, first Indian in FIFA executive panel 374, first international match 411, first World Cup match commissioner 374, India's longest unbeaten run in a year 412, most individual in international club match 407, worst defeats 412; **Indian League**, most individual goals in a match 411; **Indian Super League**, biggest margin of victory, hat-trick records, maximum titles, most goals by a team, most goals in a match, most wins by a team 411; **individual records**, back-to-back hat-tricks 412 fastest goal 410, fastest international goal, hat-trick in Olympics, hat-trick on debut, maximum caps earned (top five), maximum goals scored (top five), Maximum hat-tricks, most goals in Asian Games, most successful captain 412, youngest match winner at Nehru Cup 413, longest unbeaten streak at home 410, most clean sheets 406, most rolls from eye to eye 14; **National Football League**, first to win three, most individual goals in a match, most individual hat-tricks in NFL and I-League 411; **Olympics**, biggest margin of victory, only win in, overall performance 411; **pre-World Cup**, best performance 411, biggest margin of victory, worst defeat 412; **referee**, first in Olympics, first in World Cup 407, most matches officiated 410; **Santosh Trophy**, all-time top scorers, biggest margin of victory, highest number of goals by an individual in a single match, most individual goals in a single edition, most individual goals in finals, most wins, success for different teams 410; **tiebreaks**, first 410; **tournament**, oldest 406; **win**, longest sequence 410
foreign body, longest removed 277
foreign collaboration, first 341
forest, first healing centre 300
fort, longest fortification wall 66, with largest metal ordnance 67
fossil, first dinosaur 256, first megafossil from Himalayas 255, oldest biological 256, oldest dinosaur discovery 285
freefall, most hours logged 350
frog, flying, largest, rarest, smallest 289
fruit, first train 86

G

G20 345
garden, oldest botanical 296
gateway, tallest 67
gecko, 'flying', largest, rarest, smallest 290
gene, first national bank 257, first synthesis of workable 258
geologists, first 255, first official 256
geology, first course 255
geomagnetic, **observatory**, first 255, reversals, periodicity 256
geometry, earliest treatise, first mention of 246
geoscientific data centre, first data 256
gharana, oldest 128
glacier, largest 282
glasshouse, largest 80
gnat, first 241
goat, first cloned pashmina 97, heaviest 96
Golden Reel Award, first Asian 131
gold violin, smallest 28
golf, **Asian Games**, first sweep of gold medals 413; **Asian Tour**, lowest winning score on, most titles 416, youngest to Order of Merit 417 best world ranking 416; **British Open**, first to qualify for 413; **European Tour**, best finish in Order of Merit, 416, first win in Europe, first win on 414, least putts on, lowest winning score on, only Indian to win four events in India, only Indian to win two titles in a year, quickest to win two titles, 416; youngest to win title 417; **first**, first to represent the country at four multi-discipline Games 415, international recognition, Olympians, to win all three Nationals titles 413, first international success in U-10 category, highest golf course 416, Indian at the majors, Indian men winning international tournaments 413; **Indian Open**, winners 413, Indians topping the Asian Tour Order of Merit, 413; **Indian Tour**, five titles in a season twice on 414, lowest round on, lowest winning score

on 416, most titles in a season 414; **Japanese Tour**, only Indian to win four titles on 416; **Ladies European Tour**, best finish on the Order of Merit, first to secure her card (playing rights) winner on, First to win LET title outside India, first to win on 415; **Ladies Indian Open**, first to win 415; **Ladies PGA**, first to qualify 415, longest hole-in-one 417; **Majors**, best finish in 416, first to make the 'cut' in a, most birdies, 414, most Indian tournaments on Asian tour 413, most international titles, most lucrative season 414, oldest club 416; **Olympics**, first woman to qualify for the 415, only team title in the US 416; **PGA** best Indian performance on the tour 416, first to gain qualification for on the tour, first to play the championship 413, first to win on a Japanese tour, first to win on tour 414; **PGTI**, most career prize money won 414, youngest winner on the domestic tour 417; **prize money**, best performance based on received 416, highest earner in a domestic season, highest (women), quickest to reach the million mark in, tournament with highest 414, Rookie on a rampage, sponsorship bonanza 413; **WGC**, first to play in three events in a year 414; **World Championship**, first team to qualify for 414; **World Cup**, first participation in 414; **youngest**, to win two back-to-back international titles 417
governor, youngest 212
graffiti, first officially recognized woman artist 157
Grammy, best world music album, first award-winning Indian percussionist, only Indian to win both Oscar and 131
gramophone, first company, first record 129, first singer recorded 128, first voices, only museum 129
Gramophone recording in India 129
graveyard earliest, Necropolis 61
Gregory series, first to give 246
gun, first foundry 222
gurdwara, highest 71
gymnastics, Asian Championship, first medal 417; **Asian Games**, first medal 417; **Commonwealth Games**, first appearance in, first medal in (men), first national championship, most individual titles in the nationals, most successive titles – team 417; **Olympics**, first appearance 417, most representations 418; **World Cup**, first medal 417
gymnosperms, discovery 258

H

hall, largest chaitya 70, largest vaulted 62
hang-glider, longest-harness flight 350
harmonica, most people playing together 132
harp, first player 129
Hasselblad, first Indian to receive award 154
healthcare scheme, largest 266
helicopter, first Apache 241, First helicopter training school 236, first indigenous 309, first indigenous advanced light 240, first lifted battalion, first operations 223, first pilot 238, first school 308
heliport, first 309
helium isotope, discovery in cosmic rays 253
helmet, first bulletproof 222
hepatitis E virus, first clone 258
herbarium, first virtual 297
Herbicides, first attempt at weed control using 99
High Court, first judge 213, oldest 214, with most judges 213
highest contribution to equity trading 337
Highest single-day transactions 337
highway, first 317, highest national, longest construction in a single day, longest tunnel, shortest national 319
History of Television in India 187
hockey, Asia Cup, biggest victory margin (men)/(women), biggest win in finals 421, first win (women) 419, highest goal scorer 421; **Asian Men's Hockey** first win 420; **Asian Women's Hockey**, first win 420; **awards**, first women professional players 419, most Arjuna for any sport in a year, most FIH hockey star, 418, best performance in a foreign tour 420; **Champions Trophy**, best performance, best performance, best recovery in men's 420; **coach**, first foreign, first major success by foreign 419; **Commonwealth Games**, first success (women) 419; **FIH Hocky 5s Championship**, inaugural win 420, first domestic league (women), first national championship (men), first national championship (women) 419; first Olympian to head Indian hockey 418; **International Hockey Federation**, first Indian to head 418; **Junior Asia Cup**, first win, most capped player, most international caps (women) 420, most wins in national championship (women), most wins of national championship (men), oldest tournament (men), oldest tournament (women) 419; **Olympics**, best goalkeeping in 421, best victory margin 420, fastest goal 421, first medal and most successful team 419, most goals – team, most medals, Most Olympic goals – individual 420, oldest player, only captain in successive, only double hat-trick in, only goalkeeper in three finals, only hat-trick (women) 421, playing for teams with most golds 420, youngest to win gold 421; **World Cup**, best

performance (men), best performance (women) 420, highest goal scorer 421, most appearances, most appearances in women's, most goals 420; **Youth Asia Cup**, highest goal scorer and double hat-trick 421
homoeopathic, company 268, first, college 267, international congress 272
Honorary doctorate, first Indian sportsman and coach to receive, first Indian sportsperson to receive, 374
hospital, corporate 268, first 267, first, with stealth neuro-navigation system, corporate, with a rooftop helipad, 268, with a rooftop helipad 269
hotel, first five-star, 342
houseboat, first 79
hovercraft, first and longest deep-sea passage, first berthing platform 243
human organ, regeneration 258
hydroelectric project, first 78
Humpy, K., 393, 394, 395, 396, 397
hypothalamus, discovery of feeding centre in 271

I

IAF, first AESA radar for 240
ice-skating, oldest rink 80
idol, tallest Ganesha 73
igloo first stay 82
IIT, first 107
Imperial Civil Service, first Indian in the, 211
implant, first cochlear 273
index, first infrastructural 343
India, The Largest Producer 94
Indian Dance 126
Indian Defence Highligts 2024 226
Indian Medical Service, first to pass the examination 110
Indian Postal Order, first electronic 188
Indian Statistical Institute, first woman director 111
infantry, oldest brigade, oldest unit 221
infinite series, first study of, 246
ink, indelible, first use 200
Inland Waterways of India 320
institute, first farm machinery training and testing 98, first for population sciences 107, first for studying footwear design, first gemmological 109, first metro technology 107, first national for management 109, first national for the visually impaired, first national of Watersports 110, first of fashion technology, first of mass communication 109, first of oceanography 107, first statistical 109, first to teach modern architecture 106, first yoga 109, oldest extant for the blind 102
insulin, first to extract from plant 257
insurance, company, first general, first Indian life, first life, largest 332
Integrated Automatic Aviation Meteorological System, first 235
Intelligence Bureau, first Indian director of the 213
International Booker Prize, first Indian citizen to win Booker Prize, first novel in Indian language to win 172
International Court of Justice, first Indian president 215
International Geological Congress, first president of 256
International Society of Soil Sciences, first Indian president 89
International Subscriber Dialling (ISD), first 192
Internet, First 3G operator 194, first and only 4G 195, first provider of services, top subscription areas - wired and wireless, highest data consumption, fastest 4G service provider 194
Internet Service Provider (ISP), first private 194
iron, earliest furnace, earliest use 260, first ore deposits 256, smallest 29
iron and steel, first commercial production of 340
irrigation, earliest 86, first use of lift 99, largest groundwater system 88
island, largest, freshwater 283, ocean 283
ITLOS, first Indian judge 214, first Indian woman judge 214
IVF, first baby 266, oldest mother 266

J

jackfruit, heaviest 92
jazz, first Indo fusion album 131
jet, first 240, 309, first bomber, first indigenous tandem seat trainer 240
JK Architecture of the Year Awards
Baker, Baker, Laurie, D. Raje, Anant 60
Jnanpith, first recipients 172
job, first LGBTQIA+ fair 327
journalist, first Indian origin to win Pulitzer Prize, longest career as 179
jowar, tallest 92
judge, first transgender 215
juggling, most patterns on a balance board 14
jumping jacks, 1 hr 17, most 1 min 18, woman – 1 min 24, 17

K

kabaddi, Asian Championship, first participation in

junior 422; **Asian Games**, first appearance 421, first demonstration, most Asian titles (men and women), most titles (men), most titles (women) 422; **first nationals**, 421; **International Kabaddi Federation**, first Indian president 374, most expensive non-cricket player 422; **Olympics**, first demonstration 421; **Pro Kabaddi League**, first, first team to win three consecutive titles, most expensive foreign player, most expensive player 422; **World and Asian Championship**, most medals (women) 422; **World Cup**, most wins (men), 422
Kamal, A. Sharath 431, 432, 433, 434
Kaprekar Constant, discovery 246
Kathak, first known teacher 123, largest ensemble 125
Kathakali, thickest make-up 123
kayaking, longest, group, solo, 364
kebab, longest 45
Khan, Shah Rukh 141
Khardung La 355
kicks, most, full-contact on a kick-pad – alternate legs in 1 hr 19
kidney, heaviest removed, largest operated on 278, largest removed, 277
Kirti Chakra, first prisoner of war to receive 220
kites, most on a single line 41
Knitting, solo-marathon 14
Kodak, first express outlet 153
Kohli, Virat, 399, 403, 404
Krishnan effect, discovery, 252
Kuchipudi, first couple to win Padma Shri, first solo 123
Kumar, Uttam 138

L

laboratory, first forensic science 212
Labour Day, first 327
lagoon, largest brackish-water 282
lake, largest freshwater 283, oldest man-made 61
lamb, first from frozen embryo 96
language, oldest living 162
Largest exporter of spice 343
Largest legislative building 217
Largest office building, Surat Diamond Bourse 81
laser, first carbon dioxide 255
lawyer, first transgender 215
leaf, largest 296, largest taro, longest mango 298
LED display screen, largest on water (aboard a ship/boat/vessel), 344
Legion d'Honneur, first to win 140
legislation, first labour 328
Legislative Assembly, first state, shortest session of state legislative assembly 217
Legislative councils, most elections won 217
lemon, biggest 298
letter, first office for dead 189, first window delivery 188
library, biggest public system, first boat, First library, first mobile, first national medical, First online Braille, first operational digital network, first sports, first university 112, Ghoda, largest 113, largest university 112, oldest 111, 113, only bookshop-cum-library on a lake, only underground 112
lieutenant general, first woman 221
lighthouse, first unmanned, oldest, oldest functional, tallest, tallest from mean sea level 79
Linnean medal, first biologist to win 258
literacy, first 100 per cent literate district 102
literary, award winners, first Commonwealth writers' Prize 173, first DSC Prize for South Asian literature 171, first Grinzane Cavour, first Indian to win Prestigious Erasmus Prize, first Kamaladevi Chattopadhyay NIF Book prize 173, first Newbery Medal 172, first Ondaatje Prize 173, first Saraswati Samman, first winner of the Pulitzer Prize, highest monetary prize, JCB Prize, Rabindranath Tagore literary prize 173; **festival**, first virtual, first agency 168, first children's 165, first Yuva Puraskar 173
lithium, first resource 339
Lithograph 176
livestock, largest population 96
lizard, largest, longest tail in relation to the body, longest tongue 289, only flying, only legless 290
loan, first institution for agri 329
locomotive, first factory 314, most produced in a year 315
locust, oldest control programme 87
Lok Sabha election result partywise 206
loose bodies, most removed from a joint 279
Lothal, oldest dockyard, 60; earliest copper kiln, earliest zinc use, 260
LPG, first company to market 339, first private branded, 338
luge, youngest Olympian 422
Lunar probe, first, 262
lunges, most in 1 hr 18
lyricist, most prolific 144

M

magazine, first for visually challenged, first in Hindi 177, first in hot-air balloon 188, first sports 375, first wildlife 297, first women's in an Indian language, first women's in English 177, longest-

running Indian women's 179, most read English 178, most read Hindi 179, most read in a regional language 179, oldest children's 178
magic square, earliest 246
Mahalanobis distance, invention of 247
mail, first automatic processing centre 190, first by steamboat 187
make-up, seven basic styles in Kathakali 123
mall, first virtual 343
mammal, fastest breeders 285, fastest land, fastest water 286, largest land, largest litter, longest gestatio, longest-living, oldest living 285, only herbivorous marine 286, shortest gestation, slowest breeders 285, slowest land, slowest water 286, smallest 285
man, tallest 41
Manasara 61
mandala artwork, largest group, largest solo 158
mangoes, largest producer of 94
Mannequin, tallest 41
manufacturer, first champagne 342
manuscript, **first Mughal illuminated** 156
marathon, **4 Deserts Grand Slam**, first winner 367; **7 Emirates Run**, first to complete 367; **full**, most in a year 368; **GQ**, first to complete the run; 366; **half-marathons**, most by an individual, most consecutive distance runs, most in a year 368, most organized in a single day – multiple venues 368; **marathoner**, oldest 368, most visually impaired athletes completing 369; **Six World Marathons**, first to complete all 367; **triathlon**, first disabled 369, first Ironman 367, most completed in a year, only Asian to complete in six continents 368; **Ultraman**, first to finish the world championship, first triathlete 367; **ultramarathons**, fastest at Badwater 368, first to complete grand-to-grand 366, most in a year 368; **world challenge**, first to complete – full marathon 367
marine, first research institute 256
marker and ink, **marathon portrait solo** 159
market (bazaar), first underground 81
marshal, first 238, first field 221
martial arts, best performance in CWG, oldest competitor 423; **Judo**, first international medal, first judoka to win world title, first medal in Asian Championship (women), 423; **National**, first national, most wins in nationals, youngest champion, 423; **Wushu**, first world champion (men), first world wushu champion (women) 423
Master Craftsman Award, most national awards won in a family 157
Mastering a Language, **University** centre for Spanish, Portuguese, Italian and Latin American studies, 105, first for journalism and mass communication 111, first university to introduce Japanese language courses 105, oldest centre for Chinese studies, oldest centre for German Studies, only place to teach ancient Greek 105
mathematics, earliest mention of series, 246
Mayamata 61
mayor, youngest 211
maze, largest 62
medical, college 268, conference 272, first, organized service, laser facility 268, most innovations by a professional 270, rural college 269, school to offer oncology degrees 267, smallest robot 270, symposium 272
medicine, earliest treatise, first Persian text 266
memory, fastest solving of the mirror cube while blindfolded, fastest to arrange all elements in order, fastest to identify all the bones of the human body, fastest to identify flags of all countries of the world, fastest to recall 2,500 digit, most dinosaur names identified in a minute, **periodic table**, fastest identification 40
M&E sector, details of employment 151
mesons, discovery 253
metallurgist, first to work with plutonium 260
metal-scrap structure, tallest group, tallest solo 304, widest group 305
meteorite, largest shower 283
methane, first plant 257
metro, deepest station, deepest tunnel, first, first driverless, first underwater, largest network 317
microchips, first batch of 342
microlight, aircraft flight 350, first jump from a 348, longest cross-country expedition, most expeditions 349
microwave oven, smallest 28
military, first dog school, first intelligence school 229
milk, top producing country 95
mill, first cotton textile, oldest jute 341
minaret, first revolving 68, only shaking 69, tallest brick 62
mine, oldest gold, only diamond 340, state/UT with most, 339
mining, first coal 339, first underwater system 256
minister, **Cabinet**, longest-serving 208, shortest tenure 210, Union, first to die in harness, first to resign 208
mint, first 329
missile, first anti-ship, first corvette 234, first indigenous anti-radiation 241, first indigenously developed naval anti-ship 235, longest-range nuclear 222

mission, **first**, interplanetary 262, remote sensing 261
Mission Possible: Know Your Exams 108
mobile, app, first store 194, most downloaded, most number of downloads 195, first tower at the highest altitude 193
Mohanty, Anubhav 216
Molecular Distillation Unit, first 252
monastery, highest 71, largest 68
monument, most names engraved 79, oldest Buddhist 68
mosque, earliest 68, largest 70, only one in marble 71
Most popular payment platform 331
moth, largest 289
motorsport, first Indian to win a world title in, 375
mountain, longest land range 282
mountaineering, fastest to scale most 8,000 m peaks 371, first club, first expedition 369, first institute, first to summit four unscaled peaks above 6,000 m, fastest to scale most 8,000 m peaks, first to summit three highest peaks of South America, 370, first to summit the Volcanic Seven and youngest to climb both the Seven Summits and Volcanic Seven summits 369, first to summit three highest peaks of South America 370; **Himalaya**, most summits 370; **Mount Everest**, first to summit without supplemental oxygen, first woman, oldest to scale 370; **Seven Summit**, first to complete 369, oldest to complete 370
MSO, first to win 247
municipalities, first 211
mural, oldest extant 156
museum, conflictorium 118, first archaeological site, first culinary arts, first dinosaur, first insect, first interactive of music 115, first national of Indian cinema, first of textiles 113, first of toilets, first of utensils 115, first partition 114, first Prime Minister's 115, first public in a university, first railway 113, first science 115, first sports 114, first transport 113, first underground, first wax 114, India's first sunken 118, Largest and oldest 113, largest chain of science, largest terracotta, only election 115, only kite 114, only leprosy 118, Smritivan Earthquake 117
music, earliest form of, earliest mention of ragas, earliest notes 125, earliest reference to performances 123, earliest royal composers 125, first fusion melody 128, first medieval treatise on, first raga, first recorded, first school, first set of records 130, first to standardize 125, most events in a day 132, most prolific composer 125, oldest sabha for dance and music 128, only director couple 131; **album**, first fusion 130; **award**, first Asian to win Golden Reel 131; **festival**, first virtual 132, **instruments**, earliest 128, first electronic 129, first three-in-one classical 128, marathon duet 132, oldest 128, oldest known percussion, oldest south Indian stringed 128; **performers**, first at Royal Albert Hall 128, first at the UN 130, first duo to introduce jugalbandi 129, Longest innings as a conductor 132, most recorded artiste 130; **singing**, earliest ballad 125; **songs**, earliest form of classical, earliest Prakrit 125, first recorded 128, only multilingual classical 125
mustard, first hybrid 92
mutual fund, first domestic, first offshore, first private sector, largest 333

N

nasal polyp, largest removed 279
National Film Awards 146
Natya Shastra, first modern translation 122
Navarasas 127
navy, first academy 236, first air squadron 231, first chief of naval staff 230, first combat management system 237, first commander-in-chief 230, first exclusive base 231, first school 236, first virtual reality centre 237
NEET, first to score 100 per cent 111
news, **bulletin**, first 184
newspaper, first for visually impaired 176, first Hindi, first non English 176, first run entirely by women 177, first to be printed in colour 178, first vernacular 177, most pages in 180, most pages in a supplement, oldest extant in English, oldest extant in regional language, 179, only handwritten 177, state/UT with most registered 178; **article**, most in a year – multiple publication 180, most published in a year – single publication 179; **news agency**, first to supply news in Urdu 176
new species, first time discovery of 292
newsreader, first 185
NFAI, archival acquisition by 150
Nizamat Imambara 70
Nobel Prize, first in physics 253, first winner in economics 327
note, first 200-rupee, 329, first secured promissory 333, highest denomination rupee 329
nova, first to observe 250
NPCI 330
nuclear, first advanced heavy water 253, first implosion, first reactor, 252, first shelter 229, only safety institute 253
nukkad natak, marathon performance 132

numbers, earliest use of irrational, 246
nurse, first woman 270
nursing, first college 267

O

observatory, first solar 115
Ocean fish, largest recorded 295
oceanography, first course 256
Odissi, earliest sculptures, earliest text to mention 122
officer, first commissioned 220
official residence, largest 80
oil, first well 338
Oldest forts, Dholavira, Kalibangan 64
Olympic Games, first Indian woman to become a member of IOC's Athletes' Commission 374
Olympic Order, first Indian recipient (See also individual sports), 375
Olympics 2024 444, 447
onion, first hybrid 92
online, longest lesson 119
opera, first full-fledged, first in English by an Indian 133
operating system, most popular 195
operation, first active 241
operators' association, first 193
ordnance, first board 229
organic producers, largest number in the world 94
organisms, earliest multicellular discovered 257
organization, first all-India farmers' 327, largest media 180
Oriental Telephone Company 193
ozone, first to measure 252

P

pacemaker, first bi-ventricular 273
paddy, tallest plant 89
Padma Bhushan, youngest to receive 378
Padma Shri, first sportsman to be awarded 374
Padma Vibhushan, first woman sportsperson to get 374
painting, acrylic paint, largest portrait solo 159, earliest discovered 155, earliest rock 157, first auction of contemporary Indian abroad, first gallery 156, largest portrait (solo), largest single wall solo 158, natural colours, largest solo 159, oil paint, largest solo 158, painter, first realist 156, sand paint, marathon 159
palace, facade on a wall 64, largest chandelier 67, oldest,, site excavated, 60
panchayat, first 211
papaya, tallest plant 92
paper-making machine, first 176
paragliding, first at the Mantar XC Open Championship 348, first from a high cliff 348, first to with a prosthetic leg, first visually impaired person to 350
paramotor, first international medallist 348, longest expedition 350
Param Vir Chakra, first (Air Force) 239, first (Army) 220
parcel, first service 190
Pardo alla Carriera, first south asian to win 141
Paris Paralympics 2024 448, 451
park, first national 298, highest national, largest zoological, state/UT with most national 297
Parliament, first couple 216, first hung, first session, first visually impaired member 215, **Lok Sabha**, first deputy speaker, first dissolution, first speaker 215, highest average age, longest tenure as chairman, lowest average age, shortest term, longest term as speaker, most bills passed in a year, 216; **Rajya Sabha**, first woman secretary general 215, shortest term as speaker 216
peak, highest 283
pearl, first culture 98
pencil art, largest drawing (solo), 157, marathon session 159
Pencils, largest collection of 53
Pens, largest collection of 55
periodical, first vernacular 178, State/UT with the most newspaper and periodical publications 178
pesticide, first 99, first synthetic 99
PhD, first Indian to receive from a foreign university 110, first to obtain a doctorate, most awarded by a university in a year, most degrees obtained, most number of qualifications from most number of universities 111
philately, Federation Internationale de Philatelie (FIP), first Indian president, first exhibition, first miniature sheet, first national museum, first society, largest bureau 191
phosphocreatine, discovery 254
photographer, First Asian to win the International Photography Awards 154, first commercial, first woman 152, oldest extant portrait, 153, **studio**, earliest commercial, first personal 153
photography, earliest book 152, first course, 153, first fellow of the British Photographic Society 154, first photo-film manufacturing company, first society 153, largest unit for production, marathon (city/structures), marathon (models) 154; **album**, earliest recorded commercial 152; **awards**, first winner of the Wildlife photographer of the Year 154, **exhibition**, first permanent in space 155, first photo 152

pigeon pea, first hybrid 92
piglets, most in a single litter 96
pillar, oldest rust-free iron 60
pilot, first Indian 237, first licence 308, first naval 230, first woman naval helicopter 231, oldest to obtain commercial licence 310
pipeline, first, 338, longest underground 80, longest underwater hydrocarbon 338
plane, first indigenously assembled, first radio 308
planetarium, oldest 248
plank, longest 18
plant, at the highest altitude 296, first heavy water 335, first solar-powered thermal, 335, heaviest fruit 296, heaviest wood, largest family of 296, largest grid-connected rooftop solar 335, lightest wood 296, longest money 300, longest tapioca 298, oldest fossils 295, rare flowering 296, tallest bougainvillea, tallest coriander, tallest musk mallow, tallest prickly amaranth, tallest rose 298
plastic, first state/UT to place a ban on bags 300
plog run, most participants 304
ploughed field, earliest 86
poet, first in English in India 163
Poles, first at Antarctica, first at the Arctic, first organization to reach 'three', longest stay in Antarctica 371; **North**, first to reach by surface, first to ski to 371; **South**, 371, first route recce to 371
Pole Star, first observation of 250
police, first act, first dog squad, 212, first transgender sub-inspector 213
political economy, first book on 326
political organization, first 199
political party, first electoral win by an Indian 199, national party with most votes 200, oldest 199
pollen cryobank, first 87
poppy, first non-narcotic 92
port, first corporatized, first private sector 323, oldest operating and largest riverine 322
postal communication, earliest 187
postal inspector, first woman 188
postcard, first 188
postcards, largest, collection of matchbox theme 35
postgraduate, first degree, 110
postmaster, longest-serving 190
Postmaster General, first Indian 188
post office, first all-woman 189, first delivery peons 188, first drive-in 189, first fully-computerized 190, first mobile, first savings account, India's first 3D 189
poultry, largest company 97
power, first hydro station, first indigenous atomic plant, first nuclear plant, first private company, largest private sector thermal station, largest supplier 335, largest thermal plant 338, state with highest installed capacity of renewable 339
powerlifting, Asian Championship, best performance in Asian junior championship 423, best performance in sub-junior championship 424, most medals, most medals in one edition 423; **Asian Para Games**, first medal 424; **Commonwealth Championship**, best performance (men), first gold in Para Powerlifting, first medal in Para Powerlifting 424, most golds (individual), 423; **Olympia Pro**, back-to-back win 424; **World Championship**, best performance 423
power loom, first 342
Premchand Roychand legacy 336
president, first woman 208, longest tenure 199, most from a state, oldest 208, shortest tenure 199
press, first, first multilingual 176, first newsprint 177, first regulation 176
primate, with the longest tail 285
prime minister, born after independence, first, first deputy, first to die in harness, first to resign 209, longest tenure 199, oldest, only woman 209, shortest tenure 199, youngest 209
printing, first lithographic 176
prison, first open 212, largest complex 213
Pritzker Prize, first architect 60
Privy Council, first Indians 211
programme, first master's in Hindu studies 110
pseudonym, first 164
PSU, first to go public 333
publication, most circulated Government, state/UT with most Indian-language 178, state/UT with most Indian-language 179
public prosecutor, first 213
publisher, first independent 168, largest literary, largest trade 165
publishing house, first feminist 171
Pulitzer Prize, first to win for a health/medicine-related publication 270, winner, first for feature photography 155
push-ups, abdominal in 1 hr 18, by a woman in 1 min 19, clap in 1 min 18, contortion in 1 min, diamond in 1 min 19, fingertip-one-arm in 1 min 18, half-knuckle in 1 min, most decline – 1 min 19, most incline – 1 min 19, side-jump in 1 min, superman in 1 min, tandem in 1 min, two-finger-both arms in 1 min 18, two-thumb in 1 min 19

Q

qawwali, marathon performance 132
quantum Zeno paradox, discovery 253

quasicrystals, new class 260
queue, complex, biggest 69
quilling, largest artwork (solo) 158
quiz, first live on TV 118, first national TV quizmaster, first show on radio, longest-running open 118, longest-running school, longest-running state-level, longest-running televised, Most participants in an offline quiz – single venue – single day, most participants in a single day – online, most participants - offline quiz - multiple venues - single day 119
Quizzing in India 119

R

radiation, first synchrotron facility 253
radio, first frequency modulation (FM) service, first national of music 180, first national of play, first of talks, first phone-in 184, first private FM station 180, first private station 180, first sponsored 184, highest station, most commercial anchored 184
radio phone link, first 192
radio source, first double 252
rafting, first event in the country 362, longest white-water expedition 365, most rivers in a month 364, nonstop expedition 365
rail, first construction company 312, first green corridor 314, first indigenous carriages 312, longest rail manufactured 315, longest tunnel 314, most people at a public-service event 317, station, busiest 315, first 314, first fully solar-powered 316, first public-private partnership, 314, only listed as a UNESCO World Heritage Site 316, with longest Platform, with most platforms 315
railway station, first with a green building certification 304
rainfall, maximum, minimum area 284
raj kachori, largest 23
Rajya Sabha, first sportsman to be nominated, 374
Ramoji film city 146
Ramon Magsaysay Award, first scientist to receive 89
ramps, most, constructed – single day 31
Randonneuse 360
rapper, first female 131
Rashtriya Military College 109
Ravana, tallest effigy 41
Ravanhatha, longest 132
Reconnaissance Vehicle, first set of next-gen armoured engineer 223, first unmanned aerial squadron 231
refinery, first, largest 338, oldest running 338
regiment, first para in action 223, most decorated 220, special operations division 222
Regional Folk Theatre of India 134
registration centre, first computerized 189
rehabilitation, first low-vision centre 269
reign, shortest 198
relay, first between radio stations 184, first direct 180
relay race, longest 368
Reliance and Disney merger 195
replantation, first scalp 273
republic, earliest on the subcontinent, 198
Republic Day, first parade 198
research, early vet, first dairy institute 93, first institute for freshwater aquaculture, oldest fisheries institutes 98, institute located at highest altitude 88, largest scientific and industrial organization 255, oldest fisheries institutes 98, only centre for tropical tuber crops, only weed centre 88
reserve, first marine 297
Reserve Bank of India (RBI), first Indian governor 332
reserves, highest Forex 328
reservoir, largest water 78
restaurant, first floating, first revolving 79
retail, first chain of computers, 341
reverse dips, most in 1 min 18
revolver, first indigenous 223
rice, first Basmati hybrid 89
rifle, first indigenous sniper 223, first regiment 222
river, largest system, longest 282
road, earliest route 317
roaming, first national/international service 193
robot, first sentry 223
rocket builder, India's first private 261
roof, largest retractable 80
rookery, largest 294
ropeway, highest, longest river 83
Royal Society of London, first Indian Fellow 89
Roy, Arundhati 172
RRR 152
Rubik's cube, fastest to form the English alphabet while blindfolded 14, most solved in 1 hour 40
rugby, first international 15s victory, 375
rugby stadium model, smallest 28
rule, first colonial, longest colonial 198
runway, longest length 312

S

Sahitya Akademi, Bhasha Samman Awards, first fellowship, award, countries with most fellows 172, first recipients of, first Translation Prize 171
sailing, first around the Indian peninsula, first

catamaran expedition 362, first down Ganga river, first on Beas River, first on Brahmaputra River and longest on any Indian river 361
Sainik School, first all-girls 230
sandwich, longest 45
Sangeet Natak Akademi, first winners, first winners for creative dance 123, text, only pan-Indian text 124
Santa Claus, tallest 41
sapling, most distributed in a single day 303
saree, most styles draped 44
sarpanch, youngest 212
satellite, first centre 261, first indigenous launcher 262, first indigenous series, 261, first linkage 185, first oceanographic 262, first private launched 263, first weather-cum-communications 261, heaviest launched 263, highest-resolution imaging 261, lightest in orbit 263
satellite navigation system, first 318
saxophone, first woman professional players 129
scales, largest collection of 52
school, earliest for girls, first for hearing-impaired 102, first Gondi language 104, first Indian abroad 102, first medical , first medical to offer degrees in Oncology 106, first military, first model-training 109, first of mines 107, first Sainik school for girls, first solar-powered 104, largest chain of government, largest open 102, largest science fair – multiple venues – single day 104, largest science fair – single venue – single day, oldest extant 102, oldest of art 110, tropical medicine 106
scientist, first chartered in aviation 111
scissors, smallest 28
sculpture, largest bird 73
sculpture, marathon session 159
SDG Index 2023–24, 214
sectoral fund, first 333
seed, first company 92
seismological zones, first mention 255
selfie, most people in 154
Selling the Smell of Mangoes 177
semiconductor, first laser 252
seminal plasmin, discovery 258
serial, dialogue writer with most credited episodes 187, first, first Indian animation 185, first sci-fi 187
service, first express 190, first insured 189, first registered 190, post, under British rule 188
service provider, largest wireless 194, largest wireline 193, with number of rural subscribers - wireless 194
Shakespeare, William, only folio 164
Shakti, the band 131
shares, of most companies held by an individual 337
sheriff, first Indian 212
ship, earliest representation 322, first dedicated cadet training 234, first diesel engine 323, first fast attacker 234, first 'green' 235, first ocean minesweepers 234, first submarine depot 231, first submarine rescue 232, first to sail from India 323, oldest 322
shoe, largest donation 30
shooting, Asian Championship, first gold, first medals haul, most individual medals, world record at, world record in skeet 425; **Asian Clay Championship**, first team gold, 425; **Asian Games**, best haul 426, first gold, first medals 424, first woman to win a gold 425; **Commonwealth Games**, best haul 426, first gold 424; **Nationals**, first 425; **Olympics**, best haul 427, first ever individual gold medal 424, first ever medal 425, first finalist 424; **South Asian Games**, most career golds 425; **World Championship**, best haul 425, best haul in junior, 426, first gold, first medal, world champion with a world record, 424, youngest to win junior gold medal - men 427; **World Cup**, back-to-back golds in Junior, best haul, best performance (debut), double world record 426, first gold and silver medals, first mixed air pistol team gold medal, first pistol medal 425, first skeet gold 424, first to win two golds, gold in 425, most medals, most medals in four consecutive 428, most medals in Junior, youngest to win gold (women), 427
shrimp, top producing state/UT 98
Siachen glacier, first to walk 369
silk, only producer of all five commercial varieties 89
silver article, largest 61
simulator, first indigenous training 222
Sindhu, P.V., Badminton Star 386
sines and cosines, use in place of chords, 246
Singh, Jeev Milkha 413, 414, 416
sit-ups, abdominal in 1 min, most, 1 min 17
skydiving, first disabled in Asia 350, first woman to dive over seven continents 348, highest altitude 352, highest landing 349, most jumps, oldest woman 350
skyscraper, first 81
slide, oldest 81
SMS, first provider 192
snake, at the highest altitude, fastest, longest sea, loudest hiss 291, only 'flying' 294, only that builds a nest, only with heat sensors 291
soap, largest collection of wrappers (alphabetical) 50
soap opera, most watched daily 187
social network, largest penetration 195
society, mathematical, first 246
soil, earliest treatment experiments 98

soil sciences, first Indian society 87
solar, discovery of radio burst 249, first heated tent 304, first heater 252, largest single rooftop plant by area 304
SOS, first known use of signal 192
South Asian Games, best performance, 375
space, first Indian organization, 261, first man in 261, first private sector launches 342, first venture 261, first woman, 263
spacecraft, world's smallest launched 262
spectacle power, highest corrected using ICL surgery 279
sperm, first bank 270
spices, first research institute 87
spinal disc, largest removed 279
spinning wheel, smallest 28
Spoons, largest collection of 52
squadron, first 239, first attack helicopter 239, first bomber 239, first heavy-lift transport 239, first to have a jet bomber 239, first transport 239
squash, **Asian Championships**, first individual medals, first to win world doubles title 428; **Asian Games**, best in, 429; **Asian Junior Championship**, best performance 429, first silver, first to win title (girls), first international success (women) 428, Indian president of World Federation 374; **Junior** first world No. 1 428; **Nationals**, first champion, first doubles champion, junior and senior titles 428, most titles, most titles in a row (men), most titles in a row (women), oldest champion, youngest champion (women) 429; **professionals**, first 428; **rankings**, highest 429; **World Championships**, best performance in 429; **world ranking titles**, first to win 428, World Team Championships, best performance, youngest champion (men), youngest to represent India 429
squats, alternative in 1 min 17, jump in 1 min 18, most by a woman in 1 min, most in 1 min 17, pistol – alternating legs in 1 min 18
stamp, first 190, first autograph-inscribed, first commemorative 191, first customization of 190, first designer (pre-Independence) 191, first differently-shaped 190, first featuring wildlife 191, first Indian featuring a woman 190, first international exhibition, first of independent India, first one-rupee charity 191, first state to issue (pre-1947), first to be jointly issued with another country 190, from most countries in honour of a person, first, first state to issue (pre-1947), first Indian featuring a woman, first customization of, 189; largest, collection of ₹5 34
stand-up paddle-boarding, first surfing and competition, longest group, most 364
stars variability, discovery of 249
state, first, fully organic, to enact law on contract farming, to regulate crops 86
states, cleanest 305
state transport system, first (road) 317
state/UT, first with 100 per cent literacy, highest literacy rate, highest/lowest female literacy rate, highest percentage of graduates, lowest literacy rate, lowest percentage of graduates 102; **states**, first linguistic (post-1947), first linguistic (pre-1947), first modern Indian, first under president's rule 210, least densely populated, least populated, most densely populated, most populated 215, sharing border with most states 210, with longest international border, with the largest area, with the smallest area 210, youngest 211; **UT**, least densely populated, least populated, most densely populated 215, youngest 210
statue, largest Nandi, largest Shivalinga 73, tallest 74, tallest monolithic, tallest Shani Dev, tallest shivalinga 73
steam, engine, first builder of 333, first powered plant, 335
steamboat, first 323
steam, engine, oldest 316
steel, first manufacture 261
stepwell, deepest 61, most elaborate 82
stock exchange, first woman president of 334, highest price for membership 333, oldest 336, with most listed companies 336
stone, largest, urinary bladder removed 277
store, highest number opened in a single day, 343
strike, first labour, first organized 327, largest 328
structures, earliest 68, largest tent 81, oldest extant marble 64, tallest Durga 73, tallest hollow stone 71
stupa, largest 61
Subedar, first woman 221
submarine, first base 232, first deep-sea rescue system 236, first indigenous 234, first nuclear 231
Subscriber Trunk Dialling (STD), first 192
sugar cane, tallest 89
Suicide rate highest, lowest 211
sundial, biggest 249
superconductors, first prediction of hot 252
Super Fab lab, first 260
surface salinity, highest, lowest 284
surgeon, first, neurosurgeon 271, first psychosurgeon, first woman general, first woman neurosurgeon 270
surgery, bloodless breast, earliest cataract 272, father of plastic 271, first coronary artery bypass

273, first craniopagus 272, first, department of minimal access 269, first heart-shrink, first Maze III, first video-assisted heart, global telecast of 272, heaviest woman 279, laser on trachea 272, on world's heaviest teenager 279, open-heart separation of conjoined twins 272
survey sample, largest 266
sweeping, most people simultaneously – multiple venues 45
swimming, Angel Island marathon, first to complete the round-trip 364; **Antarctic waters**, first and youngest Asian woman to 362; **Asian Games**, first diver, first gold 430, first gold 431, first swimmer, first water polo teams 430; **Asian Indoor Games**, first medal 430, at the highest altitude 365; **Commonwealth Games**, first para swimmer to win bronze, first relay team in finals, first to participate, first to reach finals 430; **English Channel**, fastest across 365, first to swim thrice solo, first woman to cross 363, oldest to cross, longest open-sea by a paraplegic 365, first and youngest Asian woman across Antarctic waters 362, first to swim from mainland to Anacapa Island 363; **Gibraltar Strait**, fastest Asian to cross 362, first backstroke without neoprene 363, First woman to swim the 364, king of 363; **Nationals**, 200 m freestyle first under two minutes 430, first 100 m freestyle under one minute 430; **Ocean's Seven challenge**, first to complete, youngest in the world to complete 362; **Olympics**, first swimmer 429, first swimmer to make 'A' cut - men's 100 m backstroke event, first swimmer to make 'A' cut - men's 200 m butterfly event 431, first to qualify for two events 430, participation in two consecutive games 431, **Para Asian Games**, first para swimmer to win gold, first visually impaired swimmer to win a gold 430, **Paralympic Games**, first Indian para-swimmer to qualify, participation in two consecutive games 431, **paraplegic**, long distance swimming by a woman, longest open-sea swimming 365; **seven seas**, first Asian woman to swim across 362; **Triple Crown**, first to complete 364, oldest to complete 365
synagogue, largest 70, oldest active 69

T

table, largest 80
table tennis, Asian Cup, first to win medal - women 433, **Asian Juniors**, first medal 432, first pair to win mixed doubles 433; **Commonwealth Championship**,, best doubles performance 434; **Commonwealth Games**, first gold medal mixed doubles, first gold men doubles, first gold men team, first gold women doubles, first gold women team, first to regain singles gold 432, first winner men singles, first winner women singles, medallist in five successive games first 431, most medals, most medals from, most medal won by an individual player in a single edition 433, first professional, 432; **International Table Tennis Federation**, first Indian to be a member of Umpires and Referees Committee, first title-triumph in junior tour 432, longest mixed doubles reign 433, most senior/junior titles in a year 431, most team titles (men/women) 433; **National**, first champion 432, most appearances 433, most singles titles in a row 431, most state representation 433, most titles singles 434, no games conceded 431, youngest to win title 434; **Olympics**, first woman to play two, youngest to qualify 431; **ranking**, first to be World no. 1 in U-18 432, **South Asian Federation Games**, most gold medals in 433; **tournament**, most participants 434; **World Championship**, best team performance 434, first doubles pair in the quarter-finals, first to reach quarter-finals 431, second division titles 434; **World Junior Championship**, first team medal 432; **WTT Contender title**, first pair to win 432
table tennis racket, longest duration of non-stop hitting a table tennis ball 40
talkie, first, 143, first female actor 138
tallest building Lokhandwala Minerva 81
tank, earliest 222, highest battle in the world 223, indigenous 222
tea, first estate, highest garden 89, oldest research station 88
teeth, most people brushing simultaneously – multiple venues 41
telecast, first 185, first national 184
telecom, **5G service**, first carrier to demonstrate capability 192
tele-density, state/UT with highest 194
telefilm, first 187
telegram, first director general, first Indian radio telegraphy company, first Indo-European line, last 192
telephone, first automatic exchange 192, first exchange 193, first internet telephony service 194, first push-button 192
telescope, first liquid mirror only for astronomical observations, first robotic 249
television, broadcasting, first simultaneous 184, first colour, first colour transmission 185, first private producer of national news 184, first teleshopping, tallest tower 185

tempera method, earliest use 155
temperature, highest, lowest 284
temple, biggest bell, biggest lamp 69, earliest extant structure 68, largest cave temple complex 69, largest collection of, largest sun 70, most sculptures in, only rat 69, tallest single-stone shikhara 70, tallest tower 71
temple, **oldest functional Hindu** Mundeshwari Devi temple 68
Tendulkar, Sachin, 168, 374, 399, 402, 403
tennis, **Asian Games**, first doubles gold medallist 434, first singles gold, 435; **ATP Tour**, first Indian to win 2 ATP Challengers singles titles, first Indian to win ATP Challenger on European Clay, oldest player to win ATP Masters title – doubles 437; **Australian Open**, first all-Indian mixed doubles title, first junior boy's champion, first men's doubles title, first mixed doubles title, 437, best singles result 434; **Billie Jean King (Federation) Cup**, first team to qualify world play-offs, 434; **Davis Cup**, best record in Asia, first appearance, Junior regional champs, most appearances, most successful doubles player 435; **French Open**, first All-Indian men's doubles, first All-Indian mixed doubles, first and only junior champion first mixed doubles title, 436; **Nationals**, first (grass court), most titles 437; **US Open**, first and only junior boys' title, first doubles title, first mixed doubles title 437, first women's doubles title 436; **Wimbledon**, First Indian woman at Wimbledon, first junior boy's title, first junior girl's doubles title, first men's doubles title, first mixed doubles title, first seeded 436, first to play 435
terrapin, largest 294
tetracycline, discovery 255
theatre, Asia's biggest festival 135, earliest open-air 60, first commercial, first public hall, most theatrical performances 133, oldest cave, oldest children's 135
The Common Man 179
The Elephant Whisperers, (See also film) 140
The End of a Journey 315
theory, first on infinite dimensional representations 247
thermal, new method for conductivity 253
thiosulphuric acid, discovery of isomerism 255
three-point disembarkation system, first 312
tickets, most booked in advance 146
tie, most knots tied in 1 minute 14
tiger, census, largest camera trap 297
tokamak, first 254
tomb, earliest known monumental 61, first garden 63
Toothbrushes, largest collection of 54
tortoise, smallest 294
Tortoises and Turtles 294
toys, most donated – single day 31
tractor, earliest use, first semi-autonomous, largest seller, state/UT with most exports 99
trading, first automatic exchange and screen-based, 337
traffic, first advanced control system 318, first police 317
train, fastest, first air-conditioned 314, first corporatized 316, first deluxe, first double-decker, first electric 314, first passenger 312, first Vistadome 314, longest route 316
train, largest collection of HO Scale models 52
training centre, first, postal network, 188
tram, first cars 314, first company 312
transplant, **first**, double (liver and kidney) 273, heart 275, liver 274, paediatric, thumb 275, womb 274
transport, first indigenous payment eco-system for 318, first regular public system 317
tree, biggest trunk 296, fastest maturing, largest canopy, largest hollow, longest-living species 295, most, planted in 15 mins 302, planted in a quarter 303, planted in one day, planted in one hour 302, tallest 295, tallest jamun 298
trekking, Everest Base Camp, fastest by a disabled person, longest desert – group, oldest trekker 371, Snowmen's trek, first women's team to complete 370
Tropical Medicine 106
tumour, **heaviest**, brain removed 277, ovarian removed 273, **largest**, bone removed 277, breast removed 278, cystic of the liver removed 277, small-intestinal removed 278, oral (head and neck) removed in one piece, thoracic removed 277, ear removed, eye removed 279
tunnel, longest transportation railway 83
turtle, carapace, smallest, largest, rarest freshwater 294
type, earliest 176
typewriters, first, first indigenous 176

U

underwater, first clean-up 243
uniform civil code 210
union, oldest banking employees' trade 327, oldest insurance trade 327, oldest trade 327
Union Government, first non-congress 208
United Nations, first use of Hindi 210
university, first energy studies 107, first five 106, first five residential 107, first for the disabled, first law 109, first modern 104, first of fisheries and ocean

studies 107, first only for tribal students 110, first railway 107, first rural 106, first Sanskrit 104, first technical 107, first university for the study of outer space 109, first virtual medical, first women's 107, largest open 111, longest functioning ancient 104
Uranus, discovery of rings 251
uterine transplant, first woman to give birth after 266

V

vaccine, first indigenously developed, largest company 269
vanadium, discovery 256
vanilla, first cultivation 92
varieties, most of cookies prepared, most of kachori prepared, most of pakoras prepared, most of siddu prepared 45
varsity, first air 309
vessels, first 243, first indigenous offshore patrol 242, latest training 243
vest, first indigenously made bulletproof 223
veterinary, first army school 229, first surgeon 93, state with most institutions 96
viaduct, longest double-decker 316, most metro stations 317
vice president, first, 208, longest tenure 199, oldest to assume office, 208, shortest tenure 199
Victoria Cross, first 220, youngest to receive 220
video viewership, highest concurrent 195
village, earliest settlement 60, first green 300
virology, first institute of advanced 269
Vishisht Seva Medal, first couple to be awarded 239
volcano, only active 284

W

war, camel, first Bactrian to join the army, dogs, first Indian breed in active duty, first national memorial, International Scout Masters Competition (ISMC), first win 230, warfare school, first high-altitude 229
warship, first indigenous modern 234, first modern builder, first modern building yard 236, first multi 234
warship/aircraft, longest serving 232
waterfall, highest 283
wave, highest 256
weightlifting, **Asian Championship**, record in clean and jerk (women) 438; **Asian Games**, first medal (women) 438; **Asian Meet**, best performance 439; **Commonwealth Games**, back-to-back gold medals, first gold (men) 438, most medals, most medals (women), youngest winner 439; **Nationals**, oldest champion, youngest champion 439; **Olympics**, first silver, qualifying gold 438; **World and Asian meets**, most medals 439; **World Championship**, first medal 438, most gold medals 439; **World Junior Championship**, first gold 438
WhatsApp, largest user base 195
wildlife sanctuary, state/UT with most 297
Wimbledon Centre Court, smallest 29
windsurfing, marathon 365
wireless, first demonstration 253
woman, first advocate 213, first Airbus commander, first airbus pilot 311, first air marshal 238, first all-woman crew to circumnavigate the world 236, first ambassador, 211, first bachelor of medicine 110, first cabinet minister 208, first career diplomat 211; first chairperson of the International Civil Aviation Organization (ICAO) Aviation Security Committee, first chief executive officer of an airline 311, first chief Justice 214, first chief minister 210, first combatants 242, first combat pilots 238, first commercial pilot 310, first commissioned pilot by Order of Merit 238, first DG Medical services 221, first director general of CSIR 255, first doctor 110, first film-maker 142, first flight commander 238, first foreign concert tour by instrumentalist 130, first full-time finance minister 208, first ghatam player 130, first graduates 110, first hovercraft pilot 242, first IAS officer, 211, first in defence services staff 238, first in military police 221, first instrumentalist 129, first in the army 221, first IPS officer 213, first judge of the Supreme Court 213, first legislator 216, first marine pilot 323, first maritime reconnaissance pilot 230, first mayor 212, first medical officer (Air Force) 238, first nadaswaram player 130, first naval helicopter, pilot 231, first officer as 'Observers' 231, first offshore pilot 311, first pilot 242, first pilot of naval aircraft 230, first pilot to lead the Republic Day fly-past 238, first rulers 198, first sarpanch 211, first shehnai player 129, first skydiver 348, first Subedar 221, first technical university for (See also university) 107, first to obtain a PhD in a scientific discipline 110, first to obtain a pilot's licence 311, first train driver 315, first vice chancellor 110, highest number of pilots 311, law graduate 110, oldest to deliver twins 273
woollen, group-single day-single venue 31
workers, on board 327
World Archery Award, first Indian to win 378
World Bank Group, first woman managing director and chief financial officer 334
World Food Prize, first winner 89

World Transplant Games, first Indian woman to participate 375
wrestling, **Asian Championship**, best performance, best performance at Asian Championship 442, first gold (women), first Indian couple to win silver 441, most gold medals 443, most medals 442, most medals (U-15) (girls) 443; **Asian Games**, first gold 441, first gold (men), first medal 440, youngest champion 443; **Asian Games, Commonwealth Games and World Championships**, first winner of all (women) 440; **award**, first coach of the year, first junior wrestler of the year 441; **Commonwealth Championship**, most individual medals (men), most medals 442; **Commonwealth Games**, best performance (men), best performance (women), first medal 440, most consecutive title (women) 442, most gold medals (men), youngest gold medallist 443; **Greco-Roman**, first gold 441; **Greco-Roman Championship**, first medals (U-17) 441; **Junior World Champion**, first 441; **Laureus World Sports Award**, first and only woman to win 440; **Olympic and World Championship** first winner of both 439; **Olympics**, first at the, first medal (men), first woman at the 439; **World Championship**, back-to-back medals 441, best performance 442, first gold medallist 440, first medal (men), first medal (women) 439, first to win gold in U-20 (women) 441, most individual medals 442

Y

yachting, at the highest altitude 365
yak, first test-tube calf 96
yield, highest-ever crude throughput and distillate 338
yoga, **longest**, ashtavakrasana 14, bakasana, ekapada shirshasana, Hanumanasana 15, highest, performance at altitude 16, janu shirshasana 15, karna pidasana, mandukasana, mayurasana - with one hand 15, nirlamba ushtrasana 17, padhasthasana, padma mayurasana 15, padm vrischikasana 17, parshva poorna dhanurasana, paschimottanasana, purvattanasana 15, setu bandhasana 14, sirsasana 17, supta pandangushthasana 15, vishvamitrasana 14
Youngest member of the Rajya Sabha 216
YouTube, most subscribed channel, most viewed Indian video, 195
Yudh Seva Medal, first 242, first and only Sarvottam (Air Force), first woman to be awarded (Air Force) 239

Z

zentangle, largest art 157
zero, first to understand 246
zinc, earliest artefact 260
zipline, highest by a differently abled person 350
zoo, oldest 296
zoologist, first 258

ABBREVIATIONS USED IN THE BOOK

b. = born on
in. = inch/inches
ft = feet
cm = centimetre/centimetres
m = metre/metres
g = gram/grams
kg = kilogram/kilograms
hr = hour/hours
min./mins = minute/minutes
sec./secs = second/seconds
Mt = Mount

IMAGE COPYRIGHT INFORMATION

NOTE: CCA-SA refers to the Creative Commons Attribution-Share Alike Wikimedia Commons/International Wikimedia Commons licences; PD: Public Domain: (All public domain photographs have been sourced from: Wikimedia Commons/Public Domain); PIB: Press Information Bureau; GODL: Government Open Data Licence – India; GoI: Government of India.

PRELIMS 6–11

Title page: by courtesy of the record holder; **6–11**: **Contents**: images have been credited under the respective chapters below;

HUMAN STORY 12–57

Opener pics, *from left to right*: Rubiks cube: Photo by MART PRODUCTION: https://www.pexels.com/photo/a-person-playing-with-a-rubiks-cube-8471996/; Philately: Photo by Suhas Hanjar: https://www.pexels.com/photo/variety-of-vintage-coins-and-stamp-15258683/; Yoga: Photo by Prasanth Inturi: https://www.pexels.com/photo/silhouette-of-man-at-daytime-1051838/; Coin stack: Photo by Pixabay: https://www.pexels.com/photo/selective-focus-photo-of-stacked-coins-128867/; Images are by the courtesy of record holders; **20–21**: **background**: Skipping Rope: Good Mood/Shutterstock.com; **30–31**: **background**: Shutterstock.com; **32–33**: **background**: pixabay.com; **42–43**: **background**: Eggs: Shutterstock.com; **Inset**: by courtesy of the record holder; **54–55**: toothbrush: Shutterstock.com; **56–57**: **background**: Newspaper: Shutterstock.com;

STRUCTURES 58–83

Opener pic, 58–59: Anshul_Tilondiya/Pixabay; **60**: **bottom left and right**: Vickey Chauhan/Shutterstock.com; **61**: **top**: Gol Gumbaz: Waj/Shutterstock.com; **bottom**: Silver jug, Jaipur: Olga_V/Shutterstock.com; **62**: **top**: Pallava bas-relief: Nickolay Stanev/Shutterstock.com, **middle**: Bhul Bhulaiya: saiko3p/Shutterstock.com; **bottom**: Qutb Minar: Arnav Pratap Singh/Shutterstock.com; **63**: Tomb of Sikandar Lodi: Shashank Shukla Kotaha/Shutterstock.com; **64–65**: **background**, Mehrangarh fort: Roop_Dey/Shutterstock.com; **insets**: **1**: Dholavira fort: Vickey Chauhan/Shutterstock.com; **2**: Quila Mubarak, Bhatinda: Amrit Kaur/Shutterstock.com; **3**: Hoshang Shah Ghori's tomb: Wikipedia/CCA-SA 3.0/Bernard Gagnon; **4**: Hawa Mahal: Atosan/Shutterstock.com; **66–67**: **background**: Kumbhalgarh fort: Kevin Standage/Shutterstock.com; **top**: Malik-e-Maidan: Denny George/Shutterstock.com; **middle**: Buland Darwaza: Roop_Dey/Shutterstock.com; **68**: **middle**: Piprahwa Stupa: CCA-SA 3.0/JimRenge; **bottom**: Tawang Monastery: Ron Ramtang/Shutterstock.com; **69**: **top**: Meenakshi Sundareswar Temple: Bilal Aliyar m/Shutterstock.com; **bottom left**: Rat temple: bodom/Shutterstock.com; **bottom right**: Cave 16, Ellora complex: Leonid Andronov/Shutterstock.com; **70**: **middle**: Nizamat Imambara: balajisrinivasan/Shutterstock.com; **bottom**: Bara Imambara: saiko3p/Shutterstock.com; **71**:**top**: Moti Masjid: Yakov Oskanov/Shutterstock.com; **middle**: Ranganathaswamy Temple: Wikipedia/CCA-SA 4.0/RUPESH MAURYA; **bottom left**: Hemkund Sahib: StockGalery/Shtterstock.com; **bottom right**: Tangyud Monastery: raman29/Shutterstock.com; **72**: **middle left**: Basilica of Our Lady of Dolours: ebin francis/Shutterstock.com; **middle right**: St Thomas Syro-Malabar Church: AnilD/Shutterstock.com; **bottom**: Old Goa cathedral: SurabhiArtss/Shutterstock.com; **73**: Nandi statue: Renu V Nair/Shutterstock.com; **bottom**: Jatayu statue: Libin Kallada Photography/Shutterstock.com; **74, 1**: Statue of Unity: Ajay U Paul/Shutterstock.com; **2**: Bishwas Swaroopam (Shiva statue): chetansoni/Shutterstock.com; **3**: Statue of Equality: Pixel posh/Shutterstock.com; **5**: Hanuman statue, Madapam: Wikipedia/PD/MaddogMike; **6**: Panchamukhi Hanuman statue: rakesh kp/Shutterstock.com; **8**: Muthumalai Murugan statue: Camshooter Shantha Kumar/Shutterstock.com; **9**: Vaishni Devi statue: Sanket_Mishra/Shutterstock.com; **75**: **top**: Bhupen Hazarika Setu: GYAN PRATIM RAICHOUDHURY/Shutterstock.com; **bottom**: Atal Setu: Photo by Anshuman Poyrekar/Hindustan Times; **76–77**: **background**: Chenab Bridge: Louise_Michel/Shutterstock.com; **76**: **bottom**: Sudarshan Bridge: Wikipedia/ Government Open Data License - India (GODL)/ Government of India; **77**: **middle**: Howrah Bridge: Subrata1985/Shutterstock.com; **bottom**: Bongibeel Bridge: Sajijur Rahman/Shutterstock.com; **78**: **top**: Tehri Dam: Uttarakhand Dev Bhumi/Shutterstock.com; **bottom left**: Sardar Sarovar Dam: Dipesh Devdas Motivaras/Shutterstock.com; **bottom right**: Farakka Barrage: Krishna8412/Shutterstock.com; **79**: **bottom left**: Lighthouse in Thalassery, Kerala: Shutterstock.com; **80**: **top**: Sri Shanmukhananda Hall: RAMNIKLAL MODI/Shutterstock.com; **bottom**: Glass-covered hall in Davanagere: SNEHIT PHOTO/Shutterstock.com; **81**: **top**: Surat Diamond Bourse: NareshSharma/Shutterstock; **bottom**: Palika Bazar: mrinalpal/Shutterstock.com; **82**: **top**: World Peace Dome: Sarang Gharge/Shutterstock.com; **middle**: Rani ki Vav: Parikh Mahendra N/Shutterstock.com; **bottom**: Supertech demolition: PradeepGaurs/Shutterstock.com; **83**: **top left**: Gulmarg Gondola: Hari Mahidhar/Shutterstock.com; **top left**: Rajgir ropeway: SOUMEN 21/Shutterstock.com; **middle**: Brahmaputra ropeway: Talukdar David/Shutterstock.com; **bottom**: Pir Panjal Railway Tunnel: Ankit Shotra/Shutterstock.com;

AGRICULTURE 84–99

Opener pic, 84–85: CRS PHOTO/Shutterstock.com; **86**: **top**: Madhu Dandavate: Government of India, GODL–India <https://data.gov.in/sites/default/files/Gazette_Notification_OGDL.pdf>, via Wikimedia Commons; **bottom**: Mango Meadows: AjayThomas/Shutterstock.com; **87**: **top right**: Biomaterial in liquid nitrogen: Shutterstock.com; **first middle**: Sir George Campbell: public domain via Wikimedia Commons https://commons.wikimedia.org/wiki/File:Major_General_George_Campbell_of_Inverneill.JPG; **second middle**: William Carrey: SUDARSHAN BHATLA/Shutterstock.com; **bottom left**: G.B. Pant University of Agriculture and Technology: Fromshahar, CC BY-SA 3.0 <https://creativecommons.org/licenses/by-sa/3.0>, via Wikimedia Commons; **bottom right**: Locust: Shutterstock.com; **88**: **top**: Groundwater irrigation system: Shutterstock.com; **middle**: Tocklai Experimentation Station: Official anahita, CC BY 3.0 <https://creativecommons.org/licenses/by/3.0>, via Wikimedia Commons; **bottom**: Central Tuber Crops Research Institute: Akhilan, CC BY-SA 4.0 <https://creativecommons.org/licenses/by-sa/4.0>, via Wikimedia Commons; **89**: **top middle**: Dr Rattan Lal: U.S. Department of AgricultureLance Cheung/Multimedia PhotoJournalist, Public domain, via Wikimedia Commons; **top right**: Dr M.S. Swaminathan: Biswarup Ganguly, CC BY 3.0 <https://creativecommons.org/licenses/by/3.0>, via Wikimedia Commons; **bottom first**: muga silk: Shutterstock.com;

bottom second: Korakundah Tea Estate: L. Shyamal, CC BY-SA 3.0 <https://creativecommons.org/licenses/by-sa/3.0>, via Wikimedia Commons; **92**: Bt cotton crop: Shutterstock.com; **93**: **top**: Central Plantation Crops Research Institute: Pmecell, CC BY-SA 4.0 <https://creativecommons.org/licenses/by-sa/4.0>, via Wikimedia Commons; **middle**: Dr Alfred Lingard: A description of the Imperial Bacteriological Laboratory, Muktesar and (1940). "Supplement. Imperial Veterinary Research Institute 1890-1940. Golden Jubilee". Indian Farming 1 (11) (COPYRIGHT EXPIRED); **bottom**: Bhut jolokia: Shutterstock.com; **94–95**: **background image**: Shutterstock.com; **94**: mangoes: Shutterstock.com; **95**: **left**: animal husbandry: Shutterstock.com; **right**: coconut plantation: Shutterstock.com; **96**: **top**: Camels in National Research Centre on Camel: Shutterstock.com; **bottom**: Dr Verghese Kurien: Ministry of Railways (GODL-India), GODL-India <https://data.gov.in/sites/default/files/Gazette_Notification_OGDL.pdf>, via Wikimedia Commons; **97**: **representative image**: Shutterstock.com; **98**: **top**: CMFRI building: Courtesy of Central Marine Fisheries Research Institute (CMFRI), Kochi, Kerala; **middle**: Indian white shrimp: Shutterstock.com; **bottom**: Rohu fish: Shutterstock.com; **99**: **middle**: Mahindra tractors: Rangeecha/Shuttestock.com; **bottom left**: DDT molecule: Shutterstock.com; **bottom right**: Ladybird beetle: Shutterstock.com;

EDUCATION 100–119

Opener pic, 100–101: WESTOCK PRODUCTIONS/Shutterstock.com; **102**: Kendriya Vidyalaya Sangathan: AjayTvm/Shutterstock.com; **104**: Ruins of Nalanda University: Thotsaporn.S/Shutterstock.com; **105**: **background**: Jan Willem van Hofwegen/Shutterstock.com; **107**: IIT Kharagpur: mrinalpal/Shutterstock.com; **110**: NALSAR: Anjaneyadas, CC BY-SA 3.0 <https://creativecommons.org/licenses/by-sa/3.0>, via Wikimedia Commons; **111**: Calcutta Public Library: Avrajyoti Mitra, CC BY-SA 2.0 <https://creativecommons.org/licenses/by-sa/2.0>, via Wikimedia Commons; **113**: Courtesy of Shubham Badhani; **114**: Madame Tussauds: cameranest/Shutterstock.com; **116–117**: **background**: Smritivan Earthquake Museum: kiran sharma/Shutterstock.com; **118**: Humayan's Tomb: Photo by Sanjeev Verma/Hindustan Times; **119**: **top**: Derek O'Brien: Saikat Paul/Shutterstock.com; **bottom**: Amitabh Bachchan: Denis Makarenko/Shutterstock.com;

PERFORMING ARTS 120–135

Opener pic, 120–121: kitreel/Shutterstock.com; **122**: Mudiyettu: Arun Soman/Shutterstock.com; **123**: Kerala Kalamandalam: tengatt/Shutterstock.com; **124**: Kutiyattam: Santhosh Varghese/Shutterstock.com; **125**: **top**: Maharaja Swathi Thirumal: Stephen Crening, Public domain, via Wikimedia Commons; **middle**: Purandaradasa: Lefteris Papaulakis/Shutterstock.com; **bottom**: Ramanuja Iyengar: SUDARSHAN BATLA/Shutterstock.com; **126–127**: **background**: Roop_Dey/Shutterstock.com; **bottom left**: JN STUDIO/Shutterstock.com; **bottom right**: Arvind Balaraman/Shutterstock.com; **middle**: Sringara: Rajesh Narayanan/Shutterstock.com; **bottom**: Raudra Ras: Sri Devi Nrithyalaya, GFDL 1.2 <http://www.gnu.org/licenses/old-licenses/fdl-1.2.html>, via Wikimedia Commons; **128**: Lithophone: Geartooth Productions/Shutterstock.com; **129**: Gramaphone: sdf_qwe/Shutterstock.com; **130**: Nadaswaram: reddees/Shutterstock.com; **bottom left**: Ancient Veena: PRL/Shutterstock.com; **bottom right**: Carvaan: Suryanshu Awasthi/Shutterstock.com; **131**: **top**: Shakti band: Ali-Khan, CC BY-SA 3.0 <https://creativecommons.org/licenses/by-sa/3.0>, via Wikimedia Commons; **bottom**: Slumdog Millionaire: s_bukley/Shutterstock.com; **132**: Parikrama: Girish Menon/Shutterstock.com; **133**: **top**: Indian plaque showing the story of Shakuntala: Artacoana for the photographic material. User:पाटलिपुत्र for the reconstitution., Public domain, via Wikimedia Commons; **bottom**: Bal Gandharva: Mahusha, CC BY-SA 4.0 <https://creativecommons.org/licenses/by-sa/4.0>, via Wikimedia Commons; **134**: **background**: Abhishek Mittal/Shutterstock.com; **top**: Yakshagana: Bindu Kotian/Shutterstock.com; **bottom left**: Bhavai: Dmitry Rukhlenko/Shutterstock.com; Tamasha: ClipCraze/Shutterstock.com;

VISUAL ARTS 136–159

Opener pic, 136–137: Ritu Manoj Jethani/Shutterstock.com; **138**: **clockwise, from top**: Zubeida Begum: PD–India; Uttam Kumar: PD–India; *Bombay* poster: Fair Use/Kailash29792; Sadhana Bose: PD–India; Prithviraj Kapoor: GODL–India/India Post, Government of India; Ardeshir Irani: CCA-SA 4.0 International/Ashvin29/ https://commons.wikimedia.org/wiki/File:Ardeshir_Irani.jpg; **139**: **clockwise, from top**: *Ghajini* poster (Tamil): Fair Use/Kailash29792; *Ghajini* Poster (Hindi): Fair Use/DatBot; *Jawan* poster: Fair Use/Kailash29792; *Animal* Poster: Fair Use/Sush150; *Gadar 2* poster: Fair Use/Sush150; **140**: **top**: Satyajit Ray: PD–India; **bottom**: *Seeta* poster: CC0 1.0 Universal Public Domain Dedication/Georgethedragonslayer; **141**: **top left**: Shah Rukh Khan: Denis Makarenko/Shutterstock.com; | **top right**: Nadia: PD–India; **142**: **top**: Lumiere Brothers Stamp: A. Marino/Shutterstock.com; **bottom left**; Dadasaheb Phalke stamp: brandonht/Shutterstock.com; **bottom right**: *Alam Ara* shot: CCA 4.0 International/Imperial Films Company/ https://commons.wikimedia.org/wiki/File:Scene_from_%27Alam_Ara%27.png; **143**: **clockwise, from top**: Raj Kapoor stamp: GODL–India/India Post, Government of India; *Maine Pyaar Kiya* Poster: Fair Use/Theo's Little Bot; Guru Dutt stamp: GODL–India/India Post, Government of India; *Kagaz Ke Phool* poster: Fair Use/Theo's Little Bot; **145**: **from left to right**: background: Andreas Glöckner from Pixabay/Pixabay.com; Insets, top: Kamalabai Gokhale: PD–India; bottom: Fatma Begum: PD–India; **146**: **clockwise, from top**: Nithya Menon; by courtesy of PIB; Sooraj Barjatya: by courtesy of PIB; Rishab Shetty: by courtesy of PIB; Manasi Parekh: by courtesy of PIB; BookMyShow: Aniket gaikwad/Shutterstock.com; *Baahubali* poster: by courtesy of the record holder; Akanksha Sood Singh: by courtesy of PIB; Ayan Mukherji: CCA 3.0 Unported/Bollywood Hungama/ https://www.bollywoodhungama.com/news/parties-and-events/photos-varun-dhawan-karan-johar-others-grace-premiere-kill/ https://commons.wikimedia.org/wiki/File:Ayan_Mukerji_grace_the_premiere_of_Kill.jpg; **147**: **from left to right**: Kangana Ranaut: PradeepGaurs/Shutterstock.com; Hema Malini: CCA 3.0 Unported/Bollywood Hungama/ http://www.bollywoodhungama.com/celebrities/images/8210/still126937.html/https://commons.wikimedia.org/wiki/File:Hema_malini_bhungama1.jpg; Shatrugan Sinha: GODL–India/ Narendra Modi; Vyajanthimala: GODL–India/President's Secretariat; Dharmendra: GODL–India/President's Secretariat; Govinda: CCA 2.0 Generic/Laura Lee Dooley/ https://commons.wikimedia.org/wiki/File:Govinda_at_

IMAGE COPYRIGHT INFORMATION

IIFA-2014-GreenCarpet2_(323).jpg; **148**: **from top to bottom**: *Kalki 2898 AD* poster: Fair Use/Sush150: *RRR* poster: Fair Use/Krimuk2.0; *Baahubali* poster: Fair Use/DatBot; *Dhoom 3* poster: Fair Use/DatBot; *Ra.One* poster: Fair Use/77Survivor; *Enthiran* poster: Fair Use/Kailash29792; *Blue* poster: Fair Use/ Kailash29792; *Dasavatharam* poster: Fair Use/Kailash29792; **149**: **from top to bottom**: *Devdas* poster: Fair Use/Theo's Little Bot; *Lagaan* poster: Fair Use/DatBot; *Indian* poster: Fair Use/ Kailash29792; *Trimurti* Poster: Fair Use/Kailash29792; *Ajooba* poster: Fair Use/Theo's Little Bot; *Razia Sultan* poster: Fair Use/ GaiusAugustine; *Shaan* poster: Fair Use/Kailash29792; *Sholay* poster: Fair Use/Theo's Little Bot; *Mughal-e-Azam* poster: Fair Use/Theo's Little Bot; **152: clockwise, from top**: Dr Dasari Narayana Rao: GODL–India/Government of India; Vijaya Nirmala: Fair Use/Kaitha Poo Manam; *Dilwale Dulhania Le Jayenge* cut out: Shams F Amir/Shutterstock.com; *Purana Mandir* poster: Fair Use/MatthewHoobin; *Veerana* poster: Fair Use/Kailash29792; *Purani Haveli* poster: Fair Use/DatBot; **153**: **top**: Bourne and Shepherd: CCA 3.0 Unported/Biswarup Ganguly/ https://commons.wikimedia.org/wiki/File:Bourne_%26_Shepherd_-_141_SN_Banerjee_Road_-_Kolkata_2016-06-23_5137.JPG; **bottom**: Elphinstone College: PD/PD–US/Bourne and Shepherd Museum of Photographic Arts; 154: **top**: Dayanita Singh: CCA-SA 3.0 Unported/Nomu420/ https://commons.wikimedia.org/wiki/File:Dayanita_singh_book_museum_12.JPG; **bottom left**: Selfie: by courtesy of the record holder; **bottom right**: Rajesh Bedi: Photo by Ravindra Joshi/ Hindustan Times; **155**: **top**: Mohenjo Daro: Shutterstock.com; **bottom**: Ajanta Caves: Shutterstock.com; **156**: **left**: Brihadeeswara Temple: Shutterstock.com; **right**: Maharaja Ram Singh: PD–India; **157**: **top**: Vasudeo S. Gaitonde: CCA-SA 4.0 International/ सुहास बहुळकर, दीपक घारे/ https://commons.wikimedia.org/wiki/File:V._S._Gaitonde.jpg; **bottom**: by courtesy of the record holder; **158**: by courtesy of the record holders;

LITERATURE 160–173

Opener pic, **160–161**: Shutterstock.com; **162**: **from top to bottom**: *A Grammar of the Bengal* Language title page: PD–India/ Nathaniel Brassey Halhed; *Therigatha*: CCA–SA 4.0 International License/This file comes from Wellcome Images, a website operated by Wellcome Trust, a global charitable foundation based in the United Kingdom. Refer to Wellcome blog post (archive)/ https://commons.wikimedia.org/wiki/File:Illustrated_Sinhalese_covers_(inside)_showing_the_events_Wellcome_L0031774.jpg; *Ashtadhyayi*: CCA–SA 4.0 International License/Ms Sarah Welch/ https://commons.wikimedia.org/wiki/File:Panini_Astadhyayi,_Sanskrit_language,_Southern_Grantha_script.jpg; **163**: Henry Louis Vivian Derozio stamp: GODL–India/India Post, Government of India; **164**: **top**: Largest book: by courtesy of PIB; **middle**: Longest novel: Fair use/Vilasini/ https://www.goodreads.com/book/show/124223748-avakasikal/ https://en.wikipedia.org/wiki/File:Avakasikal_book_cover.png; **bottom**: Shakespeare's First Folio: PD/ William Shakespeare; **165**: **top**: Comic Con: Fair use/www.comicconindia.com/https://en.wikipedia.org/wiki/File:New_Comic_Con_Header_Final_copy.png; **bottom**: Crossword Bookstore: PradeepGaurs/Shutterstock.com; **166–167**: Higginbothams: by courtesy of the record holder; **168**: College Street: neelsky/Shutterstock.com; **169**: **from top to bottom**: Salman Rushdie: CCA-SA 3.0 Unported/Elena Ternovaja/https://commons.wikimedia.org/wiki/File:Salman_Rushdie,_2024.jpg; K.J.S. Dhillon: CCA-SA 4.0 International/ET Times/https://government.economictimes.indiatimes.com/news/governance/lt-gen-kjs-dhillon-to-take-over-as-dg-dia/74560566/https://commons.wikimedia.org/wiki/File:KJS_Dhillon.png; *The Gita For Children: Limited Celebratory Edition* cover: by courtesy of Hachette India; *They Meant Business: 50 Inspiring Stories from Indian Biz*: by courtesy of Hachette India; **170**: **top**: Sapna Book House: CCA–SA 4.0 International License/https://commons.wikimedia.org/wiki/User:Gpkp/ https://commons.wikimedia.org/wiki/File:Sapna_Book_House.jpg; **bottom**: A.H. Wheeler: CCA–SA 3.0 Unported License/https://commons.wikimedia.org/wiki/User:Abhishek727/ https://commons.wikimedia.org/wiki/File:A.H._Wheeler_%26_Co._-_Sawai_Madhopur_-_F7040_Wikipedia_Veethi.JPG; **171**: **from left to right**: *Half the Night is Gone* cover: by courtesy of Juggernaut Books; *Chronicle of a Corpse Bearer* cover: by courtesy of Aleph Book Company; *Sleeping on Jupiter* cover: by courtesy of Hachette India; *No Presents Please* cover: by courtesy of HarperCollins India; **bottom**: *Gay-neck, the story of a pigeon* cover: by courtesy of Hachette India;

MEDIA AND COMMUNICATION 174–195

Opener picture, 174–175: metamorworks/Shutterstock.com; **176**: **top**: Lord Wellesley: Thomas Lawrence, Public domain, via Wikimedia Commons; **bottom**: PTI: Funstock/Shutterstock.com; **177**: **top**: Times of India Logo: KuMaR437/Shutterstock.com; **middle**: Chintamani Ghosh: The Modern Review. September 1928, Public domain, via Wikimedia Commons; **bottom**: Samachar Darpan: Digital Library of India, Public domain, via Wikimedia Commons; **178**: **top left**: Hindu Office Front: Ravichandar84, CC BY-SA 3.0 <https://creativecommons.org/licenses/by-sa/3.0>, via Wikimedia Commons; **top right**: *Chandamama* Front Cover: Chakrapani, Public domain, via Wikimedia Commons; **bottom**: *Malyala Manorama* newspaper: Ayyappan Manikantan Nair/ Shutterstock.com; **179**: **top**: The Common Man: Gurera, CC BY-SA 4.0 <https://creativecommons.org/licenses/by-sa/4.0>, via Wikimedia Commons; **middle**: Gobind Behari Lal: The Modern Review. July 1937, Public domain, via Wikimedia Commons; **bottom**: Amtria Bazaar Patrika: Amrita Bazar Patrika, CC0, via Wikimedia Commons; **180**: **middle**: Ravi Shankar: Markgoff2972, CC BY-SA 4.0 <https://creativecommons.org/licenses/by-sa/4.0>, via Wikimedia Commons; **bottom**: Funeral of Mahatma Gandhi: Unknown author, Public domain, via Wikimedia Commons; **182–183**: All Indian Radio Center Delhi: maurya.exe/ Shutterstock.com; **184**: **top**: Doordarshan: PradeepGaurs/ Shutterstock.com; **bottom left**: Ameen Sayani: Bollywood Hungama, CC BY 3.0 <https://creativecommons.org/licenses/by/3.0>, via Wikimedia Commons; **bottom middle**: Dheeraj Kumar: Bollywood Hungama, CC BY 3.0 <https://creativecommons.org/licenses/by/3.0>, via Wikimedia Commons; **bottom right**: Siri Fort Auditorium: Nvvchar, CC BY-SA 3.0 <https://creativecommons.org/licenses/by-sa/3.0>, via Wikimedia Commons; **185**: Rameswaram TV tower: flickrPrince, CC BY-SA 3.0 <https://creativecommons.org/licenses/by-sa/3.0>, via Wikimedia Commons; **187**: **top**: television set: dkroy/ Shutterstock.com; **middle**: Satyajit Ray: Dinu Alam Newyork, CC BY-SA 4.0 <https://creativecommons.org/licenses/by-sa/4.0>, via Wikimedia Commons; **bottom left**: India Post, Government of India, GODL–India <https://data.gov.in/sites/default/files/Gazette_Notification_OGDL.pdf>, via Wikimedia Commons;

188: **top**: Madras General Post Office: Wikimedia Commons/ Fair Use/India Illustrated; **middle**: first aerial post image: SUDARSHAN BHATLA/Shutterstock.com; **bottom**: General Post Office: Saikat Paul/Shutterstock.com; **189**: **top**: Mahatma Gandhi stamps: spatuletail/Shutterstock.com; **bottom**: India's first 3D post-office: ANI Photo; **190**: **top**: Stamps to commemorate festival of India: bissig/Shutterstock.com; **middle**: stamp printed for Indipex-2011: svic/Shutterstock.com; **bottom**: Triangle stamp: SUDARSHAN BHATLA/Shutterstock.com; **191**: **top**: Rabindranath Tagore stamp: spatuletail/ Shutterstock.com; **middle**: Rhino stamp: Post of India, GODL-India <https://data.gov.in/sites/default/files/Gazette_Notification_OGDL.pdf>, via Wikimedia Commons; **bottom**: National Philatelic Museum: Bhaven Jani/Shutterstock.com; **192**: **top**: radio telephone: BrAt82/Shutterstock.com; **middle**: William Brooke O'Shaughnessy: Unknown author, Public domain, via Wikimedia Commons; **193**: **top**: Bharti Airtel store: SN040288/Shutterstock.com; **bottom**: PradeepGaurs/ Shutterstock.com; **194**: **middle**: Telstra headquarters: Doob 8, CC BY-SA 3.0 <https://creativecommons.org/licenses/by-sa/3.0>, via Wikimedia Commons; **bottom**: TCS headquarters: DSP2092, CC BY-SA 3.0, via Wikimedia Commons; **195**: **top**: Disney Hotstar: mouby studio/Shutterstock.com; **bottom**: T-series: T-Series, Public domain, via Wikimedia Commons;

GOVERNMENT 196–217

Opener pic, 196–197: PradeepGaurs/Shutterstock.com; **198**: **top**: Alexander III: TsibaevAlex/Shutterstock.com; **middle left**: The last act of Malik Naib Kafur: Wikipedia/PD/USA/Harry Marriott Burton; **middle right**: Dom Francisco de Almeida: PD/Unknown; **bottom**: First Republic Day Parade: Wikipedia/ PD/Unknown author; **199**: **top**: Dr Zakir Hussain: PD--India/ National Museum Government of India; **middle left**: A. O. Hume/ Wikipedia/PD-old/A.O. Hume; **middle right**: J. L. Nehru: istockworld/Shutterstock.com; **bottom**: Chaudhary Charan Singh: Wikipedia/Government Open Data License - India (GODL); **200**: **middle left**: First general election: Wikipedia/Photo Division, Ministry of Information & Broadcasting, Government of India; **middle right**: Indelible ink: Rahul Sapra/Shutterstock.com; **bottom**: EVS and VVPAT: GEMINI PRO STUDIO/ Shutterstock.com; **201**: Voters with voter IDs: bodom/ Shutterstock; **202–203**: **background**: Hafiz Ahmed/Shutterstock.com; **insets**: **top**: PRIYA DARSHAN/Shutterstock.com; **bottom**: Daniel J. Rao/Shutterstock.com; **204–205**: **background**: PRIYA DARSHAN/Shutterstock.com; **insets**: Old woman after casting her vote: Talukdar David/Shutterstock; Vote counting: by courtesy of PIB; **207**: **top**: **from left to right**: Shankar Lalwani: Wikipedia/CCA-SA 4.0/Harsh Jain, Narendra Modi; **inset**: Exposure Visuals/Shutterstock.com; Nitish Kumar: PradeepGaurs/Shutterstock.com, Chandrababu Naidu: Saikat Paul/Shutterstock.com; **middle**: I.N.D.I. Alliance: PradeepGaurs/ Shutterstock.com; **bottom**: Election result on TV: PradeepGaurs/ Shutterstock.com; **208**: **middle left**: Dr S. Radhakrishnan: PD--USA/White House; **middle right**: Vijaya Lakshmi Pandit: CCA-SA 3.0 NL/Dutch National archives; **209**: **left to right**: PD--USA/ US Embassy New Delhi, Wikipedia/CCA-SA 2.0/Santosh Kumar Shukla, PD/Government of India work; **bottom**: Narendra Modi: YashSD/Shutterstock.com; **210**: MGR: Jayakumar/ Shutterstock.com; **211**: **top**: West Bengal-Bangladesh border: SHEE HENG CHONG/Shutterstock.com; **middle**: Panchayat office: Abhi photo studio/Shutterstock.com; **212**; **top**: Aadhar Seva Kendra: PradeepGaurs/Shutterstock.com; **middle**: Anant Parag Khadilkar: by courtesy of the record holder; **bottom**: Dog squad: Shutterstock.com; **213**. **top**: Tihar Jail: Paulose NK/ Shutterstock.com; **bottom left**: K. Prithika Yashini: by courtesy of Ashok Kumar; **bottom right**: Shambhunath Pandit: Public Domain--India/the Supreme Court of Bangladesh; **214**: **top**: ITLOS: nitpicker/Shutterstock.com; **middle**: Justice Leila Seth: CCA-SA 3.0/Nikhil Kanekal; **bottom**: SDGs: MD Foyshal Mahmud/Shutterstock.com; **215**: Dadabhai Naoroji: PD-old-70Wikimedia commons; **216**: **top**: Anubhav Mohanty: Subhashish Panigrahi (CC BY-SA 4.0); **middle**: Dr S. Muthulakshmi Reddy: Wikipedia/PD; **bottom**: Neelam Sanjiva Reddy: reddees/ Shutterstock.com; **217**: **background**: Vidhan Soudha: Lalam photography/Shutterstock.com;

DEFENCE AND MILITARY AFFAIRS 218–243

Opener pic, 218–219: Shutterstock.com; **220**: **top**: K.M. Cariappa: GODL–India/President's Secretariat; **bottom**: Bipin Rawat: GODL–India/PIB Photo Releases; **221**: **Clockwise, from top**: S.H.F.J. stamp: GODL–India/India Post; Preeti Rajak: ANI Photo; Army Service Corps logo: CC0 1.0 Universal Public Domain Dedication/Adiiitya; Sadhna Saxena: GODL–India/ Government of India; Dr Punita Arora: GODL–India/ADG (M&C) DPR (Ministry of Defence - India): **222**: **left**: Rajputana Rifles: PD–Art/The original uploader was Idleguy at English Wikipedia; **right**: Agni V: GODL–India/PIB; **223**: Zoji La War memorial: Abhisheklegit/Shutterstock.com; **224–225**: **background**: Siachen: Shutterstock.com; **226–227**: Soldier: Pixabay.com; **229**: **from top to bottom**: Military Intelligence Training School and Depot: GODL–India/Official Twitter Account of Army Training Command, Indian Army; High Altitude Warfare School: CCA-SA 3.0 Unported licence/Ali Lokhandwala/https://commons.wikimedia.org/wiki/File:Indian_Army_-_High_Altitude_Warfare_School_(_HAWS).jpg; Military Dog School: Photo by Anshuman Poyrekar/Hindustan Times; **230**: **from top to bottom**: Ram Dass Katari: GODL–India/Indian Navy; Samvid Gurukulam Girls Sainik School: by courtesy of PIB; Admiral A.K. Chatterji: GODL–India/ Indian Navy; **231**: **top left**: INS *Chakra*: PD–US/Unknown sailor or employee of U.S. Navy; **top right**: INS *Delhi*: GODL–India/ Indian Navy; **bottom**: Southern Naval Command logo: CCA 4.0 International License/Adiiitya/https://commons.wikimedia.org/wiki/File:Southern_Naval_Command_(India).png; **232**: INS *Arihant*: CCA-SA 3.0 Unported licence/Chanakyathegreat/ https://commons.wikimedia.org/wiki/File:Arihantgoingonpatrol.png; **234**: **top**: INS *Viraat*: PDUS/PH3 SHANNON E. RENFROE, USN; **middle**: INS *Nilgiri* stamp: GODL–India/India Post; **bottom left**: INS *Kora*: GODL–India/Indian Navy; **bottom right**: INS *Talwar*: PD–US: Mass Communication Specialist 3rd Class Cheyenne Geletka; **235**: **top**: INS *Aditya*: GODL–India/Ministry of Defence; **middle**: INS *Sarvekshak*: GODL–India/Ministry of Defence; **bottom**: *Varuna*: by courtesy of PIB; **236**: **top left**: Wadia group logo: Fair use/ KarimKoueider; **top right**: Arun Prakash: CCA-SA 3.0 Unported licence/Arun Prakash/https://commons.wikimedia.org/wiki/File:Arun_Prakash.jpg; **bottom**: Naval Dockyard stamp: GODL–India/Post of India; **237**: **top**: INSV *Tarini*: GODL–India/Indian Navy; **middle**: Subrato Mukherjee: PD–India; **bottom left**: INSV Mhadei: GODL–India/Indian Navy; **bottom right**: Air Warriors: GODL–India/India Post, Government

IMAGE COPYRIGHT INFORMATION

of India; **238**: **top**: S.K. Majumdar: CCA-SA 3.0 Unported licence/ https://en.wikipedia.org/wiki/User:DebashisM/DebashisM/ https://commons.wikimedia.org/wiki/File:Majumdars.jpg; **bottom**: Women combat Pilots: GODL–India/Ministry of Defence; **239**: **middle**: Tigers of the sky stamp: GODL–India/India Post; **bottom left**: 44 Squadron: CCA–SA 4.0 International License/ Vprajkumar/https://commons.wikimedia.org/wiki/File:44-IAF.png; **bottom right**: Westland Wapiti: PD–UK/Royal Air Force; **240**: **top**: HF–24 Marut: *Flickr's The Commons*/PD/San Diego Air and Space Museum at Flickr Commons/SDASM Archives/ https://www.flickr.com/photos/sdasmarchives/7585415268/in/photolist-cyieFS-cyieCL-ajYDjd-6Y25Ws-nVnBh-aVNVZD-dq6Uh1-aVNRki-J4gbQ-7MgNBW-uGRh25-tgVhpj-chdjbU-8Kd2yq-eiCxVF-h2xJoX-bszMrV-eecZ5A-4QAmCg-A5ySJU-dSZtQH; **bottom**: HAL Tejas: GODL–India/Ministry of Defence; **241**: **top**: HAL Ajeet: CCA–SA 4.0 International License/Ank Kumar/ https://commons.wikimedia.org/wiki/File:HAL_Ajeet_based_on_Folland_Gnat_Jet_at_HAL_Museum,_Bengaluru_(Ank_Kumar).jpg; **middle**: Rudram 1: GODL–India/Defence Decode; **bottom**: Boeing Apache Helicopter: CCA–SA 2.0 Generic license/ https://www.flickr.com/people/65001151@N03/Alan Wilson from Stilton, Peterborough, Cambs, UK/ https://commons.wikimedia.org/wiki/File:Boeing_AH-64DN_Apache_%E2%80%98Q-18%E2%80%99_(35435891001).jpg; **242**: ICGS *Sachet*: GODL–India/Indian Coast Guard; **243**: **clockwise, from top**: ICGS *Kuthar*: GODL–India/Indian Navy; Indian Coast Guard logo: CCA–SA 4.0 International License/https://commons.wikimedia.org/wiki/User:Sushant_savla/https://commons.wikimedia.org/wiki/File:Indian_Coast_Guard_Logo.svg; ICGS *Kirpan*: GODL–India/Indian Navy;

SCIENCE AND TECHNOLOGY 244–263

Opener pic, 244–245: vectorfusionart/Shutterstock.com; **246**: Wikipedia/CCA-SA 4.0/Ms Sarah Welch; **247**: Wikipedia/CCA-SA 4.0/Bhanuprakash13; **248**: **top**: Birla Planetorium: Arnav Pratap Singh/Shutterstock.com; **249**: Mount Abu Infrared Observatory: mdsharma/Shutterstock.com; **250–251**: **background**: Uranus: buradaki/Shutterstock.com; **252**: **top**: Pokhran: Hindustan Times; **middle**: Trombay, the site of India's first atomic reactor (Aspara): Wikipedia/PD/USA/National Security Agency; **bottom**: Optical fibre: asharkyu/Shutterstock.com; **253**: **top**: Tata Institute of Fundemental Research: KuMaR437/Shutterstock.com; **bottom left to right**: C.V. Raman: Wikipedia/PD/Sweden/Nobel Foundation; Homi Bhaba: CCA-SA 2.0/United Nations/New York; Satyendranath Bose: Wikipedia/PD/USA/Author unknown; **254**: **top**: Aditya, first tokamak: Shutterstock.com; **255**: **top**: Prafulla Chandra Ray: Wikipedia/PD-India/w.Prafulla Chandra Ray; **middle**: Dr Kalaiselvi N.: PIB; **bottom**: Presidency University: Wikipedia/GNU Free Documentation License v.1.2/Biswarup Ganguly; **256**: **bottom left**: Fossilized dinosaur eggs: CCA-SA 3.0/Unported Wikimedia/Sballal; **bottom right**: Pramatha Nath Bose: Wikipedia/PD-India; **257**: **top**: Andhra University: Wikipedia/CCA-SA 4.0/Andhra University; **middle left**: Antarctica: Mozgova/Shutterstock.com; **inset**: Sudipta Sengupta: by courtesy of Sudipta Sengupta; **middle right**: Polypeptide-P: Daolauong Kamkhom/Shutterstock.com; **258**: **top**: AIIMS: mrinalpal/Shutterstock.com, **middle**, Kolkata zoo gate: AnilD/Shutterstock.com; **bottom**: Dr Har Gobind Khorana: Wikipedia/PD-USA/National Institute of Health; **259**: **middle**: Samarendra Kumar Mitra/Wikipedia/CCA-SA 4.0/AlokeKumarBose; **bottom left**: ISI: Wikipedia/CCA-SA 4.0/Ravi Dwivedi; **bottom right**: Dr Raj Reddy: Wikimedia/CCA-SA 4.0/Debramtobin; **260**: **middle**: KSUM: by courtesy of Fablab Kerala & Kerala Start-up Mission; **bottom**: PARAM 10000: by courtesy of Centre for Development of Advanced Computing; **261**: **top**: Lothal: Shutterstock.com; **middle**: Wootz: GNU free documentation License (GFDL); **262**: **background**: PSLV: Harshit Srivastava S3/Shutterstock.com; **263**: **bottom**: Visvesvaraya Industrial and Technological Museum: Wikipedia/CCA-SA 4.0/Amanjosan2008;

MEDICAL SCIENCES 264–279

Opener pic, 264–265: Shutterstock.com; **266**: **top**: IVF under microscope: Shutterstock.com; **bottom left**: Akshayrana69, CC BY-SA 4.0 <https://creativecommons.org/licenses/by-sa/4.0>, via Wikimedia Commons; **267**: **top right**: Microscopic image of cancer cells: Shutterstock.com; **bottom**: Rajiv Gandhi Hospital: Vkraja, CC BY-SA 4.0 <https://creativecommons.org/licenses/by-sa/4.0>, via Wikimedia Commons; **268**: **top right**: Calcutta Medical College: Bratish Kar; **top left**: Homoeopathic medicine: Shutterstock.com; **bottom first**: Dr Rafiuddin Ahmed: Dr. Joji George, CC BY-SA 4.0 <https://creativecommons.org/licenses/by-sa/4.0>, via Wikimedia Commons; **bottom second**: Dr Mukesh Batra: Bollywood Hungama, CC BY 3.0 <https://creativecommons.org/licenses/by/3.0>, via Wikimedia Commons; **bottom right**: Apollo app: sdx15/Shutterstock.com; **269**: **top**: Sir Ganga Ram stamp: A. Marino/Shutterstock.com; **middle**: AIIMS New Delhi: Vishnoi M, CC BY-SA 4.0 <https://creativecommons.org/licenses/by-sa/4.0>, via Wikimedia Commons; **bottom**: Serum Institute: MudaCom/Shutterstock.com; **270**: **top**: Kadambini Ganguly: public domain, https://commons.wikimedia.org/wiki/File:Kadambini_Ganguly.jpg#file; **bottom**: Pandit Madhusudan Gupta: S. C. Belnos, Public domain, via Wikimedia Commons (COPYRIGHT EXPIRED); **271**: **top**: PGIMER Chandigarh: PradeepGaurs/Shutterstock.com; **bottom**: Christian Medical College: Lubap at English Wikipedia, CC BY 3.0 <https://creativecommons.org/licenses/by/3.0>, via Wikimedia Commons; **272**: **top left**: Statue of Sushruta: Anuja Mukhopadhyay/Shutterstock.com; **middle left**: VAT surgery: Cancer Research UK, CC BY-SA 4.0 <https://creativecommons.org/licenses/by-sa/4.0>, via Wikimedia Commons; **273**: **top**: Dr Naresh Trehan: World Economic Forum/CCA-SA 2.0 Generic (https://commons.wikimedia.org/wiki/File:Naresh_Trehan_at_the_World_Economic_Forum_on_India_2012.jpg); **bottom**: Cochlear implant: BruceBlaus, CC BY-SA 4.0 <https://creativecommons.org/licenses/by-sa/4.0>, via Wikimedia Commons; **274–275**: **background**: Shutterstock.com; **277**: Largest bone tumour: by the courtesy of the record holder; **278**: **top**: Longest blood clot: by the courtesy of the record holder; **bottom**: Largest adrenal cyst: by the courtesy of the record holder; **279**: **top right**: public domain, Press Information Bureau; **middle and bottom left**: by the courtesy of the record holder;

THE NATURAL WORLD 280–305

Opener pic, 280–281: Shutterstock.com; **282–283**: **top**: Himalayan range: Shutterstock.com; **282**: **bottom first**: Chilika lake: Shutterstock.com; **bottom second**: Thar desert: Shutterstock.com; **283**: **middle**: Majuli island: Shutterstock.com; **bottom**: Lonar crater: Shutterstock.com; **284**: **top**: Mawsynram:

Shutterstock.com; **bottom**: Barren island: Shutterstock.com; **285**: **top right**: W.H. Sleeman: public domain via Wikimedia Commons <http://www.1902encyclopedia.com/T/THU/william-henry-sleeman.jpg by Pahari Sahib>; **top left**: Blue whale: Shutterstock.com; **bottom right**: Asian elephant: Shutterstock.com; **bottom left**: Langur: Shuterstock.com; **286**: **special box**: **top**: Dolphin: Shutterstock.com; **top right inset**: Blackbuck: Shutterstock.com; **bottom right inset**: Dugong: Shutterstock.com; **bottom left**: Loris: Shutterstock.com; **bottom left**: Manatee: Shutterstock.com; **bottom right**: Rusty-spotted cat: Shutterstock.com; **287**: **top**: Snow leopard: Shutterstock.com; **bottom**: Flying fox: Shutterstock.com; **288**: **top**: Golden birdwing butterfly: Shutterstock.com; **middle**: Peregrine falcon: Shutterstock.com; **bottom left**: Sarus crane: Shutterstock.com; **bottom right**: Flamingo: Shutterstock.com; **289**: **top left**: Blue apollo butterfly: Shutterstock.com; **top right**: Bullfrog: Shutterstock.com; **bottom**: Chameleon: Shutterstock.com; **290–291**: **top**: Mugger crocodile: Shutterstock.com; **290**: **bottom**: Gliding gecko: Shutterstock.com; **291**: **bottom**: Reticulated python: Shutterstock.com; **292: left**: Snakes: <https://www.sciencedirect.com/science/article/pii/S2287884X24000955> Journal of Asia-Pacific Biodiversity (Article: A new long-snouted vine snake species in the genus Ahaetulla Link, 1807 (Colubridae: Chrysopeleinae) from India) CC BY-NC-ND 4.0 (Non Commercial-No Derivatives 4.0 International) License; **293**: **background**: Shutterstock.com; inset: Artist Nadia Russ/Shutterstock.com; **294**: **middle**: Indian Star tortoise: Shutterstock.com; **bottom**: Olive Ridley turtles: Biswanath Swain/Shutterstock.com; **295**: **top left**: Dwarf pygmy goby fish: Shutterstock.com; **top right**: Banyan tree: Shutterstock.com; **bottom**: Seahorse: Shutterstock.com; **296**: palm tree: Shutterstock.com; **295**: **bottom left**: Rhubarb: Shutterstock.com; **bottom right**: Arignar Anna Zoological Park: Albin Raj/Shutterstock.com; **298**: Kosi river at Jim Corbett: Shutterstock.com; **299**: **top and bottom**: by courtesy of the record holders; **300**: **top**: Khonoma village: Shutterstock.com; **bottom**: Shore temple: CCA-SA 4.0 International/Swarna1311 (https://commons.wikimedia.org/wiki/File:Shore_Temple_-Mamallapuram_-Tamil_Nadu_-N-TN-C55.jpg); **302–303**: **background**: Shutterstock.com; **304**: Eiffel tower replica: Shutterstock.com; **305**: Indore: PradeepGaurs/Shutterstock.com;

TRANSPORT 306–323

Opener pic 306–307: Jimmy Kamballur/Shutterstock.com; **308**: **top left**: D.H. Puss Moth: User:MilborneOne, CC BY-SA 3.0 <http://creativecommons.org/licenses/by-sa/3.0/>, via Wikimedia Commons; **top right**: Arpingstone, Public domain, via Wikimedia Commons; **309**: **top**: IT Outage: Nicolas Economou/Shutterstock.com; **middle**: Hindustan Trainer 2: Dsrivallabha, CC BY-SA 3.0 <https://creativecommons.org/licenses/by-sa/3.0>, via Wikimedia Commons; **bottom**: Boeing 707 Gauri Shankar: Steve Fitzgerald (GFDL 1.2 <http://www.gnu.org/licenses/old-licenses/fdl-1.2.html> or GFDL 1.2 <http://www.gnu.org/licenses/old-licenses/fdl-1.2.html>), via Wikimedia Commons; **310**: **top**: Kushok Bakula Rimpochee Airport: Rangeecha/Shutterstock.com; **bottom**: Cochin International Airport: PREJU SURESH/Shutterstock.com; **311**: ICAO headquarters: Henrickson at English Wikipedia, CC BY-SA 3.0 <https://creativecommons.org/licenses/by-sa/3.0>, via Wikimedia Commons; **312**: **top**: Indigo three-point disembarkation: Rudra Narayan Mitra/Shutterstock.com; **middle**: East-Indian Railways Plaque: Goutam1962, CC BY-SA 4.0 <https://creativecommons.org/licenses/by-sa/4.0>, via Wikimedia Commons; **bottom**: Victoria Terminus: Ajay Gajanan Bhise/Shutterstock.com; **314**: **middle**: Flying Ranee promotional poster: Western Railway, Public domain, via Wikimedia Commons; **bottom**: Suyash Dwivedi, CC BY-SA 4.0 <https://creativecommons.org/licenses/by-sa/4.0>, via Wikimedia Commons; **315**: **top**: Kolkata Tram: ParthaKar49/Shutterstock.com; Kanpur Central railway station: KpinfomediaIndia, CC BY-SA 4.0 <https://creativecommons.org/licenses/by-sa/4.0>, via Wikimedia Commons; **316**: **top**: Fairy Queen engine: Santulan Mahanta from Golaghat (GLGT), Guwahati (GHY), Lucknow (LKO), New Delhi (NDLS), INDIA, CC BY 2.0 <https://creativecommons.org/licenses/by/2.0>, via Wikimedia Commons; **middle**: Tejas Express: Ministry of Railways (GODL–India), GODL–India <https://data.gov.in/sites/default/files/Gazette_Notification_OGDL.pdf>, via Wikimedia Commons; **bottom**: Guwahati Railway Station: David/Shutterstock.com; **317**: **top**: Underwater Metro: Metro Railway, Kolkata (GODL-India), GODL-India <https://data.gov.in/sites/default/files/Gazette_Notification_OGDL.pdf>, via Wikimedia Commons; **middle**: NSR bus: Unknown sourceUnknown source, Public domain, via Wikimedia Commons; **318**: **top right**: REVAi car: RevaNorge, CC BY-SA 2.0 <https://creativecommons.org/licenses/by-sa/2.0>, via Wikimedia Commons; **top left**: NCMC card: Sriram2019, CC BY-SA 4.0 <https://creativecommons.org/licenses/by-sa/4.0>, via Wikimedia Commons; **bottom**: De Dion Bouton: ronald ian smiles/Shutterstock.com; **319**: **top**: Kona Electric: haryanta.p/Shutterstock.com; TangLang La: Foto2rich/Shutterstock.com; **320**: **background**: Alan Walker2004/Shutterstock.com; **top**: Ganga Waterway: Yercaud-elango, CC BY-SA 4.0 <https://creativecommons.org/licenses/by-sa/4.0>, via Wikimedia Commons; **middle**: Brahmaputra river: simantaKphotos/Shutterstock.com; **bottom**: West-Coast canal: Robert Harding Video/Shutterstock.com; **322**: **top**: Haldia Port: IVAN KUZKIN/Shutterstock.com; **middle**: HMS Trincomalee: Ian Petticrew, CC BY-SA 2.0 <https://creativecommons.org/licenses/by-sa/2.0>, via Wikimedia Commons; **bottom**: MV Ganga Vilas: by courtesy of Antara Cruises;

BUSINESS AND ECONOMY 324–345

Opener pic, 324–325: Sutthiphong Chandaeng/Shutterstock.com; **326**: **top left**: P.C Mahalanobis: Wikipedia/Fair use/KR Bharath; **top right**: R.K Shanmukhan Shetty: Wikipedia Commons/Public domain; **middle left**: Wikipedia/government open data licence-India (GODL); **middle right**: by courtesy of PIB; **bottom left**: Arthashastra: Sumit Kherde/Shutterstock.com; **bottom right**: C. D. Deshmukh: PD–India/Photo Division, Government of India; **327**: **top**: GST Bhavan: Picxy.com/pixelmaster; **bottom**: Rail Bhawan: Arnav Pratap Singh/Shutterstock.com; **328**: **top**: Kushana coins: CCA-SA 3.0, World Imaging; **middle**: Vima Kadphises coin: CCA-SA 3.0/Classical Numismatic Group, Inc. http://cngcoins.com; **bottom left**: J. R. D. Tata: PD/http://photodivision.gov.in; **bottom right**: Coins for visually impaired: by courtesy of PM India website; **329**: NABARD: sravants/Shutterstock.com; **330–331**: **background**: Arnav Pratap Singh/Shutterstock.com; NPCI: WESTOCK PRODUCTIONS/Shutterstock.com; BHIM: Funstock/Shutterstock.com; RuPay: T. Schneider/Shutterstock.com; UPI APP: LALAKA/Shutterstock.com; **332**: State Bank of India, London branch: Roberto La Rosa/

IMAGE COPYRIGHT INFORMATION

Shutterstock.com; **333**: **top**: LIC: CCA-SA 3.0/Nitine; **bottom**: Tata Iron and Steel Company Ltd: Image Credit: Picxy.com/ Sauravmahtos; **334**: **background**: Who is Danny/ Shutterstock.com; **inset**, Naina Lal Kidwai: CCA-SA 3.0/Nitine; **335**: **middle**: Tarapur Atomic plant: GODL – India/Department of Atomic Energy; **bottom**: NTPC: mrinalpal/Shutterstock.com; **336–337**: **background**: pixxelstudio91/Shutterstock.com; **top**: Pranjal Srivastava7/Shutterstock.com; **bottom**: Rajabai Clock Tower: CCA-SA 3.0/Nikkul at English Wikipedia; NSE: R.M. Nunes/Shutterstock.com; **338**: **top**: Vindhyachal Super Thermal Power Station: CCA-SA 4.0/Jayadevp13; **bottom left**: Digboi refinery: Shutterstock.com; **bottom right**: Reliance Gas: Picxy.com/neeraz.chaturvedi; **339**: **top**: Bharat Petroleum: George Trumpeter/Shutterstock.com; **bottom**: Coal Bhawan: The Captured Creations/Shutterstock.com; **340**: Gold from mine: domnitsky/Shutterstock.com; **341**: ITC head office: Srishti Sarkar; **342**: **top**: Jessop Building: CCA 3.0/Biswarup Ganguly; **bottom**: Microchip: HAKINMHAN/Shutterstock.com; **343**: **bottom**: Shop selling spices and nuts at Khari Baoli: CCA-SA 2.0/Michael Vito; **344**: **top**: Cannes Grand Prix: Getty Images@Cannes Lions, by courtesy of Cannes Lions; **bottom**: Horlicks: Godai Das/Shutterstock.com; **345**: **background**: G20: Svet foto/Shutterstock.com; **inset**: G20: PradeepGaurs/Shutterstock.com;

ADVENTURE 346–371

Opener Pic, 346–347: Rick Neves/Shutterstock.com; **348**: **top**: Rachel Thomas: courtesy of Record Holder **middle**: BASE jump: Flying Pig Studios/Shutterstock.com; **bottom**: Ravinder Bansal: Ravinder Bansal, CC BY-SA 4.0 <https://creativecommons.org/licenses/by-sa/4.0>, via Wikimedia Commons; **349**: **top**: MiG-29 Fighter Jet: Artem Katranzhi from Bakashikha, Russia, CC BY-SA 2.0 <https://creativecommons.org/licenses/by-sa/2.0>, via Wikimedia Commons; **bottom**: Parade of Corps of Signals: Ministry of Defence (GODL–India), GODL-India <https://data.gov.in/sites/default/files/Gazette_Notification_OGDL.pdf>, via Wikimedia Commons; **350**: **middle**: Major DP Singh: Amit Vermaz, CC BY-SA 4.0 <https://creativecommons.org/licenses/by-sa/4.0>, via Wikimedia Commons; **bottom left**: Vijay Kumar Devarkhyani: courtesy of record holder; **bottom right**: Tandem Skydiving: Kells Photos/Shutterstock.com; **351**: **background**: free image from pixabay.com; **352**: **top**: Eric Paul: courtesy of Record Holder; **bottom**: Fastest GQ expedition – women: courtesy of Record Holder; **353**: Daljit Singh Matharoo: courtesy of Record Holder; **354**: **top**: Sagar Thakar and Kanak Barsadia: courtesy of Record Holder; **bottom**: Hitendra Sharma: courtesy of Record Holder; **355**: **top**: Khardung La: batsac/Shutterstock.com; **middle**: Vishvesh Dhirendrakumar Mehta: courtesy of Record Holder; **bottom**: Prashant Kumar: courtesy of Record Holder; **356**: **top**: Pallavi Fauzdar: courtesy of Record Holder; **bottom**: Akhil Bharatiya Terapanth Mahila Mandal: courtesy of Record Holder; **357**: Satabdi Dhar and Himanshu Sirohi: courtesy of Record Holder; **358–359**: **background**: Largest moving pyramid: courtesy of Record Holder; **360**: **top**: Ela Ghose: courtesy of Record Holder; **middle**: Saurabh Bharat Zagade: courtesy of Record Holder; **361**: **top left**: Monocycle: Tricky_Shark/Shutterstock.com; **top right**: INS Trishna: Ajai Singh, CC BY-SA 2.0 <https://creativecommons.org/licenses/by-sa/2.0>, via Wikimedia Commons; **bottom**: Beas: Amit kg/Shutterstock.com; **362**: Rohan Dattatrey More: courtesy of Record Holder; **363**: **top**: Gibraltar Strait: Lukas Hodon/Shutterstock.com; **bottom**: Ganga River: NG Shutterbug/Shutterstock.com; **364**: **bottom left**: stand-up paddleboarding: ninaveter/Shutterstock.com; **bottom right**: Kayaking: Mark Swaroop/Shutterstock.com; **365**: **top**: windsurfing: Daria Krav/Shutterstock.com; **bottom**: Deepa Malik: President's Secretariat (GODL-India), GODL-India <https://data.gov.in/sites/default/files/Gazette_Notification_OGDL.pdf>, via Wikimedia Commons; **366–367**: **background**: suresh Gavali/ Shutterstock.com; **top and bottom**: by courtesy of the record holders; **368**: **top**: Fauja Singh: Mithrandirthewise at en.wikipedia, Public domain, via Wikimedia Commons; **middle**: Adil Nargolwala: courtesy of Record Holder; **bottom**: Brij Mojan Sharma: courtesy of Record Holder; **369**: **top**: Praveen Kumar: courtesy of Record Holder; **bottom**: Satyarup Sidhanta: courtesy of Record Holder; **370**: Bachendri Pal: President's Secretariat (GODL-India), CC BY-SA 4.0 <https://creativecommons.org/licenses/by-sa/4.0>, via Wikimedia Commons; **middle**: Ankur Bahl: courtesy of Record Holder; **bottom**: Snowman Trek route: Rik2608, CC BY-SA 4.0 <https://creativecommons.org/licenses/by-sa/4.0>, via Wikimedia Commons; **371**: Deepa Bajaj and Ajeet Bajaj: courtesy of Record Holder;

SPORTS 372–451

Opener pic, 372–373: Shutterstock.com; **374**: **top right**: Dara Singh: Camaal Fotografia, CC BY-SA 4.0 <https://creativecommons.org/licenses/by-sa/4.0>, via Wikimedia Commons; **middle**: Balbir Singh Sr: Balbir Singh (Senior), Public domain, via Wikimedia Commons; **bottom first**: Praful Patel: World Economic Forum, CC BY-SA 2.0 <https://creativecommons.org/licenses/by-sa/2.0>, via Wikimedia Commons; **bottom second**: Priya Ranjan Dasmusi: Government Open Data License–India(GODL)/Ministry of Information and Broadcasting; **375**: **top right**: C.A. Bhavani Devi: CCA 3.0 ©Marie-Lan Nguyen/Wikimedia Commons; **middle**: Olympic Order: Pistaun, CC BY-SA 4.0 <https://creativecommons.org/licenses/by-sa/4.0>, via Wikimedia Commons; **bottom**: Commonwealth Games stamp: rook76/Shutterstock.com; **376–377**: **background**: Shutterstock.com; **378**: **top right**: Deepika Kumari: CCA-SA 3.0 Unported/Rajivranprasad; **middle first**: M.C. Mary Kom: Sudarshan Jha/Shutterstock.com; **middle second**: Pullela Gopichand: reddees/Shutterstock.com; **bottom**: Sheetal Devi: Press Information Bureau, CC BY-SA 4.0 <https://creativecommons.org/licenses/by-sa/4.0>, via Wikimedia Commons; **379**: **top**: Harvinder Singh: Prime Minister's Office (GODL-India), GODL–India <https://data.gov.in/sites/default/files/Gazette_Notification_OGDL.pdf>, via Wikimedia Commons; **middle**: Jayanta Talukdar: Government Open Data License–India(GODL)/President's Secretariat; **bottom**: Abhishek Verma: Government Open Data License–India(GODL)/President's Secretariat; **380**: **top first**: Dola Banerjee: Luis Felipe Paulinyi, Public domain, via Wikimedia Commons; **top second**: Rahul Banerjee: President's Secretariat (GODL-India), GODL-India <https://data.gov.in/sites/default/files/Gazette_Notification_OGDL.pdf>, via Wikimedia Commons; **bottom**: Jyothi Surekha Vennam: President's Secretariat (GODL-India), GODL-India <https://data.gov.in/sites/default/files/Gazette_Notification_OGDL.pdf>, via Wikimedia Commons; **381**: **top**: Milkha Singh: Sanyam Bahga, CC BY-SA 3.0 <https://creativecommons.org/licenses/by-sa/3.0>, via Wikimedia Commons; **bottom**: P.T. Usha: Ministry of Youth Affairs and Sports (GODL-India), GODL-India

<https://data.gov.in/sites/default/files/Gazette_Notification_OGDL.pdf>, via Wikimedia Commons; **382**: **top**: Anju Bobby George: CCA-SA 4.0 International/Jyothishvijay; **bottom**: Hima Das: Denis Kuvaev/Shutterstock.com; **383**: **top**: Neeraj Chopra: DD News, CC BY 4.0 <https://creativecommons.org/licenses/by/4.0>, via Wikimedia Commons; **bottom**: Shiny Wilson: Ministry of Information & Broadcasting (GODL-India), GODL-India <https://data.gov.in/sites/default/files/Gazette_Notification_OGDL.pdf>, via Wikimedia Commons; **384**: **top left**: Dutee Chand: Athletics Federation of India, CC BY-SA 4.0 <https://creativecommons.org/licenses/by-sa/4.0>, via Wikimedia Commons; **top right**: Deepa Malik: Government Open Data License–India(GODL)/Prime Minister's Office, Government of India; **bottom**: Avinash Sable: U.S. Army, CC BY 2.0 <https://creativecommons.org/licenses/by/2.0>, via Wikimedia Commons; **385**: P.V. Sindhu: Shutterstock.com; **386**: **top**: Jwala Gutta and Ashwini Ponnappa: Government Open Data License–India(GODL)/Ministry of Youth Affairs and Sports; **middle first**: Saina Nehwal: CCA-SA 3.0 Unported/Bollywood Hungama; **middle second**: K. Srikanth: Wikimedia Commons/Fair Use/Pierre-Yves Beaudouin; **bottom**: P.V. Sindhu: Government Open Data License–India(GODL)/Prime Minister's Office; **387**: **top**: Prakash Padukone: CCA-SA 3.0 Unported/Mussarat Kang; **bottom**: Dinesh Khanna: CCA-SA 4.0 International/Vkg wifi; **388**: Thomas Cup: kreasitekmedia/Shutterstock.com; **389**: **top**: Satnam Singh Bhamara: All Elite Wrestling, CC BY-SA 4.0 <https://creativecommons.org/licenses/by-sa/4.0>, via Wikimedia Commons; **middle**: Prashanti Singh: CCA-SA 3.0 Unported/Risingprincess; **bottom**: Aparna Popat: Government Open Data License–India(GODL)/President's Secretariat; **390**: **top**: Chirag Shetty and Satwiksairaj Rankireddy: ryanko/Shutterstock.com; **bottom**: Vijendra Singh: Bollywood Hungama, CC BY 3.0 <https://creativecommons.org/licenses/by/3.0>, via Wikimedia Commons; **391**: **top**: Amandeep Singh: Ministry of Youth Affairs and Sports (GODL-India), GODL-India <https://data.gov.in/sites/default/files/Gazette_Notification_OGDL.pdf>, via Wikimedia Commons; **bottom**: Antim Panghal: Prime Minister's Office (GODL-India), GODL-India <https://data.gov.in/sites/default/files/Gazette_Notification_OGDL.pdf>, via Wikimedia Commons; **392**: AIBA stamp: Pavel Kapysh/Shutterstock.com; **393**: Viswanathan Anand: Wolfgang Jekel, CC BY 2.0 <https://creativecommons.org/licenses/by/2.0>, via Wikimedia Commons; **394**: Pravin Thipsay: CCA-SA 4.0 International/Swaralithipsay; **395**: **bottom left**: D. Gukesh: CC BY-SA 2.0 Generic/Frans Peeters; **bottom right**: R. Praggnanandhaa: CC BY-SA 2.0 Generic/Frans Peeters; **396**: K. Humpy: Government Open Data License–India(GODL)/President's Secretariat; **397**: **left**: D. Harika: Artsmith.concepts, CC BY-SA 4.0 <https://creativecommons.org/licenses/by-sa/4.0>, via Wikimedia Commons; **right**: Shafali Verma: CCA-SA 4.0 International/Bahnfrend; **398**: **top right**: Smriti Mandhana: Ministry of Youth Affairs and Sports (GODL-India), GODL-India <https://data.gov.in/sites/default/files/Gazette_Notification_OGDL.pdf>, via Wikimedia Commons; **middle**: Mithali Raj: CCA-SA 3.0 Unported/Sadhguru (https://www.youtube.com/watch?v= KJF5C00BSRY); **bottom**: Jhulan Goswami: paddynapper, CC BY-SA 2.0 <https://creativecommons.org/licenses/by-sa/2.0>, via Wikimedia Commons; **399**: **top**: Sunil Gavaskar: Bollywood Hungama, CC BY 3.0 <https://creativecommons.org/licenses/by/3.0>, via Wikimedia Commons; **bottom**: Harmanpreet Kaur: CCA-SA 4.0 International/Bahnfrend; **400–401**: **background**: vikas shrivastav/Shutterstock.com; **401**: Rohit Sharma: Prime Minister's Office (GODL-India), GODL-India <https://data.gov.in/sites/default/files/Gazette_Notification_OGDL.pdf>, via Wikimedia Commons; **402**: **top right**: Anil Kumble: CCA-SA 3.0 Unported/lensbug.chandru; **middle**: Rahul Dravid: Chubby Chandru, CC BY 2.0 <https://creativecommons.org/licenses/by/2.0>, via Wikimedia Commons; **bottom**: Virendra Sehwag: Flying Cloud, CC BY 2.0 <https://creativecommons.org/licenses/by/2.0>, via Wikimedia Commons; **403**: Sachin Tendulkar: PIXATHON/Shutterstock.com; **404**: **top left**: Yuvraj Singh: Chubby Chandru, CC BY 2.0 <https://creativecommons.org/licenses/by/2.0>, via Wikimedia Commons; **top right**: MSD: Suhail Suri/Shutterstock.com; **bottom**: Virat Kohli: lensbug.chandru, CC BY 2.0 <https://creativecommons.org/licenses/by/2.0>, via Wikimedia Commons; **405**: **top**: Pankaj Advani: Benutzer:Bill da Flute, CC BY-SA 3.0 <https://creativecommons.org/licenses/by-sa/3.0>, via Wikimedia Commons; **middle**: R. Umadevi: Government Open Data License–India(GODL)/Ministry of Women and Child Development; **bottom**: Geet Sethi: President's Secretariat, GODL-India <https://data.gov.in/sites/default/files/Gazette_Notification_OGDL.pdf>, via Wikimedia Commons; **406**: Aditya Mehta: Martin Rulsch, Wikimedia Commons, CC BY-SA 4.0, CC BY-SA 4.0 <https://creativecommons.org/licenses/by-sa/4.0>, via Wikimedia Commons; **407**: **top left**: Bhupendra Nath Bose: The Modern Review. January 1912, Public domain, via Wikimedia Commons; **middle right**: S.A. Rahim: Wikimedia Commons/Fair Use/The Hindu; **middle left**: Syed Nayeemuddin: CCA-SA 3.0 Unported/Biswarup Ganguly; **bottom**: Baichung Bhutia: CCA-SA 3.0 Unported/Baichung Bhutia; **408–409**: **background**: daykung/Shutterstock.com; **409**: Sunil Chhetri: Young Nova/Shutterstock.com; **410**: Inder Singh: CCA-SA 4.0 International/Vickrem3; **411**: **top**: Bartholomew Ogbeche: CCA-SA 4.0 International/Rufyrosh; **bottom**: Ferran Corominas: Sahil200034, CC BY-SA 4.0 <https://creativecommons.org/licenses/by-sa/4.0>, via Wikimedia Commons; **412**: **left**: Chuni Goswami: Wikimedia Commons/Fair Use/Vidmarp; **right**: Wikimedia Commons/Fair Use/Unknown Author; **413**: **top**: S. Chikkarangappa: Surajlnswamy, CC BY-SA 4.0 <https://creativecommons.org/licenses/by-sa/4.0>, via Wikimedia Commons; **bottom**: Jyoti Randhawa: CCA-SA 3.0 Unported/Pvt Pauline; **414**: **top**: Jeev Milkha Singh: mooinblack/Shutterstock.com; **middle**: Rashid Khan: Yu Chun Christopher Wong/Shutterstock.com; **bottom**: Arjun Atwal: CC BY-SA 2.0 Generic/Keith Allison; **415**: Aditi Ashok: CHEN WS/Shutterstock.com; **416**: **top**: Anirban Lahiri: CCA-SA 4.0 International/Punishar; **middle**: S.S.P. Chawrasia: CCA-SA 3.0 Unported/Pvt Pauline; **bottom**: Kapil Dev: Bollywood Hungama, CC BY 3.0 <https://creativecommons.org/licenses/by/3.0>, via Wikimedia Commons; **417**: **top**: Shubhankar Sharma: Yu Chun Christopher Wong/Shutterstock.com; **bottom**: Dipa Karmakar: Ministry for Development of North-East Region (GODL-India), GODL-India <https://data.gov.in/sites/default/files/Gazette_Notification_OGDL.pdf>, via Wikimedia Commons; **418**: **top**: Dilip Tirkey: Government Open Data License–India (GODL/Ministry of Youth Affairs and Sports; **bottom**: P.R. Sreejesh: Joe Pengkalan/Shutterstock.com; **inset**: Prime Minister's Office (GODL-India), GODL-India <https://data.gov.in/sites/default/files/Gazette_Notification_OGDL.pdf>, via Wikimedia Commons; **420**: Dhyan Chand: Wikimedia Commons/Fair Use/Faizhaider; **421**: **top**: Vandana Katariya: Prime Minister's Office (GODL-India), GODL-India <https://data.gov.in/sites/default/files/Gazette_

IMAGE COPYRIGHT INFORMATION

Notification_OGDL.pdf>, via Wikimedia Commons; **bottom**: Richard J. Allen: Wikimedia Commons/Fair Use/Unknown author; **422**: **top**: Pro Kabaddi: ARTDOWN/Shutterstock.com; **bottom**: Pawan Sehrawat: President's Secretariat (GODL-India), GODL-India <https://data.gov.in/sites/default/files/Gazette_Notification_OGDL.pdf>, via Wikimedia Commons; **423**: **top right**: Sushila Devi: Prime Minister's Office (GODL-India), GODL-India <https://data.gov.in/sites/default/files/Gazette_Notification_OGDL.pdf>, via Wikimedia Commons; **middle**: Shiva Keshavan: Sandro Halank, Wikimedia Commons, CC-BY-SA 3.0, CC BY-SA 3.0 <https://creativecommons.org/licenses/by-sa/3.0>, via Wikimedia Commons; **bottom**: Pooja Kadian: Government Open Data License–India(GODL)/President's Secretariat; **424**: **top**: Abhinav Bindra: Open Government Licence version 1.0/British High Commission, India; **middle**: Farman Basha: CCA-SA 3.0 Unported/Laura Hale; **bottom**: Mairaj Ahmad Khan: CCA SA 2.0 Generic/U.S. Army; **425**: **top left**: Rahi Sarnobat: President's Secretariat (GODL-India), GODL-India <https://data.gov.in/sites/default/files/Gazette_Notification_OGDL.pdf>, via Wikimedia Commons; **middle right**: Jaspal Rana: Government Open Data License–India(GODL/Ministry of Petroleum and Natural Gas; **bottom**: Rajyavardhan Singh Rathore: Ministry of Youth Affairs and Sports (GODL-India), GODL-India <https://data.gov.in/sites/default/files/Gazette_Notification_OGDL.pdf>, via Wikimedia Commons; **426**: Ronjan Sodhi: Government Open Data License–India(GODL)/President's Secretariat; **427**: **top**: Gagan Narang: Ministry of Youth Affairs and Sports (GODL-India), GODL-India <https://data.gov.in/sites/default/files/Gazette_Notification_OGDL.pdf>, via Wikimedia Commons; **bottom**: Akhil Sheoran: Ranjith_july/Shutterstock.com; **428**: **top right**: Dipika Pallikal: julesgriff from Burlington, CT, USA, CC BY-SA 2.0 <https://creativecommons.org/licenses/by-sa/2.0>, via Wikimedia Commons; **bottom**: Joshna Chinappa: CC BY-SA 2.0 Generic/Simitha T.Singam; **429**: **right**: Bhuvaneshwari Kumari: CCA-SA 4.0 International/Tpsn98290; **left**: Saurav Ghoshal: Caravanum, CC BY-SA 2.0 <https://creativecommons.org/licenses/by-sa/2.0>, via Wikimedia Commons; **430**: **top**: Shikha Tandon: Government Open Data License–India(GODL)/President's Secretariat; **bottom**: Pratham Books from India, CC BY 2.0 <https://creativecommons.org/licenses/by/2.0>, via Wikimedia Commons; **431**: Sajan Prakash: Ministry of Youth Affairs and Sports (GODL-India), GODL-India <https://data.gov.in/sites/default/files/Gazette_Notification_OGDL.pdf>, via Wikimedia Commons; **432**: **top**: A. Sharath Kamal: Government Open Data License–India(GODL/Ministry of Youth Affairs and Sports; **bottom**: Harmeet Desai: CC BY-SA 2.0 Generic/XIAOYU TANG; **433**: **top**: Manika Batra: Government of Odisha, CC BY 4.0 <https://creativecommons.org/licenses/by/4.0>, via Wikimedia Commons; **bottom**: Mouma Das: Ministry of Youth Affairs and Sports (GODL-India), GODL-India <https://data.gov.in/sites/default/files/Gazette_Notification_OGDL.pdf>, via Wikimedia Commons; **434**: Karman Kaur Thandi: CC BY-SA 2.0 Generic/si.robi; **435**: **top left**: Somdev Devvarman: CCA-SA 3.0 Unported/Photo by DAVID ILIFF; **bottom right**: Leander Paes: Romain Biard/Shutterstock.com; **436**: **left**: Leander Paes and Mahesh Bhupathi: Public domain, via Wikimedia Commons; **right**: Sania Mirza: BUGNUT23/Shutterstock.com; **437**: **top**: Rohan Bopanna: Wikimedia CC BY-SA 2.0 Generic/si.robi; **bottom**: Yuki Bhambri: CC BY-SA 2.0 Generic/si.robi; **438**: **top right**: Saikhom Mirabai Chanu: Government Open Data License–India(GODL/Ministry of Youth Affairs and Sports); **top left**: Karnam Malleswari: Government of India, GODL-India <https://data.gov.in/sites/default/files/Gazette_Notification_OGDL.pdf>, via Wikimedia Commons; **bottom**: Jeremy Lalrinnunga: cc-by-sa 3.0 © Marcus Cyron, CC BY-SA 3.0 <https://creativecommons.org/licenses/by-sa/3.0>, via Wikimedia Commons; **439**: Yumnam Renu: Government Open Data License–India(GODL)/President's Secretariat; **440**: Vinesh Phogat: Azamat Mukanov/Shutterstock.com; **441**: Bajrang Punia: Azamat Mukanov/Shutterstock.com; **442**: **top**: Deepak Punia: Zandersyn, CC BY-SA 4.0 <https://creativecommons.org/licenses/by-sa/4.0>, via Wikimedia Commons; **bottom**: Anita Sheoran: Prime Minister's Office (GODL-India), GODL-India <https://data.gov.in/sites/default/files/Gazette_Notification_OGDL.pdf>, via Wikimedia Commons; **443**: Sushil Kumar: Ten Sports, CC BY 3.0 <https://creativecommons.org/licenses/by/3.0>, via Wikimedia Commons; **bottom**: D. Gukesh: Frans Peeters, CC BY-SA 2.0 <https://creativecommons.org/licenses/by-sa/2.0>, via Wikimedia Commons; **444–445**: **background**: Grindstone Media Group/Shutterstock.com; **446**: **top**: Aman Sehrawat: Prime Minister's Office (GODL-India), GODL-India <https://data.gov.in/sites/default/files/Gazette_Notification_OGDL.pdf>, via Wikimedia Commons; **bottom**: Manu Bhaker and Sarabjot Singh: ProPhoto1234/Shutterstock.com; **447**: Prime Minister's Office (GODL-India), GODL-India <https://data.gov.in/sites/default/files/Gazette_Notification_OGDL.pdf>, via Wikimedia Commons; **448–449**: **background**: Netrun78/Shutterstock.com; **right**: Avani Lekhara: President's Secretariat (GODL-India), GODL-India <https://data.gov.in/sites/default/files/Gazette_Notification_OGDL.pdf>, via Wikimedia Commons; **451**: public domain via PIB <https://static.pib.gov.in/WriteReadData/Gallery/PhotoGallery/2024/Sep/T20240912166184.JPG>.

PREAMBLE

Limca Book of Records ('LBR'), as a record-keeping publication, has been compiling records since 1987 and has seen over 30 editions. It is India's first and longest continuously published book of records.

It is, however, a private book, run and managed by a private organization with no public funding whatsoever. The retail price is also subsidized by the owner Coca-Cola India Private Limited ('CCIPL'). The *LBR* also accepts absolutely no funding or payment or any other charges from record applicants or record holders for entries or for claims processing or for publication acceptance.

Consequently, it is important to understand that all decisions are taken by applying a set of standards that are specific and stringent, but equally are subjective, and based on what the editors and staff of *LBR*, and Consultants ('*LBR* Team') think are most suitable for the book. And that decision is solely *LBR*'s, and *LBR* is not answerable to or the decision is not affected by any other individual, entity, or by what another entity (including other record books), may do or accept.

I. INTRODUCTION

1. *LBR* is a catalogue of achievements made by Indians. It catalogues unique milestones and landmarks including, but not limited to, firsts, bests, mosts, inventions, discoveries, and honours and awards received by Indians at home or abroad in all fields – both human and natural – that can be qualified in superlatives and that conform to the prevailing editorial policy in force during any year.

While this is primarily a catalogue of superlatives and achievements, it is also a book of records, and a work of reference, and therefore in the spirit of empirical record keeping, it will record other milestones that may not always be celebratory or laudatory and may even be negative but are notable and are records, such as 'longest trial in a court of law' or records pertaining to disasters or crime. Any such record is a statement of fact on record, and is not meant to downplay any entity, nor encourage anyone to attempt to beat such records. *LBR* does not solicit or accept claims for negative records.

LBR encompasses an extensive range of information and is thus divided into chapters and record categories. Prospective entries under these chapters and categories may include, but are not limited to, any of the following headings: a record, a quantifiable skill, a superlative or historical landmark/phenomenon/man-made or natural event/process/structure considered as remarkable as a record by the *LBR* Team

2. Anyone with a reasonable claim for a record may write to *LBR* for possible inclusion (subject to acceptance under *LBR* criteria).

3. Entry into *LBR* and attempt of any record are subject to compliance with the general Terms and Conditions (the 'Terms') as well as the specific rules and guidelines applicable to each type of record attempt or claim (the 'Attempt'). Where pre-existing terms are not there to cover a particular record or claim, a relevant policy shall be decided by the *LBR* Team and that shall be binding. Earlier policies and parameters go under continuous review and modifications, and the *LBR* Team is not bound to any previously existing parameters.

4. Individuals or groups interested in attempting to set or break a record must understand and accept *LBR*'s general policy, study the Terms and the specific Rules and Guidelines applicable to the Attempt, and sign the Disclaimer and Indemnity Form (available before the commencement of any Attempt) in order to be considered for inclusion in *LBR*. Records already set and sent for inclusion ex post facto are also bound by all these Rules and Guidelines; acceptance of all Terms and Conditions is a necessary qualifier to any record being accepted.

5. All Terms, Rules, and Guidelines apply to a person/persons making a record Attempt ('Applicant'/'Applicants') who send an Application(s) to *LBR* as well as any and every person/persons ('Participant'/'Participants') part of such an Attempt (for example, in an Attempt by a group or organization).

6. *LBR* is owned by CCIPL, which reserves the right to modify these Terms and any other Rules and Guidelines established in relation to an Attempt or general policy. CCIPL does not implement or involve itself in editorial policy and does not process submissions. *LBR* is collated and published by publishers Hachette Book Publishing India Pvt. Ltd/ Hachette India, who will process the entries, make all decisions on acceptance and inclusion, and publish the book autonomously as is required for an independent book of records. Publication dates and content design are decided and implemented in conjunction with CCIPL.

All such modifications of the Terms and Conditions, and policy, will be updated on the webpage: https://www.hachetteindia.com/home/rulesandguidelines (for the latest Rules and Guidelines, and updates), and anyone attempting to enter their record in *LBR* must review the Terms and the corresponding rules for each Attempt regularly to remain informed of any changes or modifications therein.

7. *LBR* and its representatives do NOT charge any fee or accept any money for the application, review, processing, or acceptance of records [please see clauses III.(A)18 and III.(A)19 of 'General Guidelines' pertaining to certificates and discount on sale of copies to Applicants].

NOTE: *LBR* emphasizes safety and compliance very clearly in all its guidelines. No record application is reviewed or even considered without all due process being completed in an approved submission including all safety checks and regulatory compliance (the onus of listing and procuring which lies on the Applicant(s)) being certified by the authorities in question (see also Section VIII Safety Precautions).

II. ELIGIBILITY CRITERIA

1. To be eligible for consideration by the *LBR* Team for a successful Attempt, 'Applicant(s)' must fulfil the following conditions:

a. The Applicant should be a resident Indian or non-resident Indian (NRI)/overseas citizen of India (OCI)/Person of Indian Origin (PIO) (at least one grandparent should be Indian), and must submit ID and residence proofs and other documents as required by law to establish this.

b. The Applicant must have read and consented to the Terms, the specific Rules and Guidelines applicable to the Attempt, and must have signed and submitted the Disclaimer and Indemnity Form before undertaking the Attempt.

2. The Attempt must be corroborated by a valid proof of age, i.e., above 18 years:

a. The Applicant must be above eighteen (18) years of age.

b. The Applicant must have carefully read and consented to the

Terms, and the specific Rules and Guidelines set down for the Attempt. Before engaging in the Attempt, the Applicant must have submitted the Disclaimer and Indemnity Form as well as a Certificate of Medical Fitness (with the medical practitioner's registration number mentioned on it) to attempt any physical feat or one involving mental exertion, or one deemed so by the *LBR* Team.

NOTE: The *LBR* Team may still include records related to official sports events (associated with only officially recognized national or international bodies like BCCI, IOA, ICC, FIFA, etc.), and medical science (like heaviest baby, lightest baby, etc., where the minor is not an active participant or being exhorted to perform or create a record that is beyond a minor's normal capability). Further, the *LBR* Team may choose to include certain records from the public domain, which may have the involvement of a minor. All these exceptions are subject to the sole discretion and decision of the *LBR* Team.

3. The onus and responsibility of being compliant in the particular context of a record claim lies with the Applicant, and a submission to *LBR* means that all laws, rules, regulations, permissions, and necessary approvals from the right authority have been taken. For example, a driving record means that the Applicant has the necessary and valid driving licence; or a structure erected means that the Applicants have got the necessary approvals including but not limited to all safety clearances needed (structural, mechanical, electrical, fire, etc.) or an event held means that the necessary law and order permissions, etc., have been taken. *LBR* accepts no responsibility for damage or harm to public property that may result from necessary clearances and approvals not being taken and reserves the right to prosecute Applicants found in breach of such safety standards. Above all, safety of people attending or in the vicinity is paramount.

III. GENERAL GUIDELINES

A. GENERAL

1. Standard norms and rules should be adhered to while setting national and world records. In some cases there may be additional event-specific norms that need to be observed.

2. The onus of proving a record claim rests on the Applicant. The claim, signed by the Applicant, should be backed by adequate and satisfactory documents without which it will not be accepted. Materials submitted as supporting evidence, such as press clippings, audio/video tapes, flash/pen drives, CDs, DVDs, hard drives, and photographs, become the property of the publisher, Hachette Book Publishing India Pvt. Ltd/Hachette India and the Copyright Owner, CCIPL, and only copies should be submitted with the originals kept safe by the claimant for Life after the claim has been accepted (see also Section V [Evidence]). Forms such as the Application Form duly signed by the Applicant and validating/ witnessing authorities as indicated by the *LBR* Team and/or the Rules and Guidelines need to be submitted in the original (hard copy) and a copy retained by the Applicant(s) for Life after the claim has been accepted. *LBR* does not take any responsibility for lost material(s) if the record is questioned, disputed, or objected to by any person. In case of a query or objection raised, the responsibility of providing the evidence again for reverification (see also Reverification of Evidence clause V.13) and all expenditures therein lies with the Applicant.

3. It is not necessary or binding for someone from *LBR* to be present at the recordmaking event, but proper authentication of the same must be ensured. Authentication should be by someone who is competent and in a responsible position, such as a gazetted officer, district magistrate, or principal of a government school/college, unless specified otherwise.

4. The Applicant(s) must update themselves with the latest record before making any Attempt to break it. Potential record-breakers should inform *LBR* at least 30 days in advance about the record Attempt details and procedure in order to avoid disqualification on technicalities.

5. Confirmations from Consultants are not to be treated as final. The final confirmations are only issued post ratification by the *LBR* Editorial Team. Applicants are advised to check the existing record with the *LBR* Team just before their Attempts as well, so that they may be intimated of any updates.

6. While breaking an existing record, the Applicant(s) must follow the rules, technical specifications, and set precedents. For example, if the needle-threading record specifies a no. 13 needle, no other needle may be used.

7. Records should be absolute and not technical offshoots. For example, if one is setting a typing record, it is assumed that it is normal typing. One-finger or two-finger typing will not be registered as separate records. Records have to be quantifiable and comparable, and overly specific variables may not be considered.

8. While *LBR* does accept new categories, these will have to be of high interest value and have definable and comparable parameters, and these are entirely subject to the *LBR* Team's decision. For example, even if no record exists, a 'two-hour marathon for guitar playing' will not be accepted because in this case, while doing an activity continuously for two hours maybe impressive, but does not necessarily qualify as a record with definable universal parameters.

9. Not every record set by women is eligible for entry as the sub-category 'First woman to...'.

10. Collections should have a basic 'standard'. Limited numbers of obscure articles may not be accepted unless of exceptional interest value, and that acceptance shall be the sole decision of the *LBR* Team.

11. For distance records, only basic types of vehicles are recognized: four-wheelers and plus, two-wheelers, geared bicycles, gearless bicycles, tandem bicycles, and electric vehicles. Cross-country or intra-country motoring/cycling or other vehicular records must get prior clearance from the *LBR* Team for inclusion. In speed-related records, vehicles may be categorized according to engine capacity: up to150 cc, 151–450 cc, and over 450 cc.

12. Before attempting any driving record, Applicants have to submit a copy of the following document/documents, as applicable, attested by a gazetted officer or notary public: their valid driving licence/earlier experience certificate in case of motor sport or bicycling record; pilot's licence/aero-sports course certificate/earlier experience certificate in case of aero-sports record; mountaineering/ mountain sports course certificate/earlier experience certificate in case of a mountain sports record; and water sports course certificate/

earlier experience certificate in case of a water sports record to the *LBR* office for prior approval.

13. All claimants must send in supporting photographs for their Claim to the *LBR* Team. These should be clear, and should clearly demonstrate the record. No tampering or enhancement of pictures should be done. In physical evidence with documents or photographs, these should not be stapled to the entry. Detachable clips should be used. In cases where applicable and as indicated by the *LBR* Team, time- and date-stamped video recordings of the Attempt must be provided.

14. Attempts that may result in physical harm, such as 'hitting head against a wall', or mental/emotional duress for the Applicant, such as 'isolating oneself for 100 days', will not be considered, and are entirely left to the decision of the *LBR* Team.

15. Any record in the book may be reconsidered or dropped without prior intimation.

16. Certificates issued are valid only as on or for the date or period specified and will be considered ended if surpassed by a new record, and/or change in criteria, measuring methods, or if disputed and found to be erroneous on reverification (see clause V.13). *LBR* is not bound to report an update to previous record holders.

17. For reasons of space or any other reasons, a confirmed entry may at times need to be dropped at the time of going to press. The *LBR* Team reserves the right to do so and may inform the Applicant of the change in status but is not bound to do so.

18. Record holders within India or with a postal delivery address within India are entitled to ONE complimentary copy of their certificate postage free, if eligible. Other modes of despatch may be chargeable. Further copies of certificates need to be ordered by writing to the *LBR* Team and on payment (including GST) as indicated. Record holders outside India are entitled to ONE complimentary copy of their certificate but will need to pay courier and/or postal charges (including applicable taxes/surcharges). Requests for reissue of older certificates issued in previous years are considered on a case-by-case basis and such certificates are reissued on payment within reasonable time as per printing schedules, provided the record is accessible in *LBR*'s archived editions.

19. Record holders are not entitled to any remuneration or free copies of *Limca Book of Records*. They may, however, avail a 30 per cent discount on the declared MRP/cover price of the book by writing to the *LBR* Team and following the payment process.

20. If new record holders do not receive their certificate within two months after the release of the book, they should contact the *LBR* office.

21. The *LBR* Team reserves the sole right to decide on the suitability of all records for inclusion in the book. The Team's decision on all such matters is final. Any attempt to browbeat or threaten the *LBR* Team or representatives shall result in instant disqualification.

22. OBJECTIONS/DISCREPANCIES

a. Any typographical error or inaccuracy in the statement of a record or certificate should be pointed out by the record holder immediately.
b. Objections raised by any person regarding any published entry shall be entertained only within a period of three (3) years from the date of publication or acceptance/certification of a record/entry. However, discrepancies identified by the *LBR* Team suo moto shall be addressed regardless of passage of time. Applicants must note that, in accordance with the prevailing laws, there is no limitation in respect of criminal liability should it arise. Falsification of evidence is a criminal activity.

B. CHAPTERS AND CATEGORIES

LBR reserves the right to include or exclude any chapter or category, or section or record category as otherwise listed below and is under no obligation to publish all or any of the listed chapters or categories in *LBR* or any of its publications.

The list provided here is only for illustrative and explanatory reasons, and for the clarity of persons seeking to engage in an Attempt. Further, the following list consists only of chapters and categories that have been published in current and previous editions and is non-exhaustive. *LBR* may, at its sole discretion, include additional chapters or categories, delete a chapter or category, or even merge two or more chapters or categories as the *LBR* Team deems appropriate. Any such addition, deletion, or merging of chapters or categories creates no obligation on the part of *LBR* Team and/or CCIPL to inform any person making an Attempt of such addition, deletion, or merger. Records after acceptance may also be changed or deleted if suitable circumstances warrant it, and this also shall be the sole decision of the *LBR* Team. Further, the guidelines mentioned here, pertaining to *LBR* chapters and their respective categories, are generic guidelines and in no way represent an exhaustive list for the record claim to be accepted. Specific guidelines for individual record claims will be shared on email by the *LBR* Team.

1. THE HUMAN STORY

This chapter contains records, talents, and information, and includes, but is not limited to, unique achievements, uncommon talents, collections, community development initiatives, and other human feats. Applicants under this category are required to not break any laws, and must sign and submit the Disclaimer and Indemnity Form, Self-Declaration of Medical Fitness and Certificate of Medical Fitness, as applicable, at least one month prior to the Attempt. *LBR* prohibits and will not accept any Attempt that is likely to cause harm or be of nuisance to the general public, or is likely to cause unnecessary waste of essential goods or resources such as food items, or is likely to harm the environment; and of course possible physical, mental, or emotional harm to oneself.

a. Records involving alcohol consumption as an event or performance measure will not be considered.
d. For the section on Online feats, *LBR* will accept both single and multiple sessions for a single event. The number of platforms will not be a parameter.
c. *LBR* does not have categories related to religious traditions and ceremonies, unless they form general records.
d. Records indicating or involving harm to physical or mental health, such as 'maximum blood donated in a day', or 'starving for the most number of days', or 'isolating oneself for the longest period' will not be considered.
e. For collection claims, minor changes like changes in colour and/or slight tweaks will be considered as duplicated, and will not be counted separately.

f. For claims related to 'smallest/largest/biggest' forms of an object, the form has to closely resemble the original object as a replica, and creative representations will not be accepted from both functionality and outer look and feel perspectives.
g. For claims under 'Physical Feats', the gendered categories are not applicable anymore. All attempts are comparable.

2. STRUCTURES

This chapter contains records related to general, modern, residential, religious, mechanical and historical structures, bridges, dams and flyovers, and various other specialized structures.

a. There are no set parameters of the claim regarding fastest construction as each construction would have multiple aspects of difference and the *LBR* Team does not wish to encourage the fastest construction of public services or private buildings.
b. Any structure should have the necessary permissions, and structural safety certified and the Applicant should confirm such certification.

3. AGRICULTURE

This chapter contains records and information, and it may include, but shall not be limited to, topics such as agricultural crops, farm machinery, milk and milk products, poultry, animal sciences, fisheries, agricultural research, and awards. Specific rules are to be complied with for Attempts under this chapter.

4. EDUCATION

This chapter contains records and information related to literacy, schools, higher education, archives, libraries, museums, and quizzes. *LBR* has discontinued the 'youngest' category as a record claim. Record claims with qualifications beyond postgraduation are considered. Record claims pertaining to online courses, or qualifications based on the University Grants Commission–National Eligibility Test (UGC–NET), or publication of research papers will not be considered.

5. PERFORMING ARTS

This chapter contains records related to talent and information in the fields of dance, music, and theatre (including but not limited to puppetry and other local theatre types depending on parameters), and dance drama and dance–martial arts crossovers. The records are further divided into marathon events or group events. All Attempts under this chapter are required to follow the specific rules for both types of events as provided by the *LBR* Team. Record claims pertaining to fastest performances will not be considered.

6. VISUAL ARTS

This chapter contains records and information related to cinema, photography, painting, and some categories of drawing and cartooning. The records related to national and regional commercial and art cinema is based on information collected from the National Film Archive of India (NFAI), public domain, magazines, and national newspapers. The records about box-office collection are obtained from the website www.boxofficeindia.com, the standard source in India for collecting such details, or similar sources.

a. Individual record claims for cinema may be submitted for consideration under this chapter, subject to compliance with the basic criteria laid down:
   i. The film should have been cleared by the Central Board of Film Certification (CBFC) and given a censor certificate.
   ii. Certification requirements for over-the-top (OTT) content/ films/drama series will be decided on a case-by-case basis and as per the laws of the land.
   iii. The film should be screened at film festivals or at public theatres/auditoriums.
b. Information related to painting and photography is collected from newspapers, magazines, the Internet, and any other verified source. Individual record claims may be submitted for consideration under this chapter, subject to compliance with the basic criteria laid down:
   i. No miniature paintings in any medium are considered in this chapter currently. They may be eligible for entry in the Human Story chapter depending on parameters.
   ii. All rangoli, alpana and kolam records have been categorized under one category of 'Traditional floor art'.
   iii. Considering that art is a subjective concept, the *LBR* Team reserves the final decision regarding the artwork so produced. Random repetition of patterns, block colour patches, strokes of paint, or smearing paint randomly on the canvas would lead to the rejection of the claim. Similarly, geometric shapes, haphazard lines, and arbitrary usage of colour would also lead to rejection. The artwork so produced should have a coherent sense of pattern, colour, and tone. It should depict a certain level of skill and creation of aesthetics. For photography claims, repetitive, fragmented, and haphazard images would not be considered. The images should have a coherent sense of posture, alignment, and lighting.
   iv. The largest art competition would be a single-day category following the rules of continuous events and being a maximum of 12 hours.
   v. Portrait categories: A portrait should have only a single person in the painting/mosaic. A portrait is considered to be a drawing/painting of the head and shoulder of a person for the purposes of record claims.
   vi. Origami claims have been sorted into the following categories:
      1. Largest origami mosaic – solo/group
      2. Single-item origami (single sheet, single item): A) Tallest/Longest; B) Widest
      3. Multiple-item origami (multiple sheets, multiple items): A) Tallest – solo/group; B) Widest – solo/group
      4. Marathon origami (single day, single venue) – solo
      5. Most towel origami made – solo/group – in 1 hour
   vii. Claims regarding pencil carvings (graphite) have been sorted into the following categories:
      1. Largest collection of carved pencils
      2. Most pencil carvings done – single day
      3. Most pencil carvings done – 1 hour
      4. Smallest pencil carving

7. LITERATURE

This chapter contains records and information from the field of literature. Applicants willing to undertake an Attempt under this chapter must ensure compliance with the basic criteria laid down:

a. Only published works will be considered unless the work created is an art installation or superlative, or an artefact.
b. No long ghazals/poems, rewriting of religious texts, or anthologies will be considered.
c. A work infringing copyright or violative of any other prevailing laws will not be considered.

d. General category claims: Book(s) self-published or published by a publishing house should be available for purchase at bookshops or on a recognized online platform. Sales records must be certified by publishers who have audited accounts, or by Nielsen BookScan.

8. MEDIA AND COMMUNICATIONS

This chapter contains records and information related to the broad fields of (a) media and (b) communications, and may be divided into six sections: (i) print, (ii) radio, (iii) television, (iv) post and philately, (v) telecom, and (vi) Internet, social media and applications (apps). Applicants wishing to undertake an Attempt under this chapter must ensure compliance with the specific guidelines provided by the *LBR* Team.

9. GOVERNMENT

This chapter contains information and records. This category may include, but shall not be limited to, such subjects as nationhood, parties, elections, the Parliament, states, administration, government officials, civics, judiciary, and law and order.

10. DEFENCE AND MILITARY AFFAIRS

This chapter contains records and information pertaining to all the branches of the armed or paramilitary forces and related military records. This chapter does not accept entries unless routed through the appropriate defence authority/organization with the understanding that no official secrets, or confidential information, are being revealed in the process. An independent entry by current or former defence personnel should be accompanied with a self-declaration that no official secrets or confidential information is being revealed. The chapter is otherwise compiled by the *LBR* Team from news sources originating with government ministries and information sources such as the official websites of the Indian Navy, the Indian Army, the Indian Air Force, and the Coast Guard of India as well as the Press Information Bureau, Government of India.

11. SCIENCE AND TECHNOLOGY

This chapter contains absolute records like oldest planetarium and first nuclear reactor along with discoveries and records in, but not limited to, mathematics, physics, chemistry, biology, engineering, environmental sciences, computers, information technology, and space technology. All Attempts under this chapter are required to follow the specific rules for both types of events as provided by the *LBR* Team. For a new invention to be considered as a record, it must be patented with a recognized national/international body. This chapter also includes records and relevant information compiled by the *LBR* Team.

12. MEDICAL SCIENCES

This chapter contains records and information from the field of medical sciences such as medical breakthroughs, medical camps, 'firsts', and in selective medical procedures, medical devices, and equipment.

Claims are acceptable only from registered medical practitioners and related to government-approved medical practices and institutions, such as those affiliated to the Indian Medical Association, the Ministry of Health and Family Welfare, and any others as deemed eligible by the *LBR* Team.

The *LBR* Team will reject any Attempts that may potentially or otherwise harm or endanger persons/patients, e.g., speed-related records, such as 'most kidneys transplanted in a day' or 'most LASIK surgeries performed in a day', whether at a medical centre or in camps, charitable or otherwise.

LBR may accept camp-related statistics that turn out to be records, but may not process or encourage any camps set up to create records, especially speed-related medical science Attempts because such Attempts may jeopardize patient safety and health.

For all surgery-related claims, only successful surgery applications will be accepted, where the patient has not died on the operation table.

13. THE NATURAL WORLD

This chapter contains information and records, and the entries are compiled from multiple and deemed verified reports in magazines, newspapers, and Internet resources available to *LBR* on topics including, but not limited to, geographical features, flora, fauna, environment, and conservation. Information related to flora and fauna is verified with nature conservation authorities, well-known wildlife institutions, government websites, and relevant international websites.

All claims related to rainwater harvesting and pollution control are counterchecked with government sources and/or authoritative expert bodies. Gardening records relating to non-agricultural production and claims, such as largest pumpkin, will require scale-comparative photographs as well as other indicated documentation.

14. TRANSPORT

This chapter contains records and information, and the sections under this chapter include road, rail and metro, water, and air transport. Applicants who claim records under any of these sections shall provide evidence of the same, including authentication documents as required by the *LBR* Team.

15. BUSINESS AND ECONOMY

This chapter contains records and information, and the sections under this chapter may include, but shall not be limited to, the economy, financial institutions, financial instruments, banking, industries and companies, workforce, housing and real estate, and advertising.

Applicants who claim records under any of these sections shall provide proof of the same, including authentication letters from independent observers including at least one expert in the field. Industry company data must be from authentic authorized bodies such as the Registrar of Companies and the Securities and Exchange Board of India (SEBI), or in the case of own company figures, audited figures must be submitted.

a. Claims for 'highest/lowest' sale of product(s) are not accepted.

16. ADVENTURE

This chapter may be divided into various sections, including but not limited to, aero-sports, mountaineering, road expeditions, water sports, marathons (those not classified internationally as athletics track and field events), and other adventure activities. A person undertaking an Attempt under this category may seek the *LBR* Team's guidance/assistance for specific guidelines. Potential Applicants are advised to note that such guidelines or safety advice provided by the *LBR* Team shall merely be explanatory and non-exhaustive, and will not create any responsibilities or liabilities whatsoever on behalf of the *LBR* Team and/or CCIPL.

a. For all claims related to Ironman triathlon, *LBR* refers to the International Triathlon Union and the Indian Triathlon Federation.

b. For swimming records, only solo as well as up to three-person relay crossings (each covering at least 10 km) will be considered. For marathon swimming – with permitted breaks – breaks of only 1.5 minutes will be allowed for each completed hour. Exceptions may be made for para swimmers or extremely remarkable records, subject to the discretion and decision of the *LBR* Team.

c. A minimum altitude of 6,000 m is required to review any mountaineering claim. Claims regarding Mt Kilimanjaro (5,895 m) will not be considered in accordance with this limit. All mountaineering claims must be verified by the Indian Mountaineering Foundation or a similar credible international body.

d. There are separate categories for women in solo attempts and group attempts where Applicants and, if present, Participants are women.

e. Our categories for expedition records for two-wheelers will now be subdivided as:
   i. Up to 150 cc
   ii. 151 to 450 cc
   iii. Over 450 cc

f. Adventure/Marathon and Endurance Claims:
   i. A detailed logbook must be maintained with entries in chronological order. All entries in this logbook must be witnessed and authenticated by reputed individuals/competent authorities (a gazetted officer, district magistrate, or principal of a government school/college, unless specified otherwise). A sample sheet will be given by the *LBR* Team on request. Emphasis will be on events that highlight special skills.
   ii. In cases where applicable and as indicated by the *LBR* Team, time- and date-stamped videos of the Attempt must be provided.
   iii. All adventure/endurance events come under two categories.
      1. Marathon: A five-minute break for rest after every completed hour is allowed as per prevailing international norms. These breaks may be accumulated during the course of the Attempt, but not at the beginning or end (e.g., a 15-minute break may be taken after 3 hours of non-stop action, but finishing the Attempt 15 minutes before the completion of the Attempt cannot be adjusted as break time and will not be added to the tally). The logbook must clearly indicate the rest breaks.
      2. Normal: Breaks permitted as and when necessary. **NOTE:** For marathon attempts, any claimant(s) not using the permissible breaks will still be compared with the claimant(s) using them. All attempts under the marathon categories are comparable regardless of utilizing the permitted breaks or not.
   iv. Attempts jeopardizing individual or public safety and public property are not encouraged.
   v. All adventure feats/stunts/sports, etc., require prior written approval from authorities concerned.

17. SPORTS

The Sports chapter of the *LBR* primarily contains records and sports-related statistics and information. It is prepared by independent Consultants, who are well-established journalists and/or authorities in particular sports. The Consultants in conjunction with the *LBR* Team are the final authority on all records under this chapter. In cases where an uncommon sport is involved, the decisions will be made in consultation with an expert in the field.

IV. PROCEDURE FOR RECORD ATTEMPTS

1. *LBR* recognizes two types of Attempts by individuals or groups:
   a. an Attempt to break a previously existing record; and
   b. an Attempt to set a new record.

2. The following procedure must be followed by any person willing to undertake an Attempt to be considered for entry in *LBR*. An application by the person attempting the record should be either emailed to *lbr.entries@hachetteindia.com* or couriered/mailed by registered post (see clause IV.3: Application Procedure).
   a. Such application should contain details regarding the unique achievement, or proposal to set a record, for the consideration of the *LBR* Team, along with the complete address and contact number of the person attempting the same, at least one (1) month before the Attempt in order to avoid disqualification on technicalities. For specific requirements in the procedure for an Attempt, please refer to Section III of these Rules and Guidelines/Terms.
   b. The person undertaking the Attempt must approach the *LBR* Team regarding the proper procedure and information or documents required for consideration of a successful Attempt.
   c. On completion of an Attempt, the Applicant must provide the *LBR* Team detailed and accurate documentation, as required by the *LBR* Team, and these will then be scrutinized by the *LBR* Team.
   d. All entries to an edition are confirmed only after the deadline, i.e., the last date for submission of entries. Any Application made after such a date may be considered for a subsequent edition of *LBR*.
   e. On confirmation of an entry, a certificate shall be mailed to the Applicant who carried out the successful Attempt. Such certificates shall be sent after the particular edition for which the Attempt has been considered is printed or released.
   f. For all Attempts to be undertaken, the person undertaking such an Attempt must sign and submit the Disclaimer and Indemnity Form and Certificate of Medical Fitness (in hard copy), as and when required, to the *LBR* Team, prior to the Attempt. The acceptance of any application for entry in *LBR* shall be conditional on the signing of and adherence to the Disclaimer and Indemnity Form, the Terms, and any other specific rules and guidelines established by *LBR* in relation to a particular category of Attempt.

The following rules will apply to Disclaimer Forms:
   i. Disclaimer Forms should have only one party mentioned, i.e., the record claimant. The second party is not applicable. The Disclaimer Forms should have one primary signatory whether it is a team of two or a group application. That signatory should confirm that he/she is authorized to represent the group and all communications with *LBR* will be with this one primary signatory.
   ii. Applicants may choose to get the form notarized instead

of adding witnesses. Or witnesses can be used, but verification from the notary holds more value.

iii. Disclaimer Forms have to be on a stamp paper of minimum value of ₹10.

3. APPLICATION PROCEDURE

a. All applications must be sent to the following address: Limca Book of Records (Editorial), Hachette Book Publishing India Pvt. Ltd, 4th/5th Floors, Corporate Centre, Plot No. 94, Sector 44, Gurugram 122003, Haryana, India.
Ph: +91 22 35305621, Fax: +91 124 4148900
Email: *lbr*.entries@hachetteindia.com
Hachette Book Publishing India Pvt. Ltd is a company incorporated under the Indian Companies Act, 1956, with CIN U22222DL2007PTC164081.

b. *LBR*'s primary mode of communication is email (and only via its formal email IDs), which is both retrievable and transparent as well as a formal record. No Attempt should be made based on phone or other verbal conversations, or communication on social media/messaging platforms.

c. There is no need for personal visits to the *LBR* office to hand over recordrelated applications, documentation, or evidence, and in case the Applicant does visit personally, the application and requisite documents may be handed over at the reception. *LBR* staff may not be available for personal meetings. Since all claim formats devised are such that they need written submission, everything should be clear from written communication.

d. Submissions must be in English since *LBR* is currently published in the English language (submissions in other languages shall be accepted, but they should be accompanied with an English translation).

e. The primary application shall consist of the following:
   i. Name of the Applicant
   ii. Date of birth of the Applicant
   iii. Complete postal address of the Applicant
   iv. Contact details (phone number and email ID) of the Applicant
   v. Description of the record the Applicant wishes to apply for; and event plan
   vi. Confirmation of acceptance of *LBR* procedures, Terms, and Rules and Guidelines via a formal statement on email or signed hard copy

f. These applications shall be perused by the *LBR* Team, and further correspondence shall take place between the Applicant and the *LBR* Team member concerned, from the assigned chapter/section.

g. On acceptance of the initial application, the general guidelines and record-specific guidelines shall be emailed or couriered to the Applicant by the *LBR* Team along with the procedure and documentation required.

h. On receipt of the correspondence from a member of the *LBR* Team, the Applicant shall send the following documents (in both soft and hard copies) to
the addresses mentioned in clause IV.3(a) above:
   i. A covering letter stating the Attempt details
   ii. A signed copy of the Disclaimer and Indemnity Form sent to the Applicant
   iii. A self-attested copy of the Applicant's government-approved identity proof (such as passport, voter ID card, PAN card, Aadhaar, etc.)
   iv. A self-attested copy of the Applicant's government-approved age proof (such as passport, birth certificate, ration card, etc.) together with the 'Required Documents' as indicated by the *LBR* Team.

i. On authentication and verification of the Required Documents, the Applicant shall obtain a confirmation from the *LBR* Team to proceed with the Attempt.

j. After completing the Attempt in accordance with the provisions of Sections III and IV, and collecting evidence of the Attempt in accordance with the provisions of Section V, the Applicant shall send the following to claim a record (the 'Claim'):
   i. Details of the supposed record, duly authenticated by gazetted officers, or relevant public authorities, or relevant authorities in charge, or other competent authorities. Such authentication must be on the basis of personal verification of every detail of the Claim.
   ii. Material evidence of the event, consisting of all the evidence collected by the Applicant during the Attempt. All CDs/DVDs, flash/pen drives, and other data storage media/devices sent to the *LBR* Team, as part of the application process, should have the Applicant's name and the record category written legibly on it.
   iii. Accompanying clearances, permissions and safety certifications as required.

k. Only a claim that is complete and successfully submitted shall be considered for entry in the *LBR*.

l. The application procedure should be completed within the last date of submission. Entries submitted after the deadline may be considered for the subsequent edition unless extension was granted in writing or on email for extenuating circumstances, or at the discretion of the *LBR* Team.

m. In addition to the aforementioned rules, specific requirements provided under the relevant categories must be fulfilled.

V. EVIDENCE

1. The onus of proving a record is on the Applicant. The Claim, signed by the Applicant, should be backed by adequate and satisfactory documentation without which it will not be accepted by the *LBR* Team.

2. The Applicant must, as part of the verification process, submit all supporting documents including at least two authentication letters (originals), verified, stamped, and signed by gazetted officers, preferably on their letter heads, photographs (or CD/DVD/flash/pen drive containing still photos), personal details of the Applicant, including residential address and contact details, along with a covering letter, without which the Claim will not be considered for entry.

3. Outside of moral and creative ownership rights, which will vest in the creator/artist/author, etc., the assigned copyright/publishing rights and any other intellectual property rights in and to any such material evidence shall, to the extent permitted by law, be waived unconditionally by the Applicant and transferred to *LBR* and CCIPL by the submission.

4. The evidence must only be sent after the Required Documents, as indicated by the Rules and Guidelines, have been verified (with copies/scans as stipulated) and the primary application has been duly confirmed and evidence asked for by the *LBR* Team.

5. Only the Claim may be supplemented by evidence of the record with the following to be submitted on the currently prevailing and commonly available and accessible data storage media from where it is easily retrievable, such as a flash/pen drive or hard drive, with the onus of providing a back-up copy/original being on the Applicant:

a. Press clippings of local, national or international newspapers, or press cuttings, or news reports in an electronic form, furnishing direct evidence of the record; or
b. Audio recordings from radio, or any such fact of record which could be heard, furnishing direct evidence of the record; or
c. Direct evidence/audio-visual recording of the record; or
d. Any other fact of record that may be in audio, visual, or audio-visual format, furnishing direct evidence of the record; or
e. Photographs of any such fact of record documented by photographs furnishing direct evidence of the record. (It is advisable to submit high-resolution photographs only, that are pictures 1,500 pixels wide for horizontal images and 1,500 pixels high for vertical images, of 1 Mb or more.)
f. Safety certifications, age proofs, doctor's certificates, etc. where needed.

6. If any of the evidence mentioned above is in a local language, it must be sent along with a copy of an English translation of the said document attested by a gazetted officer/notary public.

7. The evidence must be clear, distinct, and unambiguous.

8. *LBR* reserves the right to refuse the Claim if evidence sufficient to prove the record act beyond reasonable doubt is not furnished, or if safety-related documentation is unsatisfactory, or for any other reason whatsoever at *LBR*'s discretion.

9. The material evidence provided by the Applicant shall NOT be returned. The Applicant is advised to keep all original evidence along with copies (and kept safe so as to be produced in the event of a dispute or reverification).

10. In case of records where giant structures are put in place or super-sized objects are involved, the measurements shall be taken in the presence of appropriate observers and authenticators, such as gazetted officers, a principal of a government school/college, an engineering expert, or others as approved by the *LBR* Team. Structural safety certification must be provided along with the evidence.

11. Originals must not be sent, unless specifically requested by *LBR* for scrutiny. *LBR* will not keep copies longer than twelve (12) months after acceptance of the Claim, but record holders should keep their evidence to be produced for disputes for life (see below V.13: Reverification of Evidence). Evidence and documents of rejected claims will not be kept with *LBR* and will be destroyed within 7 (seven) days of the rejection mail date informing the Applicant of the decision (unless the Applicant has specified that they will pick up the submission themselves or at their cost). It is reiterated that *LBR* should be sent only copies and *LBR* does not take responsibility for safekeeping of documents.

12. All records and evidence are accepted in good faith and normal deep scrutiny. Any submission of fake evidence shall be met with a charge of cheating and other offences as mentioned in the Indian Penal Code and other applicable laws. Similarly, incomplete evidence or improper certification for any record shall see rejection, and if discovered later, may see cancellation of the record and prosecution where applicable.

13. REVERIFICATION OF EVIDENCE

a. In case a discrepancy in the record comes to light, as pointed out by any person/group or independently detected by the *LBR* Team, the onus of providing the evidence again for reverification of the record entry lies entirely with the record holder. If, in the opinion of the *LBR* Team, the discrepancy, irrespective of the reason for its coming to light, is genuine, it shall be communicated to the record holder and evidence sought for reverification. In the meantime, the record will be frozen/suspended and the certificate considered withdrawn until the evidence is reverified by a panel consisting of an *LBR* Team member and a legal consultant. Announcement of such a frozen/suspended record will appear only on the *LBR* website publicly and nowhere else. Subsequent to reverification, the record may either be restored, amended, or struck off completely.
b. *LBR* will not keep any data or records longer than one year (12 months) from acceptance in writing. In the event of any objection or discrepancy needing reverification (see sub-clause [a] above), the record holder must keep all supporting evidence safe and readily accessible.
c. In all matters pertaining to reverification of records/evidence, the *LBR*'s decision shall be final and binding

VI. ACCEPTANCE CRITERIA

1. Each Attempt must be categorized within one of the chapters or categories listed under Sections II and III.B. However, *LBR* reserves the right, to be exercised at its sole and absolute discretion, to accept applications for Attempts.

2. Records must be absolute and not technical offshoots, and they must be quantifiable, comparable, and measurable. Records should be significant in achievement and not frivolous.

3. No Claim shall be considered valid unless it is sent, along with the required evidence, in the manner prescribed in Sections IV and V.

4. *LBR* reserves the right to publish or delete any chapter, section, category, or record in the present or any future edition of *LBR*, without any notice to the Applicants. *LBR* is under no obligation to inform record holders when a record may be dropped. Such decisions shall be the sole prerogative of the *LBR* Team in the larger continuing interests of the book.

5. Records shall be considered for publishing only on the grounds of their interest value and general public acceptance.

6. Further, no entries in violation of any law, rule, regulation, guideline, or any other statutory instrument shall be accepted. No record or feat attempted shall endanger anyone or any property, and if after acceptance a record is found to have caused damage of any sort to the public or individual persons (for example, a building collapse by structural weakness or illness from some food item made, etc.), then such record may be cancelled. However, *LBR* reserves the right to include public domain records of harmful/criminal nature (for example, the first plane crash or the youngest serial killer). This in no way is to be seen as an encouragement to make such records and will not be accepted in a pre-attempt application.

7. Entries for the new edition of *LBR* will be confirmed only after the annual deadline, which is usually 31 May.

8. In all matters pertaining to the *Limca Book of Records*, the *LBR* Team's and/or CCIPL's decision shall be final and binding.

9. Record claims are accepted in good faith and may be considered records and published in the book as such unless disproved with appropriate evidence.

10. It should be borne in mind, that *LBR* by its rejecting a Claim is not stating that the Claim may not be a record, or that the achievement, if any, is belittled. It is merely stating that for its purposes and within the framework of the book, as run by its editorial policy, it does not consider the Claim suitable to feature.

11. Harassment of staff, including overt or covert threats, including threats of legal process for rejecting a Claim, or for any other reason whatsoever, or defaming *LBR* or the *LBR* Team on public platforms will not be acceptable and will be met with all the measures under law. Any such behaviour will also result in automatic disqualification of the Claim.

12. Similarly, due process and timelines shall be followed as has been communicated by the *LBR* team. Attempts to browbeat staff, or bring pressure to bear, including citing official/government/ministry 'priority', may result in rejection of the record. *LBR* does not have a fast-track system either on payment or from any either reason.

VII. STATUTORY COMPLIANCE

1. It is mandatory for Applicants to abide by all local, state, and national laws, rules, and regulations applicable in relation to the Attempt. *LBR* expressly prohibits any Attempt that involves violation of any local, state, or national laws, rules, or regulations. Applicants are under an obligation to ensure that all activities related to the Attempt are neither unlawful, nor against public decency and morality.

Applicants must note that *LBR* strongly discourages Attempts that are likely to offend the sentiments of any community. *LBR* also discourages Attempts that may cause harm to the public or animals, or cause any damage to the environment, and Applicants are requested to refrain from making such Attempts. Applicants shall bear sole responsibility for any consequences arising out of any non-compliance with any applicable laws, rules, or regulations insofar as they relate to the Attempt. *LBR* shall not be liable for any harm caused to the public or the environment in the course of the Attempt, and *LBR* shall not be responsible for any non-compliance with any applicable local, state, national, or international laws, rules, and regulations insofar as they relate to the Attempt.

2. With the submission of any Claim, a record holder agrees to abide by the Terms and Conditions, and Rules and Guidelines, in full and is thereby covenanting that the submission is true with no falsifying of evidence or no mala fide intent of any sort whatsoever.

VIII. SAFETY PRECAUTIONS

1. The Applicant is requested to take all reasonable safety precautions prior to the Attempt including, but not limited to, the testing of all equipment used for the Attempt, the utilization of prescribed safety equipment in relation to the Attempt, the presence of requisite medical personnel and treatment facilities, and any applicable safety permits required under local, state, or national laws, rules, and regulations.

2. The Applicant understands that the Attempt may be dangerous to them, other Participants, and spectators, and that they must identify such risks, with the help of professional advice, such as the risk of accident, illness, paralysis, injury, loss, or death that may be caused by negligence, forces of nature, or other agencies, known and unknown. The Applicant knowingly and freely assumes all such risks, both known and unknown, and assumes full personal responsibility for the Attempt and its consequences.

3. The Applicant shall bear sole responsibility for taking all such safety precautions and acknowledge that CCIPL, the *LBR* Team, and/or their respective directors, publishers, editors, officers, appointed representatives, Consultants, or agents shall not, in any manner whatsoever, be responsible for making any safety arrangements for the Attempt.

4. Safety certifications as stated above in various sections – are an absolute necessity.

IX. PUBLICITY

1. The Applicants undertake and irrevocably and unconditionally permit CCIPL and *LBR* to cover any Attempt through various media including newspapers, radio, television (news and other channels), Internet, mobile apps, social media, etc., and shall not raise any objection, protest, or demur whatsoever to such coverage or in this regard. Whilst *LBR* shall make all reasonable efforts, there is no obligation on the part of *LBR* to air or otherwise engage in publicizing any Attempt. The Applicants must, at the request of CCIPL/*LBR*, participate in all promotional activity (such as publicity and photography) in relation to a successful Attempt, free of charge, and consent to CCIPL and *LBR* using their name and image in all promotional materials, free of charge, should CCIPL/*LBR* Team wish to do so as mentioned under Section X below.

2. In the case of publicity-related interview and other occasions/opportunities and/or events where the participation or presence of the Applicant may be required, the *LBR*/CCIPL Team will contact the Applicant(s) in writing/on email for their consent and willingness for such an interview and/or event.

3. No applicant should issue any press release or make any statements pertaining to *LBR* or the record until such statement has been approved in writing by the *LBR* Team.

4. No unauthorized use of logo or brand names for own publicity or publicizing/displaying record should occur.

X. LICENCE TO USE NAME, IMAGE, LIKENESS, RECORD

Applicants hereby grant in perpetuity to CCIPL and *LBR*, their authorized agents, successors, and assigns, the worldwide licence to use the name, image, likeness, pictures, video recordings, audio recordings, etc., of the Applicants in relation to any Attempts undertaken by the Applicants (the 'Licensed Property'). Applicants agree and grant to CCIPL and Hachette Book Publishing India Pvt. Ltd/Hachette India a waiver of their privacy and personality rights, and grant the right to use any element of the Licensed Property for any purpose in connection with *LBR* including, but not limited to, the publication and distribution of *LBR*, the promotion of *LBR*, CCIPL, and any of its divisions or products, and the filing of copyright, trademark, and other similar registrations in relation to *LBR* that involve the Licensed Property. All material(s) submitted in connection with a potential entry in *LBR* (whether in written, audio, electronic, or visual form, or a combination of these) or any photographs, video and/or film footage, and/or audio recording taken of Applicants are assigned to *LBR* and CCIPL upon submission and become the property of *LBR* and CCIPL exclusively. *LBR* and CCIPL may use the material(s) in any medium in any reasonable manner they deem fit. Copyright in any such material(s) remains the sole property of *LBR* and CCIPL.

NOTE: Contributions: All *LBR* records and/or information if featured in our book and/or database are copyright *LBR*. *LBR* is also a fact book and therefore has facts that may be available in public domain or provided by experts/consultants/reader-contributors. Such contributions from consultants and or volunteers (which are also facts and/or public domain information) may be acknowledged once in an edition if so contracted or committed but shall have no subsequent continued acknowledgement after the first use.

XI. INTELLECTUAL PROPERTY RIGHTS

The name 'Limca' and the 'Limca' logo are registered trademarks of The Coca-Cola Company, USA, and should not be used for any publicity in relation to an Attempt, or after a Claim has been accepted, without the express permission of CCIPL. All rights, titles, and interests including, but not limited to, the Intellectual Property Rights, in *LBR* and in any and all entries received, shall vest solely and exclusively in CCIPL at all times. CCIPL or any person or entity permitted by CCIPL in this regard shall be entitled to use any information in connection with the entry in any media for future promotional, marketing, publicity, and any other purpose, without any permission and/or payment to the Applicant.

XII. RESPONSIBILITY FOR ALL ASSOCIATED COSTS AND INSURANCE

The Applicant understands and acknowledges that all expenses incurred in relation to the Attempt shall be borne solely by the Applicant. CCIPL and/or *LBR* Team shall in no manner be responsible for reimbursing any expenses incurred in the course of the Attempt, or even in the event that the Applicant is successful at the Attempt. CCIPL/*LBR* Team shall not be responsible for providing any kind of insurance in relation to any Attempt, and shall not be responsible for any emergency medical expenses or any subsequent medical expenses in the event of any incident/accident, illness, or incapacity arising out of the Attempt.

XIII. WAIVER OF CLAIMS AND INDEMNITY

1. Applicants acknowledge and consent on behalf of themselves, their heirs, successors, assignees, personal representatives, and next of kin, to WAIVE ALL CLAIMS AND RELEASE AND HOLD HARMLESS the *LBR* Team, Hachette Book Publishing India Pvt. Ltd/Hachette India and all its employees, directors, parent or affiliate organizations, Consultants, representatives, partners, CCIPL, its directors, publishers, editors, officers, employees and representatives, and its partners, affiliates, subsidiaries, advertising agencies, agents, and their respective directors, officers, employees, and representatives (the 'Released Parties'), with respect to any and all injury, disability, paralysis, death, or loss or damage to person, property, or reputations, arising out of the Attempt, to the fullest extent permitted by law. The Applicants agree to indemnify and hold the Released Parties harmless from all losses, liabilities, damages, costs, or expenses (including but not limited to reasonable legal fees and other litigation costs and expenses) incurred by any of the Released Parties as a result of any claims or suits that any Applicant(s) (or anyone claiming by, under, or through such Applicant[s]) may bring against any of the Released Parties to recover any losses, liabilities, costs, damages, or expenses that may arise during or result from the Attempt in any way.

2. Further,

a. *LBR* retains an indemnity for human error or typographical error, and the right to revise a record because of that; and the right to withdraw or modify a certificate because of such error lies with the narration of the certificate. Any such correction shall also be duly corrected by the Applicant including to any areas the Applicant may have sent publicity information.

b. The right to suspend records/certification on receipt of disputes or objections lies with the *LBR* Editorial Team. In such cases the record verification will be revisited, and the Claimant of the record must provide reverification (see Clause V.13) and, if necessary, further detailing to answer such objections. If the Claimant is not able to furnish a copy of the evidence as per the original claim, the record and certification may be cancelled.

c. The principle of acceptance is basic verification and acceptance in good faith, so records should be clear and detailed. *LBR* reserves the right to do forensic examination or reopen a record case later if found to be suspect.

d. Faking of records and evidence and misrepresenting safety or other regulatory certifications is a criminal offence and shall be dealt with strictly under the prevailing laws. The Application/Claim/Record shall be cancelled and the Applicant/record holder shall be immediately blacklisted and no further applications/claims from them shall be entertained; and the rights to legal prosecution shall be reserved.

e. For records involving mass participation/huge numbers, for example, 'most people at a concert' or 'most vehicles in a rally', the simple principle of sequentially numbered badges should be there with a logbook of a unique identifier (licence/registration number, individual ID card, or any similar clearly visible device).

f. *LBR* is a private body and its editorial criteria solely belongs to it alone and its decisions shall be the ones solely binding on any record.

XIV. SEVERABILITY

Each of the provisions contained in these Terms/Rules and Guidelines is considered to be reasonable by CCIPL, *LBR*, and the Applicants, and each clause, subclause, paragraph, and sub-paragraph shall be construed as independent of any other provision. If any provision of these Terms/Rules and Guidelines proves to be invalid, void, or illegal, it shall not in any way affect, impair, or invalidate any other provision, and the remaining provisions shall remain in full force and effect.

XV. DISPUTE

The courts of competent jurisdiction at Delhi shall have exclusive jurisdiction to determine any and all disputes arising out of, or in connection with, any Attempt undertaken or entry made for the purpose of *LBR*. Further, all issues and questions concerning the construction, validity, interpretation, and enforceability of these Terms/Rules and Guidelines, or the rights and obligations of the Applicants and/or CCIPL and/or partners of *LBR*, shall be governed and construed in accordance with the laws of the Republic of India.

Note: For general queries and/or specific guidelines pertaining to specific Claims/Records, all Applicants are requested to contact the *LBR* Team by email at *lbr*.entries@hachetteindia.com.

APPENDIX 1

The clauses below are subject to ongoing review and modifications, and Applicants may check this section from time to time to update themselves on categories that may have been discontinued, modified, or changed.

1. SPECIAL NOTE FOR PROSPECTIVE ATTEMPTS

a. There are categories in the book, marked with a single asterisks, indicating that they are one-time categories. These categories will not be carried forward into our subsequent editions and are not contestable.
b. Additional pointers to remember before sending the documentation or Claims:
    i. Applicants should not send any documents unless requested by the *LBR* Team, post-approval.
    ii. Applicants should not send any documentation if their event has not been approved for consideration by the *LBR* Team.
    iii. Documents received by *LBR* for events that are not pre-approved (in writing or on email) will not be reviewed by the *LBR* Team.

2. A NOTE FOR PAST, PRESENT, AND POTENTIAL RECORD HOLDERS

a. The name Limca and the Limca logo are registered trademarks of The Coca-Cola Company, USA, and should not be used for publicity when a record is being attempted or after the Claim has been accepted, without written permission of the publisher.
b. When records are being attempted, it is not obligatory for the *LBR* Team to provide invigilators. However, where possible they may do so.
c. All Attempts at breaking old records and setting new ones are undertaken entirely at the risk of the Applicant. Neither the *LBR* Team nor CCIPL can be held responsible by the Applicant/person undertaking an Attempt or any third party for any liability that may arise out of such an Attempt.
d. Applicants may use the name '*Limca Book of Records*' while attempting the record as long as:
    i. they do not use the logo of the *Limca Book of Records* or Limca brand or any Licensed Property of CCIPL;
    ii. they do not receive or give money in the execution of such an Attempt using *LBR* as a party or implied party or endorser; and
    iii. they do not offer Participants/partners any kind of inducement using *LBR* as a party. This is strictly prohibited and will result in the Applicant's name being blacklisted and rejected for any future application/attempts.
e. The *LBR* Team reserves the complete and incontestable right to decide which chapters, sections, photographs, categories, and records to publish or delete in future editions. *LBR* will not consider record Attempts by minors (excluding exceptions, please refer II.2.) or any Attempt that is potentially dangerous or violates a law.
f. *LBR* strives to be completely authentic. However, it sometimes happens that an earlier record may come to light or be applied for after the book is released. In such cases corrections/updates will be carried out in the next edition or as deemed fit by the *LBR* Team.
g. Records that are 'firsts' are not entitled to perpetuity and can be dropped from the book without any prior intimation.
h. For reasons of space or any other reasons whatsoever, a confirmed Claim may also be dropped. *LBR* Team members may inform the Applicant of the change in status but are not bound to do so. Such decisions are the sole prerogative of the *LBR* Team in the larger continuing interests of the book.
i. The record holders are not entitled to any prize money, gift(s) or free copies of *Limca Book of Records*.
j. In case the record is subjected to reverification, the onus to prove the same is on the Applicant. So the Applicant must retain copies of documentary, images, audio, and video evidence with them should such a situation arise. The *Limca Book of Records* holds the right to revoke any record that fails reverification and to cancel the issued certificate.
k. In all matters pertaining to *Limca Book of Records*, the *LBR* Team's decision is final.

3. DISCONTINUED CATEGORIES

a. A few categories have been discontinued and will not be featured in any subsequent editions. The website is updated regularly regarding such categories.
b. Most surgeries/medical procedures within a time duration: The category for most surgeries/medical procedures has been discontinued as the quality of the procedure may be compromised during such claims.
c. Tractor service camps: The category for most tractors serviced has been discontinued, as such claims are difficult to monitor and make it an industry-specific claim.
d. Largest blood/organ donation drives.
e. Wrist cracking/wrist rotation.

f. Most couplets written.
g. Holding most burning candles in the mouth.
h. Fastest yoga asanas.
i. Collection of error coins.
j. Longest interview.
k. Limbo skating.
l. One-hand claps.
m. Most postcards sent in a day – solo/group – single/multiple venues.
n. Largest packers and movers of household goods.
o. Most people screened/diagnosed – single/multiple venues.
p. Largest anthology
q. Collections for '786' notes.
r. Fastest construction of structures.
s. Longest preservation of food items/articles.
t. Claims related to number of research papers written or published.
u. Collections based on alphabetical order (A–Z).
v. Longest lesson.
w. Most varieties (of any dish).
x. Largest doodle art – solo/group.
y. Lowest to highest value collections.
z. Longest distance covered barefoot.

4. WHY WAS YOUR RECORD REJECTED?

Unfortunately, many applications are rejected. The following are the general reasons that lead to the rejection of applications:

a. Not accepted the Terms and Conditions and/or Rules and Guidelines; and/or submission of incomplete form.
b. Insufficient documentation: The details provided do not suffice for verification purposes.
c. Not met criteria/ ineligible: For record purposes, *LBR* has certain criteria and set categories. For instance, in physical feats it has categories for 1 minute or 1 hour claims. Any claim that does not follow the format (for example, most push-ups in 40 seconds) shall not be accepted. Claims involving minors or jeopardizing safety of minors and/or others in any way will not be accepted (please see clause II.2.).
d. Specific titles: Usually, *LBR* measures record titles by one single parameter so that anybody can attempt and break/ surpass that record. If the record claim is too specific or has multiple variables, the *LBR* Team would not consider such claims. For example, 'most push-ups in one minute' would be considered whereas 'most push-ups done in 1 (one) minute by a teacher' shall not be accepted.
e. Inappropriate/Offensive: *LBR* does not accept or encourage inappropriate or offensive claims.
f. Claims involving alcohol/smoking/substance usage: *LBR* does not encourage or accept claims involving alcohol, smoking, or substance use.
g. Animal welfare: Any claim that is not in accordance with animal rights laws or involves any mistreatment of animals is neither encouraged nor accepted in *LBR*.
h. Personality-related claims: Claims related to famous personalities, such as 'most people dressed as' or 'most times performing as' will only be considered for internationally recognized, iconic, and universally acknowledged personalities. The *LBR* Team reserves the right of discretion in any such claim.
i. Record claims involving wastage of food/medical supplies, for example, artworks made with fresh food materials would not be considered.
j. Environmentally harmful claims: *LBR* does not support any claim that may have any sort of adverse effect on the environment.
k. Fastest musicians: *LBR* does not consider claims such as fastest guitarist, fastest piano player, etc., as it is not possible to judge the quality of music produced in such claims.
l. Firsts: The firsts in a field are generally not accepted unless they mark change in trend, beginning of a new era, or change the traditional way for the matter. The *LBR* Team reserves the right to accept or reject any such claim.
m. Poetry: *LBR* does not accept claims pertaining to poetry due to its subjective nature.
n. Originality/Uniqueness-based claims: Uniqueness/originality cannot be a parameter of competence for a record. The *LBR* Team reserves the right of discretion in any such claim.
o. Sports achievements: For records directly involving performance in sports, *LBR* only accepts those which occur at a top-level professional, international, or pre-eminent amateur levels, or as per the decision of the relevant Consultant in specific cases.

Limca Book of Records
NEXT EDITION: 2026

The last date for new entries and applications (complete with relevant documentation) for the *Limca Book of Records* 2026 edition:

31 May 2025

Please address all correspondence to:

Limca Book of Records (Editorial)
Hachette Book Publishing India Pvt. Ltd
4th/5th Floors, Corporate Centre
Plot No. 94, Sector 44
Gurugram 122003, Haryana, India

Phone: +91 22 35305621

Fax: +91 124 4148900

Email: *lbr.entries@hachetteindia.com*

Websites:

https://www.coca-colaindia.com/limca-book-of-records

https://www.hachetteindia.com/home/rulesandguidelines

Note: In order to have an accessible, credible, and reproducible record of interactions, email (and where it is unavailable, registered postal mail or courier service) is the preferred form of communication and correspondence.